Economic Modeling, Analysis, and Policy for Sustainability

Anandajit Goswami
The Energy and Resources Institute (TERI), India

Arabinda Mishra
ICIMOD, Nepal

A volume in the Advances in Finance, Accounting, and Economics (AFAE) Book Series

BUSINESS SCIENCE Reference
An Imprint of IGI Global

Published in the United States of America by
Business Science Reference (an imprint of IGI Global)
701 E. Chocolate Avenue
Hershey PA, USA 17033
Tel: 717-533-8845
Fax: 717-533-8661
E-mail: cust@igi-global.com
Web site: http://www.igi-global.com

Library of Congress Cataloging-in-Publication Data

Library of Congress Cataloging-in-Publication Data

Names: Goswami, Anandajit, 1980- editor. | Mishra, Arabinda, editor.
Title: Economic modeling, analysis, and policy for sustainability / Anandajit Goswami and Arabinda Mishra, editors.
Description: Hershey, PA : Business Science Reference, [2016] | Includes bibliographical references and index.
Identifiers: LCCN 2015051236| ISBN 9781522500940 (hardcover) | ISBN 9781522500957 (ebook)
Subjects: LCSH: Sustainable development--Econometric models. | Economic development--Environmental aspects--Econometric models. | Environmental policy--Econometric models.
Classification: LCC HD75.6 .E295346 2016 | DDC 338.9/27--dc23 LC record available at http://lccn.loc.gov/2015051236

This book is published in the IGI Global book series Advances in Finance, Accounting, and Economics (AFAE) (ISSN: 2327-5677; eISSN: 2327-5685)

British Cataloguing in Publication Data
A Cataloguing in Publication record for this book is available from the British Library.

All work contributed to this book is new, previously-unpublished material. The views expressed in this book are those of the authors, but not necessarily of the publisher.

For electronic access to this publication, please contact: eresources@igi-global.com.

Advances in Finance, Accounting, and Economics (AFAE) Book Series

Ahmed Driouchi
Al Akhawayn University, Morocco

ISSN: 2327-5677
EISSN: 2327-5685

Mission

In our changing economic and business environment, it is important to consider the financial changes occurring internationally as well as within individual organizations and business environments. Understanding these changes as well as the factors that influence them is crucial in preparing for our financial future and ensuring economic sustainability and growth.

The **Advances in Finance, Accounting, and Economics (AFAE)** book series aims to publish comprehensive and informative titles in all areas of economics and economic theory, finance, and accounting to assist in advancing the available knowledge and providing for further research development in these dynamic fields.

Coverage

- Economics Geography
- Interest Rates and Annuities
- Accounting information systems
- Economics of Risks, Uncertainty, Ambiguity, and Insurance
- Economic Theory
- Economics of Agriculture and Biotechnology
- Fiscal Policy
- Banking
- Bankruptcy
- Economics of Intellectual Property Rights

IGI Global is currently accepting manuscripts for publication within this series. To submit a proposal for a volume in this series, please contact our Acquisition Editors at Acquisitions@igi-global.com or visit: http://www.igi-global.com/publish/.

The Advances in Finance, Accounting, and Economics (AFAE) Book Series (ISSN 2327-5677) is published by IGI Global, 701 E. Chocolate Avenue, Hershey, PA 17033-1240, USA, www.igi-global.com. This series is composed of titles available for purchase individually; each title is edited to be contextually exclusive from any other title within the series. For pricing and ordering information please visit http://www.igi-global.com/book-series/advances-finance-accounting-economics/73685. Postmaster: Send all address changes to above address.

Titles in this Series

For a list of additional titles in this series, please visit: www.igi-global.com

Financial Market Regulations and Legal Challenges in South Asia
Amit K. Kashyap (Nirma University, India) and Anjani Singh Tomar (Gujarat National Law University, India)
Business Science Reference • copyright 2016 • 346pp • H/C (ISBN: 9781522500049) • US $200.00 (our price)

Economics and Political Implications of International Financial Reporting Standards
Efobi Uchenna (Covenant University, Nigeria) Matthias Nnadi (Rivers State University of Science and Technology, Nigeria) Sailesh Tanna (Coventry University, UK) and Francis Iyoha (Covenant University, Nigeria)
Business Science Reference • copyright 2016 • 417pp • H/C (ISBN: 9781466698765) • US $220.00 (our price)

Handbook of Research on Impacts of International Business and Political Affairs on the Global Economy
Norhayati Zakaria (Universiti Utara Malaysia, Malaysia) Asmat-Nizam Abdul-Talib (Universiti Utara Malaysia, Malaysia) and Nazariah Osman (Universiti Utara Malaysia, Malaysia)
Business Science Reference • copyright 2016 • 450pp • H/C (ISBN: 9781466698062) • US $235.00 (our price)

Relational Methodologies and Epistemology in Economics and Management Sciences
Lucio Biggiero (Università dell' Aquila, Italy) Pier Paolo Angelini (Interuniversity Research Centre for Sustainable Development (CIRPS), Italy) Mario Basevi (Italian National Institute of Statistics, Italy) Nunzia Carbonara (Politecnico di Bari, Italy) Antonio Mastrogiorgio (Interuniversity Research Centre for Sustainable Development (CIRPS), Italy) Eliano Pessa (University of Pavia, Italy) Enrico Sevi (Università dell' Aquila, Italy) and Marco Valente (Università dell' Aquila, Italy)
Information Science Reference • copyright 2016 • 485pp • H/C (ISBN: 9781466697706) • US $200.00 (our price)

Global Perspectives on Risk Management and Accounting in the Public Sector
Augusta da Conceição Santos Ferreira (University of Aveiro, Portugal) Graça Maria do Carmo Azevedo (University of Aveiro, Portugal) Jonas da Silva Oliveira (Instituto Universitário de Lisboa (ISCTE-IUL), Portugal) and Rui Pedro Figueiredo Marques (University of Aveiro, Portugal)
Information Science Reference • copyright 2016 • 510pp • H/C (ISBN: 9781466698031) • US $225.00 (our price)

Handbook of Research on Comparative Economic Development Perspectives on Europe and the MENA Region
M. Mustafa Erdoğdu (Marmara University, Turkey) and Bryan Christiansen (PryMarke, LLC, USA)
Business Science Reference • copyright 2016 • 605pp • H/C (ISBN: 9781466695481) • US $440.00 (our price)

Handbook of Research on Financial and Banking Crisis Prediction through Early Warning Systems
Qaiser Munir (Universiti Malaysia Sabah, Malaysia)
Business Science Reference • copyright 2016 • 514pp • H/C (ISBN: 9781466694842) • US $265.00 (our price)

IGI GLOBAL
DISSEMINATOR OF KNOWLEDGE
www.igi-global.com

701 E. Chocolate Ave., Hershey, PA 17033
Order online at www.igi-global.com or call 717-533-8845 x100
To place a standing order for titles released in this series, contact: cust@igi-global.com
Mon-Fri 8:00 am - 5:00 pm (est) or fax 24 hours a day 717-533-8661

Editorial Advisory Board

List of Reviewers

Table of Contents

Detailed Table of Contents

This chapter compares two quantitative frameworks, namely, Computable General Equilibrium (CGE) and Econometric models to study the impacts of climate change on human economy. However, as is inferred from this chapter, CGE framework is fraught with unrealistic assumptions, and fails to capture impacts of climate change and extreme events on the ecosystem services. On the other hand, econometric framework can be customised and is not based on the unrealistic assumptions like CGE. The various advantages and disadvantages of the two methods have been discussed critically in the process in this chapter in light of the avowed objective of understanding sustainability science.

This paper compares the effects of a global carbon tax and a global emissions trading regime on India using a dynamic CGE framework. The sensitivity of the results to the value of a crucial elasticity parameter is also analysed. The results suggest that the choice of the mitigation policy is relatively unimportant from an efficiency perspective. However, the choice of the mitigation policy and the value of the substitution elasticity between value added and energy were found to be important determinants of welfare effects. Global climate change mitigation policies have the potential for promoting low carbon and inclusive growth in India.

This chapter captures the possible impacts of green growth strategies and interventions in terms of skilled, unskilled job creation in context of an emerging country like India. Additionally, it addresses how income generation from specific possible green growth related interventions can have a ripple effect on development indicators like literacy rates, infant mortality rates, poverty. Further it links skilled and unskilled employment generation with "Right to Livelihoods" and MGNREGA and its implications for state level fiscal subsidies. Job creation reflects economic gain for different class of households in the short and long term. This economic gain reduces the level of inter-household and intra-household inter-temporal inequality levels. In the long run, this reduction in the inequality level can create a positive impact on the social sustainability.

This chapter has adopted method of Environmental Social Accounting Matrix (ESAM) and its multiplier analysis to identify sustainable growth path for India. Given the surge of GHG emissions, all developed countries and large emerging economies like India are coming under pressure in global forum to adopt a growth path that is sustainable from the environmental point of view. In this chapter, we propose to analyse the inter-linkage between sectoral GDP growth and its implications on growth in employment, income, GHG emissions and in energy use. The results indicate that the cereal productions other than rice and wheat should be given higher priority to reduce GHG emissions. Furthermore, the findings suggest that the existing pattern of government expenditure is sub-optimal as its reallocation based on their sustainable growth index increases GDP by 1%, reduces GHG emission by 1.57% and increase employment by 2.57%.

Infrastructure projects are being planned and implemented around the world. These projects lead to economic growth and social development, but often unexpected side effects emerge. The problem is that financial analyses for infrastructure projects do not incorporate quantified economic assessments of social and environmental impacts. Equally, social and environmental assessments for infrastructure projects rarely qualify or quantify socioeconomic outcomes for investments in mitigation practices.

Our analysis builds on a review of existing methodologies and tools to propose a method for jointly applying three modeling approaches for integrated economic and spatial planning. The results of case study of the Mekong Flooded Forest landscape shows the capability of the models to anticipate desired and undesired outcomes across social, economic and environmental indicators. This shows promising potential for better informing decision making for sustainability.

In this study we have developed a macro-econometric model for a typical supply constrained African economy. This is aimed at developing a theoretical and empirical template for such policy tools which are increasingly demanded in Africa. We have concretized it by building a macro-econometric model for Rwanda. The Rwanda macro-econometric model has 107 equations of which 72 are endogenous. In addition, a supplementary ARIMA based model with 33 equations for exogenous variable is built to make the model useful for forecasting. The fiscal, balance of payment and money supply block of the model is fairly disaggregated to offer an adequate picture of the macro economy. An econometric estimation of the core behavioral equations of the model using equilibrium [error]-correction approach is made with the database that stretches from 1960 to 2009. The model is similar to successful macro models in the region such as that of the KIPPRA-Treasury model of Kenya. It can also easily be further extended to the support budgeting, forecasting and macroeconomic policy analysis work at the relevant ministries in Africa such as the Ministry of Finance in Rwanda. We have managed to successfully solve the model from 1999 to 2009 and forecast major macro outcomes from 2010 to 2014. We have also used it to conduct a policy simulation exercise which is very important for policy makers such as those in Rwanda. We hope this model offers a theoretical and empirical framework for building macro model across Africa which is increasingly being demanded in many countries.

This chapter presents a discussion on the economic governance aspect of sustainability in the context of energy policy and access. It is believed that incentives are sufficient for emergence of competitive energy markets which augment energy access. However, recent developments in Transaction Cost Economics (TCE) have shown that this need not be true when costs arising out of incomplete contracting are high. Yet, the role of transaction costs and the need to identify and model their behavior has not received adequate attention. This chapter reviews the basic tenets of TCE around natural monopoly sectors. It then illustrates in greater micro-analytic detail how transaction costs can be identified and empirically modeled in the context of industrial self-generation of electricity. The conclusion is that in the analysis of production systems, sustainability arguments are not complete unless costs arising out of inefficient contracting are accounted and an adequate economic governance apparatus is set-up.

Energy pricing in India usually hinges on political, economic or social considerations of the government. Consumer power tariff, a State subject in the country, is no exception to that. However, continued subsidising of power has led to mounting losses of discoms, mostly State-owned, sometimes to a level of insolvency. This has taken a serious toll on financial stability of distribution sector, triggering a cross-sector domino effect. This has happened in spite of regulatory oversight. This study has brought forth some compelling analyses which affirm that current crisis is the outcome of vested interests of some actors and apathy of the administration. It is seen that power tariffs have been skewed disregarding tariff guidelines, whereby liabilities of the State governments to compensate the discoms through payment of subsidies are limited. This study uncovers effective consumer power subsidy across the States, and offers insights into the consequences. This study also identifies key issues plaguing the sector, followed by a brainstorming on possible corrective action-points.

As 1.3 billion people lack access to electricity globally, the challenge of ensuring universal electricity access in accordance with the Sustainable Energy for All initiative remains herculean. This chapter maps policy linkages, identifies the gaps in policies and recommends options for developing the enabling environment. The chapter suggests that the policy environment governing electricity access at present is weak and that improvements are required to deliver a sustainable outcome. Although grid extension remains the preferred mode of electrification in many countries, it is not the least-cost option in remote areas where decentralized off-grid solutions may be required. Successful promotion of off-grid solutions would require a clear regulatory environment, a non-discriminatory support mechanism for various stages of a project, financing options, policy co-ordination and linkage with other economic activities for rural development. The chapter concludes that capacity remains weak and non-transparent policy lobbying can distort the development of an enabling environment.

This chapter by Coady and Hanedar revisits the issue of the distributional impact of energy subsidy reform. It adds to the existing literature on a number of fronts. First, based on recent estimates of efficient energy taxes for India in the literature, it calculates the domestic energy price increases required to bring energy prices to levels that reflect the true social cost of energy consumption, including domestic and global environmental damage. It then simulates the impact of these price increases on household real incomes and how this varies across household income groups. Second, it extends the analysis to the efficient pricing of coal, the most polluting of all energy sources. Third, it also identifies key sectors of the economy that are likely to be the most impacted by higher energy prices.

Policy discourse on rural energy transition within developing countries approach the issue of energy transition through linearly structured, causality based models. This work aims to explore, question the authenticity of such an approach through exploring existence of non linearity in the rural energy transition process of India. Energy transition of rural households impact social, economic and environmental domains of sustainability. For instance, a switchover of a household from smoke generating mudstoves to clean cookstoves can reduce smoke generation, chance of respiratory diseases, impacting the economic, environment and social domains of sustainability. Transition to clean cookstoves can be non-linear and such a transition in a non-linear way impacts domains of sustainability. Hence this work tries to contextualize rural energy transition process through econometric methods, spatial theory of chaos. The work concludes with the exploration of non linear aspects of rural energy transition process within the local rural context and connects it to sustainability science.

Sustainability has become an important issue worldwide because of great concerns about the unintended social, environmental, and economic effects of increasing population and economic growth, as well as consumption of natural resources. One recent concept arising from sustainability issue is sustainable entrepreneurship which integrates both the social and environmental aspects, and linking them with entrepreneurial activities. This chapter therefore suggests that efforts of developing countries at promoting entrepreneurship should go beyond engaging in business enterprises but include encouraging the use of entrepreneurial values and approaches to solve sustainability problems. Hence, this chapter is an effort at developing a framework that can be used to influence sustainable entrepreneurship behaviour of the students in developing countries.

This chapter describes one series of climate-adaptive design innovations found in Ladakh, north India. Five different water management techniques chart the region's unique and highly specialized response to water scarcity, and in so doing highlight important lessons for climate-adaptive planning elsewhere. In this case study, the dispersed, community-based water management strategies practiced in Ladakh suggest a level of design thinking that supports environmental stewardship, economic autonomy, cultural consciousness and social cohesion.

According to the United Nations Conference on Sustainable Development in Rio de Janeiro in 2012, half of humanity lives in cities. The urban population has increased from 750 million people in 1950 to 3,600 million in 2011. It is estimated that by 2030 almost 60% of the population world will reside in urban areas. In Spain already does more than 80%. This will lead to significant growth in the coming years, and cities must be prepared to serve new services on a sustainable way: from meeting the needs of potable water or clean air transport will be a challenge of extraordinary magnitude and an opportunity for the industry. The Spanish National Plan for Smart Cities is a continuation of different initiatives proposing to do a set of new political measures that involve the mobilization of resources that will put special emphasis on sustainability.

Air pollution is a serious concern not just for human health but for agriculture also. This puts significant burden on the economy of a region. This paper assesses the health and agricultural damage caused by prevailing Ozone concentrations in National Capital Region (NCR) of India. The analysis is based on modelled and validated Ozone concentrations using state of the art air quality models. Established dose response relationships are used for assessment of impact over human health and agriculture. Value of statistical life approach and minimum support prices are used for economic evaluation of health and agricultural impacts, respectively. More than 3000 mortalities and loss of more than 1300 kt of agricultural crops can be attributed to Ozone pollution. An annual economic loss of about 1.27 billion USD is estimated on account of Ozone pollution in NCR. This study calls for sustainable development of the region which promotes growth without affecting the environmental quality.

The oasean rangelands surrounding and the scattered steppic area, is commonly viewed as degraded landscapes. The dynamics of oasean ecosystems is indeed affected by human and climatic disturbances and stresses which induce desertification processes. In this context, the objectives of this research are to identify and quantify ecosystem services as a tool for measuring changes in arid lands. Monetization has enabled a more complete diagnosis of ecosystems and their ecosystem services. In this paper, we examine the economic value of the regulating and cultural ecosystem services provided by the oases of Middle Draa Valley (MDV), which is part of Biosphere Reserve of southern Moroccan Oasis (UNESCO). The economic values are standardized to US$ per hectare per year (2008-2010 period prices). The total value of regulating services is found to be 2478,9 US$/ha/year for the arable area (26000ha) and 43,14 US$/ha/year for the whole Middle Draa Valley (1500 000ha). The economic value of the cultural services in the arable area is 1776,8 US$/ha/year and 30,83US$/ha/year for the total area.

Preface

What does the word sustainability mean? This was the first question that emerged upon our mind when the idea for this edited book emerged. The question then created a chain of thoughts one upon the other guided by various layers. Once each of the layer opened, what was coming up was that the word – "Sustainability" is very much like love. It is abstract, has a soul and can be felt often tangibly as well as intangibly most of the time.

Then, we as editors questioned ourselves further in the following way – "Can sustainability be measured?" The answer to the question has been quite hazy. However, several narrations have criss-crossed our mind. Each of these narrations has a connection with the economic, environmental, social and institutional domains of sustainability. Therefore, an attempt has been made to divide the sections of the book in a way so that it captures each of these narrations encompassing the economic, environmental, social and institutional domains of sustainability.

Some of these narrations and broad intuitions are also measurable and have been reflected in the content of the chapters. However, broadly we as editors have attempted to keep the narrations open so that each discourse pertaining to the social, economic and environmental domains of sustainability finds a space in the book and in the larger context of sustainability science. Therefore there is no deliberate attempt to connect each of the chapters, so that each of the story telling in the chapter flourishes independently and takes the reader into different paths of sustainability science. Often, bridging the chapters can constrict such a journey. Hence we as editors decided to give that space and leave the journey of the chapters as free as possible giving the reader their own que to sustainability science.

So as editors, in this book we deliberately kept a wide range of chapters focussing on the basic issue of energy provision reflecting developmental dividends of emerging, developing countries. In order to explore that, the theme of energy access and sustainability science has been pondered upon. Further as part of that theme, chapters regarding decentralized energy solutions and its connections to social, economic and environmental domains of sustainability science have been explored upon.

Impact of enhancement of energy access on human development in developing countries has been sought through. Further, energy access enhancement is a time dependent process and is linked to the nature of energy transition in these countries. Often these transitions can be non linear and therefore their association with the developmental paradigm all the time cannot be linearly causal in nature too. So through the chapter focusing on nonlinear energy transition these questions have been explored. An empirical estimation of non linearity in energy transition process of India has emerged in one of the chapters.

The social and economic domains of sustainability science are also impacted by tax and subsidy regimes in energy commodities as they impact the production and consumption choices of energy. This therefore also effects the producer and consumer surplus and hence the social and economic domains of sustainability science.

So chapters focussing on tax and subsidy related reforms in fossil fuel and electricity sector have attempted to address those implications on sustainability science. While dealing with it, a theoretical paradigm of impact of transaction costs in the electricity and fossil fuel sector on the economic, social and environmental domains of sustainability has been constructed too.

On the environmental domain of sustainability, issues of air pollution and its impact on the economy and society is an important concern to be addressed. The chapter focussing on economic costs of ozone pollution is an attempt in that regard.

Having dealt with these issues, this publication realizes the importance of approaching sustainability science from a vertical and horizontal dimension. This is because sustainability as a concept has a vertical as well as a horizontal dimension. The horizontal dimension of it largely focuses on the large scale wider macroeconomic impacts from different policy measures. Chapters dealing with macroeconomic impacts of policy measures promoting sustainable, environment and natural resource balancing growth have attempted to address that. At a macroeconomic, horizontal level, the chapter applying the Computable General Equilibrium (CGE) model to address the impact of climate mitigation policy has made a conscious attempt to assess this aspect on the horizontal dimension of sustainability. As editors we have given space for analysing impact of green growth interventions on economic, social domains of sustainability through CGE model. However, every modelling paradigm, framework is fraught with certain advantages and challenges. For a strong understanding of sustainability science it is important to conduct such modelling analysis which also needs to be parallel questioned by an alternative critical thinking by questioning any modelling framework. Hence, we as editors and as a devil's advocate have tried to introduce the chapter doing a cross comparison of CGE and econometric models for understanding some important issues pertaining to climate change impacts, ecosystem services that are crucial for getting into the discipline of sustainability science.

Science of this modelling based analysis has emerged upon through empirical and facts based exploration. Moreover, the chapter poising the limitations of certain macro models to touch upon the various horizontal dimensions of sustainability science strengthens the narrative. However, we as editors, strongly believe that in a world of sustainability science where multiple truth exists, no single analysis is enough to understand the complexity of a sustainability science. .

Therefore, while, there has been a critique to some types of macro models in this edited book, at the same time a counter narrative to that is established through the chapter focussing on a macro-econometric model for a supply constrained African economy.

This is essentially done to direct on how certain macromodels can also show a direction to several aspects of sustainability science. This can also include a computable general equilibrium (CGE) model to understand the macroeconomic effects of mitigation measures, socioeconomic implications of a green growth and development path even though every CGE model has its own strengths and limitations. It can also include econometric models which can capture structural non linearities of a macroeconomy in a more robust way over a longer time frame.

Any of these models even though are not sacro sanct in their identity to explain all research questions, still do have a place for analysis in the discipline of sustainability science.

Further, the position of a modelling approach to understand certain relevant questions within the discipline of sustainability science is consolidated by the chapter focusing on a systems approach to understand food energy water nexus and issues of economic land use and policy planning. The chapter establishes the need to introduce more of systems thinking and objective analysis through macro modelling techniques in the domain of sustainability science. After scanning through this horizontal dimension of economic modelling, policy analysis of sustainability science, the book moves forward to the vertical domain.

The vertical dimension of sustainability is addressed through the narration captured in the chapters dealing with social capital, cultural capital (in a particular local context) and social enterprise. These chapters essentially potray the uniqueness of constant forge to integrate the horizontal and vertical dimensions of sustainability which are important by themselves and also needs to question each other. Further, exploration of the vertical journey takes the reader to case studies of certain pilgrimage sites and highlights how cultural characteristics of these places can act as an influential factor in the urban planning process. Such impact further, affects the economic, social domain of sustainability science through the triggering factor of culture and local anthropology. Therefore, the chapter establishes the need to strengthen an understanding of local context of culture at a downscaled location to further connect it to the broader concept of sustainability science.

However, the sojourn of this book, through the horizontal and vertical dimensions of sustainability science doesnot attempt to give answers to readers. Rather, it aims to raise more questions in their mind.

This questioning has to continue in future to get broader and clear clarity on the question of – "What is sustainability science?" This edited volume is a humble beginning to trigger more questions and exploration to start in future.

Chapter 1
Sensitivity Analysis with Calibration of Natural Resource Variables under Climate Change:
Comparing Computable General Equilibrium (CGE) and Econometric Frameworks

Nilanjan Ghosh
Observer Research Foundation, India & World Wide Fund for Nature, India

Somnath Hazra
Jadavpur University, India

ABSTRACT

This chapter compares two quantitative frameworks, namely, Computable General Equilibrium (CGE) and Econometric models to study the impacts of climate change on human economy. However, as is inferred from this chapter, CGE framework is fraught with unrealistic assumptions, and fails to capture impacts of climate change and extreme events on the ecosystem services. On the other hand, econometric framework can be customised and is not based on the unrealistic assumptions like CGE. The various advantages and disadvantages of the two methods have been discussed critically in the process in this chapter in light of the avowed objective of understanding sustainability science.

DOI: 10.4018/978-1-5225-0094-0.ch001

INTRODUCTION

Modelling climate change impacts has been one of the most prevalent exercises in the literature on climate change. Strands of literature exist on those aspects (see Stern 2013 for a detailed survey). Allegations against models are too many. Though scientists describe the scale of the risks from unmanaged climate change as potentially immense, the economic models appear to underestimate those risks due to omission of key variables at the interface of the economy and ecology.

A sensitivity analysis often emerges as a natural fall out of the modelling framework. This analysis determines how the output or the model depends on the input variables (Hamby 1994). More importantly, a sensitivity analysis measures the sensitivity of the output to the input variables. In the context of climate change, models that intend to look at impacts on economic variables often consider the change in the nature-related variables as an input, and eventually, try to obtain their economy-wide impacts. This is no mere challenge!

Though economic modelling of climate change is not a new concept but precise modelling is a major concern. The situation is complicated at both levels: conceptual and methodological. While on the one hand, the mounting global emissions and atmospheric concentrations of greenhouse gases (GHGs) is a matter of concern for the present civilisations, the potentially adverse impacts of future climate change on natural and human systems is no less concerning.

When it comes to economic modelling of climate change, the challenge depends on the research question posed. This can occur at two levels. First, it can occur at the level of understanding the impacts of climate change on the various economic sectors. The second is arriving at the economic costs of climate change considering the nature-society-economy linkages.

The approach to responding to the first question is essentially neoclassical and reductionist. However, it is the second concern that poses a bigger challenge and needs to be addressed in ways that concern itself with variables that are ecological, social, and economic. One needs to understand here that the ways climate change impacts humanity is through various forces that are multi-dimensional.

One needs to appreciate here that quantifying the economic costs of climate impacts is extremely challenging. Impacts exhibit considerable heterogeneity across multiple dimensions: the timing and geographic distribution of changes in climatic variables, the consequent changes in key physical and biogeochemical "endpoints" that might occur over time and space, and the magnitude of the resulting damages that these effects are likely to impose on the range of sectors in the economy. Each of these dimensions is subject to uncertainty, and is the focus of different analytical frameworks that utilize computational simulation models. To undertake integrated assessments of climate impacts these modelling components need to be streamlined and the interfaces between them need to be articulated and coordinated.

To assess the economic impact of climate change, the Integrated Assessment Model (IAM) was initiated in 1991 by Nordhaus but the model has received attention after the Intergovernmental Panel on Climate Change (IPCC) report on socio-economic dimensions of climate change (Weyant, et. al. 1996) came to the forefront. IAM integrates climate science and impact of climate change on economic variables. More than 20 years have gone after the introduction of climate economic model or sensitivity analysis, but there is not much improvement that has happened in the context of economic modelling of climate change.

The intention of this paper is to place a comparative picture of two types of quantitative models to assess the impacts of climate change. The two types of economic modelling are: Computational General Equilibrium Model (CGE) or Macroeconomic Model, and Econometric Modelling Approach (EMA).

The Problem at Hand

The problem is more than merely being methodological. In one sense, it is more related to choosing the right framework for research question under consideration. Even at the critical interface of climate change impacts and human society, choosing the research concern remains a big challenge for many researchers. In most cases, climate change impacts have been viewed through the lens of the neoclassical economic frameworks, which steamrolls the economy into a firm, looks at climate change either as given, or as an inevitable externality, and talks of "internalising the externality". In the initial course of development of the economics of climate change, this approach was indeed helpful. As such, reductionism helps in developing any discipline.

However, beyond a particular level, such an approach is definitely not helpful. This becomes even more problematic when one considers the policy implications of such studies. Generally, policy recommendation depends on a holistic approach considering a host of factors that affect the dynamic interface of nature, economy, and society, from the climate change perspective. But, so far climate change economics is more focused on the impact of climate change on economic sectors or variables, rather than exploring this broad framework that we are proposing.

APPLICATION OF COMPUTATIONAL GENERAL EQUILIBRIUM MODELS FOR CLIMATE CHANGE ANALYSIS

To calibrate the natural resource variables under climate change or to design an environmental policy needs exhaustive knowledge about the economy-ecosystem linkage. A mathematical formula or any deductive model can give a quantitative relation between economic activity and environmental pressure of a region. The mathematical model can also describe the size and direction of the economic impact. To study the potential impact of climate change on a regional economy, one can use the computable general equilibrium (CGE) model, which explains the relationships among government, industries and consumers across the regional economy. CGE model can determine the economic impact of production, infrastructure, human health, and capital losses from environmental catastrophes. The production will be in the form of agricultural, industrial, domestic etc.; infrastructure considers water, electricity, communication and transport; human health considers illness, effect on productivity and labour supply etc; and in coastal areas the capital losses from environmental catastrophes considers the storm surge.

The CGE model also estimates the industry wise employment changes of a region when employment changes are endogenous in the CGE model and rate of unemployment in the long run is assumed to be fixed. CGE model enables systematic representation of the climate impacts at regional and sectoral levels. In short time duration the CGE model are not able to capture the time based feedbacks of a region or over the sectors. So the CGE can give either static simulation of a current or future time period (e.g., Bosello et al. 2006; 2007a,b; Roson & Van der Mensbrugghe, 2012; Ciscar et al. 2011) or dynamic simulation through time by endogenous accumulation of capital with investment determined by current economic variables (e.g., Deke, 2001; Eboli et al., 2010; Bosello et al., 2012).

In the CGE model, the lack of available data is one of the major constraints to calibrate the proactive investment functions. In the literature, it is found that the exception has been made by Bosello et al. (2010b). They have introduced optimal growth model coupled with CGE to get the time based feedbacks and optimal level of proactive investment as adaptation.

To study the real economy, the CGE model was used for the first time by Johansen (1960). For many years after that, the framework lost its relevance especially in the context of sensitivity analysis. Again, there was a renewed interest in CGE from 1972, when the model began receiving attention, especially for policy oriented research (Shoven & Whalley, 1972; Whalley 1975, 1977; Shoven, 1976; Miller & Spencer, 1977). Over time, CGE models became very popular, especially for obtaining nation-wide or economy-wide impacts of an external stimulus of an exogenous variable.

As such, international literature is replete with attempts to evaluate the economic effects of climate change, and the costs and benefits associated with their mitigation. When it comes to studies related to the economics of climate change, climate change has often been considered as an exogenous factor in the context of modelling, and its impacts on various economic sectors are taken into consideration. This has been the norm in most of the cases of global applications of climate models. Sue Wing and Lanzi (2014) provide a comprehensive review of that, including the applications of the Integrated Assessment Models (IAM) and Global Trade Analysis Project (GTAP) models.

Some of the reviewed literature (most pertinent to this chapter content) is given in Table 1.

For India, Fischer-Vanden et al. (1997) have applied the Second Generation Model to estimate thestabilizing cost of the Indian emissions, impact of domestic carbon taxes. Bussolo and O'Connor (2001) also used a single country model to measure the impacts of climate policy on four different regions within India and with additional benefits of CO2 reduction. Murthy et al. (2007) have undertaken an activity analysis model in their study and in Ojha (2009), a CGE model to estimate the climate policy impact on poverty in India has been conducted.

ECONOMETRIC MODELLING APPROACH

Sensitivity analysis quantifies the sensitivity of a model's input variables to the parameters of defining the model. To establish a functional relationship between input and output variables, elasticity of different inputs on output is the key component. Sensitivity analysis captures the systematic changes in the quantitative assumption or computations of input variables and the corresponding response on the final outcome. Econometric models are also popular to establish the relationship between inputs and output, though mostly prominent in the context of agricultural economics (Hatirili et al 2006; Rafiee et al 2010).

Some of the researchers also developed the functional relationship between input costs and output. Mobtaker et al (2010) have made a sensitivity analysis through marginal physical productivity (MPP) technique and estimated the functional relationship between input costs and output through an econometric model. Econometric model uses the realistic equations to estimate the functional behaviour of consumers, industry, and government with a specific time-series data. The analysis is technical in nature and has a clear justification of the results. Through econometric method one can easily identify the drivers of dependent variable from the pool of independent variables and this is the problem of model selection or it can be called data mining. Through econometric techniques, the parameters of inputs or elasticity of different inputs are estimated and gives the model a robust empirical base which erases the assumptions relating to optimal behaviour. In that sense, econometric frameworks render themselves to applications to get closer to reality, and the models may be customised as per need.

Table 1. Reviewed literature

CGE Economic Modelling Studies			
Study	**Regional Scope**	**Sectoral Focus**	**Remarks**
Deke et al. (2001)	Global (11 regions)	Agriculture, Sea-level rise	Uses DART model (Klepper et al., 2003)
Darwin (1999)	Global (8 regions)	Agriculture	Uses FARM model (Darwin et al., 1995)
Darwin and Tol (2001)		Sea level rise	
Jorgenson et al. (2004)	U.S.	Agriculture, Forestry, Energy, Water, Coastal protection, Air quality, Heat stress	Uses IGEM model (Jorgenson and Wilcoxen, 1993)
Bosello et al. (2005)	Global (8 regions)	Health	Uses GTAP-EF model (Roson, 2003)
Bosello and Zhang (2006)		Agriculture	
Bosello et al. (2007a)		Energy demand	
Bosello et al. (2007b)		Sea level rise	
Berittella et al. (2006), Bigano et al. (2008)	Global (8 regions)	Tourism, Sea level rise	Couples HTM and GTAP-EF models
Eboli et al. (2010)	Global (14 regions)	Agriculture, Tourism, Energy demand, Sea level rise, Health	Uses ICES model
Bosello et al. (2010a)	Global (14 regions)		Couples AD-WITCH and ICES models to investigate adaptation
Bosello et al. (2011)	Europe (3 regions)	Ecosystem services, linkages to 5 impact sectors in Eboli et al. (2010)	Uses ICES model
Bosello et al. (2012a, b)	Global (14 regions)	Agriculture, Forestry, Tourism, Energy demand, Sea level rise, Health, Flooding	Uses ICES model
Ciscar et al. (2009, 2011, 2012)	Europe (5 regions)	Agriculture, Sea-level rise, Flooding, Tourism	Uses GEM-E3 model (Capros et al., 1997)
Calzadilla et al. (2010)	Global (16 regions)	Water Resources, Agriculture	Uses GTAP-W model (Berrittella et al. 2008)
Reilly et al. (2012)	Global (16 regions)	Agriculture, Health, Ecosystems	Uses MIT EPPA model (Paltsev et al., 2005)

Source: Fisher-Vanden et al. (2013).

There are a few studies in the Indian context on econometric applications to understand climate change impacts. On a recent count, Saravanakumar (2015) has used panel data for 39 years and 13 districts to estimate the yield sensitivity of major food crops to climate change in the South Indian state of Tamil Nadu. Prior to that, Kavikumar (2009), included spatial features in the original Ricardian model, and found that the impact of climate change on net income is lower by 3 percent in models that account for spatial features relative to those that do not. Palanisami et al. (2009) report a negative impact on production due to increases in temperature and rainfall.

A Generic Comparison of the Econometric and CGE Models

As we get into an objective comparison of the econometric frameworks, we find that both the frameworks have their own advantages. This is what we present in this section.

- **Capturing Nation-Wide Impacts:** From the perspective of capturing an economy-wide impact of climate change or any other exogenous variable, CGE definitely is a preferred modelling framework. It easily results in the sensitivity and scenario analysis. This, however, cannot be said for econometric frameworks. Econometric frameworks, under such circumstances, will rather need to be conceived of in simultaneous equation frameworks, and can at most capture the partial equilibrium. It is difficult to devise a robust framework with adequate explanatory power and degrees of freedom to capture economy-wide impact in an econometric framework. This may become even more difficult in the context of climate change in a developing nation like India, where different variables are captured at differing intervals. This may not render the creation of a proper econometric model.
- **Partial Equilibrium Framework and Unrealistic Assumptions of CGE:** However, when attempted to be captured at a partial equilibrium level, econometric model is definitely more useful than CGE models. This is more so because of unrealistic assumptions that often fraught CGE frameworks. Firstly, the econometric approach does not assume that the economy is in an optimum position in the long run, but the CGE model is based on the said assumption. This is definitely unrealistic. The extensive literature on disequilibrium economics bears clear testimony to that. The econometric modelling approach also believes that spare capacity (e.g. the unemployed workforce) can be brought into the service if the right inducement is applied. So under certain conditions, a positive outcome is possible but it is not guaranteed. In Table 2, we present the differences in various assumptions in the modelling framework of two models if contextualised similarly.
- **Data Requirements:** Both types of models are data-intensive. For a robust result, one needs sufficient number of observations in the econometric framework, with adequate degrees of freedom. In the context of developing countries, often data availability is a problem, especially in the context

Table 2. Differences in assumptions of CGE and econometric frameworks

Variables	Econometric Modelling Approach	Computable General Equilibrium (CGE) Approach
Demand and supply	Industry output is demand-driven i.e. supply adjusts to meet an increase in demand.	Assumes markets are in equilibrium, and that prices adjust until supply and demand are in balance.
Behaviour of households and firms	Behaviour of economic agents is determined by empirically estimated equations.	Agents are assumed to be rational and optimisers.
Treatment of investment	Investment demand creates an economic stimulus, leading (where there is spare capacity) to an increase in output and employment, as well as an empirically estimated increase in prices.	Interest rates (the price of investment) adjust so that additional investment fully crowds out investment that would otherwise take place.
Labour market treatment	Unemployment exists in the baseline, so policies that drive an increase in economic activity lead to increases in employment and wage rates	There is assumed to be no involuntary unemployment and an economic stimulus would only lead to an increase in wages and, therefore, inflation

Source: Pollitt et al 2014.

of time-series. This creates a bit of a problem for econometric modelling. However, the situation is neither of comfort for CGE models. While at national levels, the input-output tables might be available, they are often not available at micro-levels (e.g. district levels in India). As a result, often various methods like location quotients or assumptions make the way. This naturally results in extremely poor and undependable results.

- **Customisations:** One aspect where CGE clearly fails grossly in front of econometric frameworks is with model customisations. In a system equation framework, models may be specified as a hypothesis as per need of the project. This leeway is simply missing in CGE frameworks. Econometric model also has some criticisms and one of them is known as Lucas Critique. In econometric model it is assumed that the private agent behaviour will be the same for all set of policy conditions (Lucas, 1976). The 'Lucas critique' is a criticism of econometric policy evaluation procedures that fail to recognize that optimal decision rules of economic agents vary systematically with changes in policy.

Failure of CGE Frameworks to Accommodate Role of "Ecosystem Services" in Climate Modelling

In the new emerging paradigm of ecological economics, there are attempts to better understand the dynamic interplay of nature, economy, and society. MA (2005) opened human eyes to understand the critical roles of ecosystem services in human existence, and classified the various services into four categories, namely, provisioning (namely, food, raw materials, genetic resources, water, etc.), regulating (namely, carbon sequestration, climate regulation, waste decomposition, etc), cultural (namely, tourism, scientific discovery, etc), and supporting (nutrient recycling, soil formation, etc).

As such, the new emerging paradigm views human civilisation as an integral component of the broader social-ecological system. The human system essentially extracts from the ecosystem, and often to the extent of compromising with the integrity of ecosystem structure and functions. This affects the ecosystem service provisions, thereby affecting the human system, as humankind benefits from the services that the ecosystems naturally provide them. Social system creates economic forces and enforces economic actions due to the mismatch between needs and availability. "Actions" on the ecosystem are fundamentally meant to satisfy economic needs: Hence "Actions" are "Economic Activities". "Economic Activities" emerge as interventions on the ecosystem structure and functions, and provide ecosystem services to human society. This scheme is given in Figure 1.

CGE models or any other reductionist economics essentially treat climate change impacts as an external stimulus impeding on the human society. In many cases, they are considered as "externality" emerging from human activities. With the human civilisation steamrolled into a firm, such reductionist frameworks often talk of internalising the "externalities".

More importantly, with I-O matrix (Input Output) and Social Accounting Matrix based on I_O matrix failing to capture the critical ecosystem services, it is practically impossible to obtain the impacts of climate change or extreme events on ecosystem services, and eventually how these pervade on the society.

However, to an extent possible, such a sensitivity analysis might be possible through econometric frameworks, with consideration of time-series GIS or satellite data on land-use, land-cover and integrated spatial and econometric modelling. The challenge here will be more with model specification, rather than estimation.

Figure 1. Social-ecological system

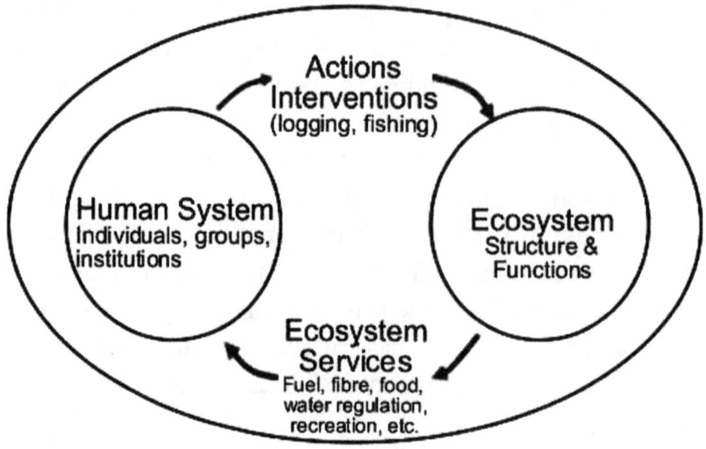

CONCLUDING REMARKS

For many, CGE or CGE-based frameworks are end in itself. This is a very wrong position for research, however normative this statement seems. As such, whether it is the econometric or the CGE frameworks, essentially these are methods to achieve certain goals: to answer certain research concerns. And research on climate change impacts needs to be policy relevant, and needs to inform as much as possible. The limitations of CGE have been described here in this paper.

Given these limitations, at a theoretical level, the concern still remains on why CGE modelling is still ubiquitously accepted, despite its very foundation in general equilibrium theory being systematically challenged over the past several decades.

It has some "away from reality" assumptions like

1. Technique of representative agents—all households, firms, agriculture, sectors, etc steamrolled into an optimising firm;
2. Their behavioural assumption as always optimising, whether it is utility or social surplus, and which, time and again, has been falsified;
3. The "well-behaved" nature of production and utility functions, i.e., satisfying the convexity properties, despite the widespread acknowledgement of non-convexities (that yield multiple equilibria);
4. The rigidity in the frameworks.

The contention of all those who feel that CGE is omnipotent fails in light of the Debreu-Sonnenschein-Mantel theorem that bears ample testimony that even complete knowledge of all supply and demand relationships in an economy is not sufficient to predict on the equilibrium conditions.

Very interestingly, so far, there hardly exists any rigorous ex post evaluation of CGE models in practice—one that can compare the predicted to actual outcomes. Therefore, there seems to be a strange silence with validity of the CGE, and practically no argument is being forwarded so far on why their predictions are any better than those derived from macro or sector-specific models, or even a random walk econometric framework.

However, when it comes to climate impact frameworks, somehow CGE frameworks are being adopted blindly, and mostly by the reductionist thought processes. There is hardly any argument that often CGE (or its variant GTAP, etc) school driver researchers listen to on inapplicability of such models in climate change research, more so when one is concerned with a broader framework of the social-ecological systems. A better understanding of ground reality is needed, and needs to be accommodated in the modelling framework to fit into the wider domain of sustainability science.

ACKNOWLEDGMENT

The authors acknowledge support of DECCMA project, and this publication is an outcome of that. Views are personal.

REFERENCES

Bosello, F., Carraro, C., & De Cian, E. (2010b). Climate Policy and the Optimal Balance between Mitigation, Adaptation and Unavoided Damage. *Climate Change Economics*, *1*(02), 71–92. doi:10.1142/S201000781000008X

Bosello, F., De Cian, E., & Roson, R. (2007a). *Climate Change, Energy Demand and Market Power in a General Equilibrium Model of the World Economy*. FEEM working paper No. 71.2007.

Bosello, F., Eboli, F., & Pierfederici, R. (2012a). *Assessing the Economic Impacts of Climate Change. An Updated CGE Point of View*. FEEM working paper, 2.2012.

Bosello F., Eboli F. & Pierfederici R. (2012b). *Assessing the Economic Impacts of Climate Change, Review of Environment, Energy and Economics*. 10.7711/feemre3.2012.02.002

Bosello, F., Nicholls, R. J., Richards, J., Roson, R., & Tol, R. S. J. (2012c). Economic impacts of climate change in Europe: Sea-level rise. *Climatic Change*, *112*(1), 63–81. doi:10.1007/s10584-011-0340-1

Bosello, F., Roson, R., & Tol, R. S. J. (2006). Economy wide estimates of the implications of climate change: Human health. *Ecological Economics*, *58*(3), 579–591. doi:10.1016/j.ecolecon.2005.07.032

Bosello, F., Roson, R., & Tol, R. S. J. (2007b). Economy wide estimates of the implications of climate change: Sea-level rise. *Environmental and Resource Economics*, *37*(3), 549–571. doi:10.1007/s10640-006-9048-5

Bussolo, M., & O'Connor, D. (2001). *Clearing the air in India: The economics of climate policy with ancillary benefits*. OECD Development Centre Working Paper No. 182. OECD.

Ciscar, J. C., Iglesias, A., Feyen, L., Szabó, L., Van Regemorter, D., Amelunge, B., & Soria, A. et al. (2011). Physical and economic consequences of climate change in Europe. *Proceedings of the National Academy of Sciences of the United States of America*, *108*(7), 2678–2683. doi:10.1073/pnas.1011612108 PMID:21282624

Deke, O., Hooss, K. G., Kasten, C., Klepper, G., & Springer, K. (2001). *Economic Impact of Climate Change: Simulations with a Regionalized Climate-Economy Model.* Kiel Institute of World Economics, Working Paper No. 1065.

Eboli, F., Parrado, R., & Roson, R. (2010). Climate-change feedback on economic growth: Explorations with a dynamic general equilibrium model. *Environment and Development Economics*, *15*(05), 515–533. doi:10.1017/S1355770X10000252

Fisher-Vanden, K. A., Shukla, P. R., Edmonds, J. A., Kim, S. H., & Pitcher, H. M. (1997). Carbon taxes and India. *Energy Economics*, *19*(3), 289–325. doi:10.1016/S0140-9883(96)01020-1

Fisher-Vanden, K. A., Wing, I., Lanzi, S., & Popp, D. (2013). Modeling climate change feedbacks and adaptation responses: recent approaches and shortcomings. *Climate Change, 117*, 481–495.

Hamby, D. M. (1994). A review of techniques for parameter sensitivity analysis ofenvironmental models. *EnvironmentalMonitoring andAssessment*, *32*(2), 135–154. doi:10.1007/BF00547132 PMID:24214086

Hatirli, S. A., Ozkan, B., & Fert, C. (2006). Energy inputs and crop yield relationship in greenhouse tomato production. *Renewable Energy*, *31*(4), 427–438. doi:10.1016/j.renene.2005.04.007

Kelly, D. L., & Kolstad, C. (1999). Integrated Assessment Models For Climate Change Control. In International Yearbook of Environmental and Resource Economics 1999/2000: A Survey of Current Issues. Cheltenham, UK: Edward Elgar.

Miller, M. H., & Spencer, J. E. (1977). The Static Economic Effects of the UK Joining the EEC: A General Equilibrium Approach. *The Review of Economic Studies*, *38*, 175–208.

Mobtaker, H. G., Akram, A., & Keyhani, A. (2010). Economic modeling and sensitivity analysis of the costs of inputs for alfalfa production In Iran: A case study from Hamedan province. *Ozean Journal of Applied Sciences*, *3*, 313319.

Murthy, M. N., Panda, M., & Parikh, K. (2007). CO2 emission reduction strategies and economic development in India. *Margin: The Journal of Applied Economic Research*, *1*(1), 85–119.

Nordhaus, W. D. (1991). To Slow or Not to Slow: The Economics of the Greenhouse Effect. *The Economic Journal*, *101*(407), 920–937. doi:10.2307/2233864

Nordhaus, W. D., & Zili, Y. (1996, February). A Regional Dynamic General-Equilibrium Model of Alternative Climate-Change Strategies. *American Economic Review*.

Ojha, V. P. (2009). Carbon emissions reduction strategies and poverty alleviation in India. *Environment and Development Economics*, *14*(3), 323–348. doi:10.1017/S1355770X0800497X

Palanisami, K., Paramasivam, P., Ranganathan, C. R., Aggarwal, P. K., & Senthilnathan, S. (2009). *Quantifying vulnerability and impact of climate change on production of major crops in Tamil Nadu, India.* In M. Taniguchi, W. C. Burnett, Y. Fukushima, M. Haigh, & Yu. Umezawa (Eds.), *Headwaters to the Ocean – Hydrological Change and Watershed Management* (pp. 509–551). London: Taylor and Francis Group.

Pindyck, R. S. (2013). Climate Change Policy: What Do the Models Tell Us? *Journal of Economic Literature*, *51*(3), 860–872. doi:10.1257/jel.51.3.860

Pollitt, H., Summerton, P., & Billington, S. (2014). *The economics of climate change policy in the UK: An analysis of the impact of low-carbon policies on households, businesses and the macro-economy*. Cambridge, UK: Cambridge Econometrics, Covent Garden.

Rafiee, S., Mousavi Avval, S. H., & Mohammadi, A. (2010). Modeling and sensitivity analysis of energy inputs for apple production in Iran. *Energy*, *35*(8), 3301–3306. doi:10.1016/j.energy.2010.04.015

Roson, R., & Van der Mensbrugghe, D. (2012). Climate change and economic growth: Impacts and interactions. *International Journal of Sustainable Economy*, *4*(3), 270–285. doi:10.1504/IJSE.2012.047933

Saravanakumar, V. (2015). *Impact of Climate Change on Yield of Major Food Crops in Tamil Nadu, India*. SANDEE Working Paper No. 91–15. South Asian Network for Development and Environmental Economics.

Shoven, J. B. (1976). The Incidence and Efficiency Effects of Taxes on Income from Capital. *Journal of Political Economy*, *84*(6), 1261–1283. doi:10.1086/260511

Shoven, J. B., & Whalley, J. (1972). A General Equilibrium Calculation of the Effects of Differential Taxation of Income from Capital in the US. *Journal of Public Economics*, *1*(3-4), 281–321. doi:10.1016/0047-2727(72)90009-6

Sue Wing, I., & Fisher-Vanden, K. (2012). Confronting the Challenge of Integrated Assessment of Climate Adaptation: A Conceptual Framework. *Climatic Change*, *117*(3), 497–514. doi:10.1007/s10584-012-0651-x

Sue Wing, I., & Lanzi, E. (2014). *Integrated Assessment of Climate Change Impacts: Conceptual Frameworks, Modelling Approaches and Research Needs*. OECD Environment Working Papers No. 66. OECD Publishing.

Weitzel, M., Ghosh, J., Peterson, S., & Pradhan, B. K. (2012). *Effects of international climate policy for India: Evidence from a national and global CGE model*. Kiel Working Paper No. 1810 November. Kiel Institute for the World Economy.

Whalley, J. (1975). A General Equilibrium Assessment of the 1973 UK Tax Reforms. *De Economía*, *42*, 139–161.

Whalley, J. (1977). The United Kingdom Tax System, 1968-1970: Some Fixed Point Indications of its Economic Impact. *Econometrica*, *45*(8), 1837–1858. doi:10.2307/1914113

Chapter 2
A CGE Analysis of the Effects of Global Climate Change Mitigation Policies on India

Basanta K. Pradhan
Institute of Economic Growth, India

Joydeep Ghosh
Independent Consultant, India

ABSTRACT

This paper compares the effects of a global carbon tax and a global emissions trading regime on India using a dynamic CGE framework. The sensitivity of the results to the value of a crucial elasticity parameter is also analysed. The results suggest that the choice of the mitigation policy is relatively unimportant from an efficiency perspective. However, the choice of the mitigation policy and the value of the substitution elasticity between value added and energy were found to be important determinants of welfare effects. Global climate change mitigation policies have the potential for promoting low carbon and inclusive growth in India.

1. INTRODUCTION

The Copenhagen Accord (2009) recognises the scientific view that the increase in average global temperature should be below 2°C over the long term in order to lower the risks of catastrophic damages to the environment and the global economy. In order to restrict global warming to 2°C, major greenhouse gas (GHG) emission reductions are needed by 2050. While most of the accumulated anthropogenic atmospheric carbon dioxide can be attributed to industrialized countries, the greater share of future emissions will come from the developing world, and India and China will contribute to a substantial part of this. Thus, participation of India and China is essential for achieving global climate policy goals. In this paper we construct scenarios using a dynamic computable general equilibrium (CGE) model to analyse the economic and environmental impacts of global climate change mitigation policies (consistent with

DOI: 10.4018/978-1-5225-0094-0.ch002

the 2°C objective) on India. The motivation behind the study was to analyse different frameworks for international cooperation for India in order to facilitate its engagement in a post-2012 global climate change abatement regime.

Policy makers in India have advocated the need to achieve high economic growth rates in order to eradicate poverty and to achieve human development goals (Planning Commission, 2011). However, the energy requirements for achieving high economic growth rates in a sustainable manner present a major policy challenge. At the same time there is increased pressure on developing countries like India to participate, through voluntary and nationally appropriate policies, in global climate change mitigation efforts (Planning Commission, 2011). India's position (Ministry of External Affairs, Government of India 2009) on climate change is based on the principle of common but differentiated responsibilities and respective capabilities and on the concept of equity (every citizen of the globe has equal entitlement to the planetary atmospheric resource). Further, India gives the highest priority to social and economic development even in the context of climate change, and has advocated the convergence of per capita emissions in the future. India believes that efforts to use cleaner technologies in developing economies should be facilitated by developed countries through the transfer of technology and financial resources to developing countries. Despite the daunting development challenges the country faces, India has established an elaborate framework to address climate related issues. Further, the country has imposed regulatory measures (such as tax on coal production) and has set a voluntary target (Copenhagen Pledge) to reduce the emission intensity of GDP by 20–25 per cent of the 2005 level by 2020.

Although India's per capita emissions are low relative to world standards, total emissions have been increasing rapidly in recent years due to high growth rates, and India is now the fourth largest CO2 emitter in the world (PBL, 2012). The average global per capita GHG emissions in 2005 was 4.22 tons of CO2-equivalent, while the corresponding figure for India was about 1.2 tons. A 2009 Ministry of Environment and Forests (MoEF) report has stated that per capita GHG emissions of India will be 2.1 tons of CO2-equivalent in 2020, and 3.5 tons of CO2-equivalent in 2030 (average of five studies). According to a CGE study by the National Council of Applied Economic Research (NCAER), that is part of the 2009 MoEF report, per capita emissions would be 2.77 tons of CO2-equivalent in 2030. The report points out that per capita emissions of India are likely to remain lower than that of developed countries despite relatively high rates of economic growth.

Environmental policies have two components:

1. Identification of an overall goal (such as emission levels); and
2. Some means to achieve that goal.

There are two main methods for achieving environmental goals (Stavins, 2000): through

1. Market-based mechanisms (such as carbon tax and emissions trading); and
2. Command-and-control policies (such as explicit directives regarding pollution levels or methods of production).

Market-based mechanisms have certain advantages over traditional command-and-control approaches for achieving environmental objectives - they can help to achieve environmental objectives at the lowest possible overall cost to society by providing incentives for the greatest reductions in pollution by those firms that can achieve these reductions most cheaply. Rather than equalising pollution levels among firms, market-based instruments equalise the incremental amount that firms spend to reduce pollution and these instruments could also provide incentives for companies to adopt cheaper and better pollution control technologies.

Market-based instruments like carbon tax and emissions trading have often been used to achieve emissions targets. Numerous studies have been conducted to analyse the impact of market-based instruments on the environment as well as the economy in general. Garbaccio et al. (1998) have examined the use of carbon taxes to reduce CO2 emissions in China. The authors found that after initial declines, GDP and consumption exceeded baseline levels and that revenue-neutral carbon taxes serve to transfer income from consumers to producers and then into increased investment. The study shows that a 'double dividend' (lower CO2 emissions and a long-run increase in GDP and consumption) could be achieved under certain assumptions (such as inelastic labour supply and revenue-neutral taxes). Parry et al. (1999) conclude that policies like carbon quotas and grandfathered carbon permits are welfare-reducing, regardless of the carbon abatement level. In contrast, carbon taxes policies can be welfare improving, because the marginal social costs of emissions reduction start at zero. Further, studies (Fisher-Vanden et al. (1997), Bernard and Vielle (2003)) have shown that carbon reduction through emissions trading is less costly (relative to carbon taxes) for the economy. Other studies have shown that by recycling carbon tax revenues to the poor (Ojha (2008)) or by subsidising production (Liang et al. (2007)) the negative effects of carbon tax policies could be alleviated. The importance of model parameters in CGE analyses of climate policies has been reported by Welsch (2007), according to whom Armington trade elasticities are a key driver in influencing the impacts of climate protection policies. Similarly, Jacoby et al. (2006) conclude that the substitution elasticity for energy and other value-added is the most important in terms of affecting the cost of a Kyoto emissions policy.

There are relatively few studies that analyse the effects of climate change mitigation policies on India in a CGE framework. Some of these studies are based on global models (see van Ruijven et al., 2012), while the other studies use national models (Fisher-Vanden et al, 1997; Ojha, 2008). Our study differs

Figure 1. CO_2 emissions for the different scenarios

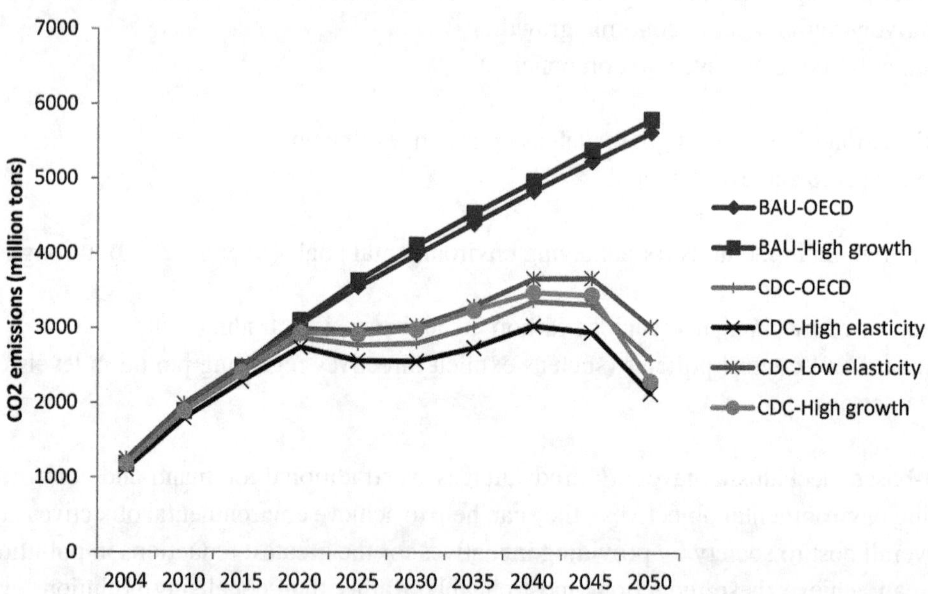

from previous studies mainly on account of the use of parameters (as discussed in greater detail later in the text) from global models that take into account the 2°C global warming target as enshrined in the Copenhagen Accord. Two types of mitigation policies are analysed in this paper – a global carbon tax and a global emissions trading regime. Specifically, we compare the economy wide effects of the two types of policies under different assumptions about economic growth rates and carbon prices. Another aspect that we focus on in this paper is the sensitivity of the results to the value of a crucial elasticity parameter. By doing this study we want to see whether global climate policies can be linked to one of India's main policy objectives, that is, promotion of low carbon and inclusive growth.

The rest of the paper proceeds as follows. Section 2 discusses the model and data. Section 3 describes the different scenarios. Section 4 is devoted to results and discussion. Section 5 concludes by mentioning the policy implications of the study.

2. MODEL AND DATA

Our model (Pradhan and Ghosh, 2012) is a single country, multi-sectoral, neoclassical-type, price-driven, recursive dynamic CGE model with a focus on the energy sector. The static part of the model is based on Lofgren et al. (2002). The structure of the energy sector is similar to models like DART (Klepper et al. 2003), EPPA (Paltsev et al. 2005) and EMPAX-CGE (RTI International 2008). Our model consists of 18 sectors - Agriculture, Coal, Oil, Gas, Manufacturing I (food and beverages, textiles, wood, minerals), Manufacturing II (paper, fertilizers, cement, iron and steel, aluminium, chemicals), Manufacturing III (plant and machinery), Oil Products, six Electricity sectors (Thermal, Carbon Capture and Storage (CCS), Hydro, Nuclear, Biomass and Other Renewables), Construction, Road Transport, Rail/Sea/Air transport, and Other Services. There are two factors of production, capital and labour.

Producers are assumed to maximize profits and to operate in perfectly competitive markets. The production structure of the fossil fuel sectors (Coal, Oil, and Gas) and the non-fossil fuel sectors (sectors other than Coal, Oil, and Gas) are modelled differently. The production structure of the fossil fuel sectors takes into account the limited availability of fossil fuels in the economy while in case of the non fossil fuel sectors this feature is not relevant and therefore not modelled. In case of the fossil fuel sectors (Figure 2), the top nest is a CES aggregation of capital-labour-aggregate intermediate input composite and the fixed fossil fuel resource (part of capital of the sector). The capital-labour-aggregate intermediate composite is a Leontief function of the capital-labour composite and aggregate intermediate input. The capital-labour composite (aggregate value added) is in turn a CES aggregation of capital and labour.

In case of the non-fossil fuel sectors (Figure 3), the top nest is a Leontief function of aggregate intermediate input and energy-capital-labour composite. The energy-capital-labour composite is a CES function of the energy composite and the capital-labour composite. The energy composite is a CES function of the non-electric composite and the electric composite. The non-electric composite is a CES aggregation of Coal, Oil, Gas, and Oil Products. The electric composite is a CES aggregation of renewable electricity composite and non-renewable electricity composite. The renewable electricity composite is a CES aggregation of Hydro, Nuclear, Biomass and Other Renewables electricity, while the non-renewable electricity composite is a CES aggregation of Thermal and CCS electricity. The capital-labour composite is a CES function of capital and labour.

Figure 2. Production structure of fossil fuel sectors (coal, oil, and gas)

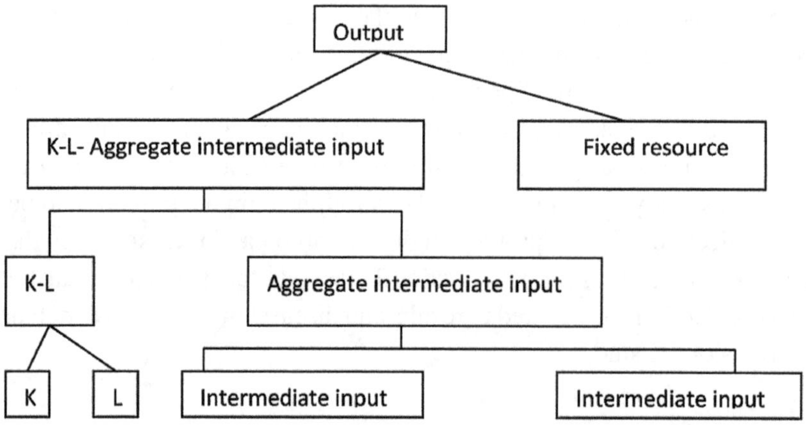

The aggregate intermediate input is a Leontief function of intermediate inputs. The main features of the production structure of the non-fossil fuel sectors are the substitution possibilities between energy, capital, and labour on one hand and the substitution possibilities between renewable and non-renewable sources of electricity on the other.

Figure 3. Production structure of non-fossil fuel sectors

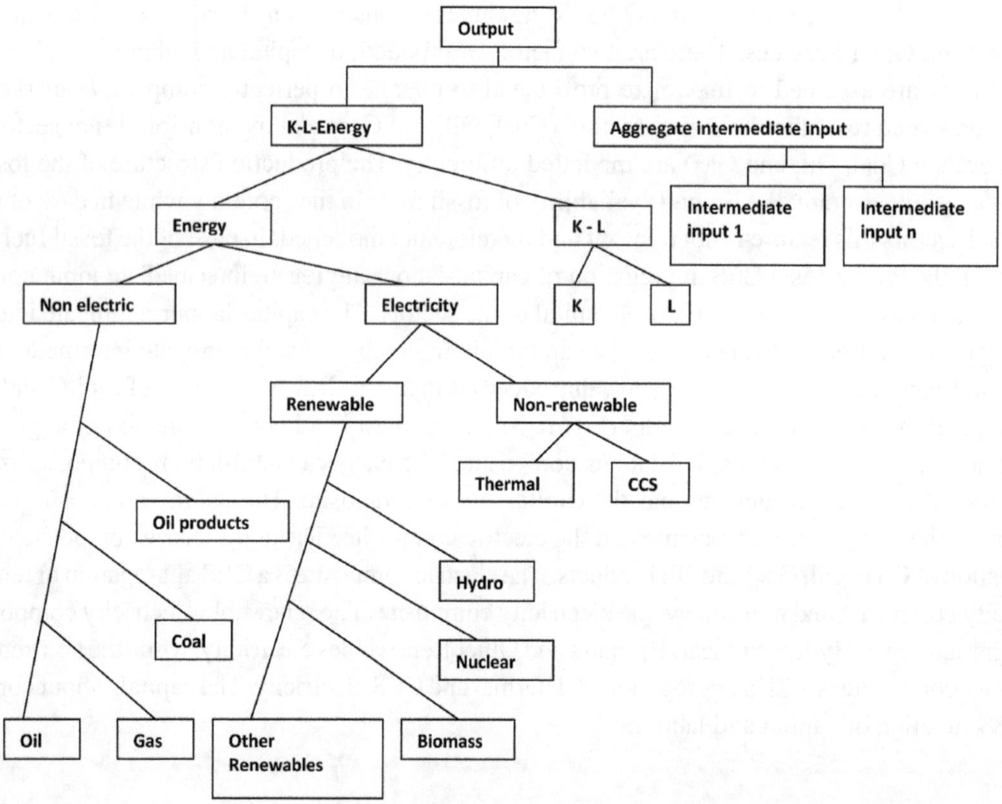

Households maximize utility subject to income and prices, and the household demand for commodities is modelled through the linear expenditure system (LES). Household income comprises of income derived from labour and capital and transfers from the government and the rest of the world. Households also save part of their income and pay taxes to the government. Further, households are classified into nine categories: five are rural (Self Employed in Non Agriculture, Agricultural Labour, Other Labour, Self Employed in Agriculture and Other Households) and four are urban (Self Employed, Regular Salaried, Casual Labour, and Other Households).

Government expenditure is on the consumption of goods and services, transfers to households and enterprises, and subsidies. Government income is from taxes (direct and indirect), capital, public and private enterprises, and rest of the world. Indirect taxes include excise duty (production tax), import and export tariffs, sales, stamp, service, and other indirect taxes. Government savings which is the difference between government expenditure and income is determined residually.

Imperfect substitution between domestic goods and foreign goods is allowed for in CGE models. In other words, producers/consumers are free to sell or buy the same goods from the domestic or foreign market based on relative prices. The Armington function is used to capture these substitution possibilities between domestic and imported goods. The import demand function, derived from the Armington function, specifies the value of imports based on the ratio of domestic and import prices. The CET function is used to capture substitution possibilities between domestic and foreign sales. The export supply function, derived from the CET function, specifies the value of exports based on the ratio of domestic prices to export prices. The elasticity of substitution determines the relative ease of substitution between domestic and foreign goods in response to changes in relative prices. World prices are assumed to be fixed in the model.

The model is Walrasian in character. Markets for all commodities and factors clear through adjustment in prices. The consumer price index (CPI) is chosen as the numeraire. Macro closures play an important role in CGE models. The closures are specified taking into account the macro economic reality of the country being modelled. Our model follows an investment-driven closure, that is, aggregate investment is fixed in the Keynesian tradition. The saving-investment balance is maintained through adjustments in aggregate savings (sum of household, government, corporate and foreign savings). The model assumes foreign savings to be fixed and the real exchange rate to be flexible. Government consumption expenditure is fixed within a period, and government savings is residually determined. Both direct and indirect tax rates are fixed. The household savings rate is also fixed. Finally, full employment along with intersectoral mobility is assumed in case of both the factors of production.

The main source of data for the analysis is a social accounting matrix (SAM) for 2003–04 developed by Ojha et al. (2009). This SAM, in turn, is based on the SAM constructed by Pradhan et al. (2006). The main difference between the two SAMs is the decomposition of the electricity sector into three separate sub-sectors - hydro, nuclear, and non-hydro - in the SAM developed by Ojha et al (2009). The non-hydro energy sector includes thermal, wind and solar electricity. However, given India's energy mix, thermal electricity is the main constituent of this group. Two modifications were made in the non-hydro sector for the purpose of this study. The first modification pertains to the disaggregation of non-hydro into Thermal and Other Renewables electricity. The second modification pertains to the creation of a sector (from Thermal) that uses CCS technology (coal) to produce electricity. The CCS electricity sector is assumed to be similar to the Thermal electricity sector but less efficient. It produces electricity using clean coal (no emissions), although at a much higher cost.

3. SCENARIOS

Initially two baseline scenarios are created keeping in view two different GDP growth paths of the economy. The first baseline scenario considers the growth projection of the Organisation for Economic Cooperation and Development (OECD) for India until 2050 (OECD 2010), while the second baseline assumes a higher growth rate relative to the OECD projection. The growth rate during 2004–10 roughly corresponds to the actual growth rate achieved during this period. The growth rate for the period 2010-15 (7.6 per cent) is based on current growth rates and the target for the Twelfth Plan (8.2 per cent). The annual growth rate during 2005–30 is 7.7 per cent in the OECD scenario and 8.3 per cent in the high growth scenario. For the entire time horizon (2005–50), the growth rate is 6.7 per cent in the OECD scenario and 7.6 per cent in the high growth scenario. The baseline (business-as-usual or BAU) scenarios are created by assuming exogenously determined growth in total factor productivity (TFP), labour force, government consumption expenditure and aggregate investment (key growth rates are presented in Appendix). Capital formation in a given period takes place by adding aggregate investment in the previous period to capital. The other assumptions are related to energy efficiency, technological developments in renewables and international prices of fossil fuels. An energy efficiency growth rate is assumed to capture future gains in energy efficiency. Future technological developments in the renewable electricity sectors are modelled by assuming efficiency growth in these sectors. Changes in the international prices (exogenous) of fossil fuels are modelled keeping in view future price projections of these commodities.

The policy regimes analyzed in the paper are compatible with meeting the 2°C target with a probability of about 50 per cent. The policy regimes are implemented through two instruments - global carbon tax (CT) and global emissions trading where the distribution of allowances to countries is based on the Common but Differentiated Convergence (CDC) approach (Hohne et al. 2006). A discussion on the policy regimes is presented in Johansson et al (2012). Global carbon tax implies the global equalization of marginal abatement costs, while the CDC approach aims at equal per capita allowances in the long run, but considers historical responsibility, in contrast to the Contraction-and-Convergence approach. The CDC approach assumes that per capita emissions of all countries converge, but developing countries start their convergence trajectories only after reaching a certain threshold. The policy regimes are implemented under both the growth trajectories – OECD growth and high growth. In addition to these four policy scenarios (CT and CDC under the two growth trajectories), we do a sensitivity analysis by changing the value of the elasticity of substitution between value added and energy in the CDC regime.

The data required to implement the policy regimes were obtained from a global climate CGE model called DART (Klepper et al. 2003; see Appendix for tax rates (carbon prices) and emission allowances by year, where only selected data are presented). The global CO_2 emissions pathways of DART follow the global CO_2 emissions pathways of the FAIR model (PBL Netherlands Environmental Assessment Agency 2005). The FAIR model was used to analyze regional emission reductions and abatement costs for different effort-sharing approaches and to construct long-term global greenhouse gas emission pathways consistent with the 2˚C target. In the CDC regime international capital flows take place because of trade in emission allowances and such flows are modeled as foreign savings (investments) in our model. The value of such flows is calculated as the difference between the allowance and emissions (under carbon tax), multiplied by the corresponding carbon tax for that year. It is to be noted that we do not model carbon trading explicitly in our model. We use carbon prices and allowances obtained from a global model (DART) to calculate the capital flows into India. In other words, there is no equalisation

Table 1. GDP growth in the different scenarios (percent)

Period	BAU-OECD	CDC-OECD	CT-OECD	CDC-High Elasticity	CDC-Low Elasticity	BAU-High Growth	CDC-High Growth	CT-High Growth
2004–10	8.5	8.5	8.5	8.4	8.6	8.5	8.5	8.5
2010–15	7.7	7.7	7.7	7.7	7.7	7.7	7.7	7.7
2015–20	8.3	8.2	8.2	8.2	8.2	9.1	9.1	9.1
2020–25	7.4	7.3	7.3	7.3	7.3	8.5	8.3	8.3
2025–30	6.9	6.7	6.7	6.7	6.7	8.0	7.9	7.8
2030–35	6.5	6.4	6.4	6.5	6.4	7.3	7.2	7.2
2035–40	6.4	6.3	6.3	6.3	6.2	7.0	6.9	6.9
2040–45	4.7	4.4	4.4	4.4	4.3	6.4	6.1	6.1
2045–50	4.3	3.0	3.0	3.0	3.1	6.0	4.1	4.1

of marginal abatement costs in our model. Thus, the difference between CT and CDC in terms of the model is that in the CT regime there is only a carbon tax, while in the CDC regime there is a carbon tax as well as capital flows. The carbon prices obtained from the global model for the two regimes (CT and CDC) differ slightly, however for the purpose of comparison we have assumed the carbon prices to be the same in this paper. The carbon prices for the different growth paths (OECD and high growth) differ. The carbon tax is applied on the consumption of Coal, Gas, and Oil Products because the consumption of these commodities is directly linked to CO_2 emissions. The policy regimes are imposed from 2013 and the time horizon is until 2050.

4. RESULTS AND DISCUSSION

In this section we present the results of the simulation runs pertaining to the different climate policy regimes. As mentioned before we run six policy scenarios – CDC under OECD and high growth, CT under OECD and high growth, and CDC under OECD using higher and lower values of the elasticity of substitution between value added and energy – and we compare each of them to the respective baselines, and also to each other. We focus our discussion mainly on the impacts on growth, welfare and CO_2 mitigation.

GDP growth rate slows down under all the climate policy scenarios (Table 1) relative to the baseline. However, the slowdown is not more than 0.4 percentage points relative to the baseline until the mid-2040s. The slowdown in GDP growth is relatively more in the later time periods (after 2045) due to relatively higher carbon prices (tax rates) in those time periods. Carbon prices rise over time, and there is significant rise in the later time periods. The economic intuition behind the rapid increase in carbon prices after 2040 is that there are many opportunities for abatement in the beginning while it becomes increasingly difficult over time to find additional abatement opportunities. Technically this stems from the CES production functions which make substitution away from a certain input increasingly expensive. As mentioned earlier, the carbon prices were obtained from a global climate model, and the carbon prices are the same in both the CT and CDC scenarios. The differences between the CT and CDC scenarios arise only due to capital flows that take place as a result of trade in emission allowances. There is not much difference in the growth rates between CDC and CT or between CDC high and CDC low elasticity scenarios, implying that the choice of the mitigation policy is not very important from an efficiency perspective. Another implication is that mitigation policies may not have a big adverse impact on overall growth unless carbon prices are very high. This result is important given India's need to generate resources to meet its development objectives.

All the climate policy regimes are characterized by high energy prices (Coal, Gas and Oil Products), higher prices in energy intensive manufacturing (Manufacturing II and III) and other energy intensive sectors like Thermal Electricity and Road Transport (see Appendix for effects on output, consumer prices, wage rates, exports and imports).The upward pressure on prices leads to lower demand in the economy and thus lower factor returns. Factor prices fall in all the climate policy scenarios. Capital is more adversely affected than labour until the 2030s, however, towards the end of the time horizon the reverse holds true. In the CDC scenario labour is hurt less and capital is hurt more relative to the CT scenario. One reason for this observation is that the damages, in terms of output, to capital intensive manufacturing is more in the CDC scenario, while the damages to labour intensive agriculture is less relative to the CT scenario. Terms of trade effects (currency appreciation) in the CDC scenario are responsible for the damage to manufacturing. The renewable energy sectors are also less adversely affected in the CDC scenario relative to the CT scenario. In other words the inflow of capital in the CDC regime increases the demand for renewable energy instead of fossil fuel based energy.

In general factor prices are relatively less adversely affected under the high elasticity scenario than under the low elasticity scenario. This is because both labour and capital intensive sectors (like agriculture, manufacturing, construction and services) are less adversely affected in the high elasticity scenario, while the fossil fuel sectors suffer higher damages. A higher value of substitution elasticity leads to higher levels of substitution away from energy to non energy inputs (labour and capital) and thus reduces abatement costs. Further, labour is less adversely affected than capital in the high elasticity scenario while it is more adversely affected than capital in the low elasticity scenario. This is because labour intensive sectors like agriculture and services are more adversely affected in the low elasticity scenario relative to the high elasticity scenario. Thus, the costs of climate policies can be substantially reduced if such policies are accompanied by growth in labour intensive sectors like agriculture and services. Government initiatives can play a pro-active role in fostering growth in labour intensive sectors and in reducing the costs of climate policies.

The exports of fossil fuels (including Oil Products) increase under the climate policy scenarios. The imposition of climate policy regimes leads to higher domestic fuel prices (except Oil because carbon taxes are not applied on this sector) thereby reducing their demand in the domestic market. Fossil fuel producers thus sell their products in the foreign market instead of the domestic market to reduce losses. In our model international prices are fixed, and therefore we do not consider the effects of changes in foreign demand (due to global climate policy) on the economy. In the presence of a global climate policy regime there could be lower demand for fossil fuels in the international market and this could affect domestic fossil fuel producers. In case of the manufacturing sectors, however, there is a decline in exports. This is due to increase in the prices of manufactured goods, as a result of high energy prices, which make them uncompetitive in the foreign market. As far as imports are concerned we find that imports of fossil fuels (including Oil Products) decline, while imports of energy intensive manufactured goods increase. Fossil fuel imports decline due to lower demand in the domestic market, while imports of energy intensive manufactured goods increase due to relatively higher prices of those goods in the domestic market as a result of climate policy. The implication is that policies that facilitate the import of energy intensive manufactured goods could be another option to reduce the costs of climate policies.

Table 2. Welfare in the different scenarios (equivalent variation percent)

	CDC-OECD	CT-OECD	CDC-High Elasticity	CDC-Low Elasticity	CDC-High Growth	CT- High Growth
2015	-0.06	-0.06	1.52	-1.65	-0.04	-0.05
2020	-0.12	-0.14	1.52	-1.78	-0.06	-0.13
2025	-0.16	-0.89	1.59	-1.94	0.16	-0.87
2030	0.13	-1.66	2.06	-1.85	0.69	-1.76
2035	-0.73	-2.02	1.42	-2.96	-0.43	-2.26
2040	-1.62	-2.13	0.76	-4.12	-1.83	-2.89
2045	-2.76	-3.06	-0.21	-5.47	-3.43	-4.06
2050	-5.30	-6.87	-2.36	-8.44	-7.14	-9.87

There is welfare loss under the climate policy regimes (Table 2). However, the welfare loss is more under the CT regime than in the CDC regime, implying that capital flows as a result of trade in emission allowances help to reduce the welfare loss. Capital flows in the CDC regime lead to a stronger currency and thereby reduce the cost of imports. There is increase in imports in the CDC regime relative to the CT regime, and the rise in imports puts a downward pressure on consumer prices leading to relatively lower welfare losses. Welfare losses are higher in the high growth scenario due to higher carbon prices relative to the OECD scenario.

Welfare losses are particularly sensitive to the value of the substitution elasticity between value added and energy. A higher value of the substitution elasticity leads to welfare gains in most periods and lower welfare losses in other periods relative to scenarios with lower elasticity values. The adverse effects on factor prices are much lower in the higher elasticity scenario, and in addition labour is hurt less than capital in this scenario. The combination of relatively lower damages to factor prices in comparison to the other scenarios, and to the price of labour relative to capital make the high elasticity scenario the best in terms of welfare implications. This scenario suggests that adverse effects on factor prices and to the price of labour in particular are mainly responsible for the welfare losses. The implication is that the choice of the mitigation policy and the value of the elasticity parameter play an important role in determining the welfare impacts.

Carbon dioxide emissions increase from about 1200 million tons (1.0 ton per capita) in 2004 to about 5600 million tons (3.5 tons per capita) in 2050 in the BAU-OECD scenario and to about 5800 million tons (3.6 tons per capita) in the BAU-High growth scenario (Figure 1). A CGE study (Ministry of Environment and Forests, 2009) by the National Council of Applied Economic Research (NCAER) which has made projections of India's GHG emissions (assuming 8 percent annual growth) until 2031 has reported that per capita CO_2 emissions of India would be 2.77 tons in 2031. In comparison, our model predicts values of 2.7 and 2.8 tons in the OECD and high growth scenarios, respectively, in 2030. The emissions path of our model is thus very similar to the NCAER projections until 2030. Further, our analysis suggests that a higher growth trajectory may not translate into significant increase in CO_2 emissions for India. This result is driven by lower energy intensity of GDP and higher share of renewables in the energy mix in the high growth scenario (see Figure 1).

The imposition of the climate policy regimes significantly brings down CO_2 emissions. However, there is an upward trend in emissions until the 2040s, and thereafter a downward trend. The choice of mitigation policy (CT vs. CDC) does not have an effect on the level of CO_2 emissions as the carbon prices are assumed to be the same in the two regimes. In reality carbon prices in the CDC regime are likely to be volatile and this could affect emission levels and capital flows. Under the climate policy regimes emissions are higher in the high growth scenario relative to the OECD scenario in most years. In the last few years of the projection period emissions are lower in the high growth scenario due to significantly higher carbon prices in the high growth scenario. The value of the substitution elasticity plays an important role in determining the level of emissions. A higher value of the elasticity leads to relatively less energy intensive production in the economy and lower CO_2 emissions.

The climate policy regimes also lead to lower energy intensity of GDP and higher share of renewables in the energy mix (Appendix). The energy intensity of GDP falls relatively more over the time horizon in the climate policy regimes than in the baselines. However, there is not much difference in the reduction in energy intensity between the alternate climate policy scenarios. The energy intensity falls relatively more in the high growth scenario than in the OECD scenario. The reduction in energy intensity is driven by the shift towards less energy intensive methods of production as well as growth in autonomous energy efficiency. The share of renewables in the energy mix increases significantly in the climate policy regimes, and the shares are relatively higher in the high elasticity and high growth scenarios. Thus, the climate policy regimes are associated with structural changes in the economy as well as changes in the energy mix.

The above discussion points out that the climate policies could adversely affect India in terms of growth and welfare. The choice of the mitigation policy is relatively unimportant from an efficiency perspective, but in terms of welfare implication an emission trading regime is a better option for India. The government could play an important role in reducing welfare losses by promoting the growth of labour intensive sectors. In the absence of growth in the labour intensive sectors of the economy the welfare losses due to climate policies could increase manifold. Significant reductions in CO_2 emissions can take place due to climate policies and such reductions could be associated with many co-benefits like less adverse effects on agriculture, human health etc. Finally, climate policies promote energy efficiency and higher deployment of renewables in the energy mix.

5. CONCLUSION

The main objective of this paper was to analyse the effects of post-Kyoto global climate policy regimes on India's GDP growth, welfare and CO_2 emissions. The climate policy regimes are global carbon tax and global emissions trading, and both of the regimes are consistent with the objective of limiting the increase in average global temperature below 2°C over the long term with 50 percent probability. The results suggest that the choice of the mitigation policy is relatively unimportant from an efficiency perspective. However, from a welfare perspective both the choice of the mitigation policy and the value of the substitution elasticity between value added and energy are important, as these two factors are associated with lower welfare losses. The emissions trading regime leads to lower welfare losses relative to the carbon tax regime. A higher value of the substitution elasticity leads to lower welfare losses (or gains in the short/medium run) relative to scenarios where a lower value of the substitution elasticity is assumed. Welfare losses could be substantially reduced by promoting the growth of labour intensive sectors (such as agriculture and services), and this result assumes importance from a policy perspective. Further, an emission trading regime leads to higher deployment of renewables in the energy mix relative to a carbon tax regime. The benefits of climate policies are not only limited to reductions in CO_2 emissions but also in increasing energy efficiency and in promoting the growth of renewables in the energy mix. Thus, global climate change mitigation policies have the potential for promoting low carbon and inclusive growth in India.

ACKNOWLEDGMENT

The study has been conducted under the POEM (Policy Options to engage Emerging Asian economies in a post-Kyoto regime) project, funded by the European Commission (Seventh Framework Programme). Seven institutions from India, China, and Europe were part of this project.

REFERENCES

Bernard, A., & Vielle, M. (2003). *Multi-Gas Strategy in Committing to the Kyoto Protocol*. IDEI Working Papers 183. Toulouse: Institut d'Économie Industrielle (IDEI).

Fisher-Vanden, K. A., Shukla, P. R., Edmonds, J. A., Kim, S. H., & Pitcher, H. M. (1997). Carbon Taxes and India. *Energy Economics*, *19*(3), 289–325. doi:10.1016/S0140-9883(96)01020-1

Garbaccio, R. F., Ho, M. S., & Jorgenson, D. W. (1998). *Controlling Carbon Emissions in China. Kennedy School of Government*. Harvard University.

Hohne, N., den Elzen, M., & Weiss, M. (2006). Common but Differentiated Convergence (CDC): A New Conceptual Approach to Long Term Climate Policy. *Climate Policy*, *6*(2), 181–199. doi:10.1080/14693062.2006.9685594

Jacoby, H., Reily, J., McFarland, J., & Paltsev, S. (2006). Technology and technical change in the MIT EPPA Model. *Energy Economics*, *28*(5-6), 610–631. doi:10.1016/j.eneco.2006.05.014

Johansson, D. J. A., Lucas, P. L., Weitzel, M., Ahlgren, E. O., Bazaz, A. B., Chen, W., …Wei, Y.M. (2012). *Multi-model analyses of the economic and energy implications for China and India in a post-Kyoto climate regime*. Working Paper 1808. Kiel, Germany: Kiel Institute for the World Economy.

Klepper, G., Peterson, S., & Springer, K. (2003). *DART 97: A Description of the Multi-regional, Multi-sectoral Trade Model for the Analysis of Climate Policies*. Working Paper 1149. Kiel, Germany: Kiel Institute for the World Economy.

Liang, Q. M., Fan, Y., & Wei, Y. M. (2007). Carbon Taxation Policy in China: How to Protect Energy and Trade Intensive Sectors? *Journal of Policy Modeling*, *29*(2), 311–333. doi:10.1016/j.jpolmod.2006.11.001

Lofgren, H., Harris, R. L., & Robinson, S. (2002) A Standard Computable General Equilibrium Model in GAMS (Microcomputers in Policy Research). Washington DC: International Food Policy Research Institute (IFPRI).

Ministry of Environment and Forests, Government of India. (2009). *India's GHG Emissions Profile: Results of Five Climate Modeling Studies*. Author.

Ministry of External Affairs, Government of India. (2009). *The Road to Copenhagen: India's Position on Climate Change Issues*. Author.

Ojha, V. P. (2008). Carbon Emissions Reduction Strategies and Poverty Alleviation in India. *Environment and Development Economics*, *14*(03), 323–348. doi:10.1017/S1355770X0800497X

Ojha, V. P., Pal, B. D., Pohit, S., & Roy, J. (2009). *Social Accounting Matrix for India*. Retrieved from ssrn.com/abstract=1457628

Organization for Economic Cooperation and Development (OECD). (2010). *Costs and Effectiveness of the Copenhagen Pledges: Assessing Global Greenhouse Gas Emissions Targets and Actions for 2020*. Author.

Paltsev, S., Reilly, J. M., Jacoby, H. D., Eckaus, R. S., McFarland, J., Sarofim, M., . . . Babiker, M. (2005). *The MIT Emissions Prediction and Policy Analysis (EPPA) Model: Version 4* (Report No. 125). Cambridge, MA: Massachusetts Institute of Technology.

Parry, I. W. H., Williams, R. C. III, & Goulder, L. H. (1999). When can Carbon Abatement Policies increase Welfare? *The Fundamental Role of Distorted Factor Markets*, *37*, 52–84.

PBL Netherlands Environmental Assessment Agency. (2012). Trends in global CO2 emissions: 2012 Report. The Hague: Author.

PBL Netherlands Envorinmental Assessment Agency. (2005). *Framework to assess international regimes for differentiation of commitments (FAIR)*. Retrieved from http://www.pbl.nl/en/publications/2005/

Planning Commission, Government of India. (2011). *Low carbon strategies for inclusive growth – An interim report, May 2011*. Author.

Pradhan, B. K., & Ghosh, J. (2012). *The impact of carbon taxes on growth, emissions and welfare in India.* Working Paper No. 315. Institute of Economic Growth (IEG).

Pradhan, B. K., Saluja, M. R., & Singh, S. K. (2006). *Social Accounting Matrix for India: Concepts, Construction and Applications*. New Delhi: Sage Publications.

RTI International. (2008). EMPAX-CGE Model Documentation (Interim Report). Research Triangle Park, NC: Author.

Stavins, R. N. (2000). Market based Environmental Policies. In P. R. Portney & R. N. Stavins (Eds.), *Public Policies for Environmental Protection*. Washington, DC: Resources for the Future.

Van Ruijven, B. J., Weitzel, M., den Elzen, M. G. J., Hof, A. F., van Vuuren, D. P., Peterson, S., & Narita, D. (2012). Emission allowances and mitigation costs of China and India resulting from different effort-sharing approaches. *Energy Policy*, *46*, 116–134. doi:10.1016/j.enpol.2012.03.042

Welsch, H. (2008). Armington Elasticities for Energy Policy Modeling: Evidence from Four European Countries. *Energy Economics*, *30*(5), 2252–2264. doi:10.1016/j.eneco.2007.07.007

APPENDIX

Table 3. Carbon prices and emission allowances for the climate policy regimes

	2015	2020	2025	2030	2035	2040	2045	2050
Carbon price ($ per ton of CO_2) - OECD	1.9	6.8	34.7	71.1	107.2	145.7	222.4	440.8
Carbon price ($ per ton of CO_2) - High growth	1.6	6.8	36.8	79.6	122.2	178.8	277.7	542.1
Allowance (million tons of CO_2) - OECD	2316	2944	3589	4233	3997	3762	3526	3290
Allowance (million tons of CO_2) - High growth	2440	3193	4036	4824	4490	4156	3821	3487

Table 4. Key growth rates

Parameter	Average Growth Rate (Percent)
Energy efficiency	1.5
Government consumption	10
Labourforce	2 in OECD scenario; 3 in high growth scenario
TFP	Agriculture 0.2, Hydro -6, Biomass 1.1, All other sectors 2.8
Investment	7 in OECD scenario; 10 in high growth scenario

Table 5. Effects on factor prices (percent change relative to baseline)

	2015	2020	2025	2030	2035	2040	2045	2050
CDC-OECD								
Labour	-0.16	-0.37	-1.60	-2.67	-3.34	-3.69	-5.44	-12.16
Capital	-0.22	-0.50	-1.97	-3.16	-3.64	-3.80	-5.35	-11.75
CT-OECD								
Labour	-0.16	-0.37	-1.66	-2.84	-3.46	-3.74	-5.47	-12.39
Capital	-0.22	-0.50	-1.85	-2.90	-3.46	-3.73	-5.31	-11.63
CDC-High Elasticity								
Labour	1.43	1.36	0.32	-0.44	-0.76	-0.69	-2.19	-8.69
Capital	0.70	0.61	-0.57	-1.45	-1.63	-1.44	-2.85	-9.20
CDC-Low Elasticity								
Labour	-1.82	-2.20	-3.66	-5.06	-6.14	-6.98	-9.03	-15.96
Capital	-1.17	-1.70	-3.49	-5.05	-5.94	-6.56	-8.37	-14.91
CDC-High Growth								
Labour	-0.13	-0.34	-1.48	-2.52	-3.17	-3.89	-5.75	-13.84
Capital	-0.18	-0.48	-1.91	-3.09	-3.42	-3.76	-5.17	-12.28
CT-High Growth								
Labour	-0.13	-0.34	-1.55	-2.73	-3.33	-3.99	-5.81	-14.19
Capital	-0.18	-0.47	-1.74	-2.72	-3.14	-3.59	-5.08	-11.96

Table 6. Effects on output (percent change relative to baseline)

	CDC-OECD		CT-OECD		CDC-High Elasticity		CDC-Low Elasticity		CDC-High Growth		CT-High Growth	
	2015	2050	2015	2050	2015	2050	2015	2050	2015	2050	2015	2050
Agriculture	0.0	-2.5	0.0	-2.8	1.2	-1.8	-1.2	-3.3	0.0	-4.1	0.0	-4.8
Coal	-3.6	-64.0	-3.6	-63.4	-7.5	-73.1	-0.2	-54.1	-3.0	-51.5	-3.0	-50.2
Oil	-0.6	-7.7	-0.6	-7.8	-3.3	-15.4	1.7	-3.9	-0.5	-18.5	-0.5	-19.0
Gas	-0.8	-2.1	-0.8	-2.0	-4.4	-6.2	2.1	-0.8	-0.7	-0.4	-0.7	-0.3
Manufacturing I	-0.1	-6.3	-0.1	-6.0	1.0	-4.5	-1.2	-8.0	-0.1	-7.5	-0.1	-7.2
Oil products	-1.2	-41.4	-1.2	-41.6	-5.4	-50.2	3.1	-33.9	-1.0	-59.3	-1.0	-59.5
Manufacturing II	-0.4	-16.6	-0.4	-14.8	0.0	-13.5	-0.8	-19.6	-0.3	-13.8	-0.3	-11.1
Manufacturing III	-0.2	-12.3	-0.2	-9.8	-0.2	-11.0	-0.2	-13.7	-0.2	-10.0	-0.2	-6.6
Hydro	-0.5	-11.2	-0.5	-12.0	-9.0	-18.7	8.4	-3.0	-0.4	-11.8	-0.4	-13.3
Renewables	-0.6	-18.3	-0.5	-19.4	-7.9	-17.8	7.6	-18.6	-0.4	-20.1	-0.5	-22.0
CCS	0.4	-6.0	0.4	-6.3	-10.9	-22.2	12.1	11.4	0.3	2.4	0.3	2.1
Thermal	-1.1	-39.0	-1.1	-39.2	-11.9	-48.0	10.2	-29.6	-0.9	-36.5	-0.9	-36.7
Nuclear	-0.9	-30.0	-0.9	-31.0	-8.1	-30.4	7.0	-29.8	-0.7	-30.8	-0.7	-32.3
Biomass	-0.1	-1.2	-0.1	-2.9	-1.4	1.0	1.2	-3.7	0.0	-3.2	0.0	-6.2
Construction	0.0	-1.1	0.0	-1.0	0.0	-0.9	0.0	-1.3	0.0	-0.7	0.0	-0.6
Road transport	-0.2	-11.7	-0.2	-12.0	0.6	-9.5	-1.0	-14.1	-0.2	-11.2	-0.2	-11.4
Rail/air/sea transport	-0.3	-10.2	-0.3	-10.0	-0.6	-8.9	0.1	-11.7	-0.2	-9.2	-0.2	-8.7
Other services	0.0	-2.8	0.0	-2.8	0.5	-2.1	-0.6	-3.6	0.0	-4.1	0.0	-4.2

Table 7. Effects on consumer prices (percent change relative to baseline)

	CDC-OECD		CT-OECD		CDC-High Elasticity		CDC-Low Elasticity		CDC-High Growth		CT-High Growth	
	2015	**2050**	**2015**	**2050**	**2015**	**2050**	**2015**	**2050**	**2015**	**2050**	**2015**	**2050**
Agriculture	-0.1	-9.4	-0.1	-9.3	-0.1	-8.3	-0.1	-10.9	-0.1	-10.8	-0.1	-10.7
Coal	5.9	347.4	5.9	347.5	-0.6	347.1	12.8	348.1	4.8	198.8	4.8	198.9
Oil	-0.6	-81.9	-0.6	-81.4	-3.5	-85.1	2.9	-76.4	-0.5	-87.4	-0.5	-86.8
Gas	1.9	25.1	1.9	26.8	-5.8	-2.4	10.2	60.4	1.6	17.2	1.6	20.2
Manufacturing I	0.0	-5.3	0.0	-5.2	-0.3	-6.0	0.2	-4.9	0.0	-6.6	0.0	-6.5
Oil products	1.5	68.4	1.5	69.1	-1.4	64.6	4.5	74.6	1.2	71.5	1.2	72.4
Manufacturing II	0.4	12.1	0.4	12.8	-0.5	2.9	1.2	21.8	0.3	8.6	0.3	9.5
Manufacturing III	0.1	2.5	0.1	3.0	-0.7	-2.5	0.9	8.0	0.1	0.4	0.1	0.9
Hydro	-0.1	-10.9	-0.1	-10.8	-0.8	-9.3	0.7	-12.9	-0.1	-11.4	-0.1	-11.2
Renewables	0.2	9.1	0.2	9.2	-0.6	7.8	0.9	10.6	0.2	8.1	0.2	8.2
CCS	-0.5	2.5	-0.5	2.6	-1.8	0.7	0.8	4.6	-0.4	-7.9	-0.4	-7.6
Thermal	0.9	56.8	0.9	57.0	-0.5	50.9	2.2	63.0	0.7	46.5	0.7	46.9
Nuclear	0.6	29.2	0.6	29.4	-1.7	27.2	2.6	31.6	0.5	26.4	0.5	26.7
Biomass	-0.1	-9.1	-0.1	-9.2	-0.2	-8.7	0.0	-9.6	-0.1	-10.5	-0.1	-10.5
Construction	0.0	-2.6	0.0	-2.6	0.0	-4.1	0.0	-1.2	0.0	-4.0	0.0	-4.0
Road transport	0.2	7.6	0.2	7.6	0.4	6.6	0.2	8.8	0.2	7.3	0.2	7.1
Rail/air/sea transport	0.1	-1.3	0.1	-1.6	0.2	-1.5	-0.2	-1.4	0.0	-3.2	0.0	-3.5
Other services	-0.1	-9.5	-0.1	-9.9	0.3	-7.8	-0.5	-11.4	-0.1	-11.1	-0.1	-11.7

Table 8. Effects on exports (percent change relative to baseline)

	CDC-OECD		CT-OECD		CDC-High Elasticity		CDC-Low Elasticity		CDC-High Growth		CT-High Growth	
	2015	**2050**	**2015**	**2050**	**2015**	**2050**	**2015**	**2050**	**2015**	**2050**	**2015**	**2050**
Agriculture	0.0	-1.5	0.0	2.9	0.2	-7.2	-0.1	4.8	0.0	-2.8	0.0	2.4
Coal	1.6	88.9	1.6	97.5	1.7	40.4	0.9	136.8	1.4	236.2	1.4	255.3
Oil	1.1	421.1	1.1	441.8	5.3	588.0	-3.9	271.3	0.9	698.8	0.9	732.5
Gas	0.6	43.0	0.6	44.5	1.6	119.8	-1.1	7.9	0.5	5.0	0.5	6.7
Manufacturing I	-0.2	-10.5	-0.2	-4.1	-0.3	-15.1	0.0	-5.5	-0.2	-11.4	-0.2	-3.3
Oil products	-1.0	41.7	-1.0	43.7	-4.0	28.2	1.8	43.7	-0.8	20.5	-0.8	22.0
Manufacturing II	-1.0	-37.9	-1.0	-32.3	-1.0	-32.8	-0.9	-42.4	-0.9	-34.0	-0.8	-26.3
Manufacturing III	-0.5	-25.1	-0.5	-17.9	-1.1	-24.8	0.2	-25.7	-0.5	-22.2	-0.4	-12.5
Road transport	-0.5	-24.6	-0.6	-21.1	-1.0	-26.2	-0.1	-23.3	-0.5	-24.8	-0.5	-20.2
Rail/air/sea transport	-0.4	-16.4	-0.4	-12.0	-2.0	-19.6	1.4	-13.1	-0.3	-14.9	-0.3	-8.8
Other services	0.0	-1.7	0.0	3.3	-0.9	-7.8	0.9	4.8	0.0	-2.5	0.0	3.8

Table 9. Effects on imports (percent change relative to baseline)

	CDC-OECD		CT-OECD		CDC-High Elasticity		CDC-Low Elasticity		CDC-High Growth		CT-High Growth	
	2015	**2050**	**2015**	**2050**	**2015**	**2050**	**2015**	**2050**	**2015**	**2050**	**2015**	**2050**
Agriculture	-0.1	-5.0	0.0	-15.6	3.9	13.3	-4.0	-21.1	0.0	-7.4	0.0	-20.6
Coal	-9.0	-94.1	-9.0	-94.1	-16.7	-95.5	-1.4	-92.3	-7.5	-94.1	-7.5	-94.1
Oil	-1.0	-34.7	-1.0	-35.4	-5.0	-44.4	3.0	-26.7	-0.8	-48.5	-0.8	-49.3
Gas	-1.1	-9.3	-1.1	-9.4	-5.6	-20.9	2.8	-2.5	-0.9	-1.4	-0.9	-1.7
Manufacturing I	0.0	-2.5	0.0	-7.6	2.3	5.4	-2.3	-10.1	0.0	-4.0	0.0	-10.5
Oil products	-1.3	-73.9	-1.3	-74.4	-6.7	-79.1	4.3	-67.4	-1.1	-84.9	-1.1	-85.3
Manufacturing II	0.2	6.5	0.2	3.5	0.9	7.0	-0.6	6.0	0.1	7.3	0.1	3.8
Manufacturing III	0.1	3.6	0.1	-0.1	0.6	6.1	-0.5	1.2	0.1	4.8	0.1	0.3
Road transport	0.1	4.1	0.1	-1.3	2.2	12.0	-2.0	-3.4	0.1	5.5	0.1	-1.2
Other services	-0.1	-4.0	-0.1	-9.4	2.1	4.7	-2.2	-12.4	-0.1	-5.9	-0.1	-12.6

Table 10. Effects on energy intensity and share of renewables (percent change between base and terminal year)

	BAU-OECD	CDC-OECD	CT-OECD	CDC-High Elasticity	CDC-Low Elasticity	BAU-High Growth	CDC-High Growth	CT-High Growth
Energy intensity of GDP	-84	-89	-89	-90	-89	-88	-91	-91
Share of renewables in energy mix	208	340	336	412	294	276	415	406

Chapter 3
Impact of Green Growth and Development Path for Skilled and Unskilled Job Creation and Economic, Social Sustainability:
Case Study of India – A Recursive Dynamic CGE Model Approach

Anandajit Goswami
The Energy and Resources Institute (TERI), India

Saswata Chaudhury
The Energy and Resources Institute (TERI), India

Tarun Garg
The Energy and Resources Institute (TERI), India

ABSTRACT

This chapter captures the possible impacts of green growth strategies and interventions in terms of skilled, unskilled job creation in context of an emerging country like India. Additionally, it addresses how income generation from specific possible green growth related interventions can have a ripple effect on development indicators like literacy rates, infant mortality rates, poverty. Further it links skilled and unskilled employment generation with "Right to Livelihoods" and MGNREGA and its implications for state level fiscal subsidies. Job creation reflects economic gain for different class of households in the short and long term. This economic gain reduces the level of inter-household and intra-household inter-temporal inequality levels. In the long run, this reduction in the inequality level can create a positive impact on the social sustainability.

DOI: 10.4018/978-1-5225-0094-0.ch003

INTRODUCTION

Policy Relevance of Green Growth Interventions for Job Creation and Development in India

In India, role of green growth in development path has been accepted and debated in recent past but for the first time it was contextualized within policy discourse of Thirteenth Finance Commission (TFC). TFC report has mentioned that growth of India should be promoted without compromising the needs of development with minimal impact on use of natural resources. An inclusive green growth pathway for a country has to generate new jobs across different sectors of the economy to promote an inclusive developmental path. Creation of job opportunity and skill enhancement within a green growth path can also have the potential to address the challenge of unemployment in India. Currently, India, has a dearth of sufficient skilled workers but the existing vocational training schemes often are successfully unable to target casual and informal workforce which contributes over 90 per cent of India's working population (Hajela, 2012). Skill shortage only aggravates the existing unemployment problem. Within current employment patterns, only about 5% of the workforce has marketable skills, as compared to 50% to 60% in some developed countries like Japan). This situation exists even though there are number of central government ministries which offer skill development initiatives through school education, institutes of higher learning, specialised vocational training institutes. Gravity of this challenge is going to increase within the backdrop of inclusion of 12 million persons who are expected to join the workforce every year (IMACS, 2010). This establishes the need of creating both jobs, skill within the Indian economy to address the future developmental goals.

Therefore, with this background it is important to assess the potential of a green growth interventions and strategies in addressing skilled, unskilled job creation in the Indian economy. This can therefore address development needs of people of the country by impacting a broad section of the population which includes women, youth, farmers, rural population and slum dwellers that can benefit from such job creation (ILO, 2010). Analysis of the quarterly survey on job creation in India shows a gap of 43.15% (Indian Express, April 2014). Therefore, this adds to the seriousness of focusing on job creation for the Indian economy as a policy imperative.

Green building and renewable energy promotion are some of the key sectors of green growth intervention other than natural resource management and resource, material and autonomous energy efficiency improvement across sectors of the economy. Creation of skilled jobs in green building and renewable energy sector can also address and strengthen implementation of measures recommended by the sub group (created in August, 2009) of the task force on "Climate Change and Green Jobs". Measures of the subgroup to create green jobs under MGNREGA (Mahatma Gandhi National Rural Employment Guarantee Act) through promotion of mitigation measures like enhancement of renewable energy and energy efficiency interventions within the country(ILO, 2010) can be strengthened by green growth promoting measures.

It will also consolidate and fast track addressal of the Article 41 of the Indian Constitution which deals with providing a non – justiciable right to work under directive principles of state policy. MGNREGA in 2005 first highlighted that the state through its economic capacity can actually convert non justiciable rights to work into justiciable ones along with a focus on skill development. A green growth and development intervention creates skilled jobs across rural households of India and therefore has a scope, potential to feed into this policy and human rights space enshrined within the constitution of India.

LITERATURE REVIEW OF BACKGROUND CONTEXT

Existing literature by World Bank (2013), Ministry of Environment and Forest (2009) indicates impact of carbon taxes on probable GDP loss, labour supply, productivity, environmental health, factor returns.

India needs to move from traditional fossil fuel based economy to a clean and renewable energy based economy to achieve inclusive energy security (TERI, 2009) which is also a key measure for a green growth path of the country in future. However, existing literature do not have a mention of impact of a green growth and development policy or intervention on the degree, level of rural and urban household skilled and unskilled job creation that can have developmental implications for the country and states of India. This chapter therefore attempts to fill up that gap in the literature through next sections. It starts with a set of research questions, followed by a model framework and final findings from the modelling analysis.

RESEARCH QUESTIONS

Key research questions which are explored in this chapter are as follows:

1. What is the impact of interventions like an increase in investment and economic activity in the green sector[1] on household level job creation across rural and urban household income classes and on state level fiscal subsidies?
2. What are the policy interventions through which potential of this job creation can be realized in the country?

Above research questions are explored by means of a below mentioned methodological process. The methodological process initiates with a model framework.

MODEL FRAMEWORK

The model framework comprises of a Social Accounting Matrix (SAM) based national level dynamic recursive Computable General Equilibrium (CGE) model. A recursive dynamic CGE model is chosen as in the policy parlance, perfect foresight approach of an inter temporal, rational expectation based CGE model might not work. Changes of policy interventions are realized in an economy with a lag and moreover there is always an interactive adaptation of policy measures by agents within an economy. A perfect foresight based dynamic CGE model will not take into account of this behavioural nature of agents in an economy. Therefore, a recursive dynamic CGE model is chosen.

This SAM for our dynamic CGE model comprises of sectors like green building, biomass, solar, hydro, wind, nuclear. 43 sectors have been included at the national level social accounting matrix (SAM). It also includes sectors like paddy, wheat, cereals, cash crops, industry, services spanning across primary, secondary and tertiary segments of the Indian economy using national accounts statistics. In order to construct this, latest input output table of 2007 – 08 released by *Ministry of Statistics and Programme Implementation (MOSPI)* has been used.

Figure 1. Model framework

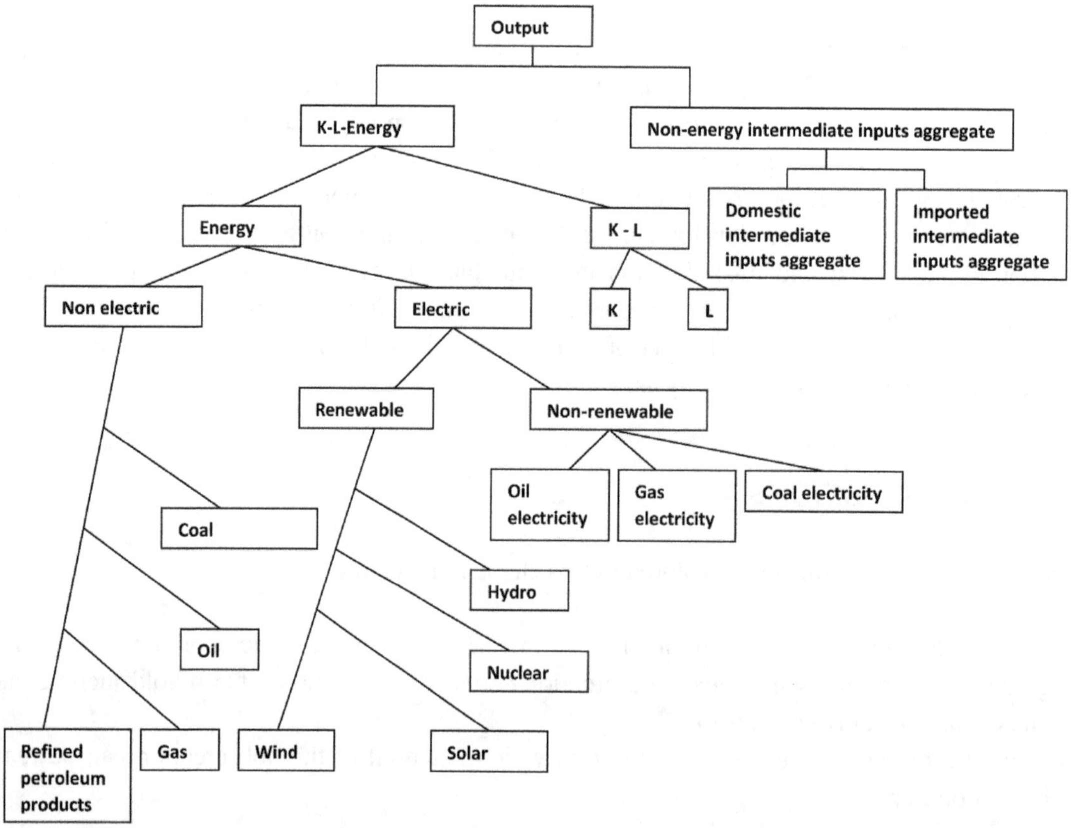

Agriculture sector data has been updated by applying latest National Account Statistics, Economic Survey data. Data regarding the fuels and petroleum products have been obtained from the latest input output table and has been validated with Ministry of Petroleum and Natural Gas reports.

Green building sector data has been built up for the CGE model by applying information from sources of GRIHA, CPWD, AFD and internal building audit reports of TERI. For household data, the decile MPCE (marginal per capita expenditure) class data from the latest NSSO round (68th round) was considered. Further, from decile class, five rural and urban classes were formed using latest NSSO round (68th round). Capital formation data was available from National Accounts Statistics. Labour data for different sectors has been collected *from Annual Survey of Industries (ASI), government of India publication for the year 2007-08*. Total labour value figures in terms of emoluments for most sectors were collected from ASI.

Labour value for remaining sectors has been calculated based on sectoral relationship. For instance, labour value of construction sector has been distributed among green, non-green construction sectors based on their composition in total construction. Within labour, a division between skilled, unskilled labour was done. In order to do that, sector specific skill – unskilled labour ratio was worked out. Further, employment levels of sectors of the economy were available from National Accounts Statistics. Using skilled – unskilled ratio, presence of skilled and unskilled labour in each sector was obtained.

Larger framework of the nesting structure of the model has been shown in Figure 1:

Table 1. Interconnection between savings, investment, employment, and sectoral outputs

A 1% increase in employment	A 1.2% increase in savings which highlights that the savings propensity of households in India can be elastic with green growth interventions	Changes in sectoral outputs of Indian economy (will emerge from CGE based endogenous model using the changes in savings as a scenario)
A 1% increase in savings	A .99% increase in investment which indicates that not all of the savings of households get translated to investment owing to different gestation lags	Changes in sectoral outputs of Indian economy (will emerge from CGE based endogenous model using the changes in investment as a scenario)
A 1% increase in employment	A 1.69% increase in investment which indicates the potential of investment and capital formation from green growth and development led employment generation	Changes in sectoral outputs of Indian economy (will emerge from CGE based endogenous model using the changes in investment as a scenario)

Source: TERI Macroeconomic Model Estimates, RBI Statistics.
Savings measured by household financial savings, investment measured by gross domestic capital formation.

In order to build in dynamism (recursive) into scenario based static CGE model, the savings and investment data of Indian economy has been considered as the model works on a saving and investment closure rule. Total public, government and household savings has been considered for savings. Gross domestic fixed capital formation has been considered as an indicator of investment variable.

Further, to validate the association between savings, investment, employment and sectoral outputs of the recursive dynamic CGE model, a time series based error corrected, cointegration method based econometric analysis is carried out to understand an elasticity of savings, investment to employment.

The interconnected impacts on selected macroeconomic variables are highlighted in the Table 1.

This nature of response between the savings and investment was also done outside the model to understand and calibrate the closure rule of the model. A responsive relationship between savings and investments outside the simulated set up of CGE is conducted to capture the structural non linearities within the economy. Further, in the simulated set up of dynamic CGE, the closure rule is defined and their responsive behavioural change in a simulated set up is cross compared with the relationship as depicted by the econometric relationship outside the dynamic CGE model. Hence, the results of the econometric relationship helps to conduct a cross validation and calibration of the simulated closure rule set up within the dynamic CGE model.

Given this broader macroeconomic context, the next section highlights the impact of green growth and development on skilled, unskilled job creation with its relevance to the national policy discourse as emerging from the national level CGE model.

NATIONAL LEVEL CGE MODEL FINDINGS PERTAINING TO SKILLED, UNSKILLED JOB CREATION, FISCAL SUBSIDIES AND ITS ORIENTATION TO A POLICY CONTEXT FOR GREEN GROWTH AND DEVELOPMENT

The dynamic CGE analysis suggests that an increase in an economic activity within solar sector can have a potential to lead to a *3.2% increase* in the national level GDP indicating the high potential of the solar sector to create economic multipliers across the economy through green growth interventions and strategies. Further, a similar increase in economic activity through investments in biomass, wind sector can lead to a *0.4% and 0.1% increase in national level GDP*. The rise in GDP will happen due to an increase in direct and indirect demands across sectors of the economy owing to a potential rise in the investment which will generate new demand for goods and services in the economy and will raise the GDP.

As per the latest Central Electricity Authority documents of 2013, there are plans to enhance capacity addition to a larger extent in the solar sector in comparison to other renewable energy sector. Therefore, this probable investment and economic activity scenario matches with the planned capacity addition declarations of the government of India at the national level.

At the national level, investments in the green sector can also have a potential to increase the factor returns *(a 20% increase in investment in the green sector can lead to a 0.2% increase in the factor returns)* and can lead to skilled, unskilled job creation within households across different income classes. For that, rural (five for rural) and urban (five for urban) households of India have been divided into five different classes based on monthly per capita expenditure data of households emerging from latest 68th round of NSSO data. CGE analysis suggests that *for a new activity generation through investments in the green building sector, approximately 7 skilled and 14 unskilled jobs can be created in the highest rural household classes for per 100 households. Skilled and unskilled job creation is 4 and 8 for the highest urban household class for per 100 household.*

Skill within the green building segment of the country is a scarce resource because of which the skilled job creation in both rural and urban households is lesser than the unskilled job creation. However, an investment in the green building sector has a spillover effect in terms of its job creation within the rural household classes. It not only generates new skilled and unskilled employment in the urban sector but it generates a higher unskilled job creation per 100 household for rural household classes. *This also hints towards some possible migration from rural to urban areas that can happen owing to unskilled job creation through investments in green building sector (assuming that the green building largely comes up in urban areas of the country). Broadly, an investment in all green sectors (as identified in the national level CGE model) leads to 174 unskilled and 87 jobs for highest rural income class (r5) and 128 unskilled and 32 skilled jobs for highest urban income class (u5). Clearly, green growth interventions have a larger spillover effect in terms of job creation for rural households in comparison to urban households (what could be the reason for higher spillover effect in Rural India? is not it conflicting with rural-urban migration?). Moreover, the degree of job creation goes up as one moves up in the income class ladder within the rural and urban households. These preliminary results also hint towards the inter and intra household growing inequality debates within the country.*

Some of the results showing household level skilled, unskilled job generation owing to green growth and development interventions in the agriculture, renewable energy provision, industry, green building sector for a reference scenario baseline case (in 2015) is indicated in Figure 2.

Over the time horizon, the level of skilled and unskilled employment generation is shown by the Figure 3. To project the future level of skilled and unskilled employment generation, three scenarios are constructed.

These scenarios include

1. Reference,
2. Policy, and
3. Ambitious scenario.

Figure 2. Rural and urban household classwise unskilled, skilled job creation (r5, u5 denotes the highest income class in the ascending order)
Source: Model Estimates.

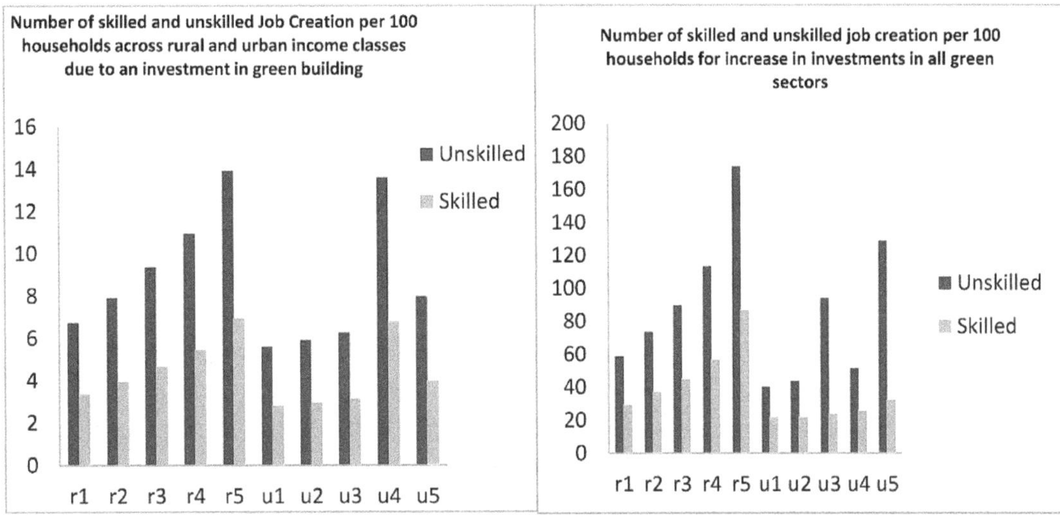

The reference scenario is the one where the business as usual practices are continuing. Policy scenario is the one where green growth intervention related declared policies are implemented along with the associated employment generation schemes. Ambitious scenario is the one where the government is a little more ambitious in terms of implementing the green growth related interventions and its associated skilled and unskilled employment generation schemes.

Figure 3. Scenariowise skilled and unskilled labour employment generation in the economy
Source: Model Estimates.

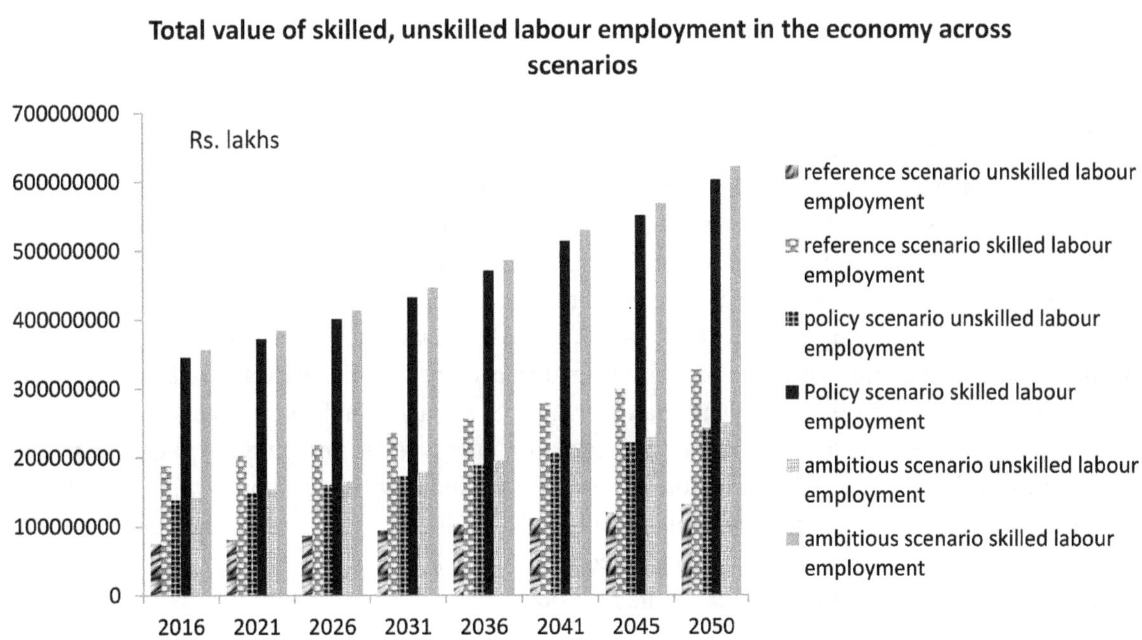

This level of employment generation along the above mentioned path (as shown in Figure 3) through interventions in renewable energy, green building, energy efficiency and natural resource management domains can have a significant contribution to the development of people and can impact the economic and social domains of sustainability.

Having outlined this above potential, the next section pans down to the specific sector of green building and its possible contribution to the employment generation opportunities within the Indian economy.

GREEN BUILDING AND EMPLOYMENT OPPORTUNITIES

The building construction industry at present contributes about 10% of GDP, and is expanding rapidly at over 9% per year spurred largely by the strong growth in the services sector[2]. This fast pace growth rate is resulting in rapid urbanization, high demand for infrastructure and buildings and thus an increasing demand for energy.

In 2020 almost 500 Million people will be living in Urban India. It is expected that 4127 Million m2 of real estate space (which includes residential, retail, offices, hotels, health care and education sectors) will be built from 2012 to 2020.[3]

Electricity consumption by buildings has grown at an average growth rate of 9% in the last 10 years (2001-11).The residential sector constitutes 24% of energy consumption in building sector and commercial sector constitutes 9% of energy consumption in building sector. As per a study conducted by TERI[4], in a conventional air conditioned commercial building, approximately

- 20% savings can be achieved by incorporating Passive design features like optimum orientation, envelope shading, daylight integration, etc.
- 30% savings can be achieved by making the building energy code compliant
- 40% savings can be achieved by incorporating Passive design features and making the building energy code compliant
- The total energy saving potential in building sector is 174000 GWH.[5]

Green buildings has various elements like insulation on wall, roof, double glaze windows, lighting controls and high performance air conditioning system for ensuring the low energy consumption in green buildings. Although market of energy efficient products is still immature in India, in the last few years there has been a noticeable improvement in the market in terms of availability of products. Energy efficient electrical appliances/equipments of many leading companies/ brands are now available in the market. With the rising demand for insulation materials, high performance glass, heat reflective paints, energy efficient masonry units, etc, the number of manufacturers and suppliers of these materials is also slowly increasing. As per the information provided by some of the leading manufacturers the sales for rockwool, polyurethane (insulation materials) has been growing at an average 18% annually and sales of Autoclaved Aerated Concrete Block has been growing at an average 15% annually, in the last 5 years.

However, there is still a huge market potential for energy efficient products, equipments and technologies, in India. As the green building movement in India will gain momentum, there will be a rise in the construction of green buildings resulting in an increase in the demand for energy efficient products in India. As per a study[6] conducted by TERI, the demand for energy efficient building materials is likely to see a rapid increase in the next decades.

Table 2. Estimated demand for energy efficient building materials

	2011 (Observed - Actual)	2020	2030
Annual demand for roof insulation (Million sqm)	3.3	9.4	22.2
Annual demand for wall insulation (Million sqm)	2.8	4.6	7.1
Annual demand for high performance glass (Million sqm)	8.5	13.8	21.2
Annual demand for T-5 (Million units)	2.16	5.94	19.44
Annual demand for LED (Million units)	1.74	4.81	15.74

Source: Authors' estimates.

The green building sector has increased the requirement of above mentioned elements thereby creating employment opportunities in the sector. However installation and commissioning of these elements require proper training of labours.

Therefore a promotion of the green building sector, can not only lead to skilled and unskilled job creation: it can also lead to energy savings. Through these set of measures, economic, environmental and social domains of sustainability can be addressed. Further, once the income of the people rise and trickle down across the households, it can lead to a rise in the literacy rates and other developmental indicators (Table 2).

Along with promotion of green building, green growth and developmental interventions also include measures like promotion of natural resource management in the agriculture sectors, autonomous energy efficiency improvement. These measures can impact developmental indicators for different time frames (2011, 2020, 2030) by different degrees.

To capture those impacts, three scenarios viz. reference, policy and ambitious are constructed to understand the different degree of impact. A back of the envelope developmental indicator function is constructed which essentially captures the changes in developmental indicators for different varying levels of income which are created and generated within the economy.

Further, such scenario specific results and directions for future policy making are explained in the Table 3. As indicated in the Table 3, green growth and development measures through agriculture and natural resource management techniques, structural changes within industry and infrastructure sector bring about a change in the poverty by uplifting people above the poverty line. This happens because the income generated from green growth interventions and new investments get distributed across the rural households. Inequality within the rural households goes down owing to that. Once the inequality levels go down, it is expected that a rise in income, creates a rise in the aspiration of households to get educated. With a rise in education, the awareness of people regarding health and better quality of life increases. This thereby positively impacts the health indicators like infant mortality rates.

From a modelling perspective, the increase in the income from green growth interventions in agriculture, renewable energy, industry, buildings sector, is fed into an interphase model (which is the back of the envelope model) as an input with development indicators as an outcome variable. In the interphase model, outputs of the CGE model (like household level income levels, skilled and unskilled job creation over time) feed in as an input. This therefore gives rise to a change in the development indicators as an output from the interphase model after considering the CGE model outputs as input variables over time.

Table 3. Scenario-wise impact of green growth and development measures on developmental indicators

Indicator	Units	Reference Scenario	Policy Scenario		Ambitious Scenario	
		2007	2020	2030	2020	2030
Literacy rate (total)	% of people ages 15 and above	62.75	66.40	70.65	71.82	78.16
Literacy rate (adult male)	% of people ages 15 and above	75.19	76.33	80.29	80.7	86.85
Literacy rate (adult female)	% of people ages 15 and above	50.82	55.91	61.5	57.43	64.9
Infant Mortality Rate	under 5 (per 1000 live births)	72.1	34.11	13.41	32.97	12.96
Poverty	millions of persons BPL	250	9.3	8.37	8.09	7.28
LCIG Report Poverty	millions of persons BPL	250		8		8
LCIG Report IMR	under 5 (per 1000 live births)			14.8		14.8
Number of skilled job creation	In lakhs	27	61	70	63	74
Number of Unskilled job creation	In lakhs	11	24	29	26	31

Source: Modeling Estimates.

A reduction in the inequality raises the aspirations of people belonging to the marginal classes of rural and urban households and they start striving for better education which gets reflected in the improved literacy rates within male and female for different scenarios over the time frame—2020 and 2030.

The dynamic CGE modeling analysis conducted indicates that job creation from green buildings has the potential to generate a savings multiplier for rural and urban households. As the economy grows with a focus on green industries, there would be demand for jobs which in turn would enhance wages and also lead more savings formation. All these in turn would have an overall impact on the economy and developmental indicators such as income, employment, improved infrastructure, and clean energy. These will have positive implications on the economic, environment and social domains of sustainability.

All these findings provide a long-term direction to the country's macro-planning and green growth and development roadmap by addressing the economic, environmental and social domains of sustainability through a progressive transformation from agriculture based economy towards green, ecologically and socially sustainable, energy efficient industry and service sector.

Green growth and development interventions is expected to create more employment for people from the agriculture sector, raise their skill levels and generate more skilled and unskilled jobs for them in the industry and service sector (which includes the construction sector) of the growing economy. This in a way in the long term will create larger economic and social sustainability which can be feed into the broader policy discourse of green job creation as explained in the next section of this chapter.

CONCLUSION AND EMERGING POLICY DIRECTIONS AND IMPLEMENTATION PLAN

The results emerging from the modelling analysis feeds into the policy discourse of green job creation that has been formulated by UNEP (United Nations Environment Programme), ILO (International Labour Organization), IOE (International Organization of Employers), ITUC (International Trade Union Confederation) in 2007.

Results of the model indicates the potential of income, skilled and unskilled employment generation from green growth interventions in the renewable energy and green building sector. Solar sector has the potential of creating economic multipliers. Green buildings can also lead to creation of skilled and unskilled employment generation. This in a way adds to the policy discourse and context of green jobs. In this regard, one needs to go back a little to the recent past and ponder upon the policy interventions made in the area of – "Climate Change and Green Jobs". The government of India had a task force established on "Climate Change and Green Jobs" in the recent past.

The Government of India task force on "Climate Change and Green Jobs" created a sub group in August 2009, which emphasized on the need to create green jobs under MGNREGA (Mahatma Gandhi National Rural Employment Guarantee Act) through promotion of mitigation measures like enhancement of renewable energy and energy efficiency interventions within the country(ILO, 2010).[7]

The national skill development corporation focuses, emphasizes on the development of resident skill for employment generation in next 10 years in India (NSDC, 2010). In order to generate employment and skill the council indicates to focus on sectors receiving the support of state and central government. It also indicates to generate skill and jobs in the area of services related to plumbing, repair mechanics and electrician services which will grow more with a rise in the green building sector of India. A green growth intervention in sectors like green building and solar sector has the scope of generating these specific skill based livelihoods.

This will then contribute to the National Skills Development Mission and its task of achieving a targeted 500 million skilled employment generation by 2022 which currently seems to be a humongous target to achieve. Even a miniscule achievement of this target through green growth interventions like promotion of green buildings will pave a long way in addressing the sustainability goals of the country in the long run. In order to achieve the long term sustainability goals of a developing country marked with distinct contrasts and inequality, this targeted implementation and achievement will be an imperative for future. This can only happen when the social, economic and environmental goals and domains of sustainability are balanced and promoted at the same time.

ACKNOWLEDGMENT

The authors will like to thank Ms. Shailly Kedia for research directions, Dr. Prodipto Ghosh, Dr. Sanjib Pohit, for CGE model building related guidance and Mr. Nitya Nanda for detailed review of the chapter. All views expressed in the chapter are personal and the authors are solely responsible for any inadvertent errors in the chapter. Authors will also like to acknowledge the support of Global Green Growth Institute in conducting this research.

REFERENCES

Authority, C. E. (2012). *All Indian Electricity Statistics*. New Delhi: Central Electricity Authority.

Commission, P. (2012). *Towards faster and more inclusive growth: an approach to the 11th five year plan*. New Delhi: Planning Commission.

Council, N. S. (2010). *Skills Gap Study of the North East*. New Delhi: National Skill Development Council.

Hajela, R. (2012). *Shortage of Skilled Workers: A Paradox of the Indian Economy. Compas: SKOPE.* University of Oxford.

Indian Express Limited. (2014). *Job creation down 43.15% in Q3 as economy slows*. Retrieved from http://indianexpress.com/article/business/business-others/job-creation-down-43-15-in-q3-as-economy-slows/

Limited, I. M. (2010). *The Skill Development Landscape in India and Implementing Quality Skills Training*. New Delhi: ICRA Management Consultancy Services Limited.

Organization, I. L. (2010). *Green jobs creation through sustainable refurbishment in the developing countries*. Geneva: ILO.

Organization, I. L. (2010). *MGNREGA: A review of decent work and green jobs in Kaimur District in Bihar*. New Delhi: International Labour Organization.

TERI. (2009). India's energy security: new opportunities for a sustainable future. New Delhi: The Energy and Resources Institute (TERI).

ENDNOTES

1 A sector that uses renewables, produces output in a resource efficient way and has a potential to generate employment and household welfare

2 Energy Assessment Guide for Commercial Buildings, April 2008, Developed and Published by: USAID ECO-III Project

3 rics.org/research

4 TERI study on 'High Performance Commercial Buildings in India' supported by Bureau of Energy Efficiency and United States Department of State.

5 Report on Overview of the Indian Building Sector, AFD report

6 'High Performance Commercial Buildings in India', project implemented by TERI and supported by the United States Department of State and Bureau of Energy Efficiency, Government of India

7 Available at http://www.ruraldiksha.nic.in/green/2011%20ILO%20Decent%20Work.pdf, pg 16.

Chapter 4
Prioritizing Sectors for Sustainable Growth in India:
An Environmental Social Accounting Matrix based Analysis

Barun Deb Pal
Institute for Social and Economic Change, India

Sanjib Pohit
CSIR-National Institute of Science Technology and Development Studies, India

ABSTRACT

This chapter has adopted method of Environmental Social Accounting Matrix (ESAM) and its multiplier analysis to identify sustainable growth path for India. Given the surge of GHG emissions, all developed countries and large emerging economies like India are coming under pressure in global forum to adopt a growth path that is sustainable from the environmental point of view. In this chapter, we propose to analyse the inter-linkage between sectoral GDP growth and its implications on growth in employment, income, GHG emissions and in energy use. The results indicate that the cereal productions other than rice and wheat should be given higher priority to reduce GHG emissions. Furthermore, the findings suggest that the existing pattern of government expenditure is sub-optimal as its reallocation based on their sustainable growth index increases GDP by 1%, reduces GHG emission by 1.57% and increase employment by 2.57%.

1. INTRODUCTION

India needs to grow fast in terms of Gross Domestic Product (GDP) in the coming decades to fulfil the basic development needs of her citizens. However, this would raise her greenhouse gas (GHG) emissions; a fact repeatedly pointed out to India by the global community in the context of climate change mitigation efforts. Thus, India's challenge is to decouple GHG emissions with its economic growth so that its GHG emissions do not increase significantly with the growth in GDP. To address this issue, In-

DOI: 10.4018/978-1-5225-0094-0.ch004

dia has laid emphasis on energy efficiency improvement and renewable energy use in its 12th five year plan period during 2012 to 2017 (Planning Commission, 2011). Though these initiatives are important to reduce GHG emissions, lack of availability of advanced technologies in the domestic economy is key constraint for their successful implementation. Therefore, decoupling GHG emissions with economic growth becomes a major policy issues in India.

There is no easy solution to address this issue. One way could be to focus on the growth of those sectors which are comparatively less GHG intensive than others.. This again poses a counter question, whether the growth of low emission intensive sectors leads to solve the issue of targeted GDP growth, employment creations, and growth in income of the households? To address this question prioritization of sectors is necessary by considering their impacts on GDP, income of the households, employment, energy use and GHG emissions. As government expenditure acts as a stimulus for a sector to grow, allocation of government budget according to the priority of the sectors could be a policy effort to decouple GHG emissions with the overall economic growth. Although the issue of prioritization has also been acknowledged by the Government of India (GOI) in its approach towards 12th five year plan to allocate government budgetary support to various sectors, no criteria for prioritization has been outlined in the plan document (Planning Commission, 2011).

Till date the issue of prioritization has been resolved by the experts with the help of cost-benefit analysis (Ortega et.al, 2014; Kendrovski et.al, 2014; Alston et.al, 1995); and most of these studies have taken into account single sector with the objective of prioritizing government interventions to achieve desired growth of the sector of concern. On the other hand, a few experts have also applied Input Output (IO) data and technique to identify key sector of the economy to emphasis the policy focus (Botric, 2013). However, key sector analysis using IO technique only takes into account monetary flow across various sector and their backward and forward linkages and leaves the environmental consequences asides. Therefore extending linkages across the sector by incorporating GHG emissions and employment in the IO framework could be a logical step to identify key sector(s) to decouple GHG emission with the economic growth in India. The linkages between economic sector and their environmental consequences has already been analysed by the experts using environmentally extended social accounting matrix (ESAM), which is an extension of IO matrix of the country of concern. The application of ESAM is popular in many countries such as Netherlands, Bolivia, Chile, China and UK.[1] Recently, similar attempt has been made in case of India by Pal and Pohit (2014). However, India is still young in application of ESAM in its environmental policy analysis. Therefore, an attempt has been made in this chapter to set criteria to prioritize sectors of Indian economy using environmentally extended social accounting matrix (ESAM) multiplier based analysis. Using ESAM multiplier we have estimated sector specific Low Carbon Development Score (LCDS) which comprises of sector specific impact on GDP growth, growth in households income, greenhouse gas (GHG) emissions, and primary energy use. The higher the value of this score, higher is their priority for government budget reallocation. Further we have analysed the impact of government budget reallocation according to the newly set criteria on GDP growth, employment growth and GHG emissions. In this way, this study provides a guideline for government budget reallocation as an alternative mechanism to low carbon economic development especially when technology adoption is not easy process.

Following this introductory section, the rest of the paper is organised as follows. The section 2 describes briefly framework of ESAM for India along with the derivation of ESAM multiplier analysis. Section 3 describes application of ESAM multiplier to estimate development score for India to identify key sectors for improvement in GHG emission intensity. Section 4 describes an illustrative example of ESAM multiplier model to analyse the impact of fiscal restructuring on economic growth and GHG emissions in India. Finally section 5 gives some concluding remarks of this study.

2. ENVIRONMENTALLY EXTENDED SOCIAL ACCOUNTING MATRIX (ESAM): FRAMEWORK AND MULTIPLIER MODEL

ESAM is an extension of a Social accounting matrix with environmental indicators. In India, the first ever ESAM have been published by Pal and Pohit (2014) for the year 2006-07. In this ESAM, authors have extended India's SAM of the year 2006-07 with sector specific GHG emission and energy resource depletion including coal, oil and land. As this is the only ESAM available for India for the year 2006-07, we have taken this ESAM as primary data base to carry out ESAM multiplier based analysis for this study purpose. As Table 1 indicates, Rows 1-6 and Columns 1-6 represent a SAM structure whereas, Rows 1-10 and Columns 1-10 represent a hypothetical ESAM.

ESAM multiplier analysis basically follows SAM multiplier analysis. Let A be the domestic expenditure coefficient matrix, X be the matrix of sector-wise gross output and Y be the matrix of exogenous variables. In this case, we have assumed government expenditure, foreign trade and gross capital formation as exogenous variables. Therefore, SAM can be written as,

$$X_{nx1} = A_{nxn} X_{nx1} + Y_{nx1} \tag{1}$$

or

$$X = \left(I - A\right)^{-1} Y \tag{2}$$

Table 1. Structure of hypothetical ESAM

			Production	Factors of production	Institutions	Tax/ Subsidies	capital account	Rest of the world	Substances (GHG)	Depletion of Natural resource		Environmental theme
										Renewal of Energy resource	Renewal of land	
			1	2	3	4	5	6	7	8	9	10
Production		1							Emission of pollutants from production			
Factors of production		2								Discovery of Energy capital	Renewal in land through conservation	
Institutions		3			SAM				Emission of pollutants from consumption			
Taxes/ Subsidies		4										
capital account		5										
Rest of the world		6										
Substances (GHG)		7	Absorption of substances in production		Absorption of substances in consumption							Accumulation of substances
Depletable Substances	Depletion of Energy Resources	8		Extraction of Energy stock								Net Reduction in natural stock
	Depletion of Land	9		Depletion of land due to land use change					Emission from land use change			Net depletion in land
Environmental theme				GHG inventory								

$$X = M \cdot Y \tag{3}$$

where, matrix M is the SAM multiplier matrix with dimension nxn, (n being the number of accounts in SAM) which shows the direct and indirect induced impact on the economy due to unitary changes in the exogenous factor. The multiplier matrix M has several blocks like, commodity to commodity block; commodity to households block; factor payment to commodity blocks and so on. Each of these blocks describes the impact on of exogenous policy change on its components. For example, households to commodity block describe the impact on of exogenous changes in any commodity producing sector on households' income[2]. However the above multiplier analysis does not consider the direct and indirect induced impact of exogenous policy changes on GHG emission. To capture the same, we have estimated pollution *trade-off* multiplier following the approach described in Kohn (1975). The pollution *trade-off* multiplier measures the direct and indirect induced impact on pollution level due to the exogenous change in the economy. Thus, the pollution trade-off multiplier helps us to understand the fall or rise in GHG emission with the fall and rise in economic output. It can be explained in other way round also like, the amount of economic growth to be sacrificed to reduce one unit GHG emission in the economy. The mathematical expression of the pollution *trade-off* multiplier is given as follows:

$$E_{nx1} = P_{nxn} * X_{nx1} \tag{4}$$

where, E is (n X 1) matrix of sector wise emission, P is the diagonal matrix of dimension n x n where diagonal elements are sector specific emission coefficient.

Replacing Equation (2) into Equation (3),

$$E = P * \left(I - A\right)^{-1} * Y \tag{5}$$

$$\frac{\partial E}{\partial Y} = P * \left(I - A\right)^{-1} = T \tag{6}$$

Here T is the pollution trade-off multiplier matrix which indicates direct and indirect induced impact on emission due to any changes the exogenous variables as mentioned in ESAM multiplier model.

3. ESTIMATION OF LOW CARBON DEVELOPMENT SCORE FOR INDIA

As noted earlier, LCDS comprises of various economic and environmental indicators. The key economic indicators selected in the study are namely GDP, employment, households' income. Meanwhile, the selected environmental indicators are like – primary energy and GHG emissions multiplier. Here, we have taken into account the multiplier effect of every sector on these indicators and add up those to estimate sector specific LCDS for India for the year 2006-07. The multiplier effects are obtained from the various blocks of SAM multiplier and pollution trade-off multiplier matrix as obtained in previous section. Table 2 given describes selected multiplier for this study, their represented blocks of multiplier matrix M and justification for their consideration for prioritization purpose using proposed development score.

Table 2. Various multipliers, their rationality, and source

Multipliers	Justification	Representative Blocks of M Matrix
GDP Multiplier	Indicates overall economic growth	**Factor:** Commodity Increase or decrease in monetary value of factor input payment (Labour, Capital Land) in response to unitary changes in exogenous variables
Households Income Multiplier	Growth in households' income is an indicator for poverty alleviation.	**Households:** Commodity Increase or decrease in monetary value of Households income in response to unitary changes in exogenous variables
Energy Multiplier	Energy use is the principal source for GHG emissions.	**Primary Energy:** Commodity Increase or decrease in monetary value of factor expenditure on energy (Coal, Oil and Gas) in response to unitary changes in exogenous variables
Employment Multiplier	Employment generation is crucial for inclusive growth in developing countries	**Sector Wise No. of Person per Unit of Output:** Commodity Increase or decrease in number of labour employment in response to unitary changes in exogenous variables
GHG emissions multiplier	GHG emission causes global climate change. India is highly vulnerable in terms of variability in agricultural production and overall economic growth due to climate change effects.	**Pollution Trade-Off Multiplier:** Increase or decrease in GHG emission, measured in terms of tons of Carbon dioxide (CO2) equivalent with the increase or decrease in sectoral output in response to unitary changes in exogenous variables.

As Table 2 shows, except employment multiplier all other multiplier values can be obtained directly from estimated SAM and GHG emissions multiplier. As the employment multiplier shows the increase in number of employment due to increase in exogenous injection to the economic activities, we need some additional information about number of employment per unit of output. Information was collated from the unit level data available from the 64th round National Sample Survey (NSS) for the year 2007 published by Government of India (NSSO, 2010).

After estimating all the multipliers required for this study, we have applied these to set criteria for prioritizing sectors of the Indian economy to achieve low carbon economic development by decoupling GHG emissions with economic growth. Once we obtain all the indicators, LCDS can be obtained as shown in Table 3.

The first 5 columns of Table 3 show the value of various multipliers. Since these multipliers are measured in different units, we have to make them unit free for any addition or subtraction purposes. To do this, we have normalized each column by considering average of each column as control total. Columns with serial no 6 to 10 show the normalized value of the respective columns with serial no 1 to 5. The values shown in the column 6 to 10 represent relative influence of each sector on each indicator as compared to the average impact on those indicators due to exogenous shock into the economy by one unit. For example, if this value is greater than one for any indicator, this implies impact of the corresponding sector on that indicator is more than the average overall impact on that indicator in the economy. Once we get this entire unit free values, we can add them to get column 11 for LCDS. Note that the higher values corresponding to GHG and energy use show the increase in GHG emissions and energy use. Therefore, considering the issue of GHG emission control, we have put negative sign before the GHG and energy values while adding for development indicator. Hence the formula of getting sustainable growth index is:

Table 3. Estimation of SGI for each sector

Sectors	ESAM Multiplier					Unit Free Score						
	GHG (Tons/ Rs.Lakh)	Employment (Person/ Rs.Lakh)	Income (Rs. Lakh)	GDP (Rs. Lakh)	Energy (Rs. Lakh)	GHG	Employment	Income	GDP	Energy	LCDS	Rank
	1	2	3	4	5	6	7	8	9	10	11	12
PAD	17.12	3.72	1.49	1.85	0.13	1.68	2.13	1.56	1.45	0.65	4.18	7
WHT	12.52	4.23	1.59	1.96	0.14	1.23	2.43	1.67	1.54	0.69	5.16	6
CER	7.1	5.6	1.55	1.87	0.09	0.7	3.22	1.63	1.47	0.43	6.3	1
CAS	7.29	4.64	1.54	1.86	0.09	0.72	2.66	1.62	1.46	0.46	5.7	2
ANH	16.78	4.03	1.32	1.74	0.06	1.65	2.31	1.38	1.37	0.31	4.12	8
FRS	1.41	2.75	0.45	0.61	0.02	0.14	1.58	0.48	0.48	0.11	2.83	13
FSH	4.31	4.22	1.34	1.77	0.09	0.42	2.42	1.41	1.39	0.43	5.38	3
COL	7	0.91	0.83	1.21	1.06	0.69	0.52	0.87	0.95	5.34	-2.85	32
OIL	1.03	1.82	0.23	0.34	1.02	0.1	1.05	0.24	0.26	5.14	-3.21	33
GAS	11.25	1.18	0.71	0.95	1.04	1.11	0.68	0.74	0.74	5.26	-3.5	34
FBV	7.08	0.6	1.12	1.46	0.08	0.7	0.35	1.18	1.15	0.42	2.81	14
TEX	6.72	0.69	1.05	1.4	0.09	0.66	0.4	1.1	1.1	0.47	2.69	17
WOD	5.09	0.72	1.09	1.44	0.07	0.5	0.42	1.14	1.13	0.37	2.87	12
MIN	1.63	1.13	0.33	0.48	0.02	0.16	0.65	0.35	0.38	0.12	1.62	23
PET	3.35	1.8	0.38	0.57	0.62	0.33	1.04	0.39	0.45	3.13	-0.79	30
CHM	5.63	2.03	0.72	1	0.09	0.55	1.17	0.75	0.78	0.46	2.71	16
PAP	6.97	0.29	0.7	0.96	0.09	0.69	0.17	0.73	0.76	0.46	1.51	25
FER	10.52	1.82	0.71	1.01	0.21	1.03	1.05	0.75	0.79	1.05	1.57	24
CEM	42.96	0.14	0.72	1.02	0.16	4.23	0.08	0.75	0.8	0.78	-2.4	31
IRS	11.41	0.44	0.74	1.03	0.18	1.12	0.25	0.77	0.81	0.89	0.86	29
ALU	3.16	0.26	0.35	0.47	0.08	0.31	0.15	0.37	0.37	0.39	0.86	28
OMN	4.19	1.14	0.5	0.69	0.06	0.41	0.66	0.52	0.54	0.31	1.79	22
MCH	4.99	0.86	0.63	0.87	0.07	0.49	0.49	0.66	0.68	0.37	1.99	21
NHY	74.63	0.28	1.03	1.49	0.35	7.34	0.16	1.08	1.17	1.77	-5.31	35
HYD	3.83	1.29	1.25	1.71	0.05	0.38	0.74	1.31	1.35	0.27	3.66	9
NUC	13.79	0.18	0.97	1.49	0.09	1.36	0.1	1.01	1.17	0.46	1.47	27
BIO	4.21	4.18	1.3	1.73	0.06	0.41	2.4	1.36	1.35	0.32	5.35	4
WAT	5.97	0.66	1.22	1.64	0.07	0.59	0.38	1.27	1.29	0.35	3.07	10
CON	7.72	1.04	1.03	1.34	0.11	0.76	0.6	1.08	1.05	0.55	2.57	18
LTR	6.51	1.7	0.91	1.23	0.2	0.64	0.98	0.96	0.96	1	2.34	19
RLY	11.22	0.71	1.09	1.44	0.11	1.1	0.41	1.15	1.13	0.54	2.18	20
AIR	14.17	0.52	1	1.33	0.12	1.39	0.3	1.05	1.05	0.62	1.47	26
SEA	5.38	0.41	1.14	1.5	0.08	0.53	0.24	1.2	1.18	0.41	2.73	15
HLM	4.56	0.44	1.18	1.53	0.07	0.45	0.25	1.24	1.2	0.36	2.95	11
SER	4.13	4.52	1.17	1.6	0.06	0.41	2.6	1.23	1.26	0.29	5.32	5

Note: Description of Sectors is given in the Appendix.

Table 4. Classification of sectors based on their priority on the basis of estimated LCDS

Category	Sector
High priority	CER, CAS, FSH, BIO, SER, WHT, PAD, ANH, HYD, WAT, HLM, WOD
Medium Priority	FRS, FBV, SEA, CHM, TEX, CON, LTR, RLY, MCH, OMN, MIN, FER
Least priority	PAP, AIR, NUC, ALU, IRS, PET, CEM, COL, OIL, GAS, NHY

Low Carbon Development Score = Employment + Households Income + GDP – GHG – Energy.

In the context of adding all the indicators to obtain LCDS for India, one may argue about the choice of weights to estimate LCDS as there is a well established method of Principle Component Analysis (PCA) to estimate weights for each indicator while estimating any index or performance score. However, the weights estimated with the help of PCA are based on the available data of the economy and reflects the existing focus of the government on the concerned indicators used for calculating indices. In case of India, it is evident from the history that the poverty alleviation, employment generation and high economic growth were major focus since its independence. The focus towards low carbon growth has become one among the policy agenda since it signed Kyoto-Protocol in UNFCCC in the year 1991. More specifically the strong policy initiatives have been taken very recently after Copenhagen summit of UNFCCC in the year 2009. Keeping these issues in mind, this study is an attempt to estimate LCDS for an ex-ante assessment of government policies for low carbon development. Hence by adding all the selected indicators we are assuming equal weights to each indicator.

The sector specific LCDS thus obtained are arranged in descending order and rank them to identify priority sectors for government budget allocation purpose to reduce GHG emission intensity in India The column 12 of the above table shows the rank of every sector on the basis of their LCDS.

For clarity of presentation, we have arranged these 35 sectors into three categories namely,

1. High priority sectors with rank is less than or equal to 12;
2. Medium Priority with rank greater than 12 and less than or equal to 24); and
3. Least priority sector with rank greater than 24 (see Table 4).

It is observed from Table 4 that the agriculture sector receives high priority on the basis of LCDS. Moreover the priorities are to be given to cereals (CER) other than paddy (PAD) and wheat (WHT), cash crop (CAS) and fisheries (FSH) as compared to paddy (PAD), animal husbandry (ANH) and wheat production. Though the paddy and wheat are main staple food for most of Indians, the significant GHG emissions from these productions results the lower value of LCDS as compared to cereals. Since cropping intensity in India is 136% and government is planning to improve it further by implementing National Food Security Mission (NFSM), Mechanization and so on. Therefore, it can be argued on the basis of results shown in Table 4 that promoting cereals (mostly pulses other than paddy and wheat in this case) and cash crops production can help to achieve higher cropping intensity in India. Again the cost of cultivation data published by Department of Agriculture, Government of India, ensures that the profit from pulses and cash crops are higher than paddy and wheat.[3] Hence, a strategic land use planning to increase area under pulses and cash crops without changing area under staple foods crops can give more return from the agriculture sector without much increase in GHG emissions. Therefore with the government policy support towards pulses and cash crops cultivation, farmers can obtain better return from crop cultivation by cultivating pulses and cash crops in at least one cropping season. As a result agricultural situation in India and income of the farmers will be improved.

On the other hand, the hydro electricity production in India also receives high priority as compared to nuclear and thermal electricity. Though the Nuclear electricity does not have significant direct impact on energy based GHG emission, its indirect induced impact as obtained through SAM multiplier increases GHG emission in India. By contrast, too much dependency on coal based power plants makes thermal electricity sector least priority category sector. Again, we have seen primary energy production sectors are least priority sector as they lead to depletion of energy resources and increase in fugitive emission in India. However, this result is not surprising as energy production sectors in the India is highly energy and emission intensive (NATCOM, 2010). On the other hand, it is evident from the studies that almost 7.5 crore Indian households (approximately 25% of Indian Population) do not have access to electricity (Planning Commission, 2011). So providing adequate electricity through renewable sources like hydro electricity generation can be an important step towards limiting GHG emissions. It is now clear from the above discussion that, the ESAM multiplier analysis may provide an indicative road map to the policy maker to achieve low carbon development in India. However, the claims made in the above paragraphs require further justification through policy impact evaluation. In this context we have brought forward in following section, an analysis on impact of fiscal reallocation among the sectors, based on their priority, on economic growth and GHG emission control in India.

4. FISCAL REALLOCATION AND ITS IMPACT IN INDIA

The 12th five year plan document published by the then Planning Commission of India has argued that government will allocate budgetary support among various sectors based on the priority basis except defence, education and health sectors (Planning Commission of India, 2011). Since government expenditure across various sectors acts as a fiscal stimulus for economic growth, we have considered this as policy instrument for our analysis. Again as we have kept government expenditure as exogenous factor in our ESAM model, it becomes easier to us to do such kind of analysis.

Now if we look at the government expenditure pattern in India of the year 2006-07, almost 80% of total government expenditure is spent on Defence, Public administration, education, and health. Out of remaining 20%, major share are spent for chemical, land transport, and construction sectors which are considered here as medium priority sectors in terms of LCDS as estimated in this study. Therefore, the current focus of the government is different than the focus required to achieve low carbon growth in India. Table 5 gives clear understanding about this fact.

It is evident from Table 5 that government of India can change its focus according to the rank of sectors in terms of development score and reallocate its budgetary support to achieve low carbon growth. The impact of such analysis is given in the following section.

Table 5. Government expenditure pattern: sectoral share

Sr. No	Sector	Share (2006-07)	Rank (2006-07)	Rank (LCDS)
1	PAD	0.0149	14	7
2	WHT	0.0077	17	6
3	CER	0.0270	12	1
4	CAS	0.0000	26	2
5	ANH	0.0495	10	8
6	FRS	0.0000	25	13
7	FSH	0.0000	27	3
8	COL	0.0009	22	32
9	OIL	0.0000	28	33
10	GAS	0.0040	19	34
11	FBV	0.0579	9	14
12	TEX	0.0478	11	17
13	WOD	0.0000	24	12
14	MIN	0.0000	29	23
15	PET	0.0613	8	30
16	CHM	0.1322	1	16
17	PAP	0.0117	16	25
18	FER	0.0000	23	24
19	CEM	0.0000	30	31
20	IRS	0.0000	31	29
21	ALU	0.0000	32	28
22	OMN	0.0785	5	22
23	MCH	0.0845	4	21
24	NHY	0.0770	6	35
25	HYD	0.0143	15	9
26	NUC	0.0022	21	27
27	BIO	0.0000	33	4
28	WAT	0.0666	7	10
29	CON	0.1074	3	18
30	LTR	0.1229	2	19
31	RLY	0.0221	13	20
32	AIR	0.0029	20	26
33	SEA	0.0067	18	15

Table 6. Impact of government expenditure reallocation on key development indicators

	Existing Condition	New Scenario	% Change
GDP (Rs. Lakh)	375954398	379422539	0.92
Household Income (Rs. Lakh)	331147217	334085182	0.89
Employment (person)	391766427	401832389	2.57
GHG emission (tons)	1845745200	1825373538	-1.10
Emission Intensity (tons/Rs.lakh)	5.09	5.00	-1.91
Energy Demand (Rs. Lakh)	26701963	26282632	-1.57
Total Value of Output (Rs. Lakh)	897371524	900034205	0.30

5. IMPACT OF RE-ALLOCATION OF GOVERNMENT BUDGET ON INDIAN ECONOMY

Here, we have followed a conservative approach by keeping aside the defence, health and education sector from budget reallocation and decided to reallocate only 20% of total government expenditure among the reaming activities listed in ESAM. This decision is corroborated with the statement made by the government of India in its 12th five year plan approach paper of reallocating budgetary support across various sectors except defence, administration, education and health (Planning commission, 2011). Here we have used the rank of the sectors as shown in Table 3 as the criteria for re-allocation. For example, sector with rank 1 according to LCDS will receive the amount same as the amount currently received by the sector which has rank 1 based on existing share of government expenditure. Once we get this re-allocated government expenditure, we put this in the column of government expenditure in our ESAM and run the multiplier analysis. The results from this multiplier analysis are shown in Table 6.

Table 6 indicates that the reallocation of existing government expenditure according to priority sectors results positive impacts on the economy. The high impacts are observed in the form of GHG emission reduction by 1.10%; emission intensity reduction by 1.91%; the primary energy demand (intermediate as well as final demand) reduction by 1.57% and the increase in employment by 2.57%. Though the impact on GDP, household's income and value of output are not significant but these are at least higher than the existing case. Hence we can argue that the existing pattern of allocating government expenditure is suboptimal and more benefit can be drawn by efficient allocation through prioritization based on sector specific implication of GDP growth, growth in households' income, GHG emission and energy consumption.

5. CONCLUSION

Decoupling GHG emissions with economic growth is an important research and policy agenda in the Indian economy to achieve low carbon economic development in future. This issue is also challenging to the researcher due to the scarcity of relevant data. In this context, this study is an attempt to bridge the gap. The result presented in this paper reveals that even if we can reallocate 20% of government expenditure spent on various sectors, we can gain almost 1% more GDP growth with substantial reduction in GHG emission and without hindering employment growth. Therefore, government can set its priority on the basis of Low Carbon Development Score and reallocate its budgetary support to achieve efficient policy outcome (Appendix).

REFERENCES

Alarcón, J., van Heemst, J., & De Jong, N. (2000). Extending the SAM with Social and Environmental Indicators: An Application to Bolivia. *Economic Systems Research, 12*(4), 473–496. doi:10.1080/09535310020003784

Alston, J. M., Norton, G. W., & Pardey, P. G. (1995). *Science under Scarcity*. New York: Cornell University Press.

Botric. (2013). *Identifying Key Sectors in Croatian Economy Based on Input-Output Tables*. EIZ-WP-1302.

Central Statistical Organization. (n.d.). *Energy Statistics of India, Government of India*. Retrieved from www.mospi.nic.in

Gallardo, A., & Mardones, C. (2013). Environmentally extended social accounting matrix for Chile. *Environment, Development and Sustainability, 15*(4), 1099–1127. doi:10.1007/s10668-012-9430-0

Jian, X. (2000). An Environmentally Extended Social Accounting Matrix. *Environmental and Resource Economics, 16*(4), 391–406. doi:10.1023/A:1008376618447

Kendrovski, V., Spasenovska, M., & Menne, B. (2014). The Public Health Impacts of Climate Change in the former Yugoslav Republic of Macedonia. *International Journal of Environmental Research and Public Health Open Access, 11*, 5975–5988.

Kohn. (1975). Input Output Analysis and air pollution control. *Economic Analysis of Environmental Problem*, 259-274. Retrieved from: http://www.nber.org/chapters/c2837

Ministry of Environment and Forests. (2009). *India's GHG emissions Profile – Results of five modelling study*. Government of India. Retrieved from www.moef.nic.in

NATCOM- Indian Network on Climate Change Assessment. (2010). *Greenhouse Gas Emission 2007*. India: Ministry of Environment and Forests, Government of India.

Ortega, S. T., Hanley, N., & Simal, P. D. (2014). A Proposed Methodology for Prioritizing Project Effects to Include in Cost-Benefit Analysis Using Resilience. *Vulnerability and Risk Perception, Sustainability, 6*, 7945-7966.

Pal, B. D., Ojha, V. P., Pohit, S., & Roy, J. (2014). GHG emission and Economic Growth. Springer.

Pal & Pohit. (2014). Environmentally Extended Social Accounting Matrix For Climate Change Policy Analysis for India. *Journal of Regional Development and Planning, 3*(1), 61–75.

Planning Commission. (2011). *Faster Sustainable and More Inclusive Growth, Approach towards 12th five year Plan*. Government of India.

Pradhan, B. K., Saluja, & Singh, S.K. (2006). A Social Accounting Matrix for India, Concepts, construction and Applications. Sage Publication.

Robert, K. (1975). Input Output Analysis and air pollution control. Economic Analysis of Environmental Problem. Retrieved from http://www.nber.org/chapters/c2837

ENDNOTES

1 For example, see Keuning (1992), Heemst and Jong (2000), Gallardo and Mardones (2013), Xie (2000) and Shmelev (2010).

2 For further detail, see Pradhan et.al (2006).

3 www.eands.dacnet.nic.in, accessed on February12, 2015.

APPENDIX

Table 7.

Sectors Code	Sector Description
PAD	Paddy Rice
WHT	Wheat
CER	Cereal, Grains etc, other crops
CAS	Cash crops
ANH	Animal husbandry & prod.
FRS	Forestry
FSH	Fishing
COL	Coal
OIL	Oil
GAS	Gas
FBV	Food & beverage
TEX	Textile & Leather
WOD	Wood
MIN	Minerals n.e.c.
PET	Petroleum & Coal Prod.
CHM	Chemical, Rubber & Plastic prod.
PAP	Paper & Paper prod.
FER	Fertilizers & Pesticides
CEM	Cement
IRS	Iron & Steel
ALU	Aluminum
OMN	Other manufacturing
MCH	Machinery
NHY	Hydro
HYD	Thermal
NUC	Nuclear
BIO	Biomass
WAT	Water
CON	Construction
LTR	Land transport
RLY	Rail Transport
AIR	Air Transport
SEA	Sea Transport
HLM	Health & medical
SER	All other services

Chapter 5
Integrated Economic and Spatial Planning for the Food–Energy–Water Nexus

Andrea Bassi
KnowlEdge Srl, Italy

Louise Gallagher
Luc Hoffmann Institute, Switzerland

ABSTRACT

Infrastructure projects are being planned and implemented around the world. These projects lead to economic growth and social development, but often unexpected side effects emerge. The problem is that financial analyses for infrastructure projects do not incorporate quantified economic assessments of social and environmental impacts. Equally, social and environmental assessments for infrastructure projects rarely qualify or quantify socioeconomic outcomes for investments in mitigation practices. Our analysis builds on a review of existing methodologies and tools to propose a method for jointly applying three modeling approaches for integrated economic and spatial planning. The results of case study of the Mekong Flooded Forest landscape shows the capability of the models to anticipate desired and undesired outcomes across social, economic and environmental indicators. This shows promising potential for better informing decision making for sustainability.

1. INTRODUCTION

Infrastructure projects are being planned and implemented around the world. They include large undertakings, such as airports and highways, as well as smaller ones, like irrigation projects; but all share the same goal: to support economic development and increase human well-being (Korytárová & Hromádka, 2014). These investment projects are driven both by the private sector - primarily for economic gains (Kateja, 2012) - and the public sector looking for social outcomes through reduced poverty, increased access to services and improvements in quality of life (Zhang & Chen, 2013). The returns for society

DOI: 10.4018/978-1-5225-0094-0.ch005

and economies –local, national and regional– on infrastructure investment are analyzed by governments and investors, but mostly focus on financial returns and desired economic outcomes, whatever these may be (Jones, Moura, & Domingos, 2014). Yet, there are unintended and unforeseen consequences of physical design and construction of infrastructure projects that impede the attainment of development goals. These are harder to measure in financial terms and therefore not considered deeply upfront in (Arce & Gullòn, 2000).

One critical example in the developing regions of the world is the relationship between infrastructure development and natural capital. Integrity of biodiversity, land and water all support a flow of inputs to our economies and societies at different scales. The complex natural systems that the world relies on for food, water, and energy are increasingly strained by climate change and the demands of a growing human population (MEA, 2005; Helm, 2014). The top pressures on "stores" of this natural capital are natural resource extraction (Behrens, Giljum, Kovanda, & Niza, 2007), infrastructure projects for transport and energy (Meunier, 2012) and expanding agricultural production and human settlements (McDonald, et al., 2014; Schäffler & Swilling, 2013). Under pressure, natural systems become less stable and resilient. This is a problem of global significance that entail risks for sectors reliant on natural inputs and impacts on the world's most vulnerable people who typically rely most directly on nature's "free" benefits.

The problem is essentially that financial analyses for infrastructure projects do not incorporate quantified economic assessments of social and environmental impacts. Equally, social and environmental assessments for infrastructure projects rarely qualify or quantify socioeconomic outcomes for investments in mitigation practices. How would land use change if the economy develops as desired? And what would be the consequences on natural resource use and on ecosystem services –particularly those related to food-energy-water? How large might the resulting cost implications be for vulnerable households? How best to plan roads, railways, power, waste management or irrigation infrastructure in a context of climate change? These are questions to which current methodologies for infrastructure assessments give unsatisfactory answers (for more information, see http://www.ruom.net/portfolio-item/inside-969-movement/).

Many tools are being put forward to inform decision-making by estimating the short, medium and longer-term outcomes of investments across social, economic and environmental dimensions (Bassi, Bečić, & Lombardi, 2014). There are a number of successful case studies of holistic infrastructure and land use planning, but far many more examples that have not found the mark. The results being produced by these tools are not all that useful for the end-users they aim to support (Rozema & Bond, In press).

In this chapter, we argue that a critical challenge to conservation science and policymaking is to overcome the silo between social, environmental and economic assessment. If an integrated approach is used, information will be generated that can effectively supports decision-making for infrastructure project (Isely, et al., 2010; Vandermeulen, Verspecht, Vermeire, Van Huylenbroeck, & Gellynck, 2011). This is because direct, indirect and induced impacts of infrastructure construction will be identified and forecasted. Desired and undesired impacts will be anticipated and quantified, across social, economic and environmental dimensions. This leads to more informed decision making, where risks of failure are reduced and where funding is more effectively used.

Our hypothesis is that existing approaches are failing to deliver the information required by key decision-makers because:

1. They do not adequately or credibly capture the cross-sectoral or systemic impacts of new infrastructure developments, and so undere4stimate costs and overestimate the benefits of these projects;
2. Tools are being applied in a top-down manner, with little participation by the end-user, or those they trust, in the design or implementation of assessments.

Our analysis builds on a review of existing methodologies and tools (Bassi, Lombardi, & Gallagher, 2014) to propose a method for jointly applying three modeling approaches for integrated economic and spatial planning. We are testing this method in the context of hydropower planning in Cambodia under Linked Indicators for Vital Ecosystem Services (LIVES) project. Here, we give preliminary results and reflect on the lessons learned six months into project implementation.

2. CHALLENGES POSED BY CURRENT METHODOLOGICAL APPROACHES TO ECONOMIC AND LAND USE POLICY AND PLANNING

2.1 Disjointed Policy Processes

Planning processes often take place in silos. For instance, many countries currently have water use planning systems that ignore rapid needs increases for irrigated croplands. These same countries are often planning to meet energy needs with mixed portfolios including hydropower but without accounting for impacts on water security, biofuels and food security. All of these plans are further compromised by their failure to systematically account for the impacts of carbon emissions and climate change on each of these processes. These planning processes require analytical models and toolkits that employ a systemic approach. On the other hand, the existing models lack the data and methodological components required to conduct an integrated policy assessment. These assessments are especially needed in a developing country policy context1. Generally, these toolkits focus on one resource (e.g. PODIUMSim and WEAP for water, LEAP and MARKAL for energy), ignoring or only partially considering the connections with other resources (UNEP, 2014).

2.2 Poor Reconciliation of Costs and Benefits at Different Scales

Almost universally, decision makers at all levels are less concerned with single issues in their own right, and much more concerned with the impact of these issues on their bottom line - economic growth, social equity, geopolitical stability and national security. In economics, we use a wide range of real-time connected economic indicators to build a robust picture of economic "stocks and flows" in a country, and we then package and communicate these complex assessments to other communities using aggregate indicators such as GDP. This is the type of integrated system we need for Food, Energy and Water; a system that provides a clear understanding of the quantity and quality of environmental "stocks and flows" on a given landscape, allowing us to link these indicators to the health, livelihoods, and security of people at the scales and in the locations that matter to decision processes.

2.3 Cost Optimization

Environmental policy theorists Baumol and Oates suggest that the substantive allocative issue with large-scale infrastructure is how to ensure that the public service or benefit that the infrastructure is to provide is obtained at the least cost to society overall (Baumol & Oates, 1988). But how is the cost estimated and how is the least cost option identified? Are all costs, across actors and sectors, and for the short, medium and longer term factored in the analysis? Impact assessments of large-scale infrastructure projects like transport corridors, power installations or waste management facilities tend to emphasize their development benefits (i.e. logistics savings, jobs, revenue) (ADB, 2009; OECD, 2002), using conventional internal rate of return or at best, cost-benefit analysis (CBA). At times, certain negative environmental externalities are estimated, such as carbon emissions, but these are rarely fully integrated in the economic analysis. Moreover, these studies fail to include other critical dimensions like loss of more immediate contributions of nature to economies and human wellbeing like reduced water availability due to deforestation, or reduced capacity for flood regulation when river banks are altered.

2.4 Location Optimization

The public infrastructure siting problem, involving "Not In My Back Yard" goods such as road networks, sewage treatment plants and power stations, has been characterized by Mitchell and Carson (1986) and Pommerehne *et al.* (1997) as one involving the allocation of an indivisible good with unequal cost sharing and limited siting alternatives. Negative externalities are concentrated on relatively few individuals living in close proximity whereas the benefits are dispersed across the wider population (Pommerehne, Hart, & Schneider, 1997; Mitchell & Carson, 1986). Modern waste disposal infrastructure is built to serve regions rather than localities to capture economies of scale. As a result, fairness judgments concerning regional risk-sharing or wider social and environmental concerns have also been documented (White & Ratick, 1989); (Snary, 2004); (Ellis, 2004).

2.5 Lack of Adequate Responses for the Complexity of the Problem

Many indicators have been developed by governments, by the academic community (i.e. Environmental Performance Index2, Environment Vulnerability Index3) or by non-governmental organization such as Global Footprint Network. These initiatives have helped to advance science of sustainability measurement but we are still far from what one would consider adequate indicators for monitoring the connectivity, stability and resilience of food, energy, and water at scales relevant to individuals, communities, and decision makers.

3. REVIEW: EXISTING TOOLS USED IN INTEGRATED ECONOMIC AND SPATIAL PLANNING

A variety of approaches have been developed to assess the impact of public policies and private investments on land use, environmental conservation, human well-being and inclusive economic growth. These can be categorised as methodological frameworks and tools (Table 1).

Table 1. Summary of strengths and weaknesses of available measurement and analysis tools

Tool	Strengths	Weaknesses
Indicators and measurement frameworks	• Allow for the quantification of problems and identification of their causes and effects; • Facilitate the assessment of the intervention options available; • Enable quantitative monitoring and evaluation of the implemented actions.	• Data not always and reliable (especially across sectors); • Need to be combined with other tools for systemic analysis (e.g., scenarios and simulations) to explicitly show how changes in one variable is connected to changes in other variables.
Spatial planning	• Supports spatially disaggregated assessment of policy impacts. • Supports the identification of the desirable locations for infrastructure projects.	• Generally a sectoral analysis. • Applicable to specific policy decisions rather than wider development planning processes.
Natural Capital & Environmental Accounting	• Facilitates the integration of environmental indicators into national accounting systems. • Promotes a more systemic view of development trends.	• Limited data on natural capital and ecosystems. • Generally focused on national trends, still mostly unused in decision making.
Natural Capital Valuation	• Provides the basis for monetizing environmental goods and services. • Makes the argument for investing in natural capital preservation.	• Difficulties in translating certain ecosystem services into a monetary value. • Lack of consistency across the existing methodologies.
Investment & Policy evaluation tools	• Assess the advantages and disadvantages of green economy investments. • Support the identification of the most promising policy options for sustainable development.	• Generally focused exclusively on economic returns. • Inadequate for long-term planning.
Scenario Creation tools	• Promote innovative thinking about possible future trends for the system as a whole. • Improve multi-stakeholder, cross-sectoral risk management.	• Generally qualitative, and often disconnected from the capability of DSS. • Require facilitation and broad stakeholder involvement to create ownership.
Scenario Forecasting tools	• Allow a quantitative, integrated assessment of development and investment plans (short to long term). • Support the monitoring and identification of potential future challenges resulting from implemented actions.	• Require technical knowledge to build models and reliable data to customize them. • Require a disciplined monitoring, analysis, and communication process. • Ineffective if not integrated in the decision-making process.

1. **Methodological Frameworks:** Using one or more tools to provide guidance to decision makers for assessing environmental, social and economic implications of their choices, as well as to evaluate gaps in the current governance and policy structure, and identify potential entry points for action. The methodological frameworks relevant to land use and economic planning include:
    a. **Economic/Technological Assessment:** Decision Support Systems (DSS), feasibility studies and economic assessment studies;
    b. **Social/Governance Assessment:** Poverty and Social Impact Analysis (PSIA) and Governance Assessments;
        i. **Environmental Assessment:** Strategic Environmental Assessment (SEA); and
        ii. Environmental Impact Assessment (EIA).
2. **Tools:** Used in applying the methodological frameworks or to answer a specific set of questions in infrastructure and/or land use planning These include
    a. **Indicators:** OECD's diagnostic indicators for green growth, the Global Green Growth Institute's green growth indicators, World Bank's Adjusted Net Savings, UNEP's Green Economy Indicators, Planetary Boundaries, Ecological Footprint;

b. **Spatial Planning Tools:** Integrated Spatial Planning (ISP), Smart Infrastructure Planner (SIP), Natural Capital Project's InVEST, and several other Geographical Information System (GIS) tools like MARXAN;
c. **Natural Capital Assessment and Environmental Accounting Tools:** System of Environmental and Economic Accounting (SEEA), The Economics of Ecosystems and Biodiversity (TEEB); Natural Capital assessment and valuation tools (InVEST, ARIES and MIMES can be used for this purpose);
d. **Investment/Policy Evaluation Tools:** Cost benefit Analysis (CBA), Multi-Criteria Analysis (MCA) and Life Cycle Assessment (LCA);
e. **Scenario Creation (Qualitative) and Forecasting (Quantitative) Tools:** Qualitative approaches like Causal Loop Diagrams, Delphi Analysis and Story and Simulation, as well as quantitative simulation models like Computable General Equilibrium, energy supply optimization, nester–or coupled–models and integrated models.

4. PROPOSED APPROACH: KNOWLEDGE INTEGRATION AS FOUNDATION

The review shows that many tools exist for land use, ecosystem service and socioeconomic modeling (Bassi, Lombardi, & Gallagher, 2014). However, little consideration has been given as to how these could be applied in parallel to yield better information for economic, land use and conservation planning.

Combining tools allows for a holistic consideration of development impacts and land-use change – planned or other – and the socioeconomic implications of such change and translates these into spatial outputs.

This is what WWF has done with the creation of the Integrated Planning for Sustainability family of models. This work actively complements other existing efforts carried out by WWF (primarily through the Natural Capital Project, as well as REDD+ and green economy initiatives), UNEP (through their green economy work as well as TEEB on natural capital valuation), as well as selected governments (of relevance to the case study presented in this chapter, among many projects carried out in over 30 countries, are the cases of Indonesia and Malaysia for national strategies, as well as Thailand, Vietnam and Myanmar for sectoral policy and sub-national, e.g. landscape and provincial, assessments).

The approach presented in this chapter is based on the research work carried out in the *Linked Indicators for Vital Ecosystem Services* project led by the Luc Hoffmann Institute. This project aims to create a replicable scientific and policy process for integrating measures of ecosystem health into policy decisions influencing food-energy-water security. The project extends existing modeling to incorporate key socio-economic and environmental dynamics to demonstrate how natural capital can be integrated into policy action in national and place-based contexts. The demonstration site is the WWF Mekong Flooded Forest (MFF) Landscape in Cambodia and Laos. This site was chosen for its unique characteristics, being an area where social well-being and economic development an intrinsically related to the environment (e.g. with high dependence on the Mekong river for water, food and energy). This means that the environment has been the main enabler for social and economic development, but it is now threatened by the creation of infrastructure that may profoundly change the local economy as well as the livelihood of local people. For this reason a systemic approach is required, for assessing the local, regional and national impacts of infrastructure projects (which may benefit the country at the expense of local communities), across social economic and environmental measures. Further, several technical and scientific sectoral studies have been carried out in the region and strong support for the development of new tools based on system analysis was expressed both by the Ministry of the Environment and by provincial authorities. The combination of these factors makes the MFF landscape an excellent application from a research point of view and from a policy/implementation perspective.

The approach proposed by the LIVES project makes use of the following modeling tools:

1. **Spatial Planning Tools:** Marxan: Used to plot out optimal physical placement of economic activities, human settlements etc., but often without reference to what this means for socioeconomic effects or monetary valuation of loss/gain in natural capital assets. They are often static assessments that do not 'speak to' decision-makers outside of land use/conservation planners.
2. **Nonmarket Environmental Valuation Methods:** (e.g. InVEST) Are used to value the external costs/benefits of losing/maintaining ecosystems and their services. Depending on the specific method applied, natural capital valuation illustrates a certain dimension of economic impacts from changes in natural capital. However producing a dollar figure to represent nature's value that stand alone and are not related to priorities for policymakers means valuation results often remain on the fringe of economic decision-making.
3. **System Dynamics Macroeconomic Models:** (e.g. Green Economy Model (GEM)4) Are used to project growth in GDP, trade trends and inform public policy. The understanding of economic growth informing those models is largely based on the neoclassical growth model and analysis of historic development paths; neither of which account for environmental costs and the impacts of lost stocks of natural assets in the conventional models used.

Figure 1 summarizes the main methodologies and models used to create IPS. InVEST, which generates spatial information and estimates natural capital and ecosystem services is used as input for estimated changes in natural capital stocks, i.e. forest land cover change, and resultant estimates of changing values in key ecosystem services as well as carbon stocks, among others (see "1"). This information coupled with socio-economic analysis is used to create the map of the system (or Causal Loop Diagram) to identify the main drivers and impacts of land use change in the region (see "2"). System Dynamics methods require an integrated mathematical model, the Green Economy Model (GEM) (see "3") that incorporates the key drivers of change and impacts, such as investments and policies. This mathematical model is calibrated using InVEST's outputs, among others through validating the direction and magnitude of relationships between biophysical variables and ecosystem service variables, i.e. changes in surface water flow corresponding to hectares of forest lost in the region as a result of road construction, among others. The results of the socio-economic analysis include the estimation of impacts on poverty (monetary and in terms of access to resources). Finally, the result of the simulations generated with GEM, the System Dynamics model, can be fed back into Marxan and InVEST to visualize spatially the indirect and induced social, economic and environmental impacts of road construction. Weighing up the various impacts, the System Dynamics model could identify specific interventions on improved sustainable agricultural practices which could be tested for likely effectiveness in maintaining key ecosystem services in the InVEST models. This is an important value-added of the System Dynamics approach since InVEST only estimates the direct impacts of land use change on ecosystem services and not on other variables like population growth rates or specific action-oriented interventions.

Figure 1. The main methodologies and models integrated in IPS: Marxan and InVest, with spatial information (1); system thinking (the soft side of System Dynamics), to identify key social, economic and environmental drivers of change (2); GEM (system dynamics), to quantify scenarios with a systemic and integrated approach (3)

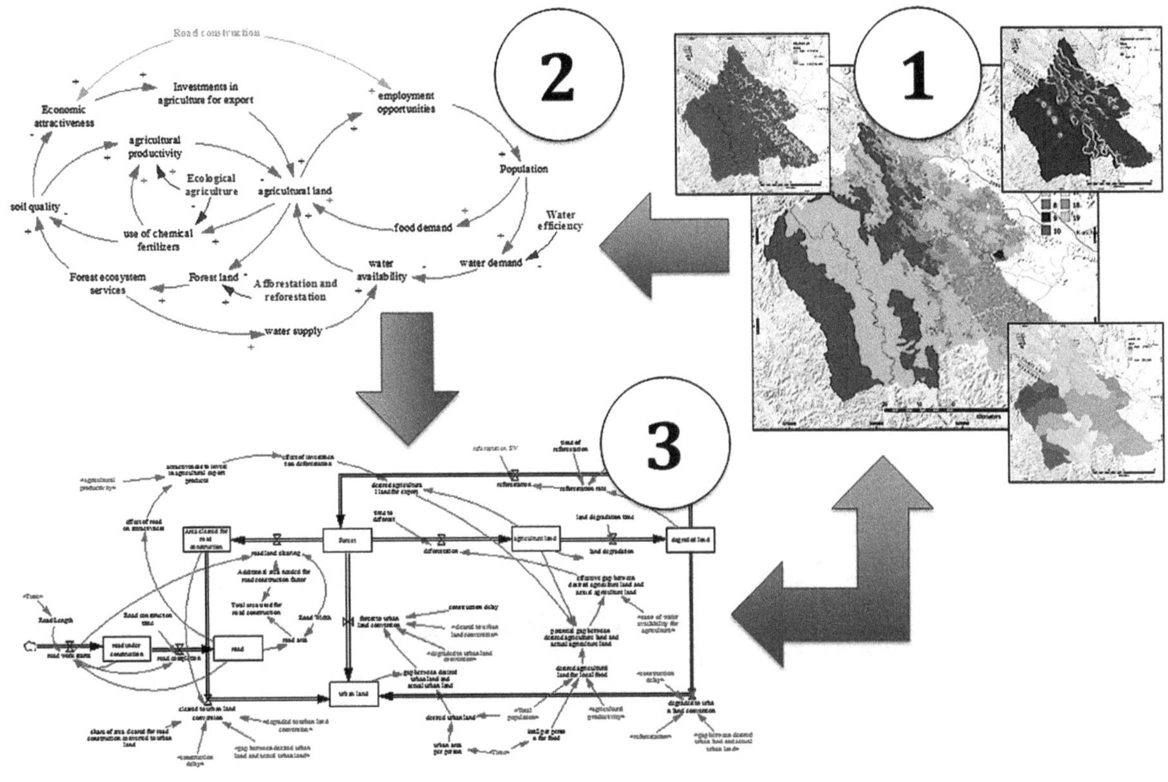

The main strength of the approach proposed is direct support to planning process, based on the incorporation of the best available science in a model that integrates social, economic and environmental dimensions and can simulate alternative scenarios projecting results over time, across sectors and actors (Figure 1).

5. FOOD-ENERGY-WATER NEXUS AT THE LANDSCAPE LEVEL

5.1 System Analysis

A Causal Loop Diagram (CLD) was created through the use of a multi-stakeholder approach to represent the many interconnections existing between food, energy and water in the SSK landscape in Cambodia (Figure 2).

The specific goal of the creation of this CLD is to explore the systemic nature of the landscape, and to support the identification of entry points for interventions (e.g. policies and investments) in order to inform policy making at the provincial and national level. These interventions are assessed using a Green Economy/Green Growth framework in which

Figure 2. Representation of the food-energy-water nexus at the landscape level

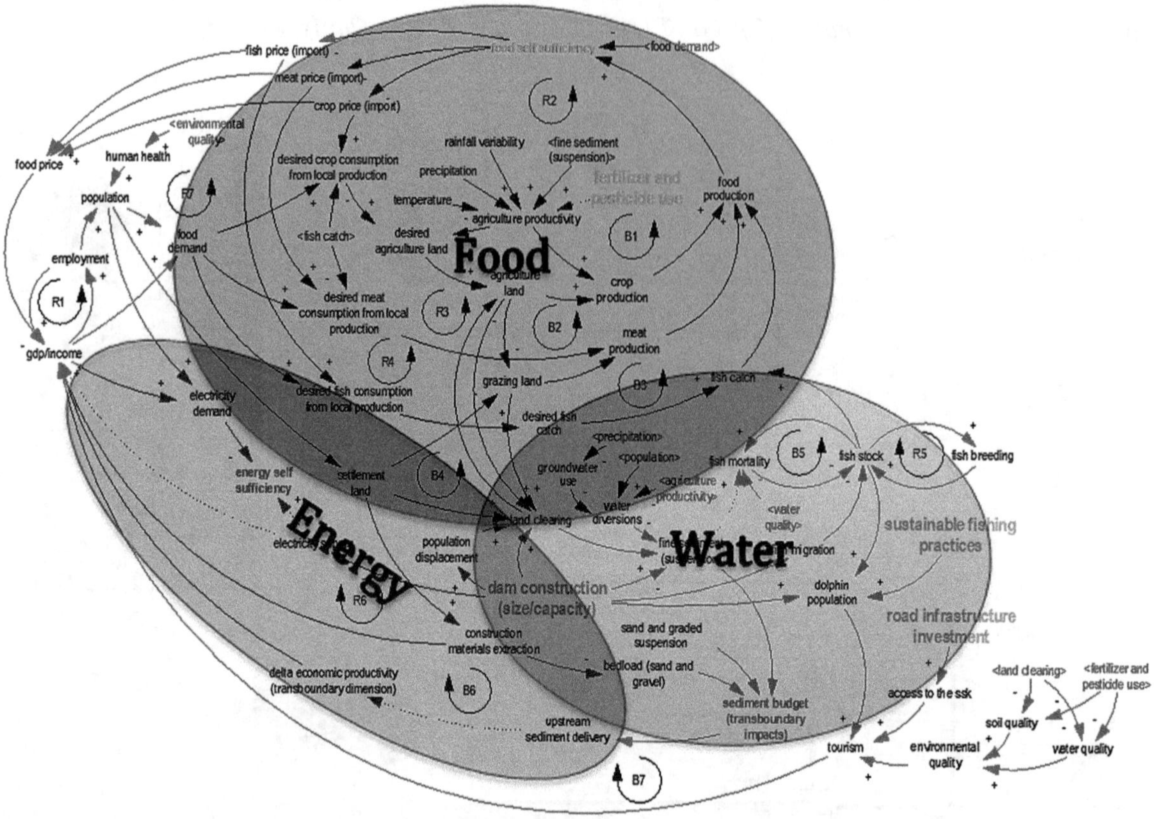

1. Issues are identified,
2. Their causes and effects are mapped using a systems approach (i.e. System Thinking), and
3. Interventions are formulated and assessed in relation to their contribution to sustainable development (SD).

At the landscape level, SD is defined as a balanced path where a healthy food-energy-water nexus effectively enables the improvement of well-being at the local and regional level.

The CLD includes several variables, all interconnected through causal relations (blue arrows) and forming many feedback loops5 (Figure 3). In particular, a few dominant feedback loops can be found in the CLD:

- **Economic Development:** With the growth in GDP and income, employment and investments will increase. As a result, employment and income will grow further (reinforcing loop, R1), and so will population, resulting in higher food and energy demand. As long as resources are available (e.g. agriculture land and fish) this feedback loop is likely to dominate the performance of the system, especially because local food production is in most cases the most economical food supply option (R2, R3 and R4).

Figure 3. The full CLD, including several reinforcing and balancing feedback loops

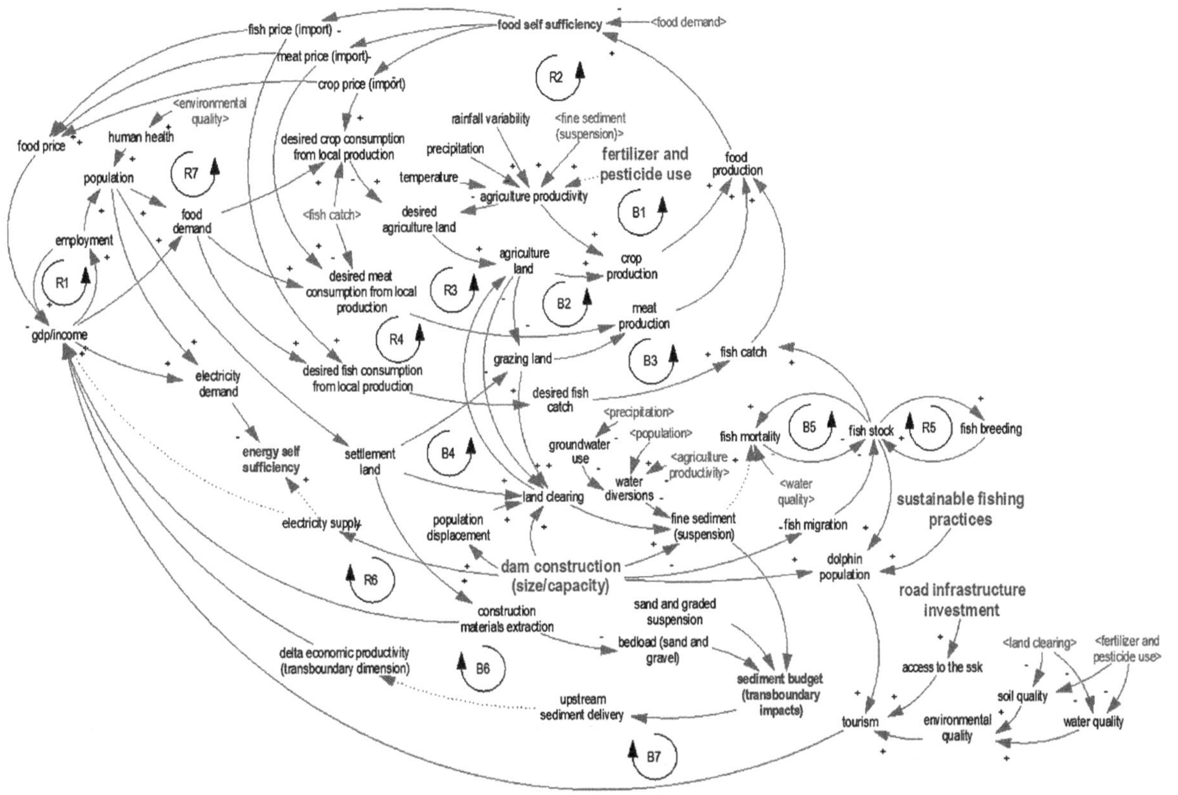

- **Natural Resources Availability:** There is finite amount of land in the landscape analyzed. Population growth and the expected increase in food demand all require land (for settlements, crop and meat production). Land scarcity, as well as land management practices (e.g. agricultural practices, affecting, among others, crop yield and water pollution) could become bottlenecks for the expansion of local food production (balancing loop, B1, B2, B3 and B4). If food self sufficiency declines, food imports will be required, reducing the strength of the economic development reinforcing feedback loop described above.
- **Pollution and Environmental Quality:** Business as usual development stimulates economic growth, but utilizes natural resources and pollutes the environment. This is the case of the use of chemical fertilizers and pesticides, which pollute water. As a consequence, human health is affected, as is biodiversity. Further, environmental quality affects soil productivity, tourism and the local population (B7), ultimately indicating that the medium to longer-term impact of unsustainable practices fully offset the short-term economic benefits they create.

The strength, and even the dominance of these feedback loops can be largely influenced by human decisions, such as the creation of a hydropower dam. In this specific case, depending on how the power generated is used, the feedback loops stimulated may be balancing or reinforcing. In fact, if electricity is entirely produced for exports, only the balancing loops of natural resource availability will be impacted (i.e. due to the deterioration of natural capital). On the other hand, if part of the energy produced is distributed locally, among the feedback loops that will be strengthened we find the economic ones, supporting socio-economic development, at least in the short term. It has to be considered in fact that an improvement in economic performance, if driving local development, will also increase food demand, which remains constrained by land and available fish stocks. As a result, it is important to balance reinforcing and balancing loops to ensure social, economic development with environmental sustainability, over the short, medium and longer term.

Importantly, the outcomes of this type of project are *direct*, *indirect* and *induced*. In fact, dam construction and operation would impact land availability for agriculture production due to controlled inundation of land (*direct*); possibly affect fish migration (*direct*), which in turn would either require fish to be imported or its consumption to be replaced with crops and meat, both requiring land (*indirect*); and finally affect economic development, negatively if other food sources are more expensive than fish (*induced*) and if the dolphin population declines or even disappears (*indirect*), affecting tourism arrivals (*induced*), and positively because of the higher access to a reliable source of electricity (*induced*).

5.2 Simulation Model[6]

5.2.1 Overview of the GEM Model Framework

The Green Economy Model (GEM) was designed explicitly to analyze green economy scenarios[7]. As a result, it includes several sectors across social, economic and environmental dimensions. The effective integration of these sectors is made through the use of stocks and flows, which bring consistency to the mathematical formulations used to create the model.

Many indicators are included in GEM applications, and particular emphasis was put into including the key capitals of sustainable development, such as social and human capital, physical (built up) capital and natural capital.

Figure 4 presents the generalized underlying structure of GEM. This diagram was developed with the input and support of several experts across countries, and builds on earlier work carried out with System Dynamics on green economy. This diagram shows how the key capitals are interconnected, and contribute to shaping future trends across social, economic and environmental indicators.

The GEM model customized at the landscape level is set up to simulate scenarios from the year 2000 to 2040. It presents annual results, but has a time step 16 times shorter. The main stocks and flows included in the model are:

- **Human Population:** Influenced by birth, death and net migration (affected by the availability of settlement land);
- **Fish Population:** Influenced by breeding, mortality, net migration (affected by dam capacity) and catch (affected by fish demand);
- **Dolphin Population:** Influenced by breeding and mortality (affected by dam capacity);
- **Land:** (Settlement, agriculture, grazing and fallow/forest land), influenced by population and food demand (i.e. crops and meat).
- **Sediments:** Influenced by water diversions (affected by population and precipitation), land clearing (affected by population and yield) and the extraction of construction materials (e.g. sand and gravel);

Figure 4. Causal Loop Diagram (CLD) representing the main variables and feedback loops of GEM applications; the GEM model framework aims to fully incorporate social and human capital, physical (built up) capital and natural capital.

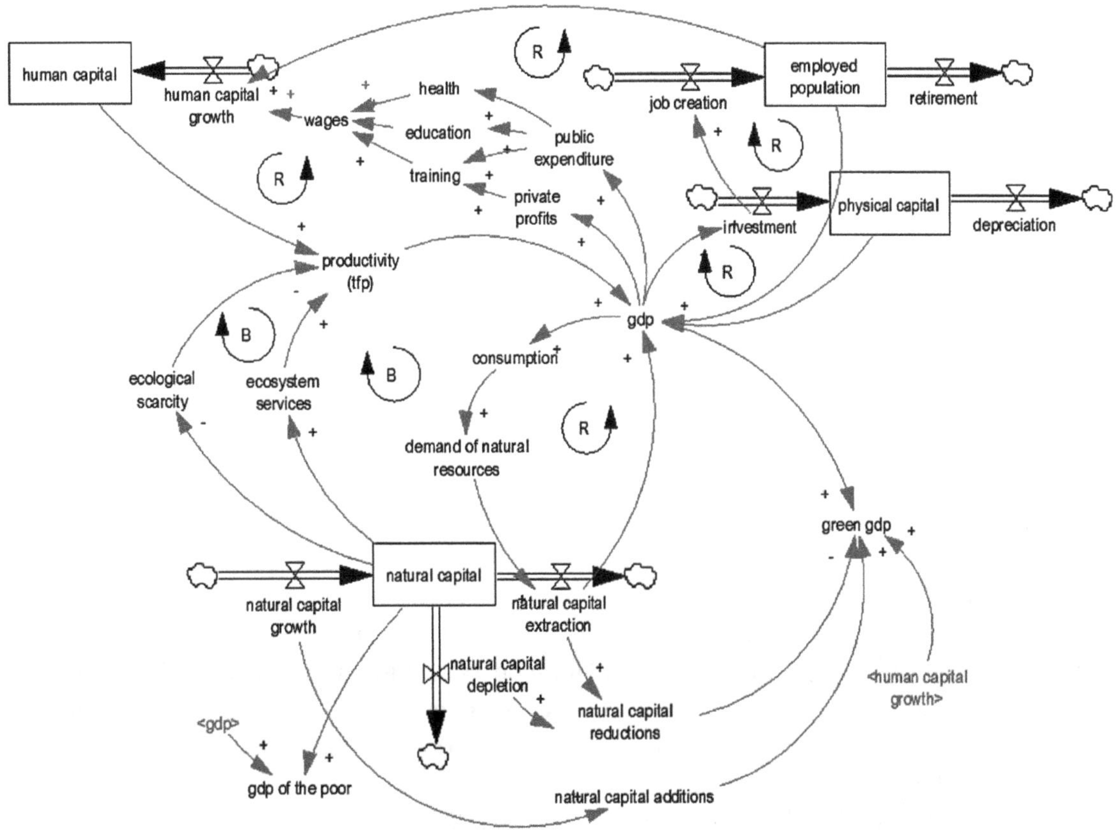

- **Hydropower Dam Capacity:** Influenced by the assumed investment in capacity expansion (the decommissioning/discard of capacity is not assumed to take place due to the long life time of capital and the simulation time reaching only 2040).
- **Road Network Length:** Influenced by the assumed investment in capacity expansion and decommissioning/discard.

The same reinforcing and balancing feedback loops presented in the CLD are also underlying the model, leading to changes in land use based on food demand and prices, which are affected by resource availability (e.g. land and fish), as well as by population and GDP.

5.2.2 Preliminary Results

The current version of the landscape model is a pilot, primarily used to explore the systemic nature of the MFF and other landscapes. It is also used to better identify the various cross-sectoral impacts of policy implementation (e.g. hydropower dam and road construction).

Figure 5. Population, land use, and daily per capita calorie intake: BAU scenario

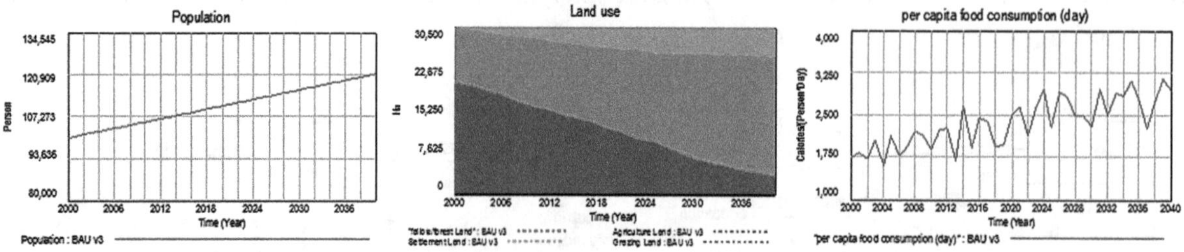

Population is projected to grow slowly but steadily, reaching 22.5% above the year 2000 by 2050. Alternative assumptions on birth and death rate could be used to project a faster demographic transition (see Text Box 1); on the other hand, the main results would not change. Even if population were to grow by 50% by 2050, GDP would be roughly similar to the BAU scenario, being curbed by the negative impact of food prices (higher than BAU) and energy availability (lower than BAU). These relations across variables are presented in more detail in the next paragraphs, for the BAU scenario.

Figure 5 shows that the growth of population is expected to profoundly change land use. Specifically, the largest impact is not due to the increase in settlement land, which represents (in the current version of the model) a rather small fraction of total land use; instead, it is the expansion of agriculture land at first, and grazing land at a later time, that leads to a marked reduction in fallow and forest land. This is due to the increase in food demand, driven by rising population and income. As a result of land use change, taking place to satisfy a growing demand for food, per capita calorie intake increases over time, reaching close to 3,000 calories per person per day (depending on the impact of climatic conditions on agricultural yield, assumed to be a random factor in the model, with an underlying growing trend of precipitation and temperature over time).

Population is one of the key drivers of economic growth in the model, as are food and energy prices and access to electricity. These are the identified primary drivers for the development of the local economy, which is greatly affected by the tourism and mining/extractive sectors as well. All other economic sectors are grouped into an *initial per capita GDP value*, which changes with population and productivity. Figure 4 presents GDP/income (left) and productivity (right), which is primarily growing due to the assumed

1. Increase in local power supply,
2. The resulting decline in electricity price (Figures 6 and 7), and
3. Road construction.

Figure 6. GDP/income, its annual growth rate, and productivity: BAU scenario

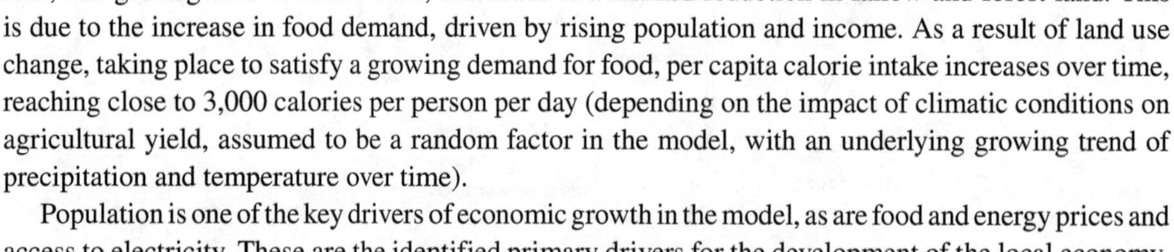

Figure 7. Electricity demand, relative energy price, and relative per capita local electricity supply: BAU scenario

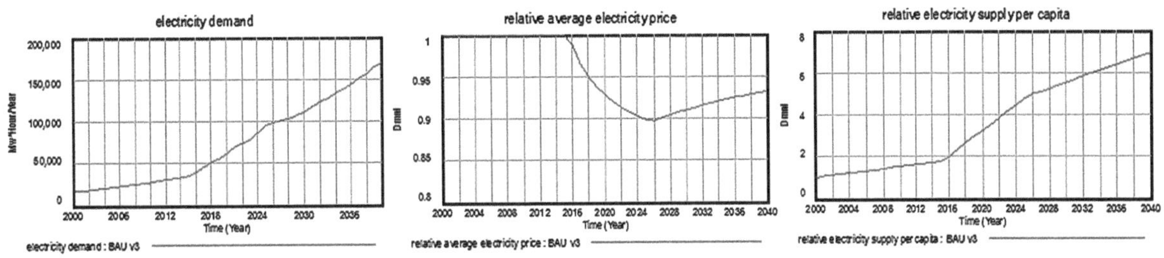

On the other hand, productivity is also impacted by the projected increase in food prices (due to the overexploitation of local natural resources -e.g. fish stock- and the need to import food). The net impact of dam and road construction can be seen in the central graph of Figure 4 (GDP/income growth rate). Without these projects both GDP/income and food demand would grow at a much slower pace.

In addition to positive economic impacts, the construction of infrastructure as assumed in the BAU scenario can lead to less than desirable indirect and induced outcomes. As shown in Figure 8 the rapid increase in food demand leads to a gradually declining food self sufficiency, making so that the local population has to rely more frequently and consistently on food imports (primarily due to the constraints encountered for fish and crop production). With the assumption that imported food products are more expensive, the average price food is projected to increase over time and negatively impact productivity.

Figure 9 shows how crop, meat and fish production respond to growing demand. Fish demand initially grows, but the depletion of the fish stock makes so that production can at best be kept constant (e.g. due to the construction of the dam, lower productivity and concerns over the collapse of the fish stock). As a result self sufficiency is projected to decline, and average prices (affected by imports) increase. Different assumptions could be tested on the impact of dam construction on the fish population, ranging from no impact to a relevant change in fish migration and population.

Desired crop production increases over time, also including an expected switch from fish to crops, and so does agriculture land. On the other hand, land availability becomes a constraint in the medium and longer term, which, coupled with declining yields due to changing climatic conditions, indicates the need to import crops more frequently and in higher quantities.

Meat demand follows the same trends observed for crops, and it increases to make up for part of the decline observed in local fish supply. Unlike agriculture land, on the other hand, there is no shortage of grazing land in the BAU simulation, due to land conversion from agriculture and fallow/forest land.

Figure 8. Food demand, self sufficiency, and relative average food price: BAU scenario

Figure 9. Desired consumption, self sufficiency, and price of fish, crops, and meat: BAU scenario

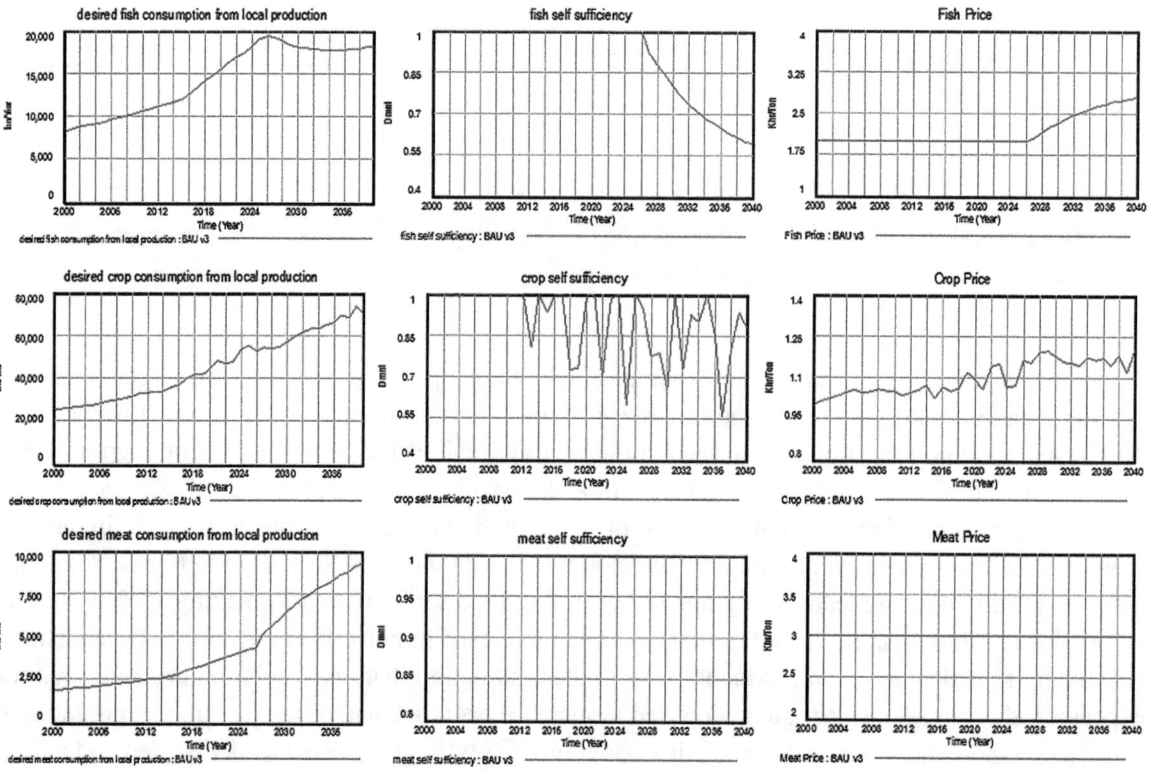

Finally, Figure 10 presents the impacts of dam construction and fish catch on the fish stock, which at first increases, then levels off due to a growing amount of catch and next declines due to overfishing. Finally, the stock seems to find an equilibrium, which corresponds to a roughly constant catch observed after 2025. The dolphin population is also assumed to be affected by dam construction (negatively) and fish population (positively) (Figure 11). A combination of these two factors leads to an initial increase and then a decline in dolphin population, which guarantees tourism arrivals. These are projected to increase due to the construction and expansion of roads and the resulting improved access to the province and the landscape.

Figure 10. Fish (tons) and dolphin population (number): BAU scenario

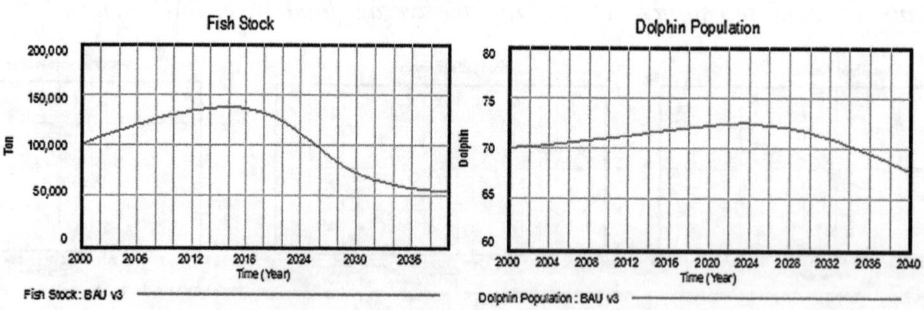

Finally, Figure 12 presents the tradeoff between the use of chemical fertilizers and pesticides used to increase agriculture yield, and their negative effect on soil quality and water pollution and overall environmental quality (which impacts resident population and the tourism sector).

5.2.3 Alternative Scenarios

The simulation of alternative scenarios helps better understand the dynamic properties of the GEM model customized at the landscape level.

Figure 11. Effects sediments and fertilizer on yield and environmental quality: BAU scenario

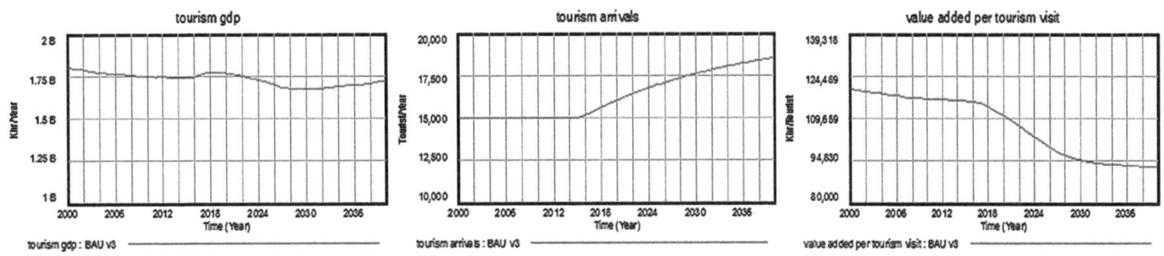

Figure 12. Tourism GDP, arrivals, and value added per visit: BAU scenario

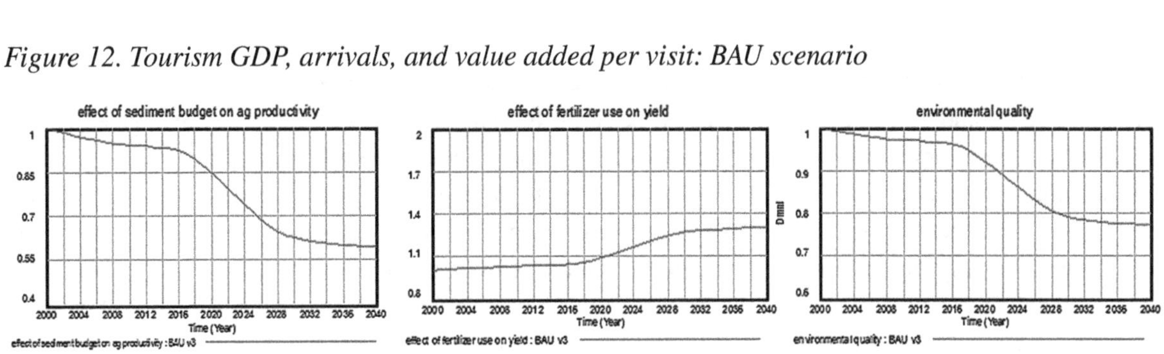

Figure 13. GDP/income growth rate (left) and relative average food price (right): BAU and alternative scenarios ("v3 no power supply" and "v3 population" respectively)

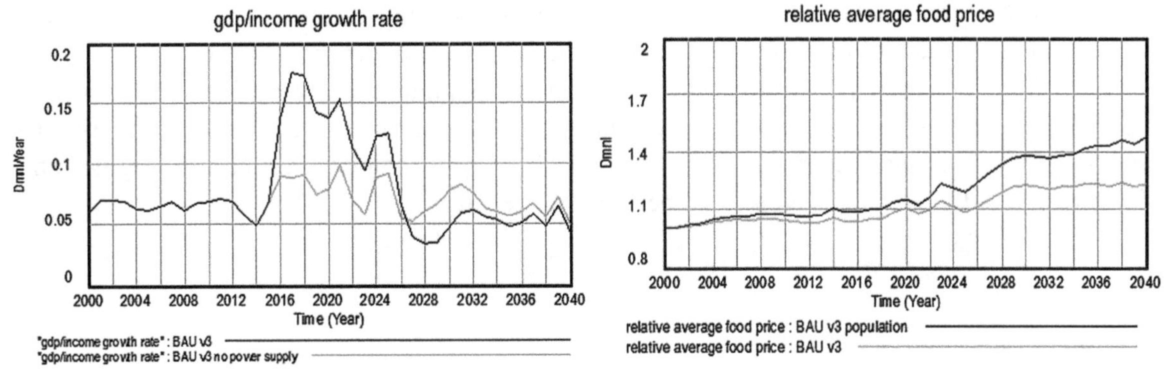

In fact, if we were to set to zero the share of power generated by the hydropower dam that is allocated to the local population (BAU v3 no power supply), we would see marked changes in local GDP/income (Figure 13, left). In the medium term the positive impact of higher electricity supply (and lower prices) would not support economic growth; on the other hand, in the longer term economic growth would be higher because of the lower increase in food prices (due to lower food demand and a lower exploitation of natural resources).

If we were to add the simulation of a higher population growth rate, in addition to the lack of electricity delivery to the local population (BAU v3 population), we would still obtain economic growth lower than BAU, but would reach similar if not higher levels of environmental degradation (i.e. due to growing food demand and finite local natural resources) which will further curb economic productivity (e.g. through higher food prices, see Figure 13, right).

6. CONCLUSION

This chapter presents the need for an integrated approach in the context of infrastructure development. If further proposes the use of System Thinking and System Dynamics to

1. Investigate the dynamic properties for the system analyzed, and
2. To project trends by using feedbacks, delays and non-linearity.

This allows to properly represent the dynamic complexity of the food-water-energy nexus at the landscape level and how the current balance between human activity and nature is influenced by the implementation of new infrastructure projects, in the short, medium and longer term.

The results presented also highlight the importance to develop tools using a participatory approach. The case study presented in this chapter shows that infrastructure (in this specific case a hydropower dam) leads to positive impacts for energy access and economic growth, as well as negative consequences on the environment. These outcomes are both direct, because of the physical presence of the dam, and indirect, because of the increased use of natural resources (e.g. fish and land) when population, GDP and income grow. These results highlight the need for a systemic analysis, where alternative and additional policy interventions can be tested to mitigate the negative impacts anticipated and further leverage the positive outcomes. In other words, sectoral planning needs to be complemented with integrated planning, with the goal to maximize a system's performance rather than individual indicators. Thus, in combination with the capability to simulate several alternative scenarios, is crucial to create local ownership of both process and model and ultimately use the results of the analysis to inform decision making.

In the context of sustainable development, which requires to simultaneously consider social, economic and environmental outcomes of policy implementation, the use of an integrated approach that considers impacts across sectors and actors, as well as over time, is a viable solution to the current fragmentation of knowledge and information and policies being developed in silos.

REFERENCES

ADB. (2009). *Asian Development Bank Support for the Transport Sector in Viet Nam*. Manila: Asian Development Bank.

Arce, R., & Gullòn, N. (2000). The application of Strategic Environmental Assessment to sustainability assessment of infrastructure development. *Environmental Impact Assessment Review*, *20*(3), 393–402. doi:10.1016/S0195-9255(00)00050-0

Bassi, A., Lombardi, N., & Gallagher, L. (2014). *Green Economy Modeling of Ecosystem Services in the Dawna Tenasserim Landscape (DTL) along the 'Road to Dawei*. WWF-Greater Mekong.

Bassi, A., Lombardi, N., & Gallagher, L. (2014). *Integrated Economic and Spatial Planning for the Food-Energy-Water Nexus*. Stocktaking Review.

Baumol, W., & Oates, W. (1988). *The Theory of Environmental Policy*. Cambridge, UK: Cambridge University Press. doi:10.1017/CBO9781139173513

Behrens, A., Giljum, S., Kovanda, J., & Niza, S. (2007). The material basis of the global economy: Worldwide patterns of natural resource extraction and their implications for sustainable resource use policies. *Ecological Economics*, *64*(2), 444–453. doi:10.1016/j.ecolecon.2007.02.034

Ellis, G. (2004). Discourses of objection: Towards an understanding of third-party rights in planning. *Environment & Planning*, *36*(9), 1549–1570. doi:10.1068/a36176

Helm, D. (2014). Taking natural capital seriously. *Oxford Review of Economic Policy*, *30*(1), 109–125. doi:10.1093/oxrep/gru005

Isely, E., Isely, P., Seedang, S., Mulder, K., Thompson, K., & Steinman, A. (2010). Addressing the information gaps associated with valuing green infrastructure in west Michigan: INtegrated Valuation of Ecosystem Services Tool (INVEST). *Journal of Great Lakes Research*, *36*(3), 448–457. doi:10.1016/j.jglr.2010.04.003

Jones, M. (2010). Accounting for the environment: Towards a theoretical perspective for environmental accounting and reporting. *Accounting Forum*, *34*(2), 123–138. doi:10.1016/j.accfor.2010.03.001

Kateja, A. (2012). Building Infrastructure: Private Participation in Emerging Economies. *Procedia: Social and Behavioral Sciences*, *37*, 368–378. doi:10.1016/j.sbspro.2012.03.302

Korytárová, J., & Hromádka, V. (2014). The Economic Evaluation of Megaprojects – Social and Economic Impacts. *Procedia: Social and Behavioral Sciences*, *119*, 495–502. doi:10.1016/j.sbspro.2014.03.055

McDonald, R., Weber, K., Padowski, J., Flörke, M., Schneider, C., Green, P., & Montgomery, M. et al. (2014). Water on an urban planet: Urbanization and the reach of urban water infrastructure. *Global Environmental Change*, *27*, 96–105. doi:10.1016/j.gloenvcha.2014.04.022

MEA. (2005). *Ecosystems and Human Well-being: General Synthesis*. Washington, DC: Island Press & World Resources Institute.

Meunier, D. (2012). Towards a Sustainable Development Approach in Transport Assessment. *Procedia: Social and Behavioral Sciences*, *48*, 3065–3077. doi:10.1016/j.sbspro.2012.06.1273

Mitchell, R., & Carson, R. (1986). *The Use of Contingent Valuation Data for Benefit-Cost Analysis in Water Pollution Control*. Washington, DC: EPA.

OECD. (2002). *Impact of Transport Infrastructure Investment on Regional Development*. Paris: OECD.

Pommerehne, W., Hart, A., & Schneider, F. (1997). Tragic choices and collective decision making: An empirical study of voter preferences for alternative collective decision-making mechanisms. *The Economic Journal*, *107*(422), 618–635. doi:10.1111/j.1468-0297.1997.tb00030.x

Rozema, J., & Bond, A. (in press). Framing effectiveness in impact assessment: Discourse accommodation in controversial infrastructure development. *Environmental Impact Assessment Review*.

Schäffler, A., & Swilling, M. (2013). Valuing green infrastructure in an urban environment under pressure—The Johannesburg case. *Ecological Economics*, *86*, 246–257. doi:10.1016/j.ecolecon.2012.05.008

Snary, C. (2004). Understanding risk: The planning officers' perspective. *Urban Studies (Edinburgh, Scotland)*, *41*(41(1)), 33–55. doi:10.1080/0042098032000155678

UNEP. (2014). *Using Models for Green Economy Policymaking*. UNEP.

Vandermeulen, V., Verspecht, A., Vermeire, B., Van Huylenbroeck, G., & Gellynck, X. (2011). The use of economic valuation to create public support for green infrastructure investments in urban areas. *Landscape and Urban Planning*, *103*(2), 198–206. doi:10.1016/j.landurbplan.2011.07.010

White, A., & Ratick, S. (1989). Risk, Compensation, and Regional Equity in Locating Hazardous Facilities. *Papers / Regional Science Association. Regional Science Association. Meeting*, *67*(1), 29–42. doi:10.1007/BF01934665

Zhang, X., & Chen, S. (2013). *A systematic framework for infrastructure development through public private partnerships*. Academic Press.

ENDNOTES

1 Currently used analytical tools include MARKAL, LEAP, WEAP and PODIUMSim. All of these are strong starting points, but none of which have the data to produce the type of real time, cross sector analyses that policy makers need to manage risks across food, energy and water.

2 http://www.yale.edu/esi/

3 http://www.vulnerabilityindex.net/

4 For more information see: http://www.ke-srl.com/KnowlEdge_Srl/Models.html

5 Feedback can be defined as *a process whereby an initial cause ripples through a chain of causation ultimately to re-affect itself*. While the causal relations provide a sense of direction, two or more variables linked through loops provide feedbacks that highlight the strength and dominance of certain parts of the system. These are the parts that generate change. In essence, feedback loops highlight the complex and dynamic structure of the system.

6 The GEM model presented in the next sections of the report should be considered a proof of concept, created to explore the feedback loops identified in the CLD. It does not use local and accurate data inputs, and behavioral validation has not been carried out. On the other hand, its structure has been validated, and it can be used to identify required data, existing equations applicable to the MFF and desired policy interventions for the simulation of scenarios.

7 For more information see: www.ke-srl.com

Chapter 6

Exogenous Shocks and Macroeconomic Policy Analysis using Applied Macro-Econometric Models in Africa: The Case of Rwanda

Alemayehu Geda
Addis Ababa University, Ethiopia

Fredrik Huizinga
Central Planning Bureau of The Netherlands, The Netherlands

Addis Yimer
Addis Ababa University, Ethiopia

ABSTRACT

In this study we have developed a macro-econometric model for a typical supply constrained African economy. This is aimed at developing a theoretical and empirical template for such policy tools which are increasingly demanded in Africa. We have concretized it by building a macro-econometric model for Rwanda. The Rwanda macro-econometric model has 107 equations of which 72 are endogenous. In addition, a supplementary ARIMA based model with 33 equations for exogenous variable is built to make the model useful for forecasting. The fiscal, balance of payment and money supply block of the model is fairly disaggregated to offer an adequate picture of the macro economy. An econometric estimation of the core behavioral equations of the model using equilibrium [error]-correction approach is made with the database that stretches from 1960 to 2009. The model is similar to successful macro models in the region such as that of the KIPPRA-Treasury model of Kenya. It can also easily be further extended to the support budgeting, forecasting and macroeconomic policy analysis work at the relevant ministries in Africa such as the Ministry of Finance in Rwanda. We have managed to successfully solve the model from 1999 to 2009 and forecast major macro outcomes from 2010 to 2014. We have also used it to conduct a policy simulation exercise which is very important for policy makers such as those in Rwanda. We hope this model offers a theoretical and empirical framework for building macro model across Africa which is increasingly being demanded in many countries.

DOI: 10.4018/978-1-5225-0094-0.ch006

1. INTRODUCTION

Macroeconomic Policy making in Africa is increasingly being informed by medium to long-term plans such as 'The Poverty Reduction Strategy Paper (PRSP)'. This is closely linked to a widely used budgeting approach called the Medium Term Expenditure Framework (MTEF). Both the realization of a strategy such as the PRSP and the use of MTEF requires an overall macroeconomic framework that ensures consistency in defining the aggregate resource envelop of a country and how it is going to be spend, as well as forecasting major macro aggregates three to four years ahead. A macroeconometric model is an invaluable instrument in achieving that. Since both the preparation of the budget and forecasting of key macro variables are made in a consistent framework, it does not allow the components of the budget to be changed in a discretionary manner (i.e. without taking the overall consistency framework into account). In addition, such forecasts could be used to monitor the economy with reference to the government's current economic strategy, and to suggest modifications, either of substance or of the tactics.

Another important justification for having macro modeling in many African countries is its capability to help policy makers take informed decisions by conducting policy analysis using policy simulation. This is crucial for policy makers because it will help them to assess the implications of proposed policy packages before their actual implementation. Policy analysis conducted with the aid of such models avoids a partial analysis, and hence partial understanding, of issues of national significance. It has the advantage of taking all possible inter-linkages in the economy that are not easily tractable by human mind. In addition, macro models are also instrumental to carry macroeconomic research by allowing macro policy research institutions to organize their research across the major components (block) of the macro model and carry out an in-depth analysis of major issues in each block such as inflation or fiscal deficit. This in turn improves the model and hence policy formulation (see Huizinga *et al*, 2001; Huizinga & Geda, 2004).

Despite such important use of macro model, the use of macro models in Africa is limited. Recently, however, many countries are showing interest to have such models. Thus, there is a need to come up with a template macro model for the majority of countries in the continent by ensuring that such model is grounded on African reality, applicable and built based on rigorous analysis. The building of the Rwandan macroeconometric model in this study is primarily motivated to develop such template model that can be used in majority of the countries in the continent. We will be doing that by (a) developing a macro econometric model well-grounded in theory and rigorous econometric analysis and (b) by illustrating the use of such model using actual macroeconomic policy issues in Rwanda with a suggested framework of innovative use of macro model by combing it with expert opinion. Our experience in building and using model in Kenya and Ethiopia shows that notwithstanding the weakness of macro models in forecasting, in practice, things are not as bad as they at first look. This is because model outcome is not meant to be used by itself, but jointly with expert opinion for additional information. This information may be based on events that have just been realized and will affect the immediate future such as a new retrenchment program or multi-year development aid programs, or drought in the horizon. Also, expert opinion from different parts of the government may be incorporated into the macro model's forecast. Examples here are specialists on government expenditure and revenue and specialist on different sectors of the economy. In turn, these specialists benefit from this exchange as well, since they get a better picture of the overall economy. In practice, adding such outside information significantly reduces the forecast uncertainty, especially for the short run (see Huizinga et al, 2001; Huizinga & Geda, 2004).

Generally, a translation has to be made from the shocks or policy proposals to be analyzed into actual input for the model, as the model is not tailor made to the often-complex shocks and policy proposals. This requires a thorough understanding of how the model works, and even then some simplifications and additional assumptions are needed to make a proper analysis. Also here, expert opinion is often necessary to do this properly. Thus, the practical use of a model of the type developed in this study requires institutional building at relevant ministries such as the Ministry of Finance and the Central bank. Such institutionalization is important not only for appropriate use of the model but also for its sustainability. It is clear that the model will only be as good as the resources, which are used in designing, operating and maintaining it. Above all, the key to the success of a macro model is to determine the measures which are necessary to sustain and institutionalize the macro model thereby ensuring that the model remains operational and is continually updated. To sum up institutionalization and sustainability requires, inter alia: accuracy and timeliness of the data, trained staff who are assigned to maintain and operate the model, expert opinion which will ensure the accuracy of the relationships specified within the model and help to design scenarios and interpret the results of the policy simulations; and the users who are expected to benefit from the analytical and forecasting activities. (See Huizinga *et al*, 2001; Huizinga & Geda, 2004).

With this background, the rest of this paper is organized as follows. In section two an attempt to offer the theoretical framework of the model will be done. We think that there are two strands of modeling practice in Africa that might be relevant in this context. One is to focus on the typical aggregate demand and aggregate supply framework. In such models the supply side is not generally emphasized. The KIPPRA-Treasury model of Kenya as well as the recent macroeconometric model of the Central Bank of Kenya are good examples of such models. Such models are generally demand driven in the spirit of Keynes (see Huizinga *et al*, 2001; Were *et al,* 2013.). Another strand of the approach is to emphasize the supply constrained nature of the African economy in question. Such assumptions generally tally with the stylized facts in the continent – we may call this a *structuralist* version of the aggregate demand-aggregate supply modeling. The theoretical framework for such models is developed in Huizinga and Geda (2004; see Geda, 2011) and applied in the macro model of the Ministry of Finance of Ethiopia as well as in Geda and Yimer (2015) for Ghana. In this paper we have followed the latter approach which we think are relevant for all most all countries in Sub Sahara Africa where the agricultural and informal sectors are crucial and generally supply constrained. Section three presents by way of illustration, discusses the use of the model for policy analysis. Section four concludes the study.

2. THE THEORETICAL FRAMEWORK AND ESTIMATED RESULTS OF THE MODEL

2.1 The Theoretical Model

The model is built along the lines of the aggregate demand – aggregate supply (AD-AS) framework but by emphasising the supply constrained nature of the economy in question[1]. This is done, unlike typical demand-driven Keynesian models, by explicitly modelling the supply side of the economy. The supply side will contain three main components: the formal sector, the informal sector and the agricultural sector. Agriculture will be subdivided into cash crops (exports) and food production for the domestic market. This could, if the need arises, readily be subdivided further by major types of agricultural products. The informal sector consists mainly of small scale industry and handicrafts, informal trade such as street vendors and informal restaurant services. The formal sector consists mainly of the government and the formal private sectors of industry and services. The latter include for instance large and medium scale manufacturing, formal trade, hotels, and restaurants, transport and communications, banking, insurance and real estate.

Thus, the real sector aspect of the model consists of an aggregate agricultural sector, an informal sector, and a formal public and private sectors. This real sector model incorporates the basic linkages within and between the three sectors as shown in Figure 1. Once we have this prototype, the model may be expanded up to the full scale of the short run model, using the AD-AS framework. The formal and informal sectors both have CES production functions. The shares of inputs are different, however. The level of capital used in the formal sector is far greater than in the informal sector. As a result, the employment response to demand fluctuations is far greater in the informal sector than in the formal sector.

The formal private sector will be modeled along neoclassical lines, based on the theory of profit maximization, described in detail in Huizinga and Geda (2004) and offered briefly in Appendix 1. With a monopolistically competitive firms in view, prices are set as a markup over costs, which consist of labor costs and the cost of intermediate goods and raw materials. Demand for labor and capital follow from a constant-elasticity-of-substitution (CES) production function which allows us to model wages and capital formation/investment.

Formal sector output in the short run is demand driven. In the longer run, there is a supply component, as investment may be used to increase capacity. The degree to which this happens depends to a large extent on factors outside the firm's control, such as the quality of infrastructure, and an overall stable economic and political climate. This is especially true if overseas physical and financial investment is to play a major role. Investment in the formal sector, therefore, has both a cyclical component following GDP and a structural component following infrastructure and overall macroeconomic stability considerations.

Demand for labor in the formal sector exhibits a large degree of labor hoarding, especially during bad agricultural seasons, when reduction in domestic demand will be mostly absorbed by a reduction in profits, and relatively little by layoffs. This is partly based on the high search costs for relatively highly skilled and therefore scarce labor force and partly based on implicit contract considerations. Skilled labor will, therefore, be relatively insulated from the cyclical variations in economic growth, both in terms of income and employment Thus, in the formal sector wages will be based on a mixture of bargaining and efficiency consideration as well as structural productivity. Wages of the unskilled are purely based on efficiency considerations, as there is an excess supply of unskilled labor. This means that wages are a markup over subsistence levels, without much regard to economic activity in the short run. (See Huizinga *et al*, 2001; Huizinga & Geda, 2004)

The agricultural sector, on the other hand, is mostly supply driven. Output is determined by land, the quality of seeds and fertilizer, labor, some capital (such as an ox in some countries), and most importantly, rainfall. Thus the modeling starts with the agricultural sector as shown in Figure 1. It has a production function based on land, labor, rainfall, and technology. Labor consists mostly of family labor, which is exogenously determined by population growth. There are strong decreasing returns to scale with respect to labor, reflecting the current excess labor supply. Since all elements of the agricultural production function are exogenous, so is total agricultural output.

Part of the labor force has moved to the urban areas to find a job in the formal and informal sector. Because of low skill level these workers start out in the informal sector. The wage rate in the informal sector is a mark-up over the subsistence level in the agricultural sector because, among other things, of efficiency wage considerations. As a result, there are always agricultural workers, especially young

Figure 1. A flow chart for Rwandan macro model: the real sector
Source: Huizinga and Geda (2004).

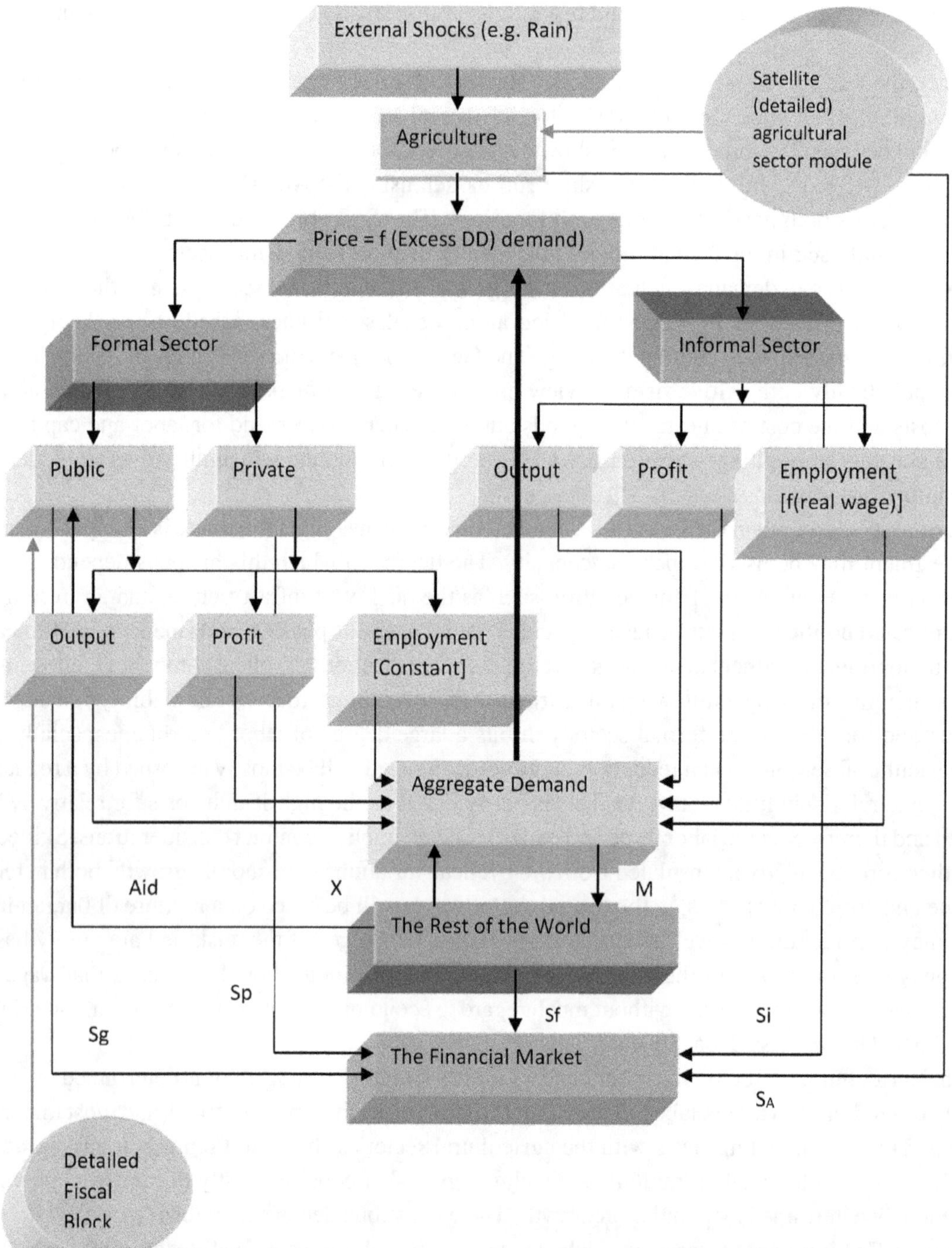

ones who would prefer to work in the informal sector and would move there if job conditions improve. Because of the constant excess supply of labor to the informal market, the wage is constant in the short run. Similarly, the wage in the formal sector is a mark-up over that in the informal sector, also based on efficiency wage considerations. Workers in the informal sector would prefer a job in the formal sector and, therefore, there is also always excess supply to the formal sector. Again we may assume that the wage in the formal sector is constant in the short run as there will be an excess supply of labor in the Lewisian (1955) sense, in a way that not all the labor is needed to produce output. This is not visible in the form of unemployment because of the family nature of farm production (i.e. there is a disguised unemployment). Still, mostly young people may leave the farm because they cannot get their own land (is very small in size even if they managed to get one due to population pressure) and search for employment in the urban informal sector, thus maintaining the excess labor supply in that informal sector (See Huizinga & Geda, 2004).

Short run aspect of the macro economy relates to modeling output volatility. This is in particular assumed to prevail in the agricultural sector. The most important determinant of cyclical variation in output is rainfall. If there is an adverse external shock such as a bad agricultural season, the supply of food to the market is sharply reduced. As a result, the price of food rises. As food is a major component of the CPI in many African countries, rainfall has a major effect on the CPI. As nominal wages are not indexed, real wages of urban workers drop sharply when there is a drought or shortage of food. This will reduce domestic demand for industrial products both from the formal and the informal sector. In the informal sector, reduced demand leads to reduced employment, which further reduces demand. In the formal sector, the effects are less dramatic. One reason is that part of the demand for the formal sector comes from abroad. Export demand is not directly affected by the drought. Another reason is that the formal sector is better able to absorb a temporary reduction in demand through a reduction in profits (in the case of the private sector) or a deficit (in the case of the government sector). The informal sector bears the brunt of the cyclical variation in economic growth. Unlike the formal sector, it cannot afford to keep employment intact during a cyclical downturn or a drought. So, a reduction in demand will reduce output, employment and investment immediately. The flip side is that it is relatively easy to reactivate economic activity if demand picks up again. Labor will be readily available and the capital stock is not a major input. So, the informal sector is completely demand driven with constant excess supply and a production function based mostly on low skilled labor (see Huizinga & Geda, 2004).

The long term growth is modeled as follows. It is reasonable to assume that through a combination of better seeds, the use of fertilizer, and better infrastructure, the output of the agricultural sector can be increased substantially. This leads, other things remaining intact, to a drop in the food prices and a rise in the real wage of the urban workers. The increase in disposable income leads to a rise in consumption demand to the formal and informal sectors. In the formal sector this leads to increased profits, investment and eventually employment. In the informal sector, it leads to increased employment and eventually increased investment and profits. The key issue in terms of poverty reduction is that the demand for labor in the formal and informal sectors continuously grows faster than the population growth, which adds to the excess supply of labor in the agricultural sector, assuming that the food sector will not constrain this growth through inflation in a familiar Kaleckian fashion (see Geda & Tafere, 2013).

In sum, the overall model for the short run consists of two blocks that form the aggregate supply side of the model: the agricultural sector whose output is determined by exogenous, but widely fluctuating supply conditions, and the formal and informal sectors which in the short run are mostly demand determined. The link between the two components is the price of food, which is set such that the demand for food in the formal and informal sectors equals the exogenous supply of food. This real sector modeling is briefly summarized by Figure 1. In the real sector modeling, the aggregate demand (consumption, investment, government spending, and exports) will determine the level of imports and total value-added. This value-added is disaggregated into agricultural, formal, and informal sector as noted. Out of the components of value-added, the value-added in the informal sector is assumed to be the residual. With this, the injection from the aggregate demand which in turn create the demand for value added is assumed to generate demand for factor inputs (capital, labour, and imports). The choice of this factor inputs is assumed to follow from an optimization problem of agents in each sector using a CES productions function as given in Appendix 1 explicitly.

The model is designed in such a way that it has a tendency to return to equilibrium with 'normal' capacity utilisation and unemployment rates in the medium and long run. The main feedback mechanisms in the real economy works through the wage-price spiral, the interest rate and the real exchange rate, which are modelled as a nominal sector of the model and depicted in Figure 2. The mechanisms in the model can be illustrated by considering a supply shock, like a favorable rainfall, that raises output in the agricultural sector. The increased supply of food leads to a lower price of food and a rise in the real wage. This leads to a rise in consumption demand to the informal and formal sectors. Both sectors increase output. The formal sector also increases investment financed in part by the increased profits. Employment in the formal sector is much less responsive in the short run. The informal sector is far more employment-based and does not feature labor hoarding, and therefore, immediately increases employment. In addition, increased demand and profits leads to more investment, but this may be less important numerically. The increase in investment and employment further increase demand to the informal and formal sector, and also demand for food from the agricultural sector. The model converges because of leakage in the form of increased savings, increased imports and increased prices in the formal sector, leading to erosion in competitiveness (See Figures 1 and 2).

Figure 2 gives an overview of the nominal side of the economy. The yellow boxes denote demand and supply in the labour, goods and services, and the money market. The green boxes denote endogenous prices and the light blue ones exogenous variables. The arrows indicate direction of causation or determination. Six prices are determined endogenously in the model (The price of goods and services; the nominal and real wage; the nominal and real exchange rates and the domestic nominal interest rate (see Huizinga & Geda, 2004; also in Geda, 2011).

Wages and prices are determined in the labour and product markets. Wages and prices also depend on each other as indicated by the double arrow, so that there is a wage-price spiral in the model. The exchange rate and the interest rate are determined in the financial market. The financial market is subdivided into the markets for domestic money and domestic bonds and the market for foreign assets. By Walras' law we only have to model two of these markets, and if these are in equilibrium, so is the third. The markets for domestic money and for foreign assets are modelled here - leaving the market for domestic bonds implicit. The exchange rate is floating (or managed floating), so that the money supply is available as an exogenous policy instrument. Money demand is determined by aggregate demand, the price level and the interest rate. The interest rate moves to clear the money market, so that the interest rate is a function of money supply, real demand and prices. The exchange rate clears the market for foreign assets. A rise in the domestic interest rate relative to foreign interest rates makes domestic assets relatively more attractive and thus causes an appreciation. The real exchange rate follows by definition from the nominal exchange rate, the domestic price level and the foreign price level (see Huizinga & Geda, 2004).

Figure 2. A flow chart for Rwandan macro model: the nominal side
Source: Huizinga and Geda (2004).

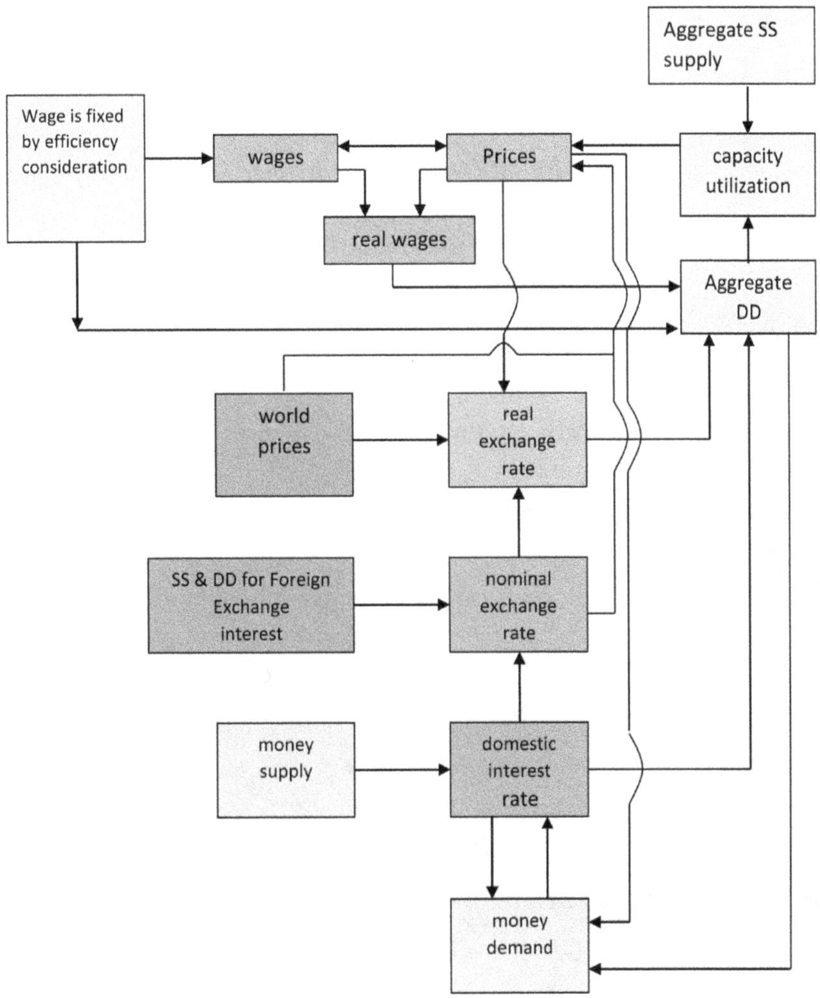

The full equations of the model including definition of symbols used in the estimated equations in the next section are offered in Appendix 1. We also would like to note that a detailed theoretical framework of the model, form where it is adopted here, is given in Huizinga and Geda (2004, also in Geda 2011) and interested readers can refer to it for detail.

2.2 Estimated Results of the Behavioral Equations of the Model

The estimated core behavioral equations of the model in error correction formulation are presented below. The full theoretical specifications of each of the estimated equations, including the definitions of symbols used here in the estimated equations, are given as Appendix 1. The t-ratios of the estimated equations are given in parenthesis. In addition various model diagnostic tests are also reported for each of the estimated equations. With the p-values of the F-statistics closer to zero, we generally reject the null of 'all variables are jointly insignificant'. On the other hand, for all other diagnostic tests reported, a P-value closer to zero means rejection of the null(i.e., our model is statistically fit to the OLS assumption). The number of lags used in the LM and Ramsey Reset test is given in the brackets. We generally found the theoretical expected sign in the estimated equations given from 1 to 13 below.

1. **Private Consumption:**

$$\Delta(LnRPC) = \underset{(-2.238)}{-3.183} + \underset{(11.931)}{0.516}\,\Delta(LnRGDI) - \underset{(-0.581)}{0.016}\,\Delta(LnDIR)$$
$$-\underset{(-2.699)}{0.259}\,LnRPC_{(-1)} + \underset{(5.911)}{0.374}\,LnRGDI_{(-1)} - \underset{(-2.033)}{0.064}\,LnDIR_{(-1)}$$

R^2=0.916,$\bar{R}^2$=0.896,DW=1.739
F-Statistic=46.025
Prob=0.000
LM Serial Correlation test (1) (obs*R-Squared) =0.242
Prob Chi-Square=0.623
White Hetroskedasticity test (obs*R-Squared) =20.076
Prob Chi-Square=0.329
Jarque-Bera Normality test=2.550
Prob=0.279
Ramsey Reset test (1)(F-Statistic)=1.175
Prob=0.29

2. **Private Investment:**

$$\Delta(LnRPRINV) = \underset{(-1.385)}{-6.586} - \underset{(-4.604)}{0.510}\,\Delta(LnRPUINV) + \underset{(4.455)}{2.130}\,\Delta(LnRGDP) -$$
$$\underset{(-2.740)}{1.695}\,\Delta(LnGDPDEF) - \underset{(-0.396)}{0.217}\,\Delta(LnINVP) - \underset{(-34.755)}{0.977}\,LnRPRINV_{(-1)} -$$
$$\underset{(-1.147)}{0.219}\,LnRPUINV_{(-1)} + \underset{(2.767)}{1.065}\,LnRGDP_{(-1)} - \underset{(-2.570)}{1.280}\,LnGDPDEF_{(-1)} -$$
$$\underset{(-6.131)}{0.966}\,LnLINVP_{(-1)} + \underset{(3.847)}{0.192}@\,trend$$

R^2=0.816, $\bar{R}^2$=0.693, DW=1.586
F-Statistic=46.025
Prob=0.000
LM Serial Correlation test (1) (obs*R-Squared) =4.099
Prob Chi-Square=0.129
White Hetroskedasticity test (obs*R-Squared) =17.953
Prob Chi-Square=0.10
Jarque-Bera Normality test=8.777
Prob=0.012
Ramsey Reset test (1)(F-Statistic)=10.922
Prob=0.005

3. Food Demand (Consumption):

$$\Delta(LnFC) = \underset{(-2.326)}{-7.717} + \underset{(0.357)}{0.118}\,\Delta(LnCPI) + \underset{(13.360)}{1.751}\,\Delta(LnRGDI) - \underset{(-2.700)}{0.416}\,LnFC_{(-1)}$$
$$+\underset{(3.074)}{0.929}\,LnCPI_{(-1)} - \underset{(-2.037)}{0.652}\,LnCP_{(-2)} + \underset{(2.957)}{1.011}\,LnRGDI_{(-1)} + \underset{(3.651)}{0.443}\,DUM_{90}$$

R^2=0.926, $\bar{R}^2$=0.902, DW=2.012
F-Statistic=37.675
Prob=0.000
LM Serial Correlation test (1) (obs*R-Squared) =0.029
Prob Chi-Square=0.863
White Hetroskedasticity test (obs*R-Squared) =9.208
Prob Chi-Square=0.2.38
Jarque-Bera Normality test=2.456
Prob=0.293
Ramsey Reset test (1)(F-Statistic)=3.780
Prob=0.066

4. Agricultural Production (Value Added):

$$\Delta(LnRAGVA) = \underset{(-1.752)}{-15.494} + \underset{(11.084)}{2.385}\,\Delta(LnAGLF) + \underset{(4.033)}{1.011}\,\Delta(LnCS)$$
$$-\underset{(-2.269)}{0.427}\,LnRAGVA_{(-1)} + \underset{(2.013)}{0.374}\,LnAGLF_{(-1)} + \underset{(4.848)}{0.549}\,LnCS_{(-1)} + \underset{3.487}{0.049}@\,trend$$

R^2=0.439, $\bar{R}^2$=0.286, DW=1.942
F-Statistic=2.869
Prob=0.032
LM Serial Correlation test (1) (obs*R-Squared) =0.661
Prob Chi-Square=0.791
White Hetroskedasticity test (obs*R-Squared) =28.367
Prob Chi-Square=0.245
Jarque-Bera Normality test=8.591
Prob=0.014
Ramsey Reset test (1)(F-Statistic)=0.103
Prob=0.752

5. **Non Agricultural Production (Value Added):**

$$\Delta(LnRNAGVA) = \underset{(-4.559)}{-10.421} + \underset{(9.409)}{3.078}\,\Delta(LnNAGLF) + \underset{(3.061)}{0.786}\,\Delta(LnCS)$$
$$- \underset{(-2.588)}{0.237}\,LnRNAGVA_{(-1)} + \underset{(2.808)}{0.966}\,LnNAGLF_{(-1)} + \underset{(3.757)}{0.235}\,LnCS_{(-1)} + \underset{(8.365)}{0.069}@trend$$

R^2=0.693, $\bar{R}^2$=0.605, DW=1.57
F-Statistic=7.890
Prob=0.000
LM Serial Correlation test (1) (obs*R-Squared) =0.521
Prob Chi-Square=0.771
White Hetroskedasticity test (obs*R-Squared) =27.348
Prob ChiSquare=0.241
Jarque-Bera Normality test=0.529
Prob=0.768
Ramsey Reset test (1)(F-Statistic)=0.103
Prob=0.752

6. **Export Demand:**

$$\Delta(LnRX) = \underset{(3.844)}{3.048} + \underset{(1.204)}{0.199}\,\Delta(LnRER) + \underset{(2.451)}{0.479}\,\Delta(LnINVGDP) + \underset{(3.713)}{0.433}\,\Delta(LnINCTRAD)$$
$$- \underset{(-11.238)}{0.532}\,LnRX_{(-1)} + \underset{(0.270)}{0.029}\,LnRER_{(-1)} + \underset{(9.347)}{0.556}\,LnINVGDP_{(-1)} + \underset{(12.447)}{0.333}\,LnINCTRAD_{(-1)}$$
$$- \underset{(-8.789)}{0.820}\,DUM_{94}$$

R^2=0.862, $\bar{R}^2$=0.801, DW=2.402
F-Statistic=14.077
Prob=0.000
LM Serial Correlation test (1) (obs*R-Squared) =2.069
Prob Chi-Square=0.150
White Hetroskedasticity test (obs*R-Squared) =4.308
Prob Chi-Square=0.890
Jarque-Bera Normality test=0.796
Prob=0.672
Ramsey Reset test (1)(F-Statistic)=0.103
Prob=0.752

7. **Import Demand:**

$$\Delta(LnRM) = \underset{(-1.918)}{-16.643} - \underset{(-1.872)}{0.503}\,\Delta(LnRER) + \underset{(0.767)}{1.288}\,\Delta(LnAID) + \underset{(1.468)}{0.579}\,\Delta(LnRGDP)$$
$$-\underset{(-2.114)}{0.448}\,LnRM_{(-1)} + \underset{(0.418)}{0.079}\,LnRER_{(-1)} + \underset{(1.440)}{0.141}\,LnAID_{(-1)} + \underset{(1.980)}{0.909}\,LnRGDP_{(-1)}$$
$$+\underset{(2.240)}{1.334}\,DUM_1 - \underset{(-1.953)}{0.045}@\,trend$$

R^2=0.682, $\bar{R}^2$=0.479, DW=1.809
F-Statistic=3.349
Prob=0.021
LM Serial Correlation test (1) (obs*R-Squared) =0.165
Prob Chi-Square=0.684
White Hetroskedasticity test (obs*R-Squared) =7.588
Prob Chi-Square=0.576
Jarque-Bera Normality test=0.100
Prob=0.951
Ramsey Reset test (1)(F-Statistic)=0.043
Prob=0.839

8. **Exchange Rate:**

$$\Delta(LnNER) = -\underset{(-1.696)}{0.523} + \underset{(8.565)}{1.203}\,\Delta(LnM) - \underset{(-6.684)}{0.140}\,\Delta(LnXA\_DS)$$
$$-\underset{(-2.726)}{0.125}\,LnNER_{(-1)} + \underset{(8.918)}{0.282}\,LnM_{(-1)} - \underset{(-13.959)}{0.245}\,LnXA\_DS_{(-1)}$$

R^2=0.570, $\bar{R}^2$=0.457, DW=1.564
F-Statistic=5.039
Prob=0.004
LM Serial Correlation test (1) (obs*R-Squared) =1.289
Prob Chi-Square=0.256
White Hetroskedasticity test (obs*R-Squared) =12.951
Prob Chi-Square=0.841
Jarque-Bera Normality test=0.532
Prob=0.766
Ramsey Reset test (1)(F-Statistic)=12.161
Prob=0.004

9. **Wage Rate:**

$$\begin{aligned}\Delta(LnNWR) = &\underset{(-2.169)}{-4.144} + \underset{(1.454)}{0.416}\,\Delta(LnCPI) - \underset{(-0.999)}{0.459}\,\Delta(LnUNEMPTRATE)\\ &+ \underset{(0.455)}{0.145}\,\Delta(LnLABPRO) - \underset{(-6.763)}{0.949}\,LnNWR(-1) + \underset{(1.40)}{0.365}\,LnCPI(-1)\\ &- \underset{(-1.990)}{1.457}\,LnUNEMPTRATE(-1) + \underset{(4.757)}{0.713}\,LnLABPRO(-1) + \underset{(1.083)}{0.050}@TREND\end{aligned}$$

R^2=0.993, $\bar{R}^2$=0.984, DW=1.781
F-Statistic=107.356
Prob=0.000
LM Serial Correlation test (1) (obs*R-Squared) =1.020
Prob Chi-Square=0.312
White Hetroskedasticity test (obs*R-Squared) =6.837
Prob Chi-Square=0.554
Jarque-Bera Normality test=0.080
Prob=0.961
Ramsey Reset test (1) (F-Statistic)=0.437
Prob=0.538

10. **Money Demand:**

$$\begin{aligned}\Delta(LnM2) = &-\underset{(-0.597)}{1.065} + \underset{(3.499)}{0.754}\,\Delta(LnCPI) - \underset{(-1.864)}{0.103}\,\Delta(LnIRD) + \underset{(9.471)}{0.507}\,\Delta(LnRGDP)\\ &- \underset{(-2.117)}{0.064}\,LnM2_{(-1)} + \underset{(2.351)}{0.113}\,LnCPI_{(-1)} - \underset{(-1.985)}{0.098}\,LnIRD_{(-1)} + \underset{(1.079)}{0.094}\,LnRGDP_{(-1)}\\ &+ \underset{(66.558)}{2.167}\,DUM_{06} + \underset{(4.449)}{0.196}\,DUM_{07}\end{aligned}$$

R^2=0.982, $\bar{R}^2$=0.975, DW=2.019
F-Statistic=128.613
Prob=0.000
LM Serial Correlation test (1) (obs*R-Squared) =0.124
Prob Chi-Square=0.725
White Hetroskedasticity test (obs*R-Squared) =8.477
Prob Chi-Square=0.487
Jarque-Bera Normality test=0.476
Prob=0.788
Ramsey Reset test (1)(F-Statistic)=1.322
Prob=0.264

11. **Consumer Price:**

$$\Delta(LnCPI) = \underset{(9.932)}{17.085} + \underset{(3.667)}{0.388}\,\Delta(LnCUR) + \underset{(1.87)}{0.031}\,\Delta(LnM2) - \underset{(-5.193)}{0.266}\,\Delta(LnFC)$$
$$+\underset{(4.632)}{0.508}\,\Delta(LnLIR) + \underset{(0.703)}{0.060}\,\Delta(LnMP) - \underset{(-4.993)}{0.467}\,LnCPI_{(-1)} + \underset{(6.064)}{0.485}\,LnCUR_{(-1)}$$
$$+\underset{(4.903)}{0.593}\,LnLIR_{(-1)} + \underset{(0.167)}{0.019}\,LnMP_{(-1)} + \underset{(2.046)}{0.062}\,LnM2_{(-1)} - \underset{(-8.682)}{0.406}\,LnFC_{(-1)}$$
$$+\underset{(1.860)}{0.046}\,DUM_{94} - \underset{(-3.578)}{0.141}\,DUM_{96} + \underset{(5.593)}{0.043}@TREND$$

R^2=0.880, $\bar{R}^2$=0.750, DW=1.576
F-Statistic=6.797
Prob=0.000
LM Serial Correlation test (1) (obs*R-Squared) =2.358
Prob Chi-Square=0.125
White Hetroskedasticity test (obs*R-Squared) =12.992
Prob Chi-Square=0.527
Jarque-Bera Normality test=0.968
Prob=0.616
Ramsey Reset test (1)(F-Statistic)=6.879
Prob=0.022

12. **Export Price:**

$$\Delta(nLXP) = -\underset{(-5.077)}{6.608} + \underset{(2.548)}{1.917}\,\Delta(LnPUC) + \underset{(2.904)}{0.514}\,\Delta(LnCUR) + \underset{(1.406)}{0.132}\,\Delta(LnRIR)$$
$$+\underset{(3.521)}{0.330}\,\Delta(LnMP) - \underset{(-5.055)}{0.919}\,LnXP_{(-1)} + \underset{(5.080)}{2.335}\,LnPUC_{(-1)} + \underset{(1.790)}{0.411}\,LnCUR_{(-1)}$$
$$+\underset{(1.998)}{0.247}\,LnRIR_{(-1)} + \underset{(0.309)}{0.054}\,LnMP_{(-1)}$$

R^2=0.754, $\bar{R}^2$=0.606, DW=2.31
F-Statistic=5.104
Prob=0.002
LM Serial Correlation test (1) (obs*R-Squared) =1.610
Prob Chi-Square=0.205
White Hetroskedasticity test (obs*R-Squared) =4.595
Prob Chi-Square=0.868
Jarque-Bera Normality test=1.961
Prob=0.375
Ramsey Reset test (1)(F-Statistic)=2.784
Prob=0.117

Table 1. Level and growth of government expenditure in the budget framework

Model Years	July 2011- June 2012	2012/13	2013/14	1014/15	Average
	2011	2012	2013	2014	
Current Expenditure(in Billion RWF)	596.3	670	782	8.57	726.3
Annual Growth		12.4	16.7	9.6	12.9
Capital Expenditure(in Billion RWF)	508.6	651.6	715	6.25	624.9
Annual Growth		28	9.8	-12.6	8.4
Total Government Expenditure	1104.9	1321.1	1497	1482	1351.3
Annual Growth		19.6	13.3	-1	10.6

13. **Investment Price:**

$$\Delta(LnINVP) = \underset{(0.065)}{0.042} - \underset{(-3.149)}{0.530}\,\Delta(LnCUR) - \underset{(-0.014)}{0.009}\,\Delta(LnPUC) + \underset{(2.667)}{0.605}\,\Delta(LnMP)$$
$$+ \underset{(2.448)}{0.106}\,\Delta(LnRIR) - \underset{(-3.163)}{0.359}\,LnINVP_{(-1)} + \underset{(1.210)}{0.127}\,LnCUR_{(-1)} + \underset{(1.062)}{0.280}\,LnPUC_{(-1)}$$
$$+ \underset{(2.486)}{0.487}\,LnMP_{(-1)} + \underset{(1.073)}{0.105}\,LnRIR_{(-1)} + \underset{(0.456)}{0.456}\,DUM_{91} - \underset{(-4.172)}{0.034}@TREND$$

R^2=0.743, $\bar{R}^2$=0.526, DW=1.822
F-Statistic=3.425
Prob=0.019
LM Serial Correlation test (1) (obs*R-Squared) =0.674
Prob Chi-Square=0.412
White Hetroskedasticity test (obs*R-Squared) =9.196
Prob Chi-Square=0.604
Jarque-Bera Normality test=0.128
Prob=0.938
Ramsey Reset test (1)(F-Statistic)=1.896
Prob=0.194

14. **Identities and Bridging Equations:** We have developed the model in EViews platform. A solution to the fully fledged model requires incorporating identities and bridging equations. The list of these equations is given in Appendix 2.

3. THE USE OF THE MODEL: A POLICY SIMULATION EXPERIMENT FOR RWANDA

In this section, we have carried out some policy simulations of the Rwandan government plan which is contained in the 'Budget Framework Paper 2012/13-2014/15' prepared by the Ministry of Finance and Economic Planning in April, 2012. The government of Rwanda is aware that its budget will have macroeconomic ramifications that may result from its policy and possible external shock such as those shows in Box 1 and Table 1. However, these probable macroeconomic risks are not quantified in the

Box 1. External and policy shocks examined in the simulation exercise

Government Policy 1
1. The Government expenditure stipulated in the budget framework contains (see Table 1): a. Change in the total government expenditure in line with the proposed budget (an annual growth of 10% during the budget period); b. Change in composition of this expenditure: Annual growth of 13 and 5% for current and capital expenditure, respectively.

Box 2.

Government Policy 2
2. **The New Wage Pay and Retention Policy:** RWF46.7 billion which is about 8% of current expenditure or 4% of the total government expenditure. 3. **The Proposed Efficiency Saving:** This is assumed to bring 4.2% cut on the allocation of each of the budge lines outlined in the budget to generate the 1.1 billion RWF proposed (which is 0.1% of the budget) for the airport project. **The External Sector Risk Stipulated in the Budget** 4. **The Probable Slowdown in the World Economy:** Impact of the global economy on the planned budget. This takes two forms: a. Change in foreign price (import price increase) 5 to 10% which is the record in the last 5 years. We simulated the relatively optimistic scenario of a 5% rise in import price. b. A decline in exports (say due to Global economic slowdown - Rwanda's trading partners' economy). The last five years show a decline in exports that varies from 2.6 to 8.4%. We took the average value of 5%. **Financing Risk** 5. **Financing Risk:** A short fall in external resources is proposed to be addressed by a possible delay in non-priority spending in the budget document. For this we simulated a decline in net-external borrowing of 10%.

Source: Compiled from Republic of Rwanda, Ministry of Finance and Economic Planning (2012) 'Consolidated Annexes to the 2012/13-2014/15 Budget Framework Paper.

budget because of lack of macroeconomic models. Thus, our focus is on macroeconomic risks, if any, this budget framework has on macroeconomic stability. Apart from showing the short-term forecasting ability of the model, we are hoping to demonstrate the use of such models to tackle real world policy problems.

The simulation exercise in relation to the scenario in Box 1 is focused on the following major macroeconomic outcomes (see Box 3) which need to be examined to see what might be their likely direction and hence the implied macroeconomic stability of the country for the realization of the proposed budget. To say that macroeconomic stability is fundamental for sustainable growth, poverty reduction and social and political stability in Africa, is perhaps to state the obvious. Thus, we have carried all the shocks outlined in Box 1. However, we have presented here only two of them (one policy and one external shock each) to save space. Interested readers can refer to our working paper for detail (see Geda & Yimer, 2013).

Box 3. Macroeconomic outcome indicators selected to gauge indicator of macroeconomics

1	GDP and GDP Growth	7	Eternal Sector/Balance of Payment
2	Investment (Private and Total)	7.1	*Export of Goods and Non-factor Services*
3	Private Consumption	7.2	Import of Good and Non-factor Services
4	Inflation (CPI)	7.3	Current/Overall Balance of Payment
5	Exchange rate (Nominal and Real)		
6	Fiscal Issues		
6.1	Government Revenue (before and after grants)		
6.2	Government Expenditure		
6.3	Government Surplus/Deficit		

Table 2. Base run and forecast values of major macroeconomic outcomes forecast

Year	Growth	Real GDP	Real Private Investment	Real Private Consumption	Real Exports	Real Imports	Total Government Expenditure	Total Revenue After Grants
2009	5.6	1366.8	104.3	1545.6	94.8	1093.3	780.4	738.0
2010	5.7	1444.8	118.2	1659.0	93.5	1134.1	909.6	897.7
2011	8.9	1574.1	135.5	1837.3	90.7	1199.3	1044.0	1063.1
2012	6.4	1675.0	145.5	2024.1	86.6	1285.3	1168.5	1219.0
2013	7.7	1803.9	162.3	2237.1	82.5	1377.9	1299.8	1382.8
2014	7.0	1930.6	175.8	2463.6	78.9	1482.5	1435.3	1552.4
Year			Gov't Fiscal Surplus After Grants (% GDP)0	Gov't Fiscal Surplus Before Grants (% GDP)	Current Account Deficit (% GDP)	BOP Overall (% of GDP)		
2009			-0.5	-17.8	-12.0	-6.8		
2010			-0.1	-15.5	-9.9	-5.3		
2011			0.1	-13.9	-8.7	-4.6		
2012			0.3	-13.4	-8.5	-4.6		
2013			0.5	-13.0	-8.4	-4.6		
2014			0.6	-12.9	-8.4	-4.8		

3.1. Forecasted and Simulation Outcomes of the Economy

3.1.1. The Base Run Values and Forecast

We commenced our policy analysis by producing what is called the base-run values of the model. The current version of the model could be solved from 1999 to 2009 and can fairly reproduce the actual figures. It can however be improved further by working with experts at the Ministry of Finance and Planning (MoFP) of Rwanda, especially by working on a consistent and detailed database.

There are two advantages of the base run (some of the major values of this base run are reported in Table 2 and Figure 3). First, it gives us the evolution of the economy without policy intervention and external shocks. This will be the bench mark to measure the effect of the government's planned activities, as has been outlined in Box 1. Second, it shows also the potential of the model for making macroeconomic forecasts which are important for the MoFP and policy makers. This forecast values are given in Table 1 and Figure 1 as illustration.

3.1.2 Simulation Outcomes of the Economy

1. **The Effect of Government Policy 1:** Planned Government Spending. We have a complete database of the macro economy from 1960-2009. We have used this database for estimation and running of the model, as we noted above. We then forecasted major economic variables from 2010 to 2014 using the model. This value, which is reported in the previous section, is thus the outcome of the

Figure 3. Base run and forecast values of major macroeconomic outcomes forecast

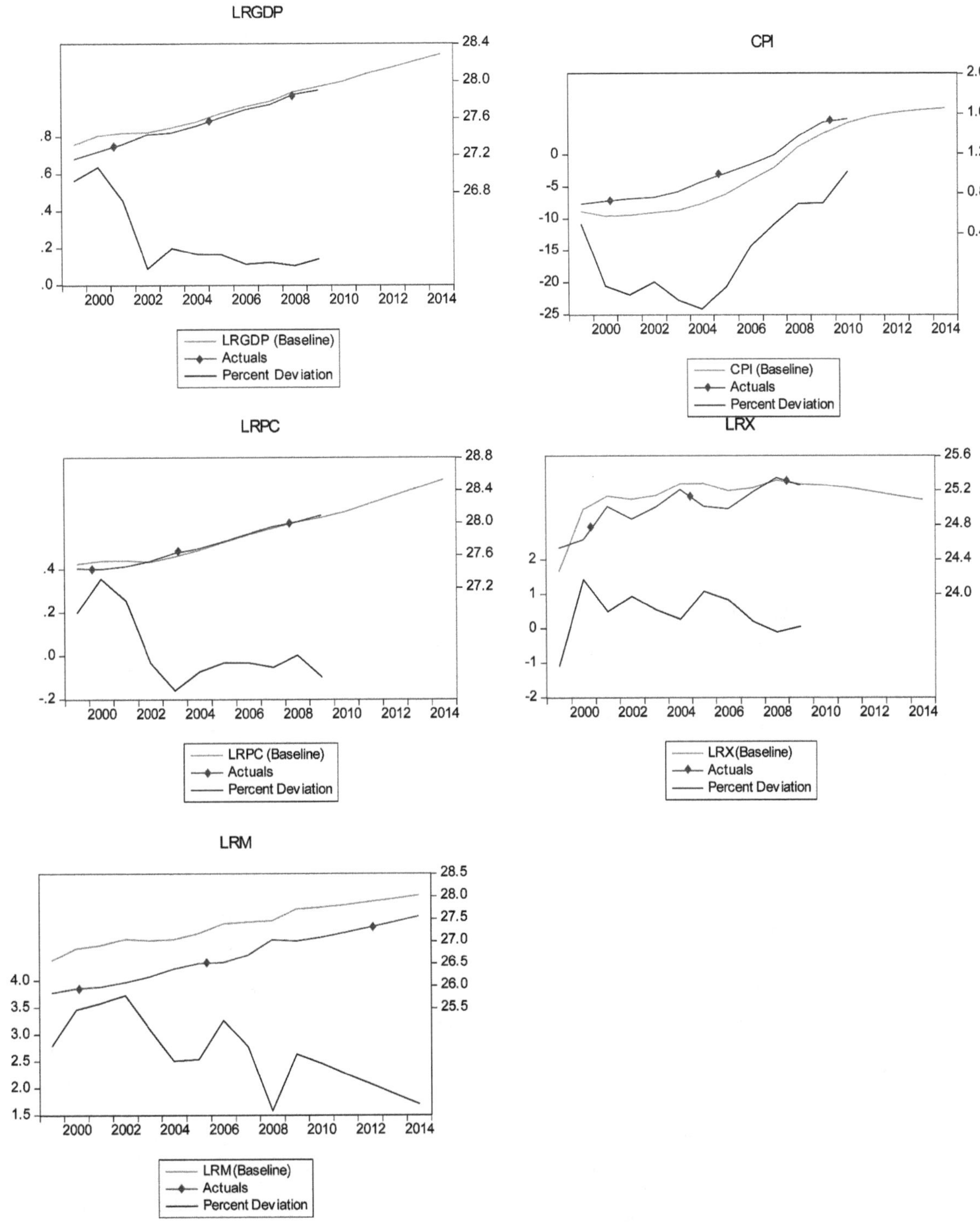

model without any policy intervention - just using the model dynamics (and hence depicts the economy's own dynamics). In this simulation we have raised the level of total public spending to the level stipulated in the new budget framework from the base run, which is a growth of about 10% per annum from 2009 to 2014. The result of this simulation is provided in Figure 4 (and Table 11 in Appendix 3).

Figure 4. The effect of the proposed government spending (deviation from base run, in %)

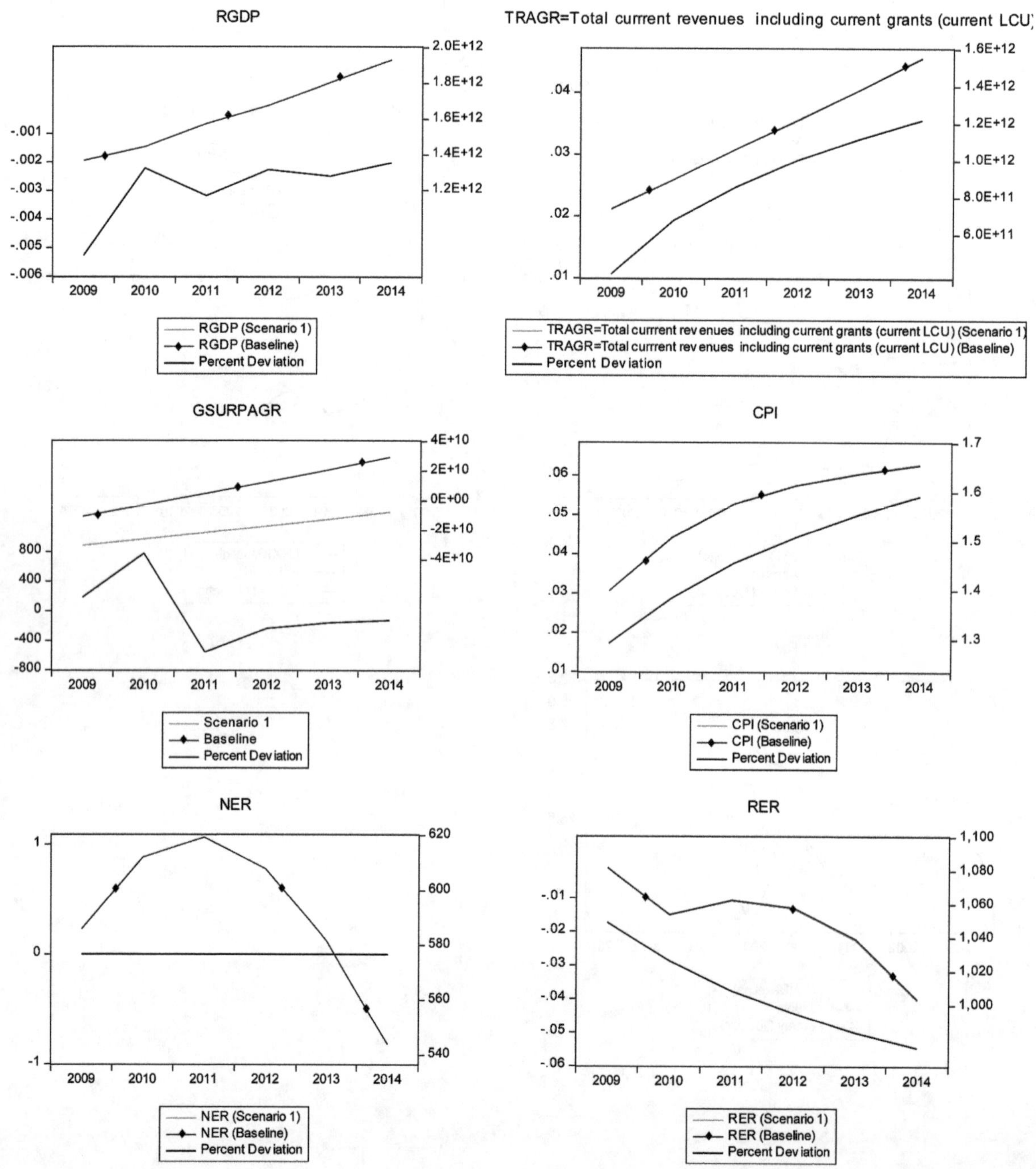

As can be gleaned from Figure 1 and Table 11, the result shows that the proposed spending during the fiscal period will generally be compatible with stable macroeconomic environment. The effect on real GDP is almost none and hence the GDP growth rate will remain as that of the base run forecast reported above. Similarly, the effect on inflation, nominal as well as real exchange rates is negligible as the deviation from the base-run being in the range of 0.01% to 0.05% with the policy. However, it has an effect in the level of fiscal deficit (after grants). The deficit will get worsened initially from -0.5% of GDP in the base run to -1.4% of GDP with the policy in the first year; and from -0.11% to -1.0% in the second year. It then stabilizes at about -0.5% of GDP by the end of the planned period. All these indicate, the government will be in stable macroeconomic environment with this planned spending.

Notwithstanding the effect of this total spending simulation above, the model shows that the composition of this spending does matter interims of its macroeconomic effect, although it is not extremely significant in terms of magnitude, as can be read from Figure 4 and its associated table, Table 12 in Appendix 3. Here, as we noted in Box 1, we varied the current expenditure by 13% per annum while the capital expenditure by 5% as stipulated in the budget framework paper (the combined effect of this is to vary the total spending by 10% and simulated above, however).

As can be read from Figure 5 (Table 12 in Appendix 3) the effect on GDP is very similar; thus, the GDP growth rate will remain as that of the base run forecast. The effect on nominal and real exchange rate also remains fundamentally unchanged. CPI (inflation), GDP and total revenue after grants have the same effect in terms of direction. However, the effect becomes stronger in this scenario. The overall magnitude of the effect however is a variation from the base run value of 0.2 to 0.55 with the policy in all cases and hence not significant. The policy will also result in an increase in money supply of 2 to 7% compared to the base run.

2. **The Effect of Government Policy 2:** The Effect of the New Wage Pay and Retention Policy. The effect of the new wage pay and retention policy is to raise the government spending (8% of current expenditure or 4% of total) as we noted above. Hence, its effect is similar to the simulation above but less potent owing to its relative magnitude. Thus, as can be gleaned from Figure 6 and the associated Table 13 in Appendix 3, its effect is to reduce GDP, private investment and real exchange rate. However, the magnitude is very small. In fact the growth rate of the economy is hardly affected compared to the base run. On the other hand, it leads to a rise in total current expenditure, inflation and the money supply as would be expected. Again the magnitude of this is not that strong and hence the stability of the macroeconomic environment will not be affected. It will have an effect to raise the fiscal deficit after grants from about -0.5% of the GDP to -3 to -5% of the GDP during the planned period (Figure 6).
3. **The Effect of the External Economy (Possible External Shock):** The effect of this probable adverse external shock is to reduce GDP (-1.3%), private investment (-5%), exports (about -4.5%) and imports (about -1%) sharply in the first period. This will lead to a sharp increase in fiscal deficit although the balance of payment is not affected that much in this period. However, this sharp decline will moderate over the course of the planned period accompanied by a decline in imports and recovery in exports. As a result the balance of payment as well as the government deficit will show a recovery. This simulation generally shows the significant macroeconomic risk implications of such an external shock and the need to be cautious to take appropriate policy response, if such an event does occur (Figure 7).

Figure 5. The effect of the composition of government proposed spending (deviation from base run, in %)

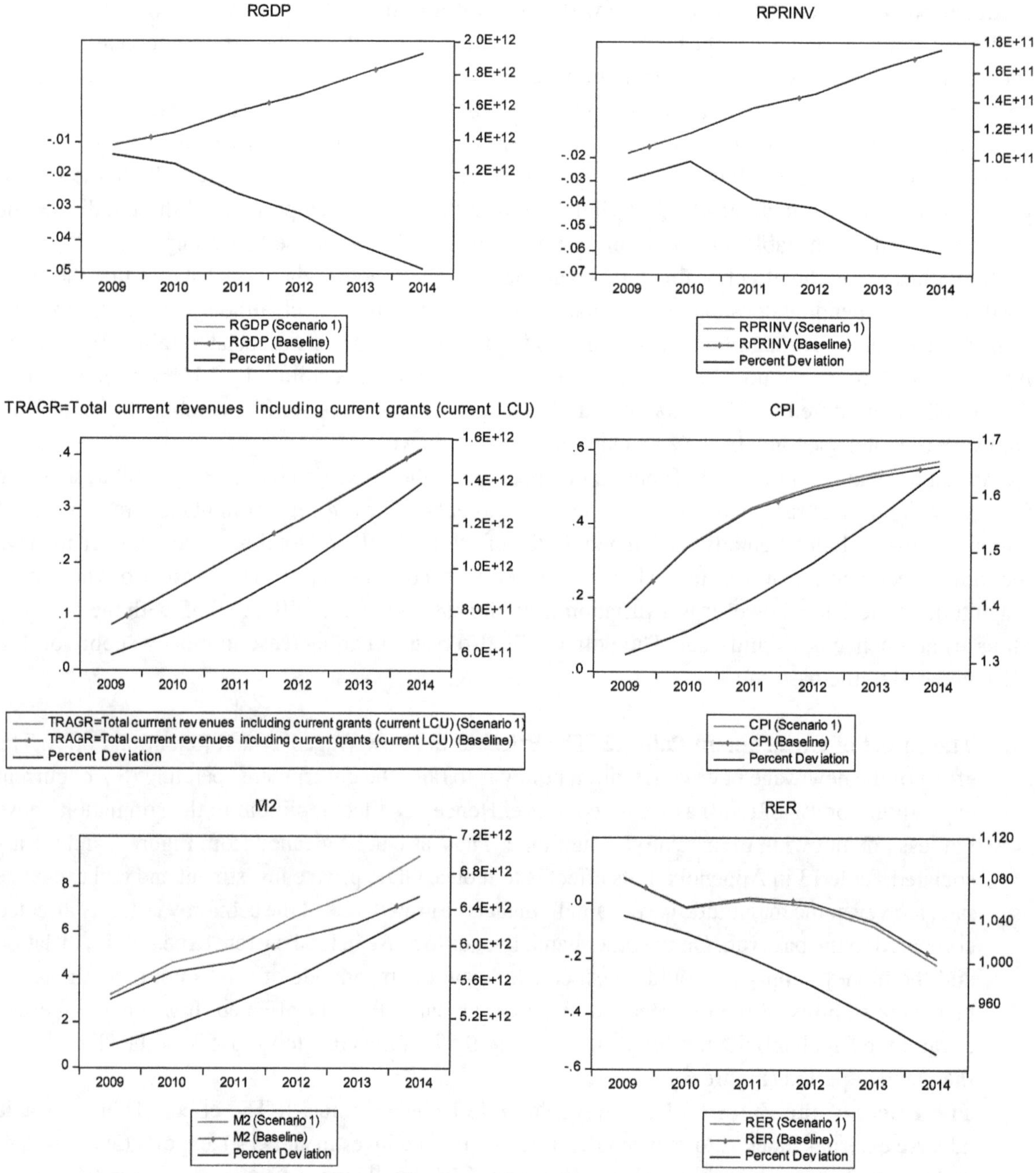

4. **The Effect of a Shortfall in External Financing:** This is a probable financing risk envisaged in the budget planning process, as is noted in Box 1. As the Figure 8 and the associated Table 15 in Appendix 3 shows, we can fairly generalize that the effect of this probable risk is negligible, in particular in real GDP growth as well as government total expenditure terms. However, its effect on government fiscal deficit as well as total government revenue (including grants) is relatively

Figure 6. The effect of the wage and pay and retention policy (deviation from base run, in %)

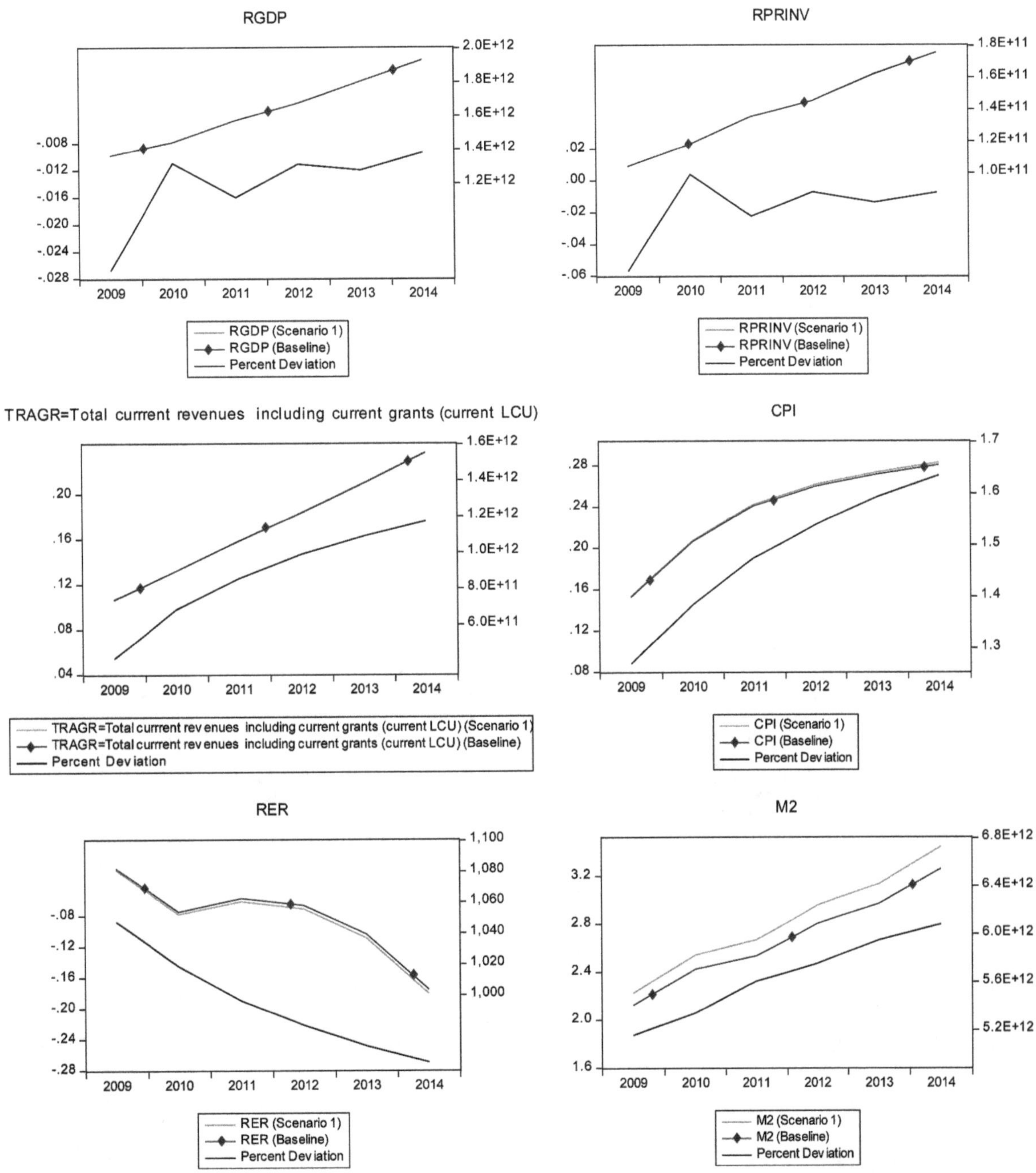

Figure 7. The effect of a possible slow down in the world economy (deviation from base run, in %)

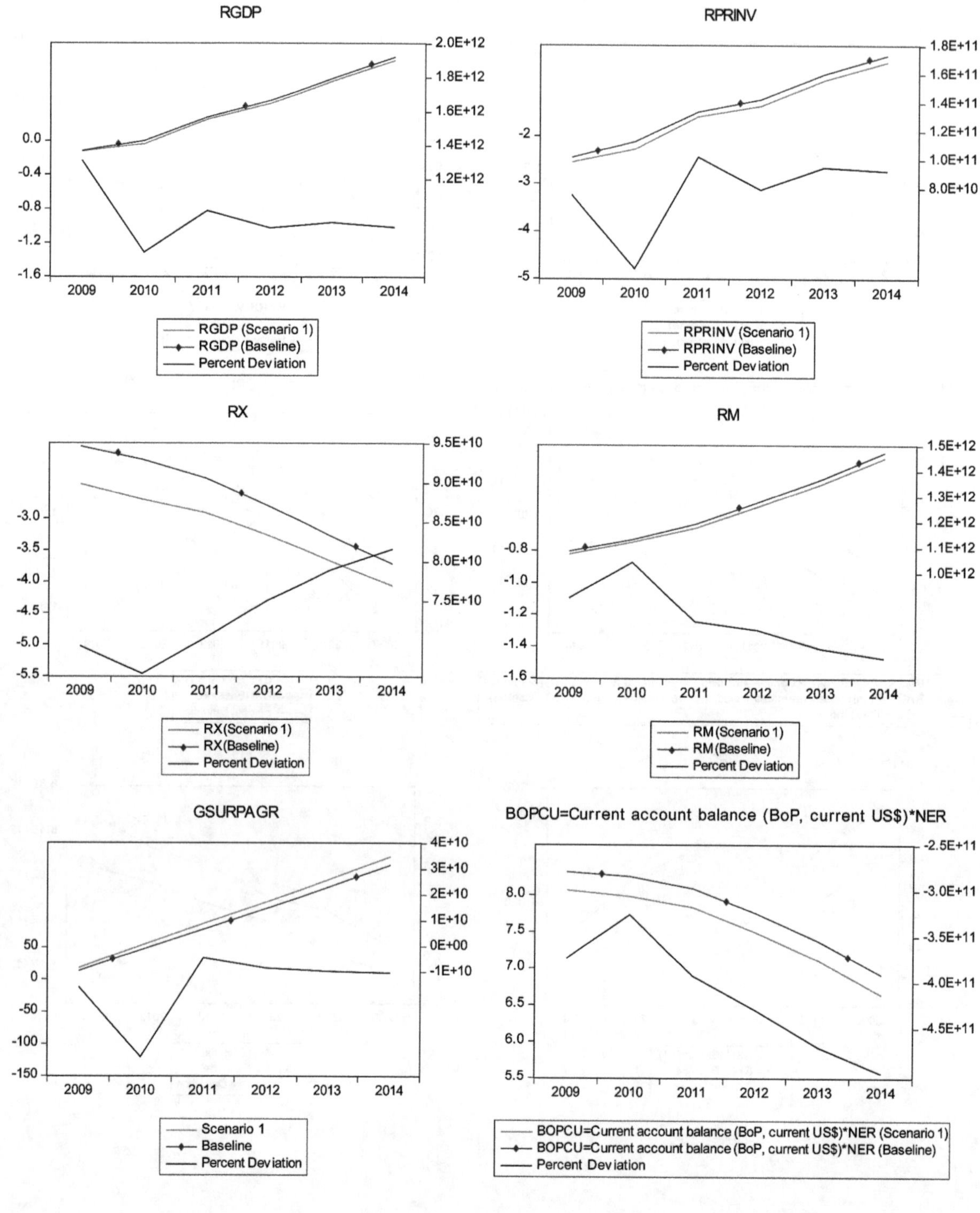

Figure 8. The effect of a shortfall in external financing (deviation from base run, in %)

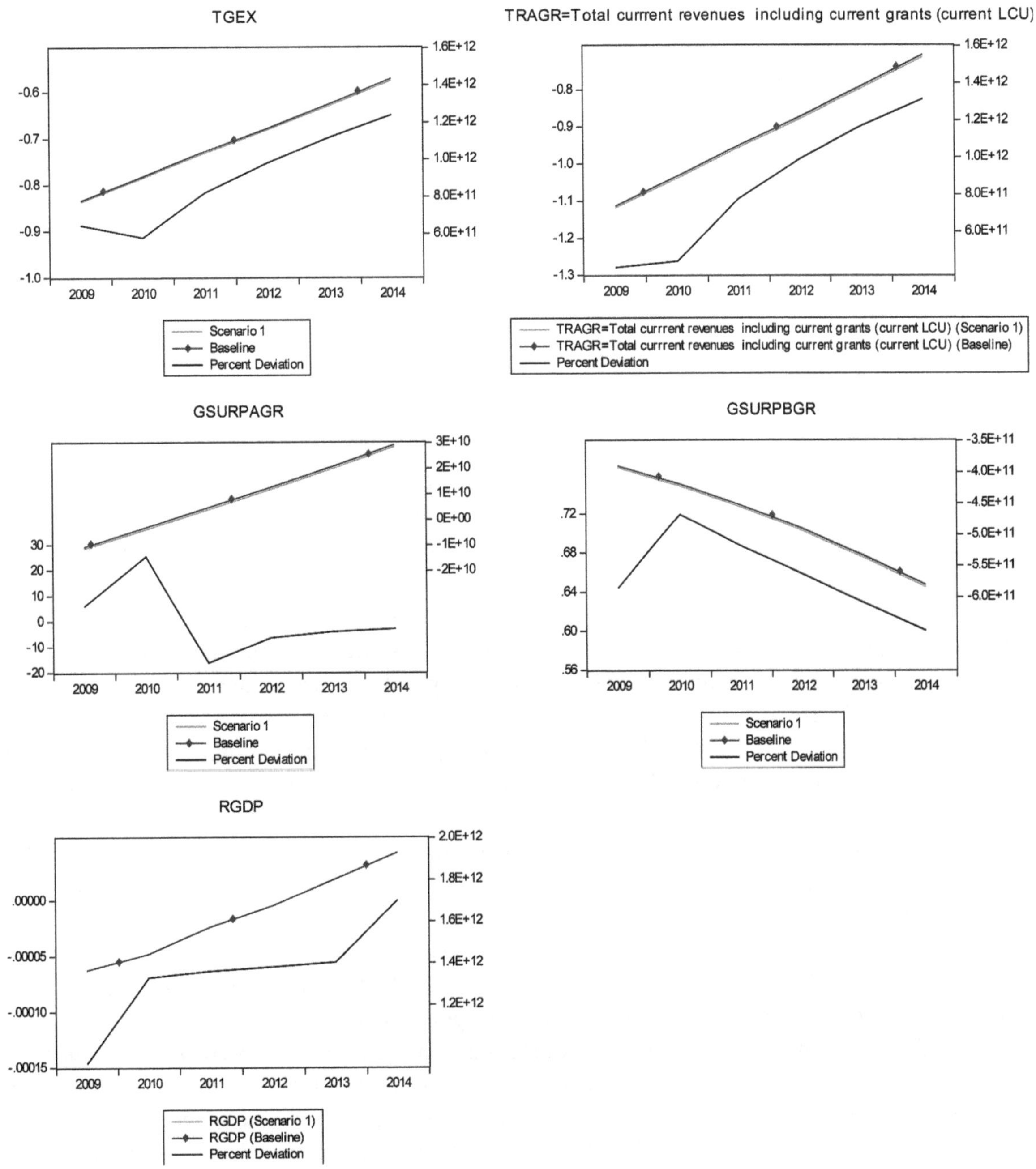

important in percentage terms (a deterioration of 6 to 25% from the base run in the first two periods). In actual terms this is not significant as it shows a deterioration of the government fiscal deficit (after grants) from -0.48% of GDP in the base run to -0.51% of GDP with the shock in the first year; and a similar deterioration from -0.11% to -0.14% of GDP in the second year. In summary, this macroeconomic risk is not significant. However, the government's strategy of 'delaying of spending' plan in such an event is an excellent cautious policy to deter any probable effect of this financing risk on the macro economy.

4. CONCLUSION

In this study we have developed a macro-econometric model for a typical supply constrained African economy such as Rwanda. This is aimed at developing a template for such policy tools which are increasingly demanded in Africa. The Rwanda macro-econometric model has 107 equations of which 72 are endogenous. In addition, a supplementary ARIMA based model of 33 equations which is necessary for handling the forecasting of exogenous variable needed for the overall forecasting ability of the model is built. The fiscal (including financing), balance of payment and money supply block of the models are fairly disaggregated to offer an adequate picture of the macro economy. A single equation equilibrium correction [error-correction] modeling framework is used for estimation of the core behavioral equations of the model. The model is similar to successful macro models in the region such that that of the KIPPRA-Treasury model as well as the Central Bank of Kenya's recent model. The model can also easily be further extended to the support budgeting, forecasting and macroeconomic policy analysis work at the relevant ministries such as the Ministry of Finance of Rwanda. We have managed to successfully solve the model from 1999 to 2009 and able to forecast major macro variables until the year 2014. The use of the model is illustrated by a real world policy analysis is about the Rwandan economy through a simulation exercise.

In the simulation exercise an attempt to understand the implications of the government of Rwanda's budget related policy as contained in its "2012/13-2014/15 Budget Framework Paper" is made. The analysis has focused in forecasting major macroeconomic outcomes in the planning period that could arise from the government's proposed policy and probable external shocks. The following major conclusion regarding the macroeconomic aspects of the economy (both prospects and risks) that might be encountered in the planning period can be read from the policy simulation exercise.

First, the forecasted macroeconomic outcome in the planning period (2012/13-2014/15) is compatible with forecast offered by the Ministry of Finance and Planning. This underscores the importance of this macro model for the future works of the Ministry (MoFP).Second, our simulation exercise revealed that the planned spending is compatible with stable macroeconomic environment. Thus, there seems to be no macroeconomic risk as it stands. Third, the Rwandan economy may face a limited macroeconomic risk if the world economy does slow down and price of imports (in particular fuel price) increase in the planning period. This requires the need to have a policy response, such as a flexible exchange rate policy, encouraging tourism etc. to contain the probable macroeconomic risks. Fourth, in terms of fiscal policy, given the level and forecast of inflation, there seems to be even a limited room for pro-poor fiscal expansion. This fiscal expansion is, however, conditional on an expansion of the food supply and hence growth in the agricultural sector. If that is not feasible, the financing strategy proposed by the government of Rwanda (i.e.; shying away from domestic debt) and delay in spending in face of shortage of external resources is a good strategy that needs to be pursued. In relation to this, the government deficit after grant is generally good. However, grants are above 10% of GDP and may lead to vulnerability. Thus, the government needs to be cautious about it. Finally, we note in conclusion the potential use of this model at the MoFP and policy making circles in Rwanda. It is an excellent macroeconomic tool for policy analysis and forecasting if, in particular, it is accompanied by expert opinion of Rwandese experts. Thus, there is a need to institutionalize it at the MoFP (or other relevant place) and build capacity of Rwandan experts for its effective use.

REFERENCES

Geda, A. (2002). *Finance and Trade in Africa: Macroeconomic Response in the World Economy Context*. London, UK: Palgrave-McMillan. doi:10.1057/9780230502543

Geda, A. (2011). *Readings on Ethiopian Economy*. Addis Ababa: Addis Ababa University Press.

Geda, A., & Tafere, K. (2011). *The Galloping Inflation in Ethiopia: A Cautionary tale for Aspiring Developmental African Countrie*. Department of Economics, Addis Ababa University.

Geda, A., & Yimer, A. (2013). *A Macroeconometric Model for Rwanda*. IAES Working Paper no 2. Retrieved from www.IAESAfrica.com

Geda, A., & Yimer, A. (2015). *A Macroeconometric Model for Ghana*. Retrieved from www.IAESAfrica.com

Huizinga, F., & Geda, A. (2004). *The Theoretical Model of the Ethiopian Ministry of Finance and Economic Development Model*. MoFED Working Paper. Ministry of Finance and Economic Development, Government of Ethiopia.

Huizinga, F., Geda, A., Ndung'u, N. S., & Karingi, S. N. (2001). *Theoretical Base for the Kenya Macro Model: The KIPPRA-Treasury Macro Model*. KIPPRA Discussion Paper No. 11. KIPPRA. Retrieved from http://www.kippra.org

Republic of Rwanda, Ministry of Finance and Economic Planning. (2012). *Consolidated Annexes to the 2012/13-2014/15 Budget Framework Paper*. Author.

Were, M., Kamau, M., Sichei, M., & Moses, K. (2013). *A Theoretical Framework for Kenya's Central Bank Macroeconometric Model*. Africa Growth Initiative Working Paper No 10.

ENDNOTES

1 This section is based on Huzinga and Geda (2005; see Geda, 2011) and it heavily draws from that. Readers are advised to consult this for a full and detailed picture of the theoretical framework. Here in an effort to save space we have attempted to give just the gist of the theoretical framework. A demand-driven version of this model's theoretical framework is given in Geda *et al* (2002) and heavily influenced the theoretical formulation of recent model of the Central Bank of Kenya (see Were *et al* 2013).

2 This may also indicate the agriculture-industry linkage which we have assumed to be negligible since the bulk of non-export agricultural output in many countries is accounted by cereals that could be taken as food.

3 Such an assumption is not only realistic but also can simplify the modeling work. In the future, and with further development of the private sector, this might be modeled using a labour bargaining model (see Huzingaet al. 2002 for such an application). In the manufacturing sector, the formal sector wage could also be thought as a mark-up over the informal sector nominal wage rate (w_I), which itself, in turn, is set as a mark-up (g_i) over the subsistence level of wage in rural areas (w_A).

APPENDIX 1: THE FULL THEORETICAL MODEL

1. INTRODUCTION

The theoretical model reported in this appendix is the basis for the empirical model developed and reported in the main text of this study. This theoretical framework draws from the theoretical framework developed by Geda and Huizinga (2004; also in Geda, 2011).

The model is based on aggregate demand – aggregate supply framework (AD-AS) that is focused on African stylized facts – in particular its structural features and the duality of its economies – thus we can call it Structural African Aggregate demand –Aggregate Supply model (SA_AD-AS model). The supply side will contain three main components: the formal sector, the informal sector and the agricultural sector – this underscores the duality of the African economy. Agriculture will be subdivided into cash crops and food production for the domestic market. This could, if the need arises, readily be subdivided further by major types of agricultural products. The informal sector consists mainly of small scale industry and handicrafts, informal trade such as street vendors and informal restaurant services. The formal sector consists mainly of the government and the formal sectors of industry and services. The latter include for instance large and medium scale manufacturing, formal trade, hotels, and restaurants, transport and communications, banking, insurance and real estate.

The formal private sector will be modeled along neoclassical lines, based on the theory of profit maximization, described below. With a monopolistically competitive firms in view, prices are set as a markup over costs, which consist of labor costs and the cost of intermediate goods and raw materials. Demand for labor and capital follow from a constant-elasticity-of-substitution (CES) production function. Demand for labor in the formal sector exhibits a large degree of labor hoarding, when reduction in domestic demand will be mostly absorbed by a reduction in profits, and relatively little by layoffs. This is partly based on the high search costs for relatively highly skilled and therefore scarce labor force and partly based on implicit contract considerations.

Formal sector output in the short run is demand driven. In the longer run, there is a supply component, as investment may be used to increase capacity. The degree to which this happens depends to a large extent on factors outside the firm's control, such as the quality of infrastructure, and an overall stable economic and political climate. This is especially true if overseas as well as public sector physical and financial investment is to play a major role. Investment in the formal sector, therefore, has both a cyclical component following GDP and a structural component following infrastructure and overall stability considerations.

The informal sector bears the brunt of the cyclical variation in economic growth. Unlike the formal sector, it cannot afford to keep employment intact during a cyclical downturn (say during a drought in some of the countries). So, a reduction in demand will reduce output, employment and investment immediately. The flip side is that it is relatively easy to reactivate economic activity if demand picks up again. Labor will be readily available and the capital stock is not a major input. So, the informal sector is completely demand driven with constant excess supply and a production function based mostly on low skilled labor.

The agricultural sector, on the other hand, is mostly supply driven. Output is determined by land, the quality of seeds and fertilizer, labor, some capital such as an ox (in an ox-plough culture), and most importantly, rainfall in small holder agriculture sector. Labor consists mostly of family labor, which is exogenously determined by population growth. There is always an excess supply of labor in the Lewisian (1955) sense, in a way that not all the labor is needed to produce output. This is not visible in the form of unemployment because of the family nature of farm production. Still, mostly young people may leave the farm because they cannot get their own land (is very small in size even if they managed to get one due to population pressure) and search for employment in the urban informal sector, thus maintaining the excess labor supply in that informal sector.

Wages will be based on a mixture of bargaining and efficiency considerations. Wages of the skilled workers will be based on structural productivity. There is a shortage of skilled labor so the unemployment rate for skilled labor will be based on search considerations, and be relatively constant. Skilled labor will, therefore, be relatively insulated from the cyclical variations in economic growth, both in terms of income and employment.

Wages of the unskilled are purely based on efficiency considerations, as there is an excess supply of unskilled labor. This means that wages are a markup over subsistence levels, without much regard to economic activity in the short run.

2. CYCLICAL VARIATION IN OUTPUT

The most important determinant of cyclical variation in output in agriculturally dominated economy is rainfall. If there is an adverse external shock such as a drought, the supply of food to the market is sharply reduced. As a result, the price of food rises.. As food is a major component of the CPI in Africa, a shock in the agricultural sector such a shortage or excess rainfall has a major effect on the CPI. As nominal wages are not indexed, real wages of urban workers drop sharply in an event of shortage of food. This will reduce domestic demand for industrial products both from the formal and the informal sector. In the informal sector, reduced demand leads to reduced employment, which further reduces demand. In the formal sector, the effects are less dramatic. One reason is that part of the demand for the formal sector comes from abroad. Export demand is not directly affected by the shock in the agricultural sector (except perhaps agricultural exports). Another reason is that the formal sector is better able to absorb a temporary reduction in demand through a reduction in profits (in the case of the private sector) or a deficit (in the case of the government).

3. LONG TERM GROWTH

A possible strategy for long term growth may be modeled as follows. It is reasonable that through a combination of better seeds, the use of fertilizer, and better infrastructure, the output of the agricultural sector can be increased substantially. This leads, other things remaining intact, to a drop in the food prices and a rise in the real wage of the urban workers. The increase in disposable income leads to a rise in consumption demand to the formal and informal sectors. In the formal sector this leads to increased profits, investment and eventually employment. In the informal sector, it leads to increased employment and eventually increased investment and profits. The key issue in terms of poverty reduction is that the demand for labor in the formal and informal sectors continuously grows faster than the population growth, which adds to the excess supply of labor in the agricultural sector, assuming that the food sector will not constrain this growth through inflation.

4. MODELING STRATEGY

The overall model for the short run consists of two blocks: the agricultural sector whose output is determined by exogenous, but widely fluctuating supply conditions, and the formal and informal sectors which in the short run are mostly demand determined and in the long run by the level of capital formation and infrastructural provision (which in turn are a function of foreign exchange generation)). The link between the two components is the price of food, which is set such that the demand for food in the formal and informal sectors equals the exogenous supply of food. Since the link between the two components of the model is basically one variable, the two model blocks may be developed almost separately. Perhaps more importantly, they may be expanded and disaggregated almost separately. For instance the agricultural sector may be disaggregated into satellite model with several sub-blocks for the different food crops, leading to a composite price for food, without affecting the overall structure of the model. Thus, if the need arises, we can model peculiar features of a country by introducing additional equations given the general template or core-model specified in this paper.

Thus, it therefore makes sense to first build a prototype of the model consisting of an aggregate agricultural sector, an informal sector, and a formal sector. This prototype model incorporates the basic linkages within and between the three sectors. Once we understand this prototype, the model may be expanded up to the full scale of the short run model, using an AD-AS framework.

5. THE PROTOTYPE MODEL

The prototype model starts with the agricultural sector. It has a production function based on land, labor, rainfall, and technology. Labor equals the agricultural population and grows with the general population growth. There are strong decreasing returns to scale with respect to labour, reflecting the current excess labor supply. Since all elements of the agricultural production function are exogenous, so is total agricultural output.

Part of the labor force has moved to the urban areas to find a job in the formal and informal sector. Because of low skill level these workers start out in the informal sector. The wage rate in the informal sector is a mark-up over the subsistence level in the agricultural sector because, among other things, of efficiency wage considerations in urban areas. As a result, there are always agricultural workers, especially young ones who would prefer to work in the informal sector and would move there if job conditions improve. Because of the constant excess supply of labor to the informal market, the wage is constant in the short run. Similarly, the wage in the formal sector is a mark-up over that in the informal sector, also based on efficiency wage considerations. Workers in the informal sector would prefer a job in the formal sector and, therefore, there is also always excess supply to the formal sector. Again we may assume that the wage in the formal sector is constant in the short run.

The formal and informal sectors both have CES production functions. The shares of inputs are different, however. The level of capital used in the formal sector is far greater than in the informal sector. As a result, the employment response to demand fluctuations is far greater in the informal sector than in the formal sector.

The mechanisms in the model can be illustrated by considering a supply shock, like a favorable rainfall, that raises output in the agricultural sector. The increased supply of food leads to a lower price of food and a rise in the real wage. This leads to a rise in consumption demand to the informal and formal sectors. Both sectors increase output. The formal sector also increases investment financed in part by the increased profits. Employment in the formal sector is much less responsive in the short run. The informal sector is far more employment - based and does not feature labor hoarding, and therefore, immediately increases employment. In addition, increased demand and profits leads to more investment, but this may be less important numerically. The increase in investment and employment further increase demand to the informal and formal sector, and also demand for food from the agricultural sector. The model converges because of leakage in the form of increased savings, increased imports and increased prices in the formal sector, leading to erosion in competitiveness. An overview of the model is presented in Figures 1 and 2 in the main text.

6. THE THEORETICAL FRAMEWORK

The Real Side

Modeling the macro economy both from the supply and the demand side requires that output derived both from the demand and the supply (output) side should be the same. In practice most countries report their data from the demand side which is not disaggregated by sector. In such situations, if the country has an input-output or a social accounting matrix, it can serve to link the national account as defined or derived from the final demand (expenditure) side to that of the same from the supply side. This is briefly outlined in the next sub-section (1.1). When such matrix is not available however, we could resort to the approach outlined in sub-section (1.1.1).

The CPS Matrix: The Link Between the Components of Aggregate Demand and Sectoral Production

The Cumulated Production Structure Matrix (CPS) provides the link between the components of aggregate demand and sectoral value added. It is the reduced form of the input-output matrix, in which the matrix of intermediate deliveries has been substituted out. It provides a direct link between the components of final demand and total sectoral production needed to produce it. For instance, the cell Y_FC in Table 1 is the value added produced by the formal sector that is used for the production of consumer goods, either directly by firms producing consumer goods or indirectly by firms producing intermediate goods used by other firms that produce consumer goods. The aggregate demand columns of the table add up to the value of the final demand component and indicate how each final demand is produced. The rows add up to the total sectoral production and indicate how sectoral production is allocated over the various final demand categories (see Table 1 and also Appendix 2).

Table 3 specifies as inputs sectoral value added, indirect taxes, and imports. Sectoral value added is then split up into labor input and capital input (using CES production function). This table gives an overview of the way the model links aggregate demand to sectoral value added and imports, and demand for labor and capital. First, final demand is modeled. Then the demand for value added by sector, indirect taxes, and the demand for imports is determined. This is done mostly based on the shares in the CPS matrix. However, special attention is given to the agricultural sector, of which the volume of production is largely exogenous. To accommodate this, the informal sector is used as a residual source of value added for each final demand component. When we have determined value added by sector, the

Table 3. Aggregate demand and aggregate supply in the CPS matrix framework

	Factor Inputs	Value-Added Plus Imports	Aggregate Demand				
			C	I	G	X_c	X_o
Formal sector value added	L_f, K_f	Y_f	Y_{fC}	Y_{fI}	Y_{FG}	Y_{fXc}	Y_{fXo}
Informal sector value added*	L_i, K_i	Y_i	Y_{iC}	Y_{iI}	Y_{iG}	Y_{iXc}	Y_{iXo}
Value added Agricultural sector (non–exports)	L_a, Ka	Y_a	Y_{aC}	Y_{aI}	Y_{aG}	Y_{aXc}	Y_{aXo}
value added Agricultural sector (exports)	L_{ax}, K_{ax}	Y_{ax}	Y_{axC}	Y_{axI}	Y_{axG}	Y_{axXc}	Y_{axXo}
Indirect taxes		T	T_C	T_I	T_G	T_{Xc}	T_{xo}
Imports		M	M_C	M_I	M_G	M_{Xc}	M_{Xo}

* Assumed as residual source of value added for each final demand component.

Xc= Export of coffee; f=formal; C,I,G & X=/ come from Table 4; Xo= Other exports; i=informal; Y,L & K = / come from Table 4; A=agriculture

demand for labor and capital is determined by sector. Total demand for labour and capital is calculated by adding demand by sector (see Appendix 2).

If we divide the columns of aggregate demand by their row totals, we get the shares of the primary inputs in aggregate demand. This share matrix is given in Table 4 and shown by the coefficient 'a' with various subscripts ($a_{ij}=d_{ij}/\sum_j d_{ij}$).

These shares indicate how important a final demand category is for a primary input. These shares provide the default way to model the demand for primary input. For instance the demand for total imports is:

$$\hat{M} = a_{mc}\hat{C} + a_{mi}\hat{I} + a_{mg}\hat{G} + a_{mxc}\hat{X}_c + a_{mxo}\hat{X}_o$$

where a_{mc} = Mc/M (See Equation (7) below).

Table 4. Shares of the primary inputs in aggregate demand

	Factor Inputs	Sectoral Inputs	Aggregate Demand				
			C	I	G	X_c	X_o
Formal sector value added	L_f, K_f	Y_f	a_{yfc}	a_{YfI}	a_{YfG}	a_{YfXc}	a_{YfXo}
Informal sector value added	L_i, K_i	Y_i	a_{YiC}	a_{YiI}	a_{YiG}	a_{YiXc}	a_{YiXo}
Agricultural sector value added*	L_a, K_a	Y_a	a_{YaC}	a_{YaI}	a_{YaG}	a_{YaXc}	a_{YiXo}
value added Agricultural sector (exports)	L_{ax}, K_{ax}	Y_{ax}	a_{YaxC}	a_{YaxI}	a_{YaxG}	a_{YaxXc}	a_{YaxXo}
Indirect taxes		T	a_{TC}	a_{TI}	a_{TG}	a_{TXc}	a_{Txo}
Imports		M	a_{mC}	a_{mI}	a_{mG}	a_{mXc}	a_{mXo}

Y= value added; I= Investment; C= consumption; G= Government expenditure; Xc= Exports of coffee; Xo= Other Exports; M= Imports; Subscripts f, I, a, and 'ax' refer to formal, informal, agricultural and agricultural exports; * Exogenous.

Table 5. From CPS matrix to price formation

Input	Cost Components of Aggregate Demand				
	C	I	G	X_c	X_o
Labor (L)	L_C	L_I	L_G	L_{Xc}	L_{Xo}
Capital (K)	K_C	K_I	K_G	K_{Xc}	K_{Xo}
Imports	M_C	M_I	M_G	M_{Xc}	M_{Xo}
Factor costs (sum of labour, capital and imports)	F_C	F_I	F_G	F_{Xc}	G_{Xo}
Indirect taxes less subsidies)	T_C	T_I	T_G	T_{Xc}	T_{Xo}
Market Price (factor cost plus indirect taxes less subsidies)	Ync	YnI	Yng	Ynx	Ynxo

The default way to model value added by sector is similar. For instance, value added in the formal sector is:

$$\hat{Y}_f = a_{yfc}\hat{C} + a_{yfi}\hat{I} + a_{yfg}\hat{G} + a_{yfxc}\hat{X}_c + a_{yfxo}\hat{X}_o$$

The value added in the agricultural sector does not follow this structure. The quantity is mainly exogenous, and fluctuates mostly with rainfall (See Appendix 2). The price of agricultural products is endogenous, so the value is endogenous as well. Because the row for agricultural production does not follow the general framework, we need another row to be a residual term for each column. For this we chose the value added in the informal sector. This is a reasonable assumption given our limited knowledge about the latter. Value added by sector is produced according to a CES production function (See Equation (1) and (2) below). Using this production function we derive the demand for capital and labor by sector.

In the Table 4, there is a direct link between final demand and labor input, capital input, indirect taxes, and imports. Table 5 gives the cost component of each final demand category and thus may be used for the cost component of the final demand pricing equations. (See section 2 below).

For modelling it is useful to distinguish between cost at factor prices and at market prices. For that we make a subtotal row for cost at factor prices. Dividing the columns of this table by the entries in the row factor costs gives the cost shares by final demand category. This is given in Table 6.

Table 6. Cost shares by final demand category

Input	Cost Components of Aggregate Demand				
	C	I	G	X_c	X_o
Labor	a_{lc}	a_{lI}	a_{lG}	a_{lXc}	a_{lXo}
Capital	a_{kc}	a_{kI}	a_{kG}	a_{kXc}	a_{kXo}
Imports	a_{mc}	a_{mI}	a_{mG}	a_{mXc}	a_{mXo}
Factor costs	1	1	1	1	1
Indirect taxes	t_c	t_I	t_G	t_{Xc}	t_{Xo}

These shares indicate how important a primary input is for the total cost of a final demand category. The default way to model the cost component is by using these shares. For instance, the cost component of the price of exports of major export commodity such as coffee, cocoa or copper is:

$$P_{xc} = cost_{xc}\left(1 + t_{xc}\right)$$

In percentage change, this is:

$$\hat{P}_{xc} = a_{lxc}(\hat{w} - \hat{h}) + a_{kxc}\hat{P}_k + a_{mxc} * \hat{P}_m + \frac{dt_{xc}}{\left(1 + t_{xc}\right)}$$

where w is wage rate and h is labour productivity, ^ indicates growth rate.

Production Functions

Supply from the agricultural sector, excluding agricultural exports, (Y_A) is assumed to come from an augmented CES production function, the argument goes, with capital such as oxen (K), labour(L_A), rainfall(R), and other productivity enhancing inputs such as fertilizer (F). The function below is specified assuming an optimizing peasant household that is endowed with K and L. The rest of the arguments are added on *ad hoc* basis (could be taken as factor augmenting).

$$Y_A = A\left[\beta_L L_A^{-\lambda} + \beta_K K_A^{-\lambda} + \beta_R R_A^{-\lambda}\right]^{-1/\lambda} \tag{1}$$

The supply in the formal (modern) sector is also formulated in a similar manner. Unlike the agricultural sector, intermediate imports (Z), instead of rain, are important in this sector, however. Adjustment to aggregate demand shock in this sector is effected through change in the level of output and profit, instead of the labour market that is assumed to be characterized by wage inflexibility owing to employment guarantee and high search cost. The supply in the sector is thus specified as,

$$Y_F = A\left[\beta_L L_F^{-\lambda} + \beta_K K_F^{-\lambda} + \beta_Z Z_F^{-\lambda}\right]^{-1/\lambda} \tag{2}$$

The capital variables in Equations (1) and (2) could be disaggregated into infrastructure and non-infrastructure if there is a need to see the effect of each component of the capital stock on output.

The informal sector is assumed to operate with limited capital. Labour is assumed as the most important input. Adjustment to demand shocks is effected through a flexible wage rate, the fairly large level of urban unemployment serving as a reservoir of labour. Thus, the supply in the informal sector (Y_I) is specified, as noted above, as a residual.

$$Y_I = Y - \left[Y_A + Y_F\right] = AL_I^{\beta_I} \tag{3}$$

where Y is the GDP.

If we modelled aggregate output from the supply side as above, and if we do not have a CPS matrix to get the aggregate demand equivalent of this supply side output, we may need to device another approach so as to reconcile it with the national account convention of getting GDP from the final demand/ expenditure side. One such device is to consider the economy as the sum of output of agricultural and non-agricultural sector, the aggregate excess demand in each of these sectors clears for agricultural prices (see Equation (13d)) and non-agricultural prices, respectively. In particular, in the latter case, since each price of the aggregate demand component is derived from optimality condition (see the nominal sector modelling in section 7 below), the final demand in nominal terms should be equal to the sum of the non-agricultural output, agricultural output and the informal sector output in nominal terms, aggregate price being the equilibrating variable. This is given as (3b) below. This way we can get the same value of output both from the demand and the supply side.

$$P^{informal}Y_{informal} = P^{GDP}Y - \left[P^{agr}Y_A + P^{formal}Y_F\right] = AL_I^{\beta_I} \tag{3a}$$

where Y is real GDP.

Note here that $P^{GDP}Y$ is the nominal GDP as defined from the demand (expenditure) side and given as the national income identity Y=C+I+G+X-M in national accounts.

Demands for Factor Inputs

Employment in the Formal Sector

Total employment is the sum of employees in the formal, informal, and agricultural sector. The supply of labour is assumed exogenous in the model (determined by population growth). The demand for labour (and hence the number of employees) in the formal sector is derived from the CES production function given in Equation (2). The optimal labour input according to this CES production function is

$$L_F = \left(\beta_L\right)^{\delta}(Y_F)\left(\frac{w}{p_y}\right)^{-\sigma} \textit{where } \sigma = \frac{1}{1+\lambda} \tag{4}$$

We have in terms of percentage changes:

$$\hat{L}_f = \hat{Y}_f - \sigma\left(\hat{w} - \hat{p}_y\right) \tag{5}$$

Total employment growth equals the growth of the economically active population. In the short run we assume there is no migration between the urban and rural sectors. Employment in rural and urban sectors both grow with total employment. In the urban sector, formal employment is given by Equation (5) and employment in the agriculture (and informal) sectors are the residual.

Investment

The investment function is derived from the conditions for an optimal level of capital stock (K) with P_k as price of capital goods. The optimal macro capital stock is given by:

$$K = \left(\beta_k\right)^{\sigma} Y \left(\frac{p_k}{p_y}\right)^{-\sigma} \tag{6}$$

From this we get,

$$\frac{\Delta K}{k_{-1}} = \hat{Y} - \sigma\left(\hat{p}_k - \hat{p}_y\right) \tag{6a}$$

or

$$\frac{i}{K_{-1}} = \hat{Y} - \sigma\left(\hat{p}_k - \hat{p}_y\right) + \delta \tag{6b}$$

It is sometimes argued that profits (π) allow internal financing of investment, which is cheaper than external financing. In addition, the capacity utilization rate (q) may play a role as a direct indicator of the difference between optimal and actual capacity. Similarly, public investment (I_g) might also have a crowding-in/out on private investment. Adding these elements, we get,

$$\begin{aligned} \frac{i}{K_{-1}} &= \hat{Y} - \sigma\left(\hat{p}_k - \hat{p}_y\right) + \delta + \lambda\left(\frac{\pi}{K}\right)_{t-1} + \mu(q-1) + \eta\hat{I}_g \\ &= \hat{Y} - \sigma\left(\hat{p}_i - \hat{p}_y\right) - \sigma\frac{dr}{r+\delta+r} + \delta + \lambda\left(\frac{\pi}{K}\right)_{t-1} + \mu(q-1) + \eta\hat{I}_g \end{aligned} \tag{6c}$$

where we used the fact that $p_k = (r+d+)p_i$. Capital is often considered a quasi fixed factor of production, because changing the capital stock takes a lot of time and involves important adjustment cost. Therefore, lags may be important in this equation. For the same reason, expectations matter as well, although they are difficult to model, and empirical models of investment with various expectations terms have not been very successful so far. If infrastructure is generally undertaken by the public section, as is usually the case in many African countries, the public investment variable in Equation (6c) could be disaggregate into infrastructure and others (which may includes human capital formation) with various lags.

Relationship with the Incremental Capital Output Ratio (ICOR)

Apart from the price terms, we have from the above equation that

$$K = \beta_k^\sigma Y$$

where β^σ_k is a constant coefficient.

This coefficient (i.e. β^σ_k) is also known as the capital output ratio. If this ratio is constant, as would be the case if relative prices are constant, the marginal capital output ratio and the average capital output ratio are the same. The marginal capital output ratio is the incremental capital output ratio (ICOR). The ICOR plays an important role in, for instance, the IMF and World Bank models and also in many planning and budgeting exercises across Africa. Thus, alternatively we may get to an investment equation using the ICOR as follows.

$$\Delta K = ICOR\left(\Delta Y\right)$$

where $\Delta K = I - d * K_{t-1}$ and 'd' is the depreciation rate

$$I = ICOR * \Delta Y + d * K_{t-1}$$
$$I = ICOR * \Delta Y + d * ICOR * Y_{t-1}$$

The first term is the accelerator term, and we see that ICOR is its coefficient. The second term is the replacement investment.

Demand for Imports

Gross output is a CES function of value added and imports. So, we get a scale variable and a price elasticity. For our scale variable we use the growth of gross output weighted by importance to total imports. We derive import, based on the CPS matrix noted above, as follows.

$$m = m_c + m_i + m_g + m_x$$
$$m = \frac{m}{C}C + \frac{m}{I}I + \frac{m}{G}G + \frac{m}{X}X \tag{7a}$$

where m_j denotes the cumulated imports content in final demand category j (j = c, i, g, x), assuming the shares (m_j/j) to be constant we get,

$$\Delta m = \left(\frac{m_c}{C}\right)_{-1}\Delta C + \left(\frac{m_i}{I}\right)_{-1}\Delta I + \left(\frac{m_g}{G}\right)_{-1}\Delta G + \left(\frac{m_x}{X}\right)_{-1}\Delta X \tag{7b}$$

or

$$\hat{m} \; = \; \hat{z}_m \; \equiv \; \frac{m_c}{m}\hat{c} \; + \; \frac{m_i}{m}\hat{i} \; + \; \frac{m_g}{m}\hat{g} \; + \; \frac{m_x}{m}\hat{x} \tag{7c}$$

This is the percentage change in imports due to output effects, assuming constant import shares, that is, constant relative prices. To add the effect of relative prices we write:

$$\hat{m} = \hat{z}_m - \sigma\left(\hat{p}_m - \hat{p}_y\right) \tag{7d}$$

where P_m denotes price of imports in local currency (Birr).

Note that, by implication, z_m is proportional to a geometric average of the components of gross output z.

$$Z_m \propto C^{\frac{m_c}{M}} I^{\frac{m_i}{M}} G^{\frac{m_g}{M}} X^{\frac{m_x}{M}} \tag{7e}$$

In empirical studies, it is often found that the elasticity of imports with respect to the scale variable z_m is larger than 1. This may be explained by a trend towards internationalization. We capture this effect with an additional parameter $\alpha \geq 1$.

$$\hat{m} = \alpha\hat{z}_m - \sigma\left(\hat{p}_m - \hat{p}_y\right) \tag{7f}$$

The price of imports equals the (exogenous) price of imports in foreign currency, $p_M(\$)$, times the exchange rate (e), times 1 plus the import tariff rate.

$$\hat{p}_m = \hat{p}_m(\$) + \hat{e} + \frac{\Delta t_m}{1 + t_{m-1}} \tag{7g}$$

Alternative Specification of Imports

An alternative way to model imports, in particular when detailed data as above is missing, is to specify imports as a function of real exchange rate and the level of income, GDP ad Aid as follows:

$$M = \beta_0 + \beta_1 \frac{\hat{p}}{P_d} + \beta_2 Y + \beta_3 AID$$

where Y is GDP; P_d domestic price; AID official aid and $\hat{p}$ as defined above.

Labour Supply and Unemployment

Labour supply is modelled exogenously as the product of the population within working age times the labour activity ratio plus employment in non-working age. The equation for labour supply is,

$$l^s = \phi population_{working\ age} + employment_{non-working\ age} \tag{8a}$$

where φ is the exogenous labour activity ratio.

The labour supply minus the labour in military service equals the economically active population (l^{econ}),

$$l^{econ} = l^s - l^{military} \tag{8b}$$

where l^{econ} is the economically active population. The number of unemployed workers *u* is given as the economically active population minus employment.

$$u = l^{econ} - l \tag{8c}$$

The unemployment rate *ur* is given by the number of unemployed divided by the labour supply.

$$ur = \frac{u}{l^s} \tag{8d}$$

Final Demand for Goods

Consumption

Consumption is determined by a model of intertemporal optimization. We present a simple version of this model. Suppose consumers maximize the following two period intertemporal problem.

$$\begin{aligned} &\arg\max(c_1, c_2) : \log c_1 + \frac{1}{1+\delta}\log c_2 \\ &subject\ to : c_1 + \frac{1}{1+r}c_2 = y_1^d + \frac{1}{1+r}y_2^{d,e} + wealth_0 \end{aligned} \tag{9a}$$

where c_i and y_i^d denote real consumption and real disposable income in period i, for i = 1, 2. The superscript *e* denotes expected value, the value of y_2 is not known in the first period, so consumers have to form expectations about it. *r* is the real interest rate and *d* the personal discount rate, $wealth_0$ denotes wealth accumulated from the past. The maximand is the present discounted value of intertemporal utility. The appropriate discount rate is the personal discount rate *d*. The right hand side of the budget constraint equals the present discounted value of resources and the left hand side the present discounted value of consumption expenditure. The budget constraint says that consumers may save and borrow, but such that the present values of their incomes and expenditures remain equal to each other.

It is generally assumed that the personal discount rate d is equal to the real interest rate r. Under this condition, the first order conditions for this problem imply,

$$c_1 = c_2 \tag{9b}$$

So the consumption levels in both periods are equal to each other. This is the basic idea of consumption smoothing over time; consumers save and borrow in order to keep their consumption levels relatively constant.

By assuming an explicit formula for expected real disposable income in period two, we can solve for c explicitly. We assume,

$$y_2^{d,e} = y_1^d\left(1+g\right) \tag{9c}$$

that is, income is assumed to grow at a rate g. Then the formula for consumption becomes,

$$c_1 = \left(1+\frac{g}{2+r}\right)y_1^d + \left(\frac{wealth_0}{2+r}\right) \tag{9d}$$

which indicates that the coefficient on current income is around 1 if g is around zero, that is, if the current level of income is at a normal level. The coefficient on wealth is around 1/2 in this model, but in a more general model with more periods, it is approximately equal to 1 divided by the number of periods. If the number of periods is very large, the coefficient equals $r/(1+r) \approx r$ (r is the real interest rate).

Since reliable data on wealth is not usually available, we left that variable out of the equation. The equation in the model (in log) is,

$$c = (\alpha 1 - \alpha 2\, r)\, y^d \tag{9e}$$

Disaggregation by Sector

In most countries in Africa, food is an essential consumption good and also a major component of total consumption. It, therefore, merits special attention. We assume that there is a minimum level of food consumption $\overline{c}_a$, which needs to be consumed to stay alive. Expenditure on this minimum food consumption is $pa^*\overline{c}_a$. Remaining nominal disposable income is denoted Y_d^* and is given by,

$$Y_d^* = Y_d - p_a\overline{c}_a \tag{9f}$$

In nominal terms consumption of food is given as,

$$p_a c_a = a_a Y_d^* + p_a\overline{c}_a \tag{9g}$$

An increase in disposable income also raises food consumption but reduces the relative share of other agricultural consumption goods.

Consumption of non-food (c_{na}) is a function of disposable income after expenditure on necessities.[2] This could be given by,

$$p_{cna}c_{na} = a_{na}Y_d^* \tag{9h}$$

where P_{cna} is price of non-food consumption.

Total consumption is given by the sum of 9g and 9h which should be equal to 9e (or one need to estimate only one of 9g or 9h, getting the 3rd as residual from total consumption, 9e).

Exports

Exports are determined by an interaction of foreign demand for the country's goods, which might be set as a function of the relative export price in local currency and the level of income of the trading partners (Y_N) which is exogenously given.

$$x = wt^{\alpha} \left(\frac{p_x}{p_{wt}}\right)^{-\sigma} \tag{10a}$$

The term in the bracket is the real exchange rate P_d being the domestic price. The above equation abstracts form quality effects or supply side effects. The effects of the supply side could be modelled by adding the capital stock to the level equation, or the investment as a ratio of the capital stock or (of value added) to the percentage change equation. The last term has indeed been highly significant in several studies of exports. Adding this effect we get for the percentage change in exports,

$$\hat{x} = \alpha\hat{wt} - \sigma(\hat{p}_x - \hat{p}_{wt}(\$) - \hat{e}) + \phi\left(\frac{i}{y}\right)_{-1} \tag{10b}$$

Disaggregation of Exports

Some goods form a major component of total exports. In addition, most African countries are price takers in the world commodity market, so that the export price and the world price are equal. Exports thus may not be demand determined but pure supply driven, based on profit motive. The profitability could be modelled as the difference between the exogenous world price and the domestic cost.

$$\hat{X}_c = \beta_3\left(\hat{P}^w + \hat{e} - \hat{cost}\right) \tag{10c}$$

For other products we may assume that demand play a role so that Equation (10b) holds. Total exports are given as the sum of the two (Equations (10b) and (10c)).

Government Spending and Revenue

Government spending (G) and revenue (T) in the model are formulated using a number of semi-behavioral equations which took the following generic form.

$$G = \sum G_i = \sum \left(\alpha_i + \beta_i Z_i\right) \tag{11}$$

$$T = \sum T_i = \sum \left(\alpha_i^* + \beta_i^* Z_i\right) \tag{12}$$

where G_i and T_i denotes the vectors of different spending and revenue categories, respectively, and Z_i a vector of determinants of G_i & T_i, α and β (α* and β*) are parameters. To capture the fiscal response to the external finance, one of the variables in the vector Z is an indicator of foreign finance, such as aid which could be disaggregated by its various forms such as grants and non-grants, if needed (see Alemayehu 2002).

7. THE NOMINAL SIDE

Price Determination in the Agricultural Sector

Supply of agriculture, as noted above, can fairly be thought as exogenous in the short run. This is because of the observed stagnant technology progress as well as the sector's dependence on rain and population growth (for labour supply), which are exogenous. The demand for agricultural goods equals

$$p_a c_a = a_a Y_d^* + p_a \overline{c}_a \tag{13a}$$

$$Supply\ equals = p_a * y_a + e p_f m_{ca}' \tag{13b}$$

where m_{ca} is the real import of consumption for agriculture (imported food), e the nominal exchange rate and p_f price of imports (foreign price).

Equating supply and demand gives,

$$p_a\left(y_a - \overline{c}_a\right) + \left(e p_f m_{ca}\right) = a_a Y_d^* \tag{13c}$$

The left hand side of this equation is the marketed surplus of agriculture plus imports of food. The right hand side shows the market demand. The price of agricultural products is, thus, given as,

$$p_a = \frac{a_a Y_d^* - \left(e p_f m_{ca}\right)}{y_a - \overline{c}_a} \tag{13d}$$

Price and Wage Determination in the Formal Sector

We assume that output prices are set by firms who operate in a market structure of monopolistic competition. That is, we assume that for each good, there exits an inverse demand curve $p^f = p^f(z)$, with p^f denoting the price at factor cost and z gross output. The price at factor cost is exclusive of indirect taxes and subsidies, and thus equals the price the firm actually receives for its product. We also assume that there exists a well behaved cost function $c = c(z)$. Profit maximization then leads to,

$$\arg\max\left(z\right):\left(1-t_{\pi}\right)\left[p^{f}\left(z\right)z-c\left(z\right)\right] \tag{14a}$$

where t_{Π} is the profit tax.

Profits are maximized by setting the price p^f equal to,

$$p^{f}=\left(1-\frac{1}{\varepsilon}\right)^{-1}mc \tag{14b}$$

where ε is the price elasticity of demand and *mc* denotes marginal cost: $mc = dc/dz$. Note that the profit tax has no influence on the price, since both marginal revenue and marginal cost are reduced by the same amount. The market price, denoted p_y, is related to the factor cost price p^f by,

$$p_{y}=p^{f}\left(1+t_{z}-s_{z}\right) \tag{14b}$$

where t_z and s_z are the indirect tax and subsidy rates.

The relation for the market price is therefore,

$$p_{y}=\left(1-\frac{1}{\varepsilon}\right)^{-1}\left(1+t_{z}-s_{z}\right)mc \tag{14c}$$

We do not observe marginal cost, however, so the above equation is not operational. Therefore, we first define capacity as the level of production with minimum average long run cost. Note that marginal cost at capacity equals this average long run cost. Using duality theory, we make a Taylor expansion of marginal cost around capacity output. We get,

$$mc=ac+\alpha z*\frac{\left(z-z^{*}\right)}{z^{*}} \tag{14d}$$

where z* equals capacity level of output and α involves derivatives of the cost function. The term z/z* is the capacity utilization rate, denoted by q.

Average cost, denoted ac, equals,

$$ac = \frac{w\left(1+s_f\right)l + p_k K + p_m m}{z} \tag{14e}$$

where w denotes the gross wage level, s_f the social security contributions rate paid by the firm, l employment, $p_k$the user cost of capital, K the capital stock, p_m the domestic currency price of imports and m imports.

The user cost of capital p_k in turn equals,

$$\begin{aligned} p_k &= \left(i - \pi + \delta + \overline{r}\right) p_i \\ &= \left(r + \delta + \overline{r}\right) p_i \end{aligned} \tag{14f}$$

where i is the nominal interest rate, π the inflation rate, δ the depreciation rate, r the real interest rate and the risk premium.p_i is the price of investment goods, that is the price of capital when bought.

The capacity utilization rate *q* should ideally be constructed using a proper explicit production or cost function. For the time being we simply assume that output fluctuates around capacity, so that we may approximate capacity by average output. This implies,

$$\frac{z - z^*}{z^*} = q - 1 = \frac{z}{z_{average}} - 1 \tag{14g}$$

The basic equation for the percentage change in value added price is then,

$$\hat{p}_y = \hat{a}c + \beta 1 \Delta\left(q-1\right) + \beta 2\left(q-1\right) + \frac{\Delta t_z - \Delta s_z}{1 + t_z - s_z} + constant \tag{14h}$$

The equation contains a constant. This is true for all behavioural equations, but for brevity's sake we leave the constants out from now on. Assuming technological progress to be labour saving, and denoting labour productivity by *h*, we get,

$$\hat{a}c = \alpha_j\left(\hat{w} - \hat{h}\right) + \alpha_k \hat{p}_k + \alpha_m \hat{p}_m \tag{14i}$$

where α_j is the share of factor j in gross output.

Influence of Competitor Prices

So far, we have abstracted from the influence of competitor prices. In the long run competitor prices should not matter much, because in equilibrium all firms will have a certain competitive rate of return on their investment. So if, say, exporting firms would continually meet foreign price reductions without accompanying reductions in their own costs, they would end up bankrupt and would disappear. In the short run, however, firms may well follow competitor prices in order to retain their market shares if foreign prices fall, or if foreign prices rise, to get a short run increase in profits when expansion of output is not possible in the short run. There is, indeed, strong evidence that export prices are especially sensitive to foreign competitor prices.

We may model this by writing,

$$\hat{p}_y^{m,s} = (1-\gamma)\hat{p}_y + \gamma\hat{p}_{comp} \\ = \hat{p}_y + \gamma\left(\hat{p}_{comp} - \hat{p}\right) \tag{14j}$$

where the superscript m,s indicates short-run market prices and y is the elasticity of final demand prices to competitor prices. Note that if $y \neq 0$, the value added price, p_y, also depends on competitor prices; a reduction in price in order to meet a reduction in competitor prices, leads to a reduction in value added and profits.

All together, we get for the final goods prices determined in the market as,

$$\hat{p}_y^{m,s} = (1-\gamma)\left(\alpha_w\left(\hat{w} - \hat{h}\right) + \alpha_k\hat{p}_k + \alpha_m\hat{p}_m + \beta 1\Delta q + \beta 2\left(q-1\right) + \frac{\Delta t_z - \Delta s_z}{1 + t_z - s_z}\right) + \gamma p_{comp} \tag{14k}$$

Price of Aggregate Goods in the Formal Sector

Price of aggregate goods basically follows the same structure as given above for single good in the formal sector. We only have to take into account that some goods are not set according to market conditions, but set directly by the government. Let the share of such goods be λ. Then we get for the price equations of aggregate goods, $\hat{p}^{ag}$.

$$\hat{p}^{ag} = (1-\lambda)\,\hat{P}_y^{m,s} + \lambda\,\hat{p}^{p} \tag{14l}$$

where the superscript p denotes policy-determined.

Substituting out the Price of Capital

There are three aggregate goods' prices in the model, one for consumer goods, a second for investment goods, and another for export goods. The straightforward thing to do is to model all three according to the above equations with coefficients that are appropriate for the separate aggregate goods. However, we do not know much about the user cost of capital, p_k. Therefore, we decided to substitute it out of the price equations. To do this, we assume that the depreciation rate is constant, so that,

$$\hat{p}_k = \frac{d\left(r + \delta + \bar{r}\right)}{r + \delta + \bar{r}} + \hat{p}_i = \frac{dr}{r + \delta + \bar{r}} + \hat{p}_i \tag{14m}$$

On the further assumption that effective indirect taxes and subsidies are zero (for instance, because indirect taxes paid on investment goods may be taken as a credit by the investing firm) and also setting *g* and *l* equal to zero for investment goods, we get,

$$\hat{p}_i = \alpha_{w,i}\left(\hat{w} - \hat{h}\right) + \alpha_{k,i}\hat{p}_k + \alpha_{m,i}\hat{p}_m + \beta 1_i \Delta q + \beta 2_i \left(q - 1\right) \tag{14n}$$

where the subscript *i* stands for investment goods. This implies,

$$\begin{aligned}\hat{p}_k &= \frac{dr}{r + \delta + \overline{r}} + \alpha_{w,i}\left(\hat{w} - \hat{h}\right) + \alpha_{k,i}\hat{p}_k + \alpha_{m,i}\hat{p}_m + \beta 1_i \Delta q + \beta 2_i \left(q - 1\right) \\ &= \frac{1}{1 - \alpha_{k,i}}\left[\frac{dr}{r + \delta + \overline{r}} + \alpha_{w,i}\left(\hat{w} - \hat{h}\right) + \alpha_{m,i}\hat{p}_m + \beta 1_i \Delta q + \beta 2_i \left(q - 1\right)\right]\end{aligned}$$

We may use this equation to substitute out the user cost of capital in the price equations. Substituting this equation into the equation for the change in short run market prices of good *j*, $\hat{p}_j^{m,s}$, we get,

$$\hat{p}_j^{m,s} = \left(1 - \gamma_j\right)\left[\alpha'_{r,j}\frac{dr}{r + \delta + \overline{r}} + \alpha'_{w,j}\left(\hat{w} - \hat{h}\right) + \alpha'_{m,j}\hat{p}_m + \beta 1'_j \Delta q + \beta 2'_j (q - 1) + \frac{\Delta t_{z,j} - \Delta s_{z,j}}{1 + t_{z,j} - s_{z,j}}\right] + \gamma_j \hat{p}_{comp} \tag{14o}$$

where

$$\alpha'_{r,j} = \alpha_{k,j}\frac{1}{1 - \alpha_{k,i}}; \alpha'_{w,j} = \alpha_{w,j} + \alpha_{k,j}\frac{\alpha_{w,i}}{1 - \alpha_{k,i}}; \alpha'_{m,j} = \alpha_{m,j} + \alpha_{k,j}\frac{\alpha_{m,i}}{1 - \alpha_{k,i}}$$

$$\beta 1'_{j'} = \beta 1_j + \alpha_{k,j}\frac{\beta 1_j}{1 - \alpha_{k,i}}; \beta 2'_j = \beta 2_j + \alpha_{k,j}$$

In the above equation we assumed that the capacity utilization rate *q* is modelled at the macro level. $\alpha'_{w,j}$ has the interpretation of the cumulated labour share in good j, including the labour content of the capital stock. Similarly, $\alpha'_{m,j}$ has the interpretation of the cumulated share of imports in the production of good *j*. The above equation thus model production as ultimately using only labour, imports and time (the effect of *r*). Given the relatively small nature of the formal sector, the high search cost for skilled labour and strong institutional impact of the public sector, the nominal wage rate in the formal sector is assumed to be fixed[3] at w_f.

Price and Wage Determination in the Informal Sector

The supply of output in the informal sector (defined as residual in Equation (3)) is assumed to depend on labour supply, rendering a horizontal supply curve at a fixed price. This nominal wage rate (w_I), is set as a mark-up (g_i) over the subsistence level of wage in rural areas (w_A).

$$w_I = w_A(1 + g_A) \quad (15)$$

The mark-up, g_A, is determined by a complex process of migration which is related to urban cost of leaving and the risk premium that the potential migrant is assumed to take. The average rural nominal wage (w_A) would serve as a proxy for the opportunity cost of the potential migrant. This cost can be approximated by the sum of average agricultural output and income. Given this nominal wage, the price in the informal sector could be set as

$$P_I = w_I(1 + g_i) \quad (16)$$

Thus, the general prices level should be a weighted average of the price in the formal and informal sector and that of the agricultural sectors:

$$P^{GDP} = \beta_1 P^{agr} + \beta_2 P^{formal} + \beta_3 P^{informal} \; where \; \beta_1 + \beta_2 + \beta_3 = 1 \quad (17)$$

The Money Market and the Exchange Rate

Money Demand and Supply and Interest Rate

The demand for money, M^d, is defined as a function of real GDP, the price level and the nominal interest. We have,

$$M^d = \alpha Y + \beta P - \gamma i \quad (18)$$

where M^d denotes nominal demand for money, Y stands for real GDP, and i the nominal interest rates on bonds (the rest of the symbols being parameters).

We assume that the exchange rate is floating (or managed floating), so that money supply is available as an exogenous policy instrument (semi-behavioural given by MS*). Equilibrium in the domestic money market then implies that,

$$i = \frac{1}{\gamma}\left(\alpha Y + \beta P - MS^*\right) \quad (18b)$$

It is reasonable to assume that the Central (National) Bank directly targets inflation, hence Equation (18b) and the money supply (in first differences) can be written as:

$$\Delta i = \frac{1}{\gamma}\left[\alpha \Delta Y + \beta \Delta P - \Delta MS^*\right] \quad (18c)$$

With the inflation targeting monetary policy rule could be given by

$$\Delta MS^{*} = \alpha \Delta Y + \beta \Delta P^{*} + \beta_1 \left[\Delta P - \Delta P^{*}\right] with\ \beta_1 < \beta \quad (18d)$$

where P* is the target level of inflation.

This gives us the interest rate equation of the model

$$\Delta i = \frac{\beta - \beta_1}{\gamma}\left[\Delta P - \Delta P^{*}\right] \quad (19)$$

Exchange Rate

The exchange rate is assumed to be determined by the supply of, and the demand for foreign exchange. The supply of foreign exchange, in turn, is determined by export earning and external finance or aid (AID), plus remittance less the government's demand for foreign exchange for its international obligations such as for debt servicing (FX^{dd}_{g}). The latter could also shows the possibility of a Dutch disease. Demand for foreign exchange is determined by the level of imports. Excess demand in this market is cleared through movement in the nominal exchange rate as given below.

$$e = \beta_0 + \beta_1 M - \beta_2 \left[X + Aid - FX_g^{dd}\right] \quad (20)$$

The real exchange is derived by definition:

$$RER = e + p_f - p_d \quad (21)$$

where RER is the real exchange rate.

APPENDIX 2: MODELING AGGREGATE DEMAND AND SUPPLY

Notwithstanding the short–run nature of this macro model, it is important to specify the supply side of this model since short-run output fluctuation in Africa depends on vagaries of nature that affects the agricultural sector. Aggregate supply of goods and services in the model emanate from its three components: the agricultural, the formal and informal sectors.

The modelling of the supply side is carried at two stages. In the first stage, we have specified a relationship between aggregate demand and aggregate supply (or value-added) using a cumulative production structure. This approach is chosen owing to the paucity of data in the disaggregation of output into the formal, informal, and agricultural sector. Thus, in this state aggregate demand (consumption, investment, government spending, and exports) will determine the level of imports and total value-added. This value-added is disaggregated into agricultural, formal, and informal sector. Out of the components of value-added, the value-added in the informal sector is assumed to be the residual. In the second stage,

Table 7. Aggregate demand, valued-added, factor inputs, and prices

Demand for Factor Inputs	Value-Added (Agg. Supply)	Aggregate Demand				
		Consumption [C]		Investment [I*]	Gov't Spending [G]	Exports [X]
		Food C_f	Non-Food (C_{nf})			
$Y_F = A\left[\beta_L L_F^{-\lambda} + \beta_K K_F^{-\lambda}\right]^{-1/\lambda}$	Y_F	c_{fa}	c_{nf}	I^*_a	G_a	X_a
$Y_I = A\left[\beta_L L_I^{-\lambda} + \beta_K K_I^{-\lambda}\right]^{-1/\lambda} = AL_i^{\beta}$	Y_I	c_{fi}	c_{ni}	I^*_i	G_i	X_i
$Y_A = A\left[\beta_L L_A^{-\lambda} + \beta_K K_A^{-\lambda} + \beta_R R_A^{-\lambda}\right]^{-1/\lambda}$	Y_A	c_{fa}	c_{na}	I^*_a	G_a	X_a
Demand for imports	M	c_{fm}	c_{nm}	I^*_m	G_m	X_m

Table 8. Cost structure: inputs and prices

Cost Components	C_f	C_{nf}	I	G	X
Labour	L_{cf}	L_{cf}	L_{I*}	L_G	L_X
Capital	K_{cf}	K_{cf}	K_{I*}	K_G	K_X
Imports	M_{cf}	M_{cf}	M_{I*}	M_G	M_X
Indirect tax	t_c	t_c	t_{I*}	t_G	t_X
Column total (Prices)	P_{cf}	P_{cnf}	P_{I*}	P_G	P_X
	P_c				

Note: P = prices; t = indirect taxes; Sectors: I (or i) = Informal; F (or f) = formal; A (or a) = Agricultural; M (or m) = imports; Demand: C = Consumption; I* = Investment; G = Pubic spending; X = Exports; Y = value-added

the injection from the aggregate demand which in turn create the demand for value added is assumed to generate demand for factor inputs (capital, labour, and imports). The choice of this factor inputs is assumed to follow from an optimization problem of agents in each sector using a CES productions function as given in Table 7. This formulation also offers the cost structure of prices for the aggregate demand components as given in Tables 7 and 8.

Table 9. Identities and bridging equations

General	The Fiscal Block Government Revenue
NGDI = NGDP - TXR RC = RPC + RGC RGDI = NGDI / GDPDEF RPRINV = NPRINV / INVP RINV = RPRINV + RPUINV PF = 0.5 * (XP + MP) RER = NER * (PF / CPI) RGDP = RPC + RINV + RGC + RX - RM RTVA = RAGVA + RNAGVA GDPDEF * RGDP = RPC * CPI + RINV * GDPDEF + RGC * CPI + RX * XP - RM * MP NGDP = GDPDEF * RGDP	TRBGR = TXR + NONTXR + CAPREV TXR = DTX + IDTX + FTRTX DTX = DTX(-1) * (NGDP / NGDP(-1)) + Discrepancy IDTX = IDTX(-1) * (FCONEX / FCONEX(-1)) + Discrepancy FCONEX = RPC * CPI + RGC * CPI FTRTX = IMPORTAX + EXPORTAX X = RX * XP M = RM * MP IMPORTAX = IMPORTAX(-1) * (M / M(-1)) + Discrepancy EXPORTAX = EXPORTAX(-1) * (X / X(-1)) + Discrepancy TRAGR = TRBGR + GR CAPREV = NETBORROWING_EXT + OTHCAPIREV
Government Expenditure, Fiscal Balance and Debt	**The Monetary Block**
TGEX = GCUREX + GCAPEX GCUREX = WS + TINTEXPE + AMORT_EXT + OTHCUREXP + Discrepancy WS = (WS(-1)) * (EMPT / EMPT(-1)) * (WRATE / WRATE(-1)) DEBT_DOM = DEBT_DOM(-1) + NETBORROWING_DOM + Discrepancy EXTDEBT = EXTDEBT(-1) + NETBORROWING_EXT TINTEXPE = INTPAYDOMDEBT + INTPAYEXTDEBT OTHCUREXP = OTHCUREXP(-1) * (NGDP / NGDP(-1)) + Discrepancy GCAPEX = GCAPEX(-1) * ((NETBORROWING_EXT + GR) / (NETBORROWING_EXT(-1) + GR(-1))) + Discrepancy GSURPAGR = 0.25 * (TRAGR - TGEX) GSURPBGR = TRAGR - TGEX - GR	GOVSUGRLessEA = GSURPAGR - NETBORROWING_EXT - AMORT_EXT TOTAL_FINANCING = - 1 * (GOVSUGRLessEA) NETBORROWING_DOM = TOTAL_FINANCING - NETBORROWING_EXT NETBORROWING_EXT = GROSSBORROWING_EXT - AMORT_EXT OFICALEXCHANGERESERVES = OFICALEXCHANGERESERVES(-1) + CHANGEINRESERVES (-1) CHANGEINRESERVES = BOPOVERALL - STATDESCREPANCY1 M2 = OFICALEXCHANGERESERVES + (DOM_CREDIT_CALIMSONGOVT(-1) + NETBORROWING_DOM) + DOMCRED_CLAIMS_OTHERS + STATDESCREPANCY2
The Balance of Payment Block	
BOPCU = 0.25 * (X - M + NDINROW + NCUTR) BOPOVERALL = BOPCU + BOPCA	

Table 10. List of variables used in the model

Name	Label
AID	Net Official Development Assistance and Official Aid Received
AGLF	Agriculture Labor Force, Absolute Value
AMORT_EXT	External Loan Amortization, Nominal
BOPCA	Balance of Payment, Capital, Nominal
BOPCU	Balance of Payment, Current, Nominal
BOPOVERALL	Balance of Payment, Overall, Nominal
CAPREV	Capital Revenue, Nominal
CHANGEINRESERVES	Changes in net reserves, Nominal
CPI	Consumer Price Index
CS	Total Capital Stock, Real
CURN	Capacity Utilization Rate, Nominal
CURR	Capacity Utilization Rate, Real
DUM_1	Period dummy,(1991-2009==1) and 0 otherwise
DUM_{90}	Impulse Saturation Dummy,1990=1 and 0 otherwise
DUM_{91}	Impulse Saturation Dummy,1991=1 and 0 otherwise
DUM_{94}	Impulse Saturation Dummy,1994=1 and 0 otherwise
DUM_{95}	Impulse Saturation Dummy,1995=1 and 0 otherwise
DUM_{96}	Impulse Saturation Dummy,1996=1 and 0 otherwise
DUM_{06}	Impulse Saturation Dummy,2006=1 and 0 otherwise
DUM_{07}	Impulse Saturation Dummy,2007=1 and 0 otherwise
DIR	Deposit Interest Rate, Nominal
DOM_CREDIT_CALIMSONGOVT	Claims on Central Government, Nominal
DEBT_DOM	Domestic Debt, Nominal
DOMCRED_CLAIMS_OTHERS	Claims on Others, Nominal
DTX	Direct Tax, Nominal
EMPT	Total Employment, Absolute Value
EXCESDDFOOD	Excess Food Demand
EXPORTAX	Export Tax, Nominal
EXTDEBT	External Debt Stock, Nominal
FCONEX	Final Consumption Expenditure, Nominal Total
FTRTX	Foreign Trade Tax, Nominal
GCAPEX	Government Capital Expenditure, Nominal
GCUREX	Government Current Expenditure, Nominal
GDPDEF	GDP Deflator, Period Average
GR	Grant, Nominal
GROSSBORROWING_EXT	Gross External Borrowing, Nominal
IDTX	Indirect Tax, Nominal
IMPORTAX	Import Tax, Nominal
INCTRAD	Income of Trading Partners, Real

continued on following page

Table 10. Continued

Name	Label
INF	Inflation(Change in CPI)
INTPAYDOMDEBT	Interest Payment on Domestic Debt, Nominal
INTPAYEXTDEBT	Interest Payment on External Debt, Nominal
INVGDP	Investment to GDP Ratio, Real
INVP	Investment Price
LnAGLF	The Natural Log of Agriculture Labour Force, Absolute Value
LnABPRO	Labor Productivity, Real
LnAID	The Natural Log of Net Official Development Assistance and Official Aid Received
LnCPI	The Natural Log of Consumer Price Index
LnCS	The Natural Log of Total Capital Stock, Real
LnCURN	The Natural Log of Capacity Utilization Rate, Nominal
LnCURR	The Natural Log of Capacity Utilization Rate, Real
LnDIR	The Natural Log of Deposit Interest Rate, nominal
LnDTX	The Natural Log of Direct Tax, Nominal
LnEMPT	The Natural Log of Total Employment, Absolute Value
LnFC	The Natural Log of Real Food Consumption
LnGDPDEF	The Natural Log of GDP Deflator, Period Average
LnINCTRAD	The Natural Log of Income of Trading Partners, Real
LnINVGDP	The Natural Log of Investment to GDP Ratio, Real
LnINVP	The Natural Log of Investment Price
LnIR	Lending Interest Rate
LnLABPRO	The Natural Log of Labor Productivity
LnM	The Natural Log of Import of Goods and Services, Nominal
LnM2	The Natural Log of Money Supply(M2)
LnMD	The Natural Log of Money Demand
LnMP	The Natural Log of Import Price
LnNAGLF	The Natural Log of Non-Agricultural Labor Force
LnNER	The Natural Log of Nominal Exchange Rate, Period Average
LnNGDP	The Natural Log of Nominal GDP
LnNPRINV	The Natural Log of Nominal Private Investment
LnNPUINV	The Natural Log of Nominal Public Investment
LnNWR	The Natural Log Nominal Wage Rate
LnPUC	The Natural Log of Per Unit Cost of Out Put
LnRAGVA	The Natural Log of Real Agricultural Value Added
LnRER	The Natural Log of Real Exchange Rate
LnRES	The Natural Log of Reserves, Nominal
LnRGC	The Natural Log of Real Government Consumption
LnRGDI	The Natural Log of Real Disposable Domestic Income

continued on following page

Table 10. Continued

Name	Label
LnRGDP	The Natural Log of Real GDP
LnRIR	The Natural Log of Real Interest Rate
LnRM	The Natural Log of Real Import of Goods and Services
LnRNAGVA	The Natural Log of Real Non-Agricultural Value Added
LnRPC	The Natural Log of Real Private Consumption
LnRPRINV	The Natural Log of Real Private Investment
LnRPUINV	The Natural Log of Real Public Investment
LnRX	The Natural Log of Real Export of Goods and Services
LnUNEMPTRATE	The Natural Log of Unemployment Rate
LnXP	The Natural Log of Export Price
M	Imports of goods and Services, (BOP, nominal)
M2	Money Supply(M2)
MD	Money Demand, Nominal
MP	Import Price
NAGLF	Non-Agricultural Labor Force, Absolute Value
NAGVA	Nominal Agricultural Value Added
NCUTR	Net current transfers (Bop, Nominal)
NDINROW	Net Direct Income(ROW, BoP, Nominal)
NER	Nominal Exchange Rate, Period Average
NETBORROWING_DOM	Net Domestic Borrowing, Nominal
NETBORROWING_EXT	Net External Borrowing, Nominal
NGDI	Nominal Domestic Disposable Income
NGDP	Nominal GDP
NGDPP	Nominal GDP Potential
NNAGVA	Nominal Non-Agricultural Value Added
NONTXR	Non-Tax Revenue, Nominal
NPRINV	Nominal Private Investment
NPUINV	Nominal Public Investment
NWR	Nominal Wage Rate
OFICALEXCHANGERESERVES	Official Exchange Reserve, Nominal
OTHCAPIREV	Other Capital Revenue
OTHCUREXP	Other Current Expenditure
PC	Nominal Private Consumption
PF	Foreign price
PUC	Per Unit Cost of Output
RAGVA	Real Agricultural Value Added
RER	Real Exchange Rate
RGC	Real Government Consumption
RGDI	Real Disposable Domestic Income

continued on following page

Table 10. Continued

Name	Label
RGDP	Real Gross Domestic Product
RGDP_BELGIUM	Real GDP of Belgium
RGDP_KENYA	Real GDP of Kenya
RGDP_SWITHERLAND	Real GDP of Switzerland
RGDPP	Real GDP Potential
RINV	Real Total Investment
RIR	Real Interest Rate
RM	Real Import of Goods and Services
RNAGVA	Real Non-Agricultural Value Added
RPC	Real Private Consumption
RPRINV	Real Private Investment
RPUINV	Real Public Investment
XP	Export Price
X	Export of goods and services,(Bop, Nominal)
WS	Wages and Salaries, Nominal
WRATE	Wage Rate, Nominal
TXR	Total Tax Revenue, Nominal
TRBGR	Total Revenue Before Grant, Nominal
TRAGR	Total Revenue After Grant, Nominal
TOTALDEBT	Total Government Debt, Nominal
TINTEXPE	Total Interest Expense, Nominal
STATDESCREPANCY 1	Statistical Discrepancies 1
STATDESCREPANCY 2	Statistical Discrepancies 2
RX	Real Export of Goods and Services
RTVA	Real Total Value Added

APPENDIX 3: SIMULATION RESULTS USING THE RWANDA MACROECONOMETRIC MODEL

Table 11. The effect of the proposed government spending (deviation from base run, in %)

Year	Growth	Gov't Fiscal Surplus After Grants (% GDP)	Gov't Fiscal Surplus Before Grants (% GDP)
2009	-0.1	-2.2	-34.3
2010	0.1	-1.8	-35.4
2011	0.0	-1.4	-35.5
2012	0.0	-1.0	-36.4
2013	0.0	-0.7	-37.0
2014	0.0	-0.4	-37.7

Table 12. The effect of the composition of government proposed spending (deviation from base run, in %)

Year	Growth	Real GDP	Real Private Investment	Total Government Expenditure	Total Revenue After Grants	Total Revenue Before Grants	Real Exchange Rate	M2 (Money Supply)	MD (Money Demand)
2009	-0.26	-0.01	-0.01	10.14	0.01	0.02	-0.02	0.37	0.02
2010	-0.05	0.00	0.00	10.16	0.02	0.04	-0.03	0.40	0.03
2011	-0.11	0.00	0.00	10.19	0.02	0.04	-0.04	0.46	0.04
2012	-0.10	0.00	0.00	10.24	0.03	0.05	-0.04	0.49	0.05
2013	-0.14	0.00	0.00	10.29	0.03	0.06	-0.05	0.53	0.05
2014	-0.11	0.00	0.00	10.34	0.04	0.06	-0.05	0.56	0.06

Table 13. The effect of the wage and pay and retention policy (deviation from base run, in %)

Year	Growth	Real GDP	Real Private Investment	Total Revenue After Grants	Total Revenue Before Grants	Current Account Deficit	BoP (Overall)	CPI (Inflation)	Real Exchange Rate	M2 (Money Supply)
2009	-0.50	-0.03	-0.06	0.05	0.10	0.02	0.03	0.09	-0.09	1.87
2010	0.29	-0.01	0.00	0.10	0.18	0.00	0.00	0.15	-0.15	2.06
2011	-0.06	-0.02	-0.02	0.13	0.23	0.00	-0.01	0.19	-0.19	2.32
2012	0.08	-0.01	-0.01	0.15	0.26	-0.01	-0.02	0.22	-0.22	2.47
2013	-0.01	-0.01	-0.01	0.16	0.29	-0.01	-0.01	0.25	-0.25	2.66
2014	0.04	-0.01	-0.01	0.18	0.32	-0.01	-0.01	0.27	-0.27	2.80

Table 14. The effect of a possible slow down in the world economy (deviation from base run, in %)

Year	Growth	Real GDP	Real Private Investment	Real Investment (Total)	Real Private Consumption	Real Exports	Real Imports	Total Government Expenditure	Total Revenue After Grants	Total Revenue Before Grants
2009	-4.30	-0.24	-3.24	-0.46	-0.46	-5.02	-1.10	-1.16	-0.60	-1.14
2010	-25.65	-1.31	-4.79	-0.76	-1.10	-5.46	-0.87	-0.29	0.48	0.87
2011	5.58	-0.83	-2.44	-0.44	-1.10	-4.90	-1.25	0.68	1.48	2.62
2012	-3.47	-1.03	-3.13	-0.58	-1.27	-4.29	-1.30	1.08	1.86	3.30
2013	0.91	-0.96	-2.66	-0.53	-1.31	-3.82	-1.41	1.39	2.13	3.78
2014	-0.87	-1.02	-2.74	-0.57	-1.38	-3.48	-1.47	1.54	2.24	4.01

Year	Gov't Fiscal Surplus After Grants (% GDP)	Gov't Fiscal Surplus Before Grants (% GDP)	Current Account Deficit	Bopca_0	BoP (Overall)	CPI (Inflation)	Real Exchange Rate	M2 (Money Supply)
2009	-11.80	-1.18	7.13	0.00	12.04	1.13	1.77	0.35
2010	-120.24	-1.69	7.73	0.00	13.69	3.02	-0.31	0.70
2011	33.18	-1.97	6.90	0.00	12.51	4.12	-1.42	1.03
2012	17.53	-2.13	6.43	0.00	11.54	4.76	-2.07	1.31
2013	12.71	-2.22	5.92	0.00	10.43	5.13	-2.45	1.60
2014	10.31	-2.28	5.56	0.00	9.54	5.36	-2.70	1.85

Table 15. The effect of a shortfall in external financing (deviation from base run, in %)

Year	Growth	Total Government Expenditure	Total Revenue After Grants	Total Revenue Before Grants	Gov't Fiscal Surplus After Grants (% GDP)	Gov't Fiscal Surplus Before Grants (% GDP)	Current Account Deficit
2009	-0.003	-0.89	-1.28	-2.42	5.92	0.64	0.00
2010	0.00	-0.91	-1.26	-2.31	25.33	0.72	0.00
2011	0.00	-0.82	-1.10	-1.97	-16.28	0.69	0.00
2012	0.00	-0.75	-0.99	-1.78	-6.39	0.66	0.00
2013	0.00	-0.70	-0.90	-1.62	-4.04	0.63	0.00
2014	0.00	-0.65	-0.83	-1.50	-2.98	0.60	0.00

Chapter 7
Modeling Transaction Costs for a Sustainable Energy Policy:
A Review and Illustration

Ranjan Kumar Ghosh
Swedish University of Agricultural Sciences (SLU), Sweden

ABSTRACT

This chapter presents a discussion on the economic governance aspect of sustainability in the context of energy policy and access. It is believed that incentives are sufficient for emergence of competitive energy markets which augment energy access. However, recent developments in Transaction Cost Economics (TCE) have shown that this need not be true when costs arising out of incomplete contracting are high. Yet, the role of transaction costs and the need to identify and model their behavior has not received adequate attention. This chapter reviews the basic tenets of TCE around natural monopoly sectors. It then illustrates in greater micro-analytic detail how transaction costs can be identified and empirically modeled in the context of industrial self-generation of electricity. The conclusion is that in the analysis of production systems, sustainability arguments are not complete unless costs arising out of inefficient contracting are accounted and an adequate economic governance apparatus is set-up.

1. INTRODUCTION

Sustainability science has emerged over the last few decades as an important area of research and enquiry which attempts to uncover the complexities around the interface of economy, society and nature (Clark & Dickson, 2003; Komiyama & Takeuchi, 2006; Orecchini, Santiangeli, & Valitutti, 2011). It is transdisciplinary in approach and oriented towards problem solving in complex situations. It is also problem driven and relies on local knowledge to contextualize the problem. The study of economic systems, on the other hand, have been rather disciplinary as it was 'developed predominantly as a science of choice' (Oliver, 2002; p.172). This was especially since Lionel Robbins defined it as the 'science which studies human behavior as a relationship between ends and scarce means which have alternative uses' (Robbins, 1932; p.16). Can contributions from the study of economic systems fit the criteria laid down by sustainability science?

DOI: 10.4018/978-1-5225-0094-0.ch007

I will argue in the affirmative because a fundamental characteristic of an economic society is exchange which is based on relationships guided by (formal or informal) contracts. While James Buchanan (1975) could have been more generous when he said 'economics as a discipline went "wrong" in its preoccupation with the science of choice and the optimization apparatus', Oliver Williamson conceded that 'the parallel development of a science of contract was neglected' (Oliver, 2002; p.172). Recently, however, institutional theorists have framed an operational contractual paradigm to include the analysis of transaction costs. The prime proposition from such is that effective economic governance minimizes the threats of post-contractual hazards. Transaction cost economics (TCE) takes a micro-analytic view of economic organization and looks at it as a contracting problem. According to a 'discriminating alignment hypothesis' (Oliver, 1998), governance structures align themselves to minimize the costs which arise out of the particular attributes of a transaction. Since TCE assumes bounded rationality (instead of the neo-classical complete rationality), under uncertainty, investment in specific assets generate difficulties which need to be governed by institutions of private ordering. However when transactions are complex and uncertainties are high, future events cannot be foreseen and hence contracts or promises are almost always incomplete. This requires adaptation after a contract has been executed. When the costs of adapting to the *ex-post* contractual changes become very high, vertical integration of production becomes the default option.

Such a study of economic governance should be a critical component of sustainability science. The conceptual framing of economic governance draws from different disciplines and is empirically tied to the problem context. In this chapter, this proposition is verified by showing how a TCE perspective applied to a familiar energy problem helps in making the policy outcomes sustainable. When it comes to energy sustainability, the indicators which have been emphasized are (Orecchini, 2011): renewability of resources; efficiency in conversion, distribution and use; lowered environmental impact; higher energy accessibility and; localized energy systems. To show how the study of economic governance through TCE helps strengthen each of these goals is beyond the scope of this chapter. So I will focus on the energy access aspect of sustainability.

It is widely accepted that efficient markets can increase electricity access. But electricity markets can develop only when contracts between producers, suppliers and buyers are credible. If the institutional environment (the mechanism of rule production and enforcement in a society) is such that contracts are not credible, then the costs imposed by ex-post changes are high (Spiller & Tommasi, 2005). The neo-classical prediction of efficient electricity markets is therefore valid only under the assumptions of zero transaction costs. When these costs are high, the failure to observe a competitive market is not surprising. In the world of positive transaction costs, efficiency is essentially relative and alternative governance structures (markets, hierarchies or hybrids) need to be subjected to a comparative analysis (Coase, 1964). TCE supplies us with the necessary elements of a framework to analyze which form of governance structure is appropriate for improved energy access. The popular neo-classical assertion is that adequate incentives are sufficient to unleash functional competition, which is a first best solution for optimal redistribution of scarce energy resources. TCE has thrived on a careful analysis of 'attributes of a transaction' and 'incompleteness of contracts' to prescribe that an optimal form of governance – spot markets, long term contracting or vertically integrated firms – is that which minimizes transaction costs arising due to specific investments, uncertainties and opportunistic behavior. Yet, the role of transaction costs and the need to identify and model their behavior has not received adequate attention as far as energy policy is concerned. The chapter deals with this as follows: section 2 presents a discussion on the basic principles of TCE and its evolution from the literature on regulation of public utilities. Section 3

Table 1. Governance structure, asset specificity, and uncertainty

		Asset Specificity		
		Low for Both Parties	**High for Both Parties**	**High for One, Low for Other**
Uncertainty	**High**	Contract/Vertical Integration	Vertical Integration	Vertical Integration
	Low	Spot Market	Long-term contract	Vertical Integration

Source: Ghosh and Kathuria (2015).

presents in micro-analytic detail how transaction costs can be identified and empirically modeled. This is illustrated through the case of industrial energy access by captive power generation in India. Section 4 ends with some conclusions.

2. THE PROBLEM OF NATURAL MONOPOLY AND TRANSACTION COST ECONOMICS

TCE originated from Coase (1937) indicating transaction costs as a reason for firms to internalize production rather than contracting everything out to the market. However, it did not provide a predictive theory of the conditions under which different transactions would be efficiently carried out either in the market or in the firm. Williamson (1979, 1985) filled this predictive gap by taking a micro-analytic view of economic organization and looking at it as a contracting problem. Transaction costs, according to Williamson are defined as the costs of writing, monitoring, verifying and enforcing a contract. He specified variables which determined whether markets or hierarchies would lower the cost of a particular transaction. The TCE theoretical framework is founded on two key assumptions of *bounded rationality* and *opportunism*. Bounded rationality (as against the complete rationality assumption of neo-classical economics) refers to the fact that people have limited cognitive memories i.e. they are intendedly rational but limitedly so. Opportunism, as Williamson calls it, is the tendency of 'self-interest seeking with guile' where actors could potentially exploit contracting partners under unforeseen favorable circumstances. Under the conditions that these assumptions hold, the interplay of three core variables of *asset specificity*, *uncertainty* and *frequency* determine what kind of transaction costs will be generated and whether a transaction will be carried out in the market or within a firm (Table 1).

While it is relatively simple to understand that if frequency of a transaction is high there is increased likelihood that a transaction will be internalized, the critical factors are uncertainty in those transactions and the specificity of assets involved. If an asset is very specific to a particular transaction and has almost zero opportunity costs outside of it, then it is efficient to vertically integrate that asset. According to Williamson, all contracts are eventually incomplete because actors are boundedly rational and can never specify entire future contingencies. So if one party makes a very specific investment, and an *ex-post* situation arises where it generates rents for the other party, then it may behave opportunistically. This is what is known as the 'fundamental transformation' (Williamson, 2002), where a contracting party with significant asset-specific investments could face an *ex-post* hold-up situation due to opportunistic behavior or contractual incompleteness. This can be easily understood, if we take the example of private investment in power generation utilities. The investments are asset-specific (with little or no alternative use), there are significant economies of scale in electricity production and the product is widely consumed. Specific investment means that a substantial portion of that is sunk (due to low potential for alternative use) and hence there is a lock-in where, once committed, the firm may be willing to operate at even lesser than average costs. Economies of scale imply that tendencies for natural monopoly will always be at the boundaries. Moreover, wide consumption means that the set of consumers will match the set of voters, thus implicating political interests. These three factors combined, increase the probability of government trying to expropriate rents through administrative means (for example, limiting pricing flexibility) (Spiller, 2010). In such a case by keeping prices low, the governments can garner political support while deflating the incentives to invest. Hence, unless there is an assurance against expropriation through regulatory commitment, investments won't take place (Spiller & Tommasi, 2005). Such an assurance comes from appropriate governance structures which align themselves to minimize these costs (Spanjer, 2009). As can be seen from Table 1, spot markets are an efficient governance solution when there are low asset specificities and uncertainty involved in the transaction. But as transactions become increasingly complex involving higher degrees of asset specificities for both contracting parties and higher levels of uncertainty, then vertical integration is an efficient governance structure or solution.

Incidentally, TCE has its roots in the debate around what is the best way to organize sectors (like electricity, railroads, water) which displayed natural monopoly characteristics – through competition or regulation. This debate pretty much dominated industrial economics throughout the 20th century. By the decade of 1960s and 1970s, a significant volume of literature grew which showed theoretically that regulation led to inefficiencies and the sector could be better organized through de-regulation and competition (Demsetz, 1968; Priest, 1993). Demsetz (1968) in particular showed that 'there were no conditions under which regulation by commission could be guaranteed to optimize social welfare' (Priest, 1993). The theory of natural monopoly states that a single firm can produce the total market demand at lower cost than any combination of two or more firms. A sustainability condition in a natural monopoly market with a single output is that average costs will fall as output expands, which means that the marginal or the incremental cost will be lower than the average cost. The usual average cost curve of a firm is as shown in Figure 1. Up to Q', the average cost of output keeps falling and displays economies of scale but beyond that the average cost curve starts rising and it becomes uneconomical for the firm to produce any output level beyond Q'. Then other firms come in to satisfy the market demand beyond that level. However, in the case of a natural monopoly the average cost of a firm keeps falling in the long run and can alone meet most of the market demand as shown in Figure 2. The argument given by economists in favor of regulation was that public utilities like, electricity, gas and water displayed natural monopoly characteristics. They could be provided at a lower cost by a single firm than by a set of competing firms (Grossman & Cole, 2003). This would avoid duplication of infrastructure and avoid sunk costs of competing firms. Natural monopoly characteristics was therefore, a case of market failure and an efficient provision of such essential commodities was possible through natural monopolies working under state monitored regulation which would restrict its market power and reduce deadweight losses (the area OAB in Figure 3). Under monopoly, the price charged by the utility would be Pm which is much higher than the competitive price P_c. However, by putting a price ceiling (by the regulator) to P_r, the area for the deadweight loss can be reduced.

Demsetz (1968) contradicted the logic that this was the best way to resolve a natural monopoly problem. In fact, Demsetz argued that monopolists are prevented by market conditions themselves to charge monopoly prices without even the need for intervention through regulation. The theory of natural monopoly predicts that two firms cannot survive when the average cost per unit keeps falling because one firm will expand production to reduce the selling price and hence eliminate the other. This helps

Figure 1. Average cost curve and economies of scale
Source: Own diagram.

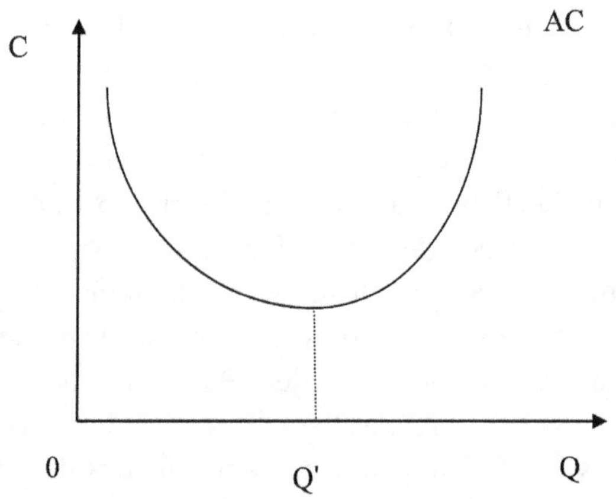

Figure 2. A monopolist's long run average cost curve (LRAC)
Source: Own diagram.

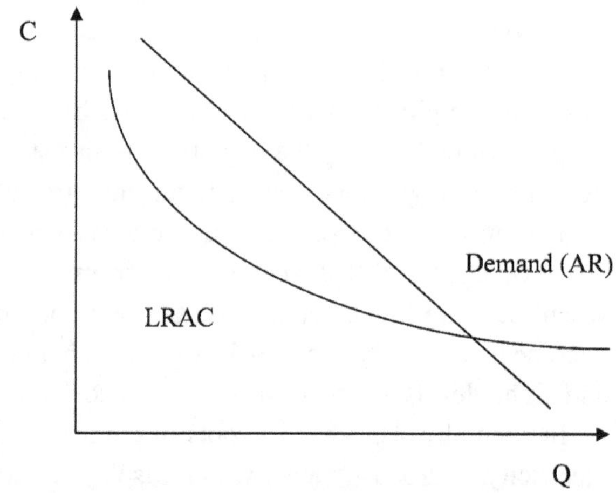

the incumbent firm achieve market power and subsequently charge monopoly price. However, Demsetz points out to at least two problems in this line of argument. First, bidding rivals need not share in the total production with the incumbent firm as they can directly contract with the buyers and the best bidder can win a patronage. Secondly, monopoly price may not be a natural outcome of an unregulated market as the number of rival bidders can be large and hence the final contracted price could be low enough to match the average cost. Therefore he proposed that even if competition cannot be introduced at the level of production, the management of a natural monopoly could be awarded to a franchisee based on

Figure 3. Problems of natural monopoly and deadweight losses
Source: Own diagram.

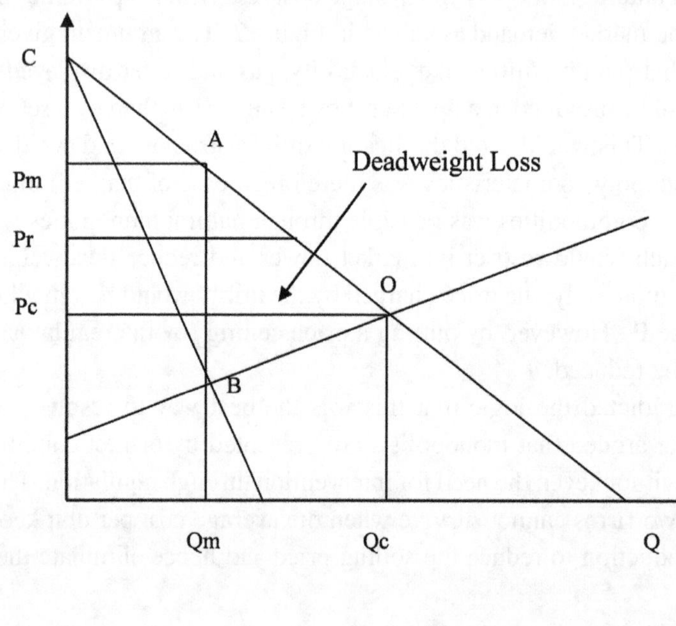

competitive bidding. This way efficiency could be increased as it would lead to low price and better management. The basic economic logic of Demsetz was to replace sitting commissions with market processes (Priest, 1993p. 304): However, Demsetz's theoretical proposition would be valid only under two assumptions. Firstly, there needs to be a legal regime where a governmental body has absolute rights over the decision to grant or deny the rights of operation to the utility. Secondly, a property rights structure whereby a governmental body owned the capital plant and would then offer franchisee rights to others.

O.E. Williamson (1976) and Goldberg (1976) posed a serious challenge to Demsetz's logic that the theory of natural monopoly is deficient and competition is possible though auctioning the right to serve (franchise bidding). They showed the limits of this proposition in the presence of specific investments and significant uncertainty for the case of cable TV franchising. In fact Williamson's paper turned out to be one of the most influential works which laid the foundation for a deeper analysis of transaction costs and comparative institutional arrangements. Williamson argued that merely showing that regulation is flawed was not sufficient to prove that it was inferior mode of organizing a transaction. One had to compare it with the deficiencies of the alternative mode which in this case was franchisee bidding. In doing so Williamson looked into contractual details in what he calls a 'micro-analytic' approach. Demsetz in his abstract analysis and in order to simplify his logic had stripped away some 'irrelevant complications' (Williamson, 1976p. 77) like uncertainty, irrational behavior or durability of distribution systems. He also assumed that there would be many non-collusive bidders for the contract and that 'long term contracts for the supply of (nonutility services) are concluded satisfactorily in the market place without the aid of regulation' (Demsetz, 1968p. 64).

But Williamson differed with the idea that contracts are complete and free of *ex-post* hazards. Whether they were once-for-all contracts, incomplete long-term contracts or re-current short term contracts, *bounded rationality* and *uncertainty* would lead to the hazards of opportunism. The contracts cannot be specified to an extent where monitoring is costless. Owing to contractual incompleteness and the hazards associated with it, Williamson proposed that regulation will be a viable alternative (Williamson, 1976p. 61-103):

At the risk of oversimplification, regulation may be described contractually as a highly incomplete form of long-term contracting in which (1) the regulatee (sic.) is assured an overall fair rate of return, in exchange for which (2) adaptations to changing circumstances are successively introduced without the costly haggling that attends such changes when parties to the contract enjoy greater autonomy... (a) n unbiased assessment of the abstract properties of alternative modes will be facilitated by examining the transactional attributes of each in micro-analytic detail. It will be useful for this purpose to regard rate of return regulation as a highly incomplete form of contracting in which the prospects for windfall gains and losses are strictly limited and, in principle and sometimes in fact, adaptations to changing circumstances are introduced in a low cost, non-acrimonious way. The frequency and extent to which such adaptations are required and the differential ease with which these are effectuated by alternative modes are important in making an informed comparative institutional choice.

Williamson not only laid down a theoretical proposal that under conditions of high transaction costs, contracts will eventually be incomplete and regulation would be a preferred mode of organizing such complex transactions, but with this paper, also opened up a new world of 'economics through the lens of contract'. The essence of this approach is a *comparative institutional assessment* which stresses that various institutional arrangements exist so as to minimize the transaction costs. This was indeed a truly 'positive' explanation of why regulation existed as it showed the limits of deregulated markets. Having reviewed the fundamental aspects of TCE, in the next section I present a practical application in the context of industrial energy access. This is done through modeling of transaction specificity which determines the electricity make-or-buy decision of manufacturing firms.

3. EMPIRICAL MODELING OF TRANSACTION COSTS: AN ILLUSTRATION

Electricity is a critical input in the supply chain of a firm and is an inevitable factor in the growth of any developing country. However across the developing world, unreliable electricity supply remains an obstacle for economic growth (Fisher-Vanden, Mansur, & Wang, 2012). Generally, firms enter into agreements with electricity distribution companies for meeting their power requirements. However, in a situation where there is a persistent demand-supply gap in the transmission grid, such agreements are usually not fulfilled[1] and firms are faced with a situation of shortage (De Nooij, Koopmans, & Bijvoet, 2007). One response to this is for the firms to opt for self-generation. While there have been previous explanations of when (or under what conditions) firms opt for self-generation, they have focused mainly on factor demand and the marginal cost structure (Lee, Anas, Verma, & Murray, 1996; Rose & McDonald, 1991). But that does not sufficiently explain divergent behavior of similarly oriented firms. Although many firms operate under a similar economic environment and have similar firm characteristics in terms of size, marginal cost structure, product profile or location, yet only a few among them opt for self-generation. The remaining, although facing similar situations of power supply uncertainty, do not opt for self-generation i.e. the 'make' option. For example, an industrial survey (see Ghosh & Kathuria, 2014 for details about the survey), finds that for firms in a similar range of size (or cost structure) and factor demand (CMD), 43% opted for self-generation whereas 57% did not.

Treating electricity provision to manufacturing firms as a transaction, I hypothesize that the observed vertical integration is a response to the transaction-specific costs imposed on the firms due to unreliable supply. As discussed in section 2, an asset is specific when it has very low value outside one particular transaction or aspect of a supply chain. If that particular transaction stops then investment in that asset becomes 'sunk' and hence it becomes highly specific in nature. Williamson has further decomposed asset specificity into a non-exhaustive list of five types:

1. Site (or location) specificity where the location of an activity cannot be changed,
2. Physical specificity where the characteristic of the good is exclusive,
3. Human asset specificity which entails non-substitutable learning effects,
4. Dedicated assets which are customer specific investments, and
5. Brand name capital (Williamson, 1985).

Electricity does not qualify strictly into any of these categories of asset specificity. Yet, its physical property is such that it requires being simultaneously produced and consumed. It is costly and inefficient (if not entirely impossible) to store electric power unlike other resources or inputs and thereby requires high levels of coordination leading to what some say 'coordination economies' (Meyer, 2012). Therefore timing, in electricity provision, is of indispensable importance. This brings the provisioning of electricity into a sixth category of asset specificity called 'temporal specificity'. Masten, Meehan, and Snyder (1991) show in the case of shipbuilding how temporal specificity can be an important factor determining organizational form. Similarly Klein, Crawford, and Alchian (1978) show how because of timing issues, newspapers tend to own their presses more than book publishers. Moreover, the substitutability of electricity as a product is rather limited and ineffective. Discontinuity in such transactions, whether due to coordination or production failures, leads to discontinuity in economic activities dependent on such transactions (Nooteboom, 1993). This dependence on the part of the economic actors (in this case industrial producers) creates transaction-specific costs (*ibid.*). Under such situation, the suppliers of electricity may behave opportunistically. Such opportunism, when the supplier is a private utility, could be the raising of prices or when the supplier is a partially deregulated state-owned utility (facing soft budget constraint), just a wave of hand i.e. unscheduled power cuts or supplying power at fluctuating voltages. This imposes costs on manufacturing firms and could force them to vertically integrate the production of electricity in order to minimize such dependence. Variations in this dependence could provide an explanation for observing divergent behavior in terms of the 'make or buy' decision. For example, a firm manufacturing a perishable good (like food or beverages) will have a different level of dependence on a continuous supply of electric power than those which are producing comparatively high storage goods. A pharmaceutical firm would risk altering the chemical composition of crucial drugs in the absence of reliable continuous electric power, which may not be the case for a textile manufacturing firm. These examples suggest that although electric power may not be a specific asset in itself, it creates a *chain of specificity* which becomes a crucial determinant in industrial behavior.

To empirically validate this hypothesis a binary choice model is used for selection. In the probit model, the dependent variable has a binary outcome of 0 when the firm does not install a CPP and 1 when it installs a CPP. This represents the 'make or buy' decision process.[2]

The basic form of a binary dependent outcome variable takes the form[3]

$$y = \begin{cases} 1 & with\ probability\ p \\ 0 & with\ probability\ 1-p \end{cases} \tag{1}$$

with the conditional probability being

$$p_i \equiv \Pr\left(y_i = 1 \mid x\right) = F\left(x_i'\beta\right) \tag{2}$$

x is the regressor vector and β is parameter vector.

$F(\cdot)$ is a cumulative distribution function which ensures that the condition $0 \leq p \leq 1$ is satisfied. Specifically when estimating a probit model the distribution function follows the standard normal cumulative distribution function (cdf).

$$\Phi\left(x'\beta\right) = \int_{-\infty}^{x'\beta} \varnothing\left(z\right) dz \tag{3}$$

and

$$\varnothing\left(z\right) = 2\pi^{-\frac{1}{2}} \exp\left(\frac{-z^2}{2}\right) \tag{4}$$

z being a real number.

Based on our discussion in the preceding section, our model for the make-or- buy decision takes the following form:

$$\Pr\left(pwr_{make} = 1 \mid x\right) = F\left(\beta_0 + \beta_i X_{ij} + \beta_k Z_{kj} + \beta_n Dummy_{nj}\right) \tag{5}$$

where,

X_{ij} is the vector of *i* power specificity related variables;
Z_{kj} is the *k* vector of firm level controls; and
$Dummy_{nj}$ are *n* dummies for distribution utility environment.

The above equation can be interpreted as giving the direction of change in probability of a firm installing its own backyard CPP. The estimation of the parameters uses a maximum likelihood procedure, also known as the Maximum Likelihood Estimation technique. It gives a value of the parameter vector $\hat{\beta}$, the Maximum Likelihood Estimator (MLE), which maximizes the probability of observing the given sample from the population. For a sample of n independent observations, the MLE maximizes (through iterative methods) the following log-likelihood function:

$$Q(\beta) = \sum_{i=1}^{n}\left[y_i \ln F\left(x_i'\beta\right) + \left(1 - y_i\right)\ln\left\{1 - F\left(x_i'\beta\right)\right\}\right] \tag{6}$$

However, interpreting the parameter values of a probit model is not straight forward (Cameron & Trivedi, 2009). The coefficients of the model (as stated in Equation 5), cannot be simply interpreted as giving the percentage change in probability of a firm going for self-generation for a unit change in the variable values. This is because the distribution function is non-linear cdf and the change in probability will vary at different points of the probability function. Therefore, the marginal effects (at mean) are calculated which give the instantaneous rate of change in the probability of observing the non-zero dependent variable, when the explanatory variable changes by a small amount holding all other variables constant at their means. This is, however, only when the explanatory variable is continuous. For categorical explanatory variables the marginal effects show the extent to which probability will be higher of observing the outcome among the categories holding the other variables at their means. In addition a two-step sample selection model is estimated using a Heckman procedure where the outcome dependent variable is the capacity of installed CPP. In a sample selection model those observations which do not opt for the 'make' are censored and the outcome equation is estimated accounting for the sample selection bias. The likelihood function for such a model is

$$L = \prod_{i=1}^{n}\left\{\Pr(y_{1i}^* \le 0)\right\}^{1-y_{1i}}\left\{f\left(y_{2i} \mid y_{1i}^* > 0\right) \times \Pr\left(y_{1i}^* > 0\right)\right\}^{y_{1i}} \tag{7}$$

The data comes from a representative primary survey of 107 firms (of which nearly 40% have gone for vertical integration). The survey (see Ghosh & Kathuria, 2014 for details about the survey and data) was conducted in the Southern Indian state of Andhra Pradesh over a period of eight months in the year 2012. This state is a leader in power sector deregulation post liberalization and an industrial state of

Table 2. Industry-wise sample stratification

Industry	Non-CPP	CPP	Total
Cement	2	7	9
Chemicals	17	6	23
Food	7	12	19
Machinery and Tools	15	2	17
Metallic (including Iron and Steel)	12	1	13
Textiles	10	2	12
Total	63	30	93

Source: Ghosh and Kathuria (2014).

prominence with one of the fastest growing captive power sectors. It has the highest share of captive generation and consumption in Southern India and fifth highest in all-India (CEA, 2010-11). Though Andhra Pradesh is a pioneer in electricity reforms, in recent times the performance of the power sector in this state has not been good, forcing power cuts and designated power holidays on the industries. The sample consists of 93 manufacturing firms, out of which 30 ($\approx$ 35%) have CPPs and 63 do not have CPPs (i.e. depend entirely on the grid for their power requirements). Table 2 shows the industry-wise sample stratification and the proportion of CPP and non-CPP firms for each category. As can be seen from the table, Chemicals, Food and Machine Tools have higher proportions in the sample. This is consistent with the fact that these industries have the highest share in the Andhra Pradesh industrial sector. Moreover, Cement and Food are the sectors where the share of firms that have gone for CPPs is very high.

The key explanatory variables are: the annual total sales of the firm which indicates the size of the firm; power specificity which measures the specificity i.e. extent of dependence on a critical input (electricity in this case); land availability which is a proxy for location; and power cuts which reflect power shortages (or supply uncertainty). Power specificity is a variable composed of a) power intensity measured as per unit expense on electricity and b) dependence on continuous supply i.e. the costs of discontinuity of the input. The reason is neither the intensity factor nor the dependency factor alone explain the specificity of electricity transaction. Together they explain transaction specificity. Additional dummies include the type of the industry and the operational environment in terms of distribution utilities. Table 3 presents the summary statistics.

Various specifications of the model were estimated and the key variables turned out to be significant[4]. Power specificity is significant and has a positive co-efficient validating our hypothesis. This shows that when firms have greater intensity for power as well as dependence on continuous supply at the same time, the likelihood for owning one's own backyard CPP will be higher. The variable for firm size is positive and statistically significant. This confirms the hypothesis that bigger the firm size, more likely that it will 'make' its own electricity. Sales-squared is significant and non-linearity is observed. It suggests that beyond a certain level of firm size, the likelihood of a firm opting for the make option will fall. This could be because very large firms have their own substations and receive electric power using very High Tension (HT) transmission lines and hence do not face any power shortage. The location indicator (presence of extra land) is significant and has a positive co-efficient. Once firms start planning to go for a CPP, availability of land may be a concern but not an insurmountable one, especially in semi-urban and rural areas. The result for power shortage variable is interesting. Although it is significant,

Table 3. Description and summary statistics of independent variables

Variable Name	Description	Obs.	Mean	SD
Power Intensity	Power expense/total expenses	93	0.08	0.09
Power Continuity	Dependency on continuous supply; = 1 if low; = 2 if medium; = 3 if high	93	2.03	0.81
Power Specificity	The transaction specificity to electricity use (product of intensity and continuity)	93	0.19	0.26
Annual Sales	Rs. Million	93	3747	9078
Power Cuts	1 if firm faces power cuts; and 0 otherwise	93	0.81	0.40
Land Availability	1if firm had extra land; and 0 otherwise	93	0.35	0.48
Industrial Type	0 if Chemicals; = 1 if Food and Beverages; = 2 if Textile; = 3 if Non-metallic; = 4 if Metallic	93	1.90	1.57

Source: Own estimations.

Notes: CPDCL - Central Power Distribution Company Limited; SPDCL – Southern Power DCL; EPDCL – Eastern Power DCL; NPDCL – Northern Power DCL.

the co-efficient turns out be negative for all the estimated models. This means that higher the level of power cuts, lower is the likelihood that they will self-generate. This is because I have clubbed, scheduled power cuts also in the category of power shortage and firms may not perceive a power cut a problem if it is scheduled (though I do not have any evidence).[5] Given the available schedule of power cut, they may have already altered their production process or kept a weekly off keeping the scheduled power cut in mind. Interestingly, all those firms which have indicated unscheduled power cuts as a problem are relatively small in size. The average sales of these firms are at least 50% of those which have reported scheduled power cuts in their region. This implies that these smaller firms may not end up having a CPP due to other constraints like scale economies. This is representative of the entire industrial population trend where the proportion of CPP firms is very low compared to non-CPP firms.

Since direct interpretation of coefficients in a probit model is not possible, Table 4 gives the marginal effects (at representative value) of the explanatory variables on the likelihood of observing self-generation. A one unit change in power specificity raises the likelihood of captive generation by 0.42. Firm size also has a positive effect. One unit change in firm size leads to approximately 0.14 increase in the probability of captive generation. Location also has a mildly strong impact on the likelihood of going for captive generation. A firm with extra land will have a 29% higher likelihood of making own power than a firm which does not have extra land. When comparing across industries, the marginal effects suggest that a food manufacturing firm will be 37% more likely to opt for a CPP as compared to a chemical firm. On the other hand, a textile, non-metallic or metallic firm will be 4.5%, 5.6% and 4.2% respectively less likely to opt for a CPP as compared to a chemical firm. On the other hand, a textile, non-metallic or metallic firm will be 15.7%, 32.4% and 15.2% respectively less likely to opt for a CPP as compared to a chemical firm.

As our results show, the power specificity variable comes out significant and matches our hypothesis in terms of the direction of the causality. Higher is the specificity, more likely the firm will opt for self-generation. Variation across industrial categories is also observed. Food manufacturing firms and chemical firms are more likely to opt for the 'make' option as compared to other industrial categories. This validates the proposition that transaction specificities would be higher for them as their dependence on continuous power supply is higher. Power shortage, firm size and location variables are also significant

Table 4. Marginal effects for the various probit specifications (N=93)

	Marginal Effect	Standard Error	z- Statistic	p-Value
Annual Sales	0.149	0.0855	1.74	0.082
Power Specificity	0.422	0.205	2.06	0.040
Land Availability	0.291	0.129	2.25	0.024
Power Cuts	-0.624	0.238	-2.62	0.009
Food Industry	0.371	0.188	1.97	0.049
Textile Industry	-0.0456	0.0357	-1.28	0.202
Non-metallic Industry	-0.0567	0.0384	-1.48	0.140
Metallic Industry	-0.0424	0.0365	-1.16	0.245
Annual Sales (Squared)	-0.0588	0.0342	-1.72	0.086

Source: Own estimations.

confirming that contextual factors influence the decision. However, operational environment does not significantly explain this divergent behavior but this could be due to insufficient operational heterogeneity.

In Heckman two-step, the selection equation is the same as the probit. In the outcome equation location variable is dropped as it is an exclusion restriction in the selection model. It is reasonably assumed that this variable only impacts the choice of whether to install a power plant or not, but does not influence its size. The variables which influence positively the capacity of CPP are firm size, power intensity and continuity. Power shortages do not have any significant influence[6].

The results point out a serious policy concern. The Indian Electricity Act (2003) incentivizes self-generation by making captive power plant establishment license free and allowing open access. This is supposed to motivate firms to produce electricity for self-consumption and earn extra revenues by selling excess power to the grid. As the results show, an increase in power shortages actually reduces the likelihood for a firm to self-generate since it is limited by scale economies and size. However, with increasing transaction-specificity firms opt for self-generation. This means that firms which have high transaction specificity but are constrained by small size, have no option but to depend on erratic grid supply. This may drive them out of production eventually thereby making such a policy unsustainable. Recent trends confirm that indeed a large number of smaller firms have shut down in many Indian states due to increased power shortages.

4. DISCUSSION AND CONCLUSION

This chapter underscores the importance of economic governance in sustainability science through the analysis of transaction costs in industrial energy access. TCE helps understand firm behavior and model its responses with greater precision. Therefore, sustainability arguments, at least in relation to production systems, are not complete unless costs arising out of inefficient contracting are accounted and an adequate economic governance apparatus is set-up. The analysis presented in this chapter has shown that there need for research on sustainable industrial behavior under conditions of shortages which are beset with incomplete or uncertain contractual relationships. Under these conditions, sensitivity to transaction cost concerns increase. The challenge lies in identifying and dealing with them through efficient governance structures. Sustainability science aims to move away from the predominant diagnostic approach of scholarship to a more pragmatic 'problem solving' approach (Komiyama & Takeuchi, 2006). A key feature of any sustainable solution is the ability for conflicting actors to realize mutual gains. The approach of economic governance provides that outlet as far as the economic aspect of sustainability is concerned.

REFERENCES

Buchanan, J. M. (1975). A contractarian paradigm for applying economic theory. *The American Economic Review*, *65*(2), 225–230.

Cameron, A. C., & Trivedi, P. K. (2009). Microeconometrics Using Stata (Vol. 5). College Station, TX: Stata Press.

CEA. (2008). *All India Electricity Statistics, General review*. New Delhi: Central Electricity Authority, Ministry of Power, Government of India.

Clark, W. C., & Dickson, N. M. (2003). Sustainability science: The emerging research program. *Proceedings of the National Academy of Sciences of the United States of America*, *100*(14), 8059–8061. doi:10.1073/pnas.1231333100 PMID:12794187

Coase, R. H. (1937). The Nature of the Firm. *Economica, 4*(16), 386-405.

Coase, R. H. (1964). The Regulated Industries: A Discussion. *The American Economic Review*, *54*, 194–197.

De Nooij, M., Koopmans, C., & Bijvoet, C. (2007). The Value of Supply Security: The Costs of Power Interruptions: Economic Input for Damage Reduction and Investment in Networks. *Energy Economics*, *29*(2), 277–295. doi:10.1016/j.eneco.2006.05.022

Demsetz, H. (1968). Why Regulate Utilities? *The Journal of Law & Economics*, *11*(1), 55–65. doi:10.1086/466643

Fisher-Vanden, K., Mansur, E. T., & Wang, Q. J. (2012). *Costly Blackouts? Measuring Productivity and Environmental Effects of Electricity Shortages. No. w17741*. National Bureau of Economic Research. doi:10.3386/w17741

Ghosh, R., & Kathuria, V. (2014). The transaction costs driving captive power generation: Evidence from India. *Energy Policy*, *75*, 179–188. doi:10.1016/j.enpol.2014.10.003

Ghosh, R., & Kathuria, V. (2015). Gas based power generation in India: Lessons from a transaction cost analysis. *Energy Strategy Reviews*, *8*, 1–7. doi:10.1016/j.esr.2015.06.001

Goldberg, V. P. (1976). Regulation and Administered Contracts. *The Bell Journal of Economics*, *7*(2), 426–448. doi:10.2307/3003265

Grossman, P. Z., & Cole, D. H. (Eds.). (2003). *The End of a Natural Monopoly: Deregulation and Competition in the Electric Power Industry* (Vol. 7). Routledge.

Klein, B., Crawford, R. G., & Alchian, A. A. (1978). Vertical Integration, Appropriable Rents, and the Competitive Contracting Process. *The Journal of Law & Economics*, *21*(1), 297–326. doi:10.1086/466922

Komiyama, H., & Takeuchi, K. (2006). Sustainability science: Building a new discipline. *Sustainability Science*, *1*(1), 1–6. doi:10.1007/s11625-006-0007-4

Lee, K. S., Anas, A., Verma, S., & Murray, M. (1996). *Why Manufacturing Firms Produce Some Electricity Internally.* World Bank Policy Research Working Paper Series 1605.

Masten, S. E., Meehan, J. W., & Snyder, E. A. (1991). The Costs of Organization. *Journal of Law Economics and Organization*, *7*(1), 1–25.

Meyer, R. (2012). Vertical Economies and the Costs of Separating Electricity Supply - A Review of Theoretical and Empirical Literature. *The Energy Journal (Cambridge, Mass.)*, *33*(4), 161–185. doi:10.5547/01956574.33.4.8

Nooteboom, B. (1993). An Analysis of Specificity in Transaction Cost Economics. *Organization Studies*, *14*(3), 443–451. doi:10.1177/017084069301400306

Orecchini, F. (2011). Energy sustainability pillars. *International Journal of Hydrogen Energy*, *36*(13), 7748–7749. doi:10.1016/j.ijhydene.2011.02.022

Orecchini, F., Santiangeli, A., & Valitutti, V. (2011). Sustainability science: Sustainable energy for mobility and its use in policy making. *Sustainability*, *3*(10), 1855–1865. doi:10.3390/su3101855

Priest, G. L. (1993). The Origins of Utility Regulation and the "Theories of Regulation" Debate. *The Journal of Law & Economics*, *36*(1), 289–323. doi:10.1086/467276

Robbins, L. (1932). *An Essay on the Nature and Significance of Economic Science*. London: Macmillan.

Rose, K., & McDonald, J. F. (1991). Economics of Electricity Self-generation by Industrial Firms. *The Energy Journal (Cambridge, Mass.)*, *12*(2), 47–66. doi:10.5547/ISSN0195-6574-EJ-Vol12-No2-4

Spanjer, A. R. (2009). Regulatory Intervention on the Dynamic European Gas Market– Neoclassical Economics or Transaction Cost Economics? *Energy Policy*, *37*(8), 3250–3258. doi:10.1016/j.enpol.2009.04.021

Spiller, P. (2010). *Transaction Cost Regulation*. Working paper 16735. National Bureau of Economic Research. Retrieved from http://www.nber.org/papers/w16735

Spiller, P., & Tommasi, M. (2005). The Institutions of Regulation: An Application to Public Utilities. In C. Menard & M. M. Shirley (Eds.), *Handbook of New Institutional Economics* (pp. 515–543). Springer.

Williamson, O. E. (1976). Franchise Bidding for Natural Monopolies-In General and with Respect to CATV. *The Bell Journal of Economics*, *7*(1), 73–104. doi:10.2307/3003191

Williamson, O. E. (1979). Transaction Cost Economics: The Governance of Contractual Relations. *The Journal of Law & Economics*, *22*(2), 233–261. doi:10.1086/466942

Williamson, O. E. (1985). *The Economic Institutions of Capitalism*. New York: Free Press.

Williamson, O. E. (1998). The Institutions of Governance. *The American Economic Review*, *88*(2), 75–79.

Williamson, O. E. (2002). The Theory of the Firm as Governance Structure: From Choice to Contract. *The Journal of Economic Perspectives, 16*(3), 171-195.

ENDNOTES

1 In an industrial survey conducted by the author, it was found that approximately 80% of the firms did not receive the full contracted maximum demand (CMD).

2 'Making' does not mean that the firm does not use grid based electric power at all. The general behavior of India firms producing their own electricity is that they use backyard power plants to partially fulfill their power requirements. According to the Electricity Act, 2003 a firm qualifies as a CPP as long as it uses at least 51% of the self-generated electricity for its production purposes. Any excess production above that is eligible to be sold back to the grid. See page 127, Power Compendium 2011, Ministry of Power, India.

3 Following notations are as per: Microeconometrics Using Stata, Cameron and Trivedi, Stata Press, 2009.

4 The results from specification and robustness tests are available from the author on request

5 When we consider 'scheduled power cuts' as part of no power problem and categorize them accordingly, the variable comes out to be positive but insignificant in all the models. The results are available on request.

6 The results of Heckman estimations are available from the author on request

Chapter 8
Consumer Power Subsidies: Brewing Crisis in India's Economy

Shyamasis Das
PWC India, India

ABSTRACT

Energy pricing in India usually hinges on political, economic or social considerations of the government. Consumer power tariff, a State subject in the country, is no exception to that. However, continued subsidising of power has led to mounting losses of discoms, mostly State-owned, sometimes to a level of insolvency. This has taken a serious toll on financial stability of distribution sector, triggering a cross-sector domino effect. This has happened in spite of regulatory oversight. This study has brought forth some compelling analyses which affirm that current crisis is the outcome of vested interests of some actors and apathy of the administration. It is seen that power tariffs have been skewed disregarding tariff guidelines, whereby liabilities of the State governments to compensate the discoms through payment of subsidies are limited. This study uncovers effective consumer power subsidy across the States, and offers insights into the consequences. This study also identifies key issues plaguing the sector, followed by a brainstorming on possible corrective action-points.

INTRODUCTION: ELECTRICITY PRICING AND SUBSIDY – A LINGERING ISSUE

Energy pricing in domestic market is a subject that usually hinges on political, economic or social considerations of the governments, especially in developing countries, and hence, naturally attaches the interests of different stakeholders. Often the governments in such countries exert their discretion to regulate domestic prices of energy commodities and resort to artificially reducing their end-user prices, commonly known as energy subsidizing. The purpose of such practice may vary from realizing certain social or economic objectives to gaining political mileage. However, this comes at a substantial cost. Apart from bringing distortion in the market, this kind of government intervention can incur revenue losses to the retailers or service providers who are mostly state-owned, or to the country's exchequer.

DOI: 10.4018/978-1-5225-0094-0.ch008

In the last decade or so, the issue of fuel subsidies in developing countries has come to the fore in policy-related discourse across different platforms including intergovernmental meetings, thinktanks, ministerial committees, *etc*. India features prominently as an economy footing one of the biggest oil subsidy bills in the world (oil subsidy, also known as under-recovery in India amounted to INR[1] 1,61,029 crores in 2012-13 (Ministry of Petroleum & Natural Gas, 2014), *i.e.* around US$ 30.13 billion[2]). Quite naturally, the issue of oil subsidies in India has drawn lot of national as well as international attention. It ought to be noted that the competent authorities in the country have initiated steps in containing or phasing out subsidies to oil products. For example, the price of gasoline has been decontrolled since June 2010. This is followed by deregulation of diesel pricing in October 2014 and initiation of direct cash transfer to households' bank accounts in case of LPG subsidy. However, a particular issue which till date has remained thorny and largely unresolved is the concern of power subsidy in India. According to the latest available report published by the Power Finance Corporation (PFC), a Government of India undertaking, on the performance of State power utilities, the aggregate losses of the utilities in financial year (FY) 2012-13 were INR 1,05,070 crores[3] (*i.e.* ~ US$ 19.66 billion) (PFC, 2015). This is a jump of about 40% over 2010-11 level and 63% increase with respect to 2009-10 (PFC, 2013). The spiraling losses of the utilities have their origin in the existing form of consumer electricity subsidies as highlighted in this study.

This apart, subsidizing power de-incentivizes efforts towards improving demand-side energy efficiency. Wasteful power consumption in residential sector encouraged by subsidized electricity tends to push up peak demand which in turn aggravates peak power shortage. During 2007-08 and 2014-15, the annual unmet peak demand in India ranged between 4.5% to 16.6%, while peak demand recorded a compound annual growth rate of about 4.5%[4] with a high base-level (108,866 MW in 2007-08). On the other hand, free or very low priced electricity in agricultural sector has done no good to improve pump efficiency in irrigation; currently the average efficiency of irrigation pumps in use is reported to be 20% to 35% whereas efficient pumps available in the market at higher costs can offer efficiency of upto 50% (Saini, 2011). In spite of the aforesaid implications and more, the administration and the political class prefer to circumvent the issue of electricity subsidy, possibly because of involvement of different stakeholders' interests. In view of the troubled state of affairs of the country's power distribution sector, it is imperative to examine the status quo.

Political Economy

India having population more than a billion (as per Census 2011) faces a variety of socio-economic challenges. Access to affordable electricity across the social strata is one such challenge. Though per capita electricity consumption in the country has witnessed a rise of 168% over the last two decades to reach 883 kWh in 2011-12 (CEA, 2013), it is still far below the global average consumption level of 2892 kWh/ capita (CEA, 2013). It is worthwhile to mention that per capita electricity consumption is considered to have a strong linkage with Human Development Index; the latter is often regarded as standard yardstick to measure human development in a country. Thus, access to affordable electricity is central to the government's policy-making with regard to electricity distribution. This has its reflection in the National Electricity Policy (2005) of the Government of India (Ministry of Power, 2005) which set affordable electricity for every household in the country with minimum per capita availability over 1000 units (kWh) as one of the key objectives. On the other hand, owing to the dependence of majority of the population's livelihood on agrarian activities (accounting 48.9% of total employment in 2011-12) (Ministry of Finance, 2014), farming community has traditionally enjoyed quite a big share of governmental largesse. Against this backdrop, the political parties, both mainstream and local, widely touted for their pro-socialist agenda and bitterly known for vote-bank politics, continue to 'promise' cheap electricity to households and farmers in their election manifestos. Quite naturally, the populist stance of the political parties, often disregarding the negative impact on the economy and the efficacy of the support schemes, is found to influence the governments to continue the provision of subsidized power to agricultural and domestic consumers. This has been possible also because most of the electricity distribution companies (discoms) in the country are public-owned.

Administering Consumer Electricity Tariff

Electricity is a concurrent subject under the Constitution of India (refer to entry number 38 of List III of the Seventh Schedule) (Ministry of Law and Justice, n.d.) which means both Central and State governments share authorities over electricity supply. With regard to framing national-level policies, enacting legislations, making schemes and matters related to transmission and distribution, the Ministry of Power holds the primary authority (Ministry of Power). However, setting consumer power tariff has been a State subject.

Relevant Tariff Regulations as per the provisions of the Electricity Act 2003 and the National Tariff Policy 2006 provide the requisite framework and direction to fix consumer electricity tariffs. The Electricity Act 2003, credited to infuse much needed reforms in India's power sector with an aim to bring accountability and transparency in power distribution, mandated unbundling of State Electricity Boards (SEBs) into independent companies with separate financial accounts. Moreover, the Act paved the way to establishment of independent Regulatory Commissions at State and Central levels to administer tariff setting process, and the Appellate Tribunal for redressal of grievances of concerned parties. The Act also laid down guidelines towards rationalization of electricity tariff.

The State Electricity Regulatory Commissions (SERCs) are bestowed with the authority to set consumer tariffs. They issue tariff orders in accordance with relevant tariff regulations. Section 61 of the Electricity Act 2003 states that the Commission shall be guided by multi-year tariff principles in determining tariffs. The adoption of Multi-Year Tariff (MYT) framework came into effect from 1st April, 2006 (Ministry of Power, 2006). Under the MYT, tariffs are set ex-ante for each financial year of a Control Period; the latter spans over five years with an exception in the 1st Control Period which could be of three years. Tariffs are drawn based on the estimated Annual Revenue Requirement (ARR) of the electricity distribution licensee (discom) in the financial year and the expected electricity sales. The ARR is estimated from the total power purchase cost (or cost of generation in case of licensee-owned power station), cost of capital, operational and maintenance cost, depreciation, interest on working capital, provision for tax, *etc*., along with the adjustment of preceding year's unaccounted expenses or revenue gaps. The adjustment is calculated during the Annual Performance Review of the discom when the audited accounts of the discom are available. The unaccounted expenses or revenue gaps are estimated from the differences between provisional ARR and actual ARR, and projected and actual electricity sales revenue. In case the revenue gap is not adjusted while determining tariff of the ensuing year, the SERC may carry forward the deficit in lieu of adding a "carrying cost" (which corresponds to the accrued interests on the amount), to be amortized in future. The SERC earmarks this revenue deficit as Regulatory Asset. However, this provision can be used only in exceptional circumstances ("natural causes or force majeure" situations).

Consumer Categories and the Provision of Subsidies

Across most of the States in India, the power consumer base can be divided into seven broad categories: Domestic (also known as Household), Commercial, Agricultural (also includes Irrigation), Industrial, Railway Traction and Outside State (includes the electricity sales outside the State of power generation). The rest of the consumers can be classified as Others which may include public lighting, public water works, *etc*[5].

Ideally, average tariff for a consumer category should be at par with the cost of supply (CoS) of electricity. The latter refers to the cost incurred by the utility companies to provide electricity to end consumers. A typical CoS comprises of cost of generation or expenditure on power purchase, operation and maintenance cost (O&M), administrative expenses, interest payment and depreciation. Where generation and distribution businesses are still managed by the same licensee, cost for power generation is considered in place of power purchase cost. The power purchase cost is the largest component of CoS, comprising 70% to 80%.

The National Tariff Policy 2006, however, allows cross-subsidising, a practice to charge higher prices to a set of consumers for a commodity or service in order to subsidise for another consumer category. The Tariff Policy stipulates that the tariffs for the consumer categories should be set within ±20% of the average CoS (Ministry of Power, 2006). Traditionally, domestic and agricultural consumers are the beneficiaries of subsidies whereas commercial and industrial consumers pay more than CoS.

On the other hand, a State government is also allowed to grant subsidy to a class of consumers. However, the Electricity Act 2003 stipulates that the government has to make the subsidy amount available to the discom upfront.

REVIEW OF THE STATE OF AFFAIRS OF THE DISTRIBUTION SECTOR

The Electricity Act 2003 is considered as a milestone in bringing reforms in the power distribution sector. Because of the anticipated far-reaching impact of the Act on the functioning of the sector, it is often assumed that its enactment marks the beginning of a new era in power distribution. This warrants an examination of the state of affairs of the sector post enactment of the Act, in contrast to the pre-Act regime.

The cumulative losses of the SEBs were reported to be about INR 25,000 crores (*i.e.* ~ US$ 4.68 billion) as in 2001–02 (World Bank, 2014). However, even after ten years since the Act came into force, financial turnaround of the sector has been elusive. The aggregate losses of the utilities witnessed a rising trend and crossed INR 1,00,000 crores [6] (*i.e.* ~ US$ 19.66 billion) in 2012-13 (PFC, 2015), a jump of 63% from the 2009-10 level (PFC, 2013). In other words, the average recovery of cost by the utilities is reportedly a mere 75% in 2012-13 (PFC, 2015) which is no improvement from 2009-10 scenario (PFC, 2013). Such financial distress has a serious spill-over effect. As distribution segment of the power sector caters directly to the end-users, any financial imbalance in this segment can create shocks across the different segments of power sector. Public power producers to whom the SEBs usually book considerable volume of outstanding bills bear the impact. The outstanding dues payable by power utilities to Central public sector undertakings amounted to more than INR 13,000 crores (*i.e.* ~ US$ 2.43 billion) as in March 2012 (Indiastat, 2012). In such a situation, the power producers find themselves in a spot. With limited open access (bulk of the power sale is tied to long-term Power Purchase Agreements) and few non-public discoms in the market, power producers often struggle to find alternative buyers for power. Such uncertainty in realizing the dues from the struggling discoms by the power producers adversely impacts the investor sentiment in the power sector.

The brewing financial crisis in the power sector also has a serious spill-over impact on the commercial lenders like banks and non-banking financial institutions. In the face of acute fund crunch, both power project developers and discoms have heavily depended on borrowings from commercial lenders. It is reported that the cumulative debt of discoms to banks and financial institutions amounted to about INR 200,000 crores (*i.e.* ~ US$ 37.42 billion) till year 2013 (Kumar & Sethi, 2014). The Reserve Bank of India in a recent publication titled "Re-emerging Stress in the Asset Quality of Indian Banks: Macro-Financial Linkages", highlighted "the risks faced by banks on their exposure to the power sector due to rising losses and debt levels in state electricity boards" (Lokare, 2014). With rising debt burden, bailouts from the State governments have often been the public discoms' last lifeline. For instance, in March 2013, the Government of Haryana agreed to absorb the debt liability of the State power utilities to the tune of more than INR 8,000 crores (*i.e.* ~ US$ 1.5 billion) (Indian Power Sector.com, 2013).

In view of the discoms staring at financial insolvency, in 2013 the Government of India announced a bail-out plan, known as Transitional Finance Mechanism (TFM) (Ministry of Power, 2013a). However, it has "turned out to be a non-starter" owing to failure of most of the States to fulfill the eligibility conditions which include charting a detailed plan to liquidate the Regulatory Assets and reduce cross-subsidy within six months from the date of approval of the restructuring. What is this notion of Regulatory Asset? It is quite odd to note that Regulatory Asset is a liability for a discom and indirectly to the State Government, and is found to be insidious in nature.

Subsidy in Light of the Current Crisis

As previously mentioned, the National Tariff Policy and the Electricity Act offer provisions of cross-subsidies within a stipulated limit (wherein the Agricultural and Domestic consumers are the primary beneficiaries) and additional subsidies from the State government, provided the government pays the subsidy amount upfront to the discom. These subsidy-related provisions intend to allow sufficient room for the government to strike a balance between public welfare and fiscal health of the sector. Needless to say, the state of affairs of the distribution sector, as described before, reflects a grim picture. Where does the problem lie?

Apparently, the "subsidy" regime may be held responsible for distorting the energy market resulting in financial loss (directly or indirectly) to the utilities or the State budget. In an attempt to uncover the actual visage of consumer power subsidy in the country, the current study finds that in some cases the State governments have fallen short of fulfilling their obligation to provide the assured subsidy amount to the discoms upfront[7]. This leads to utilities facing revenue deficit in the form of gap between the assured amount and actual subsidy received. PFC reported that the gap between subsidy booked and subsidy received was more than INR 14,000 crores (*i.e.* ~ US$ 2.80 billion) in 2009-10 which came down to about INR 4,000 crores (*i.e.* ~ US$ 0.83 billion) in 2011-12 (PFC, 2013). In 2012-13, the gap is found to be INR 864 crores, owing to a greater release of subsidy fund by the State governments. The subsidy paid by the State governments as percentage of subsidy booked by the utilities improved to about 97% in 2012-13 (PFC, 2015) from 2009-10 level of 56% (PFC, 2013). In this context, it is worthwhile to take cognizance of the fact that the losses incurred by State-owned utilities in some of the States are more than the aforesaid unrealized sum of subsidy. For example, utilities in each of these States: Andhra Pradesh, Uttar Pradesh and Rajasthan registered losses (accrual basis) more than INR 12,000 crores (*i.e.* ~ US$ 2.25 billion) in year 2012-13 (Figure 1).

Figure 1. Top six states having losses registered by utilities in 2012-13
Data source: The Performance of State Power Utilities for the years 2010-11 to 2012-13 (PFC, 2015).

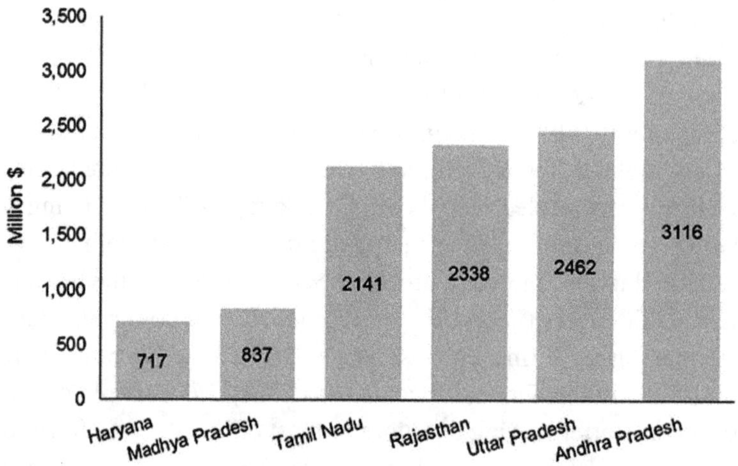

This clearly indicates that there should be other elements, apart from unrealized subsidy volume that are contributing to the mounting losses of the discoms.

The facility of Regulatory Asset which is the revenue deficit of a discom earmarked by the State Regulatory Commission for adjustment (with addition of accrued interests on the amount) while determining tariff of the ensuing year and is to be used only in exceptional circumstances (“*natural causes or force majeure*” situations), has turned out be a tool to stall tariff hike. A special World Bank study found that the annual pan-India magnitude of Regulatory Assets is to the tune of over INR 70,000 crores (i.e. ~ US$ 13 billion) and the accrued interest amount alone (“carrying cost”) can be as high as INR 9,500 crores (i.e. ~ US$ 1.78 billion) (World Bank, 2014). In contrast, the aggregate sum of subsidy booked was to the tune of INR 30,242 crores (i.e. ~ US$ 5.66 billion) in 2011-12 (PFC, 2013), less than half of the magnitude of Regulatory Assets (excluding the interest part). In spite of the National Tariff Policy 2006 stipulating that the “recovery of Regulatory Asset should be time-bound and within a period not exceeding three years at the most” (Ministry of Power, 2006), in reality hardly any State has attempted to liquidate the accumulated revenue deficit (World Bank, 2014) (ICRA Research Services, 2014).

It is an irony that Regulatory Asset has become a liability to the discoms. An obvious question arises: why Regulatory Asset is allowed to reach such a mammoth size in spite of laid-down guidelines. Apparently the reason is lack of timely cost reflective tariff revision. However, vested interests of associated actors and lapses in governance and oversight have contributed to this crisis. It is believed that the facility of Regulatory Asset is a more convenient way to stall tariff hike, than committing to pay direct “subsidy” to the discom; in the latter case, the State government has to own the monetary responsibility. This lack of timely cost reflective tariff revision not only drives up the magnitude of Regulatory Assets, the interest component accentuates the financial losses of the discoms. Therefore, it is quite clear that though on paper the scale of government-provided consumer subsidy in power sector is limited, a deeper assessment shows that the volume of effective power subsidy to consumers, resulting from the gap between actual cost of electricity supply and consumer tariff, is significantly high. It ought to be noted here that the State government is not completely insulated from this crisis. In the face of insolvency of a State-owned discom, the State government has to pitch in with financial support to the discom (it can be through revoking dues from the discom), thus, eventually absorbing the discom’s liability, fully or partly.

Box 1. Methodology for estimating consumer power subsidy

Unit subsidy (INR/kWh) = CoS per unit – Avg.tariff
CoS per unit (INR/kWh)
= (Power purchase cost + O&M +Admin. expenses + Interest payment + Depreciation)/ Total electricity sales

Avg. tariff (INR/kWh)= Revenue from electricity sales/Electricity sales
Subsidy volume = Unit subsidy X Electricity sales
Net subsidy = Gross Subsidy -- Surplus

In view of the insidious nature of power subsidy in India, it is imperative to examine effective consumer power subsidy following an internationally accepted approach.

Estimation of Consumer Subsidy in Power Sector

The shrouded subsidy regime in India's power distribution sector has prompted the current study to apply a subsidy estimation methodology which captures the consumer power subsidies in totality.

This study employs the price-gap approach of estimating consumer subsidies, a widely accepted methodology which is often used by international thinktanks such as the International Energy Agency (IEA, 2011), International Institute for Sustainable Development (Koplow, 2009), International Monetary Fund (IMF, 2013), *etc*. In this approach, the average end-user price or price paid by consumers for the commodity (or service) is compared with a reference price which corresponds to the cost of supply or service (CoS). If the end-user price is less than the reference price, the resulting gap indicates the magnitude of consumer subsidy for the commodity (or service).

In the case of consumer subsidy in power sector, the end-user price corresponds to the average electricity tariff. As the existing tariff framework in India allows separate tariffs for different consumer categories, the average tariff is considered separately for individual consumer type. The average tariff is computed from the total tariff-related revenue realized from a consumer category divided by total electricity sales to that category. The reference price corresponds to the cost of supply of electricity per unit (kWh) which takes into account power purchase cost (or cost of electricity generation in case of licensee-owned power station), operational & maintenance cost, administrative expenses, depreciation and interest payment. Box 1 shows the broad methodology for estimating consumer power subsidies.

Gross subsidy refers to the sum total of subsidies to all benefiting consumer categories. However, discoms can realize surplus revenue from commercial and industrial consumer types, commonly known as cross-subsidy. Gross subsidy less cross-subsidy gives the estimate of net subsidy.

It ought to be noted that the given methodology does not consider CoS separate for industrial (or bulk), domestic or agricultural consumers. The difference in CoS is attributed to dissimilar voltages of drawing power. The bulk consumers draw electricity at a higher voltage (also known as high tension) than domestic or agricultural consumers (low tension); hence the cost of electricity transmission is less for the former. However, it is difficult to account this difference in estimating CoS because of the common cost accounting procedure followed by the discoms in computing their annual revenue requirements. Moreover, following consultation with experts on power tariff, it is understood that the cost variation from voltage difference may not be significant. Hence, the methodology stated in Box 1 is considered to be logical with an acceptable error margin.

SUBSIDY RESULTS AND COST TO ECONOMY

Considering that power tariff is a State subject in India, this investigation intends to start with developing inventory of consumer power subsidies across the States over the recent six years starting from year 2008-09. Taking into account the available data resources, the Planning Commission's *Annual Report on The Working of State Power Utilities & Electricity Departments – 2011-12* and *2013-14* (Planning Commission, 2014) (Planning Commission, 2011) are considered as the primary data sources for the following main parameters[8]: consumer category-wise sale of electricity, cost of power supply, and consumer category-wise average tariff.

The results from the estimation include but are not limited to estimates of State-wise power subsidies for each consumer category (*viz.* Domestic, Commercial, Agricultural, Industry, Railway Traction, Outside State and Others). This is followed by drawing economic relevance of the estimated consumer power subsidies. This is performed by reflecting the derived subsidy results on key economic metrics such as state fiscal deficits, state outlay in power sector, *etc.*

The share of consumer power subsidy in the State's gross fiscal deficit is a useful indicator. Although consumer power subsidy may not always directly contribute to the State's fiscal deficit, however, the State is not insulated from this financial turmoil which is plaguing mostly the State-owned discoms. As the debt ridden State discoms reach a condition of financial insolvency, it may not be possible for the State governments to distance themselves from taking onus of the former's financial turnaround. This is also manifested in the proposed Central scheme *Financial Restructuring of the State-owned discoms* where the discoms and the State governments are required to take measures towards restructuring of discoms' debts, which will have the backing of a Transitional Finance Mechanism (TFM) from the Central government. Moreover, the State governments' support to the discoms through direct subsidy payments or in the form of soft loans or equity incurs direct cost to the State exchequer.

In the face of acute financial crunch, the discoms find themselves handicapped to invest in improving their electricity distribution infrastructures. On the other hand, the subsidies provided by the State government reduce the funding capacity of State exchequer, which may impact the State's actual budget allocation in infrastructures. This is especially relevant to the States having considerable fiscal deficits. In such a scenario where investments for improving infrastructures take a backseat, the quality of service, in this case power supply is invariably compromised. A look at some key facts reveals that in spite of introducing quite a many flagship schemes, power distribution in the country is yet to fulfill key objectives of National Electricity Policy, particularly access to electricity for all households and per capita availability of electricity to be increased to more than 1000 units by 2012. Census 2011 data shows that only 55% of rural households (67% across all households) have some kind of access to electricity in the country (Chandramouli, 2011) in spite of multiple programmes being conceived over the past decades like the Rajiv Gandhi Grameen Vidyutikaran Yojana (RGGVY). On the other hand, per capita electricity consumption is reportedly about 883 units in 2012 (CEA, 2013). Moreover, Aggregate Technical & Commercial (AT&C) loss, a key performance indicator of power distribution, reflects poor management of power distribution in the country; the average nationwide AT&C loss in year 2012-13 was reportedly around 25% (PFC, 2015), much higher than the target level of 15% (PFC, n.d). It is believed that uncertainty over recovering the cost of power supply, primarily owing to skewed power tariff and inadequate financial compensation de-incentivizes the discoms from investing in augmenting distribution infrastructure. Such possible ramification of current subsidy regime has prompted the present study to draw a comparison between subsidy volume and State outlay in power sector.

Figure 2. Consumer power subsidies - 2008-09

Source: Author's own analysis. Electricity data considered from Planning Commission's Annual Report on The Working of State Power Utilities & Electricity Departments – 2011-12 (Planning Commission, 2011). Data of GSFD sourced from RBI's annual publications (RBI, n.d.).

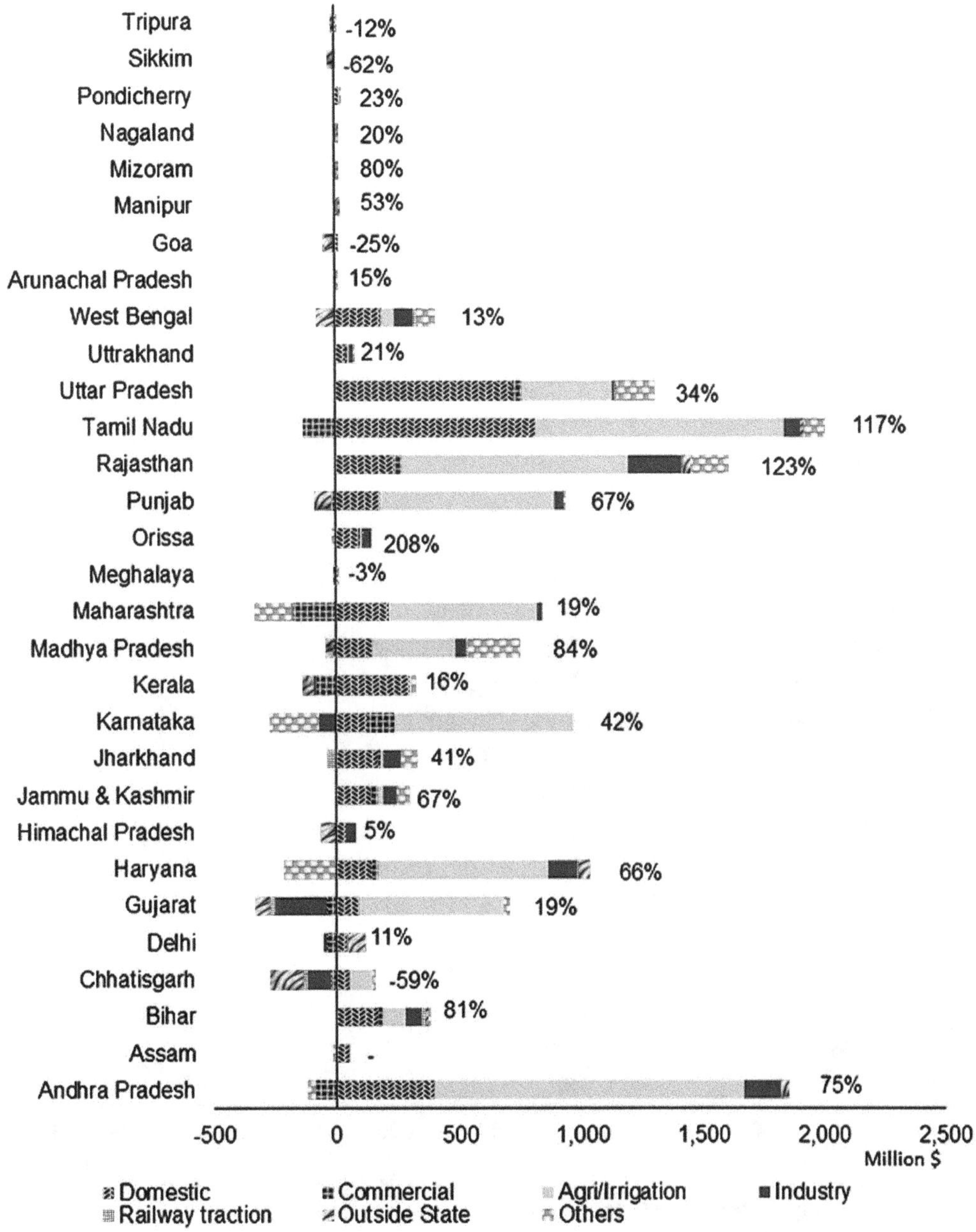

Figure 3. Consumer power subsidies - 2009-10
Source: Author's own analysis. Electricity data considered from Planning Commission's Annual Report on The Working of State Power Utilities & Electricity Departments – 2011-12 (Planning Commission, 2011). Data of GSFD sourced from RBI's annual publications (RBI, n.d.).

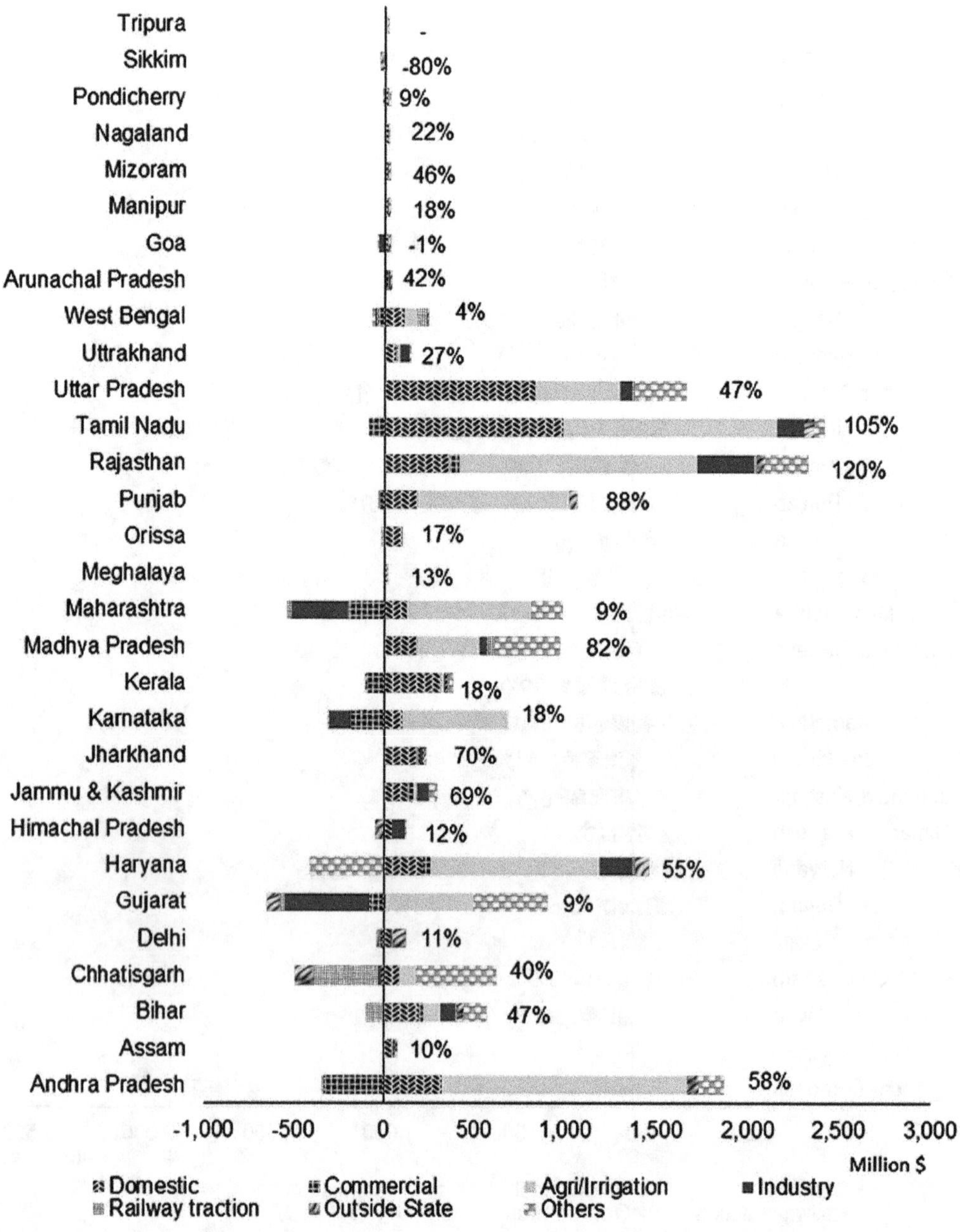

The relevant economic data are primarily sourced from the Reserve Bank of India (RBI) publications, State Economic Surveys and other reliable publicly available sources.

Figures 2 to 7 present the State-wise electricity consumption subsidies as per consumer categories over recent six years: from 2008-09 to 2013-14. The figure in percentage indicates the share of net

Figure 4. Consumer power subsidies - 2010-11

Source: Author's own analysis. Electricity data considered from Planning Commission's Annual Report on The Working of State Power Utilities & Electricity Departments – 2013-14 (Planning Commission, 2014).Data of GSFD sourced from RBI's annual publications (RBI, n.d.).

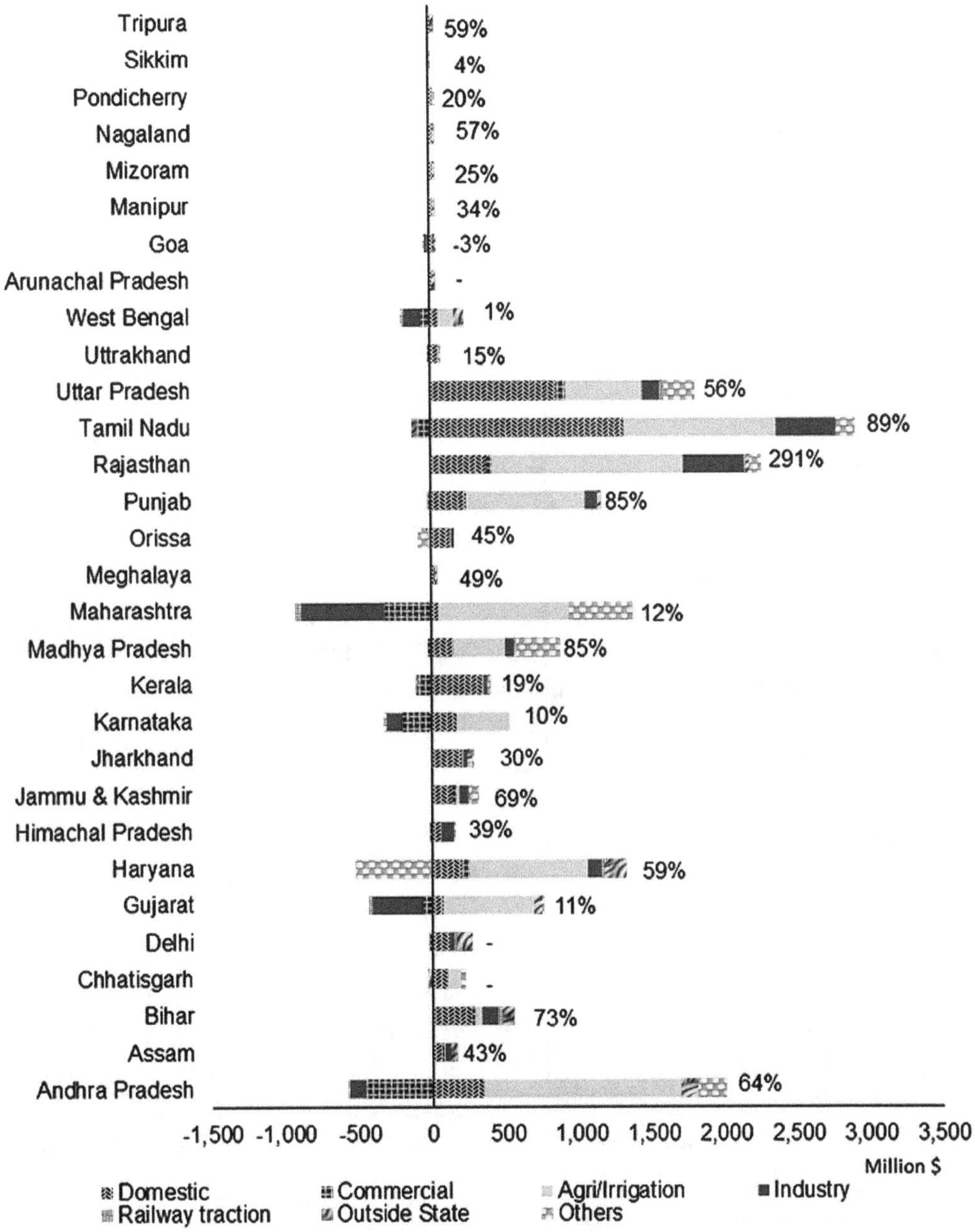

subsidy of a State in its Gross State Fiscal Deficit (GSFD). The negative (-) sign implies that there is no net power subsidy in the State. In case no value is mentioned, it means the State does not have any gross fiscal deficit in that financial year.

Figure 5. Consumer power subsidies - 2011-12

Source: Author's own analysis. Electricity data considered from Planning Commission's Annual Report on The Working of State Power Utilities & Electricity Departments – 2013-14 (Planning Commission, 2014).Data of GSFD sourced from RBI's annual publications (RBI, n.d.).

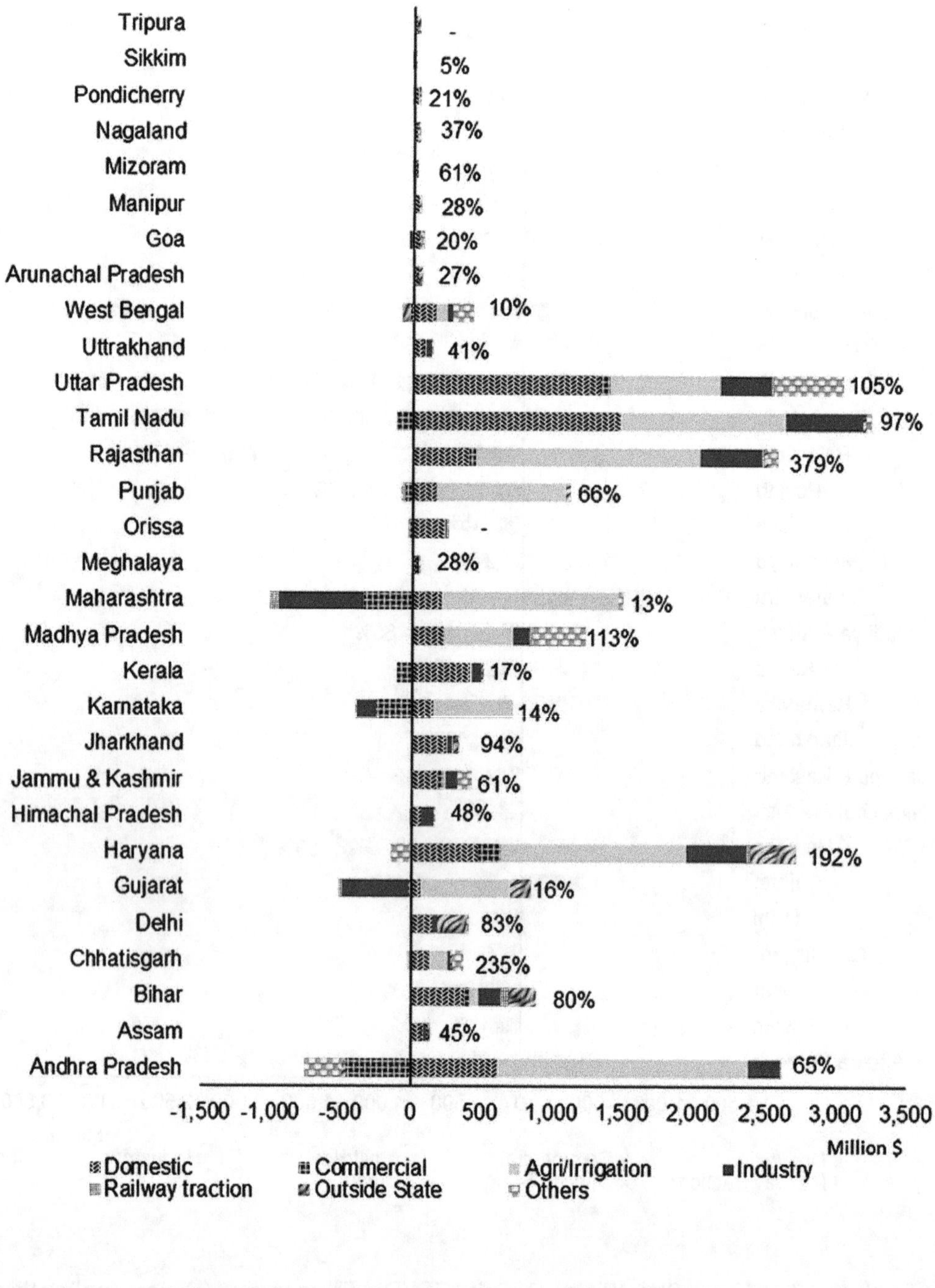

Figure 8 gives a snapshot of the subsidy volume (net subsidy after accounting cross-subsidy) at a countrywide level over the recent six years, from 2008-09 to 2013-14. The yearly subsidy magnitude is duly reflected on the country average electricity tariff[9] and CoS patterns.

Figure 6. Consumer power subsidies - 2012-13
Source: Author's own analysis. Electricity data considered from Planning Commission's Annual Report on The Working of State Power Utilities & Electricity Departments – 2013-14 (Planning Commission, 2014).Data of GSFD sourced from RBI's annual publications (RBI, n.d.). Note: This is a provisional estimate. Necessary data for the States of Delhi and Orissa were not reported.

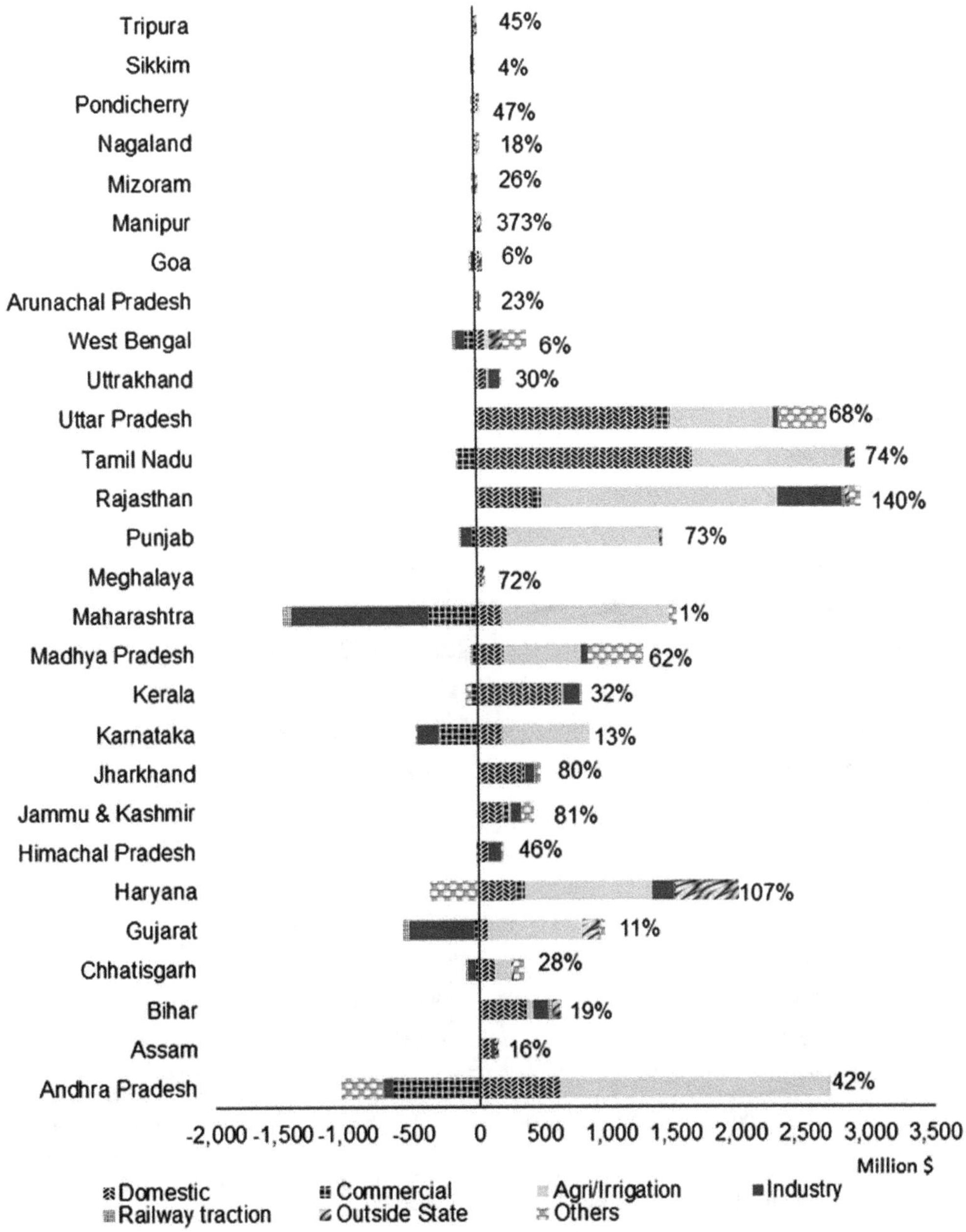

One can observe an average price-gap of more than 1 INR/ kWh (0.03 US$/ kWh) over the six years, from 2008-09 to 2013-14. Figure 8 also reflects a causal link between price-gap (cause) and subsidy volume (effect). For example, subsidy volume reached its peak (more than INR 110,000 crores) in year

Figure 7. Consumer power subsidies - 2013-14
Source: Author's own analysis. Electricity data considered from Planning Commission's Annual Report on The Working of State Power Utilities & Electricity Departments – 2013-14 (Planning Commission, 2014). Data of GSFD sourced from RBI's annual publications (RBI, n.d.). Note: This is a provisional estimate. Necessary data for the States of Delhi and Orissa were not reported.

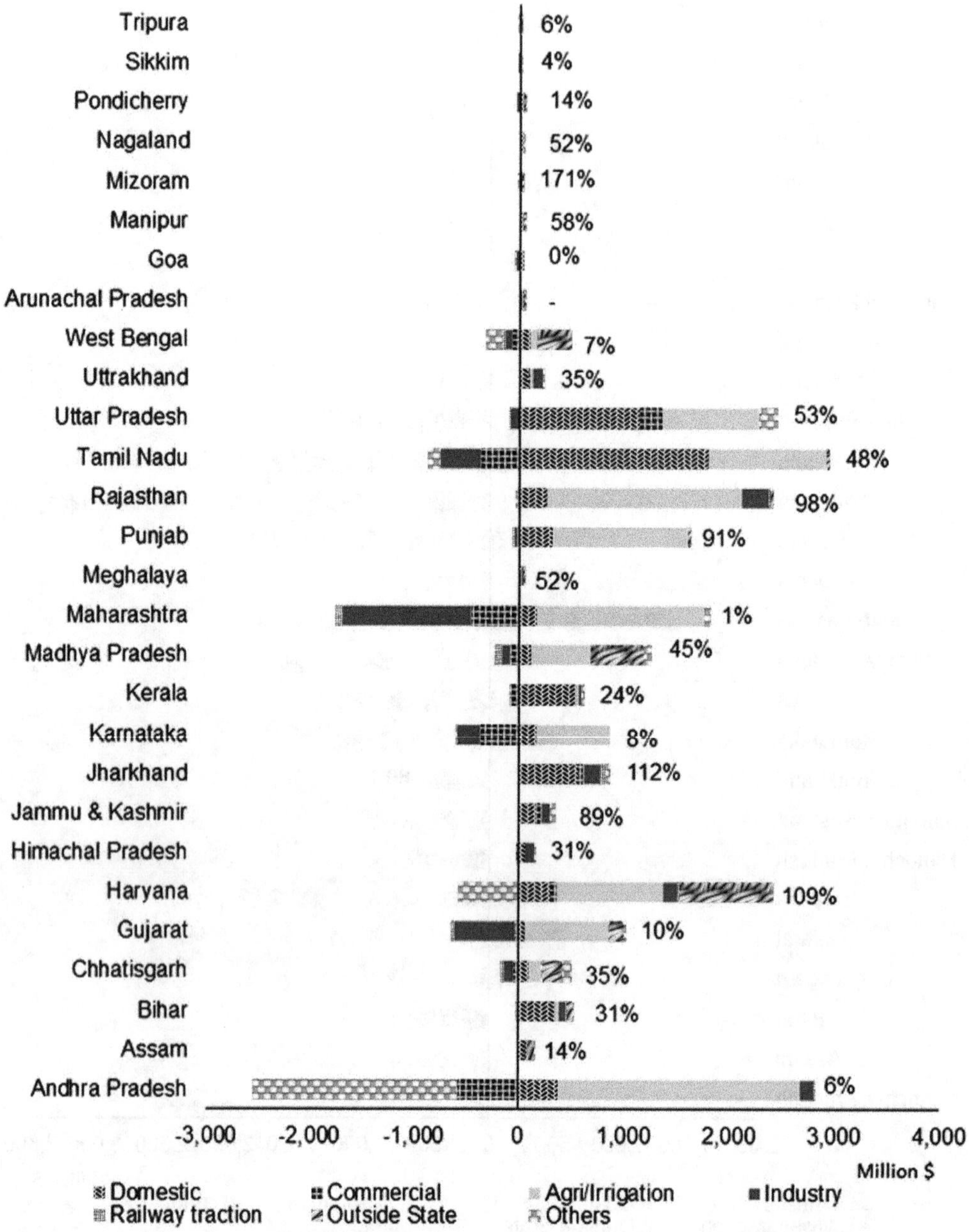

2011-12 when the difference between average CoS and tariff was at its maximum (INR 1.83/ kWh). Moreover, this shows that power subsidy requires to be better targeted rather than allowing all economic classes of the population to benefit from.

Figure 8. Country-wide consumer power subsidy volume
Source: Author's own analysis. Values of National average CoS and tariff are sourced from Planning Commission's Annual Report on The Working of State Power Utilities & Electricity Departments – 2011-12, 2013-14 (Planning Commission, 2011) (Planning Commission, 2014).

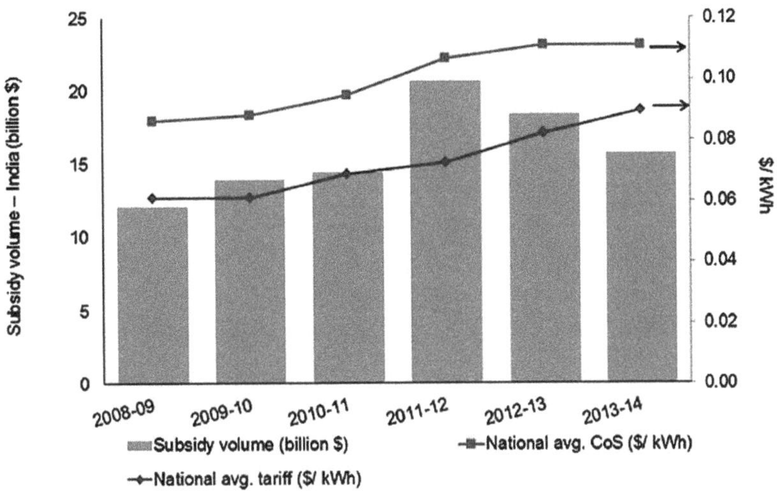

The assessment shows that cumulative subsidy volume over the six years ballooned to US$ 95.2 billion. It also reveals that the aggregate subsidy volume in recent three years (*i.e.* 2011-12, 2012-13 and 2013-14) exceeded the total State development expenditures in Energy and total State outlay for power projects over the corresponding period by 23% and whopping 500% respectively (RBI, 2014). This portrays the enormity of revenue loss that could have been utilized in T&D[10] sector, the latter reportedly starves from required investment. It is worthwhile to mention that due to transmission constraints the power exchanges in the country often fail to consummate sales-purchase deals, worth more than INR 1,000 crores (The Financial Express, 2013). Moreover, it is seen that the current transmission capacity is often unable to evacuate surplus power from one State to power deficient States. At a time when the targeted power generation capacity in the 12th Plan (2012- 2017) is set at 76 GW (Ministry of Power, 2012) with an increased share of distributed generation, ramping up the T&D infrastructure is paramount. The Working Group on Power, Government of India has estimated requirement of finance in distribution sector during the 12th Plan to the tune of INR 3.06 lakh crores (about US$ 57.26 billion) (Ministry of Power, 2012). In addition, an amount of INR 2.25 lakh crores (Ministry of Power, 2012) is reportedly required for improving power distribution infrastructure which includes smart grid, feeder separation scheme, National Electricity Fund, RGGVY and R-APDRP[11]. In light of this fund requirement, the revenue loss (about US$ 95.2 billion in six years) on account of lack of cost-reflective tariff holds significance.

As far as the share of power subsidy (net) in State's gross fiscal deficit is concerned, Andhra Pradesh, Bihar, Haryana, Jharkhand, Madhya Pradesh, Punjab, Rajasthan, Tamil Nadu and Uttar Pradesh deserve special mention (all consistently having more than 50% share during the six years' period). There are some smaller States which are also found to register high percentage of power subsidy in GSFD. However, it ought to be noted that a State with low fiscal deficit may have apparently high percentage share of subsidy. Considering this aspect, the current investigation identifies the States with high fiscal deficits and power subsidies over the period. In this exercise, those featuring in the lists of top 10 States

Figure 9. States with highest gross fiscal deficits and consumer power subsidies – 2008-09
Note: Author's own analysis.

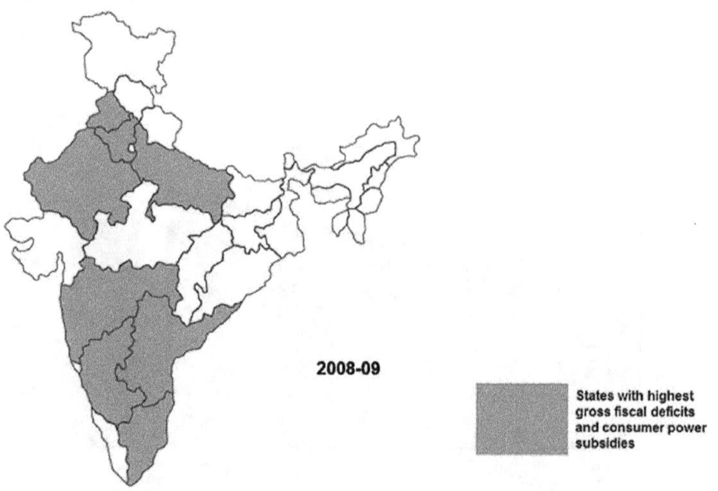

under the categories: highest gross fiscal deficits and consumer power subsidies are identified in each year. Figure 9 to Figure 14 showcase the States with highest gross fiscal deficits and consumer power subsidies over the given period.

From the figure one can see that certain States like Tamil Nadu and Uttar Pradesh were characterized with high volumes of subsidy and fiscal deficit throughout the period. Rajasthan, Punjab and Haryana also featured quite consistently in these tables.

Karnataka merits special mention here. Though it was one of the States with highest power subsidy till 2009-10, it had done well in reducing the subsidy since then. Maharashtra and Andhra Pradesh are also seen to contain subsidy in recent years.

Figure 10. States with highest gross fiscal deficits and consumer power subsidies – 2009-10
Note: Author's own analysis.

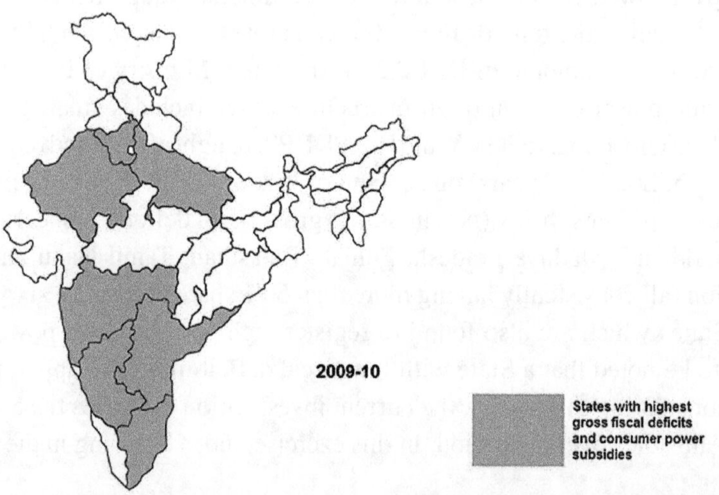

Figure 11. States with highest gross fiscal deficits and consumer power subsidies – 2010-11
Note: Author's own analysis.

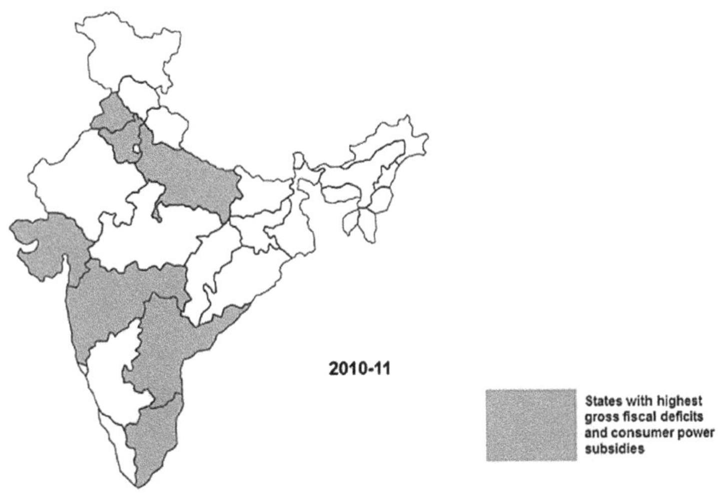

It is interesting to note that 19 out of 30 States have witnessed rise in subsidy volume over these six years[12]. One may wonder that in spite of laid-down guidelines, for example, the National Tariff Policy, discipline in tariff-setting is still elusive. The problem lies in failure of the SERCs to adhere to the stipulated guidelines. The National Tariff Policy stipulates that the SERCs should endeavor to fix the tariffs within ± 20% of the average CoS latest by the end of year 2010-2011. However, only three States: Gujarat, Maharashtra and West Bengal brought Domestic consumer tariff within the stipulated range by 2010-11. By 2013-14 total seven States: Andhra Pradesh, Gujarat, Karnataka, Madhya Pradesh, Maha-

Figure 12. States with highest gross fiscal deficits and consumer power subsidies – 2011-12
Note: Author's own analysis.

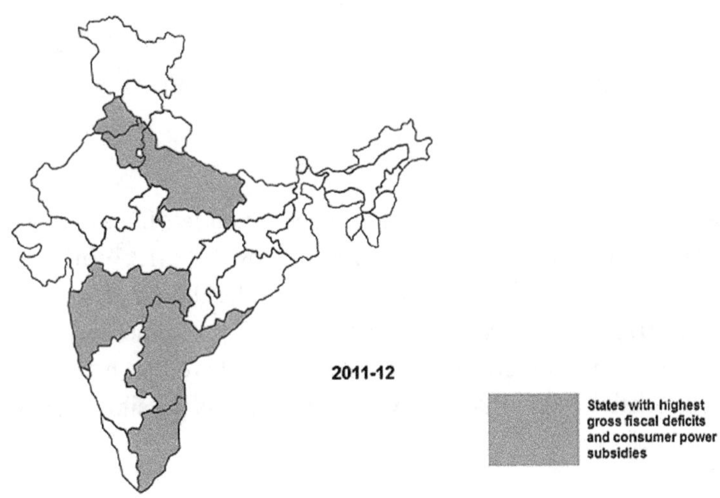

Figure 13. States with highest gross fiscal deficits and consumer power subsidies – 2012-13
Note: Author's own analysis.

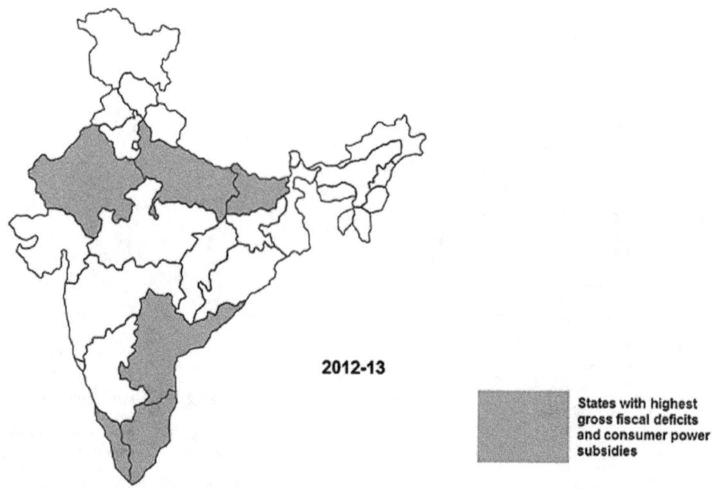

Figure 14. States with highest gross fiscal deficits and consumer power subsidies – 2013-14
Note: Author's own analysis.

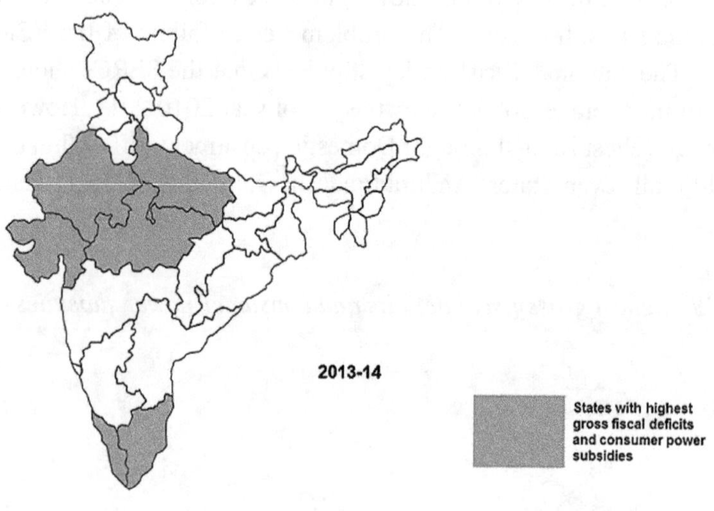

rashtra, West Bengal and Sikkim were successful to meet the target. In case of Agricultural consumer tariff, none of the States could conform to the tariff policy by 2011-12. With regard to cross-subsidy, the States also did not fare well. Only nine States could make the tariff for Commercial consumers below +20% of CoS by 2010-11, whereas tariffs for Industrial consumers were found to be within the targeted limit (+20% of CoS) in five States. It is quite evident here that non-compliance to guidelines has become a common practice rather than an exception, which is possibly responsible for brewing up the present crisis in the sector.

Figure 15. An overview of the identified ills and remedies
Note: Author's own analysis (Das & Goswami, 2015).

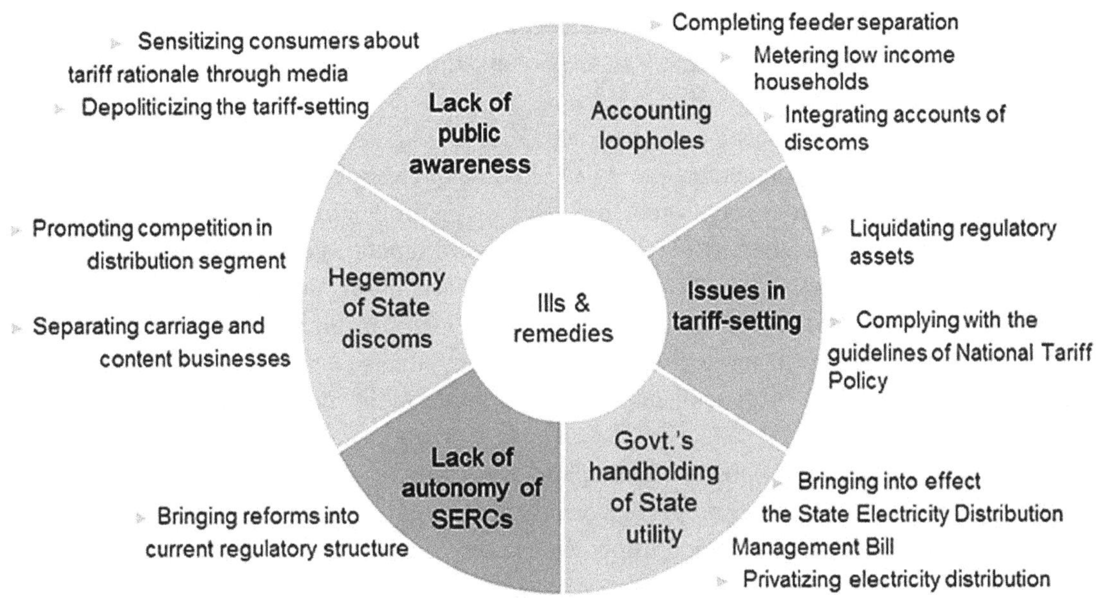

ILLS AND REMEDIES

Troubled state of affairs of India's power distribution sector is a raging issue for quite a long time. And this can be considered as the outcome of systemic lapses, ranging from operational loopholes to institutional deficiencies. Notwithstanding, the complexity of the problem prompts the concerned authorities to take a holistic approach instead of relying on *ad hoc* response to the predicament. The current investigation identifies six broad areas of concern in power distribution sector which warrant serious attention. In addition, this study puts forward a set of plausible measures for due consideration by the authorities (Figure 15).

- **Accounting Loopholes:** One of the major problems in electricity distribution in many of the States is insufficient metering of consumption. This results in under-realization of electricity charges from consumers by the discoms, which is mirrored in the average recovery of cost -- a lowly 75% in 2012-13 (PFC, 2015). Non-billing of consumption not only leads to revenue shortfalls for the discoms, but also makes it difficult to project consumption pattern and set consumer tariffs in a Multi-Year Tariff framework. It is generally found that actual power demand much exceeding the projected sales compels the discom to purchase power through short-term agreements with producers or through open access. Both these options are generally dearer than power purchase through long-term PPAs[13] and therefore, ad hoc power procurement drives up power purchase cost; the latter comprises 70 – 80% of the cost of service of a discom. As a result, in a Multi-Year Tariff regime the tariff in effect, which is set based on projected sales and ex-ante estimation of Annual Revenue Requirement, the latter being estimated from projected power purchase cost, becomes substantially out of sync with actual cost of power. This, on one hand, leaves a significant shortfall in revenue of the discom till true-up of tariff order takes place (past information shows that normally there are 2 to 3 years' gap between provisional tariff order and truing up), and on the other hand, can build up regulatory assets to avoid tariff shock. These manifest into increase in net subsidy volume.

Moreover, non-metering exaggerates the AT&C losses. Interestingly in most cases, the consumers benefiting power subsidies are found un-metered. With no credible information of actual consumption by the beneficiaries available, the SERCs rely on the utilities' inputs on consumption while setting tariffs. For example, in Karnataka electricity consumption by agriculture pumpsets and BPL[14] households, known as Bhagya Jyothi/ Kutir Jyothi (BJ/ KJ), are fully subsidized by the government. However, majority of these consumers are un-metered. Similarly, agriculture pumps (AP) in Punjab are largely beyond the purview of metering. It is "believed" that agriculture sector in the State accounts for around 30% of total electricity consumption[15].

Such lapse in measurement of power consumption, especially of subsidy beneficiaries compromises with accounting probity, essential for proper disbursement of public welfare funds. Apart from accounting problems, un-metering has cross-sectoral implications such as over usage of irrigation pumps causing rapid depletion of ground water.

Feeder separation to cater to different power requirements can limit wasteful electricity consumption to a large extent, especially in agriculture. It is often seen that State governments (*e.g.* in Karnataka) stipulate the duration of power supply (3-phase) to the irrigation pumps, along with a cap on the rated capacity of the pumps. In spirit, electricity consumptions by these pumps are subsidized by the State. Nevertheless, this power supply design has not yielded the desired result. The failure can be attributed to supply of power to rural households (2-phase supply) and the irrigation pumps through the same feeder, therefore, allowing the pumps to draw power beyond the stipulated hours. This results in greater load than the envisaged demand which in turn affects quality of power supply to the households. Separating the feeder to irrigation pumps from other uses can be a solution to this problem. However, implementation of feeder-separation requires proper design. Though some States have taken initiatives towards feeder separation, initially outcome has not been encouraging everywhere (World Bank, 2012). One major reason is lack of regularity in power supply to the irrigation pumps which makes the consumer (in this case, farmer) unsure of availability of power to run pumps. This has resulted in trust deficit among the consumers towards government schemes. Potential solution can be ensuring regularity in power supply for irrigation during a specific period of day, taking into account the farming requirement. The farmers should be consulted while designing the power supply scheme. Gujarat is the first State in the country which has successfully implemented feeder separation.

However, it should be underscored that feeder-separation should not be considered as an alternative to metering. Direct data collection at consumer level is essential for improvement of load management and better design of power subsidies in rural belts of the country. Considering the present socio-political scenario in rural areas, metering of all consumers at one go may not be easy; the States may opt for monitoring power consumption at sub-station level initially. Going forward, the concerned authority should aim to bring all consumers under the ambit of direct metering, including low-income households who are benefiting from cheaper electricity. Currently, in most of the States, the governments cap the consumption level up to which a household is entitled for subsidy; hence, metering is unavoidable. In spite of metering, discoms face difficulties to bill consumptions because of several reasons such as resistance from consumers, inadequate human resource to perform door-to-door checking and monitoring of meters, *etc*. Pre-paid meters or Advanced Metering Infrastructure (AMI) can be a solution to this monitoring problem. With maturity of the technology, its cost has become quite reasonable and is expected to come down further (World Bank, 2012). Moreover, in comparison to the cost of poorly targeted power subsidy, an initial investment in AMI implementation will help the exchequer realize long term economic benefits.

These meters will allow low-income households to draw electricity up to the threshold (monthly entitlement) of subsidised electricity, beyond which the consumer has to pay for its entire monthly consumption. This mechanism can offer multiple benefits such as arresting subsidy-related leakages and reducing AT&C losses. Moreover, this will enable the discoms to do away with the hassle of door-to-door meter checking. Initially, the mechanism can be tried in selected districts; subsequently, it can be rolled out to other places in a phased manner.

There are also some proposals wherein the State government may reimburse the low-income households their monthly expenditures towards electricity through direct benefit transfer (DBT) mechanism. This can be plausible in view of the ambitious programme *National Mission for Financial Inclusion* (also known as Pradhan Mantri Jan-Dhan Yojana) launched by the Government of India, wherein any person can open a bank account with zero balance. The Government of India has already began disbursing subsidies to domestic LPG use (upto 12 cylinders a year per household) through DBT.

Another way to contain agricultural power subsidy can be installation of solar powered pumps. This will eliminate requirement of grid power for irrigation and therefore, the State can save power subsidy to agriculture. In this regard, the Ministry of New and Renewable Energy (MNRE) have introduced Solar Pumping Programme for Irrigation and Drinking Water under Off Grid and Decentralised Solar applications scheme wherein the government has targeted to install 1,00,000 solar PV water pumping systems. The government has also allocated an initial financial support of INR 400 crores for this (MNRE, 2014). However, unplanned implementation of solar PV pumps may lead to as much ground water exploitation as free electricity has caused. One way to avoid this is to allow farmers to sell surplus solar power to grid rather than over use it for pumping; this will incentivize the farmers to use power efficiently (Tata Center, 2015).

Apart from metering, the accounting practice of discoms often raises debate regarding transparency. In recent years, we have seen certain stakeholders seeking judiciary's intervention to examine the accounts of the discoms. Such legal tussles are bound to delay the review exercise of tariff-fixing (also known as truing-up) undertaken by SERCs, potentially creating doldrums in the sector.

One plausible way to plug the loopholes can be through computerization of the accounting practice, with the help of sophisticated softwares like Enterprise Resource Planning (ERP) (Das & Goswami, 2015). This can facilitate collection, archiving and management of operational and financial data. This will benefit the SERCs in undertaking true-up of tariff-orders in a timely and transparent manner. It ought to be noted that presently R-APDRP, introduced by the Centre to facilitate State Power Utilities to reduce AT&C loss, does not include computer-based integration of financial accounts of the discoms[16].

- **Issues in Tariff-Setting:** Continued non-compliance to tariff guidelines can be considered as a major reason for today's dismal state of affairs of the distribution sector in India. One glaring example is the mounting regulatory assets, resulted from under-recovery of cost by the discoms due to lack of cost-reflective tariff revision. Though the National Tariff Policy underlines that the provision of regulatory asset can only be adopted in extra-ordinary circumstances, in practice, it has become an *unofficial* norm. This apart, few State Regulatory Commissions have adhered to the guidelines spelt out in the Tariff Policy with regard to liquidating regulatory assets. Non-compliance in tariff-determination is not just restricted to the issue of regulatory assets. Hardly the tariffs are found aligned with the cross-subsidy guidelines stipulated by the Tariff Policy.

It is paramount that the State actors recognize that carrying forward the accumulated regulatory assets can only help accentuate the current crisis. It is imperative that they explore possibilities to liquidate the mounting regulatory assets in a time-bound manner. Moreover, the SERCs should not be allowed to bypass the guidelines of the National Tariff Policy. The essentiality of cost-reflective tariff-setting should be recognized by the State actors for maintaining financial health of the discoms and the sector at large.

- **Government's Handholding of State Utility:** The Electricity Act 2003 was believed to usher in an efficient and effective paradigm in the functioning of the power distribution sector, where accountability and transparency were the cornerstones of the reform process. However, the desired outcome has remained elusive. Despite of unbundling of the SEBs, the latter has not enjoyed much functional independence; a major reason is the influence of State-appointed board members.

There is always a possibility that decisions taken by the Board are more to satisfy the political ambitions of the incumbent government which is providing unrealistically cheap power to the electorate (*i.e.* the public), than the interests of the organization or the distribution sector, which is in nutshell, to maintain balance between social obligations and organizational financial stability. In view of such systemic lacunae, the Central government has proposed a new bill known as *Model State Electricity Distribution Management Responsibility Bill, 2013* (Ministry of Power, 2013b), which aims to bring accountability and professional management of power distribution in the States (refer to the Appendix). Among other things, it has given emphasis on recasting the composition of State-owned discoms. The new Bill proposes to restrict the number of functional directors not more than 50% of the board strength. The State-nominated directors shall be limited to maximum two, and the number of independent directors shall conform to the provision of the Companies Act. However, not much progress is seen to make the Bill effective. Also, if at all gets enacted, it would be interesting to see the final form of the Bill. Doubts have been expressed in some quarters about its effectiveness; they are of the opinion that the proposed Bill may not have enough fire in terms of deterrence to non-compliance.

- **Lack of Autonomy of SERCs:** The subject of *real immunity* of the SERCs from any influence of the State governments often poses serious questions in recent times. Limited financial independence and inadequate resource and infrastructure often handicap SERCs' functioning and compromise with their autonomy. This apart, appointments to key positions in SERCs are sometimes questionable[17]. There are instances where a State official or an office-bearer in a power utility company has been immediately appointed to SERC as chairman. Moreover, in absence of any existing mechanism to oversee the activities of SERCs, integrity in their functioning has become a debatable matter. However, constituting a "super" regulatory body for oversight of the SERCs may not be practically feasible; it may add complexity to the current regulatory regime. The issue of unbiased administering of regulatory responsibilities can be addressed through introducing unambiguous guidelines pertaining to appointments to regulatory bodies, especially to avoid conflict of interests in such appointments. The new guideline may consider barring a former State official getting appointed to any position in the SERC before three years from the end of his last tenure in a government position. Similar norm should be applicable with respect to appointment of a former office-bearer of distribution licensee to the commission.

Also, a mechanism should be designed to subject the Commissions to strict compliance to applicable laws and regulations. One plausible way can be stipulating submission of 'Compliance Reports' by respective SERCs to CERC after every truing-up of tariff order. In case of non-compliance to particular clause(s) of the Electricity Act or other effective regulations, the SERCs have to show 'admissible' reasons in the *Compliance Reports*. Any default in this regard should be considered as dereliction of duty of the SERC board members, inviting disciplinary actions. Thus, one may see greater transparency and accountability in SERCs' functioning.

- **Hegemony of State Discoms:** Since inception, the State-owned discoms enjoy monopoly over power distribution in most of the States. Absence of competition in the sector, accompanied by lack of accountability in the functioning of public utilities, has resulted in inefficient delivery of service by the discoms. Hence, it is essential to encourage competition in the sector and break the stranglehold of State-owned discoms.

Interestingly, privatization of distribution sector has been tried quite some time back. However, this has remained restricted to selected circles like Delhi (in 2002) and Orissa (in 1999)[18]. The latter was the first State which embarked on privatization of the power distribution sector, with the assistance from the World Bank. The objective was to revive the ailing power sector in the State which was witnessing transmission & distribution losses as high as 43% and very low realization of billed consumer power charges, about 17% (Mahalingam, 1997). With the Orissa Electricity Reform Act 1995 coming into effect, the Orissa State Electricity Board (OSEB) underwent unbundling into four regional utilities: CESCO, WESCO, NESCO, and SOUTHCO[19]. An autonomous regulatory commission also came into existence. The transmission business remained with the publicly-owned Grid Corporation of Orissa (GRIDCO). As part of the privatization strategy, GRIDCO handed over the management contract of the central zone (comprising the circles of Bhubaneshwar, Cuttack, and Dhenkanal) to BSES (Bombay Suburban Electricity Supply Limited) for a period of three years from September 1996 with a provision of early termination. BSES was entitled to have fees comprising management fee, basic incentive fee and supplementary incentive fee. A holistic formula was prepared to compute incentive fees, taking into account different factors such as billing, collection, metering, and repair and maintenance expenditures during the period prior to the award of contract. The privatization journey did not go smoothly. GRIDCO and BSES started having disagreements. One such issue was regarding employees; the latter retained employment with Government of Orissa. Therefore, the employees were not accountable to BSES. On the other hand, BSES allegedly was not keen to invest in improving the network infrastructure as it had only management control without ownership rights. It was found that the collection was also dismal. GRIDCO undertook a review of the situation and sensed that the valuation of the Central Zone's distribution sector might get a hit if the situation was allowed to worsen. This would then pave the way for private parties to get majority stake of the distribution network at a throwaway price. This would defy the rationale of privatization which is to achieve efficiency and accountability in the functioning of the sector. The contract agreement was prematurely terminated in April 1997. Following this, the

Government of Orissa decided to give fresh lease of life to privatization of the State's power distribution by offering majority stake (51%) to private parties of all four Zones. The reasons were to salvage the sector from uncertainty amidst continued worsening condition of the State's distribution system, and to increase participation of more number of private investors with better bids leading to greater private investments in the sector. The terms and conditions were also re-laid with respect to the previous contract. Interestingly, BSES came out as successful bidder for WESCO and NESCO combined and SOUTHCO standalone, whereas in a re-bid CESCO went to AES-Jyoti. It was expected that all the Zones would see financial turnaround by 2001-02; in contrary, all of them continued suffering losses. A host of factors might have contributed to this failure: non-availability of transitional fund (the government discontinued subventions to the discoms post reforms), poor collection efficiency and high commercial losses owing to lack of metering and resistance from anti-social elements in the State, use of substandard meters, and unforeseen massive damage to distribution infrastructure due to 1999 super-cyclone. CESCO saw the exit of AES consortium in August 2001 and the management was handed over to a government appointed CEO. In the aftermath of this trouble, several committees and fact-finding teams came up with several observations (Ramanathan & Hasan, 2003). Those included unrealistic target-setting with regard to reducing T&D losses and improving collection efficiency, incorrect consumer category-wise demand projection[20], below-par management by the discoms with lack of innovative business models and insufficient working capital, inherent limitations of year-to-year tariff-setting based on cost-plus approach (causing high regulatory uncertainty), tacit political support to defaulters of bill-payment, unforeseen losses due to super-cyclone at an early stage of sector revival, and absence of moratorium on government aided debt. In March 2015 the State Regulatory Commission revoked the licenses of the three remaining private discoms because of discoms' financial instability and lack of improvement in their service, among other reasons (Business Standard, 2015). Management of power distribution has been provisionally handed over to GRIDCO.

Drawing key lessons from Orissa experience, other States including Delhi which showed interest in privatization are found to have identified some important areas for greater examination, such as baseline data, bidding process, asset valuation, regulatory uncertainty, governmental support during transition, *etc*.

Recently the Central government has gone a step further to encourage competition in the sector and improve efficiency. In December 2014, the government introduced the Electricity (Amendment) Bill, 2014. Among a host of amendments to the Electricity Act, 2003, the new Bill proposed "segregating the carriage from content in the distribution sector and determination of tariff based on market principles, while continuing with the carriage (distribution network) as a regulated activity. To protect the interest of consumers, the tariff for retail sale of electricity is proposed to be capped through the Regulator and one of the supply licensees is proposed to be a Government controlled company" (Press Information Bureau, 2014). This will benefit consumers to choose their service provider (discom), akin to the telecom sector, and consequently will encourage competition among discoms – necessary for efficient and better quality of service. However, the Ministry can only introduce requisite provision in the Act; the implementation largely depends on the State governments. Public discoms and certain quarters may offer resistance to such plan since no party would like to lose its hegemony. Some doubts have also been raised whether India's power architecture can accommodate further layers of operation. Already some States (like Tamil Nadu) have started opposing this proposal. The Bill has been referred to the Parliament Standing Committee on Energy for further examination.

Till now, other than in Mumbai where two private discoms are entitled to cater to the same neighbourhood, private discoms in other States have license of supplying power to a specific circle where no other discom is allowed to provide service. As a result, the consumers are unable to exercise their right to choose their power distributor. Allegations of financial irregularities in providing service by private discoms have reached the floor of court in recent days. For example, the three private discoms of Delhi have approached the Delhi High Court contesting the legality of the January 2014 directive of the Delhi government to audit discoms' accounts by the Comptroller and Auditor General (CAG). The matter is still sub judice. Consequently this has led to uncertainty in tariff-revision process and adversely affected the sentiments of private investors in the sector. Fair competition among discoms can potentially weed away such transparency-related issues. However, the regulator has to ensure that access to network remains non-discriminatory. Moreover, the regulator has to be wary about any kind of cartel among the private discoms. It is worthwhile to mention that recently the European Commission imposed fines to the tune of more than € 5 million on two spot power exchanges in Europe for "*having agreed not to compete with one another for their spot electricity trading services*", thus breaching the EU antitrust rules (European Commission, 2014). Envisaging some initial challenges in undertaking such big reforms, the government may start the programme in selected circles only. After garnering hands-on experience and understanding associated risks, it can be rolled out to other circles in phased manner.

- **Lack of Public Awareness:** Informed consumers are vital for quality service delivery in an economy. Notwithstanding the best of intention of a programme, there remains a possibility that it may fail owing to lack of public participation. With regard to power tariffs and subsidies, a strong and apolitical public awareness programme is essential, especially since power tariff has been a contentious issue in elections in the country. The State Regulatory Commissions should continue sensitizing public about the rationale of tariff revision. This will help avoid politicization of the issue. The Commissions can make use of the electronic and print media and information technology services for reaching out to the consumers in an effective manner.

Timely execution of the aforesaid measures is vital to fructify the target objectives. This will not only help address an issue before the latter amplifies to a crisis, the administration can benefit from avoiding losses to the exchequer as every delay results in cost escalation or loss of opportunity cost. A target-setting matrix which takes cognizance of the challenges and establishes mid- to long-term goals can be useful to avoid hiccups in implementation[21] (Figure 16). As power is a concurrent subject in India, the given measures are denoted as per the jurisdictions of the concerned authorities at State and Central levels.

CONCLUDING REMARKS

Financially viable power sector is a critical enabler of a country's economic progress. However, power distribution sector in India is turning out to be the country's Achilles heel, owing to apathy of the administration. Lack of cost-reflective consumer power tariff is responsible for causing financial instability in power distribution sector, which in turn, has triggered a cross-sector domino effect. The scale of the problem can be gauged from the cumulative losses of the utilities in the financial year 2012-13 -- a massive INR 1,00,000 crores [22] (*i.e.* ~ US$ 19.66 billion) (PFC, 2015). Consequently, the utilities are facing lack of investible surpluses, which is adversely impeding the required infrastructural augmentation and improvement. To mention its economic consequence, notwithstanding the installed power generation capacity (at 225 GW) about 67% more than recorded power demand (at 135 GW)[23], the country

Figure 16. Target-setting matrix
Note: Author's own analysis (Das & Goswami, 2015).

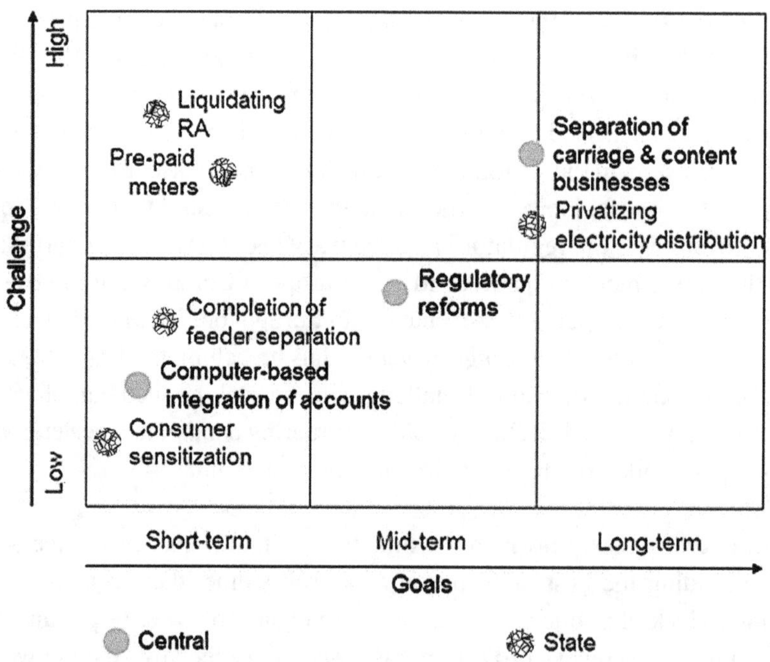

often experiences peak power deficit (FICCI- booz&co., 2013). The cost of such power shortages to the economy is reportedly about US$ 68 billion in 2012-13 (Ministry of Finance, 2013).

However, the financial crisis in power distribution sector is not a *once in a blue moon* development. The current study has come up with some compelling analyses which affirm that the situation has been allowed to aggravate in full knowledge of the concerned administration. It is seen that electricity has been forcefully undervalued by the State actors employing an insidious facility termed Regulatory Asset, whereby the liabilities of the State governments to compensate the discoms in the form of consumer power subsidies are kept low. The present investigation successfully uncovers the *effective* subsidy to power consumption across the States over a period of time. This is complemented by some thought-provoking findings, emphasizing on their economic relevance at State and National levels. The study also deliberates on some identified issues plaguing the sector, followed by a brainstorming on a set of plausible corrective action-points.

In fact, the competent authorities are not unaware of the proposed remedial measures; hitherto, the actions taken are inadequate. Nonetheless, the steps taken by the incumbent government at the Centre towards rationalising energy pricing in the country can likely be the start of a long-pending reforms process. On the power sector front, the Government of India has conceived a programme: Deendayal Upadhyaya Gram Jyoti Yojana (DDUGJY), aimed at separating feeders and implementing metering across the country; it has a budget allocation of about INR 43,000 crores (Prime Minister's Office, 2014). However, recasting debts of State utilities has remained a sticky issue – consensus on the financial restructuring package is yet to be reached. Lot of expectation is also pegged on the proposed Electricity (Amendment) Bill, 2014.

Putting a brake on the current poorly designed consumer power subsidy mechanism is all the more necessary when the Centre has taken ambitious targets to provide 24x7 power to all households, and ramp up the share of renewable energy sources (solar and wind) in India's power generation mix; as of now renewable energy options are yet to become cost competitive in coal-rich India. This apart, rationalizing power prices can offer other co-benefits such as promoting demand-side energy management; the latter can generate economy-wide multipliers.

Let's not mistake to articulate that the current crisis in the power sector is far from being doused. With no single silver bullet to revitalize the sector, this calls for a departure in the governments' (State and Centre) approach from the usual circumventing of politically-sensitive issues. A strong political will of the administration can only steer the country out of the predicament.

REFERENCES

Business Standard. (2015, March 5). *OERC cancels distribution licence of Reliance Energy's discoms in Odisha.* Retrieved June 30, 2015, from Business Standard: http://www.business-standard.com/article/companies/oerc-cancels-distribution-licence-of-reliance-energy-s-discoms-in-odisha-115030400500_1.html

CEA. (2013). *Growth of Electricity Sector in India from 1947-2013.* CEA.

CEA. (2014, January). *Central Electricity Authority: CO2 Baseline Database, version 9.* CEA.

Chandramouli, C. (2011). *Houses, Household Amenities and Assets Data 2001 - 2011 - Visualizing Through Maps.* Retrieved April 10, 2015, from Census of India: http://censusindia.gov.in/2011-Common/NSDI/Houses_Household.pdf

Das, S., & Goswami, A. (2015). *Crisis in India's Electricity Distribution Sector: Time to Reboot for a Viable Future.* New Delhi: The Energy and Resources Institute.

European Commission. (2014, March 05). *Press Release: Antitrust: Commission fines two power exchanges € 5.9 million in cartel settlement.* Retrieved June 30, 2015, from European Commission: http://europa.eu/rapid/press-release_IP-14-215_en.htm

FICCI-Booz & Co. (2013). *Power Transmission The Real Bottleneck.* New Delhi: FICCI.

ICRA Research Services. (2014). *Power Sector: Limited tariff hikes so far by SERCs for FY 2014-15, coupled with rising subsidy dependence for the sector as a whole; Subsidy estimated at Rs. 720 billion for FY 2015.* New Delhi: ICRA Research Services.

IEA. (2011). *World Energy Outlook 2011.* Paris: IEA.

IMF. (2013). *Energy Subsidy Reform: Lessons and Implications.* Washington, DC: International Monetary Fund.

Indian Power Sector.com. (2013, March 30). *Haryana government gives nod to discoms debt rejig.* Retrieved December 01, 2014, from Indian Power Sector.com: http://indianpowersector.com/home/2013/03/haryana-government-gives-nod-to-discoms-debt-rejig/#more-19450

Indiastat. (2012, March). *Socio-Economic Statistical Information about India - Power - State Electricity Boards.* Retrieved January 15, 2015, from Indiastat: http://www.indiastat.com/power/26/stats.aspx

Koplow, D. (2009). Measuring Energy Subsidies Using the Price-Gap Approach: What does it leave out? Manitoba: International Institute for Sustainable Development (IISD).

Kumar, V. R., & Sethi, M. (2014). Indian Power Utilities: A Panacea for Financial Revival. *Global Journal of Finance and Management, 67.*

Lokare, S. M. (2014, February 7). *Publications - Re-emerging Stress in the Asset Quality of Indian Banks: Macro-Financial Linkages.* Retrieved October 24, 2014, from Reserve Bank of India: http://rbi.org.in/Scripts/PublicationsView.aspx?Id=15720

Mahalingam, S. (1997, October 17). Unbundling trouble. *Frontline.*

Ministry of Finance. (2013). *Economic Survey of India - 2012-13.* New Delhi: Ministry of Finance, Govt. of India.

Ministry of Finance. (2014). Chapter 1- The State of the Economy. In Economic Survey 2013–14 (p. 5). New Delhi: Author.

Ministry of Law and Justice. (n.d.). *Seventh Schedule.* Retrieved February 26, 2015, from Ministry of Law and Justice, Govt. of India: http://lawmin.nic.in/olwing/coi/coi-english/Const.Pock%202Pg.Rom8Fsss(35).pdf

Ministry of Petroleum & Natural Gas. (2014). *Indian Petroleum and Natural Gas Statistics - 2013-14.* New Delhi: Ministry of Petroleum & Natural Gas, Govt. of India.

Ministry of Power. (2005, February 12). *National Electricity Policy.* Retrieved December 03, 2014, from Ministry of Power: http://www.powermin.nic.in/whats_new/national_electricity_policy.htm

Ministry of Power. (2006). *Tariff Policy.* New Delhi: Ministry of Power, Govt. of India.

Ministry of Power. (2012). *Report of The Working Group on Power for Twelfth Plan (2012-17).* New Delhi: Ministry of Power, Govt. of India.

Ministry of Power. (2013a). *Guidelines of Transitional Finance Mechanism under the Financial Restructuring Scheme for State Owned Discoms.* New Delhi: Ministry of Power, Govt. of India.

Ministry of Power. (2013b). *Model State Electricity Distribution Management Responsibility Bill, 2013.* New Delhi: Ministry of Power. Govt. of India.

Ministry of Power. (n.d.). *About Ministry - Responsibilities.* Retrieved June 22, 2015, from Ministry of Power, Govt. of India: http://powermin.nic.in/responsibilities

MNRE. (2014). *Supplementary guidelines for implementation of "Solar Pumping Programme for Irrigation and Drinking Water under Off Grid and Decentralised Solar applications scheme.* New Delhi: Ministry of New and Renewable Energy.

PFC. (2013). *Report on The Performance of State Power Utilities for the years 2009-10 to 2011-12.* New Delhi: Power Finance Corporation Ltd.

PFC. (2015). *Report on The Performance of State Power Utilities for the years 2010-11 to 2012-13*. New Delhi: Power Finance Corporation Ltd.

PFC. (n.d.). *R-APDRP*. Retrieved June 23, 2015, from Power Finance Corporation Limited: http://www.pfcindia.com/Content/R_APDRP.aspx

Planning Commission. (2011). *Annual Report on The Working of State Power Utilities & Electricity Departments – 2011-12*. New Delhi: Planning Commission.

Planning Commission. (2014). *Annual Report (2013-14) on The Working of State Power Utilities & Electricity Departments*. New Delhi: Planning Commission.

Press Information Bureau. (2014, December 19). *Electricity Amendment Bill, 2014 Introduced in Lok Sabha; Changes Aimed at Promoting Competition, Efficiency in Operations and Improvement in Quality of Supply of Electricity*. Retrieved June 30, 2015, from Press Information Bureau, Govt. of India: http://pib.nic.in/newsite/PrintRelease.aspx?relid=113779

Prime Minister's Office. (2014, November 20). *Deendayal Upadhyaya Gram Jyoti Yojana*. Retrieved December 30, 2014, from pmindia: http://pmindia.gov.in/en/news_updates/15461-2/

Ramanathan, K., & Hasan, S. (2003). *Privatization of electricity distribution: the Orissa experience*. New Delhi: TERI.

RBI. (2014). *State Finances - A Study of Budgets of 2013-14*. Mumbai: Reserve Bank of India.

RBI. (n.d.). *State Finances: A Study of Budgets*. Retrieved August 1st, 2014, from Reserve Bank of India: http://www.rbi.org.in/scripts/AnnualPublications.aspx?head=State+Finances+%3A+A+Study+of+Budgets

Saini, S. S. (2011, August). *Mitigation Initiatives through Agriculture Demand Side Management*. Kanpur, India: Bureau of Energy Efficiency.

Tata Center. (2015, February 28). *News+ Events*. Retrieved July 01, 2015, from Tata Center Technology+ Design: http://tatacenter.mit.edu/solar-pumps-indias-potential-to-link-electricity-access-and-irrigation-needs/

The Financial Express. (2013, July 09). *Infra woes trip transmission despite power-surplus oases*. Retrieved April 20, 2015, from The Financial Express: http://archive.financialexpress.com/news/infra-woes-trip-transmission-despite-powersurplus-oases/1139647

World Bank. (2012). *Lighting Rural India: Experience of Rural Load Segregation Schemes in States*. New Delhi: World Bank.

World Bank. (2014). *More Power to India - The Challenge of Electricity Distribution*. Washington, DC: World Bank.

KEY TERMS AND DEFINITIONS

ARR: Annual Revenue Requirement.

AT&C: Aggregate Technical & Commercial loss.

Consumer Power Subsidy: The price-gap between average consumer tariff and average cost of power supply.

CoS: Cost of Supply.

DBT: Direct Benefit Transfer.

Discom: Distribution company.

GSFD: Gross State Fiscal Deficit.

LPG: Liquid Petroleum Gas.

MYT: Multi-Year Tariff.

O&M: Operation and Maintenance cost.

PFC: Power Finance Corporation.

R-APDRP: Re-structured–Accelerated Power Development Reforms Programme.

Regulatory Asset: The revenue deficit of a discom, earmarked by the State Regulatory Commission for adjustment (with addition of accrued interests on the amount) while determining tariff of the ensuing year and is to be used only in exceptional circumstances ("natural causes or force majeure" situations).

RGGVY: Rajiv Gandhi Grameen Vidyutikaran Yojana.

SEB: State Electricity Board.

SERC: State Electricity Regulatory Commission.

Subsidy: Subsidy is defined as the price-gap between average end-use price paid by consumers and the reference price which corresponds to the total cost of supply of the commodity (or service) in the market.

TFM: Transitional Finance Mechanism.

ENDNOTES

1 Indian National Rupees

2 Exchange rate considered in this study: INR 53.44/ US$

3 Without accounting subsidy.

4 Based on data from Central Electricity Authority.

5 There is no fixed definition of the Others category. The types of consumers included in this category may vary from State to State.

6 Without accounting subsidy.

7 It is found that subsidies payable by the State governments are sometimes adjusted with the payable dues of the utilities to the States (e.g., electricity duty, interest due on State government loan) or by reducing the cost of power purchase from State-owned generating companies.

8 The study also consulted Power Finance Corporation's report: *The Performance of State Power Utilities for the years 2009-10 to 2011-12*. Certain major differences were observed in the values of average CoS with respect to Planning Commission's report. This is due to consideration of CoS at the generation end in PFC's report while the Planning Commission reported CoS data, estimated at the end-user side. The current study is of the opinion that CoS should consider all applicable cost heads till electricity supply to the consumer. Hence, the data furnished in the Planning Commission's reports are deemed more representative of the actual cost of electricity supply.

9 The country average tariff is estimated from the total annual tariff-related revenue divided by total electricity sales in the year.

10 Transmission and distribution

11 Re-structured–Accelerated Power Development Reforms Programme

12 Gross fiscal deficits have increased in 23 States.

13 Power Purchase Agreements

14 Below Poverty Level

15 The consumption pattern from 2008-09 to 2011-12 has been studied.

16 Currently, the programme has two major components: Part A to establish baseline data and IT applications for energy accounting/auditing & IT-based consumer service centers. Part B entails strengthening of distribution system.

17 Recent judgment of the Supreme Court asking the Tamil Nadu Government to appoint a retired Supreme Court or High Court judge as the chairperson of the State Regulatory Commission holds significance. The Supreme Court observed that a regulatory commission is a quasi-judicial body and hence, should have representation from judiciary.

18 Calcutta Electricity Supply Corporation operating in Kolkata is the first private discom in the country. Tata Power Company Limited is also operating in Mumbai for decades now. These happened because of historic reasons.

19 CESCO: Central Electricity Supply Company of Orissa Limited; WESCO: Western Electricity Supply Company of Orissa Limited; NESCO: North Eastern Electricity Supply Company of Orissa Limited; SOUTHCO: Southern Electricity Supply Company of Orissa Limited

20 Projected industrial power demand which cross-subsidises domestic consumption was much higher than actual, which got aggravated as industrial consumers opted for captive generation because of disadvantageous tariffs

21 Goal-setting is done based on the current state of the issues and the realizable benefits from the proposed measures.

22 Without accounting subsidy.

23 As in May 2013.

APPENDIX: SALIENT FEATURES OF THE MODEL STATE ELECTRICITY DISTRIBUTION MANAGEMENT RESPONSIBILITY BILL, 2013

1. The State government shall submit in each financial year before the State Legislature an electricity distribution management statement on the slew of measures taken related to electricity distribution. The measures will be concerning long-term planning, consumer protection, regulatory compliance, corporate governance, and financial restructuring of the State Distribution Licensee (SDL), so as to bring about the operational and financial viability of the SDL.
2. The statement shall define a set of key performance indicators (KPIs) related to each of the aforesaid aspects, giving stress to payment of dues by government departments and institutions, distribution loss cut trajectory, provisioning of subsidy, energy accounting and auditing, improvement in collection efficiency, and recovery of past receivables. The statement shall also mention the policies and strategies the State government plans to undertake to realize the KPIs.
3. The long-term planning shall require the SDL to estimate demand, AT&C loss, and availability of electricity on long-term basis and, contracts. Also, it shall have a time-bound roadmap to reduce AT&C loss.
4. With regard to compliance issue, the Bill requires the State government to evaluate twice a year the status of compliance by the SDL with the Electricity Act and Rules and Regulations, Policies, and Directives.
5. The State government and the SDL shall enter into a memorandum of understanding for setting targets for KPIs and performance evaluation of the SDL for each financial year.
6. Non-compliance of "duties" by the State government may attract appropriate action by the Central government that may render the State ineligible for power from unallocated quota, etc.

Source: Ministry of Power, Government of India (Ministry of Power, 2013b).

Chapter 9
Enabling Policies for Advancing Sustainability of Electricity Access Programs

Subhes C. Bhattacharyya
De Montfort University, UK

Debajit Palit
The Energy and Resources Institute, India

ABSTRACT

As 1.3 billion people lack access to electricity globally, the challenge of ensuring universal electricity access in accordance with the Sustainable Energy for All initiative remains herculean. This chapter maps policy linkages, identifies the gaps in policies and recommends options for developing the enabling environment. The chapter suggests that the policy environment governing electricity access at present is weak and that improvements are required to deliver a sustainable outcome. Although grid extension remains the preferred mode of electrification in many countries, it is not the least-cost option in remote areas where decentralized off-grid solutions may be required. Successful promotion of off-grid solutions would require a clear regulatory environment, a non-discriminatory support mechanism for various stages of a project, financing options, policy co-ordination and linkage with other economic activities for rural development. The chapter concludes that capacity remains weak and non-transparent policy lobbying can distort the development of an enabling environment.

INTRODUCTION

The Sustainable Energy for All initiative of the Secretary General of the United Nations (UN) in 2012 has crystallized the global attention on the energy access challenge. It is estimated that about 1.3 billion people in the World in 2012 did not have access to electricity and 2.6 billion did not have access to clean cooking energies (WEO, 2014). South Asia and Sub-Saharan Africa contribute the lion's share of non-electrified population. Out of 1.3 billion without access to electricity, around 1.1 billion people lived in rural areas, making this a predominantly rural challenge. As lack of access to energy in general

DOI: 10.4018/978-1-5225-0094-0.ch009

and electricity in particular deprives the population of the opportunity to carry out activities to meet their essential needs, energy poverty creates developmental impediments through economic and human development challenges, thereby hindering sustainable development of any country. This is supported by the observation that a generally improving human development index and higher incomes of countries are found with better energy access. Accordingly, the Sustainable Development Goals, consisting of 17 goals and 169 targets, adopted in September 2015 have included access to affordable, reliable, sustainable and modern energy for all as one of the targets to be achieved by 2030.

A critical review of electrification experience (Bhattacharyya, 2012; Alstone et al., 2015) suggests that grid extension has been pursued as the favored approach to electrification and connected billions of people with relatively low cost energy. However, in all successful cases the state has generally funded the electrification investments. In addition, subsidized tariffs are also provided in many cases to allow consumers to use a minimum amount of electricity and even cross-subsidies between different consumer categories are used to support rural electrification. However, the misdirected use of subsidy instruments has created financial distress for utilities and the governments, while the benefit has missed the targeted population. Moreover, the narrow focus on grid extension did not often result in poverty alleviation or economic development of rural areas through linkages with productive and income generating activities and the quality of supply remained poor with rural areas hardly receiving reliable and on-demand electricity supply. Accordingly, sustainability of energy access remains doubtful because of the failure to meet present needs, inability to contribute to economic development, and continued damage to the environment due to reliance on polluting energy sources.

Moreover, the central grid is unlikely to reach many unelectrified areas for a number of reasons:

1. The capital cost of grid extension is often much higher than the states or utilities can afford;
2. Managing a rapid grid extension in countries with a very low electrification rate will be practically challenging and unrealistic; and
3. Financial viability of such projects remains doubtful due to socio-economic conditions, and cost recovery issues.

Where grid extension is not feasible, decentralised off-grid solutions such as solar home systems and local mini-grids can be used. But the promotion of these solutions has suffered due to the perception of "inferior" or "temporary" nature of the solution, high cost, limited use and a step-motherly support system. Yet, (International Energy Agency & the World Bank, 2014) indicates that to achieve the universal electrification objective by the year 2030, off-grid options would have to play a significant role, with 60% of the unelectrified rural areas gaining an off-grid solution in the form of local grids or stand-alone solutions. The report estimates that an investment of $890 billion will be required between 2011 and 2030 and the business-as-usual rate of investment will not be sufficient to ensure universal electrification by 2030. Clearly then an enabling business environment has to be created to unlock the decentralized electrification opportunities.

The purpose of this chapter is to highlight the limitations of the policy environment governing electricity access at present and to suggest improvements that are required to deliver a more sustainable outcome. The term sustainability in the context of electricity access as is used here conforms to the definition given in Our Common Future (WECD, 1987) and focuses on economic, social and environmental dimensions but supplements this by including technical and governance aspects. Thus, a sustainable solution will be technically capable of meeting present and future needs, will be cost effective, socially acceptable, environment friendly and locally manageable and deployable. The policy environment discussed in this chapter covers this multi-dimensional perspective, keeping the rural and remote locations in mind. The chapter will map policy linkages, identify the gaps in policies and recommend options for developing the enabling environment. As governance has been recognized as an important element towards delivering sustainable development goals, this chapter makes a contribution to this knowledge area through a set of policy recommendations that can help achieve energy access goal (Goal 7).

DEFINING ENERGY ACCESS AND POLICY ENVIRONMENT

There is no universally accepted definition of energy access as yet. Access to electricity is usually taken to be synonymous with having an electricity connection at home or using electricity for lighting while access to cooking energy is associated with the use of non-solid fuels for cooking (International Energy Agency and the World Bank, 2014). Although such a binary household-based definition is simple to understand, they fail to reflect the multi-dimensional nature of the problem that goes beyond the household focus into the productive use of energy. Further, this multidimensional nature also has a connection with different domains of sustainability. For example, in many parts of the world, despite having access to the electricity grid, many people are unable to derive benefit from it due to erratic and minimal supply. The same is the case with improved cook stoves, which though have been disseminated widely, but its long-term operation was not given due importance and many users reverted to their traditional devices after few months of use. If the world is to achieve the target of Universal Energy Access by 2030, which among others will also require framing policies for achieving the target, then a concrete definition of 'energy access' will have to be agreed upon.

One way of understanding what energy access actually means is to consider the incremental level of access to energy services. According to this approach, there may be different levels of access to energy and the policies for achieving the universal energy access can be classified under different heads:

1. Electricity for lighting, health, education, and communication;
2. Modern fuels and technology for cooking and heating; and
3. Mechanical power for productive use.

Based on the inter-linkages between the three stages and for developing robust and inclusive policies, universal energy access can be defined as "access to clean, reliable, and affordable energy services for cooking and heating, lighting, communications, and productive uses". Apart from the incremental level of energy access, it is also necessary to include the condition of whether the delivered energy is being used for a more holistic definition of energy access. The framework for defining electricity access, adapted from TERI (2011), could be as follows:

- Is (clean) electricity available (macro-level physical dimension of the challenge, that is, rural electricity distribution backbone/micro-grids/decentralized energy options are available at all habitations?)
- If yes, is it accessible (micro-level connectivity and market dimensions, that is, infrastructure available at the door-steps, do people find it easy to take a connection, can people connect to the grid/mini-grid or buy decentralised solar devcies of their choice as and when they require?)

- If yes, is it affordable (are the product/ services packaged and customized to meet the people's "ability and willingness to spend"?)
- If yes, is it being used (human behavioural issues and other dimensions, that is, do people have reliable and safe appliances to use electricity, do they want to shift from inefficiencit devices to improved designs and so on?)

Similarly, the concept of sustainability encompasses multiple dimensions following from the definition of sustainable development presented in Our Common Future (WECD, 1987). While economic, social and environmental dimensions are retained for any sustainability analysis, additional areas such as technical and institutional/governance have also featured in project/program level studies. In addition to the understanding on sustainability, the key question also is how we understand an "enabling policy environment." It is important to note here that there is a great diversity within electricity access programs and every solution cannot be applied broadly to all of them. So how does one create an enabling environment for such a complex and diverse sector? One possible way to do this is from the point of view of the benefit to all stakeholders involved i.e. ensuring that there is some value to all stakeholders in the implementation or value chain and that it is not compromised as a result of the rigid nature of policies, which generally ends up proposing similar technological solutions or financial design which may not be applicable to the diverse range of stakeholders and situations in the electricity access sector. For example, while today there is an increased focus on private sector participation in the sector, the lack of data on when and whether the central grid will be extended to a habitation, hampers the private sector participation even if business models are developed and incentivized by policies. Similarly, it is also observed that in many cases, subsidies tend to be linked to the infrastructure development or capital cost of the power plants only, and they do not support the investor at the more critical junctures (e.g., for battery replacement in the case of off-grid solar photovoltaic power plants). As a third example, it is often observed that end-users in the case of renewable energy-based systems compare the cost of electricity from a mini-grid to that of the central grid and are therefore prone to believe that expensive power is being sold to them. Such examples demonstrate that how there are gaps still in the policy formulation for electricity access, which create situations where the different stakeholders in the entire value chain are not adequately benefitted. In other words, while evaluating these factors, it is crucial to note that the various stakeholders involved have very different expectations and these expectations must be the guiding principle for deciding how an enabling environment is to be created. Sharma & Palit (2014) argue that various stakeholders have very different expectations from electrification programs that must be taken into consideration while developing the enabling environment for an electricity access program:

- **End-Users:** Adequate and reliable electricity supply suited to their needs and paying capacities with standardized products and easy servicing.
- **Project Developers and Implementers:** Mostly would be concerned with evaluating the techno-economic viability of their projects and for adequate policy and financial support, provided at the right time to ensure external factors and ambiguity in laws do not hamper project sustainability.
- **Government:** Clear metrics for monitoring increase in access and efficient use of resources and methods by which the subsidy burden may be reduced.

The key message here is that while designing programs and enabling policies, it is important to consider that the success and sustainability of the program is defined differently for different actors and socio-economic geographies, and a "one size fits all" approach is not followed. An example here is the design of the solar PV program in Bangaladesh by Infrastructure Development Company Ltd of Bangladesh (IDCOL), which have both solar home systems as well as solar mini-grids as its component and more importantly the financiang of solar home systems and solar mini-grids are done differently with the underlining objective to ensure their economic viability and social impact in the rural areas. Furthermore, all stakeholders in the value chain of solar home systems dissemination viz. the government, IDCOL, partner organisations, the local technicians and staff of partner organisations, and the user reap benefits from the program in one way or the other, thus making the program one of the most successful and sustainable solar PV programs across the World.

Rural Electricity Access: Status and Experiences

According to (WEO, 2014), 1.3 billion people did not have access to electricity in 2012, of which 622 million resided in Africa and 620 million in developing Asia. The average global electrification rate was 82%, with a significant urban-rural disparity. 94% of the urban population had access to electricity whereas only 68% of the rural population were fortunate enough to have electricity. However, the global average masks the disparity in the access level at the regional or country level and national averages also fail to disclose the disparity that exists within a country. For example, Sub-Saharan Africa has an urban electrification rate of 59% and a rural electrification rate of 16% and it is not uncommon to find a rural electrification rate of 5 or 6% in many countries in this region. Moreover, twenty countries account for almost 80% of the people without access to electricity (see Figure 1) and a greater attention on these high-impact countries would be required to ensure universal electrification by 2030.

These numbers however, tell us little about emerging trends in global electrification. Although the figures may look bleak, the electricity access situation has been improving over the years. The Global Tracking Framework 2015 reports that the annual growth in access to electricity during the tracking

Figure 1. Top twenty countries with highest unelectrified population, in millions (WEO, 2014).

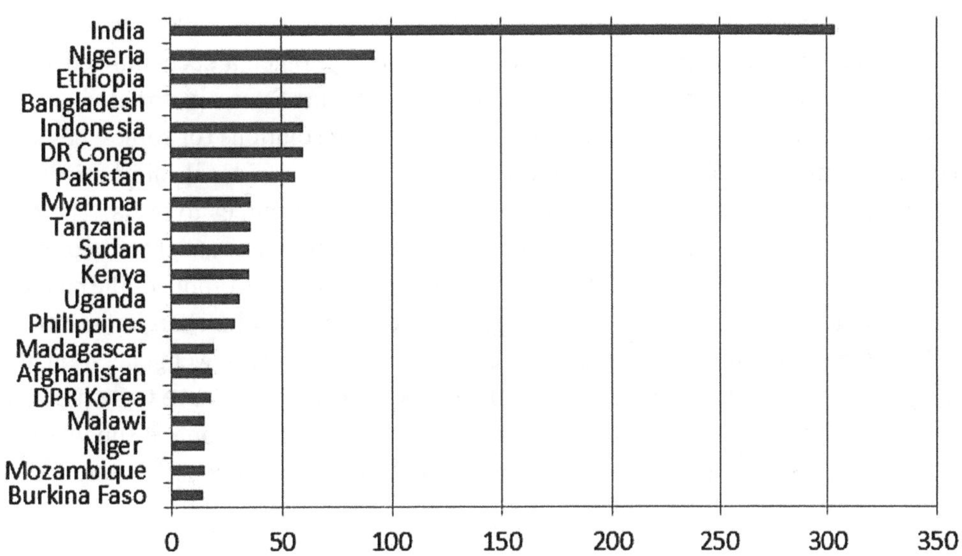

period (2010-2012) reached 0.6 percent, approaching the target growth rate of 0.7 percent required to reach universal access by 2030, and certainly much higher than the growth of 0.2 percent registered over 2000–2010. The same report also indicates that among the regions, improvements have been notable in South Asia (75 to 79 percent), Sub-Saharan Africa (32 to 35 percent) and Oceania (25 to 29 percent). Specifically, the global progress was majorly driven by significant advances in India, where 55 million people gained electricity access during 2010–12.

There is a long tradition of supporting electrification efforts throughout the world and as mentioned above significant progress has been made in terms electrification of various countries and regions. However, Palit and Chaurey (2011) suggest, with specific example from South Asian countries, that that there were no specific initiatives/schemes to improve the overall household connection level except Sri Lanka where the energy policy has specific annual targets for households level connections through grid and off-grid interventions. Similarly, Cook (2011; 2013) suggest that rural electrification schemes did not pay attention to universal access so far and a three-part solution strategy is required to solve the problem, namely a service obligation, an instrument to reduce connection and electricity charges; and greater choice of supply and suppliers. He suggests that our understanding on these issues is incomplete but the past experience shows that

- High connection and electricity charges hinder access to electricity and innovative subsidy or support mechanisms are required to address this challenge.
- The empahsis on cost recovery and reliance on the private sector is misplaced and in order to meet the needs of the poor, appropriate support for electricity supply and appliance purchase cannot be avoided.
- Simultaneously, rural areas need to be carefully selected for program implementation and embedding complimentary infrastructure into the electrification programmes is essential for successful realisation of such developmental programmes.

The lack of focus on universal electricity access in the past has constrained the population to realize their development potential and perpetuated their energy poverty.

Although electricity supply through long-distance transmission and distribution systems from central power stations is the norm, with the emergence of new generation technologies, there has been a shift to an alternative decentralized approach to delivering electricity. When a decentralized solution is not connected to the grid, it is known as an off-grid solution (see Figure 2 for a pictorial view). An off-grid electricity supply can take two forms – individual product-based solutions (or sometimes service) such as solar home systems and collective network-based solutions such as local mini/ micro-grids which distribute locally generated electricity from a single or multiple resources to users. The nature of the business varies in each case. For example, in a product-based solution, outright sale or hire-purchase transaction of an appliance supplemented by a maintenance arrangement completes the business activity. This may also include lanterns or batteries recharged and rented from solar charging stations. In a grid-based supply on the other hand, all activities of an electric utility, namely power generation, distribution, sales (billing, revenue collection, and customer relationship management) have to be performed, albeit at a smaller scale. Thus the complexity of the business evolves depending on the supply option chosen and the ability to address sustainability dimensions is also linked to the inherent features of the service.

Figure 2. Electricity supply options

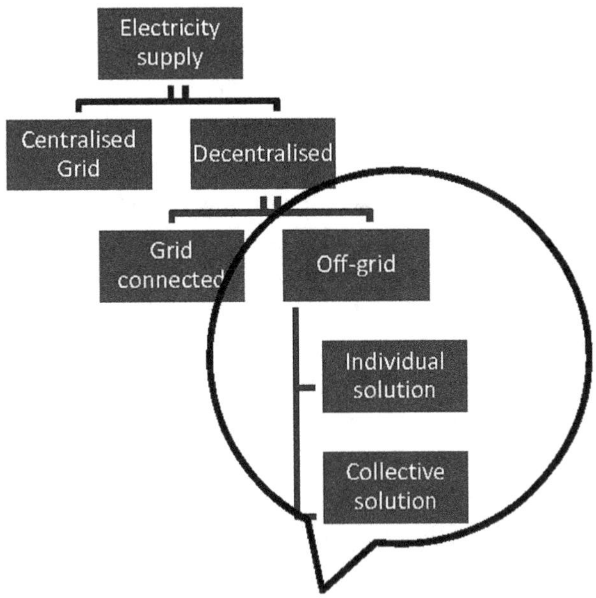

Due to relatively simple business activities involved in a product sale market, individual stand-alone options have emerged as the preferred off-grid solutions in most of the rural areas. Millions of solar home systems have been sold across the world and products like solar lamps and battery chargers have also seen a rapid growth. But their limited service hours, very limited ability to support productive application and relatively high cost of supply on per kWh basis, as compared to conventional grid, still remain a major issue for this category of items. Local grid-based solutions on the other hand have received recent attention. Bhattacharyya & Palit (2014) explain that reliable supply, possibility of inclusion of productive use of electricity, and environmental as well as energy security benefits of reliance on renewable energies make them a suitable candidate for rural electrification.

Further, very rarely traditional utilities have ventured in decentralized electrification through local mini-grids or individual product-based systems. The gap has been filled by various organisations including local communities, non-governmental organisations and the start-up companies. However, each entity is driven by its own motive and works within its own resources, skills and social constraints. Therefore, each organization is likely to appear in a niche area that suits its interests and is likely to generate sufficient benefits to it to continue with the activity.

Based on a project-level analysis in India, Mishra & Sarangi (2011) attempted to understand the basic conditions that have largely shaped off-grid project viability on a sustained basis. They found that the operational viability of off-grid projects is largely determined by policy support, social acceptance in the form of community participation, linkages with income-generating opportunities, and technological appropriateness. Interactions with stakeholders revealed that the regulatory uncertainty existing in the area of off-grid electrification stifles business growth and the ad-hoc regulatory policy arrangements produce undesirable outcomes. Similarly, Sarangi et al. (2012) highlighted that serious handicaps exist within the existing policy and legislative landscape governing the off-grid electricity sector. There is a realization within the policy circle that misplaced incentives like those available to mega power projects have yielded dampening effects on small scale decentralized energy projects. It is also contended that there exist several policy ambiguities (such as exemption from regulatory supervision for off-grid options) and inadequacies (such as no transparent grid extension policy) to address the emerging challenges confronting the sector. At the regional level, Palit and Chaurey (2011) suggest based on an analysis of off-grid electrification efforts in South Asia, that there are many challenges – technical, financial, regulatory, and institutional – hindering electricity access in the region.

Based on a review of financial flows and investment needs for energy access, Bhattacharyya, (2013) suggests that the least developed countries who are facing the greatest energy access challenge will find fund mobilisation as the most important issue. Even if they continue to invest their entire energy-related capital budget on energy access, they will not achieve universal energy access by 2030. International support will be required but the public finance may not be easily forthcoming and may not reach the countries that need them most. Therefore private investment will have to play an important role in fostering energy access but investors face major barriers particularly in the area of off-grid electrification to electrify the remote habitations. These include first generation barriers that directly affect the business prospects (and include low return, low business volume, high transaction costs, etc.), factors affecting business environment (such as regulatory and policy weaknesses), and business risks at the national level.

Using a multi-dimensional framework Bhattacharyya, (2012) finds that the present system of off-grid electrification is generally not sustainable. Most of the options are not economically sustainable in the sense that they cannot be maintained without some support. The inability of the current designs to meet future needs and poor reliability of systems also constrain their technical sustainability. However, there are also examples of off-grid projects from both developing and developed countries, which provides enough evidence that off-grid systems can also provide reliable electricity if designed accordingly (Chmiel & Bhattacharyya, 2015; Hasna & Huque, 2014; Palit et al., 2014). An off-grid project can become sustainable if it proves to be beneficial to various stakeholders simultaneously - consumers, service providers, financiers and government. This in turn requires creating a mutually beneficial system that reinforces the interactions and sustains it.

The subsequent sections present the knowledge gained from the OASYS South Asia research project[1] in terms of mini-grid-based rural electrification and highlights how such a socio-technical system can be developed and sustained.

POLICIES FOR SUSTAINING OFF-GRID ELECTRIFICATION PROJECTS

Policies at different levels influence any off-grid electrification project environment and these can be grouped under global, national and sub-national or local levels where various players are involved, often with their specific agendas (see Figure 3). At the international level, the energy access agenda is being driven by the United Nations initiative on Sustainable Energy for All. This has received support of various international, multilateral and other donor agencies and even private companies/ investors. At the national level, government ministries, regulatory agencies, banks and other bi-/multi-lateral funding agencies as well as technology providers, get involved. At the sub-national and local level, the users, electricity service providers, provincial governments, local authorities, as well as equipment suppliers and contractors participate in the project activities.

A complex web of interactions and inter-relationships develops amongst these players encompassing issues related to

Figure 3. Appropriate institutional arrangement

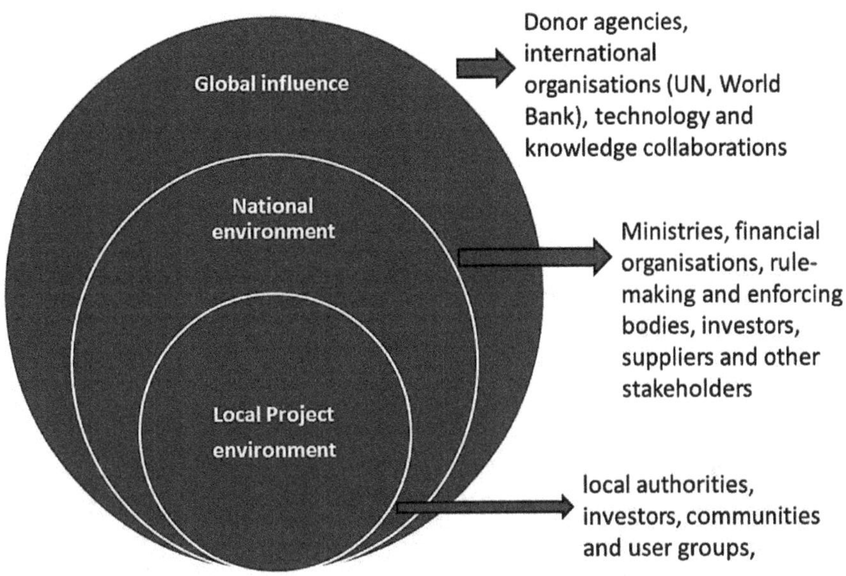

1. Credits and financing for rural areas;
2. Access to donor funding;
3. Pricing, subsidies and other support/control mechanisms for electricity and other agricultural produces;
4. Technology use and transfer;
5. Local business development;
6. Permissions and clearances from local authorities;
7. Labour and employment;
8. Land use and the like (see Figure 4).

For a successful development of the off-grid electrification sector, creating an enabling policy environment entails facilitating the interactions amongst the various stakeholders to enhance off-grid electricity access, removing barriers hindering transactions, creating opportunities for initiatives to flourish and supporting successful implementation of such initiatives to realize the goal of universal electrification.

- First, there is a need for formal recognition of off-grid options through a legal instrument that provides clear and transparent rules of the game defining the opportunities, delimiting the scope and ensuring proper governance of the delivery. In case of network-based local delivery options, an appropriate regulatory governance mechanism is required to avoid exploitation of the consumers by the monopoly suppliers while ensuring investor protection against perpetual losses. Bhattacharyya (2013) outlines three alternative regulatory arrangements in such cases, namely:
    - A generic waiver or exemption from the prevalent technical standard provisions applicable to the electricity supplier may constitute a simple solution. This can take different forms. For example, a blanket exemption for rural areas (as followed in India under the Electricity Act 2003) is a possibility. An exemption up to a given threshold (as in Mali, Senegal or Tanzania) or exemptions for specific organisations (e.g. co-operatives in Ethiopia) are other possibilities.

Figure 4. Web of policy interactions

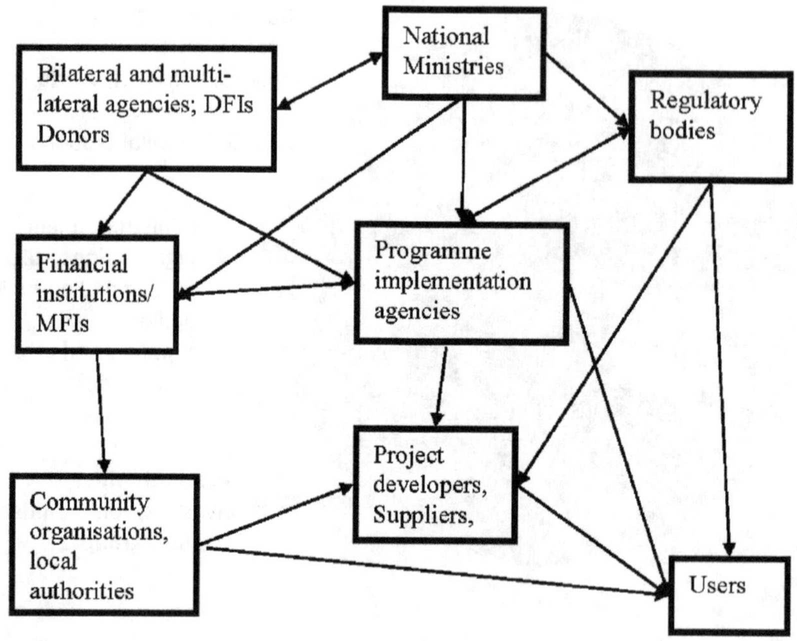

- ◦ A simplified, standardized regulatory arrangement can offer a light-touch, practical approach. Such a regulation should specify the role and duties of the provider, set the information filing requirements and ensure consumer protection mechanisms. This reduces the compliance cost and imposes lesser burden on the regulators.
- ◦ A full-fledged regulatory arrangement constitutes the most formal regulatory approach. The licensing approach or a concession approach tends to conform to this idea. But this will be a costly option and should only be adopted where benefits from the regulation outweigh the costs.

Irrespective of the regulatory arrangement selected, care needs to be taken 1) to avoid any confusion about the service area and protection against the extension of the grid within a reasonable period of time, 2) to ensure quality and reliability of service through quality standards, 3) to protect health and safety issues of anyone involved in such activities and 4) to promote standardisation of technical systems used in such activities for ease of operation, maintenance and expansion.

- Secondly, given the relatively high cost of off-grid supply and low affordability of the users, the importance of an appropriately designed financial support mechanism cannot be overemphasised. Any off-grid supply faces financial viability challenge due to the prevalence of subsidised grid electricity rates and subsidised fossil fuel supply that create a distorted playing field. Moreover, off-grid operators often do not get operating subsidies from the governments, or any cross subsidies through regulatory interventions, to provide subsidised tariffs similar to grid connections in remote areas. The subsidy policy thus discriminates between grid-connected and off-grid users. If governments want to reach the poorest section of the population, subsidies perhaps cannot be avoided but these have to be well targeted and appropriately designed. Removal of price distorting subsidies from fossil fuels, and abolition of subsidy discrimination between grid and off-grid connections can facilitate off-grid electrification. More importantly, the financial support system could be innovatively used to ensure sustainability of the off-grid operations. This requires moving away from upfront capital grants to a life-cycle investment management option. Many off-grid projects require regular capital asset replacement (batteries, gasifiers, and the like) and unless these are provided for, the project will not survive in the long-term. Very few commercial lenders provide funds to off-grid electricity businesses and consequently, lines of credit are required to support the business. This is an area that requires policy attention.

- Third, a related issue is funding investments in the off-grid areas. (Chmiel & Bhattacharyya, 2015) found that even in Isle of Eigg (in Scotland), the investment for the off-grid system came mostly from grant funds and without such funding, the project would not be affordable. Being small-scale projects, off-grid electrification projects do not attract the attention of investment banks and even bundling of projects is unlikely to make them eligible for such funding. Commercial banks do not understand the business risks in this area and being low-volume, low-return activities they find the transactions less meaningful for their business portfolio. Moreover, investors look for long maturity products to spread the cost over the lifetime of the projects but hardly any product is available in the market that goes beyond 10 years maturity. In addition, when the off-grid business is managed by a local entity (such as a community group or an NGO), their credit worthiness may be questionable and even in some cases, their legal status may be doubtful. Thus unfamiliarity with the business segment, risk perceptions, and unsuitable products make the experience frustrating for the off-grid sector. Yet, rural and agricultural banks operate in many countries and the off-grid electricity business does not involve any different risk sets than that they are familiar with. Expanding their networks, streamlining their decision-making process, strengthening their capacity and channeling additional funds through them can improve the situation. Also a long-term credit and subsidy policy for the sector can benefit the development of the sector.

Sharma & Palit (2014) explain that in OASYS South Asia project private off-grid electricity service providers such as Mera Gaon Power and Mlinda Foundation were supported through viability gap funding with some in-built flexibility to use the funding by the investor. Through a competitive bidding process, service providers were selected that provides the best value for money in terms of access provision while bridging the funding gap required by the investors. The current subsidy scheme for solar PV systems in India is linked to physical output, that is, the subsidy is received upon completion of installation. Adequate cash flow however is required when orders for equipment are placed and payments to suppliers are to be made and hence the current schemes hamper the uptake of energy access by not supporting the end-user exactly at those junctures where cash-flow limitations exist for the end-user or implementing agency. Innovative and flexible use of subsidy and funding can facilitate and promote energy access.

In conjunction with investment funding, soft credit facilities for the end users are required to enable them join the energy ladder. As electricity is a product that can only be used in conjunction with an appliance, end users need to have access to electrical appliances but their cost can be a barrier to the rural users. Similarly, the income streams in rural areas are often related to agricultural outputs and tend to be lumpy, making regular payments for services or products somewhat difficult. Micro-finance supports and customized payment options are essential to develop a viable rural electricity market. Sharma & Palit (2014) indicate that the Joint Liability Group model used in micro-finance provides a suitable mechanism to enhance credit worthiness and bankability of individual users and reduces the default risks for the lenders.

- Fourth, as donor and international funding agencies play an important role in shaping the international fund mobilization, coordination of this effort assumes importance. Poorly coordinated interventions result in inappropriate use of funds resulting in duplication of efforts, uncoordinated developments and limited real progress. In addition, tied aid can lead to non-standard systems, limited local content use and capacity development and promotes aid-dependency syndrome as well as fly-by-night expert engagement that are not helpful in the end. Sarangi, Pugazenthi, Mishra, Palit, Kishore, & Bhattacharyya (2014) suggest that adhocism and changing focus of donor funded programs are distorting the very foundation of the sector.
- Fifth, tariffs for off-grid electricity supply remains challenging. Bhattacharyya, 2015; Palit et al., 2011) find that the levelised cost of electricity from the off-grid/mini-grid options is much higher than the regulated tariff for various categories of consumers who receive grid electricity. The studies also found that capital cost subsidy will not be sufficient to ensure grid price parity and significant amount of operating cost subsidy will be required. But consumers are often willing to pay for a reliable supply and a win-win situation can arise as long as the cost of electricity remains lower than the most commonly-used alternative option. If kerosene is used for lighting, users are happy to switch for electricity if their monthly outgo does not increase. Similarly, the mini-grid based supply can be cheaper than electricity availed through diesel generators or even solar home systems. But there is no denial of the fact that even the operating cost recovery makes off-grid electricity tariff high and unless the users are able to pay such high tariffs, an off-grid system cannot become operationally viable. In many developing countries, particularly in rural areas where income may be limited and villagers may not afford to pay high charges, this remains a major challenge.

For a given capital investment, the tariff will reduce as the capacity utilization rate improves. This can be achieved either by adding an anchor load that drives the major use of electricity produced by the system or by incorporating productive uses of energy during off-peak hours. Either option can improve the financial viability of the project due to the possibility of a differential rate of electricity for these customers. Similarly, the project proponent has an improved chance of securing debt funding if the project can enter into a selling contract with a large buyer, where the buyer is credible, thereby making the contract bankable. This in turn may reduce the cost of borrowing and reduce the overall cost burden to be recovered through the tariff.

Innovative tariff design assumes great importance in this context. Instead of using kWh as the basis for charging, alternative cost recovery options need to be considered. For small users a flat rate may be appropriate but to avoid damages to the system a tripping arrangement has to be used. For consumption beyond a threshold level, a metered supply only makes sense. Even where a kWh rate is used, for cost recovery and revenue certainty, a supplementary fixed charge may also be required. Sharma & Palit (2014) shared that in the case of Mera Gaon Power (MGP), a weekly fee is charged per household which increases the affordability by distributing the cost burden. Rural consumers may not have the capacity to pay a large monthly sum and a weekly arrangement facilitates the process although it can impose additional revenue collection cost for the service provider.

- Sixth, a crucial point that emerges from this is the need to develop more integrated projects in such areas, initiatives that integrate energy and livelihoods. If new business opportunities are created, it is likely that the incomes of electricity users will increase and therefore their paying capacities for electricity would increase as well. Through this project, numerous livelihood opportunities can now be enabled, which include activities that use applications such as grinders for spices, packaging, *Saal* leaf plate making, better irrigation facilities, functioning water purifiers, and installation of fans and street lamps in community areas/ institutions such as clinics and schools. From the policy perspective therefore, it is recommended that in such cases, the electrification schemes should be designed to focus not just on the delivery of electricity infrastructure, but other crucial development infrastructure and training as well and adequate funds must be allocated toward linking different activities, such as education (computers), health (vaccine refrigerators, potable water), and agriculture (water pumping), through appropriate institutional mechanism. While electricity and other developmental interventions are included in the domain of Panchayati Raj institutions (local level administration) in India to create the necessary convergence in rural areas, the required awareness and capacity building have never been provided to these local institutions to implement and operate projects at the local level through a more decentralized planning process.

- Finally, the institutional setup for system operation and management of the system requires greater attention. Depending on the stage of development, the institutional arrangement and linkages would have to cater to the varying needs of off-grid electrification. This essentially requires a multi-tiered operational management system but a robust organisational arrangement is essential for any successful off-grid electrification. Being remote, the costs of engaging regular service and maintenance from nearby towns is high and therefore local capacities are required to be created. The capacities of the local community must be built to a level where they are able to resolve minor technical issues by themselves and have the necessary information to reach out to experts for more critical technical problems. The local institution may or may not include the main project implementing agency, but it should include the local actors. Some of these actors include members from the local community, energy entrepreneurs selected from within or outside the village, local government representatives, utility company representatives, NGO and civil society organization representatives, and independent private operators of distributed generation power plant.

The policy set outlined above suggests that careful design is essential for successful promotion of off-grid electrification options. An innovative policy framework is required to support flexible solutions to cater to the global challenge of electricity access. However, there are also barriers to the transition to such an innovative policy regime which are considered in the next section.

Issues and Challenges

A number of issues and challenges hinder the process of developing an enabling environment for promoting sustainable electricity access programs.

- *Lack of adequate capacity and awareness at various levels is an important barrier.* For example, the regulatory capacity is limited in most developing countries and the expansion of formal regulatory arrangements to mini-grid-based electrification can lead to a significant increase in the regulatory burden of the regulators, which can in turn slow down the approval and decision-making process and hinder growth of the sector. Similarly, off-grid electrification being a specialized activity requires knowledge and expertise in modern technologies, business practices and management skills to operate and manage small-scale systems in remote locations. The investors, system operators and business partners need to understand the intricacies of electricity supply business. But such knowledge may be inadequately available in rural areas. The need for skill development through a dedicated effort in parallel with policy preparation cannot be underestimated. Capacity building can take various forms and processes. Technical assistance by donor agencies for building organizational capacity or specific knowledge could come at one end of the spectrum. Local level training for technicians and local businesses through regular programs come at the other end. Various successful examples exist: for example, the Chhattisgarh Renewable Energy Development Agency has successfully sustained the pool of technicians for its solar PV mini-grids through regular training schemes. Similarly, Lighting a Billion Lives programme created a pool of trained energy entrepreneurs and technicians in rural areas, through intensive skill development efforts, to provide responsive after sales service to the solar lighting solutions installed in the rural areas of India (Chaurey et al., 2012).

- *Organizational weaknesses in policy making circles constitute another barrier.* Generally, in a multi-layered government structure, policies from the top drive the agenda but the local implementation requires a strong sense of ownership of the policies and activities and a local champion to implement the policies. However, a weak local ownership of the policies can arise due to a number of factors, including among others skewed benefit sharing, overlapping priorities or powers, dissatisfaction over earlier negotiations, additional organizational burden, and limited capacity. This can adversely influence the overall outcomes and local implementation may get affected.
- *Weak leadership is another issue.* Often policies are promoted by strong leaders who act as champions and spearhead the policy formulation, approval and its implementation. However, most governments are known for their myopic vision and the focus on a specific issue tends to be short-lived. Consequently, there is often lack of continuity and policy persistence that leads to weak performances in the long-run.
- *Non utilization of local resources to its full potential, thereby working towards local energy security, is another issue in most of the countries.* For example, Palit et al., (2014) opine that although India has been pursuing various policies on renewable energies and enhancing access, efforts in harnessing local resources for local level supply have not been very effective. The large programs have often relied on conventional technologies and fuels, whereas funding and political support have been limited for programs based on local resources. This has created failed projects and sent wrong signals although the potential remains high.
- *Lobbying for policy-making has become an important aspect in public and private decision-making process.* While the civil society participates in the lobbying process to express its views about a certain policy or action, non-transparent lobbying and capturing process for personal benefits can distort the policy-making process by protecting certain players or by offering non level-playing fields. This is however not restricted to policy-making alone. Regulatory processes, legislative actions and even investment decisions are often subjected to lobbying and the intensity of such processes can vary depending on the status of a country. This can also lead to corrupt practices and loss of social benefits. Accordingly, a transparent system for civil society participation in the decision-making process is required.

CONCLUSION AND FUTURE RESEARCH DIRECTIONS

This chapter has presented the need for creating an enabling environment for promoting electricity access solutions for remote rural areas in the developing world. As almost 20% of the global population lacks access to electricity, especially in the remote rural habitations, and given that the business as usual is unlikely to resolve this problem, concerted efforts will be required where both the public and private sector has to play their roles. However, rural electricity supply faces significant risks and business challenges due to limited system size, high cost of operation in remote areas, high transaction costs and poor paying capacity of the users. Accordingly, a conducive environment has to be offered to the investors and project developers with supportive policies to ensure delivery of electricity in accordance with the Sustainable Energy for All agenda. This chapter highlights the multiple layers of policy influence that exist in the case of rural electricity access and indicates the need for policy co-ordination at different levels. The chapter calls for regulatory certainty, suitable support mechanisms for enhancing affordability to users, low cost capital, innovative tariff design, and adequate funding support to enhance project viability. It also suggests integration of electricity access with rural development activities and an appropriate institutional arrangement for policy co-ordination and project implementation. Lack of capacity and awareness, weak organizational arrangements, poor leadership and intensive lobbying are identified as barriers that affect policy creation to sustain long-term objectives of energy for all. Addressing these challenges will be essential in order to achieve the energy access target of the Sustainable Development Goals and the policy set outlined in this chapter provides a systematic way of approaching the issue from a policy perspective.

With 70% of the population still living in rural areas of South Asia and Sub-Saharan Africa, sustainable development cannot be achieved ignoring them. Sustainable electricity in rural areas is an essential ingredient that will not only unlock the potential for economic development but also facilitate human development and social wellbeing. It can thus act as a catalyst for sustainable rural development. The enabling policy environment for sustainable off-grid electricity discussed in this chapter thus contributes to a broader rural development agenda and can also assist in achieving the sustainable development goals. Clearly, further work is required to investigate the potential of any integration of electricity with other related areas such water and food supply.

REFERENCES

Alstone, P., Gershenson, D., & Kammen, D. M. (2015). Decentralized energy systems for clean electricity access. *Nature Climate Change*, *5*(4), 305–314. doi:10.1038/nclimate2512

Bhattacharyya, S. (2012). Energy access programmes and sustainable development: A critical review and analysis. *Energy for Sustainable Development*, *16*(3), 260–271. doi:10.1016/j.esd.2012.05.002

Bhattacharyya, S. (2013). Financing energy access and off-grid electrification: A review of status, options and challenges. *Renewable & Sustainable Energy Reviews*, *20*, 462–472. doi:10.1016/j.rser.2012.12.008

Bhattacharyya, S. (2013). To regulate or not to regulate off-grid electricity access in developing countries. *Energy Policy*, *63*, 494–503. doi:10.1016/j.enpol.2013.08.028

Bhattacharyya, S. (2015). Mini-grid based electrification in Bangladesh: Technical configuration and business analysis. *Renewable Energy*, *75*, 745–761. doi:10.1016/j.renene.2014.10.034

Bhattacharyya, S., & Palit, D. (2014). *Mini-grids for rural electrification of developing countries*. London: Springer. doi:10.1007/978-3-319-04816-1

Chaurey, A., Krithika, P. R., Palit, D., Rakesh, S., & Sovacool, B. K. (2012). New partnerships and business models for facilitating energy access. *Energy Policy*, *47*, 48–55. doi:10.1016/j.enpol.2012.03.031

Chmiel, Z., & Bhattacharyya, S. (2015). Analysis of off-Grid electricity system at Isle of Eigg (Scotland): Lessons for developing countries. *Renewable Energy*, *81*, 578–588. doi:10.1016/j.renene.2015.03.061

Cook, P. (2011). Infrastructure, rural electrification and development. *Energy for Sustainable Development*, *15*(3), 304–313. doi:10.1016/j.esd.2011.07.008

Cook, P. (2013). Rural Electrification and Rural Development. In S. Bhattacharya (Ed.), *Rural Electrification through Decentralised Off-grid Systems in Developing Countries* (pp. 13–38). London: Springer-Verlag. doi:10.1007/978-1-4471-4673-5_2

Hasna, J., & Huque, A. (2014). Experience from First Solar Mini-grid Service in Bangladesh; In *Proceedings of the International Conference Innovating Energy Access for Remote Areas: Discovering Untapped Resources* (pp. 42-46). Berlin: Universitätsverlag der TU Berlin

IEA. (2011). *Energy for all: Financing access for the poor, Special early excerpt of the World Energy Outlook*. Paris: International Energy Agency.

International Energy Agency and the World Bank. (2014). *Sustainable Energy for All 2013-14: Global Tracking System Report*. Washington, DC: The World Bank.

Mishra, A., & Sarangi, G. (2011). *Off-grid energy development in India: An approach towards sustainability*. Retrieved March 28, 2015, from http://www.dmu.ac.uk/documents/technology-documents/research-faculties/oasys/project-outputs/working-papers/wp12--off-grid-approach-paper.pdf

Palit, D., Bhattacharyya, S. C., & Chaurey, A. (2014). Indian Approaches to Energy Access. In A.Halff, B. K. Sovacool, & J. Rozhon (Eds.), Energy Poverty: Global Challenges and Local Solutions. Oxford University Press. doi:10.1093/acprof:oso/9780199682362.003.0012

Palit, D., & Chaurey, A. (2011). Off-grid rural electrification experiences from South Asia: Status and best practices. *Energy for Sustainable Development*, *15*(3), 266–276. doi:10.1016/j.esd.2011.07.004

Palit, D., Malhotra, R., & Kumar, A. (2011). Sustainable model for financial viability of decentralized biomass gasifier based power projects. *Energy Policy*, *39*(9), 4893–490. doi:10.1016/j.enpol.2011.06.026

Palit, D., Sarangi, G. K., & Krithika, P. R. (2014). Energising Rural India Using Distributed Generation: The Case of Solar Mini-Grids in Chhattisgarh State, India. In S. Bhattacharyya & D. Palit (Eds.), *Mini-Grids for Rural Electrification of Developing Countries* (pp. 313–342). Springer International Publishing Switzerland; doi:10.1007/978-3-319-04816-1_12

Sarangi, G., Palit, D., & Mishra, A. (2012). Joining the dots: Regulating off-grid renewable energy sector in India. Mumbai: IGIDR.

Sarangi, G., Pugazenthi, D., Mishra, A., Palit, D., Kishore, V., & Bhattacharyya, S. (2014). Poverty amidst plenty: Renewable-energy based mini-grid electrification in Nepal. In S. Bhattachrya & D. Palit (Eds.), *Mini-grids for rural electrification of developing countries* (pp. 343–371). London: Springer. doi:10.1007/978-3-319-04816-1_13

Sharma, K., & Palit, D. (2014). Creating enabling environment for affordable delivery of sustainable electricity services. *Asia Pacific Tech Monitor*, *31*(3), 23–28.

TERI. (2011, July). Energy Access: Global and local initiatives. *The Solar Quarterly*, 26-31.

WECD. (1987). *Our Common Future, World Commission on Environment and Development*. Oxford University Press.

WEO. (2014). *World Energy Outlook 2014*. Paris: International Energy Agency.

ENDNOTE

1 https://dmu.academia.edu/OASYSSouthAsiaResearchProject

Chapter 10
The Distributional Impact of Efficient Energy Pricing in India

David Coady
International Monetary Fund, USA

Emine Hanedar
International Monetary Fund, USA

ABSTRACT

This chapter by Coady and Hanedar revisits the issue of the distributional impact of energy subsidy reform. It adds to the existing literature on a number of fronts. First, based on recent estimates of efficient energy taxes for India in the literature, it calculates the domestic energy price increases required to bring energy prices to levels that reflect the true social cost of energy consumption, including domestic and global environmental damage. It then simulates the impact of these price increases on household real incomes and how this varies across household income groups. Second, it extends the analysis to the efficient pricing of coal, the most polluting of all energy sources. Third, it also identifies key sectors of the economy that are likely to be the most impacted by higher energy prices.

1. INTRODUCTION

India has traditionally regulated domestic energy prices in an attempt to protect domestic consumers (both households and firms) from high and volatile international energy prices. However, it is widely recognized that not only are energy subsidies inefficient but the bulk of energy subsidy benefits are also captured by higher-income households (Arze del Granado, Coady and Gillingham, 2012; Coady, Flamini and Sears, 2015; Clements and others, 2013; Anand and others, 2013, 2014). Recent work has also highlighted the key role that energy subsidy reform, when combined with a scaling up of social spending, can play in achieving growth-friendly and poverty-reducing fiscal consolidation (Abdallah and others, 2015).

This chapter revisits the issue of the distributional impact of energy subsidy reform. It adds to the existing literature on a number of fronts. First, based on estimates of efficient energy taxes in Parry and others (2014) and Coady and others (2015), it calculates the domestic energy price increases required to

DOI: 10.4018/978-1-5225-0094-0.ch010

bring energy prices to levels that reflect the true social cost of energy consumption, including domestic and global environmental damage. It then simulates the impact of these price increases on household real incomes and how this varies across household income groups. Second, it extends the analysis to the efficient pricing of coal, the most polluting of all energy sources. Third, it also identifies key sectors of the economy that are likely to be the most impacted by higher energy prices.

The format of the chapter is as follows. Section II provides a brief outline of the key components of efficient energy pricing. Section III reviews recent energy price reforms in India and identifies the gap between current domestic energy prices and efficient prices and the required increase in domestic energy prices to eliminate this gap. Section IV briefly outlines the methodology used to estimate the impact of energy price increase on household real incomes and its distribution across household income groups and presents the results of our analysis. Section V summarizes our key findings and provides some concluding remarks.

2. EFFICIENT ENERGY PRICING

The efficient pricing of energy products (e.g., gasoline or coal) requires that consumers (i.e., households and firms) face a price that reflects three different components. These include—see Parry and others (2014) and Coady and others (2015) for a more detailed discussion:

- **The Supply Cost:** The supply cost of energy is the opportunity cost to a country of supplying the energy product to consumers. For internationally tradable products, such as petroleum products, the supply cost is the international price of the product adjusted for transport and distribution costs. For goods that are not internationally traded (or "non-traded"), the supply cost is the domestic cost of production ("cost-recovery price"), where costs are evaluated at efficient prices.
- **A Pigouvian Tax:** When the consumption of a good generates an external cost on society then efficient pricing requires that consumers face a price that also reflects this cost. In the absence of a well-functioning market for internalizing this cost in the consumer price, efficiency requires the imposition of a Pigouvian tax equal to the external cost generated by additional consumption. This is especially relevant for energy consumption since the consumption of fossil fuels generates a range of external costs including: costs imposed by outdoor air pollution resulting in a higher risk of mortality; costs associated with traffic congestion, accidents and road damage[1]; and the global environmental damage resulting from CO_2 emissions.
- **A Consumption Tax:** Energy consumption should also be subject to the same standard consumption tax levied on other consumption items for the purpose of raising revenue. These taxes should only be levied on final energy consumption by households with intermediate energy consumption by firms being exempt to avoid distorting firms' input choices (e.g., Diamond and Mirrlees, 1971), e.g., as with a value added tax. The base for this tax should also be the sum of the supply cost and the Pigouvian tax.

Figure 1. Evolution of energy prices and subsidies, 2004-2015 in rupees per liter, cylinder)
Source: IMF Staff estimates based on authorities' data for the price build-up. http://ppac.org.in, https://www.iocl.com/. Note: Prices for Petrol, Diesel and Kerosene are per liter, prices for LPG are per cylinder.

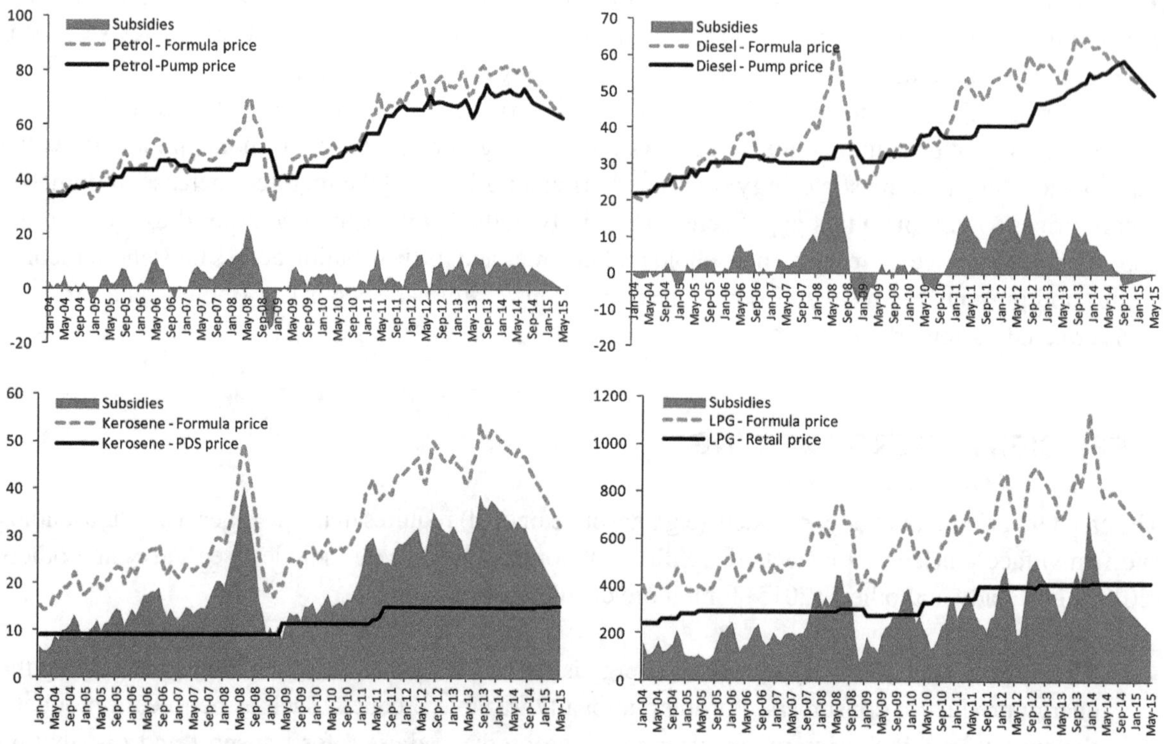

3. RECENT ENERGY PRICE REFORMS

Traditionally India has regulated the consumer price of key fuel products, including gasoline (petrol), diesel, kerosene and LPG, to protect consumers from high and volatile international oil prices. However, a range of reforms have been implemented over recent years that reduced the extent of regulation for some of these products. These include—Figure 1 shows the evolution of fuel prices and subsidies over the last decade:

- **Gasoline:** Gasoline prices were fully liberalized in June 2010. Prior to liberalization, domestic prices tended to move in line with international prices so that subsidies were generally small. The main exception was over 2007 and 2008 when international prices increased sharply but these increases were not fully passed on to domestic consumers. Over 2010 and 2011, subsequent to liberalization, gasoline prices again moved in line with international prices. However, the government suspended the formula in December 2011 and froze gasoline retail prices. The gasoline price was increased again in May 2012 and has since moved in line with international prices (GSI 2012). Excise duty on gasoline has been raised on four occasions since January 2014, most recently in January 2015.

- **Diesel:** Diesel prices were fully liberalized in October 2014. This followed a period of gradual subsidy reform. As with gasoline, diesel subsidies increased sharply over 2007 and 2008. Retail prices then moved upwards with international prices until the end of 2010, after which they diverged and diesel subsidies increased. To address rising subsides, regulated retail prices were increased in mid-September 2012. In January 2013, the government started to gradually increase retail prices by small amounts (Rs. 0.5 per liter per month) with the intention of eventual full liberalization, and also announced the sale of bulk diesel at unsubsidized prices. Since the formal liberalization of diesel prices, the excise duty on diesel has also increased on four occasions. However, there still remains a large price differential between diesel and gasoline reflecting almost entirely the preferential tax treatment of diesel—currently, diesel prices are 31 percent lower than gasoline prices.
- **Kerosene:** Most of the kerosene consumed in India is sold through the Public Distribution System (PDS) to households with ration cards. Kerosene is traditionally heavily subsidized and regulated prices have hardly changed over the last decade despite large fluctuations in international prices. Instead, the central government has attempted to contain kerosene subsidies for several years by gradually reducing the availability of kerosene through the PDS (GSI 2014). There is an ongoing policy debate around the possibility of replacing kerosene subsidies with targeted cash transfers.
- **Liquid Petroleum Gas (LPG):** The subsidy cost of LPG has been controlled through rationing the quantity (number of cylinders) available to households. In September 2012, the government restricted the amount of LPG that households could purchase at subsidized prices to 6 cylinders per year. However, following sustained political pressure, in January 2013 this ceiling was increased 9 cylinders in January 2014 and then to 12 cylinders in April 2014. In November 2014, the new government announced its intention to reduce the ceiling from March 2015. In addition, a Direct Benefit Transfer (DBT) Scheme to replace subsidies was launched in 54 districts in November 2014 and was extended to the whole country (676 districts) starting January 2015. While the retail price does not anymore include a subsidy component, LPG is still heavily subsidized through the DBT. The effective price with the DBT is the same as with the subsidies price since the coverage and amount of the DBT is not reduced. The government recently launched a public campaign to motivate consumers who can afford to pay the market price for LPG to voluntary "give up" the DBT—as of June, 2015, only 162,430 consumers opted out of the subsidy.[2]

Despite recent reforms, energy prices in India are still below their efficient levels for most energy products. Figure 2 shows the level and decomposition of the efficient energy prices and the gap between current consumer prices and efficient prices, while Table 1 presents the required price increase to reach efficient prices. The highest price increases are for kerosene sold through the PDS (as opposed to through the market) and coal, which need to be increased by around 259 percent and 455 percent respectively. Although the required price increases for diesel and gasoline are smaller they are still substantial at around 69 percent and 67 percent respectively. These are the price increases for households (final consumers), and the equivalent price increases for firms (intermediate users) are slightly smaller given that the standard sales tax does not apply; for diesel and coal, the main intermediate fuels, the required price increases are 54 percent and 404 percent respectively.

Figure 2. Efficient prices (in rupees per liter and kg, as of June 2015)
Source: Parry 2015 database available at http://www.imf.org/external/np/fad/environ/. Note: Prices for Diesel, Petrol, and Kerosene are per liter, prices for LPG and Coal are per kg.

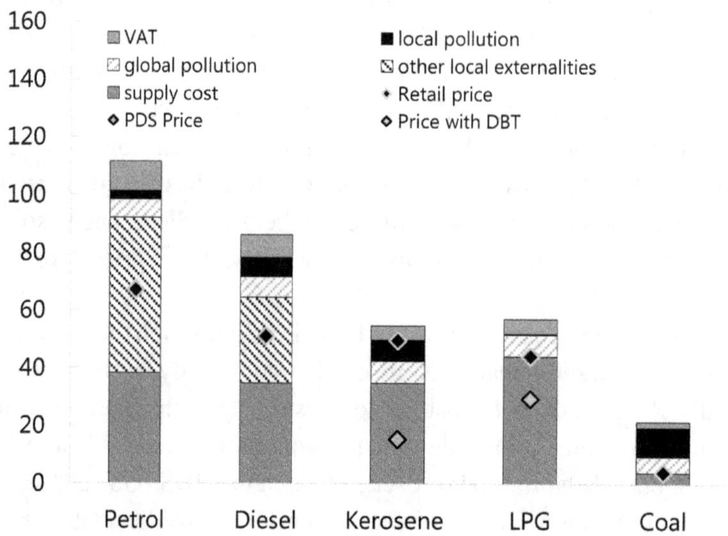

Table 1. Under-pricing of fuel products, June 2015 (in rupees per liter and kg)

	Efficient Price	Retail Price	Difference	Difference in Percentages
Petrol	111	61	45	0.67
Diesel	86	51	35	0.69
Kerosene P	55	15	39	2.59
Kerosene n	55	50	5	0.10
LPG	57	29	28	0.94
Coal	22	4	18	4.55

Source: IMF staff calculations, Indian Oil, IMF (2015) and. https://www.iocl.com/.

Notes: Prices for Petrol, Diesel and Kerosene are per liter prices for LPG and Coal are per kg. The retail price for LPG is the price of LPG that prevails net of the Direct Benefit Transfer.

4. IMPACT OF EFFICIENT PRICING

Methodology

The impact of energy subsidy reform on household real incomes can be separated into two components, the direct effect and the indirect effect (Arze del Granado, Coady, & Gillingham, 2012). The direct effect arises through the effect of higher prices for energy products consumed directly by households for cooking, heating, lighting and private transport. The indirect effect arises through the effect of higher prices for other goods and services consumed by households, which use energy products as an input and face higher production costs. The magnitude of these impacts depends on the importance of these products in total household consumption and on the extent these products are used to produce other services and goods. The distribution of the impacts across different income groups will depend on the relative importance of these factors across income groups. If the consumption baskets of higher-income groups are relatively more fuel intensive than those of lower-income groups, then the total impact will be greater for higher-income groups. The methodology used to estimate these impacts is described briefly below while a more detailed discussion can be found in Anand and others (2013, 2014).

The *direct impact* of a specific increase in the price of a fuel product, expressed as a percentage of total household consumption, can be calculated as:

Direct Impact = Budget Share * Percentage Increase in Fuel Price

For instance, if the budget share for a certain energy product is 0.03 (i.e. the household allocates 3 percent of its total consumption to this product) a doubling of this fuel price (an increase of 100 percent) will result in a decrease in real income for the household of an equivalent 3 percent. This estimate of the direct impact implicitly assumes that households do not reduce the impact by substituting away from fuel, i.e. that quantities of fuel consumed directly do not change. It is therefore often interpreted as either an estimate of the short-run impact (i.e., before households can adjust fuel consumption) or as an upper-bound of the long-run estimate.

Assessing the direct effect therefore requires data on household expenditures on energy products. The Indian National Socio-Economic Household Survey 2011/12 (the latest survey available to the authors) provides data on household expenditures for more than 600 products and services. These data are used to calculate the expenditures and the budget shares for each product. The budget share is calculated by dividing total expenditure for each product by total household consumption. Figure 3 presents the budget share for household direct consumption of fuel products and electricity for each household consumption decile. Higher-income households spend a substantially higher share of their income on energy.

Figure 3. Composition of household fuel expenditure by income group, 2011/12 (in percentages of total household income)
Source: IMF Staff estimates based on the Indian 2011-12 Household Socio-Economic Survey.

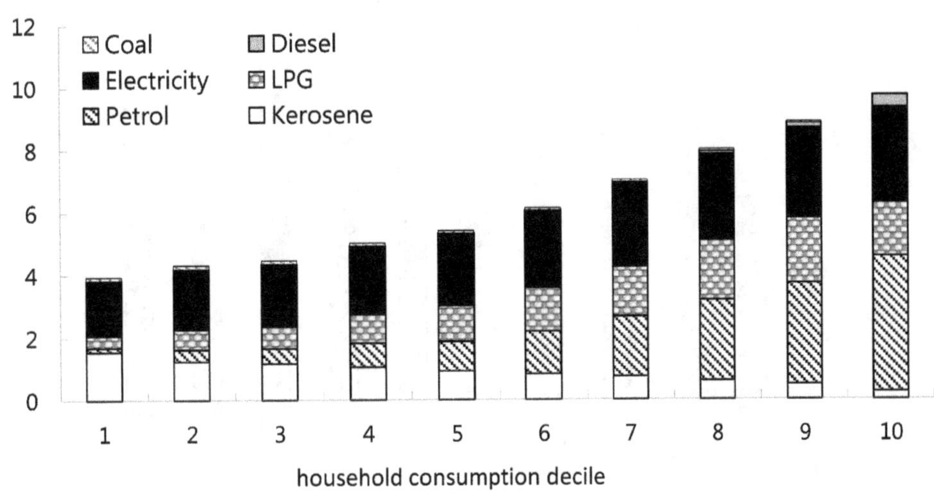

The composition of energy consumption also differs across income groups with lower-income groups allocating a relatively high share of energy expenditure to kerosene and higher-income groups relatively high shares to gasoline, diesel, LPG and electricity.

Estimating the *indirect impact* of fuel price increases requires a price-shifting model to estimate the impact of higher energy prices on the prices of other goods and services. We use the model developed by Coady and Newhouse (2006), which assumes that increases in energy production costs are fully passed forward onto the domestic output prices of goods and services. Estimating these price increases requires information on the production structure of the economy, e.g., an input-output table describing the share of different inputs in the production cost structure. In this chapter the input-output table for India for 2003/04 is used, which is disaggregated into 130 sectors. But again the implicit assumption of zero input demand price elasticity means that these estimates should also be interpreted as short-term impacts or upper-bounds on long-term impacts. The indirect impact is simulated through the increase of diesel and coal prices.[3] Once the impact of higher domestic fuel prices on the prices of other goods and services is estimated, these estimates are multiplied by the household budget shares for each of these consumption categories (taken from the household survey) to get the indirect impact of each price change.

Impact of Energy Price Reform

The total impact of higher energy prices on household real incomes, and how this varies across household income groups, is presented in Figure 4. On average, increasing energy prices to their efficient levels would decrease household real incomes by nearly 12 percent on average. The magnitude of this impact varies only slightly across income groups, but is slightly higher around 12½ percent, for the highest three income deciles.

Figure 4. Impact of energy price reform (in percent of total household consumption)
Source: IMF Staff estimates based on the Indian 2011-12 Household Socio-Economic Survey. Note: The indirect effect for diesel and coal excludes their impact through higher electricity prices, which is included under electricity.

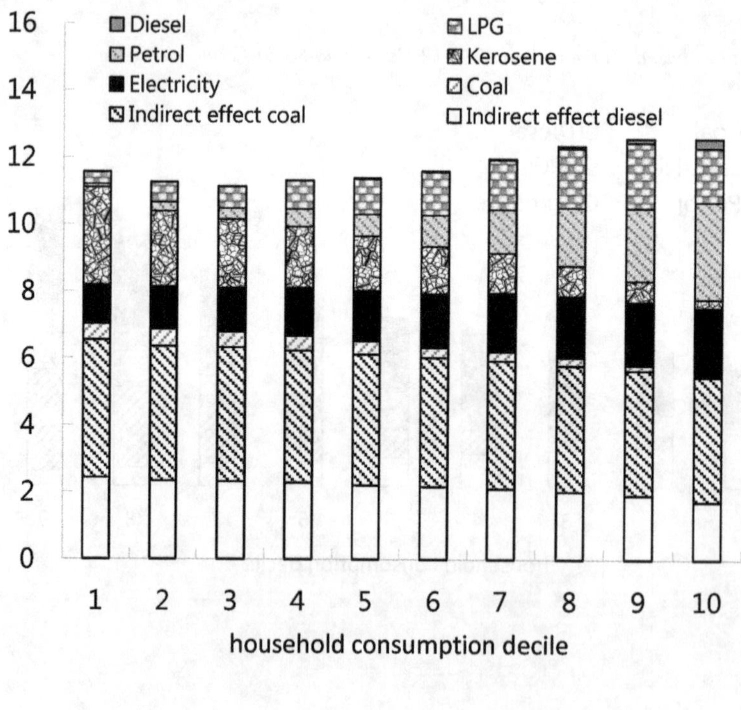

Figure 5. Effect price increase diesel and coal (in percentages)
Source: IMF Staff estimates based on the Input-Output table 2003/04 for India. Note: The price of diesel is increased by 54 percent. The price of coal is increased by 404 percent.

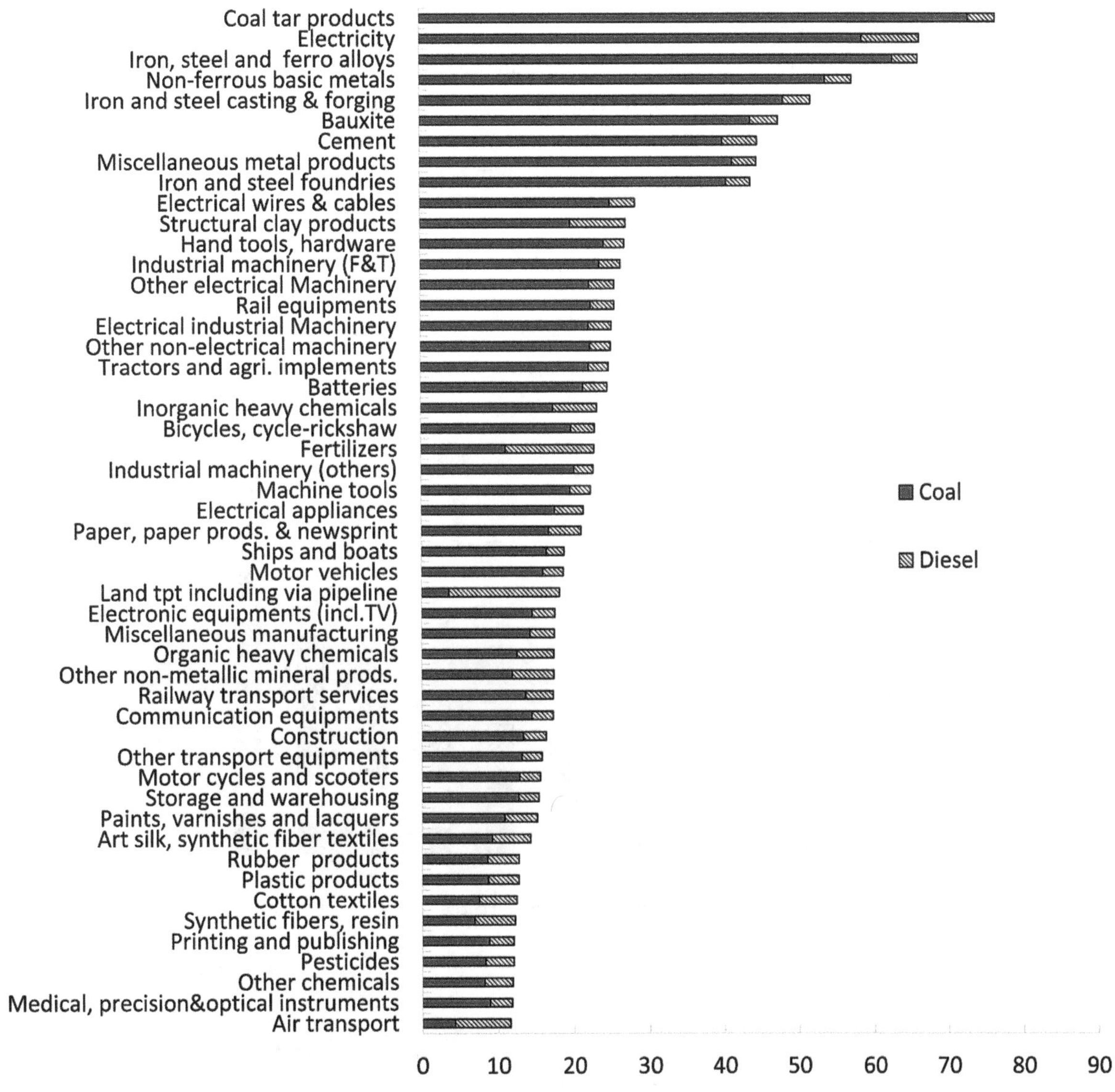

Around one third of the total impact comes through the direct effect of the price increases. Although the magnitude of the direct impact is broadly similar across income groups, its composition differs substantially. For lower-income households, the direct effect is mainly driven by the effect of the increase in kerosene prices reflecting the relative importance of kerosene prices in the budgets of these households and the large kerosene price increase. The direct effect on higher-income households is mainly driven the increase in gasoline and LPG prices reflecting their high gasoline and LPG budget shares.

Most of the indirect impact on households arises through the impact of higher coal prices (70 percent of the total indirect impact). The indirect impact – excluding the indirect effect through higher electricity prices - also varies very little across household income groups although is slightly progressive. The indirect effect arising through higher electricity prices is regressive and is mostly related to the increase in coal prices (around 90 percent). Moreover, the impact on the cost of production from higher coal and diesel prices (and therefore on their output prices given the models assumption of full shifting forward of cost increases) also varies substantially across sectors of the economy. Figure 5 presents the percentage increase in production costs for the fifty most-affected sectors. The impact of higher coal prices is substantially larger than fordiesel. With respect to the coal price increase, 4 sectors have cost increases that exceed 50 percent, and another 4 sectors have cost increases greater than 40 percent. With respect to diesel price increases, only 2 sectors show a cost increase higher than 10 percent with another 7 sectors showing cost increases above 5 percent.

Figure 6. Loss from energy price reform by household income group: a) loss in rupees per capita per month, b) share of total loss in percentages
Source: IMF Staff estimates based on the Indian 2011-12 Household Socio-Economic Survey.

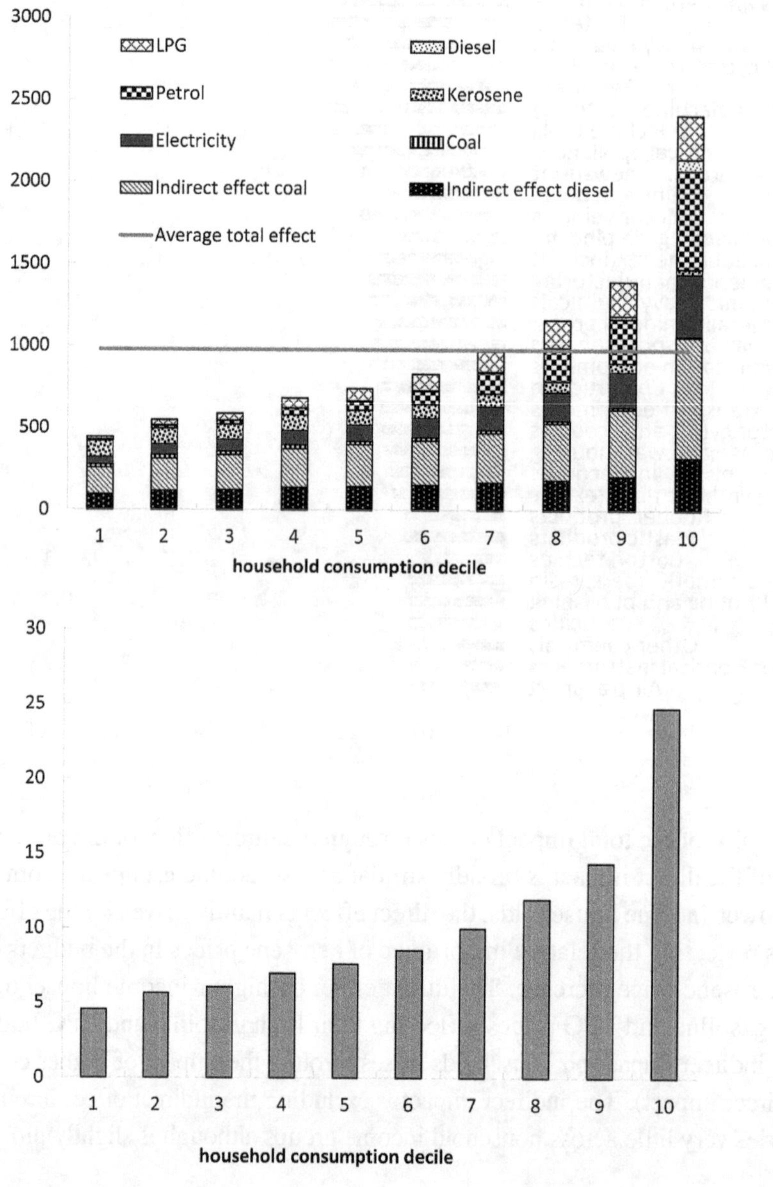

Although the impact of higher energy prices is very similar in percentage terms across income groups, the distribution of the burden is borne mainly by higher-income groups. Figure 6 shows the absolute size of the impact (Panel A) and the share of the total burden (Panel B) by income group and broken down by direct and indirect impacts and across products. Whereas the real income loss for the bottom income quintile is around Rs. 400 per capita per month, the loss for top two income quintile ranges from around Rs. 1400 to Rs. 2400 per capita per month. Reflecting this, the share of the burden borne by the bottom income quintile is around 5 percent compared to about 40 percent for the top two income quintiles.

5. CONCLUDING REMARKS

Although recent energy pricing reforms in India have substantially reduced the fiscal cost of energy subsidies, current energy prices are still substantially below their efficient levels. Efficient energy pricing requires that consumer energy prices reflect not only the supply cost of energy but also the social cost of energy consumption reflecting the environmental damage associate with energy consumption. Moving to these efficient prices would still require substantial additional increases in energy prices.

This chapter estimates the required price increases and their impact on household real incomes and its variation across household income groups. On average, the impact is large at about a 9 percent decrease in real incomes, with little variation across income groups. In addition, a number of energy-intensive sectors will experience large increases in production costs. These impacts are significant and will therefore require a package of complementary policies to mitigate the impact on households and firms and avoid an undesirable disruption of economic activity and increase in poverty. However, given the significant welfare gains to be reaped from more efficient energy pricing (i.e., from reduced environmental damage and higher fiscal revenues), there is a high social return to developing a successful reform package. For instance, Coady and others (2015) have estimated that moving to efficient pricing in India would reduce the costs associated with environmental damage (by reducing pollution and improving health as well as reducing congestion and accidents) by an equivalent of 7.6 percent of GDP and fossil-fuel related deaths by over 60 percent.

Given the large adverse impact on household real incomes, as well as the uncertainty around the precise magnitude of optimal energy taxation and household and firm behavioral responses, a gradual reform of energy pricing is desirable. This will allow households and firms time to adjust to higher energy prices and improve their energy efficiency so as to mitigate the impact of higher prices. It will also allow the government time to develop a package of complementary measures to strengthen safety nets to protect the poor as well as introduce temporary measures to improve energy efficiency in the most energy-intensive sectors of the economy. Previous studies have highlighted a range of additional measures that can facilitate successful pricing reform, including: embedding energy price reforms within a more comprehensive reform plan, developing an effective communications strategy, and depolitization of energy pricing through eventual price liberalization (Clements and others, 2013; Anand and others, 2014).

REFERENCES

Abdallah, C., Coady, D., Gupta, S., & Hanedar, E. (2015). *The Quest for the Holy Grail: Efficient and Equitable Fiscal Conoslidation in India*. IMF Working Paper (WP/15/152).

Anand, R., Coady, D., Mohommad, A., Thakoor, A., & Walsh, J. (2013). *The Fiscal and Welfare Impacts of Reforming Fuel Subsidies in India*. IMF Working Paper (WP/13/128).

Anand, R., Coady, D., Mohommad, A., Thakoor A., Walsh, J., (2014). Fiscal and Welfare Impacts of Fuel Subsidy Reform in India. *Economic & Political Weekly*, *49*(28).

Arze del Granado, J., Coady, D., & Gillingham, R. (2012). The Unequal Benefits of Fuel Subsidies: A Review of Evidence for Developing Countries. *World Development*, *40*(11), pp2234–pp2248. doi:10.1016/j.worlddev.2012.05.005

Clements, B., Coady, D., Fabrizio, S., Gupta, S., Alleyne, T., & Sdralevich, C. (2013). *Energy subsidy Reform, Lessons and Implications*. IMF.

Coady, D., Flamini, V., & Sears, L. (2015). The Unequal Benefits of Fuel Subsidies Revisited: Evidence for Developing Countries. In Inequality and Fiscal Policy. IMF Working Paper (WP/15/250)

Coady, D., & Newhouse, D. (2006). Evaluating the distribution of the real income effects of increases in petroleum product prices in Ghana. In A. Coudouel, A. Dani, & S. Paternostro (Eds.), *Analyzing the distributional impacts of reforms: Operational experience in implementing poverty and social impact analysis*. Washington, DC: World Bank.

Coady, D., Parry, I., Sears, L., & Shang, B. (2015). *How Large Are Global Energy Subsidies?* IMF Working Paper (WP/13/105).

Diamond, Peter A., & Mirrlees, James A. (1971). *Optimal Taxation and Public Production II: Tax Rules*. The American Economic Review.

Global Subsidies Initiative. (2012). *India's Fuel Subsidies: Q & A*. International Institute for Sustainable Development.

Global Subsidies Initiative. (2014a). *Subsidies to Liquefied Petroleum Gas in India: An Overview of Recent Reforms*. Author.

Global Subsidies Initiative. (2014b). *India Energy Subsidy Review: A biannual Survey of Energy Subsidy Policies*. Author.

Parry, I., Heine, D., Lis, E., & Li, S. (2014). *Getting energy prices Right, From principle to practice*. IMF.

ENDNOTES

1 Although other policy instruments such as congestion charges, speed regulations and fines, may be more efficient at addressing these external impacts (reflecting the fact that they are only indirectly linked with fuel consumption), for most countries these policy instruments are not well developed and energy consumption taxes provide a relatively efficient alternative.

2 http://www.givitup.in/

3 The optimal price for diesel and coal used as an intermediate good excludes the VAT. The required price increase is therefore less than for final consumption and is respectively 54 percent and 404 percent.

Chapter 11
Nonlinearity of Energy Transition in India and Implications for Sustainability Science:
An Exploratory Insight

Anandajit Goswami
The Energy and Resources Institute (TERI), India

Arabinda Mishra
ICIMOD, Nepal

Kaushik Bandopadhyay
TERI University, India

ABSTRACT

Policy discourse on rural energy transition within developing countries approach the issue of energy transition through linearly structured, causality based models. This work aims to explore, question the authenticity of such an approach through exploring existence of non linearity in the rural energy transition process of India. Energy transition of rural households impact social, economic and environmental domains of sustainability. For instance, a switchover of a household from smoke generating mudstoves to clean cookstoves can reduce smoke generation, chance of respiratory diseases, impacting the economic, environment and social domains of sustainability. Transition to clean cookstoves can be non-linear and such a transition in a non-linear way impacts domains of sustainability. Hence this work tries to contextualize rural energy transition process through econometric methods, spatial theory of chaos. The work concludes with the exploration of non linear aspects of rural energy transition process within the local rural context and connects it to sustainability science.

DOI: 10.4018/978-1-5225-0094-0.ch011

INTRODUCTION

Provision of minimum electricity, energy to meet basic energy service needs of rural households of India has come to forefront in several policy discourses. The need to provide basic levels of primary energy to address the minimum energy access needs of rural households have also come to fore front (Srivastava, et. al, 2012).

Within these policy discourses, need for upliftment of rural households in an energy transition ladder has emerged. From a macro level policy perspective, the larger view is that with an increase in income, households should move towards modern and cleaner forms of energy usages. This macro level perspective has stayed on in policy debates related to energy transition even though any energy transition (which is a small type of transition amongst various forms of transition) is a micro-level occurence that happens owing to interaction of several factors. A top down macro-perspective to explain household energy transition in a linear, causal way can therefore be fraught with intuitive loopholes. Energy transition impacts the social, economic and environmental domains of sustainability and at the same time these social, economic and environmental domains also impact energy transition. Therefore, the connection between rural energy transition and sustainability is not a causal phenomenon and can be nonlinear, interactive in nature while an attempt is made to associate it with the theme of sustainability.

Rural energy transition is a microlevel phenomenon of a household which is determined by several socioeconomic, political, behavioural contexts of households. It also has a continuous strategic, coordinated interaction response of households to various factors specific to households, local contextualization of macro policies, behaviour, psychology, culture, sociology. A causality based macro model to understand such a micro level change might not always be accustomed to capture necessary processes that leads to specific energy transition behaviour within rural households. However, in spite of this intuitive limitation and fallacy, energy transition processes are often attempted to be captured by a causality approach. In order to understand broader narrative of interlinkages between rural energy transition and sustainability there is a need to come out of causal process based methods and move towards understanding of nonlinearities within the energy transition process.

Causal process analysis of rural energy transition are not sensitive to nonlinear dimensions of an energy transition phenomenon. In such causal processes, mostly statistical regression techniques are applied which might not be the appropriate, intuitive transformation of normative storylines that guide an energy transition process within rural households of a developing country like India. For developing countries, complexities of such storylines are much more subtle, multidirectional and will not be captured by a linear statistical regression method. Therefore, this chapter attempts to comment on evidences of non linearity in the context of rural household energy transition of India after setting out the larger policy context. It also attempts to initiate a non-linear analytical thinking process for understanding rural energy transition of rural households of India.

The next section therefore starts with the policy context and moves onto different macrolevel perspectives on rural energy transition pattern of India emerging from Census and National Sample Survey Organization data. After setting out the macro perspectives, the different sections of the chapter moves onto a micro perspective of analysing the pattern of rural energy transition in India. As a part of such micro perspectives, the chapter assesses the context of energy poverty in different states of India. From there it narrows down to some key states which are not doing well in terms of energy poverty and access. The reason for such narrowing down is to assess what drives energy transition in these states. In order to explore that, several factors which are important at a downscaled level of a state and can impact social, economic and environmental domains of sustainability are further explored.

In order to do that, agricultural index, industry, transportation, professional services, housing loan index, trade index, finance index and other factors at each district of selected states are collated. Their relative positioning in these states are assessed as these indices in a way impact economic, environmental, social domains of sustainability and might also impact rural energy transition in these states. This is done to establish the context behind several associated factors guiding the economic, social domains of sustainability and rural energy transition context in such select states.

Once that is done, from the identified states, one of the states is chosen which is comparatively not doing well in terms of these indicators and where associated non- linear factors might guide rural energy transition. For such an investigation, within the select state, a particular fuel is chosen. The pattern of non-linearity in the specific selected fuel consumption is empirically tested across rural households of the particular state for thirty year time period using the Census data. This helps to understand if there are any evidences of non-linearity in rural energy transition of India.

Following this, the chapter further draws out narratives from this analysis for developmental policy discourse and its implications for broader social, economic and environmental domains of sustainability.

Therefore, the chapter is divided into the following sections. Section 1 starts with the policy context and moves onto the macro perspectives emerging regarding energy transition in the context of India. Thereafter, the Section 2 and 3 establishes a context of energy transition and sustainability and it is followed by the micro perspectives of such a connection at the backdrop of three states–Madhya Pradesh, Bihar and Odisha.

Finally, in the subsection of section 3, this is followed by an empirical, statistical testing of non linearity of fuelwood consumption in the context of Bihar. The last section of the chapter leads and sets the context for a developmental policy discourse that justifies need for such a discourse to understand the connection between rural energy transition and sustainability science.

POLICY CONTEXT

Rural Electrification

Rural Electrification has been considered as one of the necessary policy interventions within India to create an energy transition for select rural households of India. Need for rural electrification was mentioned in the first five year plan (1951 – 56) and it gained importance in the second and third five year plans of India.

In 1969, Rural Electrification Corporation was established within India with the support of United States Agency for International Development (USAID) and over the years it has implemented policies to facilitate rural electrification in Indian states.

Within India, maximum rural electrification was done during 5th, 6th and 7th Five-Year Plans (1974-1990). Prior to launch of Rajiv Gandhi Vidyutikaran Yojana (RGGVY), several rural electrification programmes were initiated within India. These were included under the *Minimum Needs Programme, Kutir Jyoti Scheme, Pradhan Mantri Gramodya Yojana, Accelerated Rural Electrification Programme, Rural Electricity Supply Technology Mission*.

Under all these programmes, soft loans and subsidy provisions were made to accelerate rural electrification with a specific focus on backward poverty stricken households. Hence, as a part of these programmes there was a clear direction on addressing the economic, social domains of sustainability.

Table 1. Factors from domains of sustainability determining the choice of cooking fuel

Iteration 35: log likelihood = -4.053e-13						
Iteration 36: log likelihood = -1.512e-13						
Iteration 37: log likelihood = -5.418e-14						
Iteration 38: log likelihood = -2.043e-14						
Iteration 39: log likelihood = -8.438e-15						
Iteration 40: log likelihood = -2.220e-15						
Multinomial logistic regression		Number of obs = 50				
		LR chi2(5) = 50.04				
		Prob > chi2 = 0.0000				
Log likelihood = -2.220e-15		Pseudo R2 = 1.0000				
Ckcode	**Coef.**	**Std. Err.**	**z**	**P>|z|**	**[95% Conf. Interval]**	
TCQty341	-.0019424	1258.362	-0.00	1.000	-2466.347	2466.343
hhtype	-45.93487	1.12e+08	-0.00	1.000	-2.19e+08	2.19e+08
mpceurp	.0076063	4593.685	0.00	1.000	-9003.45	9003.465
regsal	-77.55606	1.21e+08	-0.00	1.000	-2.37e+08	2.37e+08
MPCErural	-.3305957	275727.8	-0.00	1.000	-540416.8	540416.2
_cons	-167.1463	3.48e+08	-0.00	1.000	-6.81e+08	6.81e+08

(ckcode==2 is the base outcome).

This was done with an aim of providing larger access to modern forms of energy to rural households and thereby facilitate their transition to modern fuels by means of macro level policies. However, though, village electrification has increased rapidly within the country, household electrification has not happened to the same extent. Proof of this fact can be witnessed from the Table 1 which shows in terms of lighting needs, both Bihar and Odisha has still not been able to upscale their energy transition.

Provision of Clean Cooking and Electricity

Even within the policy space dealing with provision of energy to create transition of rural households towards clean cooking, Bihar and Odisha stayed below many of the Indian states like Andhra Pradesh, Kerala, Sikkim, Karnataka. Further, in terms of the physical achievement of providing electricity to different types of households: the Figure 1 suggests that there has been an underachievement in provision of electricity to households of these states too.

Hence the facts in Figure 1 indicate a disconnect between the policy space dealing with lighting and cooking choices of rural households of India and the actual energy transition happening within rural households of India that impact the social and economic domains of sustainability in the microcontext of specific rural households.

Further, a study by Hanna et. al (2012) indicates that degree, extent of energy transition of select rural households in Odisha in terms of their cooking choices depends on how households value a clean cookstove option and its effects on their health in the long term.

Figure 1. Status of electrification in states of India
Source: Energizing India, Expanding Electricity Access in Rural Areas, United Nations Development Programme (UNDP) Case Study 12, Environment and Energy.

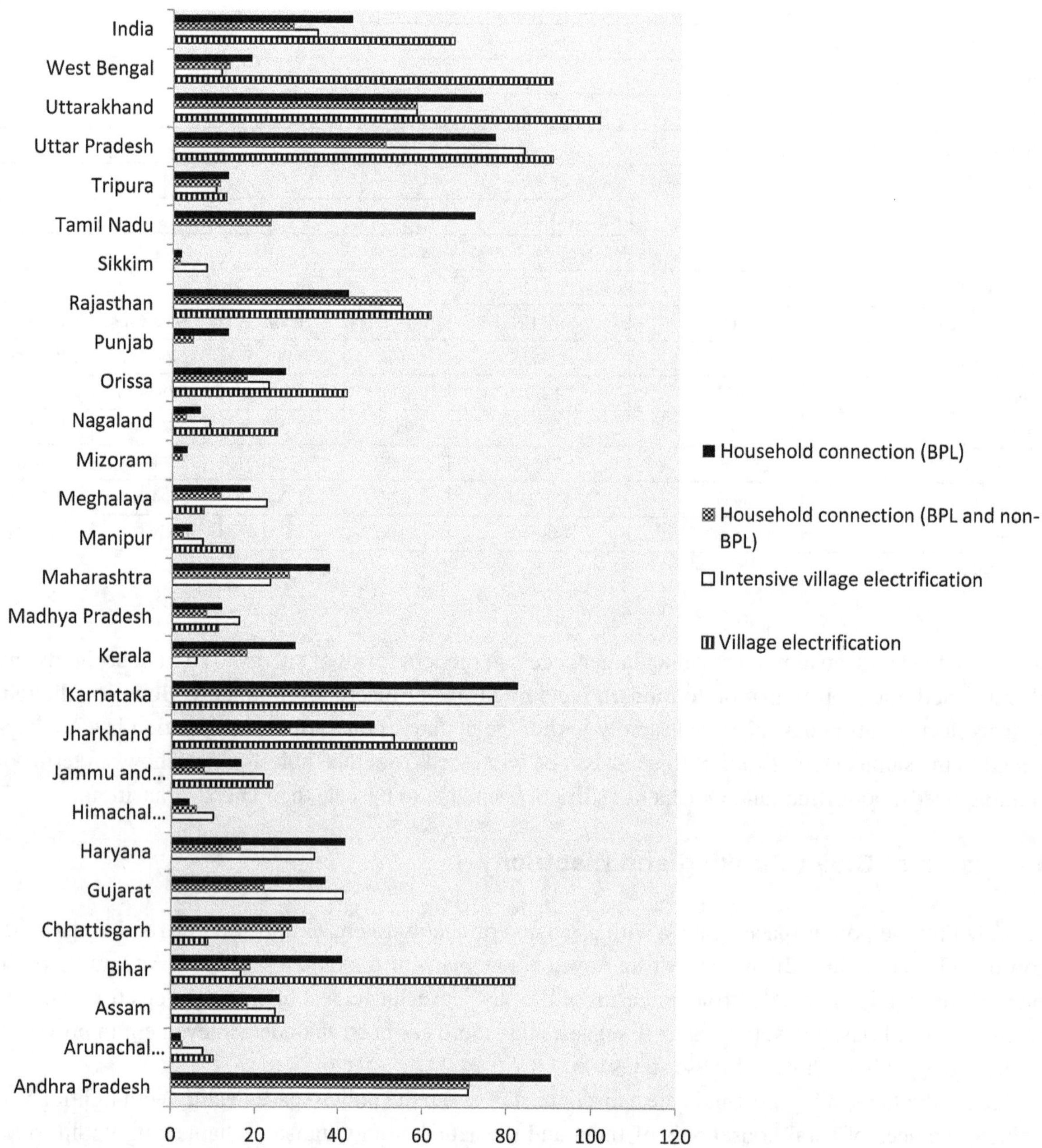

According to this study, clean cookstove usage and reduction in fuelwood use for cooking did not happen to a large extent for select rural households as in their valuation framework, stove was not going to create long term health benefits. Owing to this reason, inspite of stove breakages, rural households did not make investments in maintaining the stove for long term health benefits and gradually there was a reduction in number of meals cooked with good stoves creating a hindering factor in reducing fuelwood usage for meeting cooking needs of rural households.

With this policy context and background, section below indicates some of the perspectives from the larger evidences out of the macrodata analysis that empirically hint towards existence of non linearity in energy consumption behaviour in rural households of India.

PERSPECTIVES FROM MACROANALYSIS

Energy transition in different places of India will be dependent on the local context related to their livelihoods and income earnings, transportation, level of industrial activity (proxy of growth), availability of credits, finance and other opportunities of income generation within the local areas.

Nature of variation amongst agriculture, transportation, industrial, professional, financial and other related activities will guide the degree, nature of rural energy transition in different districts of India and will also impinge upon the economic and social domains of sustainability in a varying way while the rural households move towards an energy transition path.

In order to establish this variation within districts, across states of India mentioned in Figure 2 indicate the nature of differences in states like Uttar Pradesh (U.P.), Bihar and Madhya Pradesh (M.P.). This is done to show how within districts, the indicators that can decide the nature of rural energy transition and hence can impact on the different domains of sustainability are varying.

Figure 2. Statewise variation in economic and other related activities that can impact sustainability
Source: Based on BIU-Datanet India Estimates.

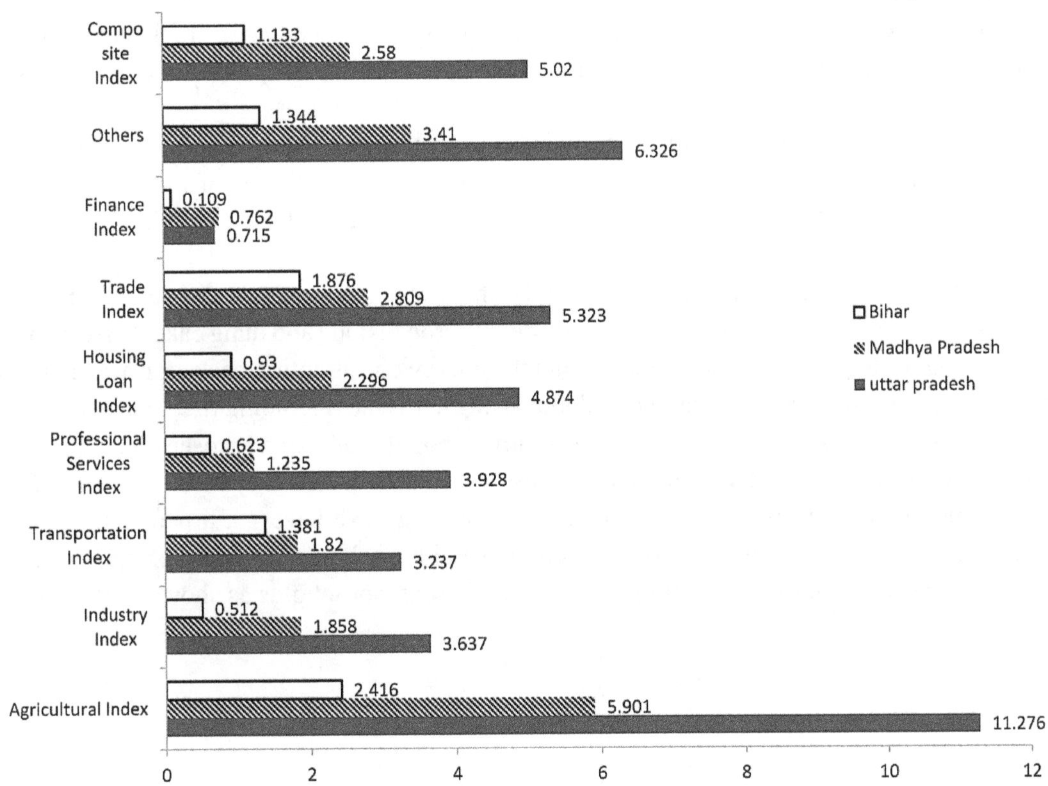

Such an exposition further highlights that sustainability domains will be impacted differentially while the select states move on its energy transition path. For each of the state indicators are constructed to show the level of economic activities viz. agricultural activity (captured by agricultural index), industry activity (captured by industry index), transportation activity (captured by transportation index) and so on.

Higher value of an indicator suggests a better position of the state in such an activity which thereby implies that such an indicator will positively impact the social and economic domain of sustainability within the state. It might therefore positively impact the social, economic domains of sustainability and contribute to the transition of rural households to modern clean fuels.

District level heterogeneities across states like U.P., Bihar and Madhya Pradesh indicate that there are socioeconomic, infrastructural and other different types of disparities that might exist even within districts of these states. These causal factors will also create varying triggering factors impacting the energy transition in these states of India.

Therefore the chapter attempts to look onto non linearity in the energy consumption behaviour of rural households in these three states of India. Analysis of NSSO 66th round data suggests that monthly per capita consumption of firewood of rural household is around 30 kg and the same for Liquefied Petroleum Gas (LPG) is around 2 kgs. These fuels are used largely for cooking purposes. Rural households are still relying on traditional fuels for cooking purposes. Approximately, 76% of rural households rely on traditional biomass for cooking and only around 12% of them rely on LPG. In comparison to this, 65% of urban households rely on LPG for cooking. Within rural households, 65% of rural households depend on electricity for lighting whereas 90% of urban households use electricity for lighting.

These observations from NSSO data are based on sampled data and can have sampling errors. Therefore there is also a need to validate these findings with household specific census observations which includes all household data.

Analysis of observations from the Census 2011 data shows that percentage of fuelwood used by rural households of India has stayed above 60% all throughout during 1990 – 2011. The percentage was higher than 80% during 1990 – 2000 and in 2004 – 05.

However, during 2011, it came down below 80%. Essentially, it highlights that biomass based fuelwood still remains the main source of energy source for rural households of India though over the years its usage has gone down. Mostly fuelwood is used for meeting cooking and lighting needs of rural households of India (Figure 3).

This is buttressed by the mentioned fact (Figure 4) which suggests that fuelwood still comprises of the larger pie of energy usage of rural households followed by crop residue and dung cake. Modern fuels like electricity, LPG occupy a much lower share within the energy consumption basket of rural households.

In addition to that, percentage of rural population using kerosene (including firewood and dung) have not substantially changed (Figure 5). Percentage of urban population using kerosene has declined from 75% to 14% whereas the same for traditional biomass energy has declined by more than 50%. Biomass based fuel options like fire-wood, crop residue and cowdung cake have got a penetration of 62.5%, 12.3% and 10.9%. However, transition to electricity in rural households has not picked up well. This is validated by the gap in the use of electricity by rural and urban households as shown in the Figure 6.

Figure 3. Households using different forms of fuels
Source: Estimated from Census 2011, the sum of the percentage of households do not add to 100% as at any point of time the same households are using a set of fuels for meeting their cooking, lighting and heating needs.

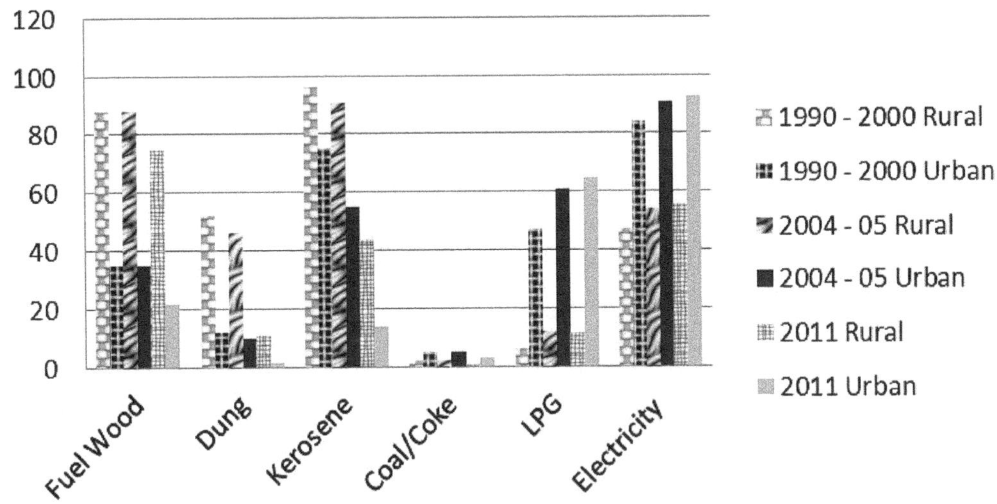

This posits an interesting question on the nature of energy transition happening in India. In terms of energy consumption for meeting lighting demands, the transition gap between urban and rural households have been estimated which is presented in the Figure 6.

In order to reduce this gap, some states need to be electrified to a larger extent. The Figure 7 suggests a mapping of states that needs to be prioritised and targeted for electrification to reduce this transition gap. Such a prioritization can be based on the degree of rural electrification status of each states of India (Figure 7).

Figure 4. Rural households using different fuel types
Source: Estimated from National Census, 2011.

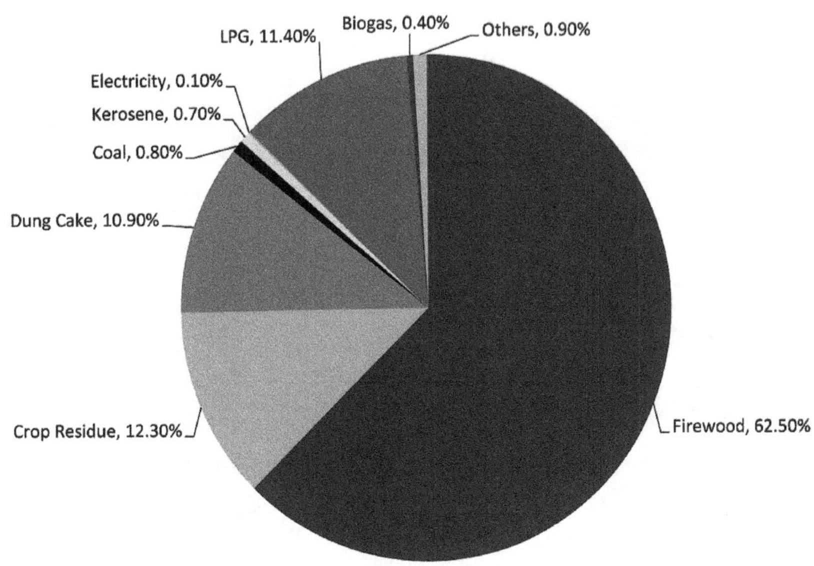

Figure 5. Urban households using different fuel types
Source: Estimated from National Census, 2011.

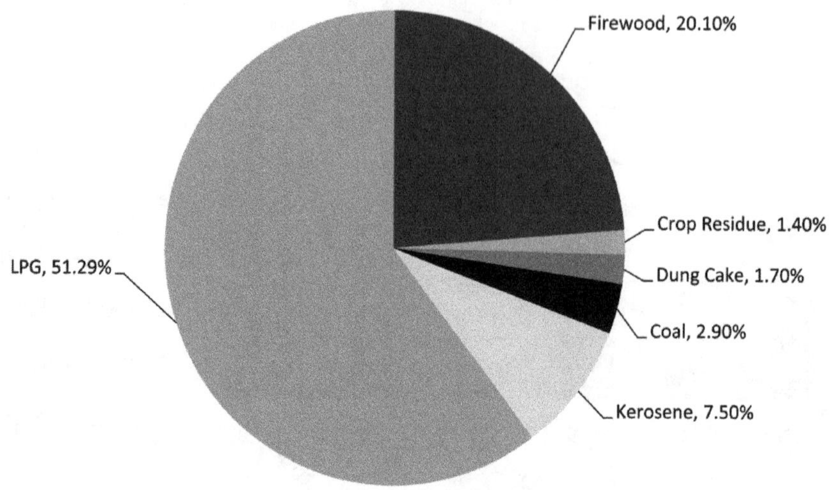

In addition to the electrification status, it is important to know whether the quality of electricity supply has any role towards a stochastic, nonlinear pattern of energy transition of rural households of India that can thereafter impact the various domains of sustainability of rural households.

Figure 6. Households using different types of fuel for lighting
Source: Estimated from National Census, 2011.

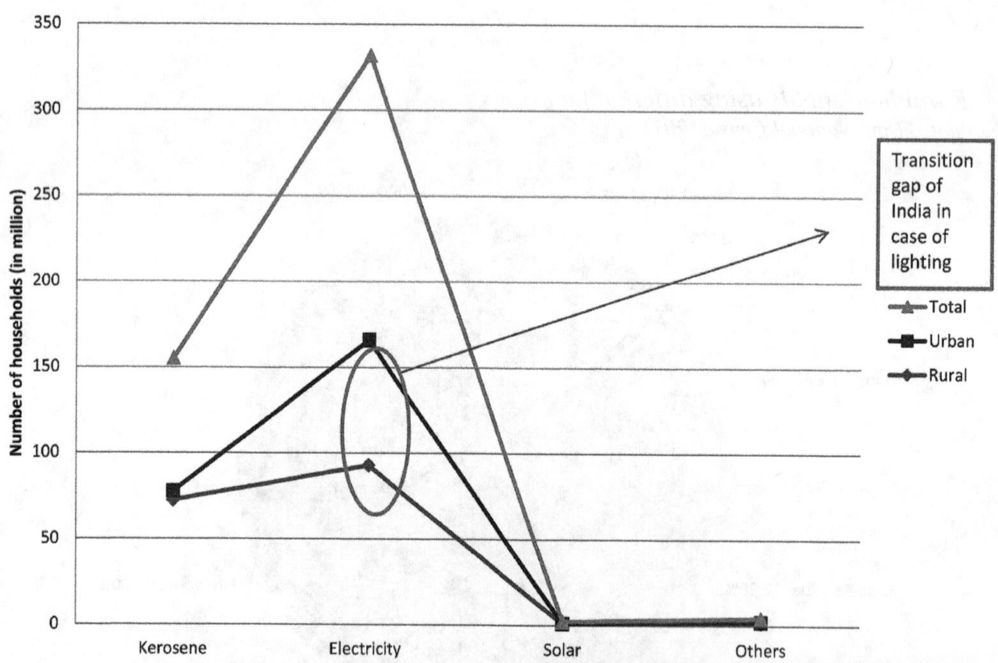

Figure 7. Statewise electrification status
Source: Estimated from Census 2011.

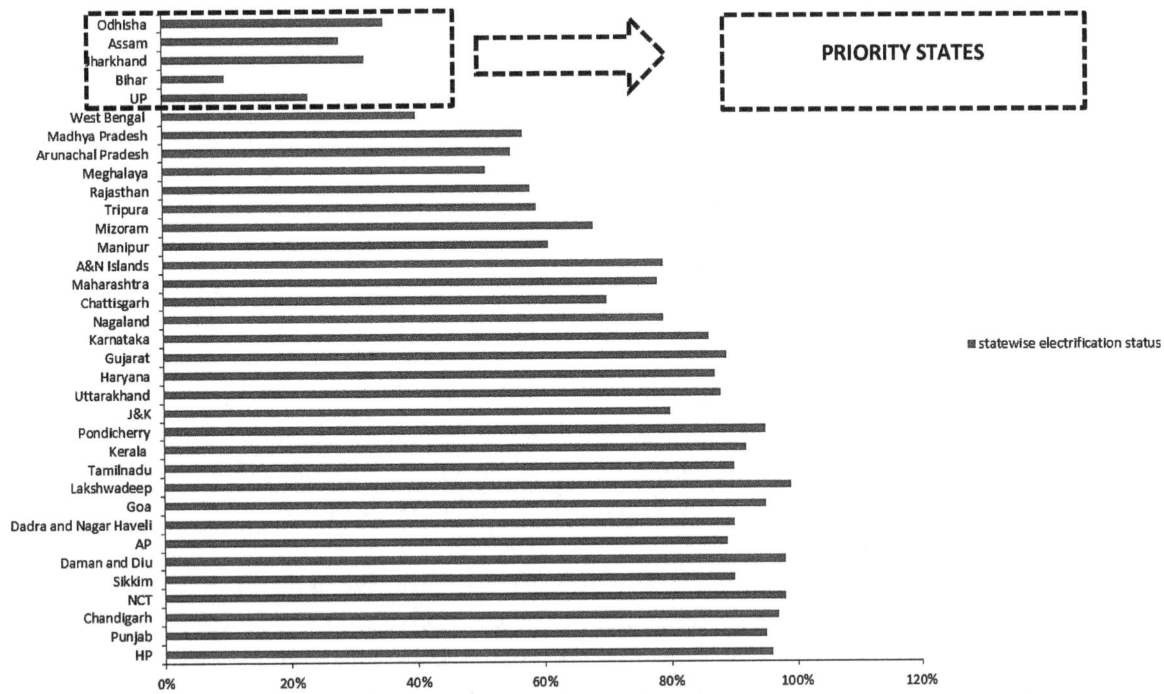

From different rounds of NSSO data it emerges that in case of cooking choices of rural households, for cooking firewood and LPG, whereas for lighting, kerosene and electricity has been largely used. Primary cooking fuel has been firewood and LPG whereas primary lighting fuel has been "Electricity and Kerosene" respectively for rural households.

Switch from firewood to LPG is occurring only among higher income classes. Thus, in case of cooking fuels data from Census, it emerges that there is no real transition happening in terms of access to modern cooking fuels. However, some fact finding from different rounds of NSSO data clearly shows a different story of transition, sustainability which in no way matches with what the literature indicates about a linear hypothesis of rural energy transition between income and switch to clean, modern fuels.

In case of kerosene and lighting usage by rural households of India, it can be found that while in the 55th round (1999-2000), switch from kerosene to clean lighting was happening around the 8th monthly per capita expenditure class (MPCE); in 61st round (2004-05) it has started happening in the 6th MPCE class; and, in the 66th round (2009-10) it is seen to be around the 3rd MPCE class (Ramji et. al. 2012).

This therefore suggests that the switch to modern lighting fuels is showing a tendency to happen in the lower income classes over time. It therefore highlights that a rural energy transition can impact social and economic domains of sustainability for lower income classes of rural households of India.

A linear relation between income of rural households of India and a switch to clean lighting sources is more prominent for fuel options of lighting. One of the reasons for this could be spill over effects of implementation of National Level Rural Electrification Program (Rajiv Gandhi Grameen Vidyutikaran Yojana or RGGVY).

However, a stark contrast in the pattern emerges in case of firewood consumption for cooking. It can be observed that, in case of firewood for cooking, household firewood consumption increases from 1999-2000 to 2004-05 and then it slightly declines in 2009-10. Actual quantity of reported consumption level in 2009-10 was higher than that reported in 1999-2000.

In comparison, electricity consumption has increased by almost 25% - 30% between1999 - 2009. However for LPG, though there have been slight marginal changes in consumption over time, it remained more or less constant. Therefore, a linear consistency in energy consumption behaviour for fire woods, electricity and LPG is not maintained. Electricity consumption still shows a linear transition path between rural household incomes and electricity consumption. But the same does not hold true for other fuel options like firewood which is used for cooking. This raises the scope of tracing out the extent and degree of non linearity in these fuel options.

This direction and conclusion can further be validated by some specific findings with respect to firewood consumption. Within low income groups per household firewood consumption has gone up from 95 kg per month (55th Round, NSSO) to about 102 kg per month (66th Round, NSSO). For medium income households, a significant increase from 107 kg per month (55th Round, NSSO) to about 125 kg per month (61st Round, NSSO) happens and then a sudden decline occurs to about 115 kg per month by the 66th Round of NSSO for the medium income households.

This shows over the years there is no general linear pattern of change in the firewood consumption behaviour within the rural households which establishes the notion of a possible presence of uncertain, non-linear stochastic element within the firewood consumption behaviour of rural households of India. There is no direct causal linear connection between income classes, firewood consumption over time.

Such a non-linear pattern holds even for LPG consumption. For instance, no income groups indicate an increase in LPG consumption from the 55th to the 61st while from the 61st to the 66th round there is a decline in LPG consumption. Unlike the other fuels, penetration of LPG has also not increased quite a lot as observed from the NSSO data. For lower Income households, LPG consumption is constant at about 6 – 8kg per month; medium income households consume about around 10kg per month; and, high income households consume about 10kg per month. There has been no significant change in LPG consumption with a change in the income classes. It therefore indicates a non-linearity in the LPG consumption behavior across the income classes over time.

From the macro data, it emerges that the change and shift towards modern forms of fuel like LPG for cooking is stochastic and does not have a deterministic relationship with an income variable. This further enhances the scope to explore the stochasticity in the LPG consumption behavior of rural households of India. However, though the above fuel specific consumption *(which hints towards a nonlinear, non-deterministic relationship between income and transition to modern form of fuel usage of rural households of India)* gives us a broad trend of how the consumption is happening, it still does not explain many hidden factors that decides the chance, possibility of a rural household making a switchover decision from one fuel to the other viz. say from firewood to LPG for cooking.

Any such switch as a part of energy transition is an outcome of several interactive mechanisms between socioeconomic, political, cultural, anthropological, behavioural variables that exists within a society and can impact a rural household. The general transition literature describes energy transition as a small transition (Den Bergh, et.al, 2006) and indicates energy transition from one point to the other as an outcome of series of interactive, coordinated strategies and as a strategic game between individuals within a society.

Therefore, any energy transition can have multiple equilibria and can be guided by nonlinearity and a steady state linear transformation visa vis income of rural households might not hold. In order to explore such multiple equilibria, there is a need to come out of the traditional theoretical paradigm and its definition of equilibrium.

Hence, at any point of time, for a macro level, several factors can be impacting such a transformation and each of the factors impact the different domains of sustainability in a differential manner. The next section therefore attempts to find out how at a national level some of these factors might be impacting the energy transition in terms of the changes in fuel choices for rural households. This is being done by means of a multinomial logit model.

Macro Econometric Analysis for Understanding the Factors Deciding the Switch from One Fuel to the Other for Rural Households of India

The objective of the macroeconometric analysis is to understand what factors determine the probability of rural households switching over from one fuel to the other. In order to do that, a multinomial logit model is established to understand the switchover pattern of rural households from one fuel to the other. Before presenting some of the findings of the broader macroanalysis, some basic assumptions and facts have to be laid out. From the set of results emerging from the multinomial logit model. In the model, the base outcome indicates the predominant cooking fuel being used by households in the sample. The data used in our multinomial logit model is taken from NSSO 66th Round.

In this case, the base outcome is 2 which means that the primary cooking fuel for most households is firewood (code=2). The multinomial logit model gives the probability of a household switching from firewood to any other outcome (code=1,...,10 except 2)1, given certain parameters, explanatory variables which are chosen in our analysis.

Explanatory variables in our analysis includes – marginal per capita expenditure, district location, internet access (proxy of technology access), availability of regular salary, household type, calorific value of fuel, type of the social group in which the rural households belong to. Each of these factors impact the social and economic domains of sustainability for rural households of India and owing to that they are being included in the model. By bringing them in the modelling, an attempt is made to understand how different indicators encompassing the social, economic domains of sustainability finally decides the extent, degree and significance of rural household energy usage.

Some of the initial findings emerging from the multinomial logit model is explained in Table 1.

Table 1 shows that the choice of cooking fuel is significantly related to use of

firewood, chips. It is also being significantly impacted by regular salary of households and marginal per capita expenditure of the rural households. This means that the chance of people in rural households of India switching to LPG from firewood is statistically significant and dependent on regular salary of the households and marginal per capita expenditure of the rural households. It clearly signifies the association between the economic domain of sustainability and the chance of people in rural households of India switching to LPG from firewood.

Marginal per capita expenditure of households is nothing but a reflection of the economic domain of sustainability of rural households. Thus, indicating that while income is significant (seen by significance of regsal), the attitude and perceptions of households regarding their development and expenditure priorities have an important role to play in the choice of the primary cooking fuel. A household may have the disposable income to spend on LPG, but unless it perceives that use of firewood has significant health impacts for them, the switch to cleaner fuels will remain to be realized and felt.

However, sustainability of rural households are also determined by location specific issues. Geographical spaces, remoteness of location often decide the social, cultural, anthropological construct of a place which thereby can impact the choice of a rural household energy transition. In order to test that, the macroeconometric model assesses the impact of districts on fuel choices for cooking. The Table 2 highlights the results.

Table 2 indicates that the type of district and geographical locations have a positive, significant impact on the use of all cooking fuels except the cooking fuel arrangement. This posits that the chance of people switching from firewood to coal, lpg, gobar gas, dung cake, charcoal, kerosene, electricity, others is dependent on the location of districts and hence it is very much geographical context specific.

The fact that fuel switching is determined by geographical contexts is a reflection of not just natural resource availability such as forests, but also of the state policies and their actual level of implementation. The positive coefficient indicates that better policy making and implementation will go a long way in determining fuel switching and household energy choices.

The modelling in Table 2 is followed by an exercise to understand the nature of impact of household size, religion, social group belonging on fuel choices made for cooking by rural households. Location of a rural household in a district, household size, religion, social group determines the social component of sustainability for rural households. The modelling exercise to understand the connection between them and the fuel choices for cooking hints towards the association between social domains of sustainability and the chance of rural energy transition.

The results in the Table 3 shows that the type and geographical location of a district impacts significantly the chance of switching to coal, lpg, gobar gas, dung cake, charcoal, kerosene, electricity, others from firewood. Location of a rural household often creates the social, anthropological and cultural construct of rural households and determine the social and economic domains of sustainability. A positive association between the type and geographical location of a district and the chance of switching to coal, lpg, gobar gas, dung cake, charcoal, kerosene, electricity, others from firewood strengthens the narrative of connection of social, economic domains of sustainability and the chance of switching to coal, lpg, gobar gas, dung cake, charcoal, kerosene, electricity, others from firewood for cooking.

In addition to this, access to new technology, internet also decides the social and cultural construct of today's modern India. It also determines the social and economic domains of sustainability by empowering rural households with more information. Therefore, through a macroecometric modelling exercise an attempt is made to explore any association between internet access and the chance of switchover from one fuel to the other by rural households of India. The Table 4 highlights such results:

Results of the macro econometric modelling conducted for lighting choices indicate that access to internet (which is a proxy of access to technology) impacts the chance of switching from electricity to other forms of lighting arrangements in a positive and significant way. Location and position of a specific district, internet access, regular salary, per capita expenditure of rural population impacts the chance of shifting towards different forms of lighting arrangements.

Hence it comes out clearly that the social, economic domains of sustainability which can be impacted by larger access to technology and internet also in a way effects the chance of switching from electricity to other forms of lighting arrangements in a positive and significant way for rural households of India.

Table 2. Impact of districts on fuel choices for cooking

Iteration 0: log likelihood = -44033.403							
Iteration 1: log likelihood = -40321.067							
Iteration 2: log likelihood = -37991.614							
Iteration 3: log likelihood = -37245.728							
Iteration 4: log likelihood = -37071.252							
Iteration 5: log likelihood = -37053.677							
Iteration 6: log likelihood = -37053.258							
Iteration 7: log likelihood = -37053.258							
Multinomial logistic regression				Number of obs = 63061			
				LR chi2(27) = 13960.29			
				Prob > chi2 = 0.0000			
Log likelihood = -37053.258				Pseudo R2 = 0.1585			
	ckcode	**Coef**	**Std. Err.**	**z**	**P>|z|**	**[95% Conf. Interval]**	
1	TCQty341	-.0000369	1.62e-06	-22.81	0.000	-.00004	-.0000337
	stat_reg	-.0006322	.0004809	-1.31	0.189	-.0015746	.0003103
	district	-.0240281	.0041777	-5.75	0.000	-.0322163	-.01584
	_cons	-1.538031	.1384941	-11.11	0.000	-1.809474	-1.266587
3	TCQty341	-.0000126	2.25e-07	-56.23	0.000	-.0000131	-.0000122
	stat_reg	.0013572	.0001302	10.43	0.000	.0011021	.0016124
	district	-.0312562	.001163	-26.88	0.000	-.0335357	-.0289768
	_cons	-.2943211	.0391099	-7.53	0.000	-.3709751	-.2176672
4	TCQty341	-5.09e-06	1.65e-06	-3.08	0.002	-8.32e-06	-1.85e-06
	stat_reg	.0064756	.0013973	4.63	0.000	.0037369	.0092142
	district	.0207977	.0084707	2.46	0.014	.0041956	.0373999
	_cons	-7.572664	.4672319	-16.21	0.000	-8.488421	-6.656906
5	TCQty341	-.0000293	7.45e-07	-39.33	0.000	-.0000308	-.0000278
	stat_reg	-.0131318	.0003528	-37.22	0.000	-.0138234	-.0124403
	district	.0139712	.0013162	10.61	0.000	.0113915	.0165509
	_cons	.6621131	.0659886	10.03	0.000	.5327778	.7914483
6	TCQty341	-.000019	7.53e-06	-2.52	0.012	-.0000338	-4.23e-06
	stat_reg	-.001482	.0033217	-0.45	0.655	-.0079924	.0050284
	district	-.0242171	.0283973	-0.85	0.394	-.0798748	.0314406
	_cons	-6.178877	.940037	-6.57	0.000	-8.021315	-4.336438
7	TCQty341	-.0000299	1.29e-06	-23.11	0.000	-.0000324	-.0000274
	stat_reg	.0050135	.0004968	10.09	0.000	.0040398	.0059872
	district	-.0189288	.0040169	-4.71	0.000	-.0268019	-.0110558
	_cons	-2.951174	.1548516	-19.06	0.000	-3.254678	-2.647671

continued on following page

Table 2. Continued

8	TCQty341	-6.35e-06	2.80e-06	-2.27	0.023	-.0000118	-8.57e-07
	stat_reg	-.0051474	.0022375	-2.30	0.021	-.0095328	-.0007621
	district	-.0903926	.031782	-2.84	0.004	-.1526842	-.0281011
	_cons	-5.08623	.5551669	-9.16	0.000	-6.174337	-3.998123
9	TCQty341	-.0000593	2.43e-06	-24.38	0.000	-.000064	-.0000545
	stat_reg	-.0044002	.0005337	-8.24	0.000	-.0054462	-.0033542
	district	.010928	.0029934	3.65	0.000	.0050611	.016795
	_cons	-.7524208	.1416224	-5.31	0.000	-1.029996	-.4748459
10	TCQty341	-.0000502	.0000134	-3.74	0.000	-.0000765	-.0000239
	stat_reg	.0038758	.0034841	1.11	0.266	-.002953	.0107045
	district	-.0235398	.0301975	-0.78	0.436	-.0827259	.0356463
	_cons	-5.820404	1.062537	-5.48	0.000	-7.902937	-3.73787

(ckcode==2 is the base outcome).

Table 3. Impact of household size, religion, social group belonging (indicating social domains of sustainability) on fuel choices for cooking

Iteration 0: log likelihood = -44029.435							
Iteration 1: log likelihood = -39149.39							
Iteration 2: log likelihood = -36672.514							
Iteration 3: log likelihood = -35982.806							
Iteration 4: log likelihood = -35891.379							
Iteration 5: log likelihood = -35886.561							
Iteration 6: log likelihood = -35886.222							
Iteration 7: log likelihood = -35886.187							
Iteration 8: log likelihood = -35886.187							
Iteration 9: log likelihood = -35886.187							
Multinomial logistic regression				Number of obs = 63051			
				LR chi2(45) = 16286.50			
				Prob > chi2 = 0.0000			
Log likelihood = -35886.187				Pseudo R2 = 0.1850			
	ckcode |	**Coef.**	**Std. Err.**	**z**	**P>|z**	**[95% Conf. Interval]**	
1	TCVal341	-.0263278	.0009804	-26.85	0.000	-.0282494	-.0244063
	district	-.0129717	.0040926	-3.17	0.002	-.0209931	-.0049503
	hhsize	.3209214	.0182286	17.61	0.000	.285194	.3566487
	rel	.0610769	.0566785	1.08	0.281	-.050011	.1721647
	socgrp	.06268	.0150464	4.17	0.000	.0331896	.0921704
	_cons	-2.918384	.1639844	-17.80	0.000	-3.239787	-2.59698

continued on following page

Table 3. Continued

3	TCVal341	-.0114961	.0001596	-72.02	0.000	-.011809	-.0111833
	district	-.0188863	.0011538	-16.37	0.000	-.0211477	-.0166249
	hhsize	.211203	.0056513	37.37	0.000	.2001267	.2222793
	rel	.3111876	.0105664	29.45	0.000	.290478	.3318973
	socgrp	.0811267	.0040286	20.14	0.000	.0732308	.0890226
	_cons	-1.292976	.0421962	-30.64	0.000	-1.37568	-1.210273
4	TCVal341	-.0145812	.0015198	-9.59	0.000	-.0175599	-.0116025
	district	.0152199	.0073121	2.08	0.037	.0008885	.0295514
	hhsize	.3585109	.0337609	10.62	0.000	.2923409	.424681
	rel	.2823244	.1038493	2.72	0.007	.0787835	.4858652
	socgrp	.1805408	.0335194	5.39	0.000	.1148441	.2462376
	_cons	-7.376072	.3716588	-19.85	0.000	-8.10451	-6.647635
5	TCVal341	-.0163797	.0003589	-45.64	0.000	-.0170831	-.0156763
	district	.0285672	.0014453	19.77	0.000	.0257345	.0314
	hhsize	.3253863	.0090127	36.10	0.000	.3077218	.3430508
	rel	.2144914	.0244959	8.76	0.000	.1664804	.2625024
	socgrp	.0657736	.0078065	8.43	0.000	.0504731	.081074
	_cons	-3.344143	.0802176	-41.69	0.000	-3.501367	-3.18692
6	TCVal341	-.022298	.006082	-3.67	0.000	-.0342185	-.0103776
	district	-.0093379	.0270732	-0.34	0.730	-.0624003	.0437245
	hhsize	.2668079	.1321562	2.02	0.043	.0077866	.5258293
	rel	.1647811	.2839186	0.58	0.562	-.3916891	.7212512
	socgrp	-.2615752	.1942988	-1.35	0.178	-.6423939	.1192434
	_cons	-6.003187	1.1337	-5.30	0.000	-8.225197	-3.781176
7	TCVal341	-.0174489	.0007041	-24.78	0.000	-.0188289	-.0160688
	district	-.0093027	.0036469	-2.55	0.011	-.0164504	-.002155
	hhsize	.1315375	.0201656	6.52	0.000	.0920136	.1710613
	rel	.1337832	.0438467	3.05	0.002	.0478452	.2197212
	socgrp	.0234344	.0141701	1.65	0.098	-.0043385	.0512073
	_cons	-2.563467	.1457515	-17.59	0.000	-2.849134	-2.277799
8	TCVal341	-.0040383	.0018485	-2.18	0.029	-.0076613	-.0004153
	district	-.0838776	.031835	-2.63	0.008	-.1462731	-.0214821
	hhsize	.0597218	.1004112	0.59	0.552	-.1370806	.2565243
	rel	.2389718	.1354301	1.76	0.078	-.0264664	.50441
	socgrp	-.0055742	.0727811	-0.08	0.939	-.1482226	.1370742
	_cons	-6.576365	.6925626	-9.50	0.000	-7.933763	-5.218968

continued on following page

Table 3. Continued

9	TCVal341	-.0252071	.0010073	-25.02	0.000	-.0271814	-.0232328
	district	.021344	.0030583	6.98	0.000	.0153498	.0273381
	hhsize	.2840084	.0196412	14.46	0.000	.2455124	.3225044
	rel	.0171794	.0700527	0.25	0.806	-.1201214	.1544801
	socgrp	.1211971	.0152938	7.92	0.000	.0912218	.1511724
	_cons	-3.686234	.1775289	-20.76	0.000	-4.034184	-3.338284
10	TCVal341	-.0180656	.0075249	-2.40	0.016	-.0328142	-.003317
	district	-.0162866	.0283093	-0.58	0.565	-.0717718	.0391986
	hhsize	-2.942599	.9925504	-2.96	0.003	-4.887962	-.9972355
	rel	.2164353	.2313151	0.94	0.349	-.236934	.6698045
	socgrp	-.1828977	.1552089	-1.18	0.239	-.4871016	.1213063
	_cons	-.0994043	1.352674	-0.07	0.941	-2.750596	2.551788

(ckcode==2 is the base outcome).

Table 4. Impact of access to internet (indicating social domains of sustainability) on fuel choices for lighting

Iteration 0: log likelihood = -6816.0365	
Iteration 1: log likelihood = -6130.8414	
Iteration 2: log likelihood = -5889.8674	
Iteration 3: log likelihood = -5800.29	
Iteration 4: log likelihood = -5778.0448	
Iteration 5: log likelihood = -5776.6798	
Iteration 6: log likelihood = -5776.6429	
Iteration 7: log likelihood = -5776.6317	
Iteration 8: log likelihood = -5776.6276	
Iteration 9: log likelihood = -5776.6261	
Iteration 10: log likelihood = -5776.6255	
Iteration 11: log likelihood = -5776.6253	
Iteration 12: log likelihood = -5776.6252	
Iteration 13: log likelihood = -5776.6252	
Iteration 14: log likelihood = -5776.6252	
Iteration 15: log likelihood = -5776.6252	
Iteration 16: log likelihood = -5776.6252	
Iteration 17: log likelihood = -5776.6252	
Iteration 18: log likelihood = -5776.6252	
Multinomial logistic regression	Number of obs = 83362
	LR chi2(30) = 2078.82
	Prob > chi2 = 0.0000
Log likelihood = -5776.6252	Pseudo R2 = 0.1525

continued on following page

Table 4. Continued

	ltcode	I Coef.	Std. Err.	z	P>lzl	[95% Conf. Interval]	
1	TCVal342	-.0079013	.0005242	-15.07	0.000	-.0089287	-.0068739
	mpcemrp	-2.81e-06	5.24e-07	-5.36	0.000	-3.83e-06	-1.78e-06
	internet	.0159915	.4663565	0.03	0.973	-.8980504	.9300333
	regsal	.449563	.0950867	4.73	0.000	.2631964	.6359295
	district	.0692122	.0016873	41.02	0.000	.0659051	.0725192
	_cons	-5.220253	.9572833	-5.45	0.000	-7.096493	-3.344012
2	TCVal342	.0003163	.0013151	0.24	0.810	-.0022612	.0028938
	mpcemrp	-7.64e-06	5.67e-06	-1.35	0.178	-.0000187	3.47e-06
	internet	15.27059	.7822492	19.52	0.000	13.73741	16.80377
	regsal	-.1264731	.7005428	-0.18	0.857	-1.499512	1.246566
	district	-.0116809	.0293811	-0.40	0.691	-.0692667	.0459049
	_cons	-38.1334	.	.	.	.	.
3	TCVal342	.000427	.0001526	2.80	0.005	.000128	.0007261
	mpcemrp	-1.45e-06	1.23e-06	-1.19	0.236	-3.86e-06	9.50e-07
	internet	.692364	1.036431	0.67	0.504	-1.339004	2.723732
	regsal	.120321	.2644442	0.45	0.649	-.3979801	.6386221
	district	.0029515	.0100343	0.29	0.769	-.0167153	.0226184
	_cons	-8.470547	2.162861	-3.92	0.000	-12.70968	-4.231418
4	TCVal342	-.0115289	.0077612	-1.49	0.137	-.0267406	.0036828
	mpcemrp	-.0000257	.0000134	-1.92	0.055	-.000052	5.99e-07
	internet	13.40294	1.059673	12.65	0.000	11.32602	15.47987
	regsal	-.8691142	.8622956	-1.01	0.313	-2.559183	.8209542
	district	-.0021839	.0345755	-0.06	0.950	-.0699507	.0655828
	_cons	-30.78222	.	.	.	.	.
6	TCVal342	-.0060312	.0021015	-2.87	0.004	-.01015	-.0019124
	mpcemrp	1.42e-07	8.94e-07	0.16	0.874	-1.61e-06	1.89e-06
	internet	15.5163	.3385512	45.83	0.000	14.85275	16.17984
	regsal	-.7845627	.3417373	-2.30	0.022	-1.454355	-.11477
	district	-.0011164	.0156026	-0.07	0.943	-.0316968	.0294641
	_cons	-36.58982	.	.	.	.	.
9	TCVal342	-.0025314	.0015691	-1.61	0.107	-.0056067	.000544
	mpcemrp	-1.43e-06	1.95e-06	-0.73	0.464	-5.26e-06	2.40e-06
	internet	15.75229	.3717001	42.38	0.000	15.02377	16.48081
	regsal	-.5751476	.3481033	-1.65	0.098	-1.257417	.1071223
	district	-.0367213	.0199011	-1.85	0.065	-.0757267	.0022842
	_cons	-37.19447	.	.	.	.	.

(ltcode==5 is the base outcome).

However, all the findings in Table 4 are broad macroeconometric model findings in the context of understanding the linkages between the social, economic domains of sustainability and rural household energy transition for cooking and lighting. This also needs to be buttressed by micro level state specific findings.

It is important to assess that rural energy transition is not straightway only dependent on income as buttressed by the macro-econometric modelling. There are several other factors like religion, district location, internet access that determines the social, economic, anthropological, cultural construct of the place and can act as a guiding factor behind rural energy transition. Many of these factors are non-linear in nature. Hence, the next section of the chapter attempts to explore micro level foundations of rural energy transition through state specific findings for a state Bihar to understand the association between social, economic domains of sustainability and rural energy transition.

The reason behind the selection of Bihar is the high percentage of energy and income poor people. Bihar has both a high percentage of income and energy poor people. The other three states which also have high levels of income and energy poor people are Madhya Pradesh, Uttar Pradesh and Odisha. Dynamics of social group, castes, religion are dominant in each of these states. As a case study, Bihar is chosen to establish the narrative, discourse pertaining to the interconnections between nonlinearity of rural energy transition and social, economic domains of sustainability.

ENERGY TRANSITION AND SUSTAINABILITY SCIENCE

As established in the above sections rural energy transition and choice of fuels can be determined by access to resources, location specificity, religion, access to internet that also in turn is linked to the social and economic domains of sustainability. This will also vary from district to district even in a particular state.

In order to establish the association between the nonlinearity of rural energy transition and the broad knowledge of sustainability science, it is important to give an evidence of what is happening in a particular state as a case study. Establishment of the local context can then largely fit into the national and international level debate pertaining to the connections of nonlinearity of rural energy transition and sustainability science. This section therefore begins by establishing the comparative position of Bihar in terms of primary energy and income poor percentage. From there onwards, it proceeds towards, how even within Bihar district wise economic, financial, infrastructure, credit related activities are varying that can impact the social, economic domains of sustainability in a varying manner and can impact the nonlinearity of rural energy transition in Bihar.

Table 5 indicates the relative position of Bihar in comparison to other states of India in terms of primary energy and income poor people using NSSO 66th Round Data.

From the broad perspective, when the lense is narrowed down to different districts of Bihar, it is found that each district of Bihar is behaving differentially in terms of agricultural activity (agricultural index), industrial activity (industry index), transportation activity (transportation index), professional services index, housing loan index, trade, finance index (encompassing all service related activities). The lower the value of these indices, the poorer is the performance of the state in each of these aspects impacting the social and economic domain of sustainability. The data applied for this analysis of the year 2011-12.

Table 5. State wise percentage distribution of primary energy and income poor population across Indian states

	Percentage Distribution	
	Primary Energy Poor	**Income Poor**
A&N Islands	0.25%	0.00%
AP	5.60%	3.95%
Arunachal Pradesh	0.51%	1.58%
Assam	1.02%	6.05%
Bihar	9.41%	9.74%
Chandigarh	0.00%	0.00%
Chhattisgarh	4.07%	3.95%
Dadra and Nagar Haveli	0.25%	0.26%
Daman & Diu	0.51%	0.26%
Delhi	2.29%	1.32%
GOA	0.25%	0.00%
Gujarat	4.33%	1.84%
Haryana	5.09%	0.26%
Himachal Pradesh	0.25%	0.26%
Jammu & Kashmir	1.78%	0.79%
Jharkhand	2.54%	5.79%
Karnataka	1.78%	5.53%
Kerala	0.25%	0.00%
Lakshadweep	0.25%	0.00%
Madhya Pradesh	10.94%	9.21%
Maharashtra	7.63%	5.26%
Manipur	1.02%	1.84%
Meghalaya	0.76%	1.58%
Mizoram	0.00%	0.53%
Nagaland	0.25%	0.00%
Odisha	2.04%	7.89%
Pondicherry	0.76%	0.53%
Punjab	3.82%	0.00%
Rajasthan	2.29%	4.21%
Sikkim	0.76%	0.26%
Tamilnadu	7.63%	5.26%
Tripura	0.00%	0.79%
Uttar Pradesh	17.30%	15.53%
Uttaranchal	0.51%	1.05%
West Bengal	3.82%	4.47%

Source: Estimates from NSSO 66th Round.

Table 6. Components of sustainability in Bihar

District	Agricultural Index	Industry Index	Transportation Index	Professional Services Index	Housing Loan Index	Trade Index	Finance Index	Others	Composite Index
Araria	0.079	0.016	0.011	0.007	0.031	0.039	0.003	0.011	0.027
Aurangabad	0.063	0.193	0.029	0.035	0.004	0.037	0	0.024	0.083
Banka	0.045	0.003	0.027	0.009	0.007	0.026	0	0.024	0.013
Begusarai	0.074	0.008	0.043	0.014	0.021	0.052	0	0.054	0.029
Bhagalpur	0.083	0.011	0.043	0.015	0.034	0.074	0	0.071	0.041
Bhojpur	0.077	0.006	0.061	0.013	0.034	0.049	0.006	0.035	0.032
Buxar	0.063	0.005	0.037	0.004	0.006	0.026	0	0.024	0.018
Darbhanga	0.048	0.007	0.026	0.013	0.039	0.049	0.001	0.032	0.03
Gaya	0.087	0.007	0.078	0.02	0.033	0.081	0.004	0.051	0.038
Gopalganj	0.061	0.015	0.024	0.038	0.112	0.039	0	0.022	0.045
Jamui	0.031	0.001	0.014	0.004	0.003	0.02	0	0.013	0.01
Jehanabad	0.024	0.001	0.02	0.004	0.003	0.023	0	0.008	0.008
Kaimur - Bhabua	0.078	0.005	0.01	0.002	0.004	0.029	0	0.012	0.016
Katihar	0.113	0.009	0.02	0.007	0.032	0.053	0	0.09	0.035
Khagaria	0.047	0.001	0.019	0.003	0.003	0.028	0	0.007	0.011
Kishanganj	0.038	0.001	0.007	0.002	0.005	0.017	0	0.006	0.01
Lakhisarai	0.027	0.001	0.008	0.002	0.002	0.017	0	0.012	0.008
Madhepura	0.045	0.003	0.009	0.005	0.002	0.028	0	0.01	0.012
Madhubani	0.063	0.003	0.031	0.015	0.015	0.035	0	0.032	0.024
Munger	0.028	0.003	0.036	0.007	0.01	0.034	0	0.021	0.016
Muzaffarpur	0.084	0.009	0.056	0.015	0.052	0.1	0.005	0.068	0.05
Nalanda	0.064	0.003	0.039	0.005	0.015	0.045	0.001	0.02	0.021
Nawada	0.029	0.001	0.016	0.003	0.004	0.02	0	0.012	0.009
West / Pashchim Champaran	0.128	0.01	0.025	0.006	0.016	0.044	0.002	0.02	0.033
Patna	0.136	0.141	0.314	0.273	0.235	0.39	0.064	0.332	0.232
East / Purba Champaran	0.108	0.006	0.047	0.011	0.014	0.075	0.001	0.051	0.035
Purnia	0.093	0.005	0.047	0.018	0.098	0.044	0.001	0.025	0.042
Rohtas	0.111	0.01	0.044	0.007	0.016	0.065	0.001	0.029	0.033
Saharsa	0.036	0.007	0.007	0.006	0.009	0.032	0.001	0.02	0.016
Samastipur	0.136	0.005	0.039	0.017	0.013	0.069	0.001	0.062	0.04
Saran	0.085	0.004	0.078	0.013	0.019	0.059	0.01	0.043	0.032
Sheikhpura	0.017	0	0.004	0.001	0.001	0.009	0	0.002	0.004
Sheohar	0.004	0	0.004	0	0	0.004	0	0.001	0.002
Sitamarhi	0.046	0.004	0.032	0.01	0.01	0.043	0.002	0.018	0.02
Siwan	0.066	0.003	0.024	0.006	0.011	0.047	0.001	0.032	0.022
Supaul	0.04	0.001	0.003	0.003	0.004	0.023	0	0.009	0.011
Vaishali	0.059	0.004	0.049	0.01	0.013	0.051	0.005	0.041	0.025

Source: BIU-Datanet India Estimates.

Districtwise Estimates of Bihar

The Table 6 highlights that places like Sheohar are at a lower end of sustainability with a composite index of .002 whereas locations like Aurangabad are doing well and better with a composite index of .08. Intuitively this also hints that rural energy transition around these locations will also not be of the same nature and they will vary. There will be a non linear relationship in the rural energy transition across these locations owing to the variation in the components of sustainability domains in these specific locations.

Another Disconnect between Income and Energy Consumption: Indicating Energy Transition and Income Change Can Be Non Linear in Bihar

The above hypothesis of non-linear relationship is further corroborated by the observed pattern between useful energy and marginal per capita consumption expenditure (MPCE) observed across districts of Bihar from the NSSO 66th Round. The Figure 8 highlights how across districts of Bihar though the MPCE is rising, the useful energy consumption is not following the same pattern.

This is however based on the sampled data of NSSO and establishes the need to look more deeply into every household over a point of time for a particular fuel choice. Therefore, in order to do that within Bihar, a specific fuel option is chosen. It pertains to fuelwood and for all households of Bihar over a thirty year time frame considering the Census data of 1991, 2001 and 2011. The next section 3.1 gives further insight on this.

Estimation of BDS Statistics: To Understand Non-Linearity in Rural Households of Bihar

In order to test non linearity in rural households of Bihar, firewood usage in all households of Bihar is analysed. Firewood is used for cooking where often stacking is observed along with biases of usage of firewood for cooking even though clean fuel forms like LPG is available.

This can happen for several reasons related to habits, socioeconomic factors, culture, anthropological aspects. Therefore, as a test of non-linearity, fuelwood was chosen for Bihar. While pondering on the issue of non linearity in fuelwood consumption the following questions are being dealt: These questions pertain to –

1. What is the nature of energy transition pathway for a rural household of Bihar?
2. Are there any kind of stable, unstable equilibrium points or pattern in the energy transition pathway of rural households of Bihar?
3. Do these points exist in case of rural households of Bihar?

In order to test non linearity *Brock, Dechert and Scheinkman (BDS)* statistics is chosen. The total population for which fuelwood consumption is studied is 1.2 crore households (12568082). The number of village units studied are 314 over a time period of 30 years. Over 30 years how these 1.2 crore households across 314 village units have behaved is being studied. The average household size in these village units have been found and assumed to be 4 – 5. This average household size data is further buttressed by metadata based literature.

Figure 8. Nature of relation between useful energy consumption and marginal per capita consumption expenditure across districts of Bihar
Source: Estimated from NSSO 66th Round.

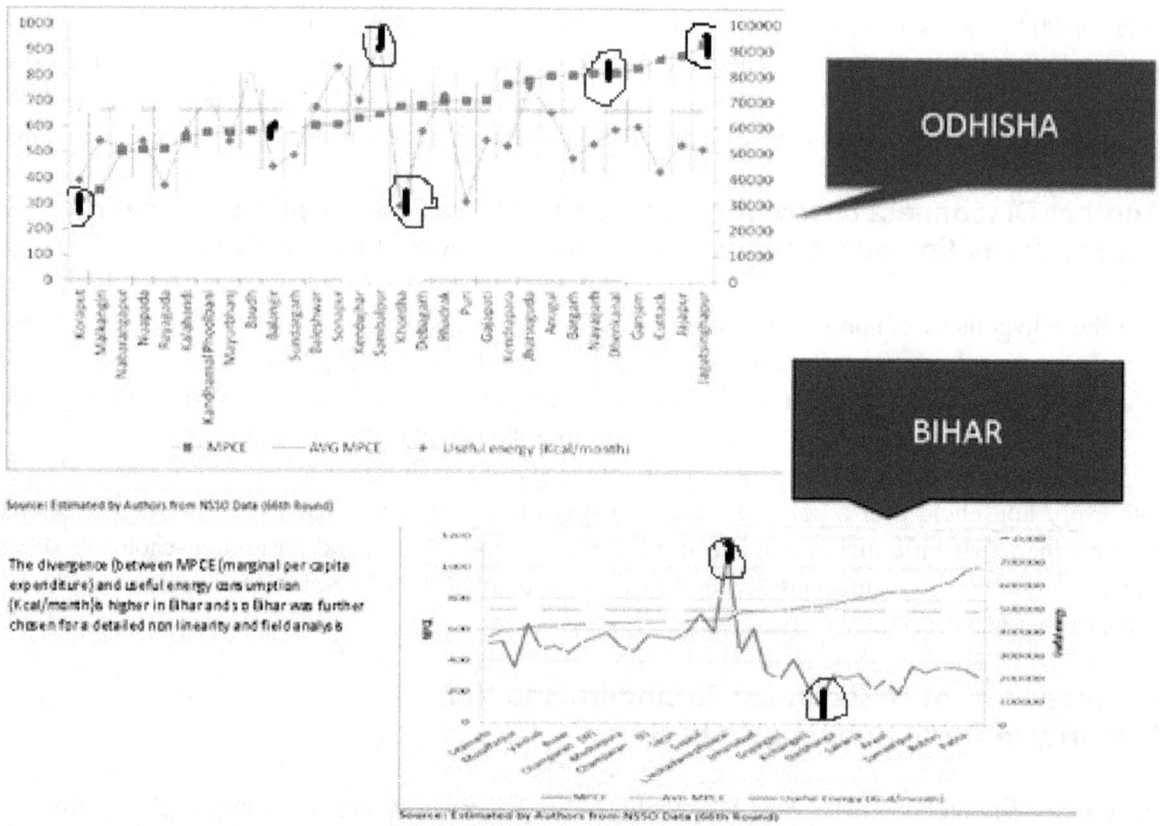

There have been distinct reasons behind the selection of BDS Statistics. This is because BDS Statistics *(W. A. Brock, W. Dechert and J. Scheinkman) detects* nonlinear serial dependence in a time series data. Here, a time series data of firewood consumption in 1.2 crore households across 314 village units and over 30 year time period is chosen.

After detrending (or first-differencing) to remove linear structure from the time series by fitting any linear model (e.g. ARMA(p,q), ARCH(q) or GARCH(p,q) models), the BDS statistics tests the null hypothesis that the remaining residuals are independent and identically distributed (i.i.d.). Rejection of the hypothesis suggests that the consumption pattern of fuelwood across households is non linear.

Figure 9. Return plot of BDS stats for firewood consumption in rural households of Bihar

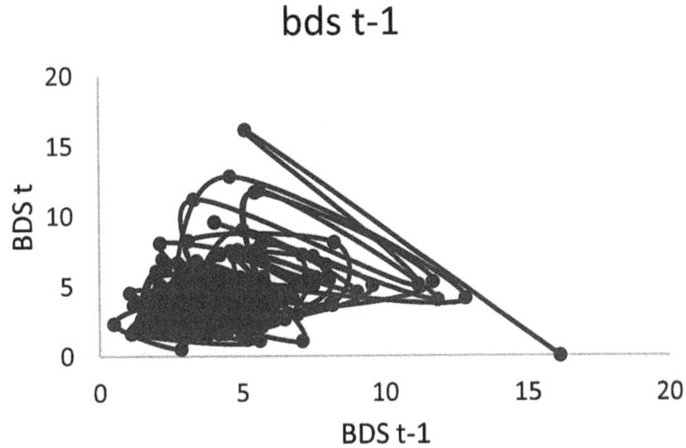

The mathematical process of the statistics is borrowed from the concept of spatial correlation of chaos theory. In this case, the households across 314 village units over 30 year time frame form a vector. The embedding dimensions of the vector comprises of the fuelwood consumption of the households of every embedding dimension. The series of scalars with fuelwood consumption of all households is converted to a series of vectors of fuelwood consumption by rural households of Bihar with overlapping entries. The correlation integral between the firewood consumption by each rural household of Bihar across 314 village units over 30 years is constructed. For every embedding dimension, atleast 1000 bootstrap simulation is done.

Finally after doing this, BDS statistics value for firewood consumption for 1.2 crore rural households across 314 village units over 30 years comes to be between 4.06 – 4.5. As the BDS Statistics for fuelwood consumption in the studied households over the time frame is greater than 1.96 which is the critical value of the statistics following the null hypothesis of no non linearity at 5% level of significance, the null hypothesis is rejected. It indicates that for fuelwood consumption across rural households of Bihar for 30 years based on the Census data, Bihar is showing a nonlinearity.

As BDS statistics is borrowed from the spatial correlation of chaos theory, the next step of the analysis was to understand the existence and nature of chaos in firewood consumption for rural households of Bihar based on Census data.

A return plot analysis of the BDS statistics over time is being conducted. The return plot analysis of BDS statistics is done to understand how the future value of this statistics (BDS t) is dependent on the past value (BDS t-1).

Existence of Chaos in Bihar in Fuelwood Consumption

The Figures 9 and 10 indicate the nature of chaotic pattern between the BDS statistics of the present and past. The return plot shown in the graph clearly highlights that the values of BDS stats over time for these rural households of Bihar have a chaotic nature of dependence between them and hence they are non linear in nature.

Figure 10. Return plot of BDS stats for firewood consumption in rural village units of Bihar at a point of time

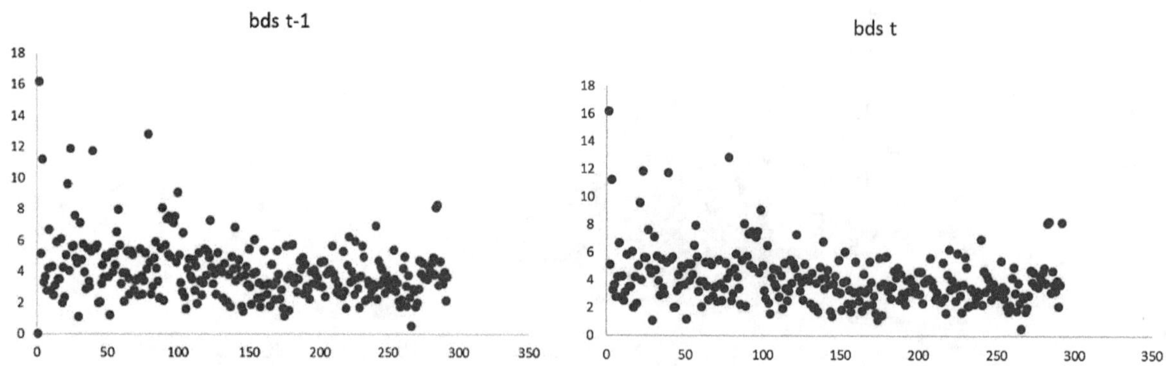

Moreover, when at any point of time (say – t-1 or t), the BDS statistics are observed for the village units (horizontal axis – 314 village units are there), there is no interdependence in the BDS stats across the village units and they also replicate a nonlinear pattern.

The return plot analysis shown in Figure 10 is also supported by the relationship between firewood consumption by number of households at different points of time.

Chaos in Firewood Consumption and Implications for Sustainability

The nature of firewood consumption across the rural households in 314 village units of Bihar over 30 years highlight the nature of interdependence between firewood consumption between the present and past in these rural households. It highlights that there is no causal dependence in firewood that is emerging

Figure 11. Chaotic nature in firewood consumption

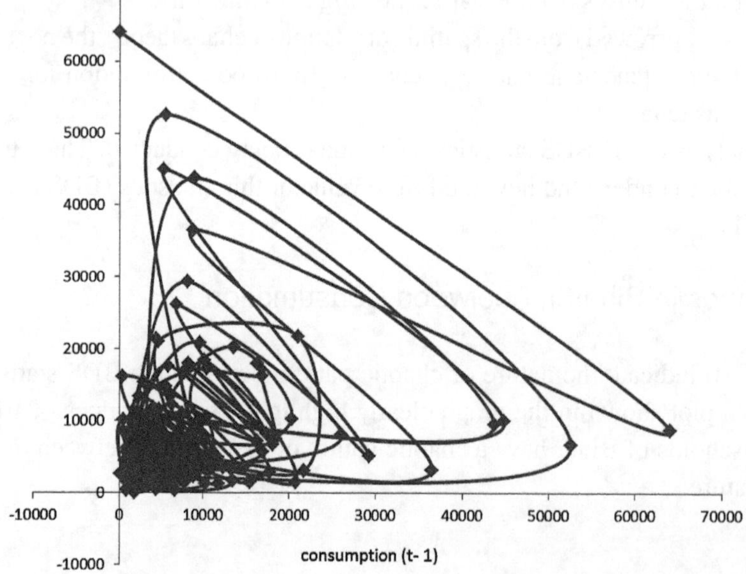

Table 7. Atkinson energy inequality index measures in Bihar

	Atkinson's Inequality Index
Biomass	0.38
Nat Avg_B	0.51
Petroleum	0.28
Nat Avg_P	0.47
Electricity	0.89
Nat Avg_E	0.70
Income	0.32
Nat Avg_Y	0.26

Source: Estimated by Authors from NSSO Data (66th Round).

in these rural households of Bihar. Further, there is no pattern of firewood consumption moving towards any equilibrium point in these rural households over a thirty year time frame. This immediately hints that the various hidden and latent socioeconomic, local context factors are playing a key role in determining this non converging pattern of the firewood consumption in the rural households of Bihar (Figure 11).

How Can the Above Consumption Pattern in Rural Households of Bihar Be Explained?

The average firewood consumption in Bihar is about 60 kg per household per month, while the average electricity consumption is about 10 kWh per household per month. Among petroleum products, the average PDS kerosene consumption per household per month is about 2.53 litres; the average market kerosene consumption is about 0.6 litres per household per month while the average LPG consumption per household per month is about 0.93 kg.

If the district level data for income and consumption of various fuels are also assessed for Bihar, one would expect to find that with higher incomes, the firewood consumption would decrease significantly while consumption of cleaner fuels such as LPG would increase. But, that is not the case for Bihar.

At a macro-level, the energy consumption in terms of Mega Joules (MJ) is higher for the districts with low incomes while the energy consumption in terms of MJ is lower for districts with higher incomes.

An analysis of the energy inequality across fuel choices in Bihar indicates that the inequality index is varying across fuels. These hints even across fuels for rural households of Bihar, inequalities are existing and it is going to have different developmental implications for households. Different social, economic, local, cultural, anthropological context and factors create this varying Atkinson Energy Inequality across fuels in rural households of Bihar. It also highlights that different domains of sustainability are interplaying in a non linear fashion guiding the access and distribution of different fuels across rural households of Bihar (Table 7).

Thus, the analysis done for these states indicate that a linear energy transition explanation might not be occurring in a specific context of rural households of Bihar. Therefore, owing to this non-linear nature, different implications on social, economic domains of sustainability and on the future developmental dividends of rural households of Bihar is bound to happen. It is therefore important to observe the pattern of non-linear rural energy transition in local contexts from a development and sustainability lense.

This therefore establishes the essence of creating a developmental policy discourse for rural energy transition and sustainability connection within rural households of India. Section 4 attempts to bring out such an essence and need which is pertinent for a developing country like India.

DEVELOPMENTAL POLICY DISCOURSE FOR RURAL ENERGY TRANSITION AND SUSTAINABILITY

In the traditional theoretical paradigm, equilibrium is seen as a generalization of human interactions. Any transition (which includes small transition like energy transition) in a theoretical framework can be conceptualised as a non-zero sum, coordination, dynamic and sequential game.

In such a case, there are repeated interactions between agents and it can lead to multiple equilibria. Any resulting equilibrium out of such interactions can be an outcome of some sort of arbitrariness and randomness. Thus each of these multiple equilibria points in a small transition process (small within the larger history of all types of transition processes that is observed in nature and society) like rural energy transition can be marked by randomness, stochasticity, non linearity. It also emerges from our case study of Bihar and it also hints on how social and economic domains of sustainability have a role to play towards such non-linear transition process in rural households of a local context of Bihar after panning down from a national level of India.

A rural energy transition sequence is an outcome of a series of repeated interaction and coordinated games as mentioned in general transition literature and it can therefore lead to non-linearity in the transition pattern.

Transition literature (Freeman and Perez, 1988, p.59 in Freeman, ed. 1996) indicates that for any period of transition the key consideration is the introduction of a deep structural change in any set up. Such a deep structural change happens only when there is a large amount of transformation that sets in the institutional and social framework (Freeman, ed. 1996). In the context of small transition process like rural energy transition, this can hold true. Specifically for a country like India with very diverse contexts in rural locations, a primary factor for transition to happen will be the initiation of a transformation within social, cultural, anthropological and institutional framework.

Such transformation in social and institutional frameworks in most cases will be non linear in nature. There are certain conceptual models in development economics that can further buttress this non linearity in social, cultural, anthropological and institutional set ups.

For instance, in order to explain this non linear nature of transition triggered by social, cultural, anthropological and institutional frameworks, false paradigm models can be looked for. False paradigm models within the developmental economics discipline of economics can help in bringing in the typical tribal, caste, cultural, institutional contexts of the locations of rural households and their role in non-linear nature of transition.

Therefore, it is certain that the area of non linearity in rural household's energy transition and its simultaneous relationship with different social, economic and environmental domains of sustainability is under-researched and has not yet begun to the extent it is supposed to be.

Somewhere, it is also being dominated by a linear top down thinking process of explaining through causal factors and relationships leading to linear energy changes. However, in reality the area of rural household energy transition is vast and needs to borrow thoughts, directions from different disciplines of psychology, false paradigm based development models complemented by social anthropology to fit into the discipline of sustainability science.

It also needs to have the quantitative and empirical backing of tools from statistics, spatial analysis paradigm of chaos theory using BDS statistical measures that can indicate the degree and nature of existence of non linearity in historical rural energy consumption data. Given the country is striving towards attaining its larger developmental goals and energy for development is also one of the foundation principles of "Sustainable Energy for All" goals of United Nations, the policy and thinking process cannot avoid exploring the non linearity questions in rural energy transition issues of a developing, multicultural country like India from a discipline of sustainability science. The sooner more research is done on this regard, the larger will be the developmental gains for rural households and the country at large!

REFERENCES

Dechert, W. D. (n.d.). Testing time series for nonlinearities: The BDS Approach, published in Nonlinear dynamics and economics. In *Proceedings of the Tenth International Symposium in Economic Theory and Econometrics*. Cambridge University Press.

Den Bergh, J., & Kemp, R. (2006). *Economics and Transitions: Lessons from Economic Sub-disciplines.* Working Paper Series # 038. United Nations University - Maastricht Economic and social Research and Training Centre on Innovation and Technology.

Freeman, C. (Ed.). (1996). *Long Wave Theory*. Cheltenham, UK: The International Library of Critical Writings in Economics Series. Edward Elgar.

Ramji, A., Soni, A., Sehjpal, R., Das, S., & Singh, R. (2012). *Rural energy access and inequalities: An analysis of National Sample Survey (NSS) data from 1999-00 to 2009-10*. The Energy and Resources Institute (TERI)-Norwegian Framework Agreement (NFA) Working Paper Series No. (4).

Srivastava, L., Goswami, A., Chaudhury, S., & Diljun, G. (2012). Energy access: Revelations from energy consumption patterns in rural India. *Energy Policy*, *1*(47), 11–20. doi:10.1016/j.enpol.2012.03.030

ENDNOTE

1 **Item 16:** Primary source of energy for cooking: coke, coal-01, firewood and chips-02, LPG-03, gobar gas-04, dung cake-05, charcoal-06, kerosene-07, electricity-08, others-09, no cooking arrangement-10,item 17: primary source of energy for lighting: kerosene-1, other oil -2, gas-3, candle-4, electricity-5, others-9, no lighting arrangement-6

Chapter 12
Ensuring Environmental Sustainability through Sustainable Entrepreneurship

Isaac Oluwajoba Abereijo
Obafemi Awolowo University – Ile-Ife, Nigeria

ABSTRACT

Sustainability has become an important issue worldwide because of great concerns about the unintended social, environmental, and economic effects of increasing population and economic growth, as well as consumption of natural resources. One recent concept arising from sustainability issue is sustainable entrepreneurship which integrates both the social and environmental aspects, and linking them with entrepreneurial activities. This chapter therefore suggests that efforts of developing countries at promoting entrepreneurship should go beyond engaging in business enterprises but include encouraging the use of entrepreneurial values and approaches to solve sustainability problems. Hence, this chapter is an effort at developing a framework that can be used to influence sustainable entrepreneurship behaviour of the students in developing countries.

INTRODUCTION

As far back as 1970s there has been a great concern about environment and development. This is because of the considerable negative effects that industrialisation is having on the natural environment in term of diminishing the vitality and sustainability of economic systems (World Resource Institute, 2004 cited by Dean and McMullen, 2007). Apart from the problems that are peculiar to local environment like air pollution, surface-water degradation, and toxic wastes in groundwater, there are negative impacts of industrialisation that are of global concern. These, according to the report of United Nations (2004), include ozone depletion, climate change, and the worldwide destruction of ocean fisheries.

The first major international gathering to discuss sustainability was the United Nations conference on the Human Environment held in Stockholm in 1972. The conference led to the establishment of the United Nations Environment Programme (UNEP) as well as the creation of numerous national envi-

DOI: 10.4018/978-1-5225-0094-0.ch012

ronmental protection agencies at country level. It was during this period that the concept of sustainable development became popular. The concept was further popularised by the report of the World Commission on Environment and Development in 1987, titled 'Our Common Future' (or Brundtland Report). This report gave the classic definition of sustainable development as development which meets the needs of the present without compromising the ability of future generations to meet their own needs (World Commission on Environment and Development, 1987). Since then, sustainable development is accepted as a convergence between the three pillars of economic development, social equity, and environmental protection (United Nations, 2010).

The concern about sustainability has also opened new opportunities for entrepreneurship and introduced a new dimension to its study. This is because entrepreneurship is believed to have potential of resolving problems of market failure inherent in the economic system, especially environmental issues. Hence, sustainable entrepreneurship, which is a spin-off concept from sustainability development, integrates both the social and environmental aspects, and linking them with entrepreneurial activities. The strategy of achieving this is the encouragement of green enterprises, which required firms to reconcile sustainability aspects with profitability.

Over the past decade, African economies have experienced rapid advancement towards integration into the global economy. This can be seen from the efforts of many of the countries undertaken significant economic reforms such as improving macroeconomic management, providing conducive private investment climate, liberalising markets as well as widening the space for entrepreneurship to drive strong and inclusive growth (Ahmed & Nwankwo, 2013). These authors however noted that there is much at stake in continuing this process of scaling up entrepreneurship as a dynamic process towards sustainable economic development. One of such is how to ensure that entrepreneurship is able to create value which is economic, social, or ecological in nature.

While the efforts of various governments, especially in developing countries, at promoting entrepreneurship is laudable one, this should however go beyond encouraging business start up where people seek advantages only for themselves or unconsciously run their businesses in a destructive way that generates imbalances. Therefore, solution to unemployment must also consider sustainable entrepreneurship, which requires the use of entrepreneurial values and approaches to solve sustainability problems. That is, application of imagination to challenging problems by conceiving, prototyping and creating solutions that deliver environmental, social and economic value (Pascual, van Klink, & Grisales, 2011). Therefore, policies and programmes of African government on entrepreneurship should be long-term and take the future into account so as to be sustainable in nature.

Though the practice of sustainable entrepreneurship is not new in African countries when considering the waste-to-wealth initiative and recycling process, but a quick look at available literature shows that not many studies are addressing the concept of sustainability entrepreneurship in this continent. This chapter is therefore an effort to fill this gap by synthesising theories from the entrepreneurship, environmental and welfare economics literatures with the view to examine the potential of entrepreneurship to create value within the dimensions of sustainability in African countries. Moreover, the chapter develops a framework which is expected to provide direction for the development of entrepreneurship education that can create and develop sustainable entrepreneurial behaviour in students, especially those in tertiary institutions. The framework can also serve as input into the formulation of policies and programmes by the government of African countries to properly lay the foundation for effective delivery of education for sustainable entrepreneurship based on the best practices in developed countries.

Since sustainable entrepreneurship is an extension of entrepreneurship, the chapter begins with the concepts related to sustainable entrepreneurship and its definition. Next, the environmental and welfare economics theory is reviewed to conceptualise how entrepreneurial action can be used to address market imperfections so that environmental and natural resources can be efficiently utilised. The chapter then provides the theoretical and empirical background for the drivers or motivation for sustainable entrepreneurship as well as how entrepreneurship education can be used to develop sustainable entrepreneurial behaviours in nascent entrepreneurs. A framework for the development of sustainable entrepreneurial behaviour is then suggested. The chapter is concluded by considering the implication of developing sustainable entrepreneurial behaviour for the entrepreneurship educators and policy makers.

THEORETICAL BACKGROUND

Concept of Entrepreneurship and Sustainability Entrepreneurship

As early as 18th century, various definitions of entrepreneurship have been put forth but with no universally accepted one. According to Venkataraman (1997), entrepreneurship is defined as the process of how opportunities to bring into existence future goods and services are discovered, created, and exploited, by whom, and with what consequences. Recent definition put forth by Stokes, Wilson and Mador (2010) defined it by encompassing all the different definitions, based on what entrepreneurs do, who they are, and what they produced. While referring to Stokes, Wilson and Mador (2010) and synthesising from studies from previous researchers, Majid and Koe (2012) then put forth a definition which is adopted in this chapter. The definition focuses on behaviour, processes and outcomes of entrepreneurs. Entrepreneurship is therefore defined as a process of identifying, evaluating and pursuing opportunities through creativity, innovativeness and transformations to produce new products, processes and values that are beneficial. This definition takes into consideration the modern school of thought on entrepreneurship which is now playing emphasis on sustainability. That is, entrepreneurial thinking process should involve identifying, evaluating and pursuing business opportunities that will be economically viable as well as preserving the environment for the next generation.

The role of entrepreneurship in economic growth is also established in the literature. But the traditional entrepreneurship education usually prescribes to students a profit-driven mentality. This, in the word of Slater and Dixon-Fowler (2010), is termed 'profit-first' mentality, which has no regard for moral considerations or social responsibilities. Recently however, the concern for society gave rise to social entrepreneurship where profit motive is not the primary consideration but on societal problems. Inspite of its non-profit motive, various case studies have shown that there are social entrepreneurs who are able to make profit while creating the social values. Some of these cases include Jacqueline Novogratz (*Acumen Fund*), Bill Drayton (*Ashoka*), Sam Goldman and Ned Tozun (*d.light*), Rafael Alvarez (*genesys works*), and Jane Chen (*embrace*) among others (see http://www.forbes.com/impact-30/list.html for more information). The success story of these social entrepreneurs is what stirs interest in the direction of concern for the environment.

The consciousness towards the environment is therefore compelling the businesses already in existence to 'green' their products or services, processes and distribution. Likewise, the new start-ups are encouraged to start out with the intention of making environmental protection an integral part of the reasons for setting it up (Santiago, 2013; Walley & Taylor, 2002). The concern for the environment and the potential of entrepreneurship to exploit the opportunities associated with environmental degradation has led to the concept of sustainable entrepreneurship. This is based on the concept of triple bottom line coined by Elkington (1994). That is, entrepreneurship that contributes equally to economy, ecology and society.

Sustainable entrepreneurship research has now emerged from the larger body of business and environment as well as corporate responsibility research. This is in response to the demand for modifications in business, social and environmental practices. Sustainable entrepreneurship, which is a concept linking development to entrepreneurship, is also variously defined in the literatures (for examples Elkington, 1998; Cohen & Winn, 2007; Dean & McMullen, 2007). But there is an agreement that the feature of sustainable entrepreneurship is based on certain fundamental aspects of entrepreneurial activities, which are personal initiative and skills, to create or discover business opportunities as well as realisation of market success. In addition to these activities, sustainable entrepreneurship also takes into account environmental and societal goals.

Therefore, the concept of sustainable entrepreneurship arises from the understanding that efforts at addressing environmental issues, such as ecosystem degradation and global climate change, requires a fundamental transformation in the way society consumes natural resources and produces energy. Hence, as put forth by Cohen and Winn (2007), sustainable entrepreneurship should result into entrepreneurial rents and also ensures social and environmental sustainability. Sustainable entrepreneurship therefore entails developing businesses which have positive relationships with the society in which it operates (Crnogaj, Rebernik, Hojnik, and Gomezelj, 2014). This means that business ventures arising from sustainable entrepreneurship must stand on the tripod of economic stability (profitability), social equity, and sustainable practice of reducing environmental degradation (Lumpkin & Katz, 2011). Hence, the principles of entrepreneurship can serve as means by which market failures such as environmental and social disruptions can be ameliorated (Crnogaj, Rebernik, Hojnik, & Gomezelj, 2014).

While synthesising the various definitions of sustainable entrepreneurship, Majid and Koe (2012) identified the main issues that sustainable entrepreneurship covers. These include what entrepreneurs can do in preserving economics, environment, social and culture in entrepreneurial ways. Hence, the authors put forth the definition of sustainable entrepreneurship as a process in which entrepreneurs exploit a business opportunity in an innovative manner for economic gains, society equity, environmental quality and cultural preservation on an equal manner. Unlike other definitions which focus on green or social domain only, the definition suggested by Majid and Koe (2012) covers the domains of economic, social, environmental and cultural. Hence, this definition is adopted for this chapter.

In conceptualising sustainable entrepreneurship, many researchers have used the triple bottom line (TBL) to describe sustainability development. The concept identified three main value creating aspects in sustainable business practices. These include economic prosperity, environmental quality, and social justice (Elkington (1997). Therefore, various models of sustainable entrepreneurship, based upon the concept of TBL, have been developed over the years. One of such models is based on the triune of social, environmental and economic to examine whether the entrepreneurs could operate an economically viable venture whilst retaining their environmental and social values (Dixon & Clifford, 2007 cited in Majid and Koe, 2012). Another is the value-based model developed by Tilley and Young (2009) which argue that sustainable entrepreneurship should be treated as the combined efforts of the 12 individual values that drive sustainability.

As it is argued in the definition of sustainable entrepreneurship, that its definition should cover the four domains of economic, social, environmental and cultural, likewise Majid and Koe (2012) proposed another model which included all these four domains in order to be regarded as true sustainable entrepreneurship. The argument is based on the thought of Nurse (2006) that sustainability issues, especially in developing countries, should not rely heavily on western scientific knowledge. This is because over dependence on western scientific concepts in managing sustainability can lead to the loss of traditional or indigenous knowledge. This traditional wisdom can actually serves as solutions for sustainable development problems in developing countries. This explains the reason why culture is included as the fourth pillar in sustainable development.

Market Imperfections and Entrepreneurial Opportunities

Central to the environmental economics is the concept of market imperfections, which is the failure of markets to efficiently allocate limited resources in a way that benefits society most. These imperfections contribute to environmental degradation. Fortunately, these market imperfections have been discovered as avenue where opportunities for the creation of radical technologies and innovative business models can be developed (Dean and McMullen, 2007; Cohen and Winn, 2007). These opportunities form the foundations for an emerging model of sustainable entrepreneurship. Exploiting these opportunities can enable existing or would-be entrepreneurs to obtain entrepreneurial rents and, at the same time, improve the social and environmental conditions. Central to the need to understand how market failure may be used to explore sources of entrepreneurial opportunities is the question Venkataraman (1997) raised about 'where opportunities to create goods and services for the future will come from'. The answer is now emerging from the understanding of how market failures can serve as entrepreneurial opportunities.

There are four of these market imperfections identified in the literature and which are also seen as sources of entrepreneurial opportunity. They are: firms are not perfectly efficient, externalities exist, pricing mechanisms work imperfectly, and information is not perfectly distributed. The theoretical background for understanding how each of these market imperfections can create entrepreneurial opportunities is based on the theoretical views on entrepreneurial opportunity, which is synthesised by Sarasvathy, Dew, Velamuri and Venkataraman (2003). First is the allocative view (opportunity recognition) which suggests that opportunities exist when there is potential to redistribute resources to benefit others without adversely affecting others. Second, there is also the discovery view (opportunity discovery) where entrepreneurial opportunities arise from information asymmetries with respect to the true value of resources and the resulting value of the combination of those resources into outputs. Lastly, the creative view (opportunity creation), that is, when opportunities are identified ex-post when entrepreneurs is seeking to maximise the utility functions of multiple stakeholders. Each of these views of entrepreneurial opportunities is useful in establishing how entrepreneurial rents can be achieved through innovations which correct the existing unsustainable use of environment.

Based on the extensive review of literature on the concept of market imperfection by Cohen and Winn (2007), the authors are able to establish the role that each of the imperfections plays in environmental degradation as well as how it can lead to any of the generic types of opportunities stated above. The first imperfection indicates the inability of firms to be perfectly efficient in their resource allocation. The outcome is that both the firms and consumers can only achieve a fraction of the potential efficiencies available from natural resources. Efforts at bringing markets closer to equilibrium will therefore require that the efficiency of resource allocation be increased. This can be achieved through opportunity identification and exploitation using entrepreneurial process. These opportunities derive from the conversion to a cyclic economy (Kirchgeorg, 1999 cited in Cohen & Winn, 2007) in which improvements in efficiency of resource use depend on recycling and recovery at every stage of the process. That is, ability to convert industrial and consumer waste into new products and services. From the above, innovating entrepreneurs who discover the potential to reduce that waste (through recycling) will be able to correct the imperfection due to inefficient resource allocation.

The second imperfection is about existence of externalities, which may be positive or negative. This imperfection suggests that the costs or benefits associated with the production or consumption activities of firms are not correctly reflected in the prices of products and services being offered by such firm. Positive externalities occur when the third party benefits without incurring the full cost associated with the value of benefit received. One example of positive externalities is when new good, resulting from research and development investment of a company, is purchased by the consumers at price below what would fully reflect the value of technological improvements (Abereijo & Ilori, 2012). On the other hand, it becomes negative when the third party suffers from the activities of a firm without receiving adequate compensations. Examples of this abound, which include impact of industrial smoke, water pollution, etc, on health and economic activities of surrounding communities. Therefore, if an entrepreneur can substitute current production processes, which results in externalities, with innovative ones, such entrepreneurs would have discovered an entrepreneurial opportunities for new business and also brought about positive environmental externalities. The types of opportunity identification that are most likely are opportunity discovery and creation. In the word of Cohen and Winn (2007), innovative firms that are able to recognise and create opportunities to reverse existing negative environmental externalities (for example, air pollution) can generate triple bottom line results. That is, their entrepreneurial actions can produce social benefits (through improvement in the quality of air within the communities) and environmental benefits (improved ecosystem functioning), and which is being done profitably. Apart from entrepreneurial opportunities resulting from improvement on production processes, there could also be an institutional entrepreneurship. This is type of entrepreneurship involves a process whereby the transaction costs associated with environmental-based externalities is reduced. Institutional entrepreneurship, as defined by Dean and McMullen (2007), is the process of reducing transactions costs through the development of economic institutions by profit-motivated economic actors. Example of institutional entrepreneurship is a legal firm who coordinates the interests of the parties that are being affected by negative externalities. By this effort, the right of the parties concerned can be enforced and the cost of bargaining and contracting with the producer of negative externalities can also be reduced (Dean & McMullen, 2007).

Moreover, the possibility of pricing mechanism working imperfectly is the third market imperfection. This imperfection arises because of the assumption of the conventional economics theory that natural resources are infinitely plentiful and that they have a market value that accurately reflect supply and demand. The reality, as put forth by Kurz and Salvadori (1997), is that many natural resources are exhaustible, undervalued and underpriced. Therefore, if the natural resources are valued more accurately and perfectly priced the demand for the use of non-renewable factors of production will decrease, while demands for more renewable factors will increase. Therefore, entrepreneurship principles can be applied whereby innovative entrepreneurs begin to discover opportunities in renewable factors of production. Example is disruptive technologies which are been sold in the market where consumers cannot buy high end products. The specific examples are Thin Film Technologies producing solar photovoltaic cell being marketed in third world countries without established power grids (Cohen & Winn, 2007).

The fourth market imperfection concerns the imperfect distribution of information. The assumption of neoclassical economics is that suppliers and buyers within free market have perfect information about prices, products and the market. But in reality, there is presence of information asymmetry, which sometimes is responsible for the unsustainable production and consumption patterns. The imperfect distribution of information are categorised into two by Dean and McMullen (2007). These are knowledge that producers have about supply and demand conditions, and knowledge that customers posses regarding the nature of product or service attributes. Some of the factors that may be responsible for imperfect information are changes in technology, tastes, and demographics. In relation to environment, imperfect information therefore exist when better channels of supply are not known or when markets for environmentally superior products are yet to be discovered. Entrepreneurial opportunities associated with this imperfect information could include the use of new product or process technologies or efficient means of supply which are not damaging to the environment. Also, identifying customers who prefer environmentally superior products or services could also serve as another source of entrepreneurial opportunities. In relation to the second category of imperfect distribution of information, opportunities can also exist for what Dean and McMullen (2007) referred to as customer-focused informational entrepreneurs. These entrepreneurs exploit opportunities by enhancing customer knowledge about the environmental attributes of products and services.

Drivers of Sustainable Entrepreneurship

The existence of numerous market imperfections, with regard to the environment and social conditions, suggests that it is not automatic that entrepreneurs will likely pursue those opportunities from which entrepreneurial rents exist. Hence, there are certain behaviours associated with individuals who prefer to pursue entrepreneurial opportunities based on market imperfections. The theoretical literatures identified certain drivers towards sustainability entrepreneurship orientation, which are categorised as being externally- or internally-driven (Kuckertz & Wagner, 2010; Gibbs, 2009; Masurel, 2007; Schlange, 2006). Government policies and or incentives as well as pressure groups constitute the external drivers, while the entrepreneurs' value system is the internal driver. Whether externally or internally driven, the response to sustainability issues also differs. Hence, Baumgartner (2009) posited that the approach could be introverted, or extroverted, or eco-efficient practices, or visionary strategy. The introverted approach involves responding to the pressures from stakeholders such as government regulation, while the extroverted approach involves highlighting the accomplishments in sustainability reports. The eco-efficient practices by firms involve adopting conservative approach of energy conservation and waste management. It is only the visionary strategy approach that actually integrates sustainability issues in business operations.

Empirically, Schick, Marven and Freimann (2002) discovered in their study that individuals categorised as eco-dedicated were influenced by their families in their childhood. Hence, some authors are of the opinion that subjects and courses that create environmental awareness, at all levels of education, could lead future entrepreneurs in the right direction (Dobson, 2007; Schaper, 2002). The findings of Schlange (2006) also confirmed that one major characteristic of sustainable entrepreneurs is a strong emphasis on ecological aspects in their business vision. It is also discovered that the main driver for a sustainable entrepreneurial motivation is structured along the social and ethical dimension. The results of study on the factors influencing propensity to sustainable entrepreneurship of SMEs in Malaysia revealed that attitudinal (attitude towards sustainability) and perceptual (perceived feasibility and desirability) factors positively and significantly influenced such propensity (Koe, Omar, Sa'ari, 2015; Koe, Omar & Majid (2014). The authors therefore concluded that effort at promoting sustainable entrepreneurship requires entrepreneurs developing sufficient sustainability capabilities, establishing a positive or favourable sustainability attitude and creating attractive sustainable entrepreneurial practices. Moreover, prior knowledge and focused attention can also contribute significantly to opportunity recognition in sustainability-related market failure (Bell and Stellingwerf (2012). Another important driver, noted by these authors, is motivations to solve the sustainability-related market failures.

The Role of Entrepreneurship Education

There is recognition in the literature that entrepreneurship education can help promote sustainable entrepreneurship. For example, Shane (2003) postulates that opportunity is likely to be exploited if an individual is better educated. This is because the information and skills acquired through education can increase expected returns for opportunity exploitation. Hence, many universities, especially in developed countries like United States of America, are incorporating sustainability into the curricula of their undergraduate studies (see McEwen, 2013 for examples of sustainability entrepreneurship education activities at the university level). It is also noted in the literature that sustainable entrepreneurship requires a new educational approach. The education should specifically focus on sustainability and be delivered in a way to stimulate sustainable entrepreneurial behaviour in students. In the word of McDonough and Braungart (2002), the goal of sustainable entrepreneurship education should be to equip the students with knowledge and skill needed to operate on renewable energy and to eliminate the concept of waste by making every waste product a raw material or input for another activity or return it into the cycle of nature. Ultimately, students of sustainable entrepreneurship should be able to apply sustainability frameworks to design new products, services, and processes (McEwen, 2013).

Among the knowledge base and skills needed are awareness of local and global environmental problems and future trends, acquisition of environmental values, and engagement in ecological or systems thinking (Richardson, Irwin and Sherwin (2005). Other skills identified by SustainAbility (2008) are the ability to seek alternative and innovative ways of meeting present needs as well as developing new business models that support the resulting innovative products and services. Also the future sustainable entrepreneurs should be able to get inspiration from the solutions already provided by the nature. This is termed biomimicry, which is an approach to innovation that seeks sustainable solution to human challenges by emulating nature's time-tested patterns and strategies (Biomimicry Institute, 2014). It is therefore important to design curricula and pedagogy that can influence the attitudes and actions of existing and, especially, the would-be entrepreneurs. The pedagogy should emphasise active, experiential, inquiry-based learning and real world problem solving in the classroom, on the campus and in the local community (McEwen, 2013). Moreover, to ensure long-term retention of the knowledge, skills and values gained the author proposed that the curriculum should provide learning experiences on real-world problems prevailing within their immediate university environment, larger community, government and industry.

Beyond the pedagogy, there are certain factors identified in the literature that may likely make entrepreneurs to discover sustainable development opportunities. These include their knowledge of the natural and communal environments in which they live as well as their perception about the threats on these environments (Patzelt and Shepherd, 2011). Other, as posited by these authors, includes the extent of their altruism toward others within the community. This again underscores the importance of approach to sustainable entrepreneurship education, which must be appropriately designed to develop these attributes.

Various approaches on education for sustainable development identified in the literature include, first, normative and zero-sum perspectives which involve awareness-building, critical thinking and introduction of tools to support environmental protection (Springett, 2005). Second approach is instrumental perspective that highlights the value of sustainability and corporate social responsibility initiatives to build competitive advantage (Kashyap et al., 2006). The more recent approach is the one that highlight the importance of entrepreneurship education to inspire and build awareness of the opportunities inherent in the sustainability arena for self-interest and to benefit diverse stakeholders (Kuckertz & Wagner, 2010). While the first and second approaches are reactive, the third is proactive in nature. That is, the third approach is meant to influence attitudes and intentions related to sustainable development. Drawing from the theory of planned behaviour, the present and future behaviour of an individual is strongly determined by behavioural intentions (Ajzen, 1991). This means that the behavioural intention of sustainable entrepreneurs will depend on attitudes, subjective norms and perceived behavioural control. The theory of planned behaviour is therefore providing the framework within which the link between education and sustainable entrepreneurship can be explored.

Relating this theory to sustainable entrepreneurship, Lourenço, Jones and Jayawarna (2013) posited that formation of sustainable entrepreneurial behaviour intention is dependent on learner's perceived benefits of learning about sustainable entrepreneurship, perceived behavioural control, and subjective norms formed through perceived ease of use of knowledge related to sustainable entrepreneurship. Therefore, it can be proposed that the intentions of would-be entrepreneurs to utilise their learning related to sustainability are influenced by their perception of learning, perception of benefits and the perceived ease with which the learning content can be applied. The empirical finding of Lourenço, Jones and Jayawarna (2013) also confirmed above theory. First, the author found that if prospective entrepreneurs perceive benefits from content related to sustainable entrepreneurship their intentions to exploit such learning will be enhanced. Second, if nascent entrepreneurs learn content related to sustainable entrepreneurship, the likelihood of exploiting such learning will also be enhanced. In summary, the major driver for would-be entrepreneurs to utilise learning is their understanding of the benefits of sustainable entrepreneurship and their perception of learning.

Another important motivation of prospective entrepreneurs to utilise learning about sustainable entrepreneurship is whether or not such entrepreneur has profit-mentality. This argument, proposed by Giacalone and Thompson (2006), is confirmed by the empirical finding of Lourenço, Jones and Jayawarna (2013). That is, profit-minded entrepreneurs will likely pursue those opportunities that promise higher entrepreneurial rents. However, Lourenço, Jones and Jayawarna (2013) discovered that, though a profit-first mentality will influence evaluation of sustainable entrepreneurship, but it is not a significant factor deterring the ability to learn material that could be in conflict with existing institutional logic of profit-first value. Hence, there is still value in introducing learning content related to sustainable entrepreneurship to would-be entrepreneurs with a profit-first mentality. It is then suggested by these authors that providing sustainability-related content in entrepreneurship education and business start-up is a valuable intervention.

The implication of the above, especially for the educators, is the need to develop competences for the delivery as well as the curriculum that can develop sustainable entrepreneurial behaviour in the students.

FRAMEWORK FOR SUSTAINABLE ENTREPRENEURSHIP

Based on the literature review, as discussed above, it is clear that the problem of environmental degradation, arising from the failure of markets, can be resolved through entrepreneurial action. That is, there are entrepreneurial opportunities associated with these market imperfections which can be exploited using entrepreneurial process. Both theoretical and empirical literatures are however suggesting that only entrepreneurs who are sustainability-oriented will likely support the idea of sustainability and exploit the opportunities associated with the market imperfections. This then indicates the importance of entrepreneurship education in fostering the entrepreneurial intentions targeted at opportunities related to sustainable development. The education will help fostering sustainable development-oriented entrepreneurial behaviour, as well as encouraging the nascent entrepreneurs to pursue business that can result in sustainable market offerings.

Considering the complexity inherent in opportunities for sustainable entrepreneurship, the contents and pedagogical input is very crucial, especially on how it can influence learners' attitudes and intentions towards sustainable development. Empirical results showed that when the techniques of delivering the education are simple and easy to learn, the perceptions of the learners about the benefits of learning sustainable entrepreneurship will be raised (Lourenco, Jones & Jayawarna, 2012). Therefore, the combined effect of understanding the benefits of sustainable entrepreneurship and perception of learning are major motivation for exploiting the learning by nascent entrepreneurs.

Figure 1 therefore shows the proposed framework for developing sustainable entrepreneurial behaviour of future entrepreneurs, especially in tertiary institutions in African countries. From this figure, the delivery approach for teaching sustainable entrepreneurship should be simple, educative (well grounded in entrepreneurship and environmental economics theories), and involves intensive hands-on experiences. This is because sustainable solutions require a lot of creativity, and as Schumpeter (1934) noted, the entrepreneurial process in sustainability involves creative destruction of conventional production methods and consumption patterns. To further stimulate the interest of students and make them appreciate the

Figure 1. Framework for the development of sustainable entrepreneurial behavior

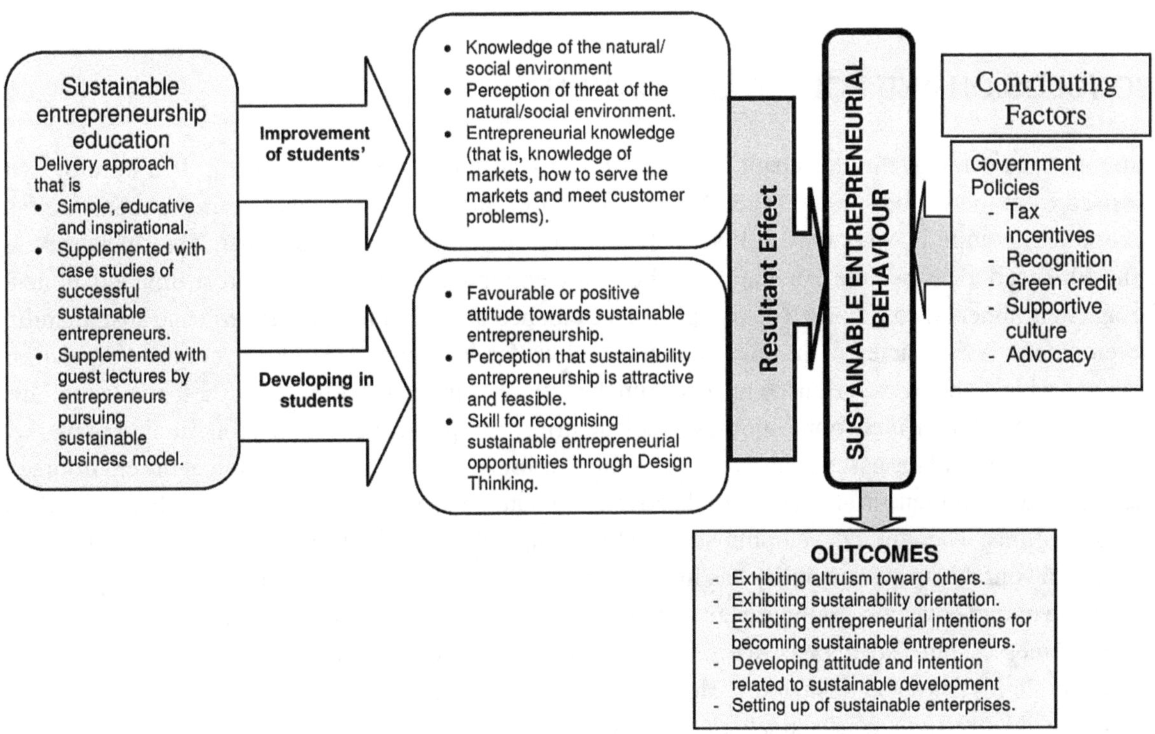

benefits associated with green business ideas there is need for industrial visit to successful businesses with best-practices. Also, the education should be supplemented with case studies of successful sustainable entrepreneurs as well as guest lectures by entrepreneurs pursuing sustainable business model.

It is expected that the approach will achieve two major goals in the learners. First, it will improve students' knowledge and perception of threats in the natural and social environments, as well as improving their entrepreneurial knowledge about the market and how to serve it, and how to meet customers' problems. Secondly, the students will develop favourable or positive attitude towards sustainable entrepreneurship, thereby perceiving sustainability entrepreneurship as being attractive and feasible. The skill for recognising sustainable entrepreneurship will also be developed in the students.

Beyond the contribution of sustainable entrepreneurship education, government policies and programmes are also important. That is, policies and programmes that can encourage and support entrepreneurial actions towards addressing environmental challenges with innovative business solutions should be put in place. Though government might not be able to decide on which market imperfections to address; efforts should however be directed at formulating policies that can foster entrepreneurial behaviour that is oriented towards sustainability, which can be in form of tax incentives, recognition, green credit, and advocacy among others.

FUTURE RESEARCH DIRECTIONS

The framework developed in this chapter is based on the results of findings in developed countries. While these findings can provide direction for sustainable entrepreneurship education, yet it is important to carry out empirical studies on the motivation and attributes of indigenous entrepreneurs in Africa who are already engaging in sustainable entrepreneurship.

CONCLUSION AND POLICY IMPLICATIONS

Attempt has been made in this chapter to contribute to sustainable entrepreneurship literature by synthesised from the various thoughts and findings from the entrepreneurship, environmental and welfare economic literature in general as well as sustainable entrepreneurship in particular. The chapter establishes the need to change the orientation of the future entrepreneurs from being profit-minded alone to being environmental conscious. That is, maintain a balance between profit generation and sustainability development. As it is noted in the environmental and welfare economics literature, majority of environmental problems being experienced results from the failure of market. Fortunately, these market failures provide avenue for business opportunities which in turn can improve the efficient functioning of market. Therefore, instead of the nascent entrepreneurs contributing further to the degradation of the environment they can use entrepreneurial process to discover, evaluate and exploit opportunities inherent in these market failures. Therefore, developing sustainability capabilities and attitude of nascent entrepreneurs which is favourable to sustainability has implication for entrepreneurship educators and policy makers.

On the part of educators, entrepreneurship education should go beyond preparing the students to start small businesses, but also emphasise transformational entrepreneurship that can bring about a complete change in their values and behaviours. Hence, the pedagogy of sustainable entrepreneurship education should be able to stimulate sustainable entrepreneurial behaviour in the students, thereby encouraging them to pursue 'green' business ideas rather than opportunistic ones that are driven by self-interest. The education should also be designed in a way that will achieve two major goals. Firstly, efforts should be geared at making the students understand and appreciate the contemporary sustainability challenges, such as climate change and depletion of non-renewable resources among others. Closely related to this is the knowledge of the potential business opportunities for sustainable entrepreneurship associated with these challenges. Consequent on the above, entrepreneurship education should be delivered in a way that will be able to develop the creative ability of students to respond to environmental and social problems as well as to discover opportunities embedded in these problems. Since one of the desired effects of entrepreneurial education is entrepreneurial inspiration, part of the delivery methodology should include case studies of successful sustainable entrepreneurs and guest lectures by entrepreneurs who are committed to pursuing sustainable business model.

Also, the policies and strategies of government should not be reactive alone, whereby established firms are made to be socially responsible, through corporate greening. It has even been found that these efforts have not meaningfully solved the environmental problems (York & Venkataraman, 2010). According to these authors, reactive policies will only bring about incremental reduction in the activities of the firms which have contributed to environmental problems. Such reduction might not be sufficient to achieve the desired economic, environmental and social sustainability. Moreover, reactive policies might not fully resolve existing market imperfections and will not encourage innovative drive necessary to discover opportunities associated with sustainability problems.

Therefore, the policies and programmes of government should support entrepreneurial actions that can encourage entrepreneurs to use entrepreneurial process to resolve environmental challenges with innovative business solutions. This could be in form of tax incentives, recognition, green credit, establishment of eco-business incubators, and patronage of green products and services from such businesses. Government should also create a platform where nascent sustainable entrepreneurs can have access to information about the existence of entrepreneurial opportunities within environmental degradation. Equally important is the effort of government to facilitate collaboration and networking with national and international organisations who can assist in the development of technologies required to solve the environmental problems.

REFERENCES

Abereijo, I. O., & Ilori, M. O. (2011). Technological spillovers from multinational companies to small and medium food companies in Nigeria. In H. Sun (Ed.), *Management of technological innovation in developing and developed countries*. Rijeka, Croatia: Intech.

Ahmed, A., & Nwankwo, S. (2013). Entrepreneurship development in Africa: An overview. *World Journal of Entrepreneurship. Management and Sustainable Development*, *9*(2/3), 82–86.

Ajzen, I. (1991). The theory of planned behaviour. *Organizational Behavior and Human Decision Processes*, *50*(2), 179–211. doi:10.1016/0749-5978(91)90020-T

Baumgartner, R. (2009). Organisational culture and leadership: Preconditions for the development of a sustainable corporation. *Sustainable Development*, *17*(2), 102–113. doi:10.1002/sd.405

Bell, J., & Stellingwerf, J. J. (2012). *Sustainable entrepreneurship: The motivations and challenges of sustainable entrepreneurs in the renewable energy industry.* (Unpublished Master Thesis). Jönköping International Business School, Sweden.

Biomimicry Institute. (2014). *What is biomimicry?* Retrieved June 29, 2015, from http://biomimicry.org/ what-is-biomimicry/

Cohen, B., & Winn, M. I. (2007). Market imperfections, opportunity and sustainable entrepreneurship. *Journal of Business Venturing*, *22*(1), 29–49. doi:10.1016/j.jbusvent.2004.12.001

Crnogaj, K., Rebernik, M., Hojnik, B. B., & Gomezelj, D. O. (2014). Building a model of researching the sustainable entrepreneurship in the tourism sector. *Kybernetes*, *43*(3/4), 377–393. doi:10.1108/K-07-2013-0155

Dean, T. J., & McMullen, J. S. (2007). Toward a theory of sustainable entrepreneurship: Reducing environmental degradation through entrepreneurial action. *Journal of Business Venturing*, *22*(1), 50–76. doi:10.1016/j.jbusvent.2005.09.003

Dixon, S. E. A., & Clifford, A. (2007). Ecopreneurship: A new approach to managing the triple bottom line. *Journal of Organizational Change Management*, *20*(3), 326–345. doi:10.1108/09534810710740164

Dobson, A. (2007). Environmental citizenship: Towards sustainable development. *Sustainable Development*, *15*(5), 276–285. doi:10.1002/sd.344

Elkington, J. (1994). Towards the sustainable corporation: Win-win-win business strategies for sustainable development. *California Management Review*, *36*(2), 90–100. doi:10.2307/41165746

Elkington, J. (1997). *Cannibals with forks – The triple bottom line of 21st century business.* Oxford, UK: Capstone.

Elkington, J. (1998). Cannibals with forks: The triple bottom line of sustainability. *Gabriola California Management Review*, *45*(4), 35–51.

Giacalone, R. A., & Thompson, K. R. (2006). Business ethics and social responsibility education: Shifting the worldview. *Academy of Management Learning & Education*, *5*(3), 266–277. doi:10.5465/AMLE.2006.22697016

Gibbs, D. (2009). Sustainability entrepreneurs, ecopreneurs and the development of a sustainable economy. *Greener Management International*, *55*, 63–78.

Kashyap, R., Mir, R., & Iyer, E. (2006). Toward a responsive pedagogy: Linking social responsibility to firm performance issues in the classroom. *Academy of Management Learning & Education*, *5*(March), 366–376. doi:10.5465/AMLE.2006.22697025

Kirchgeorg, M. (1999). Marktstrategisches kreislaufmanagement. Gabler, Germany: Wiesbaden. doi:10.1007/978-3-322-90758-5

Koe, W.-L., Omar, R., & Majid, I. A. (2014). Factors associated with propensity for sustainable entrepreneurship. *Procedia: Social and Behavioral Sciences*, *130*, 65–74. doi:10.1016/j.sbspro.2014.04.009

Koe, W.-L., Omar, R., & Sa'ari, J. R. (2015). Factors influencing propensity to sustainable entrepreneurship of SMEs in Malaysia. *Procedia: Social and Behavioral Sciences*, *172*, 570–577. doi:10.1016/j.sbspro.2015.01.404

Kuckertz, A., & Wagner, M. (2010). The influence of sustainability orientation on entrepreneurial intentions: Investigating the role of business experience. *Journal of Business Venturing*, *25*(5), 524–539. doi:10.1016/j.jbusvent.2009.09.001

Kurz, H., & Salvadori, N. (1997). Exhaustible resources in a dynamic input–output model with 'classical' features. *Economic Systems Research*, *9*(3), 235–251. doi:10.1080/09535319700000017

Lourenço, F., Jones, O., & Jayawarna, D. (2013). Promoting sustainable development: The role of entrepreneurship education. *International Small Business Journal*, *31*(8), 841-865.

Lumpkin, G. T., & Katz, J. A. (2011). An introduction to the special volume on social and sustainable entrepreneurship. In G. T. Lumpkin & J. A. Katz (Eds.), *Advances in Entrepreneurship, Firm Emergence and Growth*. Bradford, UK: Emerald. doi:10.1108/S1074-7540(2011)0000013004

Majid, I. A., & Koe, W.-L. (2012). Sustainable entrepreneurship: A revised model based on triple bottom line. *International Journal of Academic Research in Business and Social Sciences*, *2*(6), 293–310.

Masurel, E. (2007). Why SMEs invest in environmental measures: Sustainability evidence from small and medium-sized printing firms. *Business Strategy and the Environment*, *16*(3), 190–201. doi:10.1002/bse.478

McDonough, W., & Braungart, M. (2002). *Cradle to cradle: Remaking the way we make things*. New York: North Point Press.

McEwen, T. (2013). Ecopreneurship as a solution to environmental problems: Implications for college level entrepreneurship education. *International Journal of Academic Research in Business and Social Science*, *3*(5), 264–288.

Nurse, K. (2006). Culture as the fourth pillar of sustainable development. *Small States: Economic Review and Basic Statistics*, *11*, 28–40.

Pascual, O., van Klink, A., & Grisales, A. R. (2011). *Create impact! Handbook for sustainable entrepreneurship*. Retrieved March 20, 2015, from http://www.scp-centre.org/fileadmin/ content/files/6_Resources/1_Publications_pdfs/60_Creating_impact_full.pdf

Patzelt, H., & Shepherd, D. A. (2011). Recognizing opportunities for sustainable development. *Entrepreneurship Theory and Practice*, *35*(4), 631–652. doi:10.1111/j.1540-6520.2010.00386.x

Richardson, J., Irwin, T., & Sherwin, C. (2005). *Design and Sustainability: A Scoping Report for the Sustainable Design Forum*. London: Design Council.

Santiago, A. (2013). On the road to sustainability entrepreneurship: Filipino case. *World Journal of Entrepreneurship. Management and Sustainable Development*, *9*(4), 255–271.

Sarasvathy, S. D., Dew, N., Velamuri, S. R., & Venkataraman, S. (2003). Three views of entrepreneurial opportunity. In Z. Acs & D. B. Audretsch (Eds.), *Handbook of Entrepreneurial Research* (pp. 141–160). Great Britain: Kluwer Academic Publishers.

Schaper, M. (2002). The challenge of environmental responsibility and sustainable development: Implications for SME and entrepreneurship academics. In U. Fuglistaller, H.J. Pleitner, T. Volery, & W. Weber (Eds.), *Radical Change in the World – Will SMEs Soar or Crash?* (pp. 525-534). St Gallen: KMU Verlag HSG. Retrieved March 20, 2015, from www.kmu.unisg.ch/rencontres/band2002/ F_09_Schaper.pdf

Schick, H., Marxen, S., & Freimann, J. (2002). Sustainability issues for start-up entrepreneurs. *Greener Management International*, *38*(Summer), 59–70.

Schlange, L. E. (2006). *What drives sustainable entrepreneurs*? Paper presented at the Applied Business and Entrepreneurship Association International Conference, Kona, HI.

Schumpeter, J. (1934). *The theory of economic development*. Berlin: Beck Editions.

Shane, S. (2003). *A general theory of entrepreneurship. The individual-opportunity nexus*. Cheltenham: Edward Elgar. doi:10.4337/9781781007990

Slater, D. J., & Dixon-Fowler, H. R. (2010). The future of the planet in the hands of MBAs: An examination of CEO MBA education and corporate environmental performance. *Academy of Management Learning & Education*, *9*(3), 429–441. doi:10.5465/AMLE.2010.53791825

Springett, D. (2005). Education for sustainability in the business studies curriculum: A call for a critical agenda. *Business Strategy and the Environment*, *14*(3), 146–159. doi:10.1002/bse.447

Stokes, D., Wilson, N., & Mador, M. (2010). *Entrepreneurship*. Hampshire, UK: South-Western Cengage Learning.

SustainAbility. (2008). *The social intrapreneur: A field guide for corporate change makers*. Washington, DC: SustainAbility Ltd. Retrieved June 29, 2015, from http://www.echoinggreen.org/sites/default/files/ The_Social_ Intrapreneurs.pdf

Tilley, F., & Young, W. (2009). Sustainability entrepreneurs: Could they be the true wealth generators of the future? *Green Management International*, *55*, 79–92.

United Nations. (2004). *United Nations Environment Programme 2004 Annual Report*. Retrieved February 10, 2015, from http://www.unep.org/publications/contents/ pub_details_search.asp? ID=3621

United Nations. (2010). *Sustainable Development: From Brundtland to Rio 2012. Background paper prepared for consideration by the High Level Panel on Global Sustainability at its first meeting, 19 September*. Retrieved February 10, 2015, from http://www.un.org/wcm/webdav/site/climatechange/ shared/ gsp/docs/GSP1-6_Background%20on%20Sustain-able%20Devt.pdf

Venkataraman, S. (1997). The distinctive domain of entrepreneurship research: An editor's perspective. In J. Katz & J. Brockhaus (Eds.), Advances in entrepreneurship, firm emergence, and growth. Greenwich, CT: JAI Press.

Walley, E., & Taylor, D. (2002). Opportunists, champions, Mavericksy?: A typology of green entrepreneurs. *Greener Management International*, *38*(Summer), 31–43. doi:10.9774/GLEAF.3062.2002.su.00005

World Commission on Environment and Development. (1987). *Our Common Future*. Oxford, UK: Oxford University Press.

World Resources Institute. (2004). *World Resources 2002–2004*. Washington, DC: World Resources Institute.

York, J. G., & Venkataraman, S. (2010). The entrepreneur–environment nexus: Uncertainty, innovation, and allocation. *Journal of Business Venturing*, *25*(5), 449–463. doi:10.1016/j.jbusvent.2009.07.007

Chapter 13
Design for Autonomy:
Water Resources in Ladakh

Carey Clouse
University of Massachusetts – Amherst, USA

ABSTRACT

This chapter describes one series of climate-adaptive design innovations found in Ladakh, north India. Five different water management techniques chart the region's unique and highly specialized response to water scarcity, and in so doing highlight important lessons for climate-adaptive planning elsewhere. In this case study, the dispersed, community-based water management strategies practiced in Ladakh suggest a level of design thinking that supports environmental stewardship, economic autonomy, cultural consciousness and social cohesion.

INTRODUCTION

In the face of global climate change, planners and designers can provide valuable expertise to communities in transition. Indeed, changing environmental conditions will necessitate new solutions for the mitigation and adaptation of infrastructural systems, human settlement patterns, and traditional ways of conceptualizing urban life. While the impacts of a changing climate are difficult to project and plan for, instability promises to become a common challenge of the Future City. In this environment, resilient, adaptive, and flexible designs for supporting human development suggest a way forward.

This chapter describes one series of climate-adaptive design innovations found in Ladakh, north India. Five different water management techniques chart the region's unique and highly specialized response to water scarcity, and in so doing highlight important lessons for climate-adaptive planning elsewhere. In this case study, the dispersed, community-based water management strategies practiced in Ladakh suggest a level of design thinking that supports environmental stewardship, economic autonomy, cultural consciousness and social cohesion.

While social capital rarely factors into the design of water infrastructure, it can have major policy and urban planning implications. This consideration is perhaps even more relevant in the tiny high-Himalayan villages of Ladakh, where the meltwater from glaciers and snowfields has always been treated as a

DOI: 10.4018/978-1-5225-0094-0.ch013

form of the commons. In this region, subsistence agriculture practices demand a level of collaboration not often felt in more urban settings, as meltwater must be equitably divided amongst landholders, and farmers must work together to direct, store, and disperse this precious resource.

In this context, top-down government-generated planning decisions tend to be out of touch with the largely invisible social, cultural and religious processes that guide most of the decision-making and daily activities throughout the region. Unlike the high authoritarian planning schemes that have characterized other Indian cities, the water management practices described in this paper have instead been developed in and for Ladakh: they are knit into the Ladakhi cultural and social fabric, and are inextricably rooted to the region's environmental context (Scott, 1998). As a result, these design solutions are finely-tuned to the individualized needs of each community, deployed on a case-by-case basis. Whereas larger, government-sponsored infrastructural projects might lack a regional understanding of materials, construction techniques, environmental conditions or social frameworks, these design solutions reflect the context and culture that they serve.

LADAKH: CLIMATE AND CONTEXT

Located within the state of Jammu and Kashmir, in the rain shadow of north India's Himalayan range, Ladakh is a rugged and dry mountain region. Environmental conditions could be considered both extreme and inhospitable, characterized by high altitude, low humidity, and extremely low precipitation. The region is referred to as a cold desert environment, with temperature fluctuations that range from -40C to 35C and scarce rainfall, between 50 and 300mm annually (Bhasin, 1992; Demenge, 2007).

Ladakh's mountainous terrain is sparsely populated, containing some of the highest inhabited villages on earth (Norberg-Hodge, 2000). More than fifty villages exist in the region, supporting populations of 100 to 1,500 people (District Statistics & Evaluation Office, 2013). Moreover, the trans-Himalayan mountain range has effectively cut the region off from the southern portion of the subcontinent, where the "forbidding climate, remoteness and inaccessibility (has) kept Ladakh isolated, except for traders, for centuries" (Mann, 1986, 3).

In this challenging environment, strong social and cultural traditions have effectively tethered people to the land, and to each other. According to scholar R.S. Mann, Ladakhi "people feel that their adaptation (to climate) alone made them survive whenever nature posed threat (sic) to their existence" (Mann, 1986, vi). While humans have effectively and sustainably flourished in this region for more than one thousand years, existing environmental pressures, coupled with unstable weather patterns caused by a warming climate, have brought about changes to age-old patterns of living in recent years (Mingle, 2015; Rizvi, 1998).

Agriculture in Ladakh

While the region remains relatively isolated today, Ladakh has witnessed many sweeping changes over the last four decades, particularly with the rise of tourism and an increasing number of employment opportunities in the local military and government sectors. According to scholar Mohammed Deen Darokhan, this shift has also caused a deterioration in the practice of ancient farming techniques and agricultural reliance overall. Darokhan regards agriculture as "the only sustainable way of life in Ladakh," and worries that villages could "lose the genetic material and cultivation techniques due to a neglect of farming"

(Darokhan, 1999, 79). Other scholars note that agriculture is inextricably tied to land stewardship and cultural survival, as the traditional agricultural lifestyle has supported many centuries of sustainable human settlement in the region (Norberg-Hodge, 2000; Rizvi, 1998).

While these demographic shifts have become even more marked in the intervening years, culturally, socially, and even economically, traditional agrarian values persist. Most Ladakhi villagers still practice a single integrated system of subsistence agriculture and have very few opportunities for economic participation (Crook & Ostmason, 1994; Gutschow & Mankelow, 2001; Norberg-Hodge, 2000). This is the outcome of many years of farming effort, as generations of farmers have worked with natural cycles "to green the desert and bring biological diversity" to an otherwise barren landscape (Darokhan, 1999, 78). Indeed, the lush green farmlands, thick stands of willow trees, and surprisingly fertile topsoil visible in an otherwise inhospitable desert environment represent many centuries of judicious land stewardship. (Figures 1 and 2 in the Appendix) Perhaps not surprisingly, this difficult agricultural environment also reinforces the value of traditional methods, where "the adoption of agricultural innovations is slow" (Mann, 1986, 173).

The primary crops grown in Ladakh are barley, wheat, buckwheat, millet, peas, mustard seed, apricots, and livestock fodder including alfalfa (Gutschow, 1997; Humbert-Droz & Dawa, 2004; Sagwal, 1991). While agricultural production continues to support subsistence households, some farmers have shifted to cash crops in response to the large presence of the Indian military and tourist industry and their demand for potatoes and vegetables (Tiwari & Gupta, 2007).

Water in Ladakh

In Ladakh, water is primarily used for two purposes: household activities and crop irrigation. Most villages supply household water from groundwater, rather than the surface meltwater used in agriculture. In these cases groundwater is drawn from wells (using hand pumps), mountain springs, or from those two sources via tanker trucks, which refill household barrels or tube wells (Akhtar 2013; Sudhalkar, 2010). While the challenges associated with groundwater depletion in this region are significant, household water use represents but a tiny fraction of the water volume needed to support farming and animal husbandry. As such, surface water management—the collection, retention, and dispersion of flowing meltwater from glaciers and snowfields above—has become a central planning concern of the Ladakhi village. Moreover, subsistence agricultural practices, and the elaborate system of irrigation associated with them, dominate the social, economic, and physical structures of village life (Gutschow, 1997; Norberg-Hodge, 2000).

Annual precipitation is limited, and most irrigation water comes from melting snowfields and glaciers in the northern part of the watershed (Akhtar 2013). While this region hosts the headwaters of the Indus River, water used for farming must be captured as it courses down the mountains from the high Himalayan glaciers to the river below. The floodplains of the river typically lack "viable arable land" and the idea of pumping water from rivers is, in this context, too difficult (Gutschow & Mankelow, 2003, 28). Instead, villages historically drape across the sides of mountains, opportunistically sited between the high glaciers above and the river below.

While the presence or absence of glacial meltwater may initially determine the location of a village, the resulting system of irrigation infrastructure depicts a far more intentional, sophisticated and laborious planning effort. Katiyar et al. note that "Without irrigation vegetable farming is out of the question in Ladakh," and indeed this practice has emerged as a means of contending with an otherwise inhospitable climate and landscape (2012, 312). According to Tibetan scholars, skillful irrigation was present in this region in the 10th century, and in many cases early stone canal work has been improved upon for centuries (Bell, 1928).

In this climate and context, irrigation has become an elegant, efficient and equitable system in most villages, honed over many hundreds of years and kept in check by village politics and social norms. Professor and scholar Kim Gutschow describes the power dynamic created by this water management as "webs of water," which bind villagers to each other and to a communal decision making process (Gutschow 1997, 105). Sharing a single water source has led villagers to develop an advanced rotational system for water distribution as well as enduring practices for collective bargaining and oversight. In the summer months, fields might be watered every seven to ten days, depending on the crop and time of the season. If water ceases to flow at the end of the summer, everyone in the village will equally feel the effect of the drought.

Climate Change and Glaciers

According to the *Leh Handbook*, due to the region's "arctic desert condition and (the) scanty rainfall of the district, irrigation depends on the eternal glaciers" (District Statistics & Evaluation Office, 2012, 24). But glaciologists, climate scientists, and journalists agree that the glaciers appear to be eternal no more. New global weather patterns have caused large-scale changes to this landscape, resulting in an overall reduction of glacial mass across the Himalayan range. Journalist Jonathan Mingle notes that the state of "Jammu and Kashmir has lost 20 percent of its total glacial mass in the past six decades," (Mingle, 2015, 397) and cites a study of over 2,000 glaciers across the Indian Himalaya by India's Space Research Organization, which "determined that 75 percent are retreating, at an annual rate of 3.5 percent" (Mingle, 222).

A 2010 USAID report on the state of glaciers and hydrology in High Asia also explains that glacier melt is occurring, leading to impacts such as "too much water (floods), too little water (droughts/ increased aridity), or water at different times (more early in the growing season/less late in the growing season)" (Malone, 2010, 25). This is an acute problem for subsistence agricultural farmers, who rely on relatively stable weather and meltwater patterns to grow their traditional crops, and to determine when to sow, water, and harvest their fields. Unlike farmers working with electricity, pumps, and other advanced technologies, Ladakhi villagers lack access to the tools that could otherwise provide a relative safety net. Instead they have relied almost exclusively upon the glaciers high above their villages to act as a storage device for water over the course of the year.

As climate change impacts snowfall and glacial mass in the region, the water resources available to farmers appear to be shrinking (Grossman, 2105). The 2010 USAID report suggests that the drainages in this region should be addressed by "well-planned management, conservation, and efficient use of the water people currently have available to them" (Malone, 2010, 27). While one could argue that these suggestions have already guided water management practices in Ladakh for centuries, the development of new tools and techniques could help farmers plan for improved water security.

ADAPTIVE DESIGN SOLUTIONS FOR WATER MANAGEMENT

Historically, Ladakhi villlages have relied on low-tech, time-tested water management systems to funnel high glacial and snowfield meltwater down to croplands lower in the valley. The traditional canals, water diversion gates, and systems for equitable sharing, have, for centuries, effectively supported subsistence agricultural practices. As scholar Janet Rizvi notes, "The scantiness of rainfall makes Ladakhi agriculture totally dependent on irrigation; but all those sources that lie within the scope of traditional technology have been tapped (1998, 177). Indeed, many scholars suggest that Lakahi irrigation practices have already been fully optimized as a reponse to the arctic desert environment (Crook & Ostmanson, 1994; Norberg-Hodge, 2000; Rizvi 1998).

In recent years, however, the changing weather and diminishing glacial meltwater brought about by climate change has inspired improvisation on these traditional systems. In some instances, entire villages have moved to new waterside locations (Mingle, 2009). In other cases, villages have sought to improve their water management infrastructure with technical assistance from local NGOs and state government agencies. Several relatively new innovations have been adopted by Ladakhi villages, typically in the form of a design intervention that bolsters extant water infrastructure functioning.

These solutions have been developed and deployed on a case-by-case basis, often as a result of stakeholder involvement, using consensus decision-making and sweat-equity. As such, the numerous responses represent a family of design interventions that might be deployed as needed in a wide variety of water scarce environments. This body of adaptive management practices reinforce the systems already in place in Ladakh, and represent an effective small-scale planning solution for the social, cultural, environmental, economic and even religious implications of this place.

Artificial Glaciers

Artificial glaciers might be more accurately called ice dams, as they form large, layered pools of ice over the winter for spring and summer agricultural use. These large-scale landscape infrastructure projects efficiently store and manage glacial meltwater by exploiting annual freeze-thaw cycles and incorporating large storage reservoirs to contain glacial runoff (Ahmed, Higgins & Norphel, 2010). During periods of drought or when Ladakhi farmers otherwise wouldn't have access to meltwater (such as in the early spring), the artificial glaciers melt, releasing their ice stock in the form of irrigation water. The long, cascading pools are located between the high natural glaciers and the village croplands below, using gravity to move the water when farmers open regulating and diversion gates (Higgins, 2012; Norphel, 2010).

These glaciers have been placed above eight different villages in Ladakh, and range in size from a small number of pools at a single site to many dozens of reservoirs that extend over a mile in length. (Figures 3 and 4 in the Appendix) They are typically built using masonry walls with stone collected from the site and local labor, often through work parties organized by the Leh Nutrition Project (Clouse, 2014). In allowing farmers to collect water that is cascading down through the watershed during non-agricultural seasons (fall and winter), and save it for later use (spring and summer), the artificial glacier effectively increases the overall water supply available to farmers (Vince, 2009). Moreover, because these glacial pools serve the entire village and help to stretch the communal supply of water, they are collectively owned, managed, and operated by local farmers.

Ice Stupas

Ice stupas were designed by Sonam Wangchuck in 2014, as scalable ice towers that can store fall and winter water, as ice, for use during the following spring and summer. (Figure 5 in the Appendix) Much like the artificial glacier, ice stupas take advantage of annual freeze-thaw cycles, gravity-fed watersheds, and placement between high glaciers and low croplands. Unlike artificial glaciers, however, the ice stupa requires the extensive use of pipes to funnel water through trenches and up to the spout of the stupa's crown, as well as regular maintenance throughout the winter, to move pipes as ice forms.

The ice stupa has several advantages to the artificial glacier. It can be endlessly replicated across a village landscape, unlike the glacier pools, which need to be located on specific slopes and solar aspects. It is scale-able, functioning equally well for small reserves of ice as it for a large, multi-story site. In this sense it is also something that individual farmers can develop on their own accord, rather than relying on the larger village buy-in needed to implement an artificial glacier system.

However, the ice stupa connects to the social, cultural and religious fabric of Ladakh in other ways. In built prototypes over the past two years, builders have purposefully worked with the imagery of the local stone *chorten*, or *stupa*, which serves as a religious icon and prayer site. The ice forms in a similar structural shape, referencing the sacred forms of the stupas that are already built in this landscape. To emphasize this connection, the team of builders invited monks from the nearby Phyang monastery to bless the stupa, and they strung Tibetan prayer flags across the ice mass. In this way, the project developers have helped to root the radical new design intervention within the extant religious, social and cultural vocabulary of the region.

Snow Barrier Bands

Snow barrier bands perform much like the snow fences found in other parts of the world. In Ladakh, they are long, linear masonry walls built at high mountain passes in the upper portion of a watershed. The walls are typically built from stone found on the site, and are usually 3' wide, stand up to 5' tall, and can be many hundreds of feet in length. Used alone or as a part of a larger series, they help to capture snow, hold it on site at the top of the watershed, and then release it in the form of meltwater in the late spring. (Figures 6-7 in the Appendix)

In Ladakh, many ancient villages have been built on the south side of mountain ranges, in order to take advantage of passive solar heating in cold winter months. However, the winter winds blow from south to north, effectively propelling scarce winter snow from the densely populated side of the mountain range to the uninhabited northern slope. Snow barrier bands serve to stop snow before it can tip from a south-facing drainage into a north-facing drainage, thereby increasing the amount of meltwater that will be available to farmers in populated areas.

Snow barrier bands are also derivatives of ancient local building vocabularies. They incorporate masonry walls, which constitute the vast majority of traditional Ladakhi construction, from houses and temples to animal enclosure, crop protection, and fences. Because they serve an entire watershed, whole villages will work together to construct and maintain them, even though they are placed at high mountain passes. In the case of the snow barrier bands built at Warila Pass in 2013, several hundred villagers actively collaborated on the build, which was held over the course of a week at an elevation of 17,500'.

Canals/Kuhls

Water infrastructure systems, such as the *kuhls* or the primary canals that direct meltwater to village croplands, have increased in size and scope over the past decade. Kuhls have been widened, improved with impervious membranes, regulator gates, and pipes, and stretched farther than traditional technologies would have otherwise allowed. They now have been engineered to leap over ridges, cross highways, and exploit topography to carry water across many miles to towns outside of a particular drainage.

Kuhls help to address one of the major challenges for today's farmers: the inefficiency of traditional irrigation infrastructure. Ancient channels linking upper glaciers to low-lying fields have been carved out of the landscape over many hundreds of years; these are the mud, wooden, or stone lines carrying water along a path. These waterways lose a large amount of their volume to seepage; in one estimate 90% of the water routed above the village of Stongde, in the neighboring Zanskar valley, vanished before reaching fields (Crook and Ostmanson 1994). Newer, high- and medium-tech kuhls reinforce these crumbling old canals, improving water access by reducing losses due to seepage and poor engineering. (Figure 8 in the Appendix)

These new irrigation projects provide a much more efficient, and often large-scale approach, than pre-existing progenitors. However, the kuhls can still be considered relatively small-scale and supportive design interventions. While they have been built with funding from government agencies (such as the Watershed Development Agency), they often draw construction labor from adjacent villages. Moreover, kuhl construction reinforces traditional Ladakhi cultural and social frameworks, by hardening and improving existing water management systems that work within conventional agricultural concepts.

Zings

Zings are large water reservoirs, usually located just above croplands in order to store meltwater for agricultural use. The reservoirs are typically constructed from masonry or earth berms, and are then lined with concrete or mud. At the upper end they will feature a gravity-fed inlet, while the lower side will have a drain and overflow gate. Water diverted into the zings can be controlled, both to direct it in and to release it into the fields. Zings are connected to the source of the meltwater and to the fields below by the same canals that have historically supported irrigation practices in Ladakhi villages for centuries. (Figure 9 in the Appendix)

These small ponds have a limited capacity, so they cannot provide enormous stores of water. However, they do buy time, enabling farmers to irrigate fields according to their own schedule. For instance, when fields are on a rotation of a split night and day watering schedule, those who have a "night shift" can divert the water to a zing to hold it for use the following day (Gutschow, 1997). By storing water, even temporarily, above the sites where it will be used, the zings ensure that all of the water available to farmers during a season will be used, thus reducing waste.

WEIGHING THE BENEFITS

Unlike many other forward-thinking climate-adaptive design ideas, each of these five water harvesting and management solutions supports the existing agrarian lifestyles honed over centuries in Ladakhi villages. This is particularly relevant in a society where "agriculture is the backbone of every village economy, engaging up to 70% of the working force," and many Ladakhi villagers rely exclusively on local agriculture for their food supply (Pulselli & Pelliciardi, 2014, 347). Rather than reimagine the economic frameworks that will support village life in the years to come, these design interventions seek to improve the productivity of the existing system.

In assessing the economic implications of such interventions, one must first ask: Are they effective? Most hydrological models, especially those involving untested design interventions, are carried out over a series of years: indeed, one year would not adequately describe patterns or outlying factors. Current data on these five water management strategies lacks this long-term view, and several of the interventions described in this chapter lack even the most rudimentary modeling. Thus, it is still too early to be able to tell whether the interventions work as anticipated, and to what extent they improve water access for cold desert farmers.

Anecdotally, however, each of these five design interventions has been met with much interest and excitement from village farmers (Higgins, 2012). The low cost of implementation, across the board, and the relative flexibility of each of these strategies suggests radically-inclusive access for those who wish to employ these solutions. And in all cases, the water management strategies effectively improve or shore up existing systems, so they represent a relatively low-risk response to climate-change adaptation.

While traditional surface water irrigation has supported life for many hundreds of years, structural flaws are evident in the broader planning system. One of the most difficult planning challenges for Ladakhi villages is that current irrigation methods don't allow for population growth; the system assumes a fixed number of individuals or farms. With better health and life expectancy through access to new medical practices, and with the dissolution of the ancient practices of primogeniture and polyandry, the number of households in the region will likely continue to grow. Because the cultivable land in villages is fixed, individuals may need to seek employment elsewhere or import food for local consumption.

Likewise, the overall volume of water available in the watershed effectively places limits on the size and scale of an individual farmer's cropland; villagers must work together to develop an equitable division of irrigated fields. Ultimately, the volume of water coming from the high glaciers and seasonal snows may not be enough to support the crops grown below. After all, the intensive and highly productive agricultural practices of Ladakh rely heavily upon water resources, and are effectively limited by the region's supply of water.

CONCLUSION

In high mountain villages, the self-sufficiency and relative autonomy of groups have historically been prized survival traits. Small, independent villages act as distinct units, with villagers solving problems as they surface, working together to make decisions, and taking care of one another in times of need. The community-based water management framework implemented in Ladakh acknowledges that these villages have historically functioned as autonomous, self-governing populations, and seeks to reinforce age-old methods of group resilience.

Unlike the top-down planning solutions that may work well for large urbanizing populations, Ladakhi villages demand solutions that are site-specific, small, and dispersed. While broad, overarching schemes for infrastructure projects may be needed in large urban areas, in Ladakh these designs lack the physical, cultural, social, religious, and economic context that will ensure a proper fit.

The five new water management strategies for Ladakh provide a working example of the type of interventions that could work in other cold mountain environments. In suggesting a policy direction for the future, small, dispersed systems, responsive to local conditions, appear to be a promising way forward. In these examples the design intervention recognizes the relative autonomy of each village, both in terms of needs and opportunities; they engage stakeholders in the development of each system, from construction to maintenance; they layer over existing water infrastructures to improve efficiency; and they are affordable, scalable solutions, accessible to rural farming villages. These designs suggest an approach to water management that offers co-benefits: interventions are rooted in the communities they serve, connected to the cultural, social and religious context, responsive to the climate and landscape, supportive of rural self-sufficiency and independence, and affordable due to their scale and size.

In many communities water is an invisible resource: not owned, managed or operated by users, perhaps not even a significant factor of the economic, religious, or social functioning of those sites. But in the high Himalaya, water is a form of the commons that is absolutely critical to group survival, and it is made visible by the clear relevance it has to daily life. The various techniques for water planning in this desert region help to illuminate some of the opportunities and challenges inherent to climate change adaptation. In so doing, these five different designs from the Indian Himalaya suggest a model for other water-constrained mountain communities. If, indeed, instability will become the chief characteristic of the Future City, water management solutions will likewise need to become flexible, scalable, layered and dispersed. Finally, in order to effectively deploy these varied approaches, pioneering solutions also must fit in. Climate-adaptive water management practices in Ladakhi villages demonstrate the importance of integrating new design interventions with existing irrigation systems, social fabric, environmental context, religious interest and cultural identity.

REFERENCES

Acharya, S., Katiyar, A. K., Bharti, V. K., Charan, G., Prakash, B., & Srivastava, R. B. (2012). Assessment of irrigation water quality of cold arid Ladakh region. *Journal of Soil and Water Conservation*, *11*(4), 311–315.

Ahmed, N., Higgins, A. & Norphel, C. (2010). *Snow Water Harvesting in the Cold Desert Ladakh: An Introduction to the Artificial Glacier Project.* Leh: Leh Nutrition Project.

Akhtar, A., & Gondhalekar, D. (2013). Impacts of tourism on water resources in Leh town. *Ladakh Studies.*, *30*, 25–37.

Anghchok, D., & Singh, P. (2006). Traditional Irrigation and Water Distribution System in Ladakh. *Indian Journal of Traditional Knowledge*, *5*(3), 397–402.

Bell, C. (1928). *The People of Tibet.* Oxford, UK: The Clarendon Press.

Bhasin, M. K. (1992). *Cold Desert: Ladakh: Ecology and Development.* Delhi: Khamla Raj Enterprises Publications.

Clouse, C. (2014). Learning from artificial glaciers in the Himalaya: design for climate change through low-tech infrastructural devices. *Journal of Landscape Architecture*, *9*(3), 6-19.

Crook, J., & Ostmason, H. (1994). *Himalayan Buddhist Villages: environment, resources, society and religious life in Zangskar, Ladakh.* Bristol: University of Bristol Press.

Darokhan, M. D. (1999). The Development of Ecological Agriculture in Ladakh and Strategies for Sustainable Development. In Ladakh: Culture, History and Development between Himalaya and Karakoram. Delhi: Sterling Publishers.

Daultrey, S., & Gergan, R. (2011). Living with Change: Adaptation and Innovation in Ladakh. *Journal of Climate Adaptation.*

Demenge, J. (2007). *Measuring Ecological Footprints of Subsistence Farmers in Ladakh.* Paper presented at the International Ecological Footprint Conference, International Ecological Footprint Conference, Cardiff, UK.

District Statistics & Evaluation Office. (2012). *District Statistical Handbook for the Year 2011-2012.* Leh: Government of Jammu & Kashmir.

District Statistics & Evaluation Office. (2013). Ladakh Autonomous Hill District Blockwise Village Amenity Directory 2012-2013. Leh: Government of Jammu & Kashmir.

Diwedi, A. (2009). *Forests of Himalaya: Planning and Development.* Delhi: Cyber Tech Publications.

Grossman, D. (2015). As Himalayan Glaciers Melt, Two Towns Face the Fallout. *Yale Environment 360.* Retrieved 08 June 2015 From: http://e360.yale.edu/feature/as_himalayan_glaciers_melt_two_towns_face_the_fallout/2858/

Gutschow, K. (1997). Lords of the Fort, Lords of the Earth, and no lords at all: politics of irrigation in three Tibetan societies. In *Recent Research on Ladakh: Proceedings of the 6th international colloquium on Ladakh.*

Gutschow, K., & Mankelow, S. (2001). Dry Winters, Dry Summers: Water Shortages in Zanskar. *Ladakh Studies, 15*, 28–32.

Higgins, A. K. (2012). *Artificial glaciers and ice-harvesting in Ladakh, India as an adaptation to a changing climate.* (Unpublished Master's Thesis). Yale School of Forestry, New Haven, CT.

Humbert-Droz, B., & Dawa, S. (2004). *Biodiversity of Ladakh: Strategy and Action Plan.* Calcutta: ACB Publications.

Hussain, M. N., & Hussain, M. A. (2011). *Natural Resources of Jammu Kashmir and Ladakh.* Srinagar: Gulshan Books.

Malone, Elizabeth L. (2010). *Changing Glaciers and Hydrology in Asia: Addressing Vulnerabilities to Glacier Melt Impacts.* USAID Report November 2010.

Mann, R. S. (1986). *The Ladakhi: A Study in Ethnography and Change.* Delhi: Anthropological Survey of India.

Leomann Maps (n.d.). *Indian Himalaya Maps, Sheet 3.* Author.

Mingle, J. (2009, November 29). When the Glacier Left. *Boston Globe.*

Mingle, J. (2015). *Fire and Ice: Soot, Solidarity and Survival on the Roof of the World*. New York: St. Martin's Press.

Norberg-Hodge, H. (2000). *Ancient Futures: Learning from Ladakh*. London: Rider Books.

Norphel, C. (2012). *Artificial Glacier: A High Altitude Cold Desert Water Conservation Technique*. Presented at the In Defense of Liberty Conference, New Delhi, India.

Pati, D. R., & Tewari, D. D. (2009). *Conservation of Medicinal Plants*. Delhi: APH Publishing.

Pulselli, F. M., & Pelliciardi, V. (2014). Emergy Evaluation of a Mountain Socio-Economic System and Traditional Agroproduction: A Case Study in Indian Trans-Himalaya. *European Journal of Sustainable Development*, 347-356.

Rizvi, J. (1998). *Ladakh: crossroads of high Asia*. Delhi: Oxford University Press.

Sagwal, S. (1991). *Ladakh Ecology and Environment*. New Delhi: Ashish Publishing House.

Scott, J. (1998). *Seeing Like A State: How Certain Schemes to Improve the Human Condition Have Failed*. New Haven, CT: Yale University Press.

Snow Leopard Conservancy. (2010). *Ri Gyancha: a Biodiversity Resource Kit for Educators in Ladakh*. Delhi: Kalpavriksh.

Sudhalkar, A. (2010). *Adaptation to Water Scarcity in Glacier-Dependent Towns of the Indian Himalayas: Impacts, Adaptive Responses, Barriers, and Solutions*. (Unpublished master's thesis). Massachusetts Institute of Technology, Cambridge, MA.

Tiwari, S., & Gupta, R. (2007). Changing Currents: The Irrigation Practices of Leh Town. *Recent Research on Ladakh*, 217-24.

Vince, G. (2009). Glacier Man. *Science*, *326*(5953), 659–661. doi:10.1126/science.326_659 PMID:19900911

APPENDIX: FIGURES

Figure 1. Villagers work together in the fields fed by the Phuksey artificial glacier meltwater.
Credit: Carey Clouse.

Figure 2. The rugged desert agricultural landscapes of Ladakh necessitate gravity-fed irrigation strategies.
Credit: Carey Clouse.

Figure 3. Several cascading artificial glacier pools above the village of Igoo
Credit: Carey Clouse.

Figure 4. Above the village of Nang, eight artificial glacier pools are closely spaced in a narrow canyon.
Credit: Carey Clouse.

Figure 5. The ice stupa built above Phyang demonstrates the stark contrast between the stockpile of ice and the dry surrounding landscape.
Photo: SECMOL.

Figure 6. Yaks pass through a series of snow barrier bands at the top of Warila Pass, 17,500'
Credit: Carey Clouse.

Figure 7. Snow barrier bands are simple masonry walls, strategically placed within the landscape.
Credit: Carey Clouse.

Figure 8. This canal directs water from one drainage, over a ridge into another drainage above the village of Sakti.
Credit: Carey Clouse.

Figure 9. This massive reservoir contains meltwater above the village of Nang.
Credit: Carey Clouse.

Chapter 14
Smart Cities in Spain – Policy, Sustainability, and the National Plan:
New Political Measures, Agents, and Sustainability

Martín García Vaquero
IE Business School, Spain

José Manuel Saiz-Alvarez
Tecnologico de Monterrey, Mexico, & Nebrija University, Spain

ABSTRACT

According to the United Nations Conference on Sustainable Development in Rio de Janeiro in 2012, half of humanity lives in cities. The urban population has increased from 750 million people in 1950 to 3,600 million in 2011. It is estimated that by 2030 almost 60% of the population world will reside in urban areas. In Spain already does more than 80%. This will lead to significant growth in the coming years, and cities must be prepared to serve new services on a sustainable way: from meeting the needs of potable water or clean air transport will be a challenge of extraordinary magnitude and an opportunity for the industry. The Spanish National Plan for Smart Cities is a continuation of different initiatives proposing to do a set of new political measures that involve the mobilization of resources that will put special emphasis on sustainability.

Cities are engines of human and economic development. At the same time, most greenhouse gas emissions are produced in cities. Building solutions with the evolving needs and nature of citizens will create an adaptable foundation on which to shape the future of cities. Smart cities acting as catalysers of the foreseen energy, environmental and social revolution are expected to play a key role in order to achieve the new European objectives by 2020. – European Innovation Partnership on Smart Cities and Communities.

DOI: 10.4018/978-1-5225-0094-0.ch014

INTRODUCTION

According to the European 2020 Strategy Document (European Commision, 2010b), Europe is suffering a period of structural transformation in the socio-economic framework. The priorities to favor the new model that Europe needs are:

1. **Smart Growth:** Defined as the necessity of developing an economy based on knowledge and innovation;
2. **Sustainable Growth:** Achieved after to have promoted an economy that makes more efficient use of resources, is greener and more competitive;
3. **Inclusive Growth:** That is achieved when the economy reaches high employment levels while delivering social and territorial cohesion.

To this end, and in the same document, the European Commission proposes the following objectives:

1. 75% of the population between 20 and 64 years should be employed;
2. 3% of European Union's Gross Domestic Product (hereinafter, GDP) should be invested in R & D;
3. The 20/20/20 Objective (20% reduction of greenhouse gases until 20%, 20% reduction of energy consumption, and 20% increase of using renewable energy) should be achieved in terms of climate and energy;
4. The percentage of early school leavers should be under 10%, and at least 40% of the younger generation should have a tertiary degree; and
5. The risk of poverty should threaten no more than 20 million fewer people.

To achieve these objectives seven flagship initiatives are proposed: innovation, youth employment, access to internet, efficient use of resources, business competitiveness, qualification of labor and social, and territorial cohesion.

To address the main challenges in implementing the Europe 2020 Strategy, member countries have a vital instrument: the Structural Funds and the European Investment (FEIE) for period 2014-2020. Both Structural Funds and the Cohesion Fund are the financial instruments of European Union (EU) regional policy, which is intended to narrow the development disparities among regions and Member States. The Funds participate fully, therefore, in pursuing the goal of economic, social and territorial cohesion. In Spain, the Partnership Agreement to join the Europe 2020 strategy to be applied to the Foreign Earned Income Exclusion (hereinafter, FEIE), recognizes the central role that cities play as the engine of the economy, as they are places of connectivity, creativity and innovation, as well as service centers. Therefore, urban development becomes a priority area within the cohesion policy of the EU.

Given the importance of Smart Cities, it is mandatory to define and standarize indicators to measure the evolution of our cities to the challenge of achieving higher competitive rates while being sustainable cities.

Objective

The objective of this chapter is to define which are going to be the characteristics and municipal policies the Spanish cities must fulfiled in order to be transformed into Smart Cities. At this respect, ICTs play a key role to accelerate this urban change making possible a larger amount of data sharing that is necessary to transform the city. In this chapter the Spanish case will be analyzed, given its connections with Latin American and the Caribbean countries where a radical urban transformation into Smart Cities is necessary and desirable, as it is expected that 82.8% of Latin American population will be urban by the year 2025 (CEPAL, 2005, p. 29).

BACKGROUND

Smart Cities in Spain: A Must

Regarding smart cities, the economic policy carried out by the Government of Spain is reflected in the National Reform Plan (NRP) with the scope of transforming the Spanish economy. This agenda has been organized around three pillars: fiscal consolidation, sanitation, financial system to activate credit and investment, and structural reforms. The NRP 2014 integrated measures both in the medium and long terms, focused on achieving the national objectives of the Europe 2020 strategy with short-term measures registered in the areas of coordination contained in the European Commission's Communication titled "Annual Survey Growth 2014" that promotes

1. Fiscal consolidation of economic growth;
2. Competitiveness while tackling unemployment and the social consequences of the crisis, and
3. Modernization of public administration by increasing administrative efficiency by improving cooperation between different levels of government, increased use of Information and Communication Technologies (hereinafter, ICT), and eGovernment services in Europe.

In fact, the use of ICT makes the critical infrastructure components and services of a city – which include city administration, education, healthcare, public safety, real estate, transportation, and utilities – more intelligent, interconnected, and efficient (Washburn & Sindhu, 2009).

These guidelines for economic policy are reflected in industrial policy initiatives. In Spain, the industrial policy initiative is shown in the "Agenda for Strengthening the Industrial Sector in Spain" approved by the Spanish Council of Ministers on July 11, 2014. The agenda combines a series of measures at horizontal level, particularly relevant to SMEs, and others at national and international levels to get the industry achieving higher levels of sustainable economic growth.

While in the most developed countries, the industrial sector has declined both in total employment and the GDP, industry has an important role to play because of its relative size, its role in international trade flows, and the ability to drag respecting to other non-industrial activities; in particular, respecting to a very significant part of the services. The "Agenda for Strengthening the Industrial Sector in Spain" believes that the country should continue to promote the development of a strong, competitive industrial sector and international reference that contributes to the recovery of economic activity and job creation, given its effect multiplier on the rest of the economy and his greatest contribution for improving R&D

and innovation. In fact, both in the USA and in the European Union, one dollar of industrial GDP generates 1.34 of aggregate economic activity (European Commission, 2015a). All this in order to achieve the goal set by the EU included in the Europe 2020 strategy, as stated: to increase the industrial sector up to 20% of GDP in the year 2020. In 2015, the industrial sector's contribution to GDP in Spain was 15.9%. To achieve this goal, 97 measures, including those inserted into the Digital Agenda for Spain (ADPE), have been approved to promote increased productivity of industrial enterprises by incorporating ICTs, and improving production processes, especially the availability of high-speed infrastructures. Complementary to this strategy, two more plans have been approved: 2015 Smart Cities Plan, and the Digital Homes Sustainable Buildings.

Status of Smart Cities

Mainly in the XX century, municipalities and local authorities, in general, have been the main centers of economic, social and cultural development; conducive to the development of creativity and innovation environment, and particularly social innovation. According to the United Nations Conference on Sustainable Development held in Rio de Janeiro in 2012, half of humanity live in cities. The urban population has increased from 750 million, which constituted approximately in 1950, to 3,600 million in 2011. It is estimated that by 2030 almost 60% of the world population will reside in urban areas. In Spain, more than 80% live in cities, according to the Statistical Atlas of Urban Areas published by the Spanish Ministry of Development.

This will lead to significant growth in the coming years. Cities around the world must be prepared to serve sustainably, fundamentally administrative. Meet the needs of drinking water or clean air transport will be a challenge of extraordinary magnitude, and an opportunity for the industry.

Urban environments have always dealt with problems derived from social and urban structures with strong environmental impact, given their position as consumers of energy resources, and waste and pollutants emitters. Improving the good relationship with the environment, while maintaining the quality and cost of services rendered or the ability to reorganize their structures responding to new needs, are important issues to be resolved. A significant number of cities around the world have adopted new technologies for a more efficient delivery of public services management. As a result, their relations with citizens, tourists, companies, and suppliers have been redefined.

According to Manville et al. (2014), Smart Cities are defined as having at least one of these initiatives: Smart Economy, Smart People, Smart Mobility, Smart Environment, Smart Governance, and Smart Living. Considering this definition, 240 of the 468 EU cities with at least 100,000 inhabitants (51% of the total) are classified as smart cities. Spain is among the countries with the highest number of Smart Governance projects, along with France, Germany, Sweden and the United Kingdom; and Smart Mobility initiatives, along with Hungary, Romania and Italy.

Nam and Pardo (2011), cited by Manville et al. (2014), affirm that Smart Cities are about leveraging interoperability within and across policy domains of the city (e.g. transportation, public safety, energy, education, healthcare, and development). Smart City strategies require innovative ways of interacting with stakeholders, managing resources, and providing services. Of the six characteristics listed the most common projects are linked to pan-European public goods problems. Environment and Smart Mobility Smart represent, respectively, 21% and 33% initiatives, and each of the other four (Smart Governance, Smart Economy, Smart People and Smart Living) are addressed in about 10%.

There seems to be a consensus on the concept of Smart City or the minimum elements that must be present in a city to be considered as such. It can be agreed that the application of ICT to improve the quality of life of its inhabitants, and to ensure sustainable economic, social and environmental development are common elements in all definitions. Besides, the concept requires a new relationship with citizens, tourists, vendors, and government employees based on transparency, accountability, proper use, consumption of resources, and the early identification of needs.

The National Plan for Smart Cities in Spain follows the definition proposed by the Technical Group 178 of the Spanish Association for Standardization and Certification (AENOR). According this private non-profit organization created in 1986 to improve the quality and competitiveness of companies, products and services, an "Smart City is the holistic view of a city that apply ICT to improve the quality of life and accessibility of its inhabitants and ensures sustainable economic, social and environmental development in continuous improvement. A Smart City allows citizens to interact with it in a multidisciplinary and adapts to your needs in real time, as efficiently and cost, offering open data, solutions-oriented services citizens as individuals to resolve the effects of growth of cities, in public and private spheres, through the innovative integration of smart infrastructure management systems" (Marcos, 2015: p. 23).

Quantify the economic impact of the development of Smart Cities is a complex task, as it requires a cost-benefit analysis which should consider the monetization of all the associated social, magnitudes to which must be added the savings generated by the improved monitoring and management of them. Despite these difficulties, recent studies have estimated that the market for solutions for cities and additional services required for its implementation, globally could exceed EUR 400,000 million in 2020 (Spanish National Plan of Smart Cities, 2014).

Schaffers et al. (2011) affirms that in Smart Cities investments are made in human and social capital and traditional and modern communication infrastructure fuel sustainable economic growth and a high quality of life, with a wise management of natural resources, through participatory governance. In most EU countries there are Smart Cities of different sizes, and although common initiatives are at an early stage of development, large cities tend to be the most advanced ones, with perceptible increased risk of a digital divide between large and small cities.

This urban transformation results into a better quality of life and helps creating attractive environments for investment, generating growth and employment. These goals require an integrated approach that ensures the participation, cooperation, and coordination of multiple stakeholders, so that it can be deployed all their transforming potential. Solutions implemented enable smart reorganization of space and services, by reducing costs and the adjustment of supply to different citizens' needs, businesses, and tourists. Increases in effectiveness and efficiency, reduction of energy consumption and, ultimately, greater citizen satisfaction and improved social intervention capabilities are also recorded.

It is important to consider the importance of tourism in the growth strategy of many cities in Spain and Europe. Tourist arrivals offer business opportunities based on increasingly intensive use of technology needs, which advise promoting their use by public and private stakeholders, and SMEs in particular (European Commission, 2010). In Europe, there are 44 cities that have registered more than 1.5 million overnight stays per year (World Tourism Organization, 2014), representing a major challenge: managing a growing number of visitors and provide them with quality-based services.

SOLUTIONS AND RECOMENDATIONS

Smart Cities: The Spanish National Plan

The role of local authorities as guarantors of the proper provision of public services has become more complex in recent years for various reasons; among others, the maintenance of Law Regulating the Basis of Local Government of 1985, which addresses the provision of public services in different types of municipalities.

Many aspects to what should be a city, country or destination, need smart approaches. These different needs, capacities and opportunities have led to the implementation of various solutions in pace and content; uneven development observed both regarding the type of services provided, as to the way in which ICT tools developed or made for their improvement. This diversity, which has the obvious advantages of a wide range of experiences related, limits the development of standardized and replicable solutions aimed to reducing the need for financing new projects, accelerating deployments, improving results, and providing a growth opportunity for the industry.

To move forward in this process of modernization, local authorities have valued the opportunity to develop strategies for collaboration and coordination to join forces. Concepts such as sustainability, mobility or smart destination to integrate different municipalities have been allowed under one project. One of the organizations that emerged from this confluence is the Spanish Network of Smart Cities (RECI), which already has more than 60 cities. Companies and municipalities develop standards and indicators to be defined in accordance with the Technical Group for Standardization 178 of AENOR which is in charge of the Smart Cities Chapter. Other initiatives, such as the Alliance Inertia formed as a multisectoral alliance coordinated by the Commission Smartcities AMETIC, and the technology platform es.Internet, have formed groups to discuss and agree on strategies that bring business skills to the urban needs. Another initiative, called "SmartIC initiative" of CONETIC, promotes the integration of solutions implemented by SMEs for strengthening individual business skills with interoperable products and services to increase Return on Investment (ROI), and to become more visible in the Congress of Digital Cities, thanks to the Barcelona Mobile World Capital, an event held in Spain. Besides this, some valuable initiatives carried out by universities and local organizations have developed better models to be applied into Smart Cities, such as different models proposed by the Spanish Secretary of State on Telecommunications and the Information Society (SETSI), Red.es, Industrial Organization School (EOI), IDEA, and SEGITTUR. These models have contributed to develop Smart Cities in Spain, and have boosted the conversion of the Spanish tourist destinations into Smart Cities.

Complementary to these Spanish efforts to implement Smart Cities, the European Commission has created the EIP-SCC (European Innovation Partnership on Smart Cities and Communities), a meeting between cities, industry and citizens to improve life in the city through sustainable solutions. The main objective of EIP-SCC is to establish strategic partnerships between cities and industry to develop the systems and infrastructure of the cities of tomorrow and help define the next actions in the field of Smart Cities.

Spain has a good position in the deployment of these initiatives. However, it faces a great challenge due to the diversity of experiences and approaches, or the uneven connecting these projects with the city's overall strategy. On the other hand, the smart concept should not be limited to the area of large cities, as it should be extended to regions, territories, and destinations. The latter illustrates how little both the breadth and complexity of the concept are, as the geographical limits of the territory may not coincide with those of a city. Second, the development of smart tourist destinations aims tourists and improving their experience, not the territory. Finally, the interaction with tourists goes beyond a mere stay in the city.

The National Government, through the General State Administration, aims to contribute to these efforts and play a facilitating role with the approval of the "National Plan of Smart Cities", which acts as a common meeting point for multiple agents. This fact encourages the sharing of resources, experience and knowledge; facilitates the development of innovative products and services, and promotes standards and indicators that stimulate the market, promoting the growth of industry and interoperability.

Objectives of the Plan

The ultimate goal of the Smart Cities Plan is to contribute for economic development, besides maximizing the impact of public policies on ICTs to improve productivity and competitiveness to transform and modernize the Spanish economy through effective and intensive use of ICT by citizens, businesses and governments, according to the Digital Agenda applied for Spain. The weight of the industrial sector in the Spanish GDP is 20%, as reflected in the 2014 Agenda for Strengthening the Industrial Sector in Spain. To do this, it is considered essential to coordinate all policies developed by MINETUR, through the creation of a future Smart Cities Advisory Council. In fact, the Ministry of Industry, Energy and Tourism is the entity responsible for the proposal and implementation of government policy on energy, industrial development, tourism, telecommunications and information society.

The Plan, reflected in the "Agenda for Strengthening the Industrial Sector", is part of the line "Improve Competitiveness of Production Key Factors", and is the backbone of all actions focused on achieving government through the industrial subsector ICT, to improve this contribution to the national GDP, helping to increase the effectiveness and efficiency with which public services are delivered in local authorities to citizens, businesses and tourists. All of which lead to improve quality of life for Spanish towns and cities, and affect economic growth.

The expansion of ICT and improvements in local governance, with the use of governance as the basic tool of management and analysis and evaluation of public policies, acts as a way of rationalizing governmental decisions and actions as essential instruments for the Spanish local authorities to transform environments visited by citizens and tourists, in an effective, efficient and sustainable ways, through smart management systems.

It is understood that tourism should play a key role in promoting Smart Cities, especially in countries like Spain, where no city is alien to it. In 2014, Spain was the third most visited country in the world, with 65 million foreign tourists, and is the second in the world in volume of tourism revenues, which amounted to 48,928 million euros. In 2014, 25% of job creation in the Spanish economy was directly attributable to tourism. Despite having two consecutive years breaking records in the tourism sector, the first data of 2015 continues to show robust growth data.

In a context of economic recovery, it is particularly highlighted the concept of Smart tourist destination. In fact, Smart Cities Plan follows the definition proposed by the Technical Group 178 of AENOR: "An innovative tourist destination, consolidated on a cutting-edge technological infrastructure, ensuring sustainable development of the territory tourism, accessible to all, that facilitates interaction and integration between visitors and the environment and increases the quality of your experience on the destination and improve the quality of life for residents".

The presence of single characteristics of Smart Cities will generate a positive impact on the image of the city, which in the medium and long term will result into a greater influx of visitors and, consequently, greater economic benefits for citizens and businesses will be caused. Moreover, and from an environmental point of view, the increase in tourism in particular and in city services in general (transport, mobility, waste management, lighting, etc.) have a decisive impact on greenhouse gas (GHG) emissions.

Regarding mobility, new investment in infrastructures for a smart city will reduce traffic congestion, minimize the routes and times of journeys for drivers, provide tools for informing users in real-time traffic conditions, and promote public transport. In this line, it takes relevant the implementation of systems able to interact on urban mobility in cities to make significant changes in the modal split. This will cause a greater involvement related to the most efficient ways to be transported, and against the use of low-occupied private vehicles to improve citizens' quality of life as a result of moving towards low carbon dioxide emissions in the future.

Another key consideration is the relative universal accessibility universal, conditions to be met by environments, processes, goods, products and services, as well as objects, instruments, tools and devices, to be understandable, usable and practicable by all people in conditions of safety and comfort. This results in a better relationship of citizens and tourists with the city and its services. From the consideration of accessibility, also economic advantages for the industry are derived, as it expands their customer base to all people. The market potential of accessible tourism, for example, is very significant. According to a recent study on the economic impact and travel habits of accessible tourism in Europe, in 2011 there were 138.6 million people with accessibility needs in the EU, of which 35.9% were persons with disabilities between 15 and 64 years of age and 64.1% of adults over 65 years. The type of local entities that are part of our reality is different, and so are the possible solutions that can be taken to the transformation sought. The sharing of experiences and knowledge will facilitate the creation and the water transfer of common solutions. Similarly, the implementation of interoperable platforms between the towns would reach the level of the critical mass needed for certain innovations or developments to be commercially viable and exportable.

Therefore, the Plan for Smart Cities in Spain seeks to maintain and improve its leadership position in Europe of the Spanish cities and industry. Besides, the Plan is focused on achieving the following objectives:

1. *To increase the ICT contribution to the industrial sector of the GDP*. It is necessary to know the situation of the ICT sector involved in the development of cities to promote growth. Improved productivity and hence competitiveness of the industrial sector depends in part on improvements in productivity and competitiveness of the ICT sector. Investment in R&D and innovation, in necessary coordination with smart specialization strategies (European Commission, 2015) in the regions in which they are located, is a central element in the development of Smart Cities and tourist destinations.
2. *Improving the effectiveness and efficiency of local authorities in providing public services through the use of ICT*. This objective is achieved by [1] assisting local authorities in the process of transformation towards Smart Cities and tourist destinations, promoting optimal deployment of ICT resources in the provision and redefinition of public services; [2] Monitoring and promote standardization activities and standardization of technologies, metrics and services needed to set up Smart Cities, so that interoperability, creating economies of scale, and more efficient investment of resources is encouraged. These metrics are mainly concentrated in measuring citizen satisfaction

and their visitors, in time savings, reduced costs, and reduced administrative burdens. Strengthening standards and interoperability are objectives of the European Digital Agenda, so the promotion will be central part of this plan.

3. *System Governance Smart Cities*. The ultimate goal of the plan is to develop the capacity to evolve the concept of cities and tourist destinations smart technology industry. For this purpose, it is necessary to encourage the joint participation of companies, experts, industry associations, suppliers and local authorities in finding and developing solutions that enable more effective and efficient public services. The object of this plan encouraging the exchange of information and accumulated experiences, disseminate successful solutions seek the commitment of the parties and create decision rules that allow adequate progress towards the objectives established.
4. *Standardization, regulation and legislation*. They are all those measures designed to encourage or facilitate the implementation of technological infrastructure to enable more sustainable behavior in cities and their surroundings. Its main objective is the large-scale integration solutions mainly with some degree of maturity-that improve the efficiency and sustainability of the city. In this line, it is vital to create a network that supports communication between different activities and allows boosting the internal development of Smart Cities.

Structure and Actions

To achieve the objectives, the National Plan Smart Cities proposes a battery of measures structured along the following lines:

Axis I: Provide the cities the transformation towards a Smart City.

Improve the effectiveness and efficiency of local authorities in providing public services through the use of ICT governance and advance the city system and smart tourist destination. In order to achieve objectives set, all the measures to identify the situation of local authorities in relation to the concept of Smart City and destination and governance models that make it possible to implant successfully include obtaining relevant search results for citizens, visitors, businesses, suppliers and institutions.

Among other initiatives, including the implementation of the White Paper on smart cities, in order to identify and quantify all the public to solve problems, types of interventions required and metrics, as well as regulatory and planning instruments required for implementation. The necessary studies to be carried out are

1. To construct segment municipalities depending on the services provided, who provides them with what management model, at what cost and with what degree of utilization of technologies; and
2. Making a taxonomy or subsector of the ICT industry serving the cities, establishing their great magnitude and identify inhibitors and facilitators of development.

One key aspect to create Smart Cities is to identify the type brakes regulatory, technical or regulatory hindering the deployment of a city, country or smart destination. This measure must be complemented with reports on those aspects or specific conditions of smart tourist destinations, from the point of view of their different needs in terms of services provided to tourists and nature thereof.

A second key point is to promote cooperation between municipalities through creation of technological spaces with interoperable ICT environment, enabling the development of cooperative and innovative projects that facilitate experimentation, application development, exchange of good practices and sharing of technological tools.

It is important that citizens and visitors are knowledgeable about the best practices that are undertaking different initiatives, so that promotional activities must be aimed to spread the projects being worked on. Successes and reported benefits to citizens and industry are vital to give support to these initiatives.

Finally, it is important to standardize and monitor all Smart Cities initiatives by promoting standards and interoperability, as well as coordination of the agents involved. For this, the following activities can be taken place:

1. Promotion of standardization activities;
2. Creation and dissemination of the use of indicators and standards in the field of smart cities and tourist destinations;
3. Analysis of successful experiences and promote new experiences that provide metrics supported implementation; and the
4. Improvement of interoperability and innovation.

Axis II: Demonstration projects of the efficiency of ICT in reducing costs, improving citizen satisfaction and creating new business models.

The smart use of ICT can reduce costs involved in the provision of many public services. These savings are not always perceived by citizens or quantified by administrations. Part of the success of Smart City projects and, ultimately, policies that drive is linked to the ability of all actors to convey to society the importance of savings, improved service delivery, increases in the quality of life of citizens, and industrial development opportunities involved. In those cities that receive a large number of tourist arrivals, for example, ICT allow for greater efficiency in adapting and anticipating the delivery of many public services, absorbing system overhead that may entail.

The ICT sector and governments are aware of these benefits, although they are not always explicit. Moreover, there are business models that maximize these savings, and which may not be materialized. Business models capable of redefining cities to be more effective and efficient.

To encourage the emergence and spread of new business models to quantify and maximize savings derived from the smart use of technology, there are three types of public aids:

1. Loans on favorable terms, conceded after having assessed the financial adequacy of the proposed business model that fully cover the amortization period of the loan. They identify quantifiable commitments and apportioned savings and mechanisms for cooperation with other municipalities and industry, promoting interoperability, replicability, sustainability, and reuse of proposed solutions and business models;
2. Promotion of public-private cooperation by helping cities through loans and grants for projects capable of mobilizing private investment. They should be transformative initiatives to identify savings that will occur and management improvements to be achieved by better meeting the needs of citizens and businesses. In all cases, the business model must be validated in advance, and

3. Innovative public procurement through aid for cities in cooperation with industrial projects based on technologies introduced or unavailable devices.

Axis III: Development and growth of the ICT industry.

It seeks to increase the contribution of the ICT subsector serving Smart Cities of the industrial sector to the contribution of increased GDP. In order to achieve the stated objective, all actions aimed at facilitating the development of technological solutions required for the implementation of these initiatives are included. For this, as horizontal industrial policy measures, aid activities are collected with the scope of improving productivity and competitiveness and firm internationalization. The main measures are:

1. The preparation of studies for understanding the situation of ICT companies related to the field of Smart Cities, in order to define the actions to take to mitigate and / or resolve;
2. Calls for public aid to promote innovative ICT companies, which can be implanted in Smart Cities and tourist destinations development. They will be developed within the framework of the Spanish Strategic Action of Digital Economy and Society (AEESD); and
3. Development of measures for the internationalization of firms for strengthening the industrial sector.

Axis IV: Communication and dissemination of the National Plan of Smart Cities.

The scope is to ensure dissemination and understanding of the main objectives, achievements and best practices done regarding Smart Cities and smart tourist destinations. Dissemination of experiences and actions are important, so they are foreseen in the National Plan for Smart Cities in terms of key areas of action addressed and successes, advantages and benefits generated by cities, citizens, businesses and administrations, and opportunities for the industry.

Regarding the dissemination plan, its interoperability, indicators and standards related to smart cities and destinations are contemplated, as well as training of public employees, entrepreneurs and professionals of information. This strategy is complemented with communication objectives defined by ensuring understanding of the role that information technology and communications in improving the delivery of public services, and therefore to improve the quality of life of citizens, businesses and visitors. This policy is complemented with a guide for the development of cities rooted on participatory processes that integrate citizens and tourists, promote inclusion, and foster gender mainstreaming. Finally, this dissemination plan is fulfilled with the opportunity communication to guide the process of building new cities from open, interoperable and reusable solutions that ensure the efficient use of resources.

In short, this axis includes, among other initiatives, the creation, in collaboration with other public and private stakeholders, of a web portal to show local realities and best practices developed. This web portal permits the dissemination and participation in the activities and good practices of the Spanish cities with the aim of fostering continuity initiatives and generate valuable content on Smart Cities.

Complementary to this, conducting outreach activities, training and advisory services to institutions and companies on the use of mechanisms of public-private partnerships and innovative public procurement in the development of Smart Cities are important strategic measures to be carried out. Besides, developing a plan of events and professional conferences on Smart Cities (2015-2020), with the inclusion of media presence, ensures the presence in all global actions on this matter, particularly the Smart City Expo in Barcelona, Greencities & Sustainability and Mobile World Congress, will accelerate the implementation of business models aiming to transform urban areas.

- Promotion and dissemination of good practice of smart tourist destinations in Spain, thereby continuing its initiatives and helping to articulate a route network that puts together the value of its contents.
- Annual meetings infrastructure providers, ICT solutions and services can be used as a "market place" and serve to publicize the contribution of industry to the development of smart cities and tourist destinations.

Axis V: Monitoring plan, transverse action.

Ensure the achievement of the objectives of the plan and its effective and efficient implementation by conducting monitoring and evaluation in itinere of the shares, that allows to have a perfect knowledge of the progress and adapt actions to the needs and expectations of agents involved.

In this area a single measure that involves the establishment of a technical office for monitoring and evaluation of the actions undertaken included.

As transversal action, to organize and coordinate the various initiatives undertaken in the previous four axes of the plan, so that they can join forces and aligning commitments, seeking a high participation of the various stakeholders through joint working groups, public-private partnership forums, opportunities for participation and discussion sessions on the development of smart cities.

In the work of monitoring and diffusing there will be management tools implemented for monitoring the Digital Agenda for Spain. He also will work the National Observatory for Telecommunications and the Information Society (ONTSI) to obtain appropriate monitoring indicators and, in addition to work with ADPE and with the Agenda for Strengthening the Industrial Sector in Spain.

Respecting the management plan, it includes the continuous monitoring of its implementation, close with swift actions against possible deviations, evaluation and dissemination of results. This management function requires close attention to the work of revitalization and encouragement of joint ventures, experts, business associations, suppliers, and local authorities in the search for advanced technologically adapted to the needs of public service users. In this coordination, ICT have a key role to play.

Follow–Up of the Plan

To support the work of control, monitoring and dissemination of a technical office plan to follow up actions created, information is generated for its implementation to provide ongoing advice, collaboration in the design, and monitoring of impact indicators and periodical reports. Experts provide continuous support to monitor the plan by:

1. Collecting information on the progress of various measures: degree of development, outstanding actions, critical points, and possible incidents;
2. Identifying the implementation instruments and major milestones;
3. Introducing and updating information management tools;
4. Establishing impact indicators where possible;

Figure 1. Smart Cities development plan
Source: Adapted from the Spanish Smart Cities Plan.

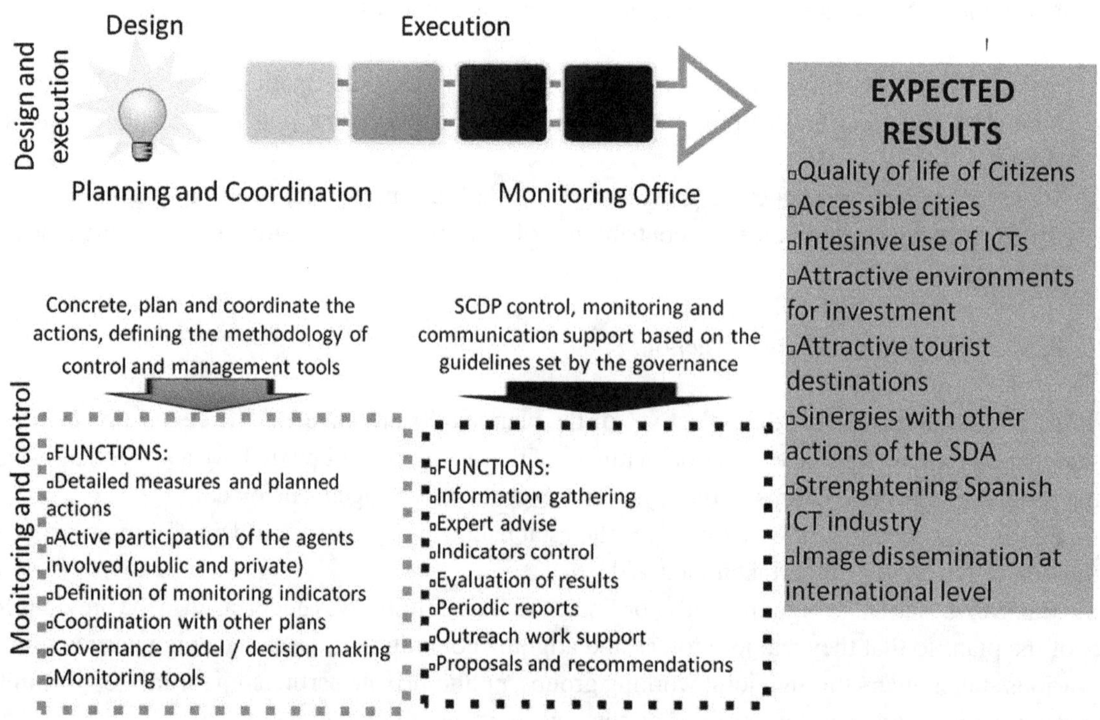

5. Coordinating efforts to avoid duplication and taking advantage of synergies;
6. Exchanging continuous information with autonomous communities and local entities;
7. Communicating with citizens and other stakeholders to monitor agents plans;
8. Disseminating measures and actions of the National Plan Smart Cities, and
9. Supporting annual review reports to assess results, redefine objectives and adjust their temporal scope (Figure 1).

Indicators of Project Evolution

The Secretary of State for Telecommunications and the Information Society (SETSI) has tracked specific plans and annual action plans as a verification of their implementation, evaluation and results dissemination. ONTSI, as the operative vehicle of SETSI, conducts regular monitoring of the key objectives through a system of indicators established by the Digital Agenda for Europe, according to their possible future revisions, and by incorporating specific indicators for the Spanish targets.

Monitoring of different axes and measures born after the launch of the Smart Cities National Plan will be made by controlling the instruments used for their implementation (mainly reporting and signed agreements), and the establishment of performance indicators of the proceedings, whenever possible.

Additionally, the first step of the plan includes the "Preparation of a White Paper on Smart Cities", whose objectives include the development of indicators to measure the achievement of the objectives proposed by the National Plan for Smart Cities.

Smart Cities and Sustainability

After a hard period of work and reflection carried out by various working groups, hundreds of indicators have been defined in Europe, so it was decided to limit the number thereof and simplify them to the maximum. Grounded on Europe 2020, they are commonly used as standards, and they are applicable and are representative for the maximum number of governments.

Each indicator has a 5-stage structure as follows:

Stage 0: Total absence of any publicly accessible on-line information service.
Stage 1: Static and open on-line information available describing the aggregate for periods (daily / weekly / monthly / yearly) and may be reused by third parties (open data) service.
Stage 2: Dynamic information available and open: on-line information describing the service in real time and can be reused by others.
Stage 3: Two-way interaction: citizens, visitors and businesses access information in real time, can be reused and also interact with the system to provide data.
Stage 4: Interoperability services: interoperability between systems that manage each of the services for automation of new procedures to optimize the resources with an impact on the cost savings or new revenue generation.

As a result, Smart Cities have the main indicators related to sustainability as follows:

1. **Smart Energy (Energy Consumption):** Measured in kWh and Euros, its service definition is defined as the total energy consumption in lighting, facilities, and public buildings. According to Europe 2014-2020, the objective is to use of resources efficiently by achieving a 20% increase in generated power obtained from renewable energy, and reduce energy consumption by 20%.
2. **Smart Water-I (Water Consumption):** Measured in cubic meters and euros, it is defined by the total consumption of water in parks and public gardens, cleaning the city, and public swimming pools. The goal, according Europe 2014-2020, is to improve water management and efficient use of resources.
3. **Smart Water-II (Water Management):** Measured by euros, supplied water in cubic meters, and treated water in cubic meters, its objective is to measure spending on drinking water delivery and disposal and treatment of sewage. As a result, an efficient use of resources and improved water management are the goals set.
4. **Smart Environment-I (Environmental Parameters):** Mainly measured by environmental parameters (decibels and carbonic dioxide) following the Europe 2014-2020 Agenda, it measures noise, air quality, and water quality to conserve and to protect environment by an efficient use of resources.
5. **Smart Environment-II (Cleaning & City):** Measured in Euros and in waste disposal service according to the Europe 2014-2020 Plan, its objective is to conserve and to protect environment by efficiently using resources. As a result, its service is defined as measuring the expenditure on cleaning and maintenance of the city.
6. **Smart Waste-I (Waste):** Measured in waste disposal service and tons of garbage collected following the Europe 2014-2020 objective for conservation and environmental protection, it measures the total expenditure on the collection and management of waste and/or solid waste.

7. **Smart Waste-II (Recycling):** Measured in euros and in the waste recycling service and tons of waste recycled, it measures the total expenditure on recycling and waste treatment following the European 2014-2020 objetive of conservation and environmental protection thanks to the efficient use of resources.
8. **Smart Mobility (Transport):** Measured by the number of public charging points and bikes in euros and spending of public transport, it has the objective of reducing greenhouse gas emissions by 20% by using sustainable transport. Consequently, public services are defined by the use of public transport, and the charging stations electric vehicle in the city and public bicycles.

CONCLUSION

The creation of Smart Cities is a must that will contribute to fight against climate change and to attain higher standard of living. As a result, conditions of life will be better for entire population, situation that will be especially benefical in the European Union where there is a direct private-public collaboration for reducing social exclusion and poverty. This social goal is directly connected with the objectives included in the European 2020 Strategy, largely rooted on competitiveness and sustainability, in the context of trying to increase social and economic wealth.

This socioeconomic wealth can be fostered by transforming cities into Smart Cities. Although some indicators are under discussion in the main entities responsible for the Smart Cities analysis, political and economic measures are generally applicable to all local authorities given their advantages in terms of wealth. Many of these indicators are seen as measurement units or consumption expenditures to be reduced or new revenues to achieve with the intensive use of new technologies, so living conditions in urban agglomerations can be ameliorated.

As Haque (2012) states, cited by Manville et al (2014), any adequate model for the Smart City must focus on the smartness of its citizens and communities and on their well-being and quality of life, as well as encourage the processes that make cities important to people and which might well sustain very different – sometimes conflicting – activities. When cities are transformed for being characterized as Smart Cities, positive externalities are created, so population is positively affected. As a result, the Mc-Clelland's N-effect is generated which will transformed the society and the economy as a whole.

In our opinion, Smart Cities are cities seeking to address public issues via ICT-based solutions on the basis of a multi-stakeholder, municipally based partnership based on public-private cooperation initiatives. The final objective is to disseminate the advantages derived from this urban transformation into cities, independently of their size, situated in developing countries. If this objective is reached, their inhabitants will enjoy higher levels of life.

FUTURE RESEARCH DIRECTIONS

In this chapter we have only analyzed the characteristics of Smart Cities in Spain, so it should be interesting to study urban transformations in other countries and regions, and especially the largest urban agglomerations situated in developing countries with the ultimate goal of ameliorating their social and economic wealth.

A second research direction will be connecting Smart Cities and social policies directed to population at risk of social exclusion. Poverty is especially intense in many urban suburbs, and mainly those situated in developing countries. The inclusion of the most vulnerable into modern societies can foster richness and a more equal and fair income distribution among the population. In this sense, ICT-based Smart Cities have an important role to achieve this goal.

Finally, a third research direction is to study the role of women and youth into Smart Cities. Given the high birth rates, especially those achieved in developing countries, young population will be increasingly higher in these countries, so urban transformation into Smart Cities are necessary and desirable. More natural resources are needed to sustain increasingly populated urban areas. As a result, the introduction of local, regional and national policies focused on creating Smart Cities will be a necessity to enhance living conditions of their residents independently where they live, as externalities are expanded independently where they are generated.

REFERENCES

Comisión Económica para América Latina (CEPAL). (2005). *Boletín demográfico*. América Latina: Proyecciones de Población Urbana y Rural (1970-2025), Santiago de Chile: CEPAL & United Nations.

EOI - PwC. (2014). Ciudades y ciudadanos en 2033. La transformación urbana de España. Madrid: Author.

European Commision. (2010b). *A European strategy for smart, sustainable and inclusive growth*. Brussels: EC.

European Commision. (2015a). *Economic Impact and Travel Patterns of Accesible Tourism in Europe - Final Report*. Brussels, Belgium: Directorate-General on Enterprise & Industry.

European Commission. (2010a). Keeping Europe, the World's Top Touristic Destination. *COM*, *352*(3), 3.

European Commission. (2014). *Estrategias Nacionales y Regionales para la Especialización Inteligente*. Brussels, Belgium.

European Commission (2015b). *Estrategias nacionales y regionals para la especialización inteligente (RIS3)*. Bruselas: Directorate-General of Regional Policy.

European Innovation Partnership on Smart Cities and Communities. (2013). *Strategic Implementation Plan*. Brussels, Belgium: Author.

European Parliament. (2014). *Mapping Smart Cities in the EU*. Brussels, Belgium: Author.

Haque, U. (2012). Surely There's a Smarter Approach to Smart Cities?. *Wired*. Available at: http://www.wired.co.uk/news/archive/2012-04/17/potential-of-smartercities-beyond-ibm-and-cisco

Komninos, N., Pallot, M., & Schaffers, H. (2012). Special Issue on Smart Cities and the Future Internet in Europe. *Journal Of The Knowledge Economy*, *4*(2), 119–134. doi:10.1007/s13132-012-0083-x

Kramer, D. (2013). Smart cities will need big data. *Physics Today*, *66*(9), 19. doi:10.1063/PT.3.2110

Kylili, A., & Fokaides, P. (2015). European smart cities: The role of zero energy buildings. *Sustainable Cities and Society*, *15*, 86–95. doi:10.1016/j.scs.2014.12.003

Manville, C. (2014). *Mapping Smart Cities in the EU*. Brussels, Belgium: Directorate-General for Internal Policies.

Marcos, T. (2015). *Las normas para las ciudades inteligentes. Informe de situación*. Madrid, Spain: AENOR.

Market Place of the European Innovation Partnership on Smart Cities and Communities. (2015). Retrieved 11 May 2015, from https://eu-smartcities.eu/

Nam, T., & Pardo, T. A. (2011). Conceptualizing Smart City With Dimensions of Technology, People, and Institutions. In *Proceedings of the 12th Annual International Digital Government Research Conference: Digital Government Innovation in Challenging Times*. ACM. Available at: http://smartcitiescouncil.com/system/files/resources/Conceptualizing%20smart%20city .pdf

Schaffers, H., Komninos, N., Pallot, M., Trousse, B., Nilsson, M., & Oliveira, A. (2011). Smart Cities and the Future Internet: Towards Cooperation Frameworks for Open Innovation, Future Internet Assembly. *LNCS, 6656*.

Spanish Ministry of Economy and Public Administration. (2014). Madrid, Spain: Acuerdo de Asociación de España.

Spanish Ministry of Industry, Energy, and Tourism. (2014). *Agenda para el fortalecimiento del sector industrial en España. Propuestas de actuación*. Madrid: Spanish Ministry of Industry, Energy, and Tourism.

Spanish Ministry of Industry, Energy, and Tourism. (2015). *Ciudades Inteligentes. Agenda Digital para España*. Madrid: Spanish Ministry of Industry, Energy, and Tourism.

Townsend, A. (2013). *Smart Cities: Big Data, Civic Hackers, and the Quest for a New Utopia*. Academic Press.

Washburn, D., & Sindhu, U. (2009). Helping CIOs Understand "Smart City" Initiatives. *Growth*. Available at: http://c3328005.r5.cf0.rackcdn.com/73efa931-0fac-4e28-ae77- 8e58ebf74aa6.pdf

World Tourism Organization (WTO). (2014). International Forum on Urban Tourism. WTO.

KEY TERMS AND DEFINITIONS

Cohesion Fund: Aimed to reduce social and economic disparities, in its actual version for 2014-2020, it aims to promote sustainable development through EU funds given mainly to Central and Eastern European Countries (CEEC) whose Gross National Income (GNI) per inhabitant is less than 90% of the EU average.

EU 2020 Strategy: Launched in 2010, Europe 2020 is the European Union's ten-year strategy for creating jobs, and smart, sustainable and inclusive economic growth.

Foreign Earned Income Exclusion: Used in many countries, thanks to agreements signed between the ministries of economy and finance, it is a fiscal instrument officially approved to avoid double taxation.

Greenhouse Effect: Mainly caused by carbone dioxide and CFC (Chlorofluorocarbons), it consists of a physical process where part of the solar radiation is kept in the lower layers of the atmosphere causing a warming of the earth's surface.

Inclusive Growth: Economic situation achieved when the economy reaches high employment levels while delivering social and territorial cohesion.

Smart City: The holistic view of an ICT-based urban agglomeration that improves the quality of life and accessibility of its inhabitants, and increasingly ensures sustainable economic, social and environmental development to increase social and economic wealth.

Structural Funds: Set from 2014 to 2020, they are financial tools set up to mainly support Europe's poorest regions to implement the EU's regional policy with the aim of reducing regional disparities in wealth, opportunities and income amog the richest and the poorest EU countries.

Sustainability Development: Formed by four interconnected domains (culture, economics, ecology and politics), it aims to preserve the planet from damage derived from non-friendly environmental economic activities.

Chapter 15
Economic Damage Due to Ozone Pollution in NCR:
Ozone Impacts

Sumit Sharma
The Energy and Resources Institute (TERI), India

ABSTRACT

Air pollution is a serious concern not just for human health but for agriculture also. This puts significant burden on the economy of a region. This paper assesses the health and agricultural damage caused by prevailing Ozone concentrations in National Capital Region (NCR) of India. The analysis is based on modelled and validated Ozone concentrations using state of the art air quality models. Established dose response relationships are used for assessment of impact over human health and agriculture. Value of statistical life approach and minimum support prices are used for economic evaluation of health and agricultural impacts, respectively. More than 3000 mortalities and loss of more than 1300 kt of agricultural crops can be attributed to Ozone pollution. An annual economic loss of about 1.27 billion USD is estimated on account of Ozone pollution in NCR. This study calls for sustainable development of the region which promotes growth without affecting the environmental quality.

INTRODUCTION

Sustainable development calls for a balance between the three legs- environmental, economic and social. While, economic growth leads to betterment on social fronts, it leaves significant footprints on the environment. One of the impacts of rapid economic growth is on quality of air which deteriorates with the release of emissions from different sources. This chapter focuses on impacts of ozone pollution on human health and agriculture in a typical urban-rural setting. The study also emphasizes on restructuring the unsustainable model of development, by reducing pollution and its impacts on social and economic dimensions.

DOI: 10.4018/978-1-5225-0094-0.ch015

Ozone is a gas which in stratosphere saves us from harmful UV radiations received from the sun. However, it is known to have a variety of impacts on humans when it is formed in the troposphere. Other than stratospheric-tropospheric exchange, Ozone is formed in the troposphere through reactions of various pre-cursors species like oxides of nitrogen (NO_x) and volatile organic compounds (VOCs) in the presence of sunlight (Sillman, 2003). Tropospheric Ozone is known to have impacts on human health and agricultural yields of various crop species. It affects the respiratory system by reducing lung function, and aggravating any pre-existing disease like asthma. Various epidemiological studies have shown that daily exposure to high Ozone concentrations may increase mortality and morbidity in a region (Halonen et al, 2010, Jerrett et al, 2009). WHO, 2008 states that 21,000 premature deaths occur annually in 25 European Union countries on and after days with high ozone levels. In view of growing evidence of health impacts of Ozone, WHO has recently revised the air quality guideline for ozone from 120 to 100 μg/m^3 (8-hr avg.) Other than health impacts, a number of studies show that Ozone can affect the plant growth in many ways. The effects are proven on their growth above the ground (Franzaring et al., 2000; Gimeno et al., 2004; Hayes et al., 2010), on their roots (Franzaring et al., 2000; Batty and Ashmore 2003), biomass partitioning (Cooley and Manning, 1987; Hayes et al.,2009), and on flowers and seeds (Rämö et al., 2007, Black et al., 2000). Ozone is known to reduce the yields of some of the important crops. A decline of 2.2–5.5% for maize, 3.9–15% for wheat and 8.5–14% for soybean can be attributed to high Ozone concentrations (Wilkinson et al, 2011). Limited research on the impacts of Ozone on materials shows that it can also significantly damage the rubber products and surface coatings (Lee, 1996). Besides, it has been found to impact the colours of textiles and paintings due to its reactivity with colors (CCME, 2003 and USEPA, 1996). Other than the environmental impacts, Ozone is a gas with significant green-house potential. It is known to have the third highest radiative forcing (between 1750-2005) just after CO_2 and methane (IPCC, 2013). In all, this is evident that ozone is an important air pollutant which causes significant impacts on human society and its economic implications need to be studied for making informed decisions for its control.

Other than stratospheric transport, ozone at ground level is formed mainly due to reactions of NO_x and VOCs in the presence of sunlight. NOx is mainly emitted from high temperature combustion in vehicles, power plants etc. However, VOCs which are the other important precursors are primarily emitted from biomass combustion in cook stoves and agricultural fields. Photo-chemical modelling is generally employed to understand the ozone formation in regions of different precursor emission intensities and meteorological conditions. Sharma et al, 2016a used emission inventories of NOx and VOCs and applied a photo-chemical model for simulating ambient ozone concentrations in National capital region (NCR) of Delhi in India. The region is known for its very high population density, vehicular congestion, industries, power plants and use of diesel generator sets. All these are important sources of ozone precursors (NOx and VOCs). Sharma et al, 2016a prepared emission inventories for these sources and simulated spatial ozone concentrations for different months of 2012. The concentrations were later validated with actual observations and were found to be violating the prescribed standards for significant period of times in the year. The study showed that high density population (in urban regions) and agricultural crops (in rural regions) in NCR are exposed to significantly high ozone concentrations. It is in this context the evaluation of the impacts on human health and agricultural productivity becomes extremely important. Hence, in the current study, we build on the last work and assess the impacts of ozone concentrations in NCR on human health and agricultural productivity. This study uses established dose response relationships to compute health and agricultural impacts in the NCR region using simulated ozone concentrations in Sharma et al, 2016a. Impacts are monetized using established economic valuation techniques and the estimates of economic damage are compared against the overall economy of the region. The study shows the application of air quality simulation tools in assessment of impacts of air pollutants like ozone in an urban-rural setting.

GROUND LEVEL OZONE

Ozone in stratosphere is known to protect us from ultra-violet light and is generally present in very low concentrations in the lower atmosphere. Ozone in lower atmosphere is formed by reactions of different compounds known as Ozone precursor species. The main precursor species are NO_2, VOCs, and CO.

Ozone Formation

Ozone is first formed in stratosphere naturally. Oxygen in stratosphere absorbs UV radiation ($\lambda < 240$ nm), and breaks into two oxygen atoms. Nascent oxygen atom combines with O_2 molecule to form Ozone with release of heat. Ozone is capable of absorbing the UV radiation with $\lambda < 290$ nm which converts back the ozone to O_2 molecules and atoms. Hence, stratospheric Ozone protects us from high-energy UV radiation. Some of stratospheric Ozone later transports to troposphere and forms OH radicals.

$$O_3 \text{ -------------}\rightarrow O_2 + O$$

$$O + H_20 \text{ --------}\rightarrow 2OH$$

Primary pollutants like VOCs and CO react with OH and forms RO_2 and OH_2. RO_2 is an organic chain with an attached O_2 (replacing H)[1]. RO_2 and OH_2 oxidizes NO to NO_2. NO_2 is photolyzed to generate atomic oxygen, which combines with oxygen to form Ozone in troposphere.

$$NO_2 \text{ ----------}h\upsilon\text{----}\rightarrow NO + O$$

$$O + O_2 \text{ -------------}\rightarrow O_3$$

Another important reaction which happens with Ozone is NO_x titration. While, Ozone is formed in the presence of sunlight, during nights, the primary NO released from sources like vehicles/power plants reacts with ozone to convert it back to Oxygen. This process is called the process of NO_x titration.

$$NO + O_3 \text{ ------}\rightarrow NO_2 + O_2$$

Solar radiation intensity, concentrations of NO_x and VOCs, and their ratios play most important role in formation of ground level ozone (Nevers, 2000, Pudasaineea et al,2006). The overall formation mechanism of Ozone is shown in Figure 1.

Figure 1. Formation of Ozone in stratosphere and troposphere
Adapted from Jacob, 2000.

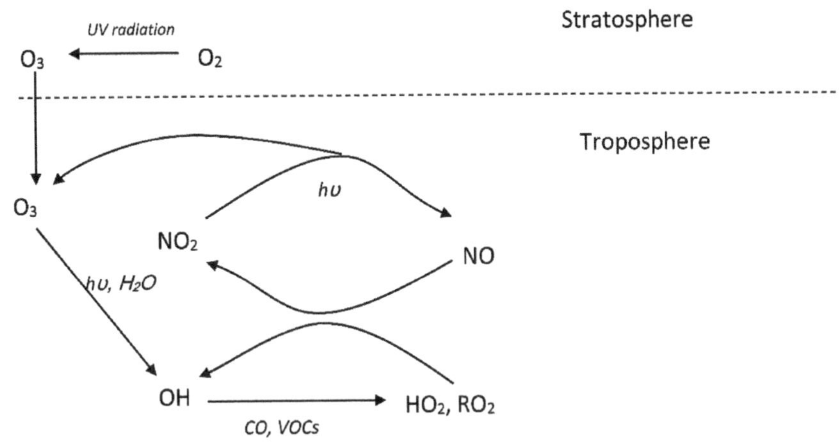

Ozone Concentrations

Since the pre-industrial era, ground level Ozone (GLO) concentrations have increased considerably in different parts of the world. Heavily populated regions of Indian sub-continent show very high concentrations of Ozone (TRS, 2008). However, this phenomenon is not restricted just to developing countries, but across the globe. Many areas in the developed world too show very high concentrations and violation of Ozone standards, not necessarily due to presence of precursor emissions but may also due to transport of Ozone from other parts of the world. Figure 2 shows the annual average concentrations of ground-level ozone (ppb) for selected cities in the world (2010), which clearly shows that Ozone concentrations in Delhi are higher than many cities in the world.

Figure 2. Annual average concentrations of ground-level ozone (ppb) for selected cities in the world (2010)
*Data source: http://www.ec.gc.ca/indicateurs-indicators/default.asp?lang=en&n=1B7C2AC9-1; *http://eng.me.go.kr/content.do?method=moveContent&menuCode=pol_cha_air_sta_cha_ozone*

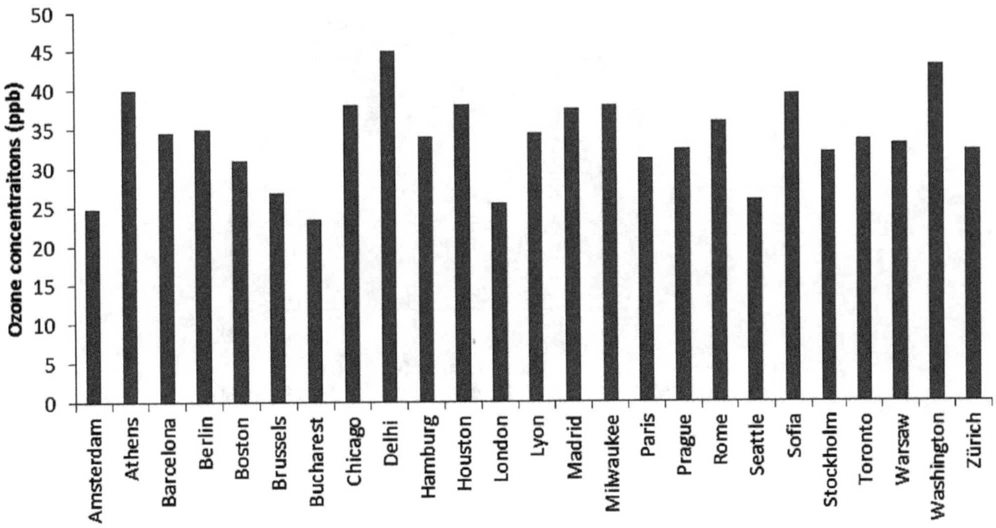

India is experiencing rapid economic growth and along with which are increasing the sources of air pollution, and hence the pollutant levels in the ambient air. While there are primary pollutants of concern like PM, NOx, SO_2, CO etc, which are emitted directly from the tail-pipe of the sources, there are secondary pollutants like Ozone, PAN, secondary particulates formed due to chemical reactions of different pollutant species under favourable meteorological conditions. Ozone is one of these pollutants formed by the reactions of different precursor species in the presence of sunlight. Chatani et al, 2014 and Sharma et al., 2016b carried out simulations of Ozone for India and has shown that concentrations are highest in the Indo-gangetic plains due to the presence of larger emission sources like residential biomass burning, transport and power plants (Figure 3). Lower concentrations are observed in cities because of titration chemistry with NOx emissions. Higher NO emissions mainly from vehicular sources lead to depletion of Ozone in the heart of the cities.

Considering the varied adeverse impacts of Ozone, it is now being regulalrly monitored in Delhi (the capital city of India). There are about 15 stations in Delhi monitoring Ozone concentrations continously. Hourly concentrations measured at some of these stations are presented in Figure 4. It is evident that at most places Ozone concentrations violate the 8-hour standard of 50 ppb or 100 μg/m³. Violatons are less in traffic locations like ITO due to the titration chemistry with NO emissions released from vehicles. However, in outskirt areas, ozone concnetrations are found to be higher. Seasonal variation of ozone concnetrations shows higher concentrations in summers and less during winters and monsoon seasons, mainly due to varying photo-chemcial activity in different months.

Figure 3. Simulated Ozone concentrations in India in June 2010
Source: TERI, 2013.

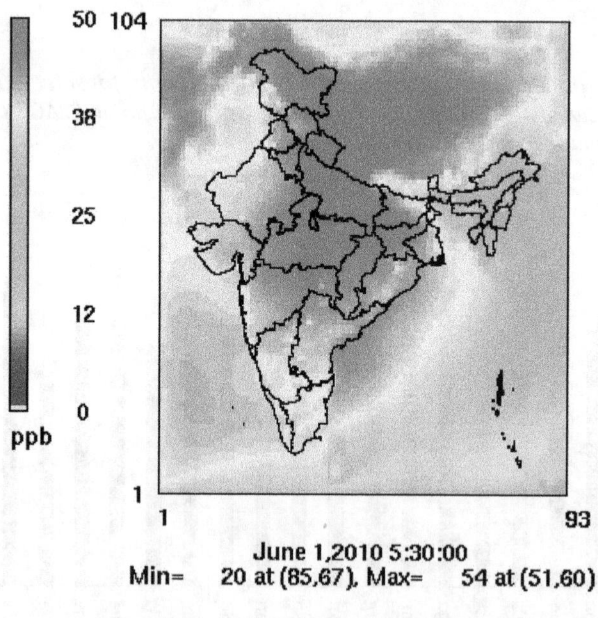

Figure 4. Hourly Ozone concentrations (μg/m³) at different locations in Delhi

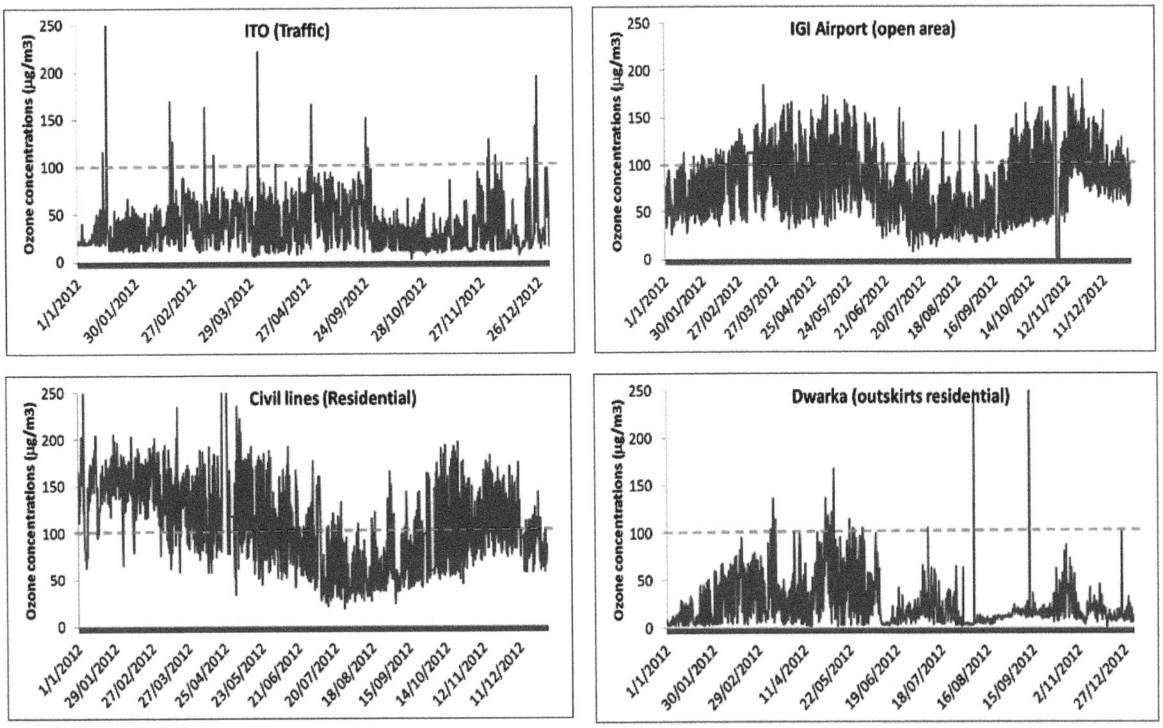

MATERIALS AND METHODS

Site Description

The NCR of Delhi has been identified as the study region for carrying out the study. The study region was chosen primarily due to the presence of high intensity sources of ozone precursor emissions, high population density, considerably high ozone concentrations, and a mix land use of urban and rural activities. National Capital Region (NCR) is an example of inter-state regional development planning with NCT-Delhi as its core and many other towns from surrounding States. The region encompasses an area of about 34,144 km² having parts of National Capital Territory of Delhi, and states of Haryana, UP, and Rajasthan. The distribution of areas and town from each of the State in tabulated in Table 1. Figure 5 shows the overall study domain and geographical extent of the NCR.

Table 1. Distribution of areas and towns from each of the State in NCR

Sub-Region	Name of the Districts	Area (in km²)
Haryana	Faridabad, Gurgaon, Mewat, Rohtak, Sonepat, Rewari, Jhajjhar, Panipat and Palwal	13,428
Uttar Pradesh	Meerut, Ghaziabad,Gautam Budha Nagar,Bulandshahr, Hapur and Baghpat	10,853
Rajasthan	Alwar	8,380
Delhi	NCT of Delhi	1,483
	Total	34,144

Figure 5. NCR region and sub-divisions
Digitized based on: http://ncrpb.nic.in/ncrconstituent.php.

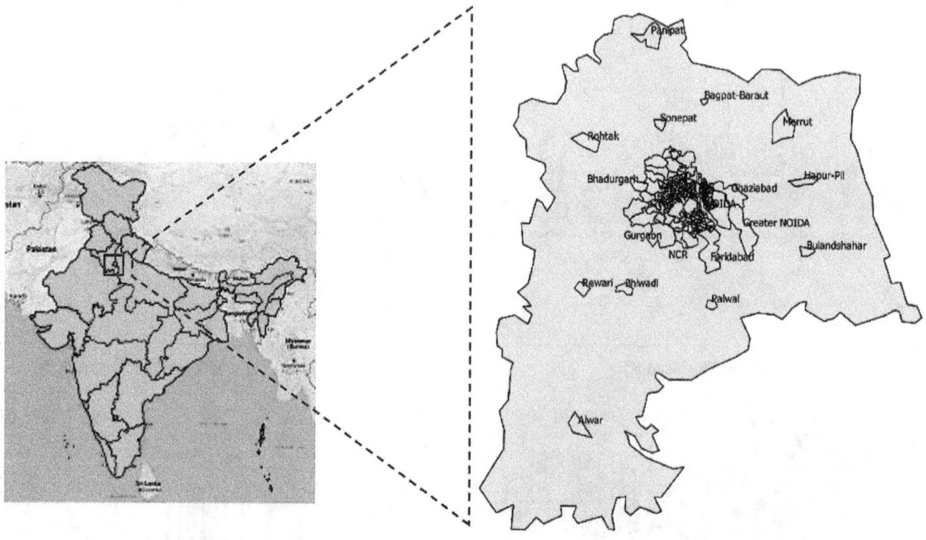

While there are obvious urban regions close to Delhi, there are rural regions too in the surroundings. In NCR, about 40% of the population lives in rural areas. In all, there are about 12.5 million vehicles registered in NCR, out of which 63% are two-wheelers. There is considerable traffic movement between different towns in the region. Other than traffic, there are industrial sources of emissions. Significant quantity of coal is consumed in industries and power plants located in the region. Other than these, frequent power cuts have led to the usage of diesel generator (DG) sets in many places of the NCR. These DG sets are known for high NOx emissions.

For the purpose of emission inventorisation and modeling the region is divided into grids of 4x4 km^2. A small grid-size of 4x4 km^2 is chosen to account for local sources and better prediction of ozone concentrations using high resolution emission and meteorological inputs.

Data Description

The data on ozone concentrations in NCR used in the present study is adopted from Sharma et al, 2016a. Spatial –temporal distribution of simulated ozone concentrations in NCR is obtained for the year 2012. These concentrations are based on emission inventories of NOx and VOCs in NCR and meteorological inputs for the year 2012. Activity data and emission factors for preparation of emission inventories are obtained from published literature and reliable government sources. Details of activity data and emission factors used for preparation of sectoral emission inventories are presented in Sharma et al, 2016a. Basic meteorological data sets for the meteorological WRF model are obtained from NCEP (rda.ucar.edu/datasets/ds083.2/) which were downscaled using the WRF model for 4x4 km^2 grids across the NCR region. Air quality modelling was carried out using CMAQ and hourly ozone concentrations are obtained for the whole year 2012 as shown in Sharma et al, 2016a.

For estimation of human exposure to ozone concentrations, population figures were collected for the whole NCR region (RGCC, 2011). District-wise population data is distributed to the grids of 4x4 km2 using GIS . Exposure to crops was estimated using production data of various crops like wheat, rice, maize etc. District wise crop production data for wheat, rice, and maize is collected from DoES, 2013 for the same year 2012. GIS is used for allocation of crop production volumes to the grids of 4x4 km^2. These datasets are used for evaluation of health and agricultural impacts as explained in the section on methodology.

Methodology

This study takes into account the socio-economic development in the region and its impact on emissions of precursors that subsequently form Ozone. Sources like vehicles, diesel generators, industries power plants have strong linkages with the social and economic development in the region. The emissions released from these sources impact the quality of air environment. The study builds on the last work (Sharma et al, 2016a) on simulation of ozone concentrations in NCR based on emission inventories of precursor species like NOx, and VOCs emitted from different sources. In the past study, the ozone concentrations were simulated by WRF-CMAQ air quality models using emissions and meteorological inputs. The modelled values were validated first by comparing with the observed ozone concentrations at different stations in the study domain. The predicted ozone values for 2012 have been used in this study for assessing the impact on human health and agricultural productivity in NCR. Established dose-response relationships were used to compute the impacts on human health and crop productivities.

The overall approach followed in this study is broadly described in Figure 6. Based on activity level information, gridded (4x4 km^2) emission inventories are prepared for different regions in the NCR, which are fed into the community multi-scale air quality (CMAQ) model (Byun et al, 1999) for air quality simulations. The model output is validated with actual observations and then the gridded ozone concentrations are put into the impact assessment models using established dose response functions. The impacts on health and agriculture have been monetized using the established methodologies for assessment of overall economic damage due to ozone. Value of statistical life (VSL) approach (World Bank, 2013) is applied for assessment of impacts on human health and minimum support prices (MSP) for various crops are used for monetization of agricultural impacts.

Figure 6. Broad approach used in this study

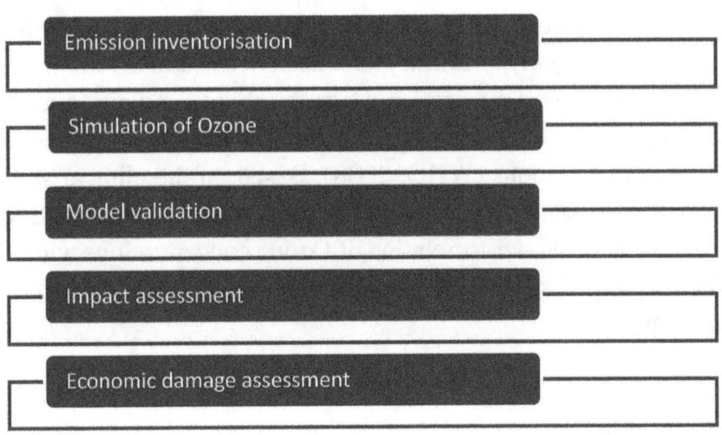

Emission inventories have been prepared for all major source – transport, industries, DG sets, power plants, agricultural burning, evaporative sources, and refuse burning. Following is the basic equation used for emission inventorisation of Ozone precursors such as NOx, NMVOCs, and CO.

Emissions = Activity levels x Emission factor x (reduction due to control technologies)

The activity data is collected from different government agencies for population, number of vehicles, fuel used in industries and power plants. As far as possible indigenous emission factors were used for emission estimation. The emission inventories were fed into the CMAQ model to predict Ozone concentrations in the NCR region for the year 2012. The modeled concentrations of Ozone were validated against actual observations from CPCB and Delhi Pollution Control Committee. As this study specifically focuses on impacts assessment of ozone pollution, the details of activity data, emission factors, precursor inventories, and results of simulation are provided separately in our other work in Sharma et al (2016a).

Impact Assessment

Ground level Ozone causes a variety number of impacts over the humans. While it impacts human health, it is more known for its detrimental impacts on agricultural activities.

Health

Ozone affects the respiratory system by reducing lung function, and aggravats any pre-existing disease like asthma. However, degree of impact depends on the exposure time and dose, climatic characteristics, and socio-economic conditions. Bush et al. 1996, Sarangapani et al., 2003 showed that Ozone is mainly absorbed in the upper respiratory tract and conducting intrathoracic airways. Ozone is found to be absorbed relatively more by children and women. After entering, Ozone may cause oxidation of some components of epithelial lining fluid (ELF) which generates bioactive compounds, such as lipid hydroperoxides, cholesterol ozonization products and can cause cell damage (Cross et al., 1998).

In the past, various epidemiological studies have shown that daily exposure to high ozone concentrations may increase mortality and morbidity in a region. Table 2 provides the results of some studies carried out to establish the health outcomes of varying Ozone concentrations. Controlled human studies and experimental animal studies have been carried out to ascertain dose-response relationships (Table 2). These studies have shown independent effects of Ozone from other pollutants. The studies have concluded that Ozone affects pulmonary function, lung permeability, causes lung inflammation, and other impacts on other related parameters. Evidently, prevailing Ozone concentrations have been conclusively linked with respiratory symptoms, increased medication usage, morbidity and mortality. Although, short term effects of Ozone are quite proven, the evidence is still not enough to establish long term effects due to exposure to high Ozone concentrations (WHO, 2008). Based on the clinical studies, there have been regional estimates made for evaluating the impact of Ozone on residing populations.

Many studies in the past have shown correlation of Ozone concentrations with increased mortalities. Figure 7 presents the findings of studies showing percentage increase in mortalities with increasing ambient Ozone concentrations.

Table 2. Key findings of the studies carried out to establish health impacts of exposure to Ozone concentrations

Study	Findings
Graham et al. 2001 Vagaggini et al. 2001	Increased neutrophil counts in nasal lavage
Montuschi et al. 2002	Increased oxidative stress
Coffey et al. 1996	Increased respiratory symptoms, bronchoalveolar cell counts, specific airway resistance
Alexis et al. 2000	Reduced airway function in asthmatics
Samet et al. 2001	Reduced pulmonary function and growth of inflammatory cells
Folinsbee et al. 2000	Airway obstruction and bronchial hyper-responsiveness.
Korrick et al. 1998 Chen et al. 1999	Decline in FEV1 and FVC
Kjaergaard et al. 2004 Braun-Fahrlander et al. 1994 Higgins et al. 1990 Grievink et al. 1998	Reduced PEF (Peak expiratory flow), FEV1 (forced expiratory volume in 1 second), and FVC (Forced vital capacity)
Vagaggini et al. 2002	Enhanced asthma due to higher counts of eosinophil and increase in bronchial obstruction.
Torres et al. 1997	Increase in Leukocytes, IL-6, and IL-8 (interleukin-8 and interleukin-6) respectively. Lymphocytes, mast cells and eosinophils also increased late after exposure.
Blomberg et al. 1999	Adhesion molecule upregulation, increased submucosal mast cell numbers, alterations to the respiratory tract lining fluid redox status, and obstructive changes in pulmonary function.
Bergamaschi et al. 2001	Significant reduction in pulmonary function tests and increased levels of Clara cell protein serum (CC16).
Ulmer et al. 1997	Negative associations between vital capacity and ozone levels the previous day.
Hiltermann et al. 1998	More intense effects of Ozone than PM_{10}, nitrogen dioxide and black smoke. Positive associations between ozone and respiratory symptoms and bronchodilator use.

Source: WHO, 2008.

Figure 7. Percentage increase in mortalities with increasing Ozone concentrations (based on different studies across the world)

Data source: Moolgavkar et al. 1995, Anderson et al. 1996, Touloumi et al. 1997, Simpson et al. 1997, Hoek et al. 1997, Zmirou et al. 1998, Loomis et al. 1999, Kwon et al. 2001, Zeghnoun et al. 2001, Goldberg et al. 2001, Saez et al. 2002, O'Neill et al. 2004, Penttinen et al. 2004, Bell et al. 2000, Gryparis et al. 2004, Schwartz et al. 2005, Bell et al. 2005, Ito et al. 2005, Levy et al. 2005.

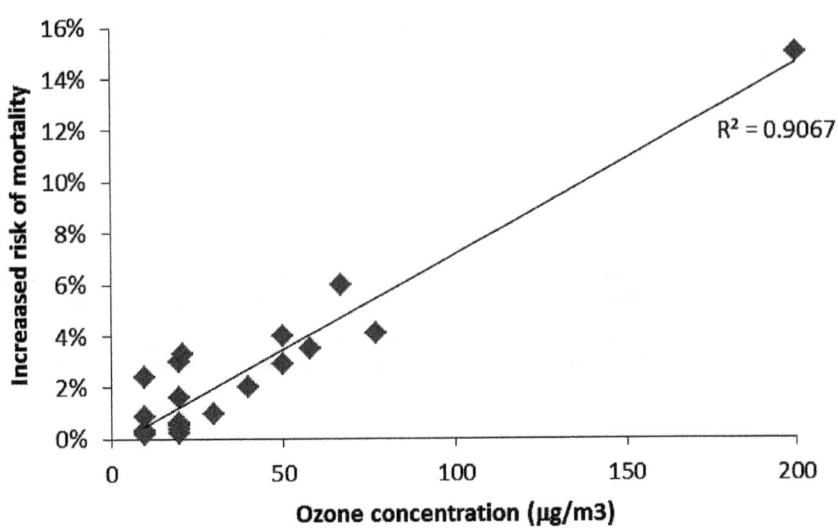

In this study, a dose response function of 0.3% increase in mortalities per 10 ppb rise in Ozone concentrations has been adopted (Bell et al, 2006). Equation (1) is used to compute the mortalities that can be attributed to Ozone pollution in NCR.

$$Increased\ mortalities = \sum_{i=1}^{n}\left[\left(\left|O3\right|i\right)\cdot P\cdot R\cdot C\right] \quad (1)$$

where i is the grid, n is the total number of grids in NCR, O_3 is Ozone concentrations, P is population, R is rate of all cause mortalities, and C is the dose response function (0.3% increase in mortalities per 10 ppb rise in Ozone concentrations)

The health impacts are monetized using the value of statistical life (VSL) approach. VSL approach is identified as a widely accepted methodology for economic evaluation of mortalities (Brent, 2014). World Bank 2013 reviews a number of VSL studies for India (Shanmugan, 1997, Madheswaran, 2007, Simon et al, 1999, Bussolo and O'Connor, 2001) and provides an estimate of about Rs17.8 million as the value of statistical life in Indian conditions. Economic damage due to health impacts of Ozone pollution in NCR is estimated by multiplying the number of attributable mortalities with the value of statistical life.

Agriculture

Other than health impacts, Ozone is also known to have impact over plants and crops. Several studies have shown that Ozone can affect the plant in many different ways (Wilkinson et al, 2011). Ozone can affect the plant through various entry routes. It can enter and affect the plant system a) through leaves via its stomata (gas-exchange pores), b) by dissolving in the water and reacting with other chemicals within the plant. This leads to reduction in the photosynthesis process and hence lesser uptake of required nutrients and hence reduced plant growth and yield. Ozone due to its oxidizing property can form compounds which can decrease the numbers of flowers and fruits in a plant. The major impacts of Ozone can then be classified into a) effects on crop yields, b)visible injuries to plants, and c) impacts on non-food plantations.

Ozone is known to reduce the yields of some of the important crops. Mills et al, 2007 categorised different crop varieties into three broad categories of ozone sensitivity-sensitive, moderately sensitive, and insensitive crops (Table 3). This is to be noted that response of wheat (which is a very important crop in Indian context) with Ozone is very highly correlated with Ozone concentrations.

Table 3. Categorization of different crops based on their sensitivities to Ozone concentrations

S. No.	Senstivity	Crops
1	Ozone sensitive crops	Wheat, water melon, pulses, cotton, turnip, tomato, onion,soybean and lettuce
2	Moderately sensitive crops	Sugar beet, potato, oilseed rape, tobacco, rice, maize, grape and broccoli
3	Ozone resistant crops	Barley and fruit represented by plum and strawberry

Source: Mills et al, 2007.

Fuhrer et al, 2003 also reviewed the various impacts of Ozone on different crop varieties. Heagle et al., 1999 reported lower micronaire, elongation, uniformity and yellowness, and increased fiber length and brightness for wheat. Bosac et al., 1998 stated the reduction in oil, protein, and carbohydrate contents of the rapeseed. Studies of ozone's influence on crop yields differ in their results based on prevailing meteorological and soil conditions . Heagle 1989 showed that dicot species like soybean, cotton and peanut are impacted more than monocot species like sorghum, field corn and winter wheat.

In this study, the district wise crop production data for wheat, rice, and maize is collected from DoES, 2013 for 2012. Grid-wise (4x4 km^2) crop productions are estimated using GIS in the study domain. In this study, AOT40 exposure metrics [Mills et al., 2007, Van Dingenen et al, 2009, Ghude et al, 2014] and concentration response (CR) functions are used to quantify relative yields (RY) which are affected by prevailing Ozone concentrations in NCR. AOT40 metrics has been used previously in many global studies and recently has been used by Ghude et al, 2014 for assessment of yield losses in India due to Ozone. The AOT40 values are estimated using Equation 2 and CR function used in the study are shown in Equations 3-5. Equation 6 is then used to compute the agricultural yield loss of different crops using relative yield loss (RYL= 1-RY)

$$AOT40\left(ppmh\right) = \sum_{i=1}^{n}\left[\left(\left|O3\right|i\right) - 0.04\right] for\ O3 > 0.04ppm \tag{2}$$

$$RY\left(Wheat\right) = -0.0161 \cdot AOT40 + 0.99 \tag{3}$$

$$RY\left(Rice\right) = -0.0039 \cdot AOT40 + 0.94 \tag{4}$$

$$RY\left(Maize\right) = -0.0036 \cdot AOT40 + 1.02 \tag{5}$$

$$Crop\ yield\ loss = Crop\ production \times RYL \,/\, \left(1 - RYL\right) \tag{6}$$

AOT40 values are computed using the modelled Ozone concentrations in each grid. Based on AOT40 values and agricultural crop production in each grid of the study domain, the crop yield losses are computed. The crop growing seasons for wheat, rice (kharif), and maize (kharif) crops are taken as December-February, July-September, and July-September, respectively. Total loss of crop yields are estimated by adding up the yield losses all the grid cells in NCR region.

The economic damage due to agricultural yield lossess is computed using the minimum support prices (MSP) for different crops to derive the conservative estimates (Equation 7). The MSP for wheat, rice and maize are adopted as Rs 1450 per 100 kgs for wheat, rs 1410 per 100 kgs for rice and rs 1310 for 100 kgs for maize.

$$Economic\ loss = Crop\ yield\ loss \times MSP \tag{7}$$

In all, this study estimates the impacts of ground level ozone, which is formed due to the precursor emissions released by different sources having strong linkages with socio-economic growth in the region. Finally, the study estimates the socio-economic impact of ozone pollution in terms of health effects and agricultural losses.

MODELLED OZONE CONCENTRATION IN NCR OF DELHI

Emission inventories of different Ozone precursors are fed into the WRF-CMAQ models to predict Ozone concentrations in the NCR for 2012. Season-wise averages for winters (December-February), summers (March-June), monsoon (July-August), and postmonsoon (September-November) are presented in Figure 8a-d. The details of the modelling results are presented in Sharma et al, 2016a.

Figure 8. Simulation results of Ozone concentrations in NCR during 2012

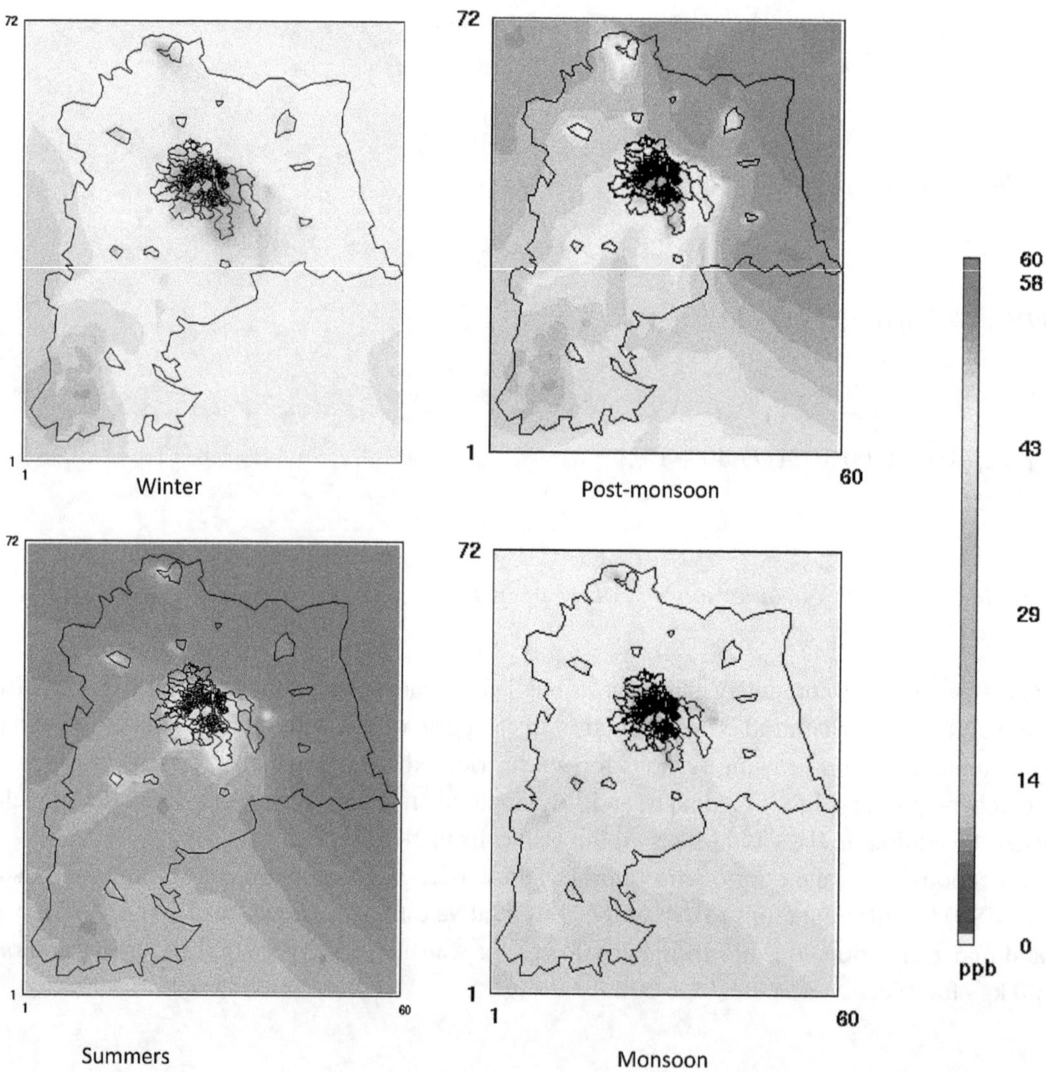

Figure 9. Shares of the three crops in the production and crop losses due to Ozone concentrations in NCR in 2012

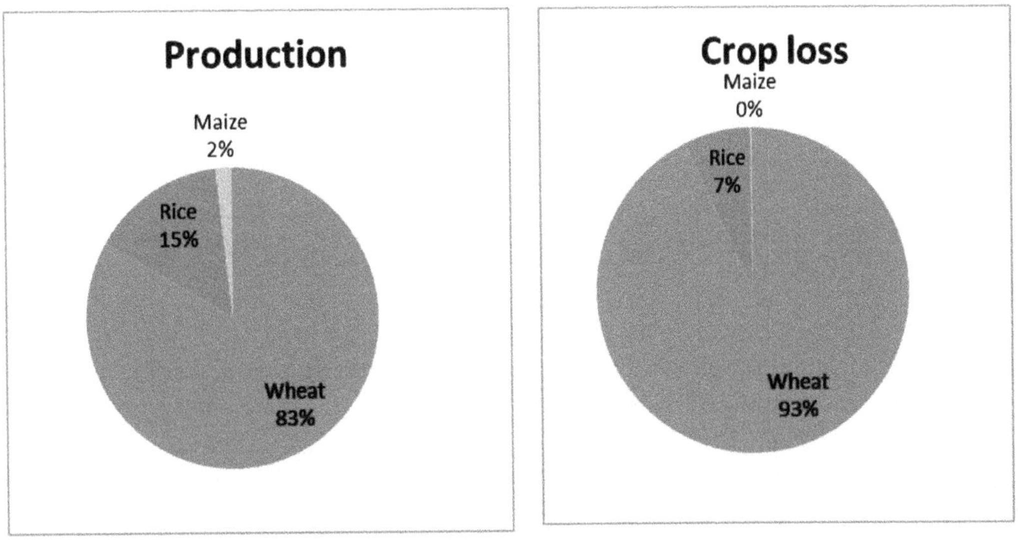

The concentrations are found to be highest during summers due to higher number of sunny days and higher solar radiations helping in Ozone formation. The concentrations are low within the city of Delhi and surrounding urban regions mainly due to titration chemistry with NOx emissions. However, in regions far from the city limits, the Ozone concentrations are higher. More importantly, this is the region with lower population densities, but with most of the agricultural activities. Concentrations are lowest in monsoon and winter seasons mainly on account of lower photo-chemical activity.

IMPACTS OF OZONE CONCENTRATIONS IN NCR

Based on the modelled and validated Ozone concentrations and dose response functions, the agricultural and health impacts of Ozone in NCR are computed for the year 2012.

The health impact assessment suggests that Ozone pollution in NCR is responsible for additional 3193 mortalities. Out of these, about 38% mortalities are in Delhi region. Although, the concentrations are lower within the city of Delhi in comparison to rest of NCR, high population density leads to higher cumulative exposure. Rural regions in NCR show higher Ozone concentrations, but due to lesser population densities show considerable lower exposures.

Agricultural crop losses due to Ozone pollution are estimated for all grids in the study domain. The production and agricultural yield losses for wheat, rice and maize in NCR for the year 2012 are presented in Table 4. Almost, 1329 kt of grains are lost on account of Ozone pollution in the region. Wheat which is the primary crop grown in the region shows highest yield loss of 23%, i.e. a crop loss of about 1232 kt. Rice and maize are the other crops which show considerable losses.

Figure 9 shows the shares of the three crops in the production and crop losses due to Ozone concentrations in NCR. Wheat accounts for 83% of the three crops produced in the region, however, its share goes upto 93% in losses due to lager impacts by Ozone.

Table 4. Production (kt), % yield loss, and total crop loss (kt) attributable to Ozone pollution in NCR

S.No	Crop	Production (kt)	% Yield Loss	Crop Loss (kt)
1	Wheat	5375	23%	1232
2	Rice	954	10%	96
3	Maize	112	1%	1
	Total	6441		1329

ECONOMIC DAMAGE OF OZONE CONCENTRAITONS IN NCR

The economic damage of Ozone pollution in NCR is estimated for health and agricultural losses. The value of statistical life approach shows that 3193 mortalities in NCR in 2012 attributed to Ozone pollution led to an economic loss of Rs 5682 crores (0.95 billion USD) annually. For Delhi alone, the loss is estimated out to be Rs 1975 crores (0.33 billion USD). Although, the concentrations in Delhi are comparatively lower than the overall NCR region, but presence of huge population base in the city provides higher exposures and hence higher impacts over health. These figures amount to 1.6% of the overall GDP of Delhi.

Economic damage due to crop losses are estimated using the minimum support prices for the three crops considered in the study. The agricultural crop losses led to an economic damage of Rs 1922 crores (0.32 billion USD). Wheat has the maximum share of 93%, followed by rice 7%.

Overall, the losses due to health and agricultural impacts of Ozone pollution amount to about 7605 crores (1.27 billion USD) in 2012 in the NCR region. This is about 2.2% of the total GDP of Delhi.

CONCLUSION

Ozone is a pollutant of global concern. In India, although the attention is currently paid to particulate matter pollution, but the effects of Ozone cannot be neglected. Ozone is widely known to adversely impact human health and agriculture, and this study estimates these impacts over the highly polluted NCR region (including the city of Delhi) in India. A simulation based approach is used to assess spatial and temporal variations of Ozone across the study domain for the year 2012. The population and agricultural production databases were overlaid on the Ozone concentrations map of NCR and impacts were estimated using established dose-response functions. The study shows that more than 3000 mortalities and loss of more than 1300 kt of agricultural crops (wheat, rice and maize) can be attributed to Ozone pollution in the region. The study also finds that the concentrations of Ozone are higher in regions outside the urban limits mainly due to the chemistry. However, because most of the agricultural activities being carried out in rural regions of NCR, the agricultural losses are high. A yield loss of 23%, 10%, and 1% have been estimated for wheat, rice and maize crops. On the other hand, while the concentrations are low inside the city limits, the presence of huge population bases leads to more exposure and hence adverse health impacts due to Ozone. Overall, the economic damage due to Ozone pollution is estimated to be about 1.27 billion USD in 2012 for the whole NCR region.

The study shows significant impacts of Ozone pollution in the region and hence calls for immediate and proactive actions before the situation worsens in future. There is an urgent need to control the emissions of precursors such as NOx and NMVOCs. NOx is primarily emitted from high temperature combustion in vehicular engines, power plants and DG sets. There is a need to advance the current legislations for emission control for different sectors in the region. Advancement of vehicular emission norms to BS-V/BS-VI could certainly lead to reduced NOx emissions from transport sector. Enhancement of public transport systems should lead to reduced energy demands from the sector and hence reduced emissions. NOx standards for coal based power plants need to be introduced. Power supplies need to be improved to reduce the usage of DG sets in the regions which are an important source of NOx. For control of NMVOCs, evaporative emissions need to be controlled by moving towards low-solvent based products (paints, printing inks, personal products etc). Biomass burning needs to be reduced by higher penetration of LPG and improved cook-stoves. Ozone is also transported in NCR from regions outside, and hence regional, scale efforts will be required for its control.

Overall, this study highlights the need for control of ozone pollution by reducing precursor emissions so that environmental quality (air quality in this context) can be conserved. The study also shows that the betterment in environmental quality may lead to significant economic benefits by reducing the impacts.

This study highlights the key sustainability issue of deteriorating air quality and more specifically, the impacts of ground level ozone on health and agriculture. The precursors of ozone are released from different sources which have close linkages with socio-economic growth in the region. However, it has been found that pollution itself hampers the socio-econmic growth of the region by affecting the health and agricultural productivity. The study emphasizes on adoption of more sustainable model of development to reduce impacts on environment and eventually on the socio-economic development.

REFERENCES

Alexis, N., Urch, B., & Tarlo, S. (2000). Cyclooxygenase metabolites play a different role in ozone induced pulmonary function decline in asthmatics compared to normals. *Inhalation Toxicology, 12*(12), 1205–1224. doi:10.1080/08958370050198548 PMID:11114789

Anderson, H. R., Ponce de Leon, A., & Bland, J. M. (1987). Air pollution and daily mortality in London: 1987–92. *BMJ, 1996*(312), 665–669. PMID:8597732

Anderson, H. R., Ponce de Leon, A., & Bland, J. M. (2004). *Meta-analysis of time-series studies and panel studies of particulate matter (PM) and ozone (O3).* Report of a WHO task group. Copenhagen WHO Regional Office for Europe, 2004. Retrieved from http://www.euro. who.int/document/e82792.pdf

Batty, K., & Ashmore, M. R. (2003). Lower threshold ozone exposures for effects on roots than shoots in wetland species. In *Establishing ozone critical levels II, 2003 451 UNECE Workshop Report.* IVL report B1523 IVL Swedish Environmental Research Institute.

Bell. M.L., Dominici, F., Samet, J.M. (1997). Ozone and short-term mortality in 95 urban communities, 1987–2000. *JAMA, 2004*, 292:2372.

Bell, M. L., Dominici, F., & Samet, J. M. (2005). A meta-analysis of time-series studies of ozone and mortality with comparison to the national morbidity, mortality, and air pollution study. *Epidemiology (Cambridge, Mass.)*, *16*(4), 436–445. doi:10.1097/01.ede.0000165817.40152.85 PMID:15951661

Bell, M. L., Peng, R. D., & Dominici, F. (2006, April). The exposure-response curve for ozone and risk of mortality and the adequacy of current ozone regulations. *Environmental Health Perspectives*, *114*(4), 532–536. doi:10.1289/ehp.8816 PMID:16581541

Bergamaschi, E., De Palma, G., Mozzoni, P., Vanni, S., Vettori, M. V., Broeckaert, F., & Mutti, A. et al. (2001). Polymorphism of quinone-metabolizing enzymes and susceptibility to ozone-induced acute effects. *American Journal of Respiratory and Critical Care Medicine*, *163*(6), 1426–1431. doi:10.1164/ajrccm.163.6.2006056 PMID:11371413

Black, V.J., Black, C.R., Roberts, J.A., & Stewart, C.A. (2000). *Impact of ozone on the reproductive*. Academic Press.

Blomberg, A., Mudway, I. S., Nordenhäll, C., Hedenström, H., Kelly, F. J., Frew, A. J., & Sandström, T. et al. (1999). Ozone-induced lung function decrements do not correlate with early airway inflammatory or antioxidant responses. *The European Respiratory Journal*, *13*(6), 1418–1428. doi:10.1183/09031936.99.13614299 PMID:10445622

Bosac, C., Black, V. J., Roberts, J. A., & Black, C. R. (1998). Impact of ozone on seed yield and quality and seedling vigour in oilseed rape (Brassica napus L.). *Plant Physiology*, *153*(1-2), 127–134. doi:10.1016/S0176-1617(98)80055-2

Braun-Fahrländer, C., Künzli, N., Domenighetti, G., Carell, C. F., Anderson, H. R., Strachan, D., & Ruffin, D. et al. (1994). Acute effects of ambient ozone on respiratory function of Swiss schoolchildren after a 10-minute heavy exercise. *Pediatric Pulmonology*, *17*(3), 169–177. doi:10.1002/ppul.1950170306 PMID:8196997

Brent, R. J. (2014). *Cost_Benefit Analysis and Health Care Evaluations* (2nd ed.). Edward Elgar Publishing Limited.

Bush, M. L., Raybold, T., Abeles, S., Hu, S. C., Ben-Jebria, A., & Ultman, J. S. (1996). Longitudinal distribution of ozone absorption in the lung: Gender differences and intersubject variability. *Journal of Applied Physiology*, *81*, 1651–1657. PMID:8904582

Bussolo, M., & O'Connor, D. (2001). *Clearing Air in India: The Economics of Climate Policy with Ancillary Benefits*. Development Centre Working Paper 182, CD/DOC 14. Organisation for Economic Cooperation and Development (OECD).

Byun, D. W., & Ching, J. K. S. (Eds.). (1999). Science algorithms of the EPA Models-3 community multiscale air quality (CMAQ) modeling system. NERL, Research Triangle Park, NC EPA/ 600/R-99/030.

CCME. (2003). *Effects of o3 on materials: update in support of the Canada-wide standards for particulate matter and O3*. Canadian Council of Ministers of the Environment.

Chatani, S., Amann, M., Goel, A., Hao, J., Klimont, Z., Kumar, A., & Zhao, B. et al. (2014). Photochemical roles of rapid economic growth and potential abatement strategies on tropospheric ozone over South and East Asia in 2030. *Atmospheric Chemistry and Physics*, *14*(17), 9259–9277. doi:10.5194/acp-14-9259-2014

Chen, P. C., Lai, Y. M., Chan, C. C., Hwang, J. S., Yang, C. Y., & Wang, J. D. (1999). Short-term effect of ozone on the pulmonary function of children in primary school. *Environmental Health Perspectives*, *107*(11), 921–925. doi:10.1289/ehp.99107921 PMID:10544161

Coffey M.J., Wheeler,C.S., Gross,K.B., & Eschenbacher,W.L.(1996). Increased 5-lipoxygenase metabolism in the lungs of human subjects exposed to ozone. *Toxicology*, *114*, 187–197.

Cooley, D. R., & Manning, W. J. (1987). The impact of ozone on assimilate partitioning in plants– a review. *Environmental Pollution*, *47*(2), 95–113. doi:10.1016/0269-7491(87)90040-6 PMID:15092712

Cross, C. E., van der Vliet, A., Louie, S., Thiele, J. J., & Halliwell, B. (1998). Oxidative stress and antioxidants at biosurfaces: Plants, skin, and respiratory tract surfaces. *Environmental Health Perspectives*, *106*(Suppl. 5), 1241–1251. doi:10.1289/ehp.98106s51241 PMID:9788905

DoES. (2013). *District-wise, season-wise crop production statistics*. Directorate of Economics and Statistics (DoES), Government of India. Retrieved from https://data.gov.in/catalog/district-wise-season-wise-crop-production-statistics#web_catalog_tabs_block_10

Folinsbee, L. J., & Hazucha, M. J. (2000). Time course of response to ozone exposure in healthy adult females. *Inhalation Toxicology*, *12*(3), 151–167. doi:10.1080/089583700196211 PMID:10715622

Franzaring, J., Tonneijck, A. E. G., Kooijman, A. W. N., & Dueck, T. A. (2000). Growth responses to ozone in plant species from wetlands. *Environmental and Experimental Botany*, *44*(1), 39–48. doi:10.1016/S0098-8472(00)00052-6 PMID:10927127

Ghude, S. D., Jena, C., Chate, D. M., Beig, G., Pfister, G., Kumar, R., & Ramanathan, V. (2014). Reductions in India's crop yield due to ozone. *Geophysical Research Letters*, *41*(15), 5685–5691. doi:10.1002/2014GL060930

Gimeno, B. S., Bermejo, V., Sanz, J., & de, . (2004b). Assessment of the effects of ozone exposure and plant competition on the reproductive ability of three therophytic clover species from Iberian pastures. *Atmospheric Environment*, *38*(15), 2295–2303. doi:10.1016/j.atmosenv.2003.10.062

Goldberg, M. S., Burnett, R. T., Bailar, J. C. III, Brook, J., Bonvalot, Y., & Tamblyn, R. (2001). Associations between daily cause-specific mortality and concentrations of ground-level ozone in Montreal, Quebec. *American Journal of Epidemiology*, *154*(9), 817–826. doi:10.1093/aje/154.9.817 PMID:11682364

Graham, R. M., Friedman, M., & Hoyle, G. W. (2001). Sensory nerves promote ozoneinduced lung inflammation in mice. *American Journal of Respiratory and Critical Care Medicine*, *164*(2), 307–313. doi:10.1164/ajrccm.164.2.2007115 PMID:11463606

Grievink, L., Jansen, S. M., Van't Veer, P., & Brunekreef, B. (1998). Acute effects of ozone on pulmonary function of cyclists receiving antioxidant supplements. *Occupational and Environmental Medicine*, *55*(1), 13–17. doi:10.1136/oem.55.1.13 PMID:9536157

Gryparis, A., Forsberg, B., Katsouyanni, K., Analitis, A., Touloumi, G., Schwartz, J., & Dörtbudak, Z. et al. (2004). Acute effects of ozone on mortality from "the air pollution and health: A European approach" project. *American Journal of Respiratory and Critical Care Medicine*, *170*(10), 1080–1087. doi:10.1164/rccm.200403-333OC PMID:15282198

Halonen, J. I., Lanki, T., Tiittanen, P., Niemi, J. V., Loh, M., & Pekkanen, J. (2010). Ozone and cause-specific cardiorespiratory morbidity and mortality, Research report. *Journal of Epidemiology and Community Health*, *64*(9), 814–820. doi:10.1136/jech.2009.087106 PMID:19854743

Hayes, F., Mills, G., & Ashmore, M. (2009). Effects of ozone on inter- and intra-species competition and photosynthesis in mesocosms of Lolium perenne and Trifolium repens. *Environmental Pollution*, *157*(1), 208–214. doi:10.1016/j.envpol.2008.07.002 PMID:18774210

Hayes, F., Mills, G., Jones, M. L. M., & Ashmore, M. (2010). Does a simulated upland community respond to increasing background, peak or accumulated exposure of ozone? *Atmospheric Environment*, *44*(34), 4155–4164. doi:10.1016/j.atmosenv.2010.07.037

Heagle, A. S. (1989). Ozone and crop yield. *Annual Review of Phytopathology*, *27*(1), 397–423. doi:10.1146/annurev.py.27.090189.002145

Heagle, A. S., Miller, J. E., Booker, F. L., & Pursley, W. A. (1999). Ozone stress, carbon dioxide enrichment, and nitrogen fertility interactions in cotton. *Crop Science*, *39*(3), 731–741. doi:10.2135/cropsci1999.0011183X003900030021x

Higgins, I. T., D'Arcy, J. B., Gibbons, D. I., Avol, E. L., & Gross, K. B. (1990). Effect of exposures to ambient ozone on ventilatory lung function in children. *The American Review of Respiratory Disease*, *141*(5_pt_1), 1136–1146. doi:10.1164/ajrccm/141.5_Pt_1.1136 PMID:2339836

Hiltermann, T. J. N., Stolk, J., van der Zee, S. C., Brunekreef, C. R., de Bruijne, P. H., & Fischer, C. B. (1998). Asthma severity and susceptibility to air pollution. *The European Respiratory Journal*, *11*, 686–693. PMID:9596122

Hoek, G., Schwartz, J. D., Groot, B., & Eilers, P. (1997). Effects of ambient particulate matter and ozone on daily mortality in Rotterdam, The Netherlands. *Archives of Environmental Health*, *52*(6), 455–463. doi:10.1080/00039899709602224 PMID:9541366

IPCC. (2013). IPCC Fifth Assessment Report. *Climatic Change*, 2013.

Ito, K., De Leon, S. F., & Lippmann, M. (2005). Associations between ozone and daily mortality: Analysis and meta-analysis. *Epidemiology (Cambridge, Mass.)*, *16*(4), 446–457. doi:10.1097/01.ede.0000165821.90114.7f PMID:15951662

Jacob, D. J. (2000). Heterogeneous chemistry and tropospheric ozone. *Atmospheric Environment*, *34*(12-14), 2131–2159. doi:10.1016/S1352-2310(99)00462-8

Jerrett, M., Burnett, R. T., Pope, C. A. III, Kasuhiko, I., Thurston, G., Krewski, D., & Thun, M. et al. (2009). Long-term ozone exposure and mortality. *The New England Journal of Medicine*, *360*(11), 1085–1095. doi:10.1056/NEJMoa0803894 PMID:19279340

Korrick, S. A., Neas, L. M., & Dockery, D. W. (2004). Ozone exposure decreases the effect of a deep inhalation on forced expiratory flow in normal subjects. *Journal of Applied Physiology*, *96*(5), 1651–1657. doi:10.1152/japplphysiol.00507.2003 PMID:14688031

Korrick, S. A., Neas, L. M., Dockery, D. W., Gold, D. R., Allen, G. A., Hill, L. B., & Speizer, F. E. et al. (1998). Effects of ozone and other pollutants on the pulmonary function of adult hikers. *Environmental Health Perspectives*, *106*(2), 93–99. doi:10.1289/ehp.9810693 PMID:9435151

Kwon, H.J., Cho, S.H, Nyberg, F., & Pershagen, G. (2001). Effects of ambient air pollution on daily mortality in a cohort of patients with congestive heart failure. *Epidemiology, 12*, 413–419.

Lee, D. S., Holland, M. R., & Falla, N. (1996, April). The potential impact of O3 on materials in the U.K. *Atmospheric Environment*, *30*(7), 1053–1065. doi:10.1016/1352-2310(95)00407-6

Levy, J. I., Chemerynski, S. M., & Sarnat, J. A. (2005). Ozone exposure and mortality: An empiric bayes metaregression analysis. *Epidemiology (Cambridge, Mass.)*, *16*(4), 458–468. doi:10.1097/01.ede.0000165820.08301.b3 PMID:15951663

Loomis, D., Castillejos, M., Gold, D. R., McDonnell, W., Borja-Aburto, V. H., & O'Neill, M. S. (1999). Air pollution and infant mortality in Mexico City. *Epidemiology (Cambridge, Mass.)*, *10*(2), 118–123. doi:10.1097/00001648-199903000-00006 PMID:10069245

Madheswaran, S. (2007). Measuring the Value of Statistical Life: Estimating Compensating Wage Differential among Workers in India. *Social Indicators Research*, *84*(1), 83–96. doi:10.1007/s11205-006-9076-0

Mills, G., Buse, A., Gimeno, B., Bermejo, V., Holland, M., Emberson, L., & Pleijel, H. (2007). A synthesis of AOT40-based response functions and critical levels of ozone for agricultural and horticultural crops. *Atmospheric Environment*, *41*(12), 2630–2643. doi:10.1016/j.atmosenv.2006.11.016

Mills, G., Buse, A., Gimeno, B., Bermejo, V., Holland, M., Emberson, L., & Pleijel, H. (2007). A synthesis of AOT40-based response functions and critical levels of ozone for agricultural and horticultural crops. *Atmospheric Environment*, *41*(12), 2630–2643. doi:10.1016/j.atmosenv.2006.11.016

Montuschi, P., Ragazzoni, E., & Valente, S. (2002). Ozone-induced increase in exhaled 8-isoprostane in healthy subjects is resistant to inhaled budesonide. *Free Radical Biology & Medicine*, *33*(10), 1403–1408. doi:10.1016/S0891-5849(02)01084-5 PMID:12419472

Moolgavkar, S. H., Luebeck, E. G., Hall, T. A., & Anderson, E. L. (1995). Air pollution and daily mortality in Philadelphia. *Epidemiology (Cambridge, Mass.)*, *6*(5), 476–484. doi:10.1097/00001648-199509000-00003 PMID:8562622

Nevers, N. D. (2000). *Air Pollution Control Engineering* (2nd ed.). New York: McGraw-Hill Companies, Inc.

O'Neill, M. S., Loomis, D., & Borja-Aburto, V. H. (2004). Ozone, area social conditions, and mortality in Mexico City. *Environmental Research*, *94*(3), 234–242. doi:10.1016/j.envres.2003.07.002 PMID:15016589

Penttinen, P., Tiittanen, P., & Pekkanen, J. (2004). Mortality and air pollution in metropolitan Helsinki, 1988–996. *Scandinavian Journal of Work, Environment & Health*, *30*(Suppl. 2), 19–27. PMID:15487682

Pudasainee, D., Sapkota, B., Shrestha, M. L., Kaga, A., Kondo, A., & Inoue, Y. (2006). Short communication Ground level O3 concentrations and its association with NOx and meteorological parameters in Kathmandu valley, Nepal. *Atmospheric Environment*, *40*, 8081–8087. doi:10.1016/j.atmosenv.2006.07.011

Rämö, K., Kanerva, T., Ojanperä, K., & Manninen, S. (2007). Growth onset, senescence, andreproductive development of meadow species in mesocosms exposed to elevated O3 and CO2. *Environmental Pollution*, *145*(3), 850–860. doi:10.1016/j.envpol.2006.03.054 PMID:16815612

RGCC. (2011). *Census of India – 2011*. New Delhi: Registrar General and Census Commissioner, Govt. of India.

Sáez, M., Tobias, A., Antó, J. M., Spix, C., de Leon, A. P., Tobias, A., & Bacharova, L. et al. (2002). A combined analysis of the short-term effects of photochemical air pollutants on mortality within the EMECAM project. *Environmental Health Perspectives*, *110*(3), 221–228. doi:10.1289/ehp.02110221 PMID:11882471

Samet, J. M., Hatch, G. E., Horstman, D., Steck-Scott, S., Arab, L., Bromberg, P. A., & Devlin, R. B. et al. (2001). Effect of antioxidant supplementation on ozone-induced lung injury in human subjects. *American Journal of Respiratory and Critical Care Medicine*, *164*(5), 819–825. doi:10.1164/ajrccm.164.5.2008003 PMID:11549539

Sarangapani, R., Gentry, P. R., Covington, T. R., Teeguarden, J. G., & Clewell, H. J. III. (2003). Evaluation of the potential impact of age- and genderspecific lung morphology and ventilation rate on the dosimetry of vapors. *Inhalation Toxicology*, *15*(10), 987–1016. doi:10.1080/08958370390226350 PMID:12928976

Schwartz, J., Gryparis, A., Forsberg, B., Katsouyanni, K., Analitis, A., & Touloumi, G. (2005). How sensitive is the association between ozone and daily deaths to control for temperature? *American Journal of Respiratory and Critical Care Medicine*, *171*(6), 627–631. doi:10.1164/rccm.200407-933OC PMID:15579726

Shanmugan, K. R. (1997). The Value of Life: Estimates from Indian Labour Market. *The Indian Economic Journal*, *44*(4), 105–114.

Sharma, S. & Khare, M., (2016a). *Ozone precursor inventories and simulation in NCR*. Unpublished.

Sharma, S., Chatani, S., Mahtta, R., Goel, A., & Kumar, A. (2016b). Sensitivity analysis of ground level ozone in India using WRF-CMAQ Models. *Atmospheric Environment*, *131*, 29–40.

Sillman, S. (2003). Tropospheric ozone and photochemical smog. In B. Sherwood Lollar (Ed.), Treatise on Geochemistry (Vol. 9). Elsevier.

Simon, N., Cropper, M., Alberini, A., & Arora, A. (1999). *Valuing Mortality Reductions in India: A Study Compensating Wage Differentials*. The World Bank Policy Paper.

Simpson, R. W., Williams, G., Petroeschevsky, A., Morgan, G., & Rutherford, S. (1997). Associations between outdoor air pollution and daily mortality in Brisbane, Australia. *Archives of Environmental Health*, *52*(6), 442–454. doi:10.1080/00039899709602223 PMID:9541365

TERI. (2013). Creation of energy scenario in the future to improve air quality in East and South Asia. The Energy and Resources Institute.

Torres, A., Soler, N., & Ewig, S. (1997). Airway inflammation in smokers and nonsmokers with varying responsiveness to ozone. *American Journal of Respiratory and Critical Care Medicine*, *156*(3), 728–736. doi:10.1164/ajrccm.156.3.9601054 PMID:9309986

Touloumi, G., Spix, C., Ponce de León, A., Le Moullec, Y., & Bacharova, L. (1997). Short-term effects of ambient oxidant exposure on mortality: a combined analysis within the APHEA project. Air Pollution and Health: a European Approach. *American Journal of Epidemiology*, *146*(2), 177–185. doi:10.1093/oxfordjournals.aje.a009249 PMID:9230780

TRS. (2008). *Ground-level ozone in the 21st century: future trends, impacts and policy implications, RS Policy document 15/08, Issued: October 2008 RS1276*. London: The Royal Society.

Ulmer, C., Kopp, M., Ihorst, G., Frischer, T., Forster, J., & Kuehr, J. (1997). Effects of ambient ozone exposures during the spring and summer of 1994 on pulmonary function of schoolchildren. *Pediatric Pulmonology*, *23*(5), 344–353. doi:10.1002/(SICI)1099-0496(199705)23:5<344::AID-PPUL6>3.0.CO;2-K PMID:9168508

U.S. Protection Agency, (1996). *Air Quality Criteria for O_3 and Related Photochemical Oxidants*. EPA 600/P-93/004bF.

Vagaggini, B., Taccola, M., Cianchetti, S., Carnevali, S., Bartoli, M. L., Bacci, E., & Paggiaro, P. L. et al. (2002). Ozone exposure increases eosinophilic airway response induced by previous allergen challenge. *American Journal of Respiratory and Critical Care Medicine*, *166*(8), 1073–1077. doi:10.1164/rccm.2201013 PMID:12379550

Vagaggini, B., Taccola, M., Conti, I., Carnevali, S., Cianchetti, S., Bartoli, M. L., & Paggiaro, P. L. et al. (2001). Budesonide reduces neutrophilic but not functional airway response to ozone in mild asthmatics. *American Journal of Respiratory and Critical Care Medicine*, *164*(12), 2172–2176. doi:10.1164/ajrccm.164.12.2009090 PMID:11751182

Van Dingenen, R., Dentener, F. J., Raes, F., Krol, M. C., Emberson, L., & Cofala, J. (2009). The global impact of O3 on agricultural crop yields under current and future air quality legislation. *Atmospheric Environment*, *43*(3), 604–618. doi:10.1016/j.atmosenv.2008.10.033

WHO. (2008). *Health risks of ozone from long-range transboundary air pollution*. Geneva: World Health Organization.

Wilkinson, S., Mills, G., Illidge, R., & Davies, W. J. (2011). How is O3 pollution reducing our food supply? *Journal of Experimental Botany*. doi:10.1093/jxb/err317

World Bank. (2013). *India Diagnostic Assessment of Select Environmental Challenges An Analysis of Physical and Monetary Losses of Environmental Health and Natural Resources* (Vol. 1). The World Bank.

Zeghnoun, A., Czernichow, P., Beaudeau, P., Hautemanière, A., Froment, L. É. T., Tertre, A. L., & Quénel, P. (2001). Short-term effects of air pollution on mortality in the cities of Rouen and Le Havre, France, 1990–1995. *Archives of Environmental Health*, *56*(4), 327–335. doi:10.1080/00039890109604464 PMID:11572276

Zmirou, D., Schwartz, J., Saez, M., Zanobetti, A., Wojtyniak, B., & Touloumi, G. (1998). Time-series analysis of air pollution and cause-specific mortality. *Epidemiology (Cambridge, Mass.)*, *9*(5), 495–503. doi:10.1097/00001648-199809000-00005 PMID:9730027

ENDNOTE

1 E.g propane (C_3H_8) when reacts with OH, $C_3H_7O_2$ (RO2) is formed.

Chapter 16
Economic Value of Regulating and Cultural Ecosystem Services of Oasean Biome:
Case Study in Middle Draa Valley

Ahmed Karmaoui
Independent Researcher, Morocco

ABSTRACT

The oasean rangelands surrounding and the scattered steppic area, is commonly viewed as degraded landscapes. The dynamics of oasean ecosystems is indeed affected by human and climatic disturbances and stresses which induce desertification processes. In this context, the objectives of this research are to identify and quantify ecosystem services as a tool for measuring changes in arid lands. Monetization has enabled a more complete diagnosis of ecosystems and their ecosystem services. In this paper, we examine the economic value of the regulating and cultural ecosystem services provided by the oases of Middle Draa Valley (MDV), which is part of Biosphere Reserve of southern Moroccan Oasis (UNESCO). The economic values are standardized to US$ per hectare per year (2008-2010 period prices). The total value of regulating services is found to be 2478,9 US$/ha/year for the arable area (26000ha) and 43,14 US$/ha/year for the whole Middle Draa Valley (1500 000ha). The economic value of the cultural services in the arable area is 1776,8 US$/ha/year and 30,83US$/ha/year for the total area.

INTRODUCTION

Many of ecosystem services (or ecosystem functions) are critical to our survival (climate regulation, air purification, crop pollination) while others enhance it (aesthetics) (Kremen, 2005). After the Millennium Ecosystem Assessment (MEA) classification, the ecosystem provides a varied range of services and dis-services to local populations, which include: provisioning, regulating, cultural and supporting services. Daily et al (1997) had emphasized that most ecosystem services were the result of a complex interaction between natural cycles operating over a wide range of space and time scales. The status and

DOI: 10.4018/978-1-5225-0094-0.ch016

trends of these ecosystem services vary by the type and intensity of the pressures to which they are exposed. Natural resource degradation is now manifesting in the different ecosystems. It is induced by both climatic factors and by human actions, exacerbated by socio-economic context marked by extreme poverty. Successive droughts in the study area, in recent years have also severely limited the production of the medium (karmaoui et al., 2015). The rapid increase in population in recent years (karmaoui et al., 2014) and the radical change that occurred in their lifestyle generated a strong pressure on natural resources. In fact, the oasean area (Draa Valley) is considered among the most barren of the country (Harakat 2007). The palm groves of the region recorded a constant decline of yields; they are threatened with extinction, particularly under the effect of soil degradation (Maroufi 2008). By Appling the environment vulnerability index at local scale, Karmaoui., et al., (2014) demonstrates that this area is vulnerable under climate change and anthropogenic impacts.

Ecosystem degradation of the Middle Draa Valley leads to the loss of ecosystem services and negative impacts on livelihoods. In fact, human domination of the biosphere has led to rapid alterations in the composition, structure and function of ecosystems (Vitousek et al., 1997). Interest in ecosystem services in both the research and policy communities has grown rapidly (Braat & De Groot, 2012; Costanza & Kubiszewski, 2012). Ecosystem service valuation has been a hot topic in ecological economic research (Sawut, 2013). Previous work describes and categorizes ecosystem services, identifies methods for economic valuation, maps the supply and demand for services, assesses threats to them, and estimates economic values (Daily, 1997; Daily et al., 2000; Heal, 2000; Millennium Ecosystem Assessment, 2003; Biggs et al., 2004; De Groot et al., 2012; Costanza et al., 2014).

The oasean ecosystem oasis system is organized in three cultures strata so hot and humid microclimate perfectly suitable for a relative rich biodiversity (karmaoui et al., 2015), dominated by the date palm that protects several local species from the sun.

In biodiversity terms, understanding the value of species that support particular ecological functions requires an understanding of both their substitutability and complementarity in the performance of those functions (Perrings, 2010). The simplification of agroecosystems to privilege particular crops or livestock strains necessarily affects the array of services that system delivers, partly because the number of functions performed increases with the number of species (Hector & Bagchi, 2007).

This chapter will detail various regulating and cultural services provided by Middle Draa Valley Oases. The paper's priority is to identify and quantify regulating and cultural ecosystem services and their associated values. This study will be the basis for future estimate ecosystem values 'before and after' environmental changes.

MATERIAL AND METHODS

Study Area

The study area is situated on the southern east of Morocco (lat. 5°30'-7°00'W, long. 29°00'-31°00'N), with a total area of 15 000 km^2 (Figure 1). The study area has an arid continental climate with high temperatures, especially between June and September (43 to 50 ° C) (Ait Hamza et al., 2009), average annual precipitation of 80 mm, and a high rates of evapotranspiration, especially during the summer. The Agriculture and farming are the main economic activities in the area (MPZ, 2011; Chelleri et al., 2014; Karmaoui et al., 2014).

Figure 1. Middle Draa Valley area
Source: Processed and modified from the digital IMPETUS atlas 2.1).

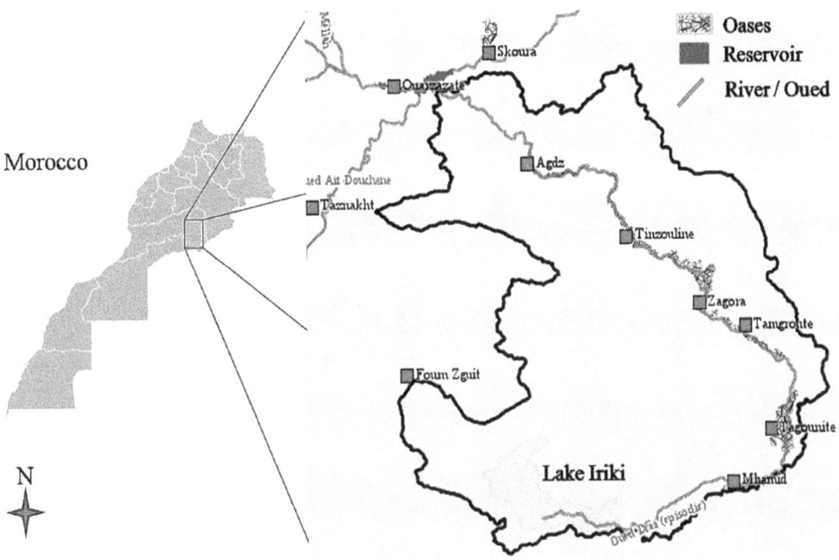

Figure 2 shows the extrapolation of the most productive part of the study area represented by six palm groves aligned as a necklace. These oases are located along the Draa Wadi (temporary river) fed by Mansour Eddahbi Reservoir.

Method

Following the reports of the Millennium ecosystem assessment (MEA, 2005), there is a clear consensus that services provided by ecosystems contribute much to the well-being of individuals, of communities and of the economy. The literature on ecosystem services has grown exponentially (Fisher et al., 2009). At present ecosystem services are increasingly reaching economic decision-making through the widespread promotion of Market Based Instruments for conservation such as Markets for Ecosystem Services (Bayon, 2004). In recent scientific literature, there are a variety of methods for estimating the value of ecosystem services (ES). The selection of appropriate valuation methods is in part determined by the type of ecosystem service being valued (Brander, 2013). In this study, we estimate the economic value of regulating and cultural services using the following methods (Brander, 2013).

- **Market Prices:** Use prices that are directly observed in markets (ex: ES that are traded directly in markets).
- **Replacement Cost:** Estimate the cost of replacing an ES with a man-made service (ex: ES that have a manmade equivalent that could be used and provides similar benefits to the ecosystem service).
- **Restoration Cost:** Estimate the cost of replacing an ES with a man-made service (ex: Any ES that can be provided by restored ecosystems)
- **Travel Cost:** Use data on travel costs and visit rates to estimate demand for recreation sites (example: Recreation sites)

Figure 2. Six aligned oases along Draa Wadi
Source: Processed and modified from the digital IMPETUS atlas 2.1).

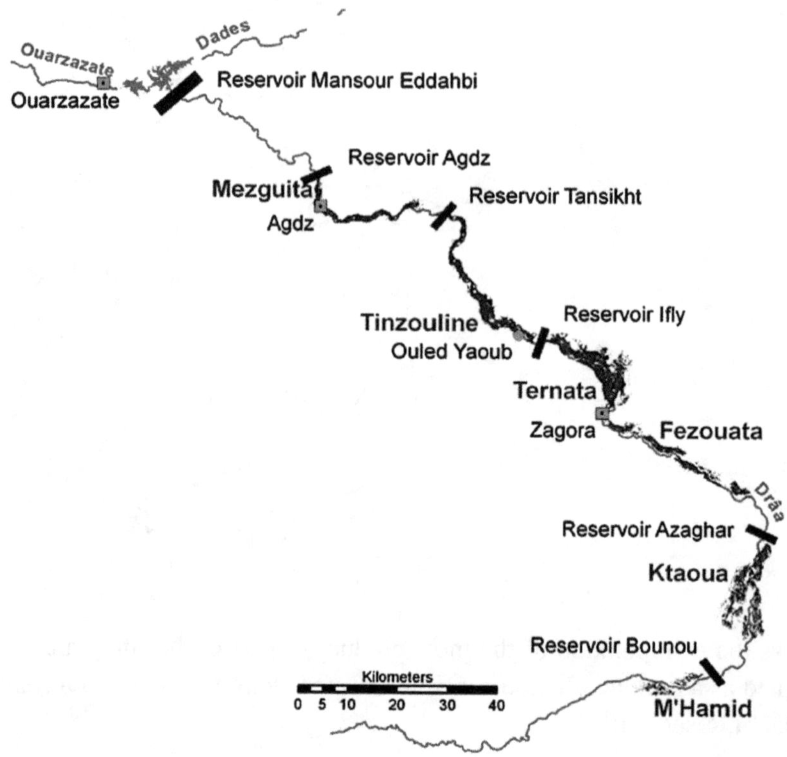

- **Contingent Valuation:** Ask people to state their willingness to pay for an ES through surveys (ex: All ecosystem services)

The Appendix provides a brief explanation of each economic valuation method, setting out the approach, applicability to different ecosystem services, example, applications, and limitations. We collect the data from a variety of sources, including bibliographic data, government ministries, and environmental organizations. Information was also gathered and classified in ecosystem services categories. The data gathered pertained to the particular indicator to be calculated and represented the 8 last years; a program of field trips and a socio-economic and ecological survey supplemented by unstructured interviews in the study area. Figure 3 gathers some methods and approached to valuing ecosystem services.

The Total Value (V) of Ecosystem Services ES (EQ1) in $/ha/year for ecosystem type k is V (ES)k (Glaves & Egan, 2013):

$$V\left(SEk\right)=\sum_{i=1}^{n}A\left(LUi\right)\times V\left(SEki\right)$$

Figure 3. Estimating total economic value (TEV) of benefits
Source: Glaves & Egan, 2013.

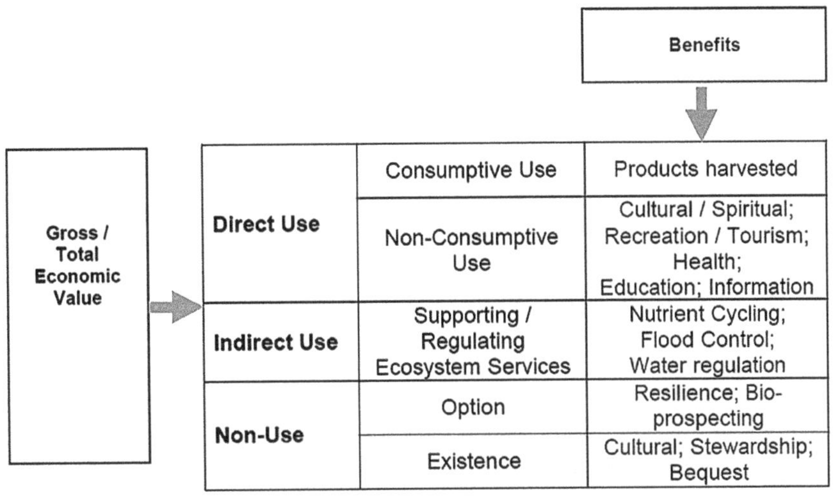

where:

A (LUi) = Area of i (Land Use in hectares)
V (ESki) = Annual value of k ES (Ecosystem Services) for each i LU (in \$/ha/yr).

RESULTS

This paper will detail several regulating and cultural services provided by Middle Draa Valley Oases. The indirect use value represents the value generated by oasean biome and which affects human well-being, but that is not conveyed in traditional markets (direct use value, such as the quantities of dates sold at the market). The regulating services provided by oasean agrosystem include building climate control, prevention of extreme events, biological control, etc; however, the cultural services (immaterial services) include educational and aesthetic services, creativity, cultural values and knowledge.

Detail of the Economic Values of Regulating Ecosystem Services of the Oasean Biome

Contingent Valuation of Regulating Services of Climate

We give an estimate of CO_2 emissions due to electricity consumption in Middle Draa Valley and the corresponding kg of CO_2 per kWh. To calculate regulating climate service, we convert kWh to kg of carbon saved. The conversion factor is 0.542 kg CO_2 saved for each kWh produced from a carbon free source (DECC, 2010). The factor is based on the carbon emissions generated by the current UK power stations per kWh generated. This factor now includes other green house gasses such as methane and nitrous oxide which are converted to their carbon dioxide equivalents so the value is really kg CO_2 eq. per kWh. In

Table 1. Quantity in tones of carbon fixed

	Number	Unit Price	Total in Dh/an	Total en $
Electric energy consumed	25113,6 tonnes	1tonn/80 euro	22099968	2651996,16

(1Dh=1MAD = 0.12 US $; www.oanda.com; Sept. 28, 2013)

Table 2. Water resource of the Middle Draa Valley

	Average Year		Dry Year	
	Mm^3	%	Mm^3	%
Total exploited resources	265	100	230	100

(Source: cited by Heidecke, 2009).

Middle Draa Valley, the population consumes about 46335000kw/an (MPZ, 2011). So, 46335000kw/an * 0,542 kg CO_2 = 25113570 kg CO_2 what gives 25113,6 tones of CO2 produced in this valley (Table 1).

For the cost, 80 € per ton is a very high cost since the production of a kWh of electricity from the combustion of coal generates about one kilogram of CO_2. It will therefore pay about 8 € cents extra per kWh for removing CO_2 generated by this energy chain is about twice the cost per kWh of electricity of nuclear origin.

Water Regulation (Water Purification and Waste Treatment)

Oases play a role in water purification by trapping or transforming excess nutrients, through physical, geochemical and biological processes. To valuate this service, we used replacement cost approach that estimate the cost of replacing an ecosystem services with a man-made service which provides similar benefits to the ecosystem service. This value is calculated basing on the cost of treatment of a total annual water exploited; that is around 250Mm^3 per year (Table 2).

On average, the Middle Draa Valley operates approximately 250 million m^3 per year (Table 3) and the purification cost is estimated at 1.5dh / 1m^3, giving a total cost of wastewater treatment as 250 000 000 * 1,5= 375 000 000 Dhs per year and 45000000 *US $*.

Contingent Valuation of Disease Control Service

Hygiene (collection and treatment of waste) and sanitation gives the value of control of diseases (trachoma, leishmaniasis ...). For the Middle Draa Valley, 9490 tons of domestic waste and two tones of medical and pharmaceutical waste are generated per year (estimated as part of the study of vulnerability

Table 3. Economic value of water purification

	Number/Quantity	Unit price	Total in dh/an	Total in *US* $
Total exploited resources	250 Mm^3	1.5dh/1m^3	375 000 000	46 000 000

(1Dh=1MAD = 0.12 US $; www.oanda.com; Sept. 28, 2013).

Table 4. Budget of the planting program vitro-plants

Year	Vitro-Plant Number	Unit Price	Total in dh/an	Total in US $
2010	5500	300-350	1 650 000	
2011	6511	300-350	1 953 300	
2012	7300	300-350	2 190 000	
Mean value			1 931 100	231 732

(ORMVAO, 2012).

in the Middle Draa Valley (Karmaoui et al., 2014). The total value of disease control service is based on waste generated and on the following costs of waste management (SWWEP, 2010):

- Average cost of collection to disposal / treatment: 440 DHs TTC / tone.
- Average cost of collection - transfer: 370 DHs / tone.
- Average cost of burial: 70 DHs / ton.
- The cost of disposal of medical and pharmaceutical waste between 5000 and 9000 DH / tone.

These data provide a total value of (9490tones*880Dh) + (2tones*6500Dh) = 8364200Dhs/year (1 003 704$/year).

Contingent Valuation of Pest Control Service

To evaluate this service, we used firstly, the cost of pesticides for weed control and secondly, the cost of vitro-plants used in the program of fighting against the Bayoud disease (*Fusarium oxysporum F. sp. Albedinis*), a soil fungus that attacks the finest date palm trees. This disease caused over the past decade the degradation of 34% of Moroccan oases space devoted for date production (PACC, 2011).

Regarding the cost of pesticides used, we used the quantity of pesticides which is estimated to 1kg per hectare per year. The average cost is estimated to 75Dhs per kg, so 75Dhs * 26000ha gives the value 1950 000Dhs/year.

Respecting the fight against the Bayoud disease, the planting program vitro-plants, aims to rehabilitate the palm groves. A budget of over 2 million DH is allocated to this project (Table 4). The unit price is 300-350 Dhs for an amount of vitro plants. The annual value devoted to rehabilitate the palm groves of Middle Draa Valley is 1 931 100Dhs/year.

So, the economic value of the pest control is presented in the Table 5, which brings together, ecosystem service, the number and quantity of each service and the unit price and the total value of this service.

Table 5. Economic value of the pest control

	Number/Quantity	Unit Price (Dh)	Total in Dh/an	Total in US $
Pest control	26000	75dh/ha/an	1 950 000	234 000
Bayoud control	6437	300-350	1 931 100	231 732
Total economic value of pest control			3881100	465732

Table 6. Economic value of pollination

Ecosystem Service	Quantity/ Production	Unit Price	Total in Dh/an	Total in US $
Pollinisation	1772 kg	200dh	35 440 000	4 252 800

Table 7. Economic value of Program of action against the silting in Middle Draa Valley

	2012	2013	2014	2015	2016	Average
Total	2 650 000	2 200 000	2 700 000	2 700 000	2 350 000	2520000

Erosion Control

This is a service of water retention, which provides flood mitigation in lower flow rates and spread over time. Oases (wetland) provide a storage capacity of about 500 to 700 million m^3. The evaluation of this service is very contingent nature of demand and required, as is the case here, to precisely identify the area to be protected and the risk in the absence of the oasis. The High Commission for Water, Forests and the Fight against Desertification (HCEFLCD) decided to mobilize 4.2 million Moroccan Dirham for fight against soil erosion in upstream of "Mansour Eddahbi" This budget, which will be spread over the period 2004-2014, what gives 420000Dhs (504 00$) per year, providing for the construction of approximately 16700 m^3 of palisades (MAP - Maghreb Arabe Presse (www.map.co.ma, accessed 18-10-2014). In addition to the fight against land erosion, the construction of these fences will help clean the mud piled in Mansour Eddahbi Dam.

Pollination

Globally, 35% of the food depends on pollinators. Bees represent 80% of these pollinators (http://www.paysan-breton.fr). So, bees are an essential part of the biodiversity; they provide transport pollen to fertilize plants, crops, and fruit trees. 80% of crops (mainly fruit, vegetables, oilseeds and protein) are dependent on insect pollinators (Terzo & Rasmont, 2007). In 2005, the contribution of pollinators including bees major world crops is estimated at € 153 billion, or 9.5% of global food production (http://agriculture.gouv.fr/Abeilles-et-biodiversite). We hold to that, on a study conducted as part of the FAO program (Bradbear, 2010) which is the basis for an estimate of pollination service across Africa. After this study, the importance of bee pollination in Western Europe is 30-50 times higher than the monetary value of honey harvests. In Africa, bee pollination is estimated to be 100 times greater than the value of the crop of honey, depending on the culture (Bradbear, 2010 (FAO)). The Middle Draa produces about 1772 kg per year that we multiplied by the market price multiplied by the factor 100 (100 times), which gives a value of 4 252 800US$/year (35440000Dh/year) (Table 6).

Soil Quality Control

The valuation of the soil quality control is based on the value of the program dedicated to fight against the sand dune Sanding (Program of action against the silting of the High Commissioner Water and Forestry). Table 7 gives the economic value used for this program in the Middle Draa valley through the decimal program (DREF SO AGADIR 2009).

Table 8. Impact of soil salinity on use of available crop area

	Without Salinity			With Salinity		
	Normal	Medium	Low	Normal	Medium	Low
Total water use (Mm3)	233.8	186.6	98.7	218.0	137.6	29.6
Use of available crop area (%)	63.9	50.7	26.0	47.7	32.0	6.1
Agric. Profits total (MDH)	260.4	189.6	79.6	171.0	119.4	20.5

(Heidecke, 2009).

To protect the Middle Draa Valley, the government deploys an annual budget of about 302 400 US $/year (2520000 Dhs/year).

Soil Salinity Control

We estimated the soil salinity control, using the basin-wide simulation results for normal, medium and low water availability without and including salinity effects (Heidecke, 2009). After the table 8, the salinity causes a decrease of 35% of total agricultural profits (70,2 Million Dhs: 8,5 Million USD); passing from 189.6 Million Dhs (22,9USD) without salinity to 119.4Million Dhs (14,4USD) with salinity; based on the value (USD/Dhs = 0, 12108).

Combining the values of each regulating service in this paper (Table 9), the total value of the regulating services provided by Middle Draa Valley is estimated to 64 444 632 in USD/year and 2478, 63 USD/ha/year for the six palm groves only and 43 USD/ha/year (43,14US$/ha/year) for the total area of Middle Draa Valley (1 500 000ha).

Table 9. Summary of regulating services of the MDV

Ecosystem Service	Total in Dh	Total in $
Air regulating	22 099 968	2651996
Erosion control	420000	50400
Soil fixation	2350000	2520000
Soil salinity	70200000	8500000
Purification of water and waste treatment	375000000	45000000
Disease control	8364200	1003704
Pest control	3881100	465732
Pollination	35440000	4252800
Total	**517755268**	**64 444 632**

1Dh=1MAD = 0.12 US $; www.oanda.com; Sept. 28, 2013.

Detail of the Economic Values of Cultural Ecosystem Services of the Oasean Biome

Cultural services are the services that produce cultural, educational and aesthetic. In fact, these services relate to immaterial values that appropriate the human being from nature and biodiversity. This type of services can be affected by the loss of such an iconic species. In terms of lifestyle, the relationship between humans and the natural environment is creative cultural values and knowledge. In this section, we will evaluate the educational and scientific values and the value of non-use of the biodiversity.

Scientific Values

The scientific value is the interest in terms of environmental research and education. It focuses on research units which are interested in environmental well considered, and the number of studies that have been conducted on the environmental well evaluated. To evaluate this service, we used the project of adaptation to climate change for resilient oases which was carried out under the African Adaptation Programme and funded by Japan and gathered 20 states. This project was launched in 2008 by the United Nations Development Programme (UNDP), in partnership with the World Food Programme (WFP), The United Nations Children's Fund (UNICEF) and the United Nations Industrial Development Organization (UNIDO). With a budget of $ 92.1 million, this project is to support these African countries to enable them to develop the necessary capacity to implement consistent for adaptation and climate risk reduction strategies (APA, 2012). After the official site of the UNDP-APP (African Adaptation Programme) (https://www.undp-aap.org/sites/undp-aap.org), the budget allocated to each country was 2 975 000 dollars for a period of three years from November 2009. This project, starting completed in December 2012, and concerns four oasean basins (Guelmime-Tata, Draa, Ziz-Ghriss and Dadès) and covering the territory of six provinces: Errachidia, Tinghir, Ouarzazate, Zagora, Tata and Guelmim. So, Zagora (Middle Draa Valley) benefits from a value of 495833$US.

Value of Non-Use of the Biodiversity

The calculation of the value of non-use is achieved by the approach of transport costs: leisure, tourism and ecotourism based on expenses from the country of origin. Tourism is an economic activity developing in the area; it depends directly on the quality of the natural environment (landscapes, opportunities for recreation ...), the cultural diversity and hospitality infrastructure. The values attached to the oasis ecosystem led to the development of tourism (Table 10), but with significant impacts on ecosystems.

Table 10. Evolution of the number of visitors

	2003	2004	2005	2006	2007
Zagora	53950	71685	78384	83784	76490

Source: Ministère du Tourisme, 2011, cited by Chelleri *et al.*, 2014.

Table 11. Infrastructure of tourism sector in Middle Draa Valley

Classified Hotels	Number	Number of Rooms	Number of Beds	Suites
4 stars	4	460	851	17
3 stars	2	41	84	5
2 stars	7	170	336	2
1 stars	1	56	110	0

Source: MPZ, 2011.

Table 12. Evolution of overnight stays

Nationality	Overnight Stays		Average	Air Ticket		In Dh	T Value in $
	2010	2011		In €	In $		
France	35140	21 535	28337,5	517	697,95	5790,4	19778158,1
Spain	6746	3 791	5268,5	270	364,5	3024	1920368,25
Italy	5251	3 420	4335,5	370	499,5	4144	2165582,25
Germany	4857	3 031	3944	1050	1417,5	11760	5590620
Holland	2700	2 077	2388,5	570	769,5	6384	1837950,75
UK	1848	1 462	1655	250	337,5	2800	558562,5
Belgium	1740	1 099	1419,5	340	459	3808	651550,5
Suiss	1363	1 026	1194,5	800	1080	8960	1290060
Portugal	1284	623	953,5	300	405	3360	386167,5
Total	71868	49 584	60726			**25317792,5**	**34179019,875**

Source: MPZ, 2011.
1Dh=1MAD = 0.12 US $; www.oanda.com; Sept. 28, 2013.

Table 13. Economic value of tourism service

	Transport Value $	Hotel Value $	Total Tourism Value
Total Tourist value	10323420	34179019,9	44502439,9

The hotel infrastructure includes 14 classified hotels (Table 11). For unclassified Hotels: There are more than 14, for a total number of 193 rooms and 338 beds.

The Table 12 shows the evolution of overnight stays classified by their country of origin.

For example, tourist arrived in Ouarzazate in 2009 spend an average of 1.70 days. 500Dhs for 1 night (average price of a classified hotel): 850Dh for 1, 7 days. The average of arrived tourists is 60726 (Table 13). So, 60726 * 850 = 51617100Dhs/year (6194052US$).

Middle Draa Valley is characterized by its diverse scenic landscape, archaeological sites (Table 14), the hospitality of its people, the richness and diversity of folklore and authenticity of its architectural heritage and its important number of *Kasbahs* (type of medina, Islamic city, or fortress).

Table 14. the archaeological sites of the Middle Draa Valley

Kasbah	Gorges	Sand Dunes	Palm Groves	Rock Carvings	Zaouïas	Popular Arts
32 Kasbats	Draa; Saghro; and the gate of Bab-N-Ali.	Of Amzrou; Tinfou; M'hamid; Ait Ichou in Tazarine; N'bch; of Chgaga.	Mezguita; Tinzouline Tarnata; Fezouata; Ktaoua; M'hamid; Tazarine.	Tazarine and Tinzouline.	Naciria in Tamgroute; Tagmedarte Sidi Salah in Tgounite; El Kadiria in Tamsla.	Ahidous; Ahouach; Saber dance; Roukba; Guedra; Rasma.

(MPZ, 2011).

For the cultural diversity, the number of Zaouias in the Middle Draa Valley is around 43 Zaouias, four are the most radiant. Regarding the folk arts, this Valley is famous for its diversity of folk art; for example, Zagora Province celebrates a large number of events of a spiritual nature "Moussems": local religious and commercial festivals), which is a definite asset for the promotion of tourism in the region.

Value of Ecotourism and Leisure

To estimate the economic value of ecotourism and leisure linked to Moussems celebration in Middle Draa Valley that have 32 Kasbahs (residence for the local tribe) and celebrates 30 Moussems (MPZ, 2011), we used the price (Restoration cost: provided by restored ecosystems) of the Iriki national Park project (amenagement and development of ecotourism Iriki national Park). Value only for Iriki Lake Project is represented as follows (SCID, 2007):

- **Study for the Park:** 400000DH.
- **Study of Reintroducing Animals:** 50000DH.
- **Ecotourism Study:** 600000DH.
- Construction, development and various infrastructure equipment (pens, water point monitoring station, information center, track ..) 8950000DH.

The total project cost is10 million Dhs. Thereafter, the ecotourism and leisure services generate an economic value of 1 200 000$. The Table 15 gathers the total values of the cultural services provided by the oases of Middle Draa Valley.

Table 15. Summary of cultural services

Cultural Ecosystem Services	Total Value	Values in $/ha/Year for the 6 Palm Groves (26 000ha)	Values in $/ha/Year For the Whole Area of MDV (1 500 000ha)
Scientific values	495 833	19	0,33
Biodiversity value	44 502 439,9	1711,6	29,7
Ecourism and leisure	1 200 000	46,2	0,8
Total	46198272,9	1776,8	30,83

1Dh=1MAD = 0.12 US $; www.oanda.com; Sept. 28, 2013. MDV: Middle Draa Valley.

The Economic Value of Supporting Services of the Oasean Biome

Supporting services, such as nutrient cycling, are classified in the MEA classification were not included in this research. We have not estimate the typology of supporting services because these services are considered as a subset of ecosystem processes (TEEB, 2010). The argument is that it is by definition intermediate services and, for this reason; they do not belong to the set of final services.

The Table 16 shows a general summary brings together the estimated values of the regulating and cultural services calculated in this paper at palm grove scale and at the whole area of Middle Draa Valley.

DISCUSSION

The Middle Draa Valley oases have adapted to harsh conditions for centuries (karmaoui et al., 2015b: In press). The oases, which now represent a real growth potential in seemingly hostile environments, are adaptive models and tools to fight against desertification (RADDO, 2011). Despite its importance, during the last 50 years extreme events (mainly droughts and floods) have become increasingly frequent, and have a considerable threat on this agro-system and on the associated ecosystem services. In fact, the oasean ecosystems currently face new challenges like reduced production resulting from Bayoud disease, soil salinization, soil encroachment, water erosion and drought (Chelleri *et al.,* 2014; Karmaoui *et al.,* 2014). Daily 1997 were defined ecosystem services as the conditions and processes through which natural ecosystems and the species that comprise them

Table 16. General summary brings together the estimated values of the regulating and cultural services

Cultural Ecosystem Services	**Total Value**	**Values in $/ha/Year for the 6 Palm Groves (26 000ha)**	**Values in $/ha/Year For the Whole Area of MDV (1 500 000ha)**
Regulating Services	**Total in $**	**/26000**	**/1 500 000**
Air regulating	2 651 996	102	1,77
Erosion control	50 400	2	0.03
Soil fixation	2 520 000	97	1,7
Soil salinity	8 500 000	327	5,7
Purification of water and waste treatment	45 000 000	1730,7	30
Disease control	1 003 704	38,6	0,67
Pest control	465 732	18	0,3
Pollination	4 252 800	163,6	3
Total for regulating services	64 444 632	2478,9	43,14
Cultural Services	**Total in $**	**/26 000**	**/1 500 000**
Scientific values	495 833	19	0,33
Biodiversity value	44 502 439,9	1711,6	29,7
Ecourism and leisure	1 200 000	46,2	0,8
Total for cultural services (/26000)	46 198 273	1776,8	30,83

sustain and fulfill human life. The economic valuation of these services is becoming increasingly important to understand the multiple benefits provided by ecosystems (Sawut, 2013). The quantification of ecosystem services value of oasean system was carried for the first time in desert oasis in Ugan-Kuqa River Delta Oasis, China in 2013. The quantification is considered as a key area for investigation in related academic fields in recent decades (Costanza et al., 1997; Daily, 1997; Wilson & Carpenter, 1999). Our case study is the first attempt of its kind in the area of Moroccan pre-Sahara. The oasean ecosystem services valuation helps to sensitize both citizens and public decision makers in the interest of collective action to preserve these types of ecosystems. The obtained values help to illustrate also, the importance of this oasean biome, which currently have nationally among the most degraded habitats, and yet provide the company with valuable services such as the regulation of water quality and protection against flooding. The economic evaluation is then perfectly able to actively contribute to awareness of economic agents, including policy makers, the preservation of these ecosystems. The comparison of the above results with result at global scale (Inland wetlands, rivers/lakes, woodlands and Grass lands) developed by De Groot et al., in 2012 is showed in the table 18. The economic value of the most productive part of the Draa valley (the six palm groves) is greater than the value of rivers/ lakes, Woodlands and grasslands; while the whole Draa Valley generates a low economic value compared to previous ecosystems except the woodlands which is the lowest.

After Table 17, the low economic value of the entire Middle Draa Valley is justified by the arid climate and the poor quality of the complex water-soil. While the economic value of six palm groves is

Table 17. Summary of monetary values for each service per biome, inland wetlands, rivers/lakes, woodlands, grass lands; values in $/ha/year

	Inland Wetlands	Rivers/ Lakes	Woodlands	Grass Lands	Oases* (/26000ha)	VDM** (/1500000ha)
Regulating services	17.364	187	51	159	2478,9	43,14
Climatic regulation	488		7	40	102	1,77
Disturbance moderation	2986					
Regulation water flows	5606					
Waste treatment	3015	187		75	1730,7	30
Erosion prevention	2607		13	44	426	7,4
Nutrient cycling	1713					
Pollination			31		163,6	3
Biological control	948				56,6	0,97
Cultural services	4203	2166	7	193	1776,8	30,83
Esthetic information	1292			167	1757,8	30,5
Recreation	2211	2166	7	26		
Inspiration	700				19	0,33
Spiritual experience						
Cognitive development						
Total economic value	21 567	2 353	58	352	4 255,7	73,97

After De Groot, (2012) and for oases (our case study).

Where *: Estimated values from the regulating and cultural services of the six palm groves of the Middle Draa Valley. **: Estimated values of the regulating and cultural services of the whole Middle Draa Valley.

very important, given the potential of the structure and function of these palm groves and consequently their ecosystem services.

Regulating Services

The regulating services correspond to control of certain environmental parameters such as the flow of rivers or air quality. These services help to avoid many natural disasters like floods. The role of oasean ecosystems in the regulation of water and air quality is clear. They involve several mechanisms among which are:

- The oasean ecosystem plays an important role by acting as a regulator of atmospheric temperatures by the influence of the moist air of Draa Oued.
- Vegetation provides a suitable habitat for many insects and birds. On the other hand, the canopy as a whole regulates water quality.
- By their root system, trees of acacia forest ecosystems protect the soil against water erosion.
- The edges of Oued Draa, the vessels offer an amount of food and suitable habitat for small animals. These are eaten by birds and juvenile fish. This is one reason why some species of fish spend time in their development cycle in the diversion dams.
- Organisms in water perform functions assimilative water and contribute to the quality of the water, holding, recycling or destroying harmful substances or excessive, through their metabolic processes.

Cultural Services

These are the intangible benefits that we can obtain from ecosystems through spiritual and aesthetic values, and recreation. Tourism in the region of Middle Draa Valley is a developing sector and is supported by the state, spending sizable funds for its promotion by the government. This valley holds significant potential for tourism, the availability of infrastructure to receive them. For the local population, tourism is the basic source of income generated by the possible sale of some art or payment for services of a tour guide. The oasean ecosystem with these components provided a rich source of inspiration for education, art, folklore, national symbols and architecture.

Supporting Services

The supporting services are necessary for the production of all other ecosystem services (nutrient cycling, soil formation, primary production, etc). The ecosystem of the Middle Draa Valley provides services that are not directly used by humans and other supporting services. The phenomenon of photosynthesis for example allows plants to capture carbon dioxide (CO2) and release oxygen (O2) into the atmosphere, developing the essential organic matter to the survival of consumers (humans, and biodiversity, etc). The vegetation plays an important role in determining the soil and, therefore, regulates siltation and siltation of streams. Biological processes involved in the flood waters receded and phases generate substances that enter the food chain. Socio-ecological systems in the oases are vulnerable to climate variability and change that causes water shortage, insufficient food, conflict / insecurity, poor harvests, human and animal diseases, lack employment. This is accelerated by factors such as household size, labor, land fragmentation and isolation from markets. Habitats of the Middle Draa Valley are highly productive systems of ecological goods and services.

Oases ecosystems have the particularity to depend on farming practices which impact significantly the quantity and quality of ecosystem services. The total economic value of the services is high when the number of evaluated services is important. From this economic assessment of the oasean services, we find that, the total economic value of non-market goods from these services is lower than the market goods. Produced values were obtained by comparison with an alternative position which is most often here in the total disappearance of the service in question on a unit area of the ecosystem.

CONCLUSION

The oasis is characterized by organizational cultures strata so hot and humid microclimate perfectly suitable for diversified agricultural production, dominated by the date palm that protects from the sun on the lower floors of fruits, tree crops such as henna or grenades and gardening or forage crops. The oasis is a genetic reservoir suitable for local species to adapt to climate change. The oasis is a space of refuge for people, plants and animals and the existence of the oasis and its operation are related to the presence and use of water in desert environments. Unfortunately, this resource is largely non-renewable, which led to the deterioration of their quality (salinity) and the risk of exhaustion. The oasis environments contain an extremely rich and suited to their particular soil and climatic conditions (Resistance to salinity, resistance to certain pathogens...).

The total value of regulating services is estimate to be 2478,9 $/ha/year in the six palm groves of Middle Draa Valley and 43,14 $/ha/year in the entire study area (1500000ha). Otherwise, the total value of cultural services is estimate to 1776,8 $/ha/year for arable area (26000ha) and 30,83 $/ha/year for the whole study area. This relative potential wealth of ecosystem services produced contributes to the well-being of society through the production of food goods quality, landscape amenities and regulating services.

REFERENCES

APA (Africa Adaptation Programme). (2012). *Handbook on Capitalisation of Experiences 2012*. Knowledge Management and Adaptation to Climate Change. UNDP.

Bayon, R. (2004). *Making Environmental markets work: lessons from early experience with sulfur, carbon, wetlands, and other related markets. Forest Trends*. Katoomba.

Biggs, R., Bohensky, E., Desanker, P. V., Fabricius, C., Lymann, T., & Misselhorn, A. A. et al. (2004). *Nature Supporting People: The South African Millennium Ecosystem Assessment*. Pretoria, South Africa: Council for Scientific and Industrial Research.

Braat, L., & de Groot, R. (2012). The ecosystem services agenda: Bridging the worlds of natural science and economics, conservation and development, and public and private policy. *Ecosyst. Serv*, *1*(1), 4–15. doi:10.1016/j.ecoser.2012.07.011

Bradbear. (2010). *(FAO): Produits forestiers non ligneux 19. Le rôle des abeilles dans le développement rural Manuel sur la récolte, la transformation et la commercialisation des produits et services dérivés des abeilles*. Academic Press.

Brander, L. (2013). *Guidance manual on value transfer methods for ecosystem services. United Nations Environment Programme*. Nairobi: UNEP.

Claire, K. (2005). Managing ecosystem services: What do we need to know about their ecology? *Ecology Letters*, *8*(5), 468–479. doi:10.1111/j.1461-0248.2005.00751.x PMID:21352450

Costanza, R., d'Arge, R., de Groot, R., Faber, S., Grasso, M., Hannon, B., … van den Belt, M. (1997). The value of the world's ecosystem services and natural capital. *Nature, 387*, 253-260.

Costanza, R., de Groot, R., Sutton, P., van der Ploeg, S., Anderson, S. J., & Kubiszewski, I. et al. (2014). Changes in the global value of ecosystem services. *Global Environmental Change*, *26*, 152–158. doi:10.1016/j.gloenvcha.2014.04.002

Costanza, R., & Kubiszewski, I. (2012). The authorship structure of ecosystem services as a transdisciplinary field of scholarship. *Ecosyst. Serv*, *1*(1), 16–25. doi:10.1016/j.ecoser.2012.06.002

Daily, G. C. (1997). *Nature's Services: Societal Dependence on Natural Ecosystems*. Washington, DC: Island Press.

Daily, G. C., Soderqvist, T., Aniyar, S., Arrow, K., Dasgupta, P., & Ehrlich, P. R. et al. (2000). Ecology: The value of nature and the nature of value. *Science*, *289*(5478), 395–396. doi:10.1126/science.289.5478.395 PMID:10939949

De Groot, R., Brander, L., van der Ploeg, S., Costanza, R., Bernard, F., & Braat, L. et al. (2012). Global estimates of the value of ecosystems and their services in monetary units. *Ecosystem Services*, *1*(1), 50–61.

DECC. (2010). *Guidelines to Defra / DECC's GHG Conversion Factors for Company Reporting*. Produced by AEA for the Department of Energy and Climate Change (DECC) and the Department for Environment, Food and Rural Affairs (Defra) Version 1.2.1 FINAL Updated: 06/10/2010. Retrieved from http://www.rensmart.com

DREF SO AGADIR. (2009). *Projets de développement forestier et de LCD dans la région Souss-Massa-Draa*. Province de ZAGORA.

Fisher, B., Turner, R. K., & Morling, P. (2009). Defining and classifying ecosystem services for decision making. *Ecological Economics*, *68*(3), 643–653. doi:10.1016/j.ecolecon.2008.09.014

Glaves, P., & Egan, D. (2013). Some Methods and Approached to Valuing Ecosystem Services. Academic Press.

Harakat, I. (2007). *Les acteurs de la coopération et la dimension socio-économique de la désertification dans le sud du Maroc: cas de Zagora. Mémoire de maitrise en science politique*. Université du Québec MONTREAL.

Heal, G. (2000). *Nature and the Marketplace: Capturing the Value of Ecosystem Services*. Covelo, CA: Island Press.

Hector, A., & Bagchi, R. (2007). Biodiversity and ecosystem multifunctionality. *Nature*, 448. PMID:17625564

Heidecke. (2009). *Economic analysis of water use and management in the Middle Drâa valley in Morocco vorgelegt am 22*. Academic Press.

Karmaoui, A., Messouli, M., Yacoubi, K.M., & Ifaadassan, I. (2014). Environmental Vulnerability to Climate Change and Anthropogenic Impacts in Dryland. *J Earth Sci Clim Change, S11*. doi:10.4172/2157-7617.S11-002

Maroufi, A. (2008). Désertification et migration: un défi pour le développement durable au Maroc. Le cas de ZAGORA. Secrétaire Général du CMEPE / MAROC. *Sustainable Mediterranean, 54*(4).

Millennium Ecosystem Assessment. (2003). *Ecosystems and Human Well-Being: A Framework For Assessment*. Washington, DC: Island Press.

MPZ. (2011). *Monographie de la province de Zagora*. Royaume du Maroc Ministère de l'intérieur Province De Zagora.

ORMVAO. (2012). *Bilans des activités de 2013 de l'office régional de mise en valeur agricole de Ouarzazate*. Author.

PACC. (2011). *Oasis et Zones Arides Résilientes Territoires Engagés*. Retrieved from www.oasisadaptation.com

Perrings, C. (2010). *Biodiversity, Ecosystem Services, and Climate Change. The Economic Problem. Environmental Economics Series*. The International Bank for Reconstruction and Development.

Sawut, M., Eziz, M., & Tiyip, T. (2013). The effects of land-use change on ecosystem service value of desert oasis: A case study in Ugan-Kuqa River Delta Oasis, China. *Canadian Journal of Soil Science, 93*(1), 99–108. doi:10.4141/cjss2012-010

SCID (Système de circulation de l'information sur la désertification au Maroc). (2007). Haut Commissariat des Eaux et Forêts et la Lutte contre la Désertification. Fiche de projet de protection des oasis du sud. Author.

SWWEP. (2010). *Profil du pays sur la situation de la gestion des déchets solides au Maroc*. Retrieved from www.SWEEP-NET.ORG.http://www.sweep-net.org/ckfinder/userfiles/files/country-profiles/country%20profile%20Maroc%20fr.pdf

TEEB. (2010). L'Économie des écosystèmes et de la biodiversité: Intégration de l'Économie de la nature. Une synthèse de l'approche, des conclusions et des recommandations de la TEEB. Programme des Nations Unies pour l'environnement.

Terzo, M., & Rasmont, P. (2007). Abeilles sauvages, bourdons et autres insectes pollinisateurs.

Vitousek, P. M., Mooney, H. A., Lubchenco, J., & Melillo, J. M. (1997). Human domination of Earth's ecosystems. *Science*, *277*(5325), 494–499. doi:10.1126/science.277.5325.494

Wilson, M. A. and Carpenter, S. (1999). Economic valuation of freshwater ecosystem services in the United States: 1971-1997. *Ecol. Appl.*, *9*, 772-783.

Zainabi, A. (2003). *La Vallée du Draa. Developement Alternatif et Action Communautaire*. Background paper WDR.

APPENDIX

Table 18. Primary valuation methods, typical applications, examples, and limitations

Method	Approach	Applications	Example Ecosystem	Service Limitations
Market prices	Use prices that are directly observed in markets	ES that are traded directly in markets	Timber and fuel wood from forests; clean water from wetlands	Market prices can be distorted e.g. by subsidies. Most ES not traded in markets
Public pricing ES for which there	Use public expenditure or monetary incentives (taxes/ subsidies) for ES as an indicator of value	ES for which there are public expenditures	Watershed protection to provide drinking water; Purchase of land for protected area	No direct link to preferences of beneficiaries
Replacement cost	Estimate the cost of replacing an ES with a man-made service	ES that have a manmade Equivalent that could be used and provides similar benefits to the ecosystem service.	Coastal protection by dunes; water storage and filtration by wetlands	No direct relation to ES benefits. Over-estimates value if society is not prepared to pay for man-made replacement. Under-estimates value if man-made replacement does not provide all of the benefits of the original ecosystem.
Restoration cost	Estimate cost of restoring degraded ecosystems to ensure provision of ES	Any ES that can be provided by restored ecosystems	Coastal protection by dunes; water storage and filtration by wetlands	No direct relation to ES benefits. Over-estimates value if society is not prepared to pay for restoration. Under-estimates value if restoration does not provide all of the benefits of the original ecosystem.
Net factor income	Revenue from sales of environment related good minus cost of other inputs	Ecosystems that provide an input in the production of a marketed good	Filtration of water by wetlands; commercial fisheries supported by coastal wetlands	Tendency to over-estimate values since method attributes all normal profit to the ES
Production function	Estimate value of ES as input in production of marketed good	Ecosystems that provide an input in the production of a marketed good	Soil quality or water quality as an input to agricultural production	Technically difficult. High data requirements
Hedonic pricing	Estimate influence of environmental characteristics on price of marketed goods	Environmental characteristics that vary across goods (usually houses)	Urban open space; air quality	Technically difficult. High data requirements. Limited to ES that are spatially related to property locations.
Travel cost	Use data on travel costs and visit rates to estimate demand for recreation sites	Recreation sites	Outdoor open access recreation	Technically difficult. High data requirements. Limited to valuation of recreation. Complicated for trips with multiple purposes or to multiple sites.
Contingent valuation	Ask people to state their willingness to pay for an ES through surveys	All ecosystem services	Species loss; natural areas; air quality; water quality landscape aesthetics	Expensive and technically difficult to implement. Prone to biases in design and analysis
Choice modelling	Ask people to make trade-offs between ES and other goods to elicit willingness to pay	All ecosystem services	Species loss; natural areas; air quality; water quality; landscape aesthetics	Expensive and technically difficult to implement. Prone to biases in design and analysis
Group / participatory valuation	Ask groups of stakeholders to state their willingness to pay for an ES through group discussion	All ecosystem services	Species loss; natural areas; air quality; water quality; landscape aesthetics	Prone to biases due to group dynamics

(Brander, 2013).

Chapter 17
Significance of Cultural Dimensions in Urban Planning Process for Sustainability of Pilgrimage Towns in India

Varma Anurag
TERI University, India

Shaleen Singhal
TERI University, India

ABSTRACT

This chapter raises the significance of integration of cultural attributes in the urban planning process for sustainability of pilgrimage towns. It identifies the spatial connotations of cultural practices, processes and events to review synergies between culture and urban planning. Two Indian pilgrimage towns of Vrindavan and Haridwar with congruent cultural context but diverse urban setting have been examined. Eight significant diverse attributes of both case studies are discussed for examining linkages of cultural dimensions with urban planning, and sustainability of indigenous urbanism of Indian pilgrimage towns. Recent policy initiatives in India envision an increasing inclusion of cultural and heritage aspects in urban development, but are constrained by paucity of empirical spatial research on Indian pilgrimage towns.

INTRODUCTION

The sustainability debate increasingly focuses on urban development and sustainability is being considered unattainable without achieving sustainable urban development (UN-HABITAT, 2002). Further, Sustainable Development Goals (SDG's) adopted in the 2030 Agenda for Sustainable Development at the United Nations Sustainable Development Summit includes making "cities inclusive, safe, resilient and sustainable" as a goal (UN, 2015). At global scale, UN-Habitat summarizes climate change, gaps in energy supply, food security, changing demographics, size of cities and towns, income inequality and managing the cultural diversity as critical issues facing urbanism. In context of developing countries,

DOI: 10.4018/978-1-5225-0094-0.ch017

additional challenges of urban growth, urban informality, growth in peri-urban areas, linking of green and brown agendas and institutional and professional capacity building are identified issues to be addressed (UN-HABITAT, 2009). Emergence of alternative paradigms of urban development with greater inclusivity is envisaged in response to homogenizing influence of globalization in the developing countries.

With a shift in goals and emergent challenges, urban planning praxis and theory explore alternative urban and spatial planning paradigms. The attributes of sustainability imperative are variously interpreted in urban planning domain, and diverse approaches to achieve urban sustainability include conceptualization of eco-villages, eco-cities (Register, 1987) and eco^2 cities (Suzuki, Dastur, & Moffat, 2010); new urbanism (Talen, 2013) and sustainable urbanism (Farr, 2008); compact cities, green cities and resilient cities amongst others. Simultaneously, in response to globalization the place-based factors of local contexts are assuming significance in urban and spatial planning paradigms (WHO, 1999) (UN-DESA). Embedded in the local discourse, culture has emerged as a significant local, place-based determinant in urban planning process necessary for achieving sustainable urban development. UNESCO has initiated preparation of a ‘Global Report on Culture and Sustainable Urban Development’ for negotiations in the post 2015 Agenda which aims to provide guidelines and recommendations aimed to foster culture-based urban sustainable development initiatives at the international, national, regional and local levels (UNESCO, 2015). Significantly, the SDG’s have adopted ‘inclusive and sustainable urbanization’ and to ‘protect and safeguard the world’s cultural and natural heritage’ for making cities resilient and sustainable (UN, 2015) amongst other adopted goals. However, presently the linkage between cultural heritage and sustainable urbanization to make cities resilient and sustainable is tenuous and its progress is confounded by abstractions in definitions of both culture and sustainability, insufficient empirical evidence and a near absence of integrated conceptual framework (Parr, 2000). This chapter examines this gap through an exploratory study situated in context of pilgrimage towns in India.

Pilgrimage towns in India are characterized by high visitations of pilgrims, which stress the prevailing environmental services and result in degradation of built environment. The need for pilgrimage infrastructure results in urban growth; which, in absence of appropriate planning regulations, threatens cultural and environmental sustainability of the pilgrimage town (Shinde, 2012). Culture-led and event based urban regeneration strategies have been identified as a key theme for urban regeneration (Singhal, McGreal, & Berry, 2013) A recent Government of India scheme - Heritage City Development and Augmentation Yojana (HRIDAY) - recognizes the need to undertake strategic and planned development for sustainable development of heritage cities in India. Most of the cities shortlisted for the scheme involve an element of sacrality and attract pilgrims at varying scales. The scheme envisages to “preserve and revitalize soul of the heritage city to reflect the city’s unique character….and facilitate inclusive heritage linked urban development” (Ministry of Urban Development, Government of India, 2015).

This chapter explores the relevance of identifying place-specific cultural characteristics and establish the need for its embedding in urban planning process at pilgrimage towns in India; fundamentally premised on significance of culture for sustainable urban development. The links between cultural characteristics - values, aspirations, activities, processes and patterns of a place, and urban planning are examined at two Hindu pilgrimage towns – Vrindavan and Haridwar - to predicate the relevance of culture to sustainable urban planning at pilgrimage towns in India. The case study towns exhibit congruence in terms of their religious significance, well-regarded sacredness, riverine geography and primacy of pilgrimage - and divergence in terms of presiding deity and associated rituals, cultural vitality, demographic patterns, urbanization trends and urban scale of the town. Briefly, the two selected case-study towns have convergent cultural backgrounds but divergent urban context.

The inter-linkages between culture, urban planning and sustainable urban development are gleaned from a review of available literature and inquiries during personal visits to the case-study towns. Synthesis of the information contributes towards emergence of a conceptual approach towards theoretically establishing the role of culture in urban planning process for sustainable urban development. The conceptual approach requires additional empirical data for its affirmation, and may have methodological synergies with investigations at similar Hindu pilgrimage towns in India, viz. Varanasi, Mathura, Rishikesh, Chitrakoot etc.

The chapter is organized in four sections wherein Section 1 provides a context to the theme being investigated. Section 2 reviews the inter-relationship between culture, sustainability and urban planning which provides a theoretical narrative supporting inclusion of culture as a major determinant of sustainable urban development. Section 3 briefly reviews distinctive characteristics of Indian urban conditions and pilgrimage towns to contextualize the case studies in a place-specific milieu. It also presents a review of two case study pilgrimage towns in India focussing on their cultural characteristics and synergy with urban planning. Section 4 includes discussions and conclusions, wherein an analysis and interpretation of two case studies lead to identification of attributes for examination of the inter-linkages between culture, urban planning and sustainability.

THEMATIC INTER-LINKAGES BETWEEN CULTURE, URBAN PLANNING AND SUSTAINABILITY

Development divorced from its human or cultural context is growth without a soul. – (Our Creative diversity, UNESCO 1995)

Multiple interpretations of culture necessitate a broad conceptualization of the embodied meaning in context of this study. Accordingly, culture is perceived as a 'way of life' and a way of living together (UNU-IAS and IICRC, 2002), as a generic nomenclature for 'diverse set of activities and pursuits' (Sen, Culture, freedom and independence, 1998) that embodies the following aspects:

- Values and aspirations of the community, or linked to the place;
- The processes and mediums through which the values and aspirations are received and transmitted;
- The tangible and intangible manifestations of these values (Hawkes, 2001);
- Uniqueness of each culture, sensitivity towards the differentiation and respect for it also encourages cultural diversity and heterogeneity (Sen, 1998) (Nadarajah, 2007).

These following sub-sections explore the inter-linkages between the three concepts of 'culture', 'urban development' and 'sustainability', to deduce its implications for urban planning at Hindu pilgrimage towns in India. The theoretical linkages between the three concepts are established by a review of cross-sectorial development literature (Figure 1). Sustainability as conceptualized in the Brundtland Commission Report focuses on the environment and ecological strategies to ensure inter-generational parity. The three recognized pillars of sustainable development include economic development, social justice and ecological responsibility; though their weightages vary and are largely determined by the local context and philosophy driving development. The three pillars are in dialectical tension, and in praxis, sustainable development appears as a shifting adjustment among them (Hawkes, 2001). Earlier,

Figure 1. Thematic linkages between culture, urban planning and sustainability

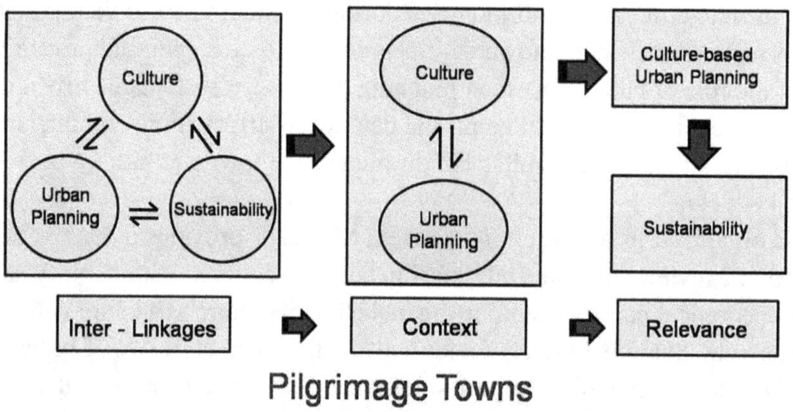

the prime determinants were the economic development and its environmental implications, with little consideration of cultural aspects, which was considered as included in the social criteria. The linkage of culture with either sustainability or urban planning and development is still an emerging area of research; with nebulous and meagre structured information available from either global research or praxis (Duxbury & Jeannotte, 2010) (Nadarajah, 2007).

Culture, Development, and Sustainable Development

The inclusion of culture in development is examined from existing literature and structured under three broad themes of development goals, public policy and action and cross-disciplinary linkages (Figure 2). Evidently, the role of culture first gained recognition in the development realm (Bandarin, Hosagrahar, & Albernaz, 2011), and later progressively gathered increasing acceptability in sustainable development domain. Increasing emphasis on human-centric development paradigms led to initiation and progressive integration of culture in sustainable development discourse, and latter sustainable development frameworks. As evidence of increasing theoretical significance, culture is advanced as the 'fourth pillar of sustainability', and its centrality as a catalyst, driver and enabler (UNESCO, 2013) for sustainable development is being acknowledged. The inclusion of culture for sustainable development is supported based on its relevance for:

- "Human capacity expansion" (Sen, 1990), and increasing emphasis of development towards 'enlarging people's choices' (World Commission on Culture and Development, 1996);
- Social and cultural fulfilment of an individual (UNESCO, 1998) perceived as objectives of human development
- Strengthening the cultural-aesthetic dimension of sustainable development (Tutzinger Manifesto, 2001);
- Emphasis on the significance of society's values, and the necessity of its finding an avenue for expression (Hawkes, 2001) and
- Cross-sectorial linkages with disaster resilience and climate change, social development, economic development, peace & reconciliation, environmental sustainability, sustainable urban development (UNESCO, 2013) (UN, 2014), poverty reduction and education (UN, 2014).

Figure 2. Increasing inclusion of 'Culture' in 'Development' and 'Sustainable Development' discourse

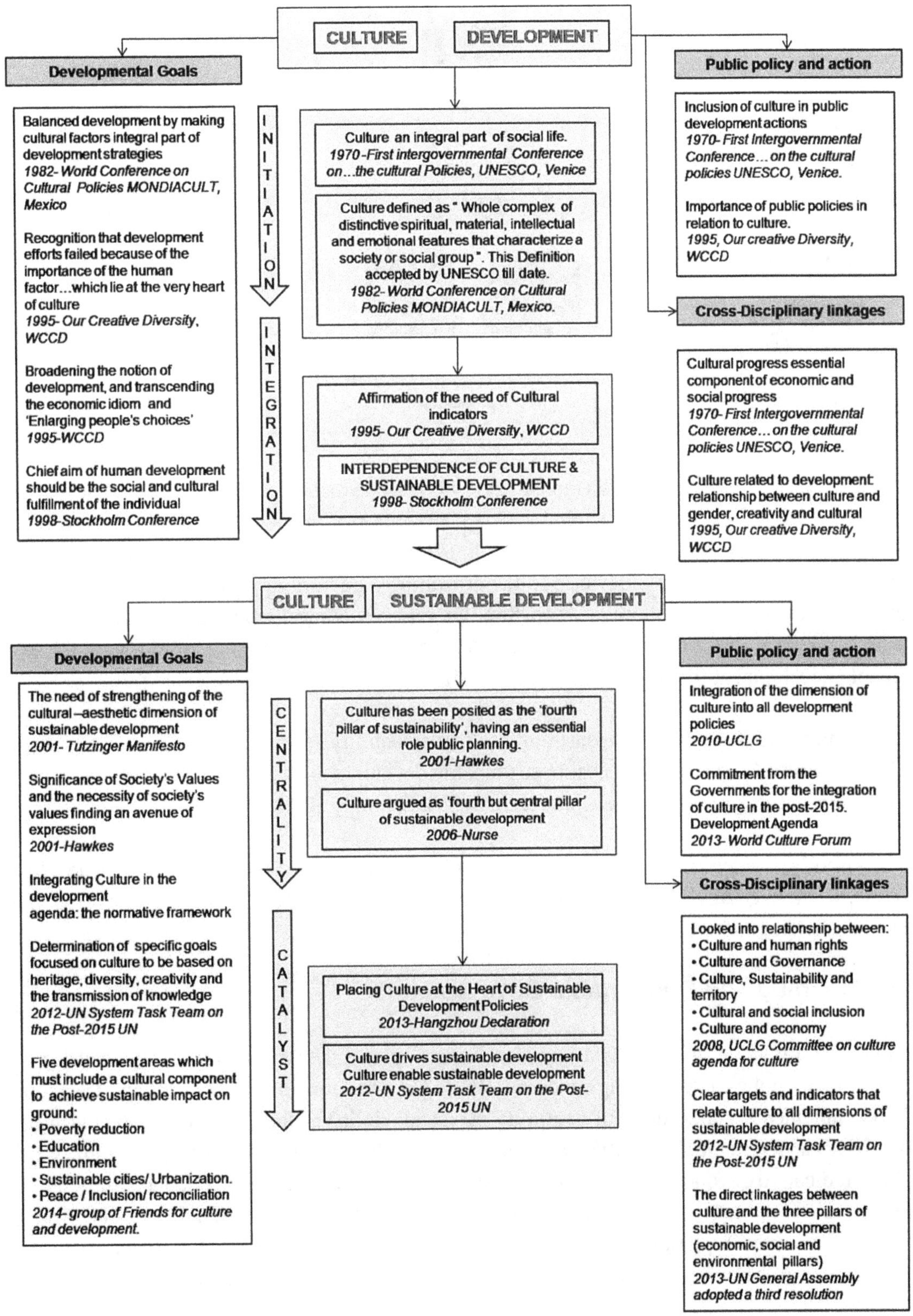

Figure 3. Three approaches on role of culture in global sustainable development
(Roders, 2013).

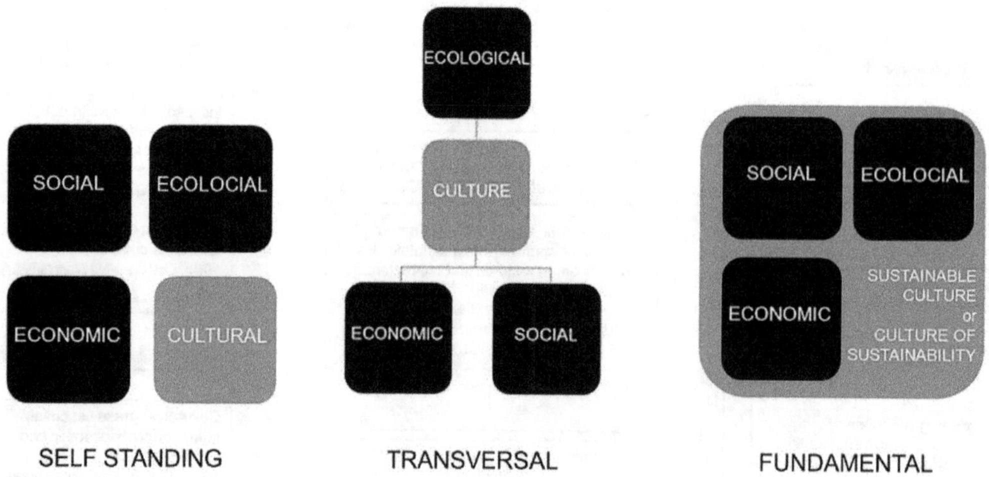

This research envisages culture as a repository of knowledge that helps a society to mediate challenges and positions culture as a resource, capital and capacity inherent in a local situation (Mercer, 2002).

The proposal for inclusion of culture as the fourth pillar of sustainability has led to a theoretical conceptualization of its critical relevance to the prevailing paradigm of sustainable development. This has included positioning of culture as a fourth pillar vis a vis other three pillars in the sustainable development paradigm. Accordingly, three conceptual possibilities of engaging culture with the existing sustainable development framework are conceptualized (Soini, 2013) as below:

- **Self-Standing:** Culture as the fourth pillar of sustainability
- **Transversal:** Culture as a catalyst in sustainable development
- **Fundamental:** Culture as a new paradigm of sustainability (Figure 3).

Concurrently, a wider role of culture in sustainability is also being advanced in the urban development discipline, wherein culture is seen as an invaluable tool for sustainable urban development (UNESCO, 2015).

Urban Planning and Sustainable Development

Brundtland Commission's report – Our Common Future –places the issue of sustainable development at the core of urban policy and planning concerns (World Commission on Environment and Development, 1987). Complementary assertions of centrality of sustainability to the urban development processes (Berke, 2002) and sustainability initiatives centring on building sustainable cities (Yanarella & Levine, 1992) are indicative of conceptual connect of sustainability with the urban. Yet concentration of urban population and its quest for economic growth has substantial adverse implications of environmental degradation, resource depletion, deteriorating ecosystems and climate change (Dixon, 2011) and the urban planning process grapples for appropriate sustainable responses. In this context, Global Report on Human Settlements focuses on need of a new perspective for urban planning, and begun differently by setting the goal of sustainable urbanization as liveable, productive and inclusive cities, towns and villages (UN-HABITAT, 2009).

Inquiry into antecedents of contemporary urban planning paradigms reinforces need for emergence of new perspectives to deal with contemporary sustainability challenges. The concept of sustainability is historically considered intrinsic to the process of urban planning with implicit theoretical linkages. It has been established that urban settlements were perceived holistically as constituents of a larger ecosystem by Alberti, Marsh 1865, Olmstead and Vaux 1887, Patrick Geddes 1915, Mumford 1968, Lynch 1981, McHarg 1969, Jacobs 1961 etc., an aspect that has well been documented by Spirn (2012) for the Anglo-American context (Spirn, 2012). Evolution of contemporary urban planning practices traces its roots in the concepts of modern urban planning in Western Europe in latter 19th century, primarily as a response to the Industrial Revolution. Urban development was perceived as an exercise in design and physical planning of human settlement with complex social, economic or political matters eluding it. At earlier stages, urban planning focussed on improvement of liveability criteria in its spatial territory, and harboured a fixation for the visual. The urban planning concepts of the industrial towns gradually spread the globe through processes of colonialism, market expansion and intellectual exchange; and embedded itself into local planning practices at dispersed location and diverse contexts (UN-HABITAT, 2009). Progressively, urban planning focussed on automobile-centric transportation, landuse and zoning based on spatial segregation of usages, and design standardization. Cities and settlements conforming to these urban planning principles were devoid of cultural diversity in response to the local place, values, and context; and alienated the people from their habitat. Tracing these antecedents in the Indian urban experience, Menon strongly advocates professional engagement with specific complexities of traditional Indian urbanism as both a socio-cultural construct and technical entity (Menon, 1999).

In response to this context, "New Urbanism" gained prominence as an alternative to traditional US suburban design in the 1980's. It was presented as a model for sustainable urban development to address wider concerns as placeless sprawl, environmental deterioration, loss of agricultural lands and wilderness and erosion of society's built heritage. Offering spatial planning solutions, it strongly advocated the principles of: i) compact development for preservation of environmentally sensitive areas; ii) infill development to revitalize city centres; interconnected streets friendly to pedestrians and cyclists; iii) mixed land uses rather than single-use pods; iv) discreet placement of garages and parking spaces to avoid auto-dominated landscapes; v) transit-oriented development (TOD); vi) well-designed and sited civic buildings and public gathering places; vii) the use of building and street and building typologies to create coherent urban form; viii) high-quality parks and conservation lands used to define and connect neighbourhoods and districts; and ix) architectural design that shows respect for local history and regional character (Ellis, 2002). Though the sustainability criteria attracted professionals in addressing wider urban planning concerns, evidently the solutions continued to focus on issues concerning the visual urban form. The social, cultural and economic dimensions of sustainable development were either relegated or simply considered beyond the scope of the movement (White & Ellis, 2007).

It becomes important to explore the nature of urbanization and contextualize its wider inter-linkages at varying scales - metropolitan, small urban centre, town, and their surrounding rural area. Mostafavi expands the context of the urban in 'Ecological Urbanism' - a framework that deals with these complex economic, political, social and cultural perspectives through conjoining of ecology and urbanism (Mostafavi, 2010). Sustainable urban development and management is identified as a critical aspect influencing sustainability and crucial to quality of life of people (UN, 2015). As urban development focuses on sustainability, the planning process is required to meet not only the challenges of urban design but also many other social, environmental, economic, health and climate issues.

Culture, Urban Development, and Sustainability

In recognition of cities as active players for promotion of sustainable development and the significance of the urban context therein, culture is increasingly imagined as a key tool for sustainable urban development (UNESCO, 2015). In beginning of 2000, the Kanazawa Initiative examined the role of culture in building sustainable cities at four different Asian countries. The research involved empirical exploration into the nature of urbanization and its linkages with sustainability from a local culture perspective in different cities. Recognition of the varying urban contexts, and sensitivity to the diversity led to evolution of four culture-centric approaches for sustainable urban development (Nadarajah, 2007) that focussed on:

- Internal cultural transformation approach;
- The multiculturalism and enlightened localism approach;
- The urban cultural identity approach;
- The cultural mode of production approach.

The inter-linkages between culture and sustainable urban development are nebulous in contemporary urban context ((Rana & Piracha, 2007) (White & Ellis, 2007), and requires additional evidence and empirical data for its affirmation. The conceptualization has been recently enunciated and theoretical frameworks or methodologies for conducting research are emergent only. Further empirical research supported by evidence-based case studies in diverse contexts will significantly contribute to establish culture as a tool for sustainable urban development. Examination of the role of culture in urban planning and its relation to sustainable development is emerging as a key area of investigation. In this background, cultural mapping is emerging as a mode of enquiry and methodological tool for diagnosing potential role of culture in the urban planning processes (Evans, 2015). In practice though, culture is seldom used as a key urban development variable, and is characteristically referred in its intersections with other key (economic, environmental, social) development variables.

CHARACTERISTIC INDIAN URBANISM AND PILGRIMAGE TOWNS

Indian urban conditions are characterized by abundant diversity that results from a combination of multiple planning processes and spatial overlapping - vernacular, indigenous urbanism, formal planned and extra-legal 'pirate modernities' (Sundaram, 2010). They distinctly exhibit spatial juxtaposition of the planned and the un-planned (extra-legal) activities in, as theorized - 'static city' and 'kinetic city' respectively (Mehrotra, 2008) (Gupte, Mehrotra, & Shetty, 2010). The static city is usually permanent whereas kinetic city is impermanent, in a realm outside the planning framework, and usually extra-legal. Un-planned activities are a formidable presence in Indian urban conditions and are normally ignored or not included in the formal planning process (Roy, 2009). Largely manifested in the interstitial spaces of a city – road edges, slums and informal settlements the un-planned is constantly in a state of adversarial relationship with the planning process. The need of urban planning to negotiate contrasting urban conditions of neat suburban developments and heterogeneous traditional settlements, city of 'haves' and 'have-nots', automobile and the bicycle etc. has been emphasized (Menon). It is essential to closely assess the nature of Indian urbanism situated in the larger Indian background characterized by heterogeneity, plurality and multiculturalism.

These generic conditions appropriately describe the urban conditions for Indian pilgrimage towns. Both the case studies are constituted of the traditional core of the city, which is culturally vibrant, dense with high numbers of pilgrim visitations and inadequate hygiene and infrastructure. Pilgrimage related activities related to rituals, practices, and ritual offerings like flowers and prasad, accommodation, fooding and transportation, function largely at the periphery of the mainstream planning, informally and extra-legally. However, an inquiry into the indigenous urbanism as manifested in these sacred spaces offers an opportunity of its use as catalysts to revitalize the civic environment. A relevant approach for study of Indian heritage (traditional pilgrimage) towns from a cultural perspective has been postulated in the 'Architectural Knowledge Systems' (Thakur, 2002) that approaches study of Indian historic towns in a people-time-place continuum framework; thus implying an assimilative and holistic enquiry into the anthropological, historical and the geographical narrative of the city. The emergent Indian Cultural Landscape (ICL) is termed as the 'intellectual landscape' - a repository of knowledge, where collective memory, information and imagination shape the landscape (Thakur, 2011). Accordingly, the place may be conceived as an overlay of cultural layers in a temporal perspective, which may be unpeeled distinctively for each settlement.

Pilgrimage has had a long tradition and continuity as large civil society movement for religious/spiritual experiences in the Hindu tradition of India (Singh, 2013). The number of pilgrims has increased manifold due to improvement in the communications and transportation system over time. Massive influx of pilgrims coupled with poor environmental infrastructure, lack of hygiene, weak governance apparatus, inadequate awareness, capacities and capabilities of the citizens or governance authorities creates problems related to health, safety and experiential aspects at the pilgrimage town. The resulting transformations are socially and environmentally detrimental for the pilgrimage town and diminish the quality of experience of the pilgrims (Shinde, 2012). Unless timely planned sensitively, the pilgrimage towns fail to offer any significant experience to pilgrims or a liveable quality of life to the residents; the town loses meaning for people and ceases to be sustainable. Aware that religious beliefs and traditions are the raison d'etre of pilgrimage towns; the following section investigates the potential role of culture in urban planning process for sustainable urban development through case studies of two Hindu pilgrimage towns. The methodology includes literature review, observations and unstructured interviews conducted at case study towns to identify cultural characteristics in its intersections with the urban planning, and inter alia sustainability of the urban development process.

Case Study of Vrindavan

Vrindavan is a small town in District Mathura within the administrative division of Agra - a city situated in Western Uttar Pradesh. Administered locally by a municipality, Vrindavan has a population of around 63,000 people distributed in 25 wards. A proposal to include seventeen more villages within the jurisdiction of Vrindavan municipality and its potential upgrade to a level of Municipal Corporation also emerges from information gathered locally during a field visit.

Notionally at centre of the sacred geography of Braj Kshetra (region) circumscribed by 84kos (252kms), Vrindavan is believed to be the place where Lord Krishna spent his early childhood. The cultural identity of Vrindavan is embodied in its religious values being a *dham* – abode of God (Brahmachari, 2011), and an eternal home to the divine Radha-Krishna who are perceived as a living presence in Vrindavan. Lost to the world as a Vrinda (Tulsi) vana (forest) on banks of River Yamuna until Sixteenth century, Vrindavan re-emerged when visited in by Chaitanya Mahaprabhu and Vallabhacharya, famous Vaishnava gurus and proponent of Bhakti movement (Entwistle, 1987). Mahaprabhu and later his disciples – the Chhat (six) Goswamis (priests), physically construed the entire town driven by divine inspiration, vision, consciousness and memory of its association with events in life of Lord Krishna. Largely because of its associative sacredness, Vrindavan soon became a leading centre of pilgrimage, Vaishnavism and Vaishnava learning. Intrinsically steeped in the metaphor of Radha-Krishna, the spiritual culture is the wellspring of many performing art forms like painting, sculpture, theatre, music, braj bhasha (language) poetry and dance. 'Raas Lila', the divine dance signifies unison of God with his devotees and related allegories are favourite themes of prominent classical dance forms all over India. Over six million pilgrims visit the sacred town of Vrindavan annually (Shinde, 2012) which acts as a testimony to the universal significance of the intrinsic cultural values associated with the place.

Vrindavan's spatial growth was predominantly guided by the Goswamis, who as religious heads exercised considerable influence over happenings in the town and region. Contemporary Mughal, Rajput and Jat patrons generously extended donation of land parcels and funding for establishment of Vrindavan as a spatio-cultural-religious town from neighbouring territories. The growth expanded outwards from banks of river Yamuna. Temples, temple precincts, ashrams, dharamshalas (charitable rest houses), ghats (stepped bathing places along rivers) and princely estates were constructed with considerable architectural elegance, skill and craftsmanship. In accordance to the traditional and scriptural knowledge, considerable significance and reverence was attached to natural elements such as vanas (sacred groves), kunds (man-made water tanks), river Yamuna and sacred hills.

Architectural appurtenances were evidently employed to enhance beauty and utility of kunds, riverfront, and community-protected groves, forests and hills. The built fabric comprised of considerable architectural heritage (Figure 4) and ritual symbols are largely encompassed within a 10km pradakshina path (circumambulatory route), and part of the inscribed area is declared as a heritage area. The traditional ecological beliefs, sanctity of river Yamuna, and recognition of value and conservation of architectural heritage have been intrinsic to the way of life of the residents'. These values can be potentially leveraged to direct urban planning initiatives for addressing challenges posed by ecological imbalance, environmental degradation, obsolescence of built fabric and deterioration of quality of life of residents.

Collective memory, community values and beliefs underpin the temporal activities of the town, leading to distinct activity patterns and urban morphologies. Faith-driven residents or pilgrims converge at specific temples or river ghats for darshan of deities and/or ritual performances at varying periodicity. Extremely populated during the festivals, events and auspicious cycles of visitation, movement between the significant activity nodes and landmarks usually follow a pattern. Tradition of daily parikrama (circumambulation) along the pradakshina path is also a regular activity with many residents and pilgrims visiting Vrindavan. Pilgrimage movements along these networks present a livelihood option to the residents who develop trade and services' establishments. A mixed landuse pattern emerges with a rich mosaic of activities that impart vibrancy to the place, and simultaneously congests meagre spatial capacity available. Awareness of the temporal spatial patterns of human ritualistic activities and movements at a local area level becomes a significant consideration for urban planning interventions.

Figure 4. Built heritage of considerable architectural merit at Vrindavan: the Yamuna riverfront

Lord Krishna is believed to permanently reside at Vrindavan, and the people reinforce His Grace and living presence by organizing community events and activities regularly. Colloquially Braj is known for celebrating more festivals than days in a year. The festivals, fairs and events are organized at varying scales ranging from a local to global scale and attract participation accordingly. The major congregation amongst others are the annual festivals of Janamashtmi and Holi with a national catchment, recitation of Srimad Bhagavatam katha (scriptural discourse) with a regional catchment, and sankirtan (congregational singing of devotional songs with music accompaniment) at local level that occurs daily. The community activities – participants include local populace and visiting pilgrims - are of profound cultural significance for perpetuation of traditions known to contribute positively to the well-being of the community. Temporal patterns of participatory community activities and the imperative to provide accessibility, sufficiency, safety and hygiene for continued enactment of these activities are key considerations for evolving urban planning strategies (Figure 5 & 6). Urban planning in accordance to the existing patterns of the community and the pilgrims activities reduces conflicts, and enables not only an enhanced quality of life for the residents but improves the pilgrim experience as well.

Vrindavan has a population of sixty three thousand people in the 2011 census, and a thriving pilgrimage-based cultural economy with about six lac visitors annually. Though most of the earnings accrue to religious actors and institutions, the pilgrimage activity also supports several allied activities, some rooted in traditional cultural economy. The allied activities include carving of stone statues, mukuts (crowns) and decorative clothes for deities, sanjhi and local cuisine amongst others (Figure 7 & 8). Presently, the production is undertaken usually in households informally at disjointed locations. Aggregation of the production activities through spatial planning may foster innovation by peer learning, economies of scale and better connect with the demand side. Thus, mapping of the processes and practices of cultural economy and assessment of its potential to generate sustainable livelihoods is an important component of urban planning initiative.

Figure 5. Temporal spatial patterns of pilgrimage activity as at streets leading to temples with prasad shops

Numerous NGO's and community-based organizations related to tradition-based cultural domains have emerged to address divergent issues in Vrindavan. These issues primarily include revitalization of the holy river Yamuna and its ghats, conservation and restoration of built heritage, facilitating and promoting pilgrimage and community activities, propagation of traditionally community activities like sankirtan, Srimad Bhagavatam katha, revitalization of pradakshina path (circumambulation route), innovation and promotion of local arts and crafts, veneration and protection of cow and promoting traditional cow-based economy. A few of these organizations are crucibles of local practices and repositories of traditional knowledge; and are immense resource for cultural mapping and interpretative efforts. Local spiritual leaders and influential citizens, with urban development concerns usually place-based and lo-

Figure 6. Congregational activites at temples

Figure 7. Spatial patterns of production and access to cultural products as decorative clothes for dieties

cal, patronize numerous significant organizations. A few enjoy easy access to the decision makers and exercise considerable influence on the residents and non-residents from across the globe. The significant numbers and outreach of these organizations presents a medium with a high capacity for mediation of local issues with official urban planning process. The participation of these organizations in urban planning framework can impart considerable insights in arriving at development objectives of local community in response to the needs and aspirations of their communities. There is a serious disquiet over the sporadic urban development in response to endogenous triggers and an inclusion of all stakeholders in the development process can potentially render the framework sustainable.

Figure 8. Mukut (crown) making for dieties

To sustain and enhance the rich cultural and historical significance through urban and spatial planning process, Uttar Pradesh Urban Planning and Development Act, 1973 mandates the Development Authorities for preparation and implementation of the master and the zonal plans. Vrindavan is regulated by the Master Plan 2021 that recommends the conservation of ancient religious, cultural and archaeological buildings, areas and precincts. The master plan delineates a heritage zone that includes built heritage and the cultural precincts in view of specific cultural considerations (MVDA, 2009). The heritage zone falls in the municipal area, and under the administrative jurisdiction of the municipality. Special development controls and guidelines are recommended in the building byelaws for physical development in the heritage zone. Zonal plans are mandated to include specific spatial recommendations for development of site plans and use/activity plans for achieving objectives envisaged in the master plan. The zonal plans for Vrindavan are not yet formulated, and thus the objectives envisaged in the master plan are under achieved.

The Vrindavan Eco-city project highlighted the people's concern about protection of cultural and traditional values (Kulshrestha, 2007); and field interactions reveal a real desire for engagement with the cultural aspects by the authorities as well. However, the role of the state witnesses a multitude of implementation agencies (Shinde, 2012), wherein overlapping responsibilities and jurisdictions are barriers in holistic fulfilment of objectives envisaged in master plan. Coherent action is also constrained by a lack of capacity and expertise in the prevailing planning system to evolve context specific urban planning strategies. Vrindavan Eco-city project concluded that a participatory approach to planning and development appeared replicable.

It is thus gleaned that richness of traditions and cultural practices finding expression through the urban planning process is circumvented due to disregard of the cultural dimension in implementation tools viz. master/zonal plan, urban planning laws, planning regulations and conflicting institutional responsibilities. It is also implicit that culturally aware state, institutions and citizenry, conscious of traditional values accorded to the river Yamuna, hills forests, sacred groves, water bodies, temples etc.; are better positioned to imagine potential contribution of indigenous urbanism towards contemporary urban development. A cultural orientation is required for capacity building of individuals and institutions to understand and sustain the embedded patterns of urbanism as cultural expressions, and leverage them as catalysts to advance a sustainable urban development trajectory.

Case Study of Haridwar

Haridwar is an ancient tirtha, a sacred geography and one of the seven sacred cities that offer moksha (salvation) according to the Skandpurana. The region is known as Kedarkhand – the abode of Kedar (Lord Shiva); and the legendary association is reinforced by the presence of Daksha Mahadeo's temple at Kankhal (near Haridwar), earlier known in legends as Prajapati Daksha's capital. As suggested by the Puranas, Haridwar is the site for Bhagirathi's penance, which led to the descent of (river) Ganga. An event of immense cultural significance in the national consciousness, a sketch depicting the descent of river Ganga was enshrined in the Indian Constitution reinforcing its significance. Earlier known variously as Mayapur, Kapilasthana, it is called Har-dwar (gateway to Shiva) by the Saivites and Hari-dwar (gateway to Vishnu) by the Vaishnavites. Puranas and Mahabharata confirm the sanctity of Haridwar, and as a paramount pilgrim destination, its appeal has been non-sectarian and supra regional.

The importance of Haridwar centres on sacrality and reverence accorded to river Ganga that finds frequent mention in the scriptures. Devotees address the river as Ganga Maa (mother) and venerate her. The river is identified as an embodiment of sacredness, and its holy water is known to offer moksha –

freedom from the cycles of birth and death. River Ganga descends to the plains at Haridwar flowing between two hills – 'neel' and 'bilwa', and is also known as the 'Gangadwar' - dwar (gateway) to a network of sacred pilgrimage spots in the Himalayas – Kedarnath, Badrinath, Gangotri and Yamunotri. Natural scenic beauty, enchanting ghats, picturesque sites, Sivalik forests, mandirs, ashrams and akharas have long been a primary attraction for pilgrims and travellers. Haridwar is a centre for traditional learning and ayurvedic knowledge, is home to erudite scholars and sanyasis of many orders. It also hosts Kumbh mela (fair) - a religious event of utmost national significance - every twelve years, with an approximate 30-50 million pilgrims visiting Haridwar during Kumbh mela in 2010. Kumbh mela is organized in an area equivalent to 130sq.kms extending much beyond Haridwar.

Situated at the right bank of river Ganga, Haridwar was earlier an area of wilderness that attracted pilgrims primarily for religious activities. It was known as 'Tapovan'- a meditational retreat - and scarce physical growth or development maintained its serenity. The sanctity attracted many seekers and devotees to the place, and livelihoods were organized strictly on basis of Vedic tenets. Mayapur – earlier prevalent name of Haridwar - was known as a riparian settlement and River Ganga was considered sacrosanct and worshipped. The physical location of earliest Mayapur is uncertain and is conjectured by findings from archaeological remnants, interpretation of texts and descriptions left by travellers. Rituals were conducted in 'purnyashalas' (charitable establishments) at Haridwar constructed by the wealthy patrons or kings and resided at ashrams or dharamshalas at Kankhal or Jwalapur located close to Haridwar. Core of the traditional town at its present location is believed to have developed over ruins of an earlier settlement, though scarce evidences are available of the antiquity and architectural heritage.

Morphologically, Haridwar has evolved along the river Ganga on the land at its right bank and the adjacent 'Neel' parbat (hill). The growth of the town is guided by constraints in the availability of land, being bound by presence of river Ganga and 'Neel' on opposite sides. The spatial patterns in the traditional core area evolved linearly in response to its geography (Figure 9), and ritual and pilgrimage cycles; with the riverfront comprised of ghats assuming significance as hub of the town. Importantly, main worship and ritual areas developed along the riverbank and supporting livelihoods emerged within this area. Dharamshalas (charitable rest houses) were built along the river, and provided independent ghats and ritual bathing areas for the residents. Consequently, a mixed land use emerged at the traditional pilgrimage core that supported residential, commercial and religious activities. The number of pilgrims and their ritual and non-ritual activities exhibit variations in magnitude based on three temporal cycles i) The daily performance, ii) Performances during the auspicious occasions and festivals and iii) Every six years during the Kumbh/Ardh-Kumbh festival.

The cultural identity of Haridwar as a traditional centre of ritual-pilgrimage converges around river Ganga (Figures 10 and 11), and now mutated to a populous, physically dense, amorphous urban settlement with juxtaposition of varied activities – ritual, pilgrimage, livelihoods and trading in same urban space. The core pilgrimage area is proportionately insignificant to the spatial expanse of the town, and experiential aspects of the pilgrims' are qualitatively diminished. The unplanned transformations of built fabric, change in usages and activities, and lack of environmental services in the core ritual-pilgrimage area results in an unsustainable physical environment leading to gentrification from the traditional core. Contemporary urban development subsumes the indigenous patterns of urbanism, and traditional identity of Haridwar as a pilgrim town is being progressively obliterated.

Figure 9. Linear morphological spatial growth along the river visible at riverfront of River Ganga at Haridwar

Figure 10. Cultural identity of Haridwar as a pilgrimage town centred on River Ganga exemplified by ritual bathing in River Ganga

Presently, Haridwar town is headquarter of Haridwar district and is comprised of three tehsils. The current population of Haridwar urban agglomeration exceeds three lacs in 2011 census and continues to exhibit significant growth rates. Current developments include housing and commercial development at the periphery of the core area, and an industrial estate in proximity; resulting in heterogeneity of activities compounded with diluted emphasis on traditional ritual-pilgrimage based activities.

Figure 11. River Ganga being venerated as a symbol of purity

Pilgrimage is prime cultural activity that contributes to the local economy. Religious actors and organizations benefit directly by the economic support and donations by the pilgrims, whereas immense indirect benefits accrue to other stakeholders in catering to pilgrims' requirements of accommodation, travel etc. Religious tourism and other tourism activities have also proliferated. Other heterogeneous economic activities like manufacturing have also developed; hence, direct benefits of cultural economy are relegated to relative insignificance. It is significant however, that cultural products are symbols to link memories to a place; and its high associative value be favourably considered to promote spatial provisions in urban planning.

Prominent NGOs, community based organizations active in the cultural domains focus on varying issues of making the Ganga clean, facilitating performance of traditional rituals, promotion of afforestation and conservation of forests, protection of natural heritage – flora and fauna, and protection of built heritage. Few large social and quasi-religious organizations are involved in research and synthesis of aspects related to traditional knowledge and local practices, and are potential resources for cultural mapping. Most organizations view the contemporary urban development as driven more by concerns of economic development that is evidently at crossroads with the cultural values of society. They stress on the critical need for mechanisms to integrate the embodied knowledge of the community, and mediation of cultural and traditional practices in the urban planning paradigm.

The urban and spatial planning processes to sustain the rich cultural and historical heritage of Haridwar are mandated through formulation of Master Plan. Additionally, 'A City Development Plan (CDP)' focussing on the municipal area in Haridwar was prepared under the ambitious Jawaharlal Nehru National Urban Renewal Mission (JNNURM) in 2007. The Haridwar Master Plan 2025 recommends cognisance of cultural aspects related to the historic-religious aspects of Haridwar in framing objectives for its future urban development. The vision statement of CDP Haridwar envisages it as a 'city of Hope, faith and Spirituality…an international destination of pilgrimage and tourism, in keeping with its rich cultural heritage' (GHK International, UK, 2007). Concurrently, Haridwar is identified as a potential site for urbanization and industrial growth due to availability of flat terrain in the hilly state of Uttarakhand. The urban planning and development strategies and policies are more reactive to existing urban situation with negligible evident efforts to centre-stage cultural aspects despite recognition of their primacy for urban growth.

To reinforce traditional identity in this transformed scenario, potential contribution of indigenous spatial patterns evolved through traditional spiritual-pilgrimage based cultural activities needs understanding as an important consideration in urban planning domain. Identification of activity patterns corresponding to the local activities and events and its inter-linkage with activity nodes emergent spatial patterns and the temporal variations are imperative for facilitation of traditional ritual-pilgrimage activities that are critical for reiteration of cultural identity of people. In view of the identified development objectives and context of accelerated urban growth, it is critical for urban planning initiatives at Haridwar to recognize the significance of the cultural values inherent in the city, spatial patterns of cultural activities, architectural heritage and ecological aspects of physical growth.

DISCUSSIONS AND CONCLUSION

This chapter explores potential of cultural characteristics of a place to inform urban planning domain for evolving sustainable trajectories of urban development for pilgrimage towns in India. Theoretical linkages between the three variables gleaned from literature advocates inclusion of cultural aspects in urban planning considerations as critical for sustainable urban development – a learning well advised for sensitization of planning professionals. Integrative frameworks to empirically evaluate potential contribution of culture to urban planning may be theoretically situated in existing frameworks for examining contribution of culture to a wider development processes.

UNESCO has developed an analytical framework to explain and quantify how culture contributes to development processes, wherein direct references to urban planning processes are absent. It identifies twenty-two indicators from seven dimensions to elucidate on linkages between culture and development; and data is being generated in seventeen countries (UNESCO, 2011) . Spain has developed a strategy for culture and development cooperation, which identifies a theoretical framework to include principles, approaches and concepts guiding the cooperation. It also envisages regulatory, institutional, methodological, instrumental and implementation frameworks within the scope of its strategy (AECID, 2007). Information from similar such interventions need to be cumulated to deduct its potential linkage to the urban planning and potential impact on sustainability issues. Paucity of empirical studies focussing on potential contribution of culture to the urban planning and sustainability domains renders formulation of integrated cooperation strategies elusive. Conducting empirical field studies and gathering evidence of inclusion of cultural dimensions in urban planning process to produce a sustainable development trajectory offers substantial research opportunities in varying urban and cultural contexts.

In contemporary Indian urban scenario, Jawaharlal Nehru National Urban Renewal Mission (JN-NURM) initiated by the Government of India in 2005 conveys the intent to engage with Indian urbanism, and included urban planning interventions within its scope indirectly. Significantly, the criteria for selection of the towns eligible for funding under JNNURM scheme included cities/urban agglomeration of religious, historic or tourist importance. It is noticeable that a supplement Heritage toolkit (JNNURM, 2006) was prepared as an afterthought in cognisance of the specific cultural requirements for preparation of the City Development Plan (CDP) envisaged in the scheme. Similarly, a recent Government of

India scheme - Heritage City Development and Augmentation Yojana (HRIDAY) - recognizes the need to undertake strategic and planned development for sustainable development of heritage cities in India. Two above schemes convey implicit priority accorded by the Government of India to engage with indigenous urbanism at heritage cities.

This chapter attempts to bridge theoretical gaps in examining potential contribution of culture to urban planning processes for achieving a trajectory of sustainable development by initiating a conceptual approach to advance the intent. Timely in the context of recent Government of India schemes (HRIDAY), a study of these linkages is confounded by challenges faced in engagement with indigenous Indian urbanism characterized by hybridity, plurality and informality. Empirical studies exploring the linkages between three variables viz. culture, urban planning and sustainable urban development in Indian cities are extremely rare, and sketchy where available.

This study examines the linkages to assess conceptually the potential role of culture in urban planning process at two existing pilgrimage towns in India – Vrindavan and Haridwar - and its influence on sustainability. Prime cultural characteristics of both the case studies are closely linked to their homogenous Hindu identity, and in being significant pilgrimage destinations. The primacy of deities - Krishna in Vrindavan and Ganga in Haridwar – result in diversity of beliefs, rituals and activities. Religious and ritual activities are raison d'etre of pilgrim towns - hinging on Parikrama (circumambulation) and visitations to temples in Vrindavan, and on a holy dip in river Ganga at Haridwar. The legends of Lord Krishna's life have found expression in various cultural forms viz. dance, drama etc. which are performed and participated en-masse by the community and visitors in Vrindavan whereas Haridwar was predominantly known for being a taposthali steeped in asceticism.

Figure 12. Attributes reflecting linkages between culture, urban planning and sustainable development

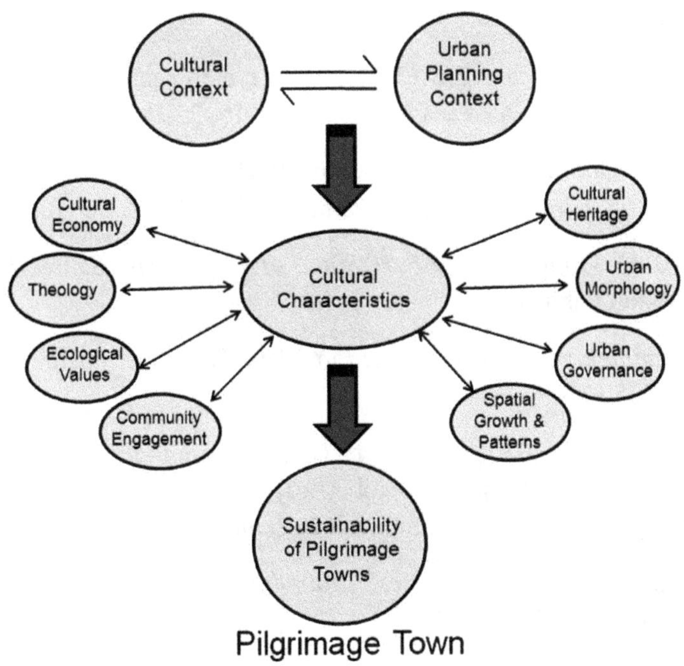

The diversity of the belief system and concomitant activities, varying geographical settings, activity nodes and their inter-linkages resulted in evolution of varying spatial and morphological patterns at the two towns. Keeping in perspective the diversity in the manifest natural, urban and cultural contexts and variance in their interface with the urban planning and sustainability domains, the study evolves a conceptual approach for inclusion of culture characteristics leading to sustainable urban development of pilgrim towns.

The case studies identify eight diverse attributes significant for examination of the linkage between the cultural dimension of pilgrimage towns with urban planning and sustainable urban development. The identified attributes are urban morphology, spatial growth, theological values, ecological values, urban governance, community engagement, cultural heritage and cultural economy (Figure 12). Prima facie, the case studies also reveal that the inter-relation between the three variables is itself not static; and temporal, positional and structural transformations therein can be analysed through careful analysis of the eight attributes. Similarly, in spite of broad similarities in cultural attributes of the case studies, the inter-relationship varies in its causality at the two towns. Accordingly, inclusion of culture in urban planning domain anticipates advancing a flexible framework for sustainable development, wherein the dynamic inter-relationships between variables continue on the sustainable trajectory.

Case studies at Vrindavan and Haridwar reiterate the need of additional research and empirical evidence to examine the ingenious urban linkages with other Hindu pilgrimage towns like Varanasi, Rishikesh, and Mathura etc. to establish a spectrum of indigenous urbanisms and establish conclusively inter-linkages between culture, urban planning and sustainable development.

REFERENCES

AECID. (2007). *Spanish Strategy for Culture and Development Cooperation*. Madrid: Ministry of Foreign Affairs and Cooperation.

Bandarin, F., Hosagrahar, J., & Albernaz, F. S. (2011). Why development needs culture. *Journal of Cultural Heritage Management and Sustainable Development*, *1*(1), 15–25. doi:10.1108/20441261111129906

Berke, P. R. (2002, August). Does Sustainable Development Offer a New Direction for Planning? Challenges for the Twenty-First Century. *Journal of Planning Literature*, *17*(1), 21–36. doi:10.1177/088122017001002

Brahmachari, R. D. (2011). *Vraja Mandala Parikrama: And the Twelve Sacred Forests of Vrindavana*. New Delhi: Vedanta Vision Publications.

Dixon, T. (2011). *Sustainable Urban Development to 2050: Complex transitions in the Built Environment of Cities*. Retrofit 2050.

Duxbury, N., & Jeannotte, M. S. (2010, September). *Culture, Sustainability, and Communities: Exploring the Myths*. Officina do Ces. Retrieved October 2013, from http://202.154.59.182/ejournal/files/Culture,%20sustainability%20and%20communities%20Exploring%20the%20myths.pdf

Duxbury, N., & Jeannotte, M. S. (2010). *Culture, Sustainability, and Communities: Exploring the Myths*. Coimbra, Portugal: Oficina do CES n.° 353.

Ellis, C. (2002). The New Urbanism: Critiques and Rebuttals. *Journal of Urban Design*, *7*(3), 261–291. doi:10.1080/1357480022000039330

Entwistle, A. (1987). *Braj: Centre of Krishna Pilgrimage*. Groningen: Egbert Forsten Publishing.

Evans, G. (2015). *Cultural Mapping and Planning for Sustainable Communities* (W. G.-P. Nancy Duxbury, Ed.). New York: Routledge.

Farr, D. (2008). *Sustainable Urbanism: Urban Design with Nature*. Hoboken, N.J.: Wiley.

Gupte, R., Mehrotra, R., & Shetty, P. (2010). archplus.net/home. Retrieved April 2014, from archplus.net: http://www.archplus.net/home/news/7,1-3904,1,0.html?referer=102

Hawkes, J. (2001). *The Fourth Pillar of Sustainability: Culture's essential role in public planning*. Victoria: Cultural Development Network Common Ground.

GHK International, UK. (2007). *City Development Plan: Haridwar Revised*. Jawaharlal Nehru National Urban Renewal Mission (JNNURM), Urban Development Department, Government of Uttarakhand. JNNURM.

JNNURM. (2006). *JNNURM: A supplement to toolkit on formulation of City Development Plan - Focus on Heritage*. Ministry of Urban Development & Ministry of Housing and urban Poverty Alleviation, Government of India.

Kulshrestha, S. K. (2007). Vrindavan Eco-city In Making: Working Together for Sustainable Development. *ISOCARP Congress 2007*. Retrieved from http://www.isocarp.net/Data/case_studies/1032.pdf

Mehrotra, R. (2008). Negotiating the Static and Kinetic Cities. In A. Huyssen (Ed.), *Other Cities, Other Worlds: Urban Imaginaries in a Globalizing Age* (pp. 205–218). Durham, NC: Duke University Press. doi:10.1215/9780822389361-009

Menon, A. K. (1999). Imagining the Indian City. In V. Prakash (Ed.), *Theatres of decolonization: (architecture), agency, (urbansim): proceedings of the second "Other Connections" Conference*. Washington, DC: University of Washington.

Menon, A. K. (n.d.). *The complexity of Indian urbanism*. Retrieved March 2014, from http://www.india-seminar.com/2007/579/579_a_g_krishna_menon.htm

Mercer, C. (2002). *Towards Cultural Citizenship: Tools for Cultural Policy and Development*. Hedemora: The Bank of Sweden Tercentenary Foundation & Gidlundds Forlag.

Ministry of Urban Development, Government of India. (2015). *Heritage City Development and Augmentation Yojana. Government of India, Ministry of Urban Development*. New Delhi: National Institute of Urban Affairs.

Mostafavi, M. (2010). Why Ecological Urbanism? Why now? In M. Mostafavi & G. Doherty (Eds.), *The Ecological Urbanism* (pp. 12–51). Baden, Switzerland: Lars Muller Publisher.

MVDA. (2009). *Mathura Vrindavan Punarikshit Mahayojana 2021 - Part A (Master Plan Report). In Agra Regional Planning Division, Mathura Vrindavan Development Authority*. MVDA.

Nadarajah, M. (2007). Common themes and differences: Approaches to culture in sustainability of Cities. In M. Nadarajah, & A. T. Yamamoto (Eds.), Urban Crisis: Culture and the Sustainability of Cities (pp. 107-132). Paris: United Nations University Press.

Nadarajah, M. (2007). *Conclusion*. United Ntions University Press.

Nurse, K. (2006). *Culture as the Fourth Pillar of Sustainble Development*. Institute of International Relations.

Parr, S. F. (2000). *In search of Indicators of culture and development: progress and proposals*. France: UNESCO.

Rana, R. S., & Piracha, A. L. (2007). Cultural Frameworks. In M. Nadarajah & A. T. Yamamoto (Eds.), *Urban Crisis: Culture and the Sustainability of Cities* (pp. 33–36). Hong Kong: United Nations Univerity Pres.

Register, R. (1987). *Eco-city Berkeley: Building Cities for a Healthy Future*. Berkeley, CA: Berkeley Hills Books.

Roders, A. P. (2013). How can Urbanization be Sustainable? A reflection on the role of city resources in Global Sustainable Development. *BDC, 13*(1), 79-91.

Roy, A. (2009). Why India Cannot Plan Its Cities: Informality, Insurgence and the Idiom of Urbanization. *Planning Theory, 8*(76), 76–87. doi:10.1177/1473095208099299

Sen, A. (1990). Development as capacity expansion. In K. Griffin & J. Knight (Eds.), *Human Development and the international development strategy for the 1990's* (pp. 41–58). London: Macmillan.

Sen, A. (1998). Culture, freedom and independence. In *World Culture Report 1998: culture, creativity and markets* (pp. 317–321). UNESCO.

Shinde, K. (2012). Policy, planning, and management for religious tourism in Indian pilgrimage sites. *Journal of Policy Research in Tourism, Leisure and Events, 4*(3), 289–291. doi:10.1080/19407963.2012.726107

Shinde, K. A. (2012). Place-making and environmental change in a Hindu pilgrimage site in India. *Geoforum, 43*(1), 116–127. doi:10.1016/j.geoforum.2011.07.014

Shinde, K. A. (2012). Place-making and environmental change in a Hindu pilgrimage site in India. *Geoforum, 43*(1), 116–127. doi:10.1016/j.geoforum.2011.07.014

Singh, R. P. (2013). Green Pilgrimage Initiatives. In *Hindu Tradition of Pilgrimage: Sacred Space and System* (pp. 333–368). New Delhi: Dev Publishers and Distributors.

Singhal, S., McGreal, S., & Berry, J. (2013). An evaluative model for city competitiveness: Application to UK cities. *Land Use Policy, 30*(1), 214–222. doi:10.1016/j.landusepol.2012.03.018

Soini, K. (2013, November). *Culture challenging and contributing to Sustainable Development*. COST IS 1007. Retrieved from http://www.culturalsustainability.eu/Soini_14112013.pdf

Spirn, A. W. (2012). *Ecological Urbanism: A framework for the design of Reilient Cities*. Retrieved from www.annewhistonspirn.com/pdf/spirn_ecological_urbanism-2011.pdf

Sundaram, R. (2010). *Externailities, Urbanism and Pirate Modernities: India.* Rising Powers Working Paper. E.S.R.C (Economic and Social Research Council.

Suzuki, H., Dastur, A., & Moffat, S. (2010). *Eco2 Cities: Ecological Cities as Economic Cities*. Washington, DC: The World Bank. doi:10.1596/978-0-8213-8046-8

Talen, E. (2013). *Charter of the New Urbanism* (2nd ed.). New York: McGraw-Hill Education.

Thakur, N. (2002). *The Architectural Knowledge Systems Approach.* Architecturez Imprints.

Thakur, N. (2011). Indian Cultural Landscapes: Religious pluralism, tolerance and ground reality. *Journal of SPA: New Dimensions in Research of Environments for Living "The Scared", 3.*

Tutzinger Manifesto. (2001). Aesthetics of Sustinability. *TUTZINGER MANIFESTO for the strengthening of the cultural-aesthetic dimension of sustainable development*. Retrieved November 2013, from http://www.kupoge.de/ifk/tutzinger-manifest/pdf/tuma-gb.pdf

UN-DESA. (n.d.). *Challenges and way forward in the urban sector: Sustainable Development in the 21st century (SD21).* United Nations Department of Economic and Social Affairs.

UN-HABITAT. (2002). *Sustainable Urbanization: Achieving Agenda 21*. UN-HABITAT DFID.

UN-HABITAT. (2009). *Planning Sustainable Cities: Global Report on Human Settlements*. London: Earthscan.

UNESCO. (1982). *Mexico City Declaration on Cultural Policies*. Mexico City: UNESCO.

UNESCO. (1998). *Intergovernmental Conference on Cultural Policies for Development.* Action Plan on Cultural Policies for Development. Retrieved February 2014, from http://portal.unesco.org/culture/en/files/35220/12290888881stockholm_actionplan_rec_en.pdf/stockholm_actionplan_rec_en.pdf

UNESCO. (2001). *UNESCCO Universal Declaration on Cultural Diversity*. UNESCO.

UNESCO. (2011). *UNESCO Culture for Development Indicator Suite: Analytical Framework.* UNESCO. Retrieved from http://www.unesco.org/new/fileadmin/MULTIMEDIA/HQ/CLT/pdf/Conv2005_CDindicators_Analytical_en.pdf

UNESCO. (2012, May). Retrieved March 2014, from https://en.unesco.org/post2015/sites/post2015/files/Think%20Piece%20Culture.pdf

UNESCO. (2013a). *Culture: Key to sustainable development. Hangzhoou*. UNESCO.

UNESCO. (2013b, December 13). Retrieved January 2014, from http://www.unesco.org/new/en/culture/themes/dynamic-content-single-view/news/un_general_assembly_adopts_by_consensus_a_new_resolution_on_culture_and_development/#.U6FJMvmSxqU

UNESCO. (2015). Retrieved 08 15, 2015, from http://www.unesco.org/new/fileadmin/MULTIMEDIA/HQ/CLT/images/Concept_Note_Report_CultureandCities.pdf

United Cities and Local Governments. (2010). *Culture: The Fourth Pillar of Sustainable Development.* Mexico City: UCLG.

United Nations. (2013). *Yangzhou Recommendations on Sustainable Cities and Urbanization. Recommendations.* Yangzhou: Yangzhou Municipal People's Government, United Nations Department of Economic and Social Affairs.

UNRISD UNESCO. (1996). Towards a World Report on Culture and Development: Constructing cultural statistics and indicators. UNRISD UNESCO.

UNU-IAS and IICRC. (2002). *Kanazawa Resolutions on culture in sustainability of cities.* Kanazawa: IICRC.

White, S. S., & Ellis, C. (2007). Sustainability. The Environment, and New Urbanism: An Assessment and Agenda for Research. *Journal of Architecture and Planning Research, 24*(2), 125-142.

WHO. (1999). *Towards a new planning process: A guide to reorienting urban planning towards Local Agenda 21.* WHO Regional Office.

World Commission on Culture and Development. (1996). *Our creative diversity.* UNESCO.

World Commission on Environment and Development. (1987). *Our Common Future.* Oxford, UK: Oxford University Press.

World Summit on Sustainable Development. (2002). *Report of the World Summit on Suatinable Development Johannesburg.* New York: United Nations.

Yanarella, E. J., & Levine, R. S. (1992). Does Sustainable Development Lead to Sustainability. *Futures, 24*(8), 759–774. doi:10.1016/0016-3287(92)90105-O

Compilation of References

Abdallah, C., Coady, D., Gupta, S., & Hanedar, E. (2015). *The Quest for the Holy Grail: Efficient and Equitable Fiscal Conoslidation in India*. IMF Working Paper (WP/15/152).

Abereijo, I. O., & Ilori, M. O. (2011). Technological spillovers from multinational companies to small and medium food companies in Nigeria. In H. Sun (Ed.), *Management of technological innovation in developing and developed countries*. Rijeka, Croatia: Intech.

Acharya, S., Katiyar, A. K., Bharti, V. K., Charan, G., Prakash, B., & Srivastava, R. B. (2012). Assessment of irrigation water quality of cold arid Ladakh region. *Journal of Soil and Water Conservation*, *11*(4), 311–315.

ADB. (2009). *Asian Development Bank Support for the Transport Sector in Viet Nam*. Manila: Asian Development Bank.

AECID. (2007). *Spanish Strategy for Culture and Development Cooperation*. Madrid: Ministry of Foreign Affairs and Cooperation.

Ahmed, N., Higgins, A. & Norphel, C. (2010). *Snow Water Harvesting in the Cold Desert Ladakh: An Introduction to the Artificial Glacier Project*. Leh: Leh Nutrition Project.

Ahmed, A., & Nwankwo, S. (2013). Entrepreneurship development in Africa: An overview. *World Journal of Entrepreneurship. Management and Sustainable Development*, *9*(2/3), 82–86.

Ajzen, I. (1991). The theory of planned behaviour. *Organizational Behavior and Human Decision Processes*, *50*(2), 179–211. doi:10.1016/0749-5978(91)90020-T

Akhtar, A., & Gondhalekar, D. (2013). Impacts of tourism on water resources in Leh town. *Ladakh Studies.*, *30*, 25–37.

Alarcón, J., van Heemst, J., & De Jong, N. (2000). Extending the SAM with Social and Environmental Indicators: An Application to Bolivia. *Economic Systems Research*, *12*(4), 473–496. doi:10.1080/09535310020003784

Alexis, N., Urch, B., & Tarlo, S. (2000). Cyclooxygenase metabolites play a different role in ozone induced pulmonary function decline in asthmatics compared to normals. *Inhalation Toxicology*, *12*(12), 1205–1224. doi:10.1080/08958370050198548 PMID:11114789

Alstone, P., Gershenson, D., & Kammen, D. M. (2015). Decentralized energy systems for clean electricity access. *Nature Climate Change*, *5*(4), 305–314. doi:10.1038/nclimate2512

Alston, J. M., Norton, G. W., & Pardey, P. G. (1995). *Science under Scarcity*. New York: Cornell University Press.

Anand, R., Coady, D., Mohommad, A., Thakoor A., Walsh, J., (2014). Fiscal and Welfare Impacts of Fuel Subsidy Reform in India. *Economic & Political Weekly*, *49*(28).

Anand, R., Coady, D., Mohommad, A., Thakoor, A., & Walsh, J. (2013). *The Fiscal and Welfare Impacts of Reforming Fuel Subsidies in India.* IMF Working Paper (WP/13/128).

Anderson, H. R., Ponce de Leon, A., & Bland, J. M. (2004). *Meta-analysis of time-series studies and panel studies of particulate matter (PM) and ozone (O3).* Report of a WHO task group. Copenhagen WHO Regional Office for Europe, 2004. Retrieved from http://www.euro. who.int/document/e82792.pdf

Anderson, H. R., Ponce de Leon, A., & Bland, J. M. (1987). Air pollution and daily mortality in London: 1987–92. *BMJ, 1996*(312), 665–669. PMID:8597732

Anghchok, D., & Singh, P. (2006). Traditional Irrigation and Water Distribution System in Ladakh. *Indian Journal of Traditional Knowledge, 5*(3), 397–402.

APA (Africa Adaptation Programme). (2012). *Handbook on Capitalisation of Experiences 2012.* Knowledge Management and Adaptation to Climate Change. UNDP.

Arce, R., & Gullòn, N. (2000). The application of Strategic Environmental Assessment to sustainability assessment of infrastructure development. *Environmental Impact Assessment Review, 20*(3), 393–402. doi:10.1016/S0195-9255(00)00050-0

Arze del Granado, J., Coady, D., & Gillingham, R. (2012). The Unequal Benefits of Fuel Subsidies: A Review of Evidence for Developing Countries. *World Development, 40*(11), pp2234–pp2248. doi:10.1016/j.worlddev.2012.05.005

Authority, C. E. (2012). *All Indian Electricity Statistics.* New Delhi: Central Electricity Authority.

Bandarin, F., Hosagrahar, J., & Albernaz, F. S. (2011). Why development needs culture. *Journal of Cultural Heritage Management and Sustainable Development, 1*(1), 15–25. doi:10.1108/20441261111129906

Bassi, A., Lombardi, N., & Gallagher, L. (2014). *Green Economy Modeling of Ecosystem Services in the Dawna Tenasserim Landscape (DTL) along the 'Road to Dawei.* WWF-Greater Mekong.

Bassi, A., Lombardi, N., & Gallagher, L. (2014). *Integrated Economic and Spatial Planning for the Food-Energy-Water Nexus.* Stocktaking Review.

Batty, K., & Ashmore, M. R. (2003). Lower threshold ozone exposures for effects on roots than shoots in wetland species. In *Establishing ozone critical levels II, 2003 451 UNECE Workshop Report.* IVL report B1523 IVL Swedish Environmental Research Institute.

Baumgartner, R. (2009). Organisational culture and leadership: Preconditions for the development of a sustainable corporation. *Sustainable Development, 17*(2), 102–113. doi:10.1002/sd.405

Baumol, W., & Oates, W. (1988). *The Theory of Environmental Policy.* Cambridge, UK: Cambridge University Press. doi:10.1017/CBO9781139173513

Bayon, R. (2004). *Making Environmental markets work: lessons from early experience with sulfur, carbon, wetlands, and other related markets. Forest Trends.* Katoomba.

Behrens, A., Giljum, S., Kovanda, J., & Niza, S. (2007). The material basis of the global economy: Worldwide patterns of natural resource extraction and their implications for sustainable resource use policies. *Ecological Economics, 64*(2), 444–453. doi:10.1016/j.ecolecon.2007.02.034

Bell, J., & Stellingwerf, J. J. (2012). *Sustainable entrepreneurship: The motivations and challenges of sustainable entrepreneurs in the renewable energy industry.* (Unpublished Master Thesis). Jönköping International Business School, Sweden.

Bell. M.L., Dominici, F., Samet, J.M. (1997). Ozone and short-term mortality in 95 urban communities, 1987–2000. *JAMA, 2004*, 292:2372.

Bell, C. (1928). *The People of Tibet*. Oxford, UK: The Clarendon Press.

Bell, M. L., Dominici, F., & Samet, J. M. (2005). A meta-analysis of time-series studies of ozone and mortality with comparison to the national morbidity, mortality, and air pollution study. *Epidemiology (Cambridge, Mass.)*, *16*(4), 436–445. doi:10.1097/01.ede.0000165817.40152.85 PMID:15951661

Bell, M. L., Peng, R. D., & Dominici, F. (2006, April). The exposure-response curve for ozone and risk of mortality and the adequacy of current ozone regulations. *Environmental Health Perspectives*, *114*(4), 532–536. doi:10.1289/ehp.8816 PMID:16581541

Bergamaschi, E., De Palma, G., Mozzoni, P., Vanni, S., Vettori, M. V., Broeckaert, F., & Mutti, A. et al. (2001). Polymorphism of quinone-metabolizing enzymes and susceptibility to ozone-induced acute effects. *American Journal of Respiratory and Critical Care Medicine*, *163*(6), 1426–1431. doi:10.1164/ajrccm.163.6.2006056 PMID:11371413

Berke, P. R. (2002, August). Does Sustainable Development Offer a New Direction for Planning? Challenges for the Twenty-First Century. *Journal of Planning Literature*, *17*(1), 21–36. doi:10.1177/088122017001002

Bernard, A., & Vielle, M. (2003). *Multi-Gas Strategy in Committing to the Kyoto Protocol*. IDEI Working Papers 183. Toulouse: Institut d'Économie Industrielle (IDEI).

Bhasin, M. K. (1992). *Cold Desert: Ladakh: Ecology and Development*. Delhi: Khamla Raj Enterprises Publications.

Bhattacharyya, S. (2012). Energy access programmes and sustainable development: A critical review and analysis. *Energy for Sustainable Development*, *16*(3), 260–271. doi:10.1016/j.esd.2012.05.002

Bhattacharyya, S. (2013). Financing energy access and off-grid electrification: A review of status, options and challenges. *Renewable & Sustainable Energy Reviews*, *20*, 462–472. doi:10.1016/j.rser.2012.12.008

Bhattacharyya, S. (2013). To regulate or not to regulate off-grid electricity access in developing countries. *Energy Policy*, *63*, 494–503. doi:10.1016/j.enpol.2013.08.028

Bhattacharyya, S. (2015). Mini-grid based electrification in Bangladesh: Technical configuration and business analysis. *Renewable Energy*, *75*, 745–761. doi:10.1016/j.renene.2014.10.034

Bhattacharyya, S., & Palit, D. (2014). *Mini-grids for rural electrification of developing countries*. London: Springer. doi:10.1007/978-3-319-04816-1

Biggs, R., Bohensky, E., Desanker, P. V., Fabricius, C., Lymann, T., & Misselhorn, A. A. et al. (2004). *Nature Supporting People: The South African Millennium Ecosystem Assessment*. Pretoria, South Africa: Council for Scientific and Industrial Research.

Biomimicry Institute. (2014). *What is biomimicry?* Retrieved June 29, 2015, from http://biomimicry.org/ what-is-biomimicry/

Black, V.J., Black, C.R., Roberts, J.A., & Stewart, C.A. (2000). *Impact of ozone on the reproductive*. Academic Press.

Blomberg, A., Mudway, I. S., Nordenhäll, C., Hedenström, H., Kelly, F. J., Frew, A. J., & Sandström, T. et al. (1999). Ozone-induced lung function decrements do not correlate with early airway inflammatory or antioxidant responses. *The European Respiratory Journal*, *13*(6), 1418–1428. doi:10.1183/09031936.99.13614299 PMID:10445622

Bosac, C., Black, V. J., Roberts, J. A., & Black, C. R. (1998). Impact of ozone on seed yield and quality and seedling vigour in oilseed rape (Brassica napus L.). *Plant Physiology*, *153*(1-2), 127–134. doi:10.1016/S0176-1617(98)80055-2

Bosello F., Eboli F. & Pierfederici R. (2012b). *Assessing the Economic Impacts of Climate Change, Review of Environment, Energy and Economics*. 10.7711/feemre3.2012.02.002

Bosello, F., De Cian, E., & Roson, R. (2007a). *Climate Change, Energy Demand and Market Power in a General Equilibrium Model of the World Economy*. FEEM working paper No. 71.2007.

Bosello, F., Eboli, F., & Pierfederici, R. (2012a). *Assessing the Economic Impacts of Climate Change. An Updated CGE Point of View*. FEEM working paper, 2.2012.

Bosello, F., Carraro, C., & De Cian, E. (2010b). Climate Policy and the Optimal Balance between Mitigation, Adaptation and Unavoided Damage. *Climate Change Economics*, *1*(02), 71–92. doi:10.1142/S201000781000008X

Bosello, F., Nicholls, R. J., Richards, J., Roson, R., & Tol, R. S. J. (2012c). Economic impacts of climate change in Europe: Sea-level rise. *Climatic Change*, *112*(1), 63–81. doi:10.1007/s10584-011-0340-1

Bosello, F., Roson, R., & Tol, R. S. J. (2006). Economy wide estimates of the implications of climate change: Human health. *Ecological Economics*, *58*(3), 579–591. doi:10.1016/j.ecolecon.2005.07.032

Bosello, F., Roson, R., & Tol, R. S. J. (2007b). Economy wide estimates of the implications of climate change: Sea-level rise. *Environmental and Resource Economics*, *37*(3), 549–571. doi:10.1007/s10640-006-9048-5

Botric. (2013). *Identifying Key Sectors in Croatian Economy Based on Input-Output Tables*. EIZ-WP-1302.

Braat, L., & de Groot, R. (2012). The ecosystem services agenda: Bridging the worlds of natural science and economics, conservation and development, and public and private policy. *Ecosyst. Serv*, *1*(1), 4–15. doi:10.1016/j.ecoser.2012.07.011

Bradbear. (2010). *(FAO): Produits forestiers non ligneux 19. Le rôle des abeilles dans le développement rural Manuel sur la récolte, la transformation et la commercialisation des produits et services dérivés des abeilles*. Academic Press.

Brahmachari, R. D. (2011). *Vraja Mandala Parikrama: And the Twelve Sacred Forests of Vrindavana*. New Delhi: Vedanta Vision Publications.

Brander, L. (2013). *Guidance manual on value transfer methods for ecosystem services. United Nations Environment Programme*. Nairobi: UNEP.

Braun-Fahrländer, C., Künzli, N., Domenighetti, G., Carell, C. F., Anderson, H. R., Strachan, D., & Ruffin, D. et al. (1994). Acute effects of ambient ozone on respiratory function of Swiss schoolchildren after a 10-minute heavy exercise. *Pediatric Pulmonology*, *17*(3), 169–177. doi:10.1002/ppul.1950170306 PMID:8196997

Brent, R. J. (2014). *Cost_Benefit Analysis and Health Care Evaluations* (2nd ed.). Edward Elgar Publishing Limited.

Buchanan, J. M. (1975). A contractarian paradigm for applying economic theory. *The American Economic Review*, *65*(2), 225–230.

Bush, M. L., Raybold, T., Abeles, S., Hu, S. C., Ben-Jebria, A., & Ultman, J. S. (1996). Longitudinal distribution of ozone absorption in the lung: Gender differences and intersubject variability. *Journal of Applied Physiology*, *81*, 1651–1657. PMID:8904582

Business Standard. (2015, March 5). *OERC cancels distribution licence of Reliance Energy's discoms in Odisha*. Retrieved June 30, 2015, from Business Standard: http://www.business-standard.com/article/companies/oerc-cancels-distribution-licence-of-reliance-energy-s-discoms-in-odisha-115030400500_1.html

Bussolo, M., & O'Connor, D. (2001). *Clearing Air in India: The Economics of Climate Policy with Ancillary Benefits*. Development Centre Working Paper 182, CD/DOC 14. Organisation for Economic Cooperation and Development (OECD).

Bussolo, M., & O'Connor, D. (2001). *Clearing the air in India: The economics of climate policy with ancillary benefits*. OECD Development Centre Working Paper No. 182. OECD.

Byun, D. W., & Ching, J. K. S. (Eds.). (1999). Science algorithms of the EPA Models-3 community multi-scale air quality (CMAQ) modeling system. NERL, Research Triangle Park, NC EPA/ 600/R-99/030.

Cameron, A. C., & Trivedi, P. K. (2009). Microeconometrics Using Stata (Vol. 5). College Station, TX: Stata Press.

CCME. (2003). *Effects of o3 on materials: update in support of the Canada-wide standards for particulate matter and O3*. Canadian Council of Ministers of the Environment.

CEA. (2008). *All India Electricity Statistics, General review*. New Delhi: Central Electricity Authority, Ministry of Power, Government of India.

CEA. (2013). *Growth of Electricity Sector in India from 1947-2013*. CEA.

CEA. (2014, January). *Central Electricity Authority: CO2 Baseline Database, version 9*. CEA.

Central Statistical Organization. (n.d.). *Energy Statistics of India, Government of India*. Retrieved from www.mospi.nic.in

Chandramouli, C. (2011). *Houses, Household Amenities and Assets Data 2001 - 2011 - Visualizing Through Maps*. Retrieved April 10, 2015, from Census of India: http://censusindia.gov.in/2011-Common/NSDI/Houses_Household.pdf

Chatani, S., Amann, M., Goel, A., Hao, J., Klimont, Z., Kumar, A., & Zhao, B. et al. (2014). Photochemical roles of rapid economic growth and potential abatement strategies on tropospheric ozone over South and East Asia in 2030. *Atmospheric Chemistry and Physics*, *14*(17), 9259–9277. doi:10.5194/acp-14-9259-2014

Chaurey, A., Krithika, P. R., Palit, D., Rakesh, S., & Sovacool, B. K. (2012). New partnerships and business models for facilitating energy access. *Energy Policy*, *47*, 48–55. doi:10.1016/j.enpol.2012.03.031

Chen, P. C., Lai, Y. M., Chan, C. C., Hwang, J. S., Yang, C. Y., & Wang, J. D. (1999). Short-term effect of ozone on the pulmonary function of children in primary school. *Environmental Health Perspectives*, *107*(11), 921–925. doi:10.1289/ehp.99107921 PMID:10544161

Chmiel, Z., & Bhattacharyya, S. (2015). Analysis of off-Grid electricity system at Isle of Eigg (Scotland): Lessons for developing countries. *Renewable Energy*, *81*, 578–588. doi:10.1016/j.renene.2015.03.061

Ciscar, J. C., Iglesias, A., Feyen, L., Szabó, L., Van Regemorter, D., Amelunge, B., & Soria, A. et al. (2011). Physical and economic consequences of climate change in Europe. *Proceedings of the National Academy of Sciences of the United States of America*, *108*(7), 2678–2683. doi:10.1073/pnas.1011612108 PMID:21282624

Claire, K. (2005). Managing ecosystem services: What do we need to know about their ecology? *Ecology Letters*, *8*(5), 468–479. doi:10.1111/j.1461-0248.2005.00751.x PMID:21352450

Clark, W. C., & Dickson, N. M. (2003). Sustainability science: The emerging research program. *Proceedings of the National Academy of Sciences of the United States of America*, *100*(14), 8059–8061. doi:10.1073/pnas.1231333100 PMID:12794187

Clements, B., Coady, D., Fabrizio, S., Gupta, S., Alleyne, T., & Sdralevich, C. (2013). *Energy subsidy Reform, Lessons and Implications*. IMF.

Clouse, C. (2014). Learning from artificial glaciers in the Himalaya: design for climate change through low-tech infrastructural devices. *Journal of Landscape Architecture*, *9*(3), 6-19.

Coady, D., Flamini, V., & Sears, L. (2015). The Unequal Benefits of Fuel Subsidies Revisited: Evidence for Developing Countries. In Inequality and Fiscal Policy. IMF Working Paper (WP/15/250)

Coady, D., Parry, I., Sears, L., & Shang, B. (2015). *How Large Are Global Energy Subsidies?* IMF Working Paper (WP/13/105).

Coady, D., & Newhouse, D. (2006). Evaluating the distribution of the real income effects of increases in petroleum product prices in Ghana. In A. Coudouel, A. Dani, & S. Paternostro (Eds.), *Analyzing the distributional impacts of reforms: Operational experience in implementing poverty and social impact analysis*. Washington, DC: World Bank.

Coase, R. H. (1937). The Nature of the Firm. *Economica, 4*(16), 386-405.

Coase, R. H. (1964). The Regulated Industries: A Discussion. *The American Economic Review, 54*, 194–197.

Coffey M.J., Wheeler,C.S., Gross,K.B., & Eschenbacher,W.L.(1996). Increased 5-lipoxygenase metabolism in the lungs of human subjects exposed to ozone. *Toxicology, 114*, 187–197.

Cohen, B., & Winn, M. I. (2007). Market imperfections, opportunity and sustainable entrepreneurship. *Journal of Business Venturing, 22*(1), 29–49. doi:10.1016/j.jbusvent.2004.12.001

Comisión Económica para América Latina (CEPAL). (2005). *Boletín demográfico*. América Latina: Proyecciones de Población Urbana y Rural (1970-2025), Santiago de Chile: CEPAL & United Nations.

Commission, P. (2012). *Towards faster and more inclusive growth: an approach to the 11th five year plan*. New Delhi: Planning Commission.

Cook, P. (2011). Infrastructure, rural electrification and development. *Energy for Sustainable Development, 15*(3), 304–313. doi:10.1016/j.esd.2011.07.008

Cook, P. (2013). Rural Electrification and Rural Development. In S. Bhattacharya (Ed.), *Rural Electrification through Decentralised Off-grid Systems in Developing Countries* (pp. 13–38). London: Springer-Verlag. doi:10.1007/978-1-4471-4673-5_2

Cooley, D. R., & Manning, W. J. (1987). The impact of ozone on assimilate partitioning in plants– a review. *Environmental Pollution, 47*(2), 95–113. doi:10.1016/0269-7491(87)90040-6 PMID:15092712

Costanza, R., d'Arge, R., de Groot, R., Faber, S., Grasso, M., Hannon, B., … van den Belt, M. (1997). The value of the world's ecosystem services and natural capital. *Nature, 387*, 253-260.

Costanza, R., de Groot, R., Sutton, P., van der Ploeg, S., Anderson, S. J., & Kubiszewski, I. et al. (2014). Changes in the global value of ecosystem services. *Global Environmental Change, 26*, 152–158. doi:10.1016/j.gloenvcha.2014.04.002

Costanza, R., & Kubiszewski, I. (2012). The authorship structure of ecosystem services as a transdisciplinary field of scholarship. *Ecosyst. Serv, 1*(1), 16–25. doi:10.1016/j.ecoser.2012.06.002

Council, N. S. (2010). *Skills Gap Study of the North East*. New Delhi: National Skill Development Council.

Crnogaj, K., Rebernik, M., Hojnik, B. B., & Gomezelj, D. O. (2014). Building a model of researching the sustainable entrepreneurship in the tourism sector. *Kybernetes, 43*(3/4), 377–393. doi:10.1108/K-07-2013-0155

Crook, J., & Ostmason, H. (1994). *Himalayan Buddhist Villages: environment, resources, society and religious life in Zangskar, Ladakh*. Bristol: University of Bristol Press.

Cross, C. E., van der Vliet, A., Louie, S., Thiele, J. J., & Halliwell, B. (1998). Oxidative stress and antioxidants at biosurfaces: Plants, skin, and respiratory tract surfaces. *Environmental Health Perspectives, 106*(Suppl. 5), 1241–1251. doi:10.1289/ehp.98106s51241 PMID:9788905

Daily, G. C. (1997). *Nature's Services: Societal Dependence on Natural Ecosystems*. Washington, DC: Island Press.

Daily, G. C., Soderqvist, T., Aniyar, S., Arrow, K., Dasgupta, P., & Ehrlich, P. R. et al. (2000). Ecology: The value of nature and the nature of value. *Science*, *289*(5478), 395–396. doi:10.1126/science.289.5478.395 PMID:10939949

Darokhan, M. D. (1999). The Development of Ecological Agriculture in Ladakh and Strategies for Sustainable Development. In Ladakh: Culture, History and Development between Himalaya and Karakoram. Delhi: Sterling Publishers.

Das, S., & Goswami, A. (2015). *Crisis in India's Electricity Distribution Sector: Time to Reboot for a Viable Future*. New Delhi: The Energy and Resources Institute.

Daultrey, S., & Gergan, R. (2011). Living with Change: Adaptation and Innovation in Ladakh. *Journal of Climate Adaptation*.

De Groot, R., Brander, L., van der Ploeg, S., Costanza, R., Bernard, F., & Braat, L. et al. (2012). Global estimates of the value of ecosystems and their services in monetary units. *Ecosystem Services*, *1*(1), 50–61.

De Nooij, M., Koopmans, C., & Bijvoet, C. (2007). The Value of Supply Security: The Costs of Power Interruptions: Economic Input for Damage Reduction and Investment in Networks. *Energy Economics*, *29*(2), 277–295. doi:10.1016/j.eneco.2006.05.022

Dean, T. J., & McMullen, J. S. (2007). Toward a theory of sustainable entrepreneurship: Reducing environmental degradation through entrepreneurial action. *Journal of Business Venturing*, *22*(1), 50–76. doi:10.1016/j.jbusvent.2005.09.003

DECC. (2010). *Guidelines to Defra / DECC's GHG Conversion Factors for Company Reporting*. Produced by AEA for the Department of Energy and Climate Change (DECC) and the Department for Environment, Food and Rural Affairs (Defra) Version 1.2.1 FINAL Updated: 06/10/2010. Retrieved from http://www.rensmart.com

Dechert, W. D. (n.d.). Testing time series for nonlinearities: The BDS Approach, published in Nonlinear dynamics and economics. In *Proceedings of the Tenth International Symposium in Economic Theory and Econometrics*. Cambridge University Press.

Deke, O., Hooss, K. G., Kasten, C., Klepper, G., & Springer, K. (2001). *Economic Impact of Climate Change: Simulations with a Regionalized Climate-Economy Model*. Kiel Institute of World Economics, Working Paper No. 1065.

Demenge, J. (2007). *Measuring Ecological Footprints of Subsistence Farmers in Ladakh*. Paper presented at the International Ecological Footprint Conference, International Ecological Footprint Conference, Cardiff, UK.

Demsetz, H. (1968). Why Regulate Utilities? *The Journal of Law & Economics*, *11*(1), 55–65. doi:10.1086/466643

Den Bergh, J., & Kemp, R. (2006). *Economics and Transitions: Lessons from Economic Sub-disciplines*. Working Paper Series # 038. United Nations University - Maastricht Economic and social Research and Training Centre on Innovation and Technology.

Diamond, Peter A., & Mirrlees, James A. (1971). *Optimal Taxation and Public Production II: Tax Rules*. The American Economic Review.

District Statistics & Evaluation Office. (2012). *District Statistical Handbook for the Year 2011-2012*. Leh: Government of Jammu & Kashmir.

District Statistics & Evaluation Office. (2013). Ladakh Autonomous Hill District Blockwise Village Amenity Directory 2012-2013. Leh: Government of Jammu & Kashmir.

Diwedi, A. (2009). *Forests of Himalaya: Planning and Development*. Delhi: Cyber Tech Publications.

Dixon, T. (2011). *Sustainable Urban Development to 2050: Complex transitions in the Built Environment of Cities*. Retrofit 2050.

Dixon, S. E. A., & Clifford, A. (2007). Ecopreneurship: A new approach to managing the triple bottom line. *Journal of Organizational Change Management*, *20*(3), 326–345. doi:10.1108/09534810710740164

Dobson, A. (2007). Environmental citizenship: Towards sustainable development. *Sustainable Development*, *15*(5), 276–285. doi:10.1002/sd.344

DoES. (2013). *District-wise, season-wise crop production statistics*. Directorate of Economics and Statistics (DoES), Government of India. Retrieved from https://data.gov.in/catalog/district-wise-season-wise-crop-production-statistics#web_catalog_tabs_block_10

DREF SO AGADIR. (2009). *Projets de développement forestier et de LCD dans la région Souss-Massa-Draa*. Province de ZAGORA.

Duxbury, N., & Jeannotte, M. S. (2010). *Culture, Sustainability, and Communities: Exploring the Myths*. Coimbra, Portugal: Oficina do CES n.º 353.

Duxbury, N., & Jeannotte, M. S. (2010, September). *Culture, Sustainability, and Communities: Exploring the Myths*. Officina do Ces. Retrieved October 2013, from http://202.154.59.182/ejournal/files/Culture,%20sustainability%20and%20communities%20Exploring%20the%20myths.pdf

Eboli, F., Parrado, R., & Roson, R. (2010). Climate-change feedback on economic growth: Explorations with a dynamic general equilibrium model. *Environment and Development Economics*, *15*(05), 515–533. doi:10.1017/S1355770X10000252

Elkington, J. (1994). Towards the sustainable corporation: Win-win-win business strategies for sustainable development. *California Management Review*, *36*(2), 90–100. doi:10.2307/41165746

Elkington, J. (1997). *Cannibals with forks – The triple bottom line of 21st century business*. Oxford, UK: Capstone.

Elkington, J. (1998). Cannibals with forks: The triple bottom line of sustainability. *Gabriola California Management Review*, *45*(4), 35–51.

Ellis, C. (2002). The New Urbanism: Critiques and Rebuttals. *Journal of Urban Design*, *7*(3), 261–291. doi:10.1080/1357480022000039330

Ellis, G. (2004). Discourses of objection: Towards an understanding of third-party rights in planning. *Environment & Planning*, *36*(9), 1549–1570. doi:10.1068/a36176

Entwistle, A. (1987). *Braj: Centre of Krishna Pilgrimage*. Groningen: Egbert Forsten Publishing.

EOI - PwC. (2014). Ciudades y ciudadanos en 2033. La transformación urbana de España. Madrid: Author.

European Commision. (2010b). *A European strategy for smart, sustainable and inclusive growth*. Brussels: EC.

European Commision. (2015a). *Economic Impact and Travel Patterns of Accesible Tourism in Europe - Final Report*. Brussels, Belgium: Directorate-General on Enterprise & Industry.

European Commission (2015b). *Estrategias nacionales y regionals para la especialización inteligente (RIS3)*. Bruselas: Directorate-General of Regional Policy.

European Commission. (2010a). Keeping Europe, the World's Top Touristic Destination. *COM*, *352*(3), 3.

European Commission. (2014). *Estrategias Nacionales y Regionales para la Especialización Inteligente*. Brussels, Belgium.

European Commission. (2014, March 05). *Press Release: Antitrust: Commission fines two power exchanges € 5.9 million in cartel settlement*. Retrieved June 30, 2015, from European Commission: http://europa.eu/rapid/press-release_IP-14-215_en.htm

European Innovation Partnership on Smart Cities and Communities. (2013). *Strategic Implementation Plan*. Brussels, Belgium: Author.

European Parliament. (2014). *Mapping Smart Cities in the EU*. Brussels, Belgium: Author.

Evans, G. (2015). *Cultural Mapping and Planning for Sustainable Communities* (W. G.-P. Nancy Duxbury, Ed.). New York: Routledge.

Farr, D. (2008). *Sustainable Urbanism: Urban Design with Nature*. Hoboken, N.J.: Wiley.

FICCI-Booz & Co. (2013). *Power Transmission The Real Bottleneck*. New Delhi: FICCI.

Fisher, B., Turner, R. K., & Morling, P. (2009). Defining and classifying ecosystem services for decision making. *Ecological Economics*, *68*(3), 643–653. doi:10.1016/j.ecolecon.2008.09.014

Fisher-Vanden, K. A., Wing, I., Lanzi, S., & Popp, D. (2013). Modeling climate change feedbacks and adaptation responses: recent approaches and shortcomings. *Climate Change*, *117*, 481–495.

Fisher-Vanden, K. A., Shukla, P. R., Edmonds, J. A., Kim, S. H., & Pitcher, H. M. (1997). Carbon taxes and India. *Energy Economics*, *19*(3), 289–325. doi:10.1016/S0140-9883(96)01020-1

Fisher-Vanden, K., Mansur, E. T., & Wang, Q. J. (2012). *Costly Blackouts? Measuring Productivity and Environmental Effects of Electricity Shortages. No. w17741*. National Bureau of Economic Research. doi:10.3386/w17741

Folinsbee, L. J., & Hazucha, M. J. (2000). Time course of response to ozone exposure in healthy adult females. *Inhalation Toxicology*, *12*(3), 151–167. doi:10.1080/089583700196211 PMID:10715622

Franzaring, J., Tonneijck, A. E. G., Kooijman, A. W. N., & Dueck, T. A. (2000). Growth responses to ozone in plant species from wetlands. *Environmental and Experimental Botany*, *44*(1), 39–48. doi:10.1016/S0098-8472(00)00052-6 PMID:10927127

Freeman, C. (Ed.). (1996). *Long Wave Theory*. Cheltenham, UK: The International Library of Critical Writings in Economics Series. Edward Elgar.

Gallardo, A., & Mardones, C. (2013). Environmentally extended social accounting matrix for Chile. *Environment, Development and Sustainability*, *15*(4), 1099–1127. doi:10.1007/s10668-012-9430-0

Garbaccio, R. F., Ho, M. S., & Jorgenson, D. W. (1998). *Controlling Carbon Emissions in China. Kennedy School of Government*. Harvard University.

Geda, A., & Yimer, A. (2013). *A Macroeconometric Model for Rwanda*. IAES Working Paper no 2. Retrieved from www.IAESAfrica.com

Geda, A., & Yimer, A. (2015). *A Macroeconometric Model for Ghana*. Retrieved from www.IAESAfrica.com

Geda, A. (2002). *Finance and Trade in Africa: Macroeconomic Response in the World Economy Context*. London, UK: Palgrave-McMillan. doi:10.1057/9780230502543

Geda, A. (2011). *Readings on Ethiopian Economy*. Addis Ababa: Addis Ababa University Press.

Geda, A., & Tafere, K. (2011). *The Galloping Inflation in Ethiopia: A Cautionary tale for Aspiring Developmental African Countrie*. Department of Economics, Addis Ababa University.

GHK International, UK. (2007). *City Development Plan: Haridwar Revised.* Jawaharlal Nehru National Urban Renewal Mission (JNNURM), Urban Development Department, Government of Uttarakhand. JNNURM.

Ghosh, R., & Kathuria, V. (2014). The transaction costs driving captive power generation: Evidence from India. *Energy Policy*, *75*, 179–188. doi:10.1016/j.enpol.2014.10.003

Ghosh, R., & Kathuria, V. (2015). Gas based power generation in India: Lessons from a transaction cost analysis. *Energy Strategy Reviews*, *8*, 1–7. doi:10.1016/j.esr.2015.06.001

Ghude, S. D., Jena, C., Chate, D. M., Beig, G., Pfister, G., Kumar, R., & Ramanathan, V. (2014). Reductions in India's crop yield due to ozone. *Geophysical Research Letters*, *41*(15), 5685–5691. doi:10.1002/2014GL060930

Giacalone, R. A., & Thompson, K. R. (2006). Business ethics and social responsibility education: Shifting the worldview. *Academy of Management Learning & Education*, *5*(3), 266–277. doi:10.5465/AMLE.2006.22697016

Gibbs, D. (2009). Sustainability entrepreneurs, ecopreneurs and the development of a sustainable economy. *Greener Management International*, *55*, 63–78.

Gimeno, B. S., Bermejo, V., Sanz, J., & de, . (2004b). Assessment of the effects of ozone exposure and plant competition on the reproductive ability of three therophytic clover species from Iberian pastures. *Atmospheric Environment*, *38*(15), 2295–2303. doi:10.1016/j.atmosenv.2003.10.062

Glaves, P., & Egan, D. (2013). Some Methods and Approached to Valuing Ecosystem Services. Academic Press.

Global Subsidies Initiative. (2012). *India's Fuel Subsidies: Q & A*. International Institute for Sustainable Development.

Global Subsidies Initiative. (2014a). *Subsidies to Liquefied Petroleum Gas in India: An Overview of Recent Reforms*. Author.

Global Subsidies Initiative. (2014b). *India Energy Subsidy Review: A biannual Survey of Energy Subsidy Policies*. Author.

Goldberg, M. S., Burnett, R. T., Bailar, J. C. III, Brook, J., Bonvalot, Y., & Tamblyn, R. (2001). Associations between daily cause-specific mortality and concentrations of ground-level ozone in Montreal, Quebec. *American Journal of Epidemiology*, *154*(9), 817–826. doi:10.1093/aje/154.9.817 PMID:11682364

Goldberg, V. P. (1976). Regulation and Administered Contracts. *The Bell Journal of Economics*, *7*(2), 426–448. doi:10.2307/3003265

Graham, R. M., Friedman, M., & Hoyle, G. W. (2001). Sensory nerves promote ozoneinduced lung inflammation in mice. *American Journal of Respiratory and Critical Care Medicine*, *164*(2), 307–313. doi:10.1164/ajrccm.164.2.2007115 PMID:11463606

Grievink, L., Jansen, S. M., Van't Veer, P., & Brunekreef, B. (1998). Acute effects of ozone on pulmonary function of cyclists receiving antioxidant supplements. *Occupational and Environmental Medicine*, *55*(1), 13–17. doi:10.1136/oem.55.1.13 PMID:9536157

Grossman, D. (2015). As Himalayan Glaciers Melt, Two Towns Face the Fallout. *Yale Environment 360.* Retrieved 08 June 2015 From: http://e360.yale.edu/feature/as_himalayan_glaciers_melt_two_towns_face_the_fallout/2858/

Grossman, P. Z., & Cole, D. H. (Eds.). (2003). *The End of a Natural Monopoly: Deregulation and Competition in the Electric Power Industry* (Vol. 7). Routledge.

Gryparis, A., Forsberg, B., Katsouyanni, K., Analitis, A., Touloumi, G., Schwartz, J., & Dörtbudak, Z. et al. (2004). Acute effects of ozone on mortality from "the air pollution and health: A European approach" project. *American Journal of Respiratory and Critical Care Medicine*, *170*(10), 1080–1087. doi:10.1164/rccm.200403-333OC PMID:15282198

Gupte, R., Mehrotra, R., & Shetty, P. (2010). archplus.net/home. Retrieved April 2014, from archplus.net: http://www.archplus.net/home/news/7,1-3904,1,0.html?referer=102

Gutschow, K. (1997). Lords of the Fort, Lords of the Earth, and no lords at all: politics of irrigation in three Tibetan societies. In *Recent Research on Ladakh: Proceedings of the 6th international colloquium on Ladakh.*

Gutschow, K., & Mankelow, S. (2001). Dry Winters, Dry Summers: Water Shortages in Zanskar. *Ladakh Studies, 15*, 28–32.

Hajela, R. (2012). *Shortage of Skilled Workers: A Paradox of the Indian Economy. Compas: SKOPE.* University of Oxford.

Halonen, J. I., Lanki, T., Tiittanen, P., Niemi, J. V., Loh, M., & Pekkanen, J. (2010). Ozone and cause-specific cardiorespiratory morbidity and mortality, Research report. *Journal of Epidemiology and Community Health, 64*(9), 814–820. doi:10.1136/jech.2009.087106 PMID:19854743

Hamby, D. M. (1994). A review of techniques for parameter sensitivity analysis ofenvironmental models. *Environmental Monitoring and Assessment, 32*(2), 135–154. doi:10.1007/BF00547132 PMID:24214086

Haque, U. (2012). Surely There's a Smarter Approach to Smart Cities?. *Wired.* Available at: http://www.wired.co.uk/news/archive/2012-04/17/potential-of-smartercities-beyond-ibm-and-cisco

Harakat, I. (2007). *Les acteurs de la coopération et la dimension socio-économique de la désertification dans le sud du Maroc: cas de Zagora. Mémoire de maitrise en science politique.* Université du Québec MONTREAL.

Hasna, J., & Huque, A. (2014). Experience from First Solar Mini-grid Service in Bangladesh; In *Proceedings of the International Conference Innovating Energy Access for Remote Areas: Discovering Untapped Resources* (pp. 42-46). Berlin: Universitätsverlag der TU Berlin

Hatirli, S. A., Ozkan, B., & Fert, C. (2006). Energy inputs and crop yield relationship in greenhouse tomato production. *Renewable Energy, 31*(4), 427–438. doi:10.1016/j.renene.2005.04.007

Hawkes, J. (2001). *The Fourth Pillar of Sustainability: Culture's essential role in public planning.* Victoria: Cultural Development Network Common Ground.

Hayes, F., Mills, G., & Ashmore, M. (2009). Effects of ozone on inter- and intra-species competition and photosynthesis in mesocosms of Lolium perenne and Trifolium repens. *Environmental Pollution, 157*(1), 208–214. doi:10.1016/j.envpol.2008.07.002 PMID:18774210

Hayes, F., Mills, G., Jones, M. L. M., & Ashmore, M. (2010). Does a simulated upland community respond to increasing background, peak or accumulated exposure of ozone? *Atmospheric Environment, 44*(34), 4155–4164. doi:10.1016/j.atmosenv.2010.07.037

Heagle, A. S. (1989). Ozone and crop yield. *Annual Review of Phytopathology, 27*(1), 397–423. doi:10.1146/annurev.py.27.090189.002145

Heagle, A. S., Miller, J. E., Booker, F. L., & Pursley, W. A. (1999). Ozone stress, carbon dioxide enrichment, and nitrogen fertility interactions in cotton. *Crop Science, 39*(3), 731–741. doi:10.2135/cropsci1999.0011183X003900030021x

Heal, G. (2000). *Nature and the Marketplace: Capturing the Value of Ecosystem Services.* Covelo, CA: Island Press.

Hector, A., & Bagchi, R. (2007). Biodiversity and ecosystem multifunctionality. *Nature*, 448. PMID:17625564

Heidecke. (2009). *Economic analysis of water use and management in the Middle Drâa valley in Morocco vorgelegt am 22.* Academic Press.

Helm, D. (2014). Taking natural capital seriously. *Oxford Review of Economic Policy, 30*(1), 109–125. doi:10.1093/oxrep/gru005

Higgins, A. K. (2012). *Artificial glaciers and ice-harvesting in Ladakh, India as an adaptation to a changing climate.* (Unpublished Master's Thesis). Yale School of Forestry, New Haven, CT.

Higgins, I. T., D'Arcy, J. B., Gibbons, D. I., Avol, E. L., & Gross, K. B. (1990). Effect of exposures to ambient ozone on ventilatory lung function in children. *The American Review of Respiratory Disease*, *141*(5_pt_1), 1136–1146. doi:10.1164/ajrccm/141.5_Pt_1.1136 PMID:2339836

Hiltermann, T. J. N., Stolk, J., van der Zee, S. C., Brunekreef, C. R., de Bruijne, P. H., & Fischer, C. B. (1998). Asthma severity and susceptibility to air pollution. *The European Respiratory Journal*, *11*, 686–693. PMID:9596122

Hoek, G., Schwartz, J. D., Groot, B., & Eilers, P. (1997). Effects of ambient particulate matter and ozone on daily mortality in Rotterdam, The Netherlands. *Archives of Environmental Health*, *52*(6), 455–463. doi:10.1080/00039899709602224 PMID:9541366

Hohne, N., den Elzen, M., & Weiss, M. (2006). Common but Differentiated Convergence (CDC): A New Conceptual Approach to Long Term Climate Policy. *Climate Policy*, *6*(2), 181–199. doi:10.1080/14693062.2006.9685594

Huizinga, F., & Geda, A. (2004). *The Theoretical Model of the Ethiopian Ministry of Finance and Economic Development Model.* MoFED Working Paper. Ministry of Finance and Economic Development, Government of Ethiopia.

Huizinga, F., Geda, A., Ndung'u, N. S., & Karingi, S. N. (2001). *Theoretical Base for the Kenya Macro Model: The KIPPRA-Treasury Macro Model.*KIPPRA Discussion Paper No. 11. KIPPRA. Retrieved from http://www.kippra.org

Humbert-Droz, B., & Dawa, S. (2004). *Biodiversity of Ladakh: Strategy and Action Plan.* Calcutta: ACB Publications.

Hussain, M. N., & Hussain, M. A. (2011). *Natural Resources of Jammu Kashmir and Ladakh.* Srinagar: Gulshan Books.

ICRA Research Services. (2014). *Power Sector: Limited tariff hikes so far by SERCs for FY 2014-15, coupled with rising subsidy dependence for the sector as a whole; Subsidy estimated at Rs. 720 billion for FY 2015.* New Delhi: ICRA Research Services.

IEA. (2011). *Energy for all: Financing access for the poor, Special early excerpt of the World Energy Outlook.* Paris: International Energy Agency.

IEA. (2011). *World Energy Outlook 2011.* Paris: IEA.

IMF. (2013). *Energy Subsidy Reform: Lessons and Implications.* Washington, DC: International Monetary Fund.

Indian Express Limited. (2014). *Job creation down 43.15% in Q3 as economy slows.* Retrieved from http://indianexpress.com/article/business/business-others/job-creation-down-43-15-in-q3-as-economy-slows/

Indian Power Sector.com. (2013, March 30). *Haryana government gives nod to discoms debt rejig.* Retrieved December 01, 2014, from Indian Power Sector.com: http://indianpowersector.com/home/2013/03/haryana-government-gives-nod-to-discoms-debt-rejig/#more-19450

Indiastat. (2012, March). *Socio-Economic Statistical Information about India - Power - State Electricity Boards.* Retrieved January 15, 2015, from Indiastat: http://www.indiastat.com/power/26/stats.aspx

International Energy Agency and the World Bank. (2014). *Sustainable Energy for All 2013-14: Global Tracking System Report.* Washington, DC: The World Bank.

IPCC. (2013). IPCC Fifth Assessment Report. *Climatic Change*, 2013.

Isely, E., Isely, P., Seedang, S., Mulder, K., Thompson, K., & Steinman, A. (2010). Addressing the information gaps associated with valuing green infrastructure in west Michigan: INtegrated Valuation of Ecosystem Services Tool (INVEST). *Journal of Great Lakes Research*, *36*(3), 448–457. doi:10.1016/j.jglr.2010.04.003

Ito, K., De Leon, S. F., & Lippmann, M. (2005). Associations between ozone and daily mortality: Analysis and meta-analysis. *Epidemiology (Cambridge, Mass.)*, *16*(4), 446–457. doi:10.1097/01.ede.0000165821.90114.7f PMID:15951662

Jacob, D. J. (2000). Heterogeneous chemistry and tropospheric ozone. *Atmospheric Environment*, *34*(12-14), 2131–2159. doi:10.1016/S1352-2310(99)00462-8

Jacoby, H., Reily, J., McFarland, J., & Paltsev, S. (2006). Technology and technical change in the MIT EPPA Model. *Energy Economics*, *28*(5-6), 610–631. doi:10.1016/j.eneco.2006.05.014

Jerrett, M., Burnett, R. T., Pope, C. A. III, Kasuhiko, I., Thurston, G., Krewski, D., & Thun, M. et al. (2009). Long-term ozone exposure and mortality. *The New England Journal of Medicine*, *360*(11), 1085–1095. doi:10.1056/NEJMoa0803894 PMID:19279340

Jian, X. (2000). An Environmentally Extended Social Accounting Matrix. *Environmental and Resource Economics*, *16*(4), 391–406. doi:10.1023/A:1008376618447

JNNURM. (2006). *JNNURM: A supplement to toolkit on formulation of City Development Plan - Focus on Heritage*. Ministry of Urban Development & Ministry of Housing and urban Poverty Alleviation, Government of India.

Johansson, D. J. A., Lucas, P. L., Weitzel, M., Ahlgren, E. O., Bazaz, A. B., Chen, W., …Wei, Y.M. (2012). *Multi-model analyses of the economic and energy implications for China and India in a post-Kyoto climate regime*. Working Paper 1808. Kiel, Germany: Kiel Institute for the World Economy.

Jones, M. (2010). Accounting for the environment: Towards a theoretical perspective for environmental accounting and reporting. *Accounting Forum*, *34*(2), 123–138. doi:10.1016/j.accfor.2010.03.001

Karmaoui, A., Messouli, M., Yacoubi, K.M., & Ifaadassan, I. (2014). Environmental Vulnerability to Climate Change and Anthropogenic Impacts in Dryland. *J Earth Sci Clim Change, S11*. doi:10.4172/2157-7617.S11-002

Kashyap, R., Mir, R., & Iyer, E. (2006). Toward a responsive pedagogy: Linking social responsibility to firm performance issues in the classroom. *Academy of Management Learning & Education*, *5*(March), 366–376. doi:10.5465/AMLE.2006.22697025

Kateja, A. (2012). Building Infrastructure: Private Participation in Emerging Economies. *Procedia: Social and Behavioral Sciences*, *37*, 368–378. doi:10.1016/j.sbspro.2012.03.302

Kelly, D. L., & Kolstad, C. (1999). Integrated Assessment Models For Climate Change Control. In International Yearbook of Environmental and Resource Economics 1999/2000: A Survey of Current Issues. Cheltenham, UK: Edward Elgar.

Kendrovski, V., Spasenovska, M., & Menne, B. (2014). The Public Health Impacts of Climate Change in the former Yugoslav Republic of Macedonia. *International Journal of Environmental Research and Public Health Open Access*, *11*, 5975–5988.

Kirchgeorg, M. (1999). Marktstrategisches kreislaufmanagement. Gabler, Germany: Wiesbaden. doi:10.1007/978-3-322-90758-5

Klein, B., Crawford, R. G., & Alchian, A. A. (1978). Vertical Integration, Appropriable Rents, and the Competitive Contracting Process. *The Journal of Law & Economics*, *21*(1), 297–326. doi:10.1086/466922

Klepper, G., Peterson, S., & Springer, K. (2003). *DART 97: A Description of the Multi-regional, Multi-sectoral Trade Model for the Analysis of Climate Policies.* Working Paper 1149. Kiel, Germany: Kiel Institute for the World Economy.

Koe, W.-L., Omar, R., & Majid, I. A. (2014). Factors associated with propensity for sustainable entrepreneurship. *Procedia: Social and Behavioral Sciences*, *130*, 65–74. doi:10.1016/j.sbspro.2014.04.009

Koe, W.-L., Omar, R., & Sa'ari, J. R. (2015). Factors influencing propensity to sustainable entrepreneurship of SMEs in Malaysia. *Procedia: Social and Behavioral Sciences*, *172*, 570–577. doi:10.1016/j.sbspro.2015.01.404

Kohn. (1975). Input Output Analysis and air pollution control. *Economic Analysis of Environmental Problem*, 259-274. Retrieved from: http://www.nber.org/chapters/c2837

Komiyama, H., & Takeuchi, K. (2006). Sustainability science: Building a new discipline. *Sustainability Science*, *1*(1), 1–6. doi:10.1007/s11625-006-0007-4

Komninos, N., Pallot, M., & Schaffers, H. (2012). Special Issue on Smart Cities and the Future Internet in Europe. *Journal Of The Knowledge Economy*, *4*(2), 119–134. doi:10.1007/s13132-012-0083-x

Koplow, D. (2009). Measuring Energy Subsidies Using the Price-Gap Approach: What does it leave out? Manitoba: International Institute for Sustainable Development (IISD).

Korrick, S. A., Neas, L. M., & Dockery, D. W. (2004). Ozone exposure decreases the effect of a deep inhalation on forced expiratory flow in normal subjects. *Journal of Applied Physiology*, *96*(5), 1651–1657. doi:10.1152/japplphysiol.00507.2003 PMID:14688031

Korrick, S. A., Neas, L. M., Dockery, D. W., Gold, D. R., Allen, G. A., Hill, L. B., & Speizer, F. E. et al. (1998). Effects of ozone and other pollutants on the pulmonary function of adult hikers. *Environmental Health Perspectives*, *106*(2), 93–99. doi:10.1289/ehp.9810693 PMID:9435151

Korytárová, J., & Hromádka, V. (2014). The Economic Evaluation of Megaprojects – Social and Economic Impacts. *Procedia: Social and Behavioral Sciences*, *119*, 495–502. doi:10.1016/j.sbspro.2014.03.055

Kramer, D. (2013). Smart cities will need big data. *Physics Today*, *66*(9), 19. doi:10.1063/PT.3.2110

Kuckertz, A., & Wagner, M. (2010). The influence of sustainability orientation on entrepreneurial intentions: Investigating the role of business experience. *Journal of Business Venturing*, *25*(5), 524–539. doi:10.1016/j.jbusvent.2009.09.001

Kulshrestha, S. K. (2007). Vrindavan Eco-city In Making: Working Together for Sustainable Development. *ISOCARP Congress 2007.* Retrieved from http://www.isocarp.net/Data/case_studies/1032.pdf

Kumar, V. R., & Sethi, M. (2014). Indian Power Utilities: A Panacea for Financial Revival. *Global Journal of Finance and Management*, *67*.

Kurz, H., & Salvadori, N. (1997). Exhaustible resources in a dynamic input–output model with 'classical' features. *Economic Systems Research*, *9*(3), 235–251. doi:10.1080/09535319700000017

Kwon, H.J., Cho, S.H, Nyberg, F., & Pershagen, G. (2001). Effects of ambient air pollution on daily mortality in a cohort of patients with congestive heart failure. *Epidemiology, 12*, 413–419.

Kylili, A., & Fokaides, P. (2015). European smart cities: The role of zero energy buildings. *Sustainable Cities and Society*, *15*, 86–95. doi:10.1016/j.scs.2014.12.003

Lee, K. S., Anas, A., Verma, S., & Murray, M. (1996). *Why Manufacturing Firms Produce Some Electricity Internally.* World Bank Policy Research Working Paper Series 1605.

Lee, D. S., Holland, M. R., & Falla, N. (1996, April). The potential impact of O3 on materials in the U.K. *Atmospheric Environment*, *30*(7), 1053–1065. doi:10.1016/1352-2310(95)00407-6

Leomann Maps (n.d.). *Indian Himalaya Maps, Sheet 3*. Author.

Levy, J. I., Chemerynski, S. M., & Sarnat, J. A. (2005). Ozone exposure and mortality: An empiric bayes metaregression analysis. *Epidemiology (Cambridge, Mass.)*, *16*(4), 458–468. doi:10.1097/01.ede.0000165820.08301.b3 PMID:15951663

Liang, Q. M., Fan, Y., & Wei, Y. M. (2007). Carbon Taxation Policy in China: How to Protect Energy and Trade Intensive Sectors? *Journal of Policy Modeling*, *29*(2), 311–333. doi:10.1016/j.jpolmod.2006.11.001

Limited, I. M. (2010). *The Skill Development Landscape in India and Implementing Quality Skills Training*. New Delhi: ICRA Management Consultancy Services Limited.

Lofgren, H., Harris, R. L., & Robinson, S. (2002) A Standard Computable General Equilibrium Model in GAMS (Microcomputers in Policy Research). Washington DC: International Food Policy Research Institute (IFPRI).

Lokare, S. M. (2014, February 7). *Publications - Re-emerging Stress in the Asset Quality of Indian Banks: Macro-Financial Linkages*. Retrieved October 24, 2014, from Reserve Bank of India: http://rbi.org.in/Scripts/PublicationsView.aspx?Id=15720

Loomis, D., Castillejos, M., Gold, D. R., McDonnell, W., Borja-Aburto, V. H., & O'Neill, M. S. (1999). Air pollution and infant mortality in Mexico City. *Epidemiology (Cambridge, Mass.)*, *10*(2), 118–123. doi:10.1097/00001648-199903000-00006 PMID:10069245

Lourenço, F., Jones, O., & Jayawarna, D. (2013). Promoting sustainable development: The role of entrepreneurship education. *International Small Business Journal*, *31*(8), 841-865.

Lumpkin, G. T., & Katz, J. A. (2011). An introduction to the special volume on social and sustainable entrepreneurship. In G. T. Lumpkin & J. A. Katz (Eds.), *Advances in Entrepreneurship, Firm Emergence and Growth*. Bradford, UK: Emerald. doi:10.1108/S1074-7540(2011)0000013004

Madheswaran, S. (2007). Measuring the Value of Statistical Life: Estimating Compensating Wage Differential among Workers in India. *Social Indicators Research*, *84*(1), 83–96. doi:10.1007/s11205-006-9076-0

Mahalingam, S. (1997, October 17). Unbundling trouble. *Frontline*.

Majid, I. A., & Koe, W.-L. (2012). Sustainable entrepreneurship: A revised model based on triple bottom line. *International Journal of Academic Research in Business and Social Sciences*, *2*(6), 293–310.

Malone, Elizabeth L. (2010). *Changing Glaciers and Hydrology in Asia: Addressing Vulnerabilities to Glacier Melt Impacts*. USAID Report November 2010.

Mann, R. S. (1986). *The Ladakhi: A Study in Ethnography and Change*. Delhi: Anthropological Survey of India.

Marcos, T. (2015). *Las normas para las ciudades inteligentes. Informe de situación*. Madrid, Spain: AENOR.

Market Place of the European Innovation Partnership on Smart Cities and Communities. (2015). Retrieved 11 May 2015, from https://eu-smartcities.eu/

Maroufi, A. (2008). Désertification et migration: un défi pour le développement durable au Maroc. Le cas de ZAGORA. Secrétaire Général du CMEPE / MAROC. *Sustainable Mediterranean*, *54*(4).

Masten, S. E., Meehan, J. W., & Snyder, E. A. (1991). The Costs of Organization. *Journal of Law Economics and Organization*, *7*(1), 1–25.

Masurel, E. (2007). Why SMEs invest in environmental measures: Sustainability evidence from small and medium-sized printing firms. *Business Strategy and the Environment*, *16*(3), 190–201. doi:10.1002/bse.478

McDonald, R., Weber, K., Padowski, J., Flörke, M., Schneider, C., Green, P., & Montgomery, M. et al. (2014). Water on an urban planet: Urbanization and the reach of urban water infrastructure. *Global Environmental Change*, *27*, 96–105. doi:10.1016/j.gloenvcha.2014.04.022

McDonough, W., & Braungart, M. (2002). *Cradle to cradle: Remaking the way we make things*. New York: North Point Press.

McEwen, T. (2013). Ecopreneurship as a solution to environmental problems: Implications for college level entrepreneurship education. *International Journal of Academic Research in Business and Social Science*, *3*(5), 264–288.

MEA. (2005). *Ecosystems and Human Well-being: General Synthesis*. Washington, DC: Island Press & World Resources Institute.

Mehrotra, R. (2008). Negotiating the Static and Kinetic Cities. In A. Huyssen (Ed.), *Other Cities, Other Worlds: Urban Imaginaries in a Globalizing Age* (pp. 205–218). Durham, NC: Duke University Press. doi:10.1215/9780822389361-009

Menon, A. K. (n.d.). *The complexity of Indian urbanism*. Retrieved March 2014, from http://www.india-seminar.com/2007/579/579_a_g_krishna_menon.htm

Menon, A. K. (1999). Imagining the Indian City. In V. Prakash (Ed.), *Theatres of decolonization: (architecture), agency, (urbansim): proceedings of the second "Other Connections" Conference*. Washington, DC: University of Washington.

Mercer, C. (2002). *Towards Cultural Citizenship: Tools for Cultural Policy and Development*. Hedemora: The Bank of Sweden Tercentenary Foundation & Gidlundds Forlag.

Meunier, D. (2012). Towards a Sustainable Development Approach in Transport Assessment. *Procedia: Social and Behavioral Sciences*, *48*, 3065–3077. doi:10.1016/j.sbspro.2012.06.1273

Meyer, R. (2012). Vertical Economies and the Costs of Separating Electricity Supply - A Review of Theoretical and Empirical Literature. *The Energy Journal (Cambridge, Mass.)*, *33*(4), 161–185. doi:10.5547/01956574.33.4.8

Millennium Ecosystem Assessment. (2003). *Ecosystems and Human Well-Being: A Framework For Assessment*. Washington, DC: Island Press.

Miller, M. H., & Spencer, J. E. (1977). The Static Economic Effects of the UK Joining the EEC: A General Equilibrium Approach. *The Review of Economic Studies*, *38*, 175–208.

Mills, G., Buse, A., Gimeno, B., Bermejo, V., Holland, M., Emberson, L., & Pleijel, H. (2007). A synthesis of AOT40-based response functions and critical levels of ozone for agricultural and horticultural crops. *Atmospheric Environment*, *41*(12), 2630–2643. doi:10.1016/j.atmosenv.2006.11.016

Mingle, J. (2009, November 29). When the Glacier Left. *Boston Globe*.

Mingle, J. (2015). *Fire and Ice: Soot, Solidarity and Survival on the Roof of the World*. New York: St. Martin's Press.

Ministry of Environment and Forests, Government of India. (2009). *India's GHG Emissions Profile: Results of Five Climate Modeling Studies*. Author.

Ministry of Environment and Forests. (2009). *India's GHG emissions Profile – Results of five modelling study*. Government of India. Retrieved from www.moef.nic.in

Ministry of External Affairs, Government of India. (2009). *The Road to Copenhagen: India's Position on Climate Change Issues*. Author.

Ministry of Finance. (2013). *Economic Survey of India - 2012-13*. New Delhi: Ministry of Finance, Govt. of India.

Ministry of Finance. (2014). Chapter 1 - The State of the Economy. In Economic Survey 2013–14 (p. 5). New Delhi: Author.

Ministry of Law and Justice. (n.d.). *Seventh Schedule*. Retrieved February 26, 2015, from Ministry of Law and Justice, Govt. of India: http://lawmin.nic.in/olwing/coi/coi-english/Const.Pock%202Pg.Rom8Fsss(35).pdf

Ministry of Petroleum & Natural Gas. (2014). *Indian Petroleum and Natural Gas Statistics - 2013-14*. New Delhi: Ministry of Petroleum & Natural Gas, Govt. of India.

Ministry of Power. (2005, February 12). *National Electricity Policy*. Retrieved December 03, 2014, from Ministry of Power: http://www.powermin.nic.in/whats_new/national_electricity_policy.htm

Ministry of Power. (2006). *Tariff Policy*. New Delhi: Ministry of Power, Govt. of India.

Ministry of Power. (2012). *Report of The Working Group on Power for Twelfth Plan (2012-17)*. New Delhi: Ministry of Power, Govt. of India.

Ministry of Power. (2013a). *Guidelines of Transitional Finance Mechanism under the Financial Restructuring Scheme for State Owned Discoms*. New Delhi: Ministry of Power, Govt. of India.

Ministry of Power. (2013b). *Model State Electricity Distribution Management Responsibility Bill, 2013*. New Delhi: Ministry of Power. Govt. of India.

Ministry of Power. (n.d.). *About Ministry - Responsibilities*. Retrieved June 22, 2015, from Ministry of Power, Govt. of India: http://powermin.nic.in/responsibilities

Ministry of Urban Development, Government of India. (2015). *Heritage City Development and Augmentation Yojana. Government of India, Ministry of Urban Development*. New Delhi: National Institute of Urban Affairs.

Mishra, A., & Sarangi, G. (2011). *Off-grid energy development in India: An approach towards sustainability*. Retrieved March 28, 2015, from http://www.dmu.ac.uk/documents/technology-documents/research-faculties/oasys/project-outputs/working-papers/wp12--off-grid-approach-paper.pdf

Mitchell, R., & Carson, R. (1986). *The Use of Contingent Valuation Data for Benefit-Cost Analysis in Water Pollution Control*. Washington, DC: EPA.

MNRE. (2014). *Supplementary guidelines for implementation of "Solar Pumping Programme for Irrigation and Drinking Water under Off Grid and Decentralised Solar applications scheme*. New Delhi: Ministry of New and Renewable Energy.

Mobtaker, H. G., Akram, A., & Keyhani, A. (2010). Economic modeling and sensitivity analysis of the costs of inputs for alfalfa production In Iran: A case study from Hamedan province. *Ozean Journal of Applied Sciences*, *3*, 313319.

Montuschi, P., Ragazzoni, E., & Valente, S. (2002). Ozone-induced increase in exhaled 8-isoprostane in healthy subjects is resistant to inhaled budesonide. *Free Radical Biology & Medicine*, *33*(10), 1403–1408. doi:10.1016/S0891-5849(02)01084-5 PMID:12419472

Moolgavkar, S. H., Luebeck, E. G., Hall, T. A., & Anderson, E. L. (1995). Air pollution and daily mortality in Philadelphia. *Epidemiology (Cambridge, Mass.)*, *6*(5), 476–484. doi:10.1097/00001648-199509000-00003 PMID:8562622

Mostafavi, M. (2010). Why Ecological Urbanism? Why now? In M. Mostafavi & G. Doherty (Eds.), *The Ecological Urbanism* (pp. 12–51). Baden, Switzerland: Lars Muller Publisher.

MPZ. (2011). *Monographie de la province de Zagora*. Royaume du Maroc Ministère de l'intérieur Province De Zagora.

Murthy, M. N., Panda, M., & Parikh, K. (2007). CO2 emission reduction strategies and economic development in India. *Margin: The Journal of Applied Economic Research*, *1*(1), 85–119.

MVDA. (2009). *Mathura Vrindavan Punarikshit Mahayojana 2021 - Part A (Master Plan Report). In Agra Regional Planning Division, Mathura Vrindavan Development Authority*. MVDA.

Nadarajah, M. (2007). Common themes and differences: Approaches to culture in sustainability of Cities. In M. Nadarajah, & A. T. Yamamoto (Eds.), Urban Crisis: Culture and the Sustainability of Cities (pp. 107-132). Paris: United Nations University Press.

Nadarajah, M. (2007). *Conclusion*. United Ntions University Press.

Nam, T., & Pardo, T. A. (2011). Conceptualizing Smart City With Dimensions of Technology, People, and Institutions. In *Proceedings of the 12th Annual International Digital Government Research Conference: Digital Government Innovation in Challenging Times*. ACM. Available at: http://smartcitiescouncil.com/system/files/resources/Conceptualizing%20 smart%20city .pdf

NATCOM- Indian Network on Climate Change Assessment. (2010). *Greenhouse Gas Emission 2007*. India: Ministry of Environment and Forests, Government of India.

Nevers, N. D. (2000). *Air Pollution Control Engineering* (2nd ed.). New York: McGraw-Hill Companies, Inc.

Nooteboom, B. (1993). An Analysis of Specificity in Transaction Cost Economics. *Organization Studies*, *14*(3), 443–451. doi:10.1177/017084069301400306

Norberg-Hodge, H. (2000). *Ancient Futures: Learning from Ladakh*. London: Rider Books.

Nordhaus, W. D., & Zili, Y. (1996, February). A Regional Dynamic General-Equilibrium Model of Alternative Climate-Change Strategies. *American Economic Review*.

Nordhaus, W. D. (1991). To Slow or Not to Slow: The Economics of the Greenhouse Effect. *The Economic Journal*, *101*(407), 920–937. doi:10.2307/2233864

Norphel, C. (2012). *Artificial Glacier: A High Altitude Cold Desert Water Conservation Technique*. Presented at the In Defense of Liberty Conference, New Delhi, India.

Nurse, K. (2006). Culture as the fourth pillar of sustainable development. *Small States: Economic Review and Basic Statistics*, *11*, 28–40.

Nurse, K. (2006). *Culture as the Fourth Pillar of Sustainble Development*. Institute of International Relations.

O'Neill, M. S., Loomis, D., & Borja-Aburto, V. H. (2004). Ozone, area social conditions, and mortality in Mexico City. *Environmental Research*, *94*(3), 234–242. doi:10.1016/j.envres.2003.07.002 PMID:15016589

OECD. (2002). *Impact of Transport Infrastructure Investment on Regional Development*. Paris: OECD.

Ojha, V. P., Pal, B. D., Pohit, S., & Roy, J. (2009). *Social Accounting Matrix for India*. Retrieved from ssrn.com/abstract=1457628

Ojha, V. P. (2009). Carbon emissions reduction strategies and poverty alleviation in India. *Environment and Development Economics*, *14*(3), 323–348. doi:10.1017/S1355770X0800497X

Orecchini, F. (2011). Energy sustainability pillars. *International Journal of Hydrogen Energy*, *36*(13), 7748–7749. doi:10.1016/j.ijhydene.2011.02.022

Orecchini, F., Santiangeli, A., & Valitutti, V. (2011). Sustainability science: Sustainable energy for mobility and its use in policy making. *Sustainability*, *3*(10), 1855–1865. doi:10.3390/su3101855

Organization for Economic Cooperation and Development (OECD). (2010). *Costs and Effectiveness of the Copenhagen Pledges: Assessing Global Greenhouse Gas Emissions Targets and Actions for 2020*. Author.

Organization, I. L. (2010). *Green jobs creation through sustainable refurbishment in the developing countries*. Geneva: ILO.

Organization, I. L. (2010). *MGNREGA: A review of decent work and green jobs in Kaimur District in Bihar*. New Delhi: International Labour Organization.

ORMVAO. (2012). *Bilans des activités de 2013 de l'office régional de mise en valeur agricole de Ouarzazate*. Author.

Ortega, S. T., Hanley, N., & Simal, P. D. (2014). A Proposed Methodology for Prioritizing Project Effects to Include in Cost-Benefit Analysis Using Resilience. *Vulnerability and Risk Perception, Sustainability*, *6*, 7945-7966.

PACC. (2011). *Oasis et Zones Arides Résilientes Territoires Engagés*. Retrieved from www.oasisadaptation.com

Pal & Pohit. (2014). Environmentally Extended Social Accounting Matrix For Climate Change Policy Analysis for India. *Journal of Regional Development and Planning*, *3*(1), 61–75.

Pal, B. D., Ojha, V. P., Pohit, S., & Roy, J. (2014). GHG emission and Economic Growth. Springer.

Palanisami, K., Paramasivam, P., Ranganathan, C. R., Aggarwal, P. K., & Senthilnathan, S. (2009). *Quantifying vulnerability and impact of climate change on production of major crops in Tamil Nadu, India.*In M. Taniguchi, W. C. Burnett, Y. Fukushima, M. Haigh, & Yu. Umezawa (Eds.), *Headwaters to the Ocean – Hydrological Change and Watershed Management* (pp. 509–551). London: Taylor and Francis Group.

Palit, D., Bhattacharyya, S. C., & Chaurey, A. (2014). Indian Approaches to Energy Access. In A.Halff, B. K. Sovacool, & J. Rozhon (Eds.), Energy Poverty: Global Challenges and Local Solutions. Oxford University Press. doi:10.1093/acprof:oso/9780199682362.003.0012

Palit, D., & Chaurey, A. (2011). Off-grid rural electrification experiences from South Asia: Status and best practices. *Energy for Sustainable Development*, *15*(3), 266–276. doi:10.1016/j.esd.2011.07.004

Palit, D., Malhotra, R., & Kumar, A. (2011). Sustainable model for financial viability of decentralized biomass gasifier based power projects. *Energy Policy*, *39*(9), 4893–490. doi:10.1016/j.enpol.2011.06.026

Palit, D., Sarangi, G. K., & Krithika, P. R. (2014). Energising Rural India Using Distributed Generation: The Case of Solar Mini-Grids in Chhattisgarh State, India. In S. Bhattacharyya & D. Palit (Eds.), *Mini-Grids for Rural Electrification of Developing Countries* (pp. 313–342). Springer International Publishing Switzerland; doi:10.1007/978-3-319-04816-1_12

Paltsev, S., Reilly, J. M., Jacoby, H. D., Eckaus, R. S., McFarland, J., Sarofim, M., . . . Babiker, M. (2005). *The MIT Emissions Prediction and Policy Analysis (EPPA) Model: Version 4* (Report No. 125). Cambridge, MA: Massachusetts Institute of Technology.

Parr, S. F. (2000). *In search of Indicators of culture and development: progress and proposals*. France: UNESCO.

Parry, I. W. H., Williams, R. C. III, & Goulder, L. H. (1999). When can Carbon Abatement Policies increase Welfare? *The Fundamental Role of Distorted Factor Markets*, *37*, 52–84.

Parry, I., Heine, D., Lis, E., & Li, S. (2014). *Getting energy prices Right, From principle to practice*. IMF.

Pascual, O., van Klink, A., & Grisales, A. R. (2011). *Create impact! Handbook for sustainable entrepreneurship.* Retrieved March 20, 2015, from http://www.scp-centre.org/fileadmin/ content/files/6_Resources/1_Publications_pdfs/60_Creating_impact_full.pdf

Pati, D. R., & Tewari, D. D. (2009). *Conservation of Medicinal Plants.* Delhi: APH Publishing.

Patzelt, H., & Shepherd, D. A. (2011). Recognizing opportunities for sustainable development. *Entrepreneurship Theory and Practice, 35*(4), 631–652. doi:10.1111/j.1540-6520.2010.00386.x

PBL Netherlands Environmental Assessment Agency. (2012). Trends in global CO2emissions: 2012 Report. The Hague: Author.

PBL Netherlands Envorinmental Assessment Agency. (2005). *Framework to assess international regimes for differentiation of commitments (FAIR).* Retrieved from http://www.pbl.nl/en/publications/2005/

Penttinen, P., Tiittanen, P., & Pekkanen, J. (2004). Mortality and air pollution in metropolitan Helsinki, 1988–996. *Scandinavian Journal of Work, Environment & Health, 30*(Suppl. 2), 19–27. PMID:15487682

Perrings, C. (2010). *Biodiversity, Ecosystem Services, and Climate Change. The Economic Problem. Environmental Economics Series.* The International Bank for Reconstruction and Development.

PFC. (2013). *Report on The Performance of State Power Utilities for the years 2009-10 to 2011-12.* New Delhi: Power Finance Corporation Ltd.

PFC. (2015). *Report on The Performance of State Power Utilities for the years 2010-11 to 2012-13.* New Delhi: Power Finance Corporation Ltd.

PFC. (n.d.). *R-APDRP.* Retrieved June 23, 2015, from Power Finance Corporation Limited: http://www.pfcindia.com/Content/R_APDRP.aspx

Pindyck, R. S. (2013). Climate Change Policy: What Do the Models Tell Us? *Journal of Economic Literature, 51*(3), 860–872. doi:10.1257/jel.51.3.860

Planning Commission, Government of India. (2011). *Low carbon strategies for inclusive growth – An interim report, May 2011.* Author.

Planning Commission. (2011). *Annual Report on The Working of State Power Utilities & Electricity Departments – 2011-12.* New Delhi: Planning Commission.

Planning Commission. (2011). *Faster Sustainable and More Inclusive Growth, Approach towards 12th five year Plan.* Government of India.

Planning Commission. (2014). *Annual Report (2013-14) on The Working of State Power Utilities & Electricity Departments.* New Delhi: Planning Commission.

Pollitt, H., Summerton, P., & Billington, S. (2014). *The economics of climate change policy in the UK: An analysis of the impact of low-carbon policies on households, businesses and the macro-economy.* Cambridge, UK: Cambridge Econometrics, Covent Garden.

Pommerehne, W., Hart, A., & Schneider, F. (1997). Tragic choices and collective decision making: An empirical study of voter preferences for alternative collective decision-making mechanisms. *The Economic Journal, 107*(422), 618–635. doi:10.1111/j.1468-0297.1997.tb00030.x

Pradhan, B. K., & Ghosh, J. (2012). *The impact of carbon taxes on growth, emissions and welfare in India.* Working Paper No. 315. Institute of Economic Growth (IEG).

Pradhan, B. K., Saluja, & Singh, S.K. (2006). A Social Accounting Matrix for India, Concepts, construction and Applications. Sage Publication.

Pradhan, B. K., Saluja, M. R., & Singh, S. K. (2006). *Social Accounting Matrix for India: Concepts, Construction and Applications*. New Delhi: Sage Publications.

Press Information Bureau. (2014, December 19). *Electricity Amendment Bill, 2014 Introduced in Lok Sabha; Changes Aimed at Promoting Competition, Efficiency in Operations and Improvement in Quality of Supply of Electricity*. Retrieved June 30, 2015, from Press Information Bureau, Govt. of India: http://pib.nic.in/newsite/PrintRelease.aspx?relid=113779

Priest, G. L. (1993). The Origins of Utility Regulation and the "Theories of Regulation" Debate. *The Journal of Law & Economics*, *36*(1), 289–323. doi:10.1086/467276

Prime Minister's Office. (2014, November 20). *Deendayal Upadhyaya Gram Jyoti Yojana*. Retrieved December 30, 2014, from pmindia: http://pmindia.gov.in/en/news_updates/15461-2/

Pudasainee, D., Sapkota, B., Shrestha, M. L., Kaga, A., Kondo, A., & Inoue, Y. (2006). Short communication Ground level O3 concentrations and its association with NOx and meteorological parameters in Kathmandu valley, Nepal. *Atmospheric Environment*, *40*, 8081–8087. doi:10.1016/j.atmosenv.2006.07.011

Pulselli, F. M., & Pelliciardi, V. (2014). Emergy Evaluation of a Mountain Socio-Economic System and Traditional Agroproduction: A Case Study in Indian Trans-Himalaya. *European Journal of Sustainable Development*, 347-356.

Rafiee, S., Mousavi Avval, S. H., & Mohammadi, A. (2010). Modeling and sensitivity analysis of energy inputs for apple production in Iran. *Energy*, *35*(8), 3301–3306. doi:10.1016/j.energy.2010.04.015

Ramanathan, K., & Hasan, S. (2003). *Privatization of electricity distribution: the Orissa experience*. New Delhi: TERI.

Ramji, A., Soni, A., Sehjpal, R., Das, S., & Singh, R. (2012). *Rural energy access and inequalities: An analysis of National Sample Survey (NSS) data from 1999-00 to 2009-10*. The Energy and Resources Institute (TERI)-Norwegian Framework Agreement (NFA) Working Paper Series No. (4).

Rämö, K., Kanerva, T., Ojanperä, K., & Manninen, S. (2007). Growth onset, senescence, andreproductive development of meadow species in mesocosms exposed to elevated O3 and CO2. *Environmental Pollution*, *145*(3), 850–860. doi:10.1016/j.envpol.2006.03.054 PMID:16815612

Rana, R. S., & Piracha, A. L. (2007). Cultural Frameworks. In M. Nadarajah & A. T. Yamamoto (Eds.), *Urban Crisis: Culture and the Sustainability of Cities* (pp. 33–36). Hong Kong: United Nations Univerity Pres.

RBI. (2014). *State Finances - A Study of Budgets of 2013-14*. Mumbai: Reserve Bank of India.

RBI. (n.d.). *State Finances: A Study of Budgets*. Retrieved August 1st, 2014, from Reserve Bank of India: http://www.rbi.org.in/scripts/AnnualPublications.aspx?head=State+Finances+%3A+A+Study+of+Budgets

Register, R. (1987). *Eco-city Berkeley: Building Cities for a Healthy Future*. Berkeley, CA: Berkeley Hills Books.

Republic of Rwanda, Ministry of Finance and Economic Planning. (2012). *Consolidated Annexes to the 2012/13-2014/15 Budget Framework Paper*. Author.

RGCC. (2011). *Census of India – 2011*. New Delhi: Registrar General and Census Commissioner, Govt. of India.

Richardson, J., Irwin, T., & Sherwin, C. (2005). *Design and Sustainability: A Scoping Report for the Sustainable Design Forum*. London: Design Council.

Rizvi, J. (1998). *Ladakh: crossroads of high Asia*. Delhi: Oxford University Press.

Robbins, L. (1932). *An Essay on the Nature and Significance of Economic Science*. London: Macmillan.

Robert, K. (1975). Input Output Analysis and air pollution control. Economic Analysis of Environmental Problem. Retrieved from http://www.nber.org/chapters/c2837

Roders, A. P. (2013). How can Urbanization be Sustainable? A reflection on the role of city resources in Global Sustainable Development. *BDC, 13*(1), 79-91.

Rose, K., & McDonald, J. F. (1991). Economics of Electricity Self-generation by Industrial Firms. *The Energy Journal (Cambridge, Mass.)*, *12*(2), 47–66. doi:10.5547/ISSN0195-6574-EJ-Vol12-No2-4

Roson, R., & Van der Mensbrugghe, D. (2012). Climate change and economic growth: Impacts and interactions. *International Journal of Sustainable Economy*, *4*(3), 270–285. doi:10.1504/IJSE.2012.047933

Roy, A. (2009). Why India Cannot Plan Its Cities: Informality, Insurgence and the Idiom of Urbanization. *Planning Theory*, *8*(76), 76–87. doi:10.1177/1473095208099299

Rozema, J., & Bond, A. (in press). Framing effectiveness in impact assessment: Discourse accommodation in controversial infrastructure development. *Environmental Impact Assessment Review*.

RTI International. (2008). EMPAX-CGE Model Documentation (Interim Report). Research Triangle Park, NC: Author.

Sáez, M., Tobias, A., Antó, J. M., Spix, C., de Leon, A. P., Tobias, A., & Bacharova, L. et al. (2002). A combined analysis of the short-term effects of photochemical air pollutants on mortality within the EMECAM project. *Environmental Health Perspectives*, *110*(3), 221–228. doi:10.1289/ehp.02110221 PMID:11882471

Sagwal, S. (1991). *Ladakh Ecology and Environment*. New Delhi: Ashish Publishing House.

Saini, S. S. (2011, August). *Mitigation Initiatives through Agriculture Demand Side Management*. Kanpur, India: Bureau of Energy Efficiency.

Samet, J. M., Hatch, G. E., Horstman, D., Steck-Scott, S., Arab, L., Bromberg, P. A., & Devlin, R. B. et al. (2001). Effect of antioxidant supplementation on ozone-induced lung injury in human subjects. *American Journal of Respiratory and Critical Care Medicine*, *164*(5), 819–825. doi:10.1164/ajrccm.164.5.2008003 PMID:11549539

Santiago, A. (2013). On the road to sustainability entrepreneurship: Filipino case. *World Journal of Entrepreneurship. Management and Sustainable Development*, *9*(4), 255–271.

Sarangapani, R., Gentry, P. R., Covington, T. R., Teeguarden, J. G., & Clewell, H. J. III. (2003). Evaluation of the potential impact of age- and genderspecific lung morphology and ventilation rate on the dosimetry of vapors. *Inhalation Toxicology*, *15*(10), 987–1016. doi:10.1080/08958370390226350 PMID:12928976

Sarangi, G., Palit, D., & Mishra, A. (2012). Joining the dots: Regulating off-grid renewable energy sector in India. Mumbai: IGIDR.

Sarangi, G., Pugazenthi, D., Mishra, A., Palit, D., Kishore, V., & Bhattacharyya, S. (2014). Poverty amidst plenty: Renewable-energy based mini-grid electrification in Nepal. In S. Bhattachrya & D. Palit (Eds.), *Mini-grids for rural electrification of developing countries* (pp. 343–371). London: Springer. doi:10.1007/978-3-319-04816-1_13

Sarasvathy, S. D., Dew, N., Velamuri, S. R., & Venkataraman, S. (2003). Three views of entrepreneurial opportunity. In Z. Acs & D. B. Audretsch (Eds.), *Handbook of Entrepreneurial Research* (pp. 141–160). Great Britain: Kluwer Academic Publishers.

Saravanakumar, V. (2015). *Impact of Climate Change on Yield of Major Food Crops in Tamil Nadu, India*. SANDEE Working Paper No. 91–15. South Asian Network for Development and Environmental Economics.

Sawut, M., Eziz, M., & Tiyip, T. (2013). The effects of land-use change on ecosystem service value of desert oasis: A case study in Ugan-Kuqa River Delta Oasis, China. *Canadian Journal of Soil Science*, *93*(1), 99–108. doi:10.4141/cjss2012-010

Schaffers, H., Komninos, N., Pallot, M., Trousse, B., Nilsson, M., & Oliveira, A. (2011). Smart Cities and the Future Internet: Towards Cooperation Frameworks for Open Innovation, Future Internet Assembly. *LNCS, 6656*.

Schäffler, A., & Swilling, M. (2013). Valuing green infrastructure in an urban environment under pressure — The Johannesburg case. *Ecological Economics*, *86*, 246–257. doi:10.1016/j.ecolecon.2012.05.008

Schaper, M. (2002). The challenge of environmental responsibility and sustainable development: Implications for SME and entrepreneurship academics. In U. Fuglistaller, H.J. Pleitner, T. Volery, & W. Weber (Eds.), *Radical Change in the World – Will SMEs Soar or Crash?* (pp. 525-534). St Gallen: KMU Verlag HSG. Retrieved March 20, 2015, from www.kmu.unisg.ch/rencontres/band2002/ F_09_Schaper.pdf

Schick, H., Marxen, S., & Freimann, J. (2002). Sustainability issues for start-up entrepreneurs. *Greener Management International*, *38*(Summer), 59–70.

Schlange, L. E. (2006). *What drives sustainable entrepreneurs*? Paper presented at the Applied Business and Entrepreneurship Association International Conference, Kona, HI.

Schumpeter, J. (1934). *The theory of economic development*. Berlin: Beck Editions.

Schwartz, J., Gryparis, A., Forsberg, B., Katsouyanni, K., Analitis, A., & Touloumi, G. (2005). How sensitive is the association between ozone and daily deaths to control for temperature? *American Journal of Respiratory and Critical Care Medicine*, *171*(6), 627–631. doi:10.1164/rccm.200407-933OC PMID:15579726

SCID (Système de circulation de l'information sur la désertification au Maroc). (2007). Haut Commissariat des Eaux et Forêts et la Lutte contre la Désertification. Fiche de projet de protection des oasis du sud. Author.

Scott, J. (1998). *Seeing Like A State: How Certain Schemes to Improve the Human Condition Have Failed*. New Haven, CT: Yale University Press.

Sen, A. (1990). Development as capacity expansion. In K. Griffin & J. Knight (Eds.), *Human Development and the international development strategy for the 1990's* (pp. 41–58). London: Macmillan.

Sen, A. (1998). Culture, freedom and independence. In *World Culture Report 1998: culture, creativity and markets* (pp. 317–321). UNESCO.

Shane, S. (2003). *A general theory of entrepreneurship. The individual-opportunity nexus*. Cheltenham: Edward Elgar. doi:10.4337/9781781007990

Shanmugan, K. R. (1997). The Value of Life: Estimates from Indian Labour Market. *The Indian Economic Journal*, *44*(4), 105–114.

Sharma, S. & Khare, M., (2016a). *Ozone precursor inventories and simulation in NCR*. Unpublished.

Sharma, K., & Palit, D. (2014). Creating enabling environment for affordable delivery of sustainable electricity services. *Asia Pacific Tech Monitor*, *31*(3), 23–28.

Sharma, S., Chatani, S., Mahtta, R., Goel, A., & Kumar, A. (2016b). Sensitivity analysis of ground level ozone in India using WRF-CMAQ Models. *Atmospheric Environment*, *131*, 29–40.

Shinde, K. (2012). Policy, planning, and management for religious tourism in Indian pilgrimage sites. *Journal of Policy Research in Tourism, Leisure and Events*, *4*(3), 289–291. doi:10.1080/19407963.2012.726107

Shinde, K. A. (2012). Place-making and environmental change in a Hindu pilgrimage site in India. *Geoforum*, *43*(1), 116–127. doi:10.1016/j.geoforum.2011.07.014

Shoven, J. B. (1976). The Incidence and Efficiency Effects of Taxes on Income from Capital. *Journal of Political Economy*, *84*(6), 1261–1283. doi:10.1086/260511

Shoven, J. B., & Whalley, J. (1972). A General Equilibrium Calculation of the Effects of Differential Taxation of Income from Capital in the US. *Journal of Public Economics*, *1*(3-4), 281–321. doi:10.1016/0047-2727(72)90009-6

Sillman, S. (2003). Tropospheric ozone and photochemical smog. In B. Sherwood Lollar (Ed.), Treatise on Geochemistry (Vol. 9). Elsevier.

Simon, N., Cropper, M., Alberini, A., & Arora, A. (1999). *Valuing Mortality Reductions in India: A Study Compensating Wage Differentials*. The World Bank Policy Paper.

Simpson, R. W., Williams, G., Petroeschevsky, A., Morgan, G., & Rutherford, S. (1997). Associations between outdoor air pollution and daily mortality in Brisbane, Australia. *Archives of Environmental Health*, *52*(6), 442–454. doi:10.1080/00039899709602223 PMID:9541365

Singhal, S., McGreal, S., & Berry, J. (2013). An evaluative model for city competitiveness: Application to UK cities. *Land Use Policy*, *30*(1), 214–222. doi:10.1016/j.landusepol.2012.03.018

Singh, R. P. (2013). Green Pilgrimage Initiatives. In *Hindu Tradition of Pilgrimage: Sacred Space and System* (pp. 333–368). New Delhi: Dev Publishers and Distributors.

Slater, D. J., & Dixon-Fowler, H. R. (2010). The future of the planet in the hands of MBAs: An examination of CEO MBA education and corporate environmental performance. *Academy of Management Learning & Education*, *9*(3), 429–441. doi:10.5465/AMLE.2010.53791825

Snary, C. (2004). Understanding risk: The planning officers' perspective. *Urban Studies (Edinburgh, Scotland)*, *41*(41(1)), 33–55. doi:10.1080/0042098032000155678

Snow Leopard Conservancy. (2010). *Ri Gyancha: a Biodiversity Resource Kit for Educators in Ladakh*. Delhi: Kalpavriksh.

Soini, K. (2013, November). *Culture challenging and contributing to Sustainable Development*. COST IS 1007. Retrieved from http://www.culturalsustainability.eu/Soini_14112013.pdf

Spanish Ministry of Economy and Public Administration. (2014). Madrid, Spain: Acuerdo de Asociación de España.

Spanish Ministry of Industry, Energy, and Tourism. (2014). *Agenda para el fortalecimiento del sector industrial en España. Propuestas de actuación*. Madrid: Spanish Ministry of Industry, Energy, and Tourism.

Spanish Ministry of Industry, Energy, and Tourism. (2015). *Ciudades Inteligentes. Agenda Digital para España*. Madrid: Spanish Ministry of Industry, Energy, and Tourism.

Spanjer, A. R. (2009). Regulatory Intervention on the Dynamic European Gas Market– Neoclassical Economics or Transaction Cost Economics? *Energy Policy*, *37*(8), 3250–3258. doi:10.1016/j.enpol.2009.04.021

Spiller, P. (2010). *Transaction Cost Regulation*. Working paper 16735. National Bureau of Economic Research. Retrieved from http://www.nber.org/papers/w16735

Spiller, P., & Tommasi, M. (2005). The Institutions of Regulation: An Application to Public Utilities. In C. Menard & M. M. Shirley (Eds.), *Handbook of New Institutional Economics* (pp. 515–543). Springer.

Spirn, A. W. (2012). *Ecological Urbanism: A framework for the design of Reilient Cities*. Retrieved from www.annewhistonspirn.com/pdf/spirn_ecological_urbanism-2011.pdf

Springett, D. (2005). Education for sustainability in the business studies curriculum: A call for a critical agenda. *Business Strategy and the Environment*, *14*(3), 146–159. doi:10.1002/bse.447

Srivastava, L., Goswami, A., Chaudhury, S., & Diljun, G. (2012). Energy access: Revelations from energy consumption patterns in rural India. *Energy Policy*, *1*(47), 11–20. doi:10.1016/j.enpol.2012.03.030

Stavins, R. N. (2000). Market based Environmental Policies. In P. R. Portney & R. N. Stavins (Eds.), *Public Policies for Environmental Protection*. Washington, DC: Resources for the Future.

Stokes, D., Wilson, N., & Mador, M. (2010). *Entrepreneurship*. Hampshire, UK: South-Western Cengage Learning.

Sudhalkar, A. (2010). *Adaptation to Water Scarcity in Glacier-Dependent Towns of the Indian Himalayas: Impacts, Adaptive Responses, Barriers, and Solutions*. (Unpublished master's thesis). Massachusetts Institute of Technology, Cambridge, MA.

Sue Wing, I., & Lanzi, E. (2014). *Integrated Assessment of Climate Change Impacts: Conceptual Frameworks, Modelling Approaches and Research Needs*. OECD Environment Working Papers No. 66. OECD Publishing.

Sue Wing, I., & Fisher-Vanden, K. (2012). Confronting the Challenge of Integrated Assessment of Climate Adaptation: A Conceptual Framework. *Climatic Change*, *117*(3), 497–514. doi:10.1007/s10584-012-0651-x

Sundaram, R. (2010). *Externailities, Urbanism and Pirate Modernities: India*. Rising Powers Working Paper. E.S.R.C (Economic and Social Research Council.

SustainAbility. (2008). *The social intrapreneur: A field guide for corporate change makers*. Washington, DC: SustainAbility Ltd. Retrieved June 29, 2015, from http://www.echoinggreen.org/sites/default/files/ The_Social_ Intrapreneurs.pdf

Suzuki, H., Dastur, A., & Moffat, S. (2010). *Eco2 Cities: Ecological Cities as Economic Cities*. Washington, DC: The World Bank. doi:10.1596/978-0-8213-8046-8

SWWEP. (2010). *Profil du pays sur la situation de la gestion des déchets solides au Maroc*. Retrieved from www.SWEEP-NET.ORG.http://www.sweep-net.org/ckfinder/userfiles/files/country-profiles/country%20profile%20Maroc%20fr.pdf

Talen, E. (2013). *Charter of the New Urbanism* (2nd ed.). New York: McGraw-Hill Education.

Tata Center. (2015, February 28). *News+ Events*. Retrieved July 01, 2015, from Tata Center Technology+ Design: http://tatacenter.mit.edu/solar-pumps-indias-potential-to-link-electricity-access-and-irrigation-needs/

TEEB. (2010). L'Économie des écosystèmes et de la biodiversité: Intégration de l'Économie de la nature. Une synthèse de l'approche, des conclusions et des recommandations de la TEEB. Programme des Nations Unies pour l'environnement.

TERI. (2009). India's energy security: new opportunities for a sustainable future. New Delhi: The Energy and Resources Institute (TERI).

TERI. (2011, July). Energy Access: Global and local initiatives. *The Solar Quarterly*, 26-31.

TERI. (2013). Creation of energy scenario in the future to improve air quality in East and South Asia. The Energy and Resources Institute.

Terzo, M., & Rasmont, P. (2007). Abeilles sauvages, bourdons et autres insectes pollinisateurs.

Thakur, N. (2011). Indian Cultural Landscapes: Religious pluralism, tolerance and ground reality. *Journal of SPA: New Dimensions in Research of Environments for Living "The Scared", 3*.

Thakur, N. (2002). *The Architectural Knowledge Systems Approach*. Architecturez Imprints.

The Financial Express. (2013, July 09). *Infra woes trip transmission despite power-surplus oases*. Retrieved April 20, 2015, from The Financial Express: http://archive.financialexpress.com/news/infra-woes-trip-transmission-despite-powersurplus-oases/1139647

Tilley, F., & Young, W. (2009). Sustainability entrepreneurs: Could they be the true wealth generators of the future? *Green Management International*, *55*, 79–92.

Tiwari, S., & Gupta, R. (2007). Changing Currents: The Irrigation Practices of Leh Town. *Recent Research on Ladakh*, 217-24.

Torres, A., Soler, N., & Ewig, S. (1997). Airway inflammation in smokers and nonsmokers with varying responsiveness to ozone. *American Journal of Respiratory and Critical Care Medicine*, *156*(3), 728–736. doi:10.1164/ajrccm.156.3.9601054 PMID:9309986

Touloumi, G., Spix, C., Ponce de León, A., Le Moullec, Y., & Bacharova, L. (1997). Short-term effects of ambient oxidant exposure on mortality: a combined analysis within the APHEA project. Air Pollution and Health: a European Approach. *American Journal of Epidemiology*, *146*(2), 177–185. doi:10.1093/oxfordjournals.aje.a009249 PMID:9230780

Townsend, A. (2013). *Smart Cities: Big Data, Civic Hackers, and the Quest for a New Utopia*. Academic Press.

TRS. (2008). *Ground-level ozone in the 21st century: future trends, impacts and policy implications, RS Policy document 15/08, Issued: October 2008 RS1276*. London: The Royal Society.

Tutzinger Manifesto. (2001). Aesthetics of Sustinability. *TUTZINGER MANIFESTO for the strengthening of the cultural-aesthetic dimension of sustainable development*. Retrieved November 2013, from http://www.kupoge.de/ifk/tutzinger-manifest/pdf/tuma-gb.pdf

U.S. Protection Agency, (1996). *Air Quality Criteria for O_3 and Related Photochemical Oxidants*. EPA 600/P-93/004bF.

Ulmer, C., Kopp, M., Ihorst, G., Frischer, T., Forster, J., & Kuehr, J. (1997). Effects of ambient ozone exposures during the spring and summer of 1994 on pulmonary function of schoolchildren. *Pediatric Pulmonology*, *23*(5), 344–353. doi:10.1002/(SICI)1099-0496(199705)23:5<344::AID-PPUL6>3.0.CO;2-K PMID:9168508

UN-DESA. (n.d.). *Challenges and way forward in the urban sector: Sustainable Development in the 21st century (SD21)*. United Nations Department of Economic and Social Affairs.

UNEP. (2014). *Using Models for Green Economy Policymaking*. UNEP.

UNESCO. (1982). *Mexico City Declaration on Cultural Policies*. Mexico City: UNESCO.

UNESCO. (1998). *Intergovernmental Conference on Cultural Policies for Development*. Action Plan on Cultural Policies for Development. Retrieved February 2014, from http://portal.unesco.org/culture/en/files/35220/12290888881stockholm_actionplan_rec_en.pdf/stockholm_actionplan_rec_en.pdf

UNESCO. (2001). *UNESCCO Universal Declaration on Cultural Diversity*. UNESCO.

UNESCO. (2011). *UNESCO Culture for Development Indicator Suite: Analytical Framework*. UNESCO. Retrieved from http://www.unesco.org/new/fileadmin/MULTIMEDIA/HQ/CLT/pdf/Conv2005_CDindicators_Analytical_en.pdf

UNESCO. (2012, May). Retrieved March 2014, from https://en.unesco.org/post2015/sites/post2015/files/Think%20Piece%20Culture.pdf

UNESCO. (2013a). *Culture: Key to sustainable development. Hangzhoou*. UNESCO.

UNESCO. (2013b, December 13). Retrieved January 2014, from http://www.unesco.org/new/en/culture/themes/dynamic-content-single-view/news/un_general_assembly_adopts_by_consensus_a_new_resolution_on_culture_and_development/#.U6FJMvmSxqU

UNESCO. (2015). Retrieved 08 15, 2015, from http://www.unesco.org/new/fileadmin/MULTIMEDIA/HQ/CLT/images/Concept_Note_Report_CultureandCities.pdf

UN-HABITAT. (2002). *Sustainable Urbanization: Achieving Agenda 21*. UN-HABITAT DFID.

UN-HABITAT. (2009). *Planning Sustainable Cities: Global Report on Human Settlements*. London: Earthscan.

United Cities and Local Governments. (2010). *Culture: The Fourth Pillar of Sustainable Development*. Mexico City: UCLG.

United Nations. (2004). *United Nations Environment Programme 2004 Annual Report*. Retrieved February 10, 2015, from http://www.unep.org/publications/contents/ pub_details_search.asp? ID=3621

United Nations. (2010). *Sustainable Development: From Brundtland to Rio 2012. Background paper prepared for consideration by the High Level Panel on Global Sustainability at its first meeting, 19 September*. Retrieved February 10, 2015, from http://www.un.org/wcm/webdav/site/climatechange/ shared/gsp/docs/GSP1-6_Background%20on%20 Sustain-able%20Devt.pdf

United Nations. (2013). *Yangzhou Recommendations on Sustainable Cities and Urbanization. Recommendations*. Yangzhou: Yangzhou Municipal People's Government, United Nations Department of Economic and Social Affairs.

UNRISD UNESCO. (1996). Towards a World Report on Culture and Development: Constructing cultural statistics and indicators. UNRISD UNESCO.

UNU-IAS and IICRC. (2002). *Kanazawa Resolutions on culture in sustainability of cities*. Kanazawa: IICRC.

Vagaggini, B., Taccola, M., Cianchetti, S., Carnevali, S., Bartoli, M. L., Bacci, E., & Paggiaro, P. L. et al. (2002). Ozone exposure increases eosinophilic airway response induced by previous allergen challenge. *American Journal of Respiratory and Critical Care Medicine*, *166*(8), 1073–1077. doi:10.1164/rccm.2201013 PMID:12379550

Vagaggini, B., Taccola, M., Conti, I., Carnevali, S., Cianchetti, S., Bartoli, M. L., & Paggiaro, P. L. et al. (2001). Budesonide reduces neutrophilic but not functional airway response to ozone in mild asthmatics. *American Journal of Respiratory and Critical Care Medicine*, *164*(12), 2172–2176. doi:10.1164/ajrccm.164.12.2009090 PMID:11751182

Van Dingenen, R., Dentener, F. J., Raes, F., Krol, M. C., Emberson, L., & Cofala, J. (2009). The global impact of O3 on agricultural crop yields under current and future air quality legislation. *Atmospheric Environment*, *43*(3), 604–618. doi:10.1016/j.atmosenv.2008.10.033

Van Ruijven, B. J., Weitzel, M., den Elzen, M. G. J., Hof, A. F., van Vuuren, D. P., Peterson, S., & Narita, D. (2012). Emission allowances and mitigation costs of China and India resulting from different effort-sharing approaches. *Energy Policy*, *46*, 116–134. doi:10.1016/j.enpol.2012.03.042

Vandermeulen, V., Verspecht, A., Vermeire, B., Van Huylenbroeck, G., & Gellynck, X. (2011). The use of economic valuation to create public support for green infrastructure investments in urban areas. *Landscape and Urban Planning*, *103*(2), 198–206. doi:10.1016/j.landurbplan.2011.07.010

Venkataraman, S. (1997). The distinctive domain of entrepreneurship research: An editor's perspective. In J. Katz & J. Brockhaus (Eds.), Advances in entrepreneurship, firm emergence, and growth. Greenwich, CT: JAI Press.

Vince, G. (2009). Glacier Man. *Science*, *326*(5953), 659–661. doi:10.1126/science.326_659 PMID:19900911

Vitousek, P. M., Mooney, H. A., Lubchenco, J., & Melillo, J. M. (1997). Human domination of Earth's ecosystems. *Science, 277*(5325), 494–499. doi:10.1126/science.277.5325.494

Walley, E., & Taylor, D. (2002). Opportunists, champions, Mavericksy?: A typology of green entrepreneurs. *Greener Management International, 38*(Summer), 31–43. doi:10.9774/GLEAF.3062.2002.su.00005

Washburn, D., & Sindhu, U. (2009). Helping CIOs Understand "Smart City" Initiatives. *Growth*. Available at: http://c3328005.r5.cf0.rackcdn.com/73efa931-0fac-4e28-ae77- 8e58ebf74aa6.pdf

WECD. (1987). *Our Common Future, World Commission on Environment and Development.* Oxford University Press.

Weitzel, M., Ghosh, J., Peterson, S., & Pradhan, B. K. (2012). *Effects of international climate policy for India: Evidence from a national and global CGE model.* Kiel Working Paper No. 1810 November. Kiel Institute for the World Economy.

Welsch, H. (2008). Armington Elasticities for Energy Policy Modeling: Evidence from Four European Countries. *Energy Economics, 30*(5), 2252–2264. doi:10.1016/j.eneco.2007.07.007

WEO. (2014). *World Energy Outlook 2014*. Paris: International Energy Agency.

Were, M., Kamau, M., Sichei, M., & Moses, K. (2013). *A Theoretical Framework for Kenya's Central Bank Macroeconometric Model.* Africa Growth Initiative Working Paper No 10.

Whalley, J. (1975). A General Equilibrium Assessment of the 1973 UK Tax Reforms. *De Economía, 42*, 139–161.

Whalley, J. (1977). The United Kingdom Tax System, 1968-1970: Some Fixed Point Indications of its Economic Impact. *Econometrica, 45*(8), 1837–1858. doi:10.2307/1914113

White, S. S., & Ellis, C. (2007). Sustainability. The Environment, and New Urbanism: An Assessment and Agenda for Research. *Journal of Architecture and Planning Research, 24*(2), 125-142.

White, A., & Ratick, S. (1989). Risk, Compensation, and Regional Equity in Locating Hazardous Facilities. *Papers / Regional Science Association. Regional Science Association. Meeting, 67*(1), 29–42. doi:10.1007/BF01934665

WHO. (1999). *Towards a new planning process: A guide to reorienting urban planning towards Local Agenda 21.* WHO Regional Office.

WHO. (2008). *Health risks of ozone from long-range transboundary air pollution.* Geneva: World Health Organization.

Wilkinson, S., Mills, G., Illidge, R., & Davies, W. J. (2011). How is O3 pollution reducing our food supply? *Journal of Experimental Botany*. doi:10.1093/jxb/err317

Williamson, O. E. (2002). The Theory of the Firm as Governance Structure: From Choice to Contract. *The Journal of Economic Perspectives, 16*(3), 171-195.

Williamson, O. E. (1976). Franchise Bidding for Natural Monopolies-In General and with Respect to CATV. *The Bell Journal of Economics, 7*(1), 73–104. doi:10.2307/3003191

Williamson, O. E. (1979). Transaction Cost Economics: The Governance of Contractual Relations. *The Journal of Law & Economics, 22*(2), 233–261. doi:10.1086/466942

Williamson, O. E. (1985). *The Economic Institutions of Capitalism.* New York: Free Press.

Williamson, O. E. (1998). The Institutions of Governance. *The American Economic Review, 88*(2), 75–79.

Wilson, M. A. and Carpenter, S. (1999). Economic valuation of freshwater ecosystem services in the United States: 1971-1997. *Ecol. Appl., 9*, 772-783.

World Bank. (2012). *Lighting Rural India: Experience of Rural Load Segregation Schemes in States*. New Delhi: World Bank.

World Bank. (2013). *India Diagnostic Assessment of Select Environmental Challenges An Analysis of Physical and Monetary Losses of Environmental Health and Natural Resources* (Vol. 1). The World Bank.

World Bank. (2014). *More Power to India - The Challenge of Electricity Distribution*. Washington, DC: World Bank.

World Commission on Culture and Development. (1996). *Our creative diversity*. UNESCO.

World Commission on Environment and Development. (1987). *Our Common Future*. Oxford, UK: Oxford University Press.

World Resources Institute. (2004). *World Resources 2002–2004*. Washington, DC: World Resources Institute.

World Summit on Sustainable Development. (2002). *Report of the World Summit on Suatinable Development Johannesburg*. New York: United Nations.

World Tourism Organization (WTO). (2014). International Forum on Urban Tourism. WTO.

Yanarella, E. J., & Levine, R. S. (1992). Does Sustainable Development Lead to Sustainability. *Futures*, *24*(8), 759–774. doi:10.1016/0016-3287(92)90105-O

York, J. G., & Venkataraman, S. (2010). The entrepreneur–environment nexus: Uncertainty, innovation, and allocation. *Journal of Business Venturing*, *25*(5), 449–463. doi:10.1016/j.jbusvent.2009.07.007

Zainabi, A. (2003). *La Vallée du Draa. Developement Alternatif et Action Communautaire*. Background paper WDR.

Zeghnoun, A., Czernichow, P., Beaudeau, P., Hautemanière, A., Froment, L. É. T., Tertre, A. L., & Quénel, P. (2001). Short-term effects of air pollution on mortality in the cities of Rouen and Le Havre, France, 1990–1995. *Archives of Environmental Health*, *56*(4), 327–335. doi:10.1080/00039890109604464 PMID:11572276

Zhang, X., & Chen, S. (2013). *A systematic framework for infrastructure development through public private partnerships*. Academic Press.

Zmirou, D., Schwartz, J., Saez, M., Zanobetti, A., Wojtyniak, B., & Touloumi, G. (1998). Time-series analysis of air pollution and cause-specific mortality. *Epidemiology (Cambridge, Mass.)*, *9*(5), 495–503. doi:10.1097/00001648-199809000-00005 PMID:9730027

About the Contributors

Anandajit Goswami Anandajit Goswami is an economist by training and has research interests on the interfaces of economic modelling, ecological, resource, macro, micro, international trade and developmental economics, and sustainability science from an interdisciplinary lens. Currently, he is associated as a Fellow with the Green Growth and Development Division of TERI. He has been working with The Energy and Resources Institute (TERI) since 2004 and has led research projects pertaining to trade and sustainable development, economic modelling supported by ICTSD (International Centre for Trade and Sustainable Development), UNCTAD (United Nations Conference on Trade and Development). He has also worked with UNECA (United Nations Economic Commission for Africa) and has led research projects of TERI with partners in Africa. He has been engaged in various South South Cooperation knowledge exchange process, some of which have been supported by UNECA, UNIDO (United Nations Industrial Developmental Organization), Ministry of External Affairs, Government of India, Ministry of Water and Energy, Government of Ethiopia, Horn of Africa Regional Environment Centre and Network, Addis Ababa University. He has published papers in peer reviewed journals and contributed chapters to books. He has co-authored a booklet on South South Cooperation and Knowledge Exchange issues and edited a booklet related to regulatory issues on biofuels. He has been giving talks on "Economics of Sustainability" in South South Knowledge exchange programmes. Other than this, he has contributed popular articles in newspapers and blogs for Economist, Reuters Foundation. Presently, Anandajit is a member of International and Indian Society for Ecological Economics. He is an associate faculty at TERI University and has obtained Masters in International Economics with Specialization in World Economy from the Jawaharlal Nehru University, New Delhi.

* * *

Isaac O. Abereijo holds a doctoral degree in Technology Management from Obafemi Awolowo University, Ile Ife, Nigeria. He is an Associate Professor at the Institute for Entrepreneurship and Development Studies of the same university, where he teaches and carries out researches on entrepreneurship studies and small business development. His areas of specialisation are technological entrepreneurship and innovation as well as small business development. He has published in local and international journals in the areas of small business finances and technological innovation. Among the international conferences and workshops attended are Price Babson Symposium for Educators, USA (2014), Incubator Manager Training workshop on Managing the Incubator, South Africa (2011) Brown International Advanced Research Institute (BIARI) on Technology Entrepreneurship and Management, USA (2009), and Global Conference on Business and Finance, Costa Rica (2006).

Andrea M. Bassi is the founder and CEO of KnowlEdge Srl and an Extraordinary Professor at Stellenbosch University, in South Africa. Dr. Bassi is a project leader and researcher, with over 10 years of experience, supporting more than 30 governments and several international organizations primarily on green economy strategies & scenarios, climate mitigation & adaptation and sustainable development. Dr. Bassi holds a Ph.D. and M.Phil. in System Dynamics at the University of Bergen, Norway, a M.Sc. in Business and Economics at LIUC, Italy, and a postgraduate course in modeling the environment at the Universitad Politecnica de Catalunia in Spain.

Subhes Bhattacharyya of Institute of Energy and Sustainable Development of De Montfort University is an internationally renowned energy specialist with more than 25 years of experience. He leads a consortium of research organisations from the UK and India working on off-grid electricity access in South Asia. He has written widely on energy issues in developing countries and particularly on energy access. He is the author of a best-selling book on energy economics and has edited books on rural electrification through decentralised off-grid systems and mini-grids for rural electrification of developing countries.

Carey Clouse is an Assistant Professor of Architecture and Landscape Architecture at the University of Massachusetts, Amherst. She holds a post-professional degree (SMArchS) in Architecture and Urbanism from the Massachusetts Institute of Technology and a BArch from the University of Oregon. In addition to teaching, she is co-partner of Crookedworks, an award-winning architecture firm.

David Coady is Division Chief of the Expenditure Policy Division at the Fiscal Affairs Department (FAD) of the IMF. Prior to that, he was Lead Social Spending Expert in FAD, Deputy Division Chief of the Expenditure Policy Division (FAD), Research Fellow at the International Food Policy Research Institute, and a lecturer in economics in the University of London. He earned his Ph.D. in economics from the London School of Economics in 1992. His research interests include development and public economics, and he has worked extensively on policy issues related to the efficiency and distributional implications of public policies including indirect taxes, public sector pricing, social spending, and the evaluation of safety net programs. He has recently co-edited books on *The Economics of Public Health Care Reform in Advanced and Emerging Economies* and on *Energy Subsidy Reform: Lessons and Implications*. His research has been published in leading economic journals, including the *Economic Journal, Economica, Review of Income and Wealth, International Tax and Public Finance, American Journal of Agricultural Economics, World Development,* and *World Bank Research Observer.*

Shyamasis Das, leveraging on more than 5 years' professional experience in Energy Management, Public Policy and Climate Change Advisory, has an ideal techno-economic profile and hands-on experience in dealing with energy policies and regulations. He collaborates with Multilateral and Bilateral Organizations, Ministries, Public Agencies, Corporate Houses and NGOs, and is credited with accomplishing quite a many critical assignments with high-profile clients such as the World Bank Group, GGGI, DFID, Central and State Ministries, Govt. of India, Indian Railways and major MNCs. He is also the principal author of international publications on public policies and energy-related issues. Before his stint in TERI as an Associate Fellow, he has worked with Ernst & Young, GIZ- International Services, and Enerdata (France). Shyamasis has undertaken MSc. on Energy Management in France.

Louise A. Gallagher is an environmental economist with broad range of experience in policy analysis, market transformation and environmental finance. Her technical expertise includes valuation of natural capital and environmental externalities and applying this information in decision-making. She holds a PhD in Environmental Studies specializing in environmental economics and policy from University College Dublin. Louise is the Research Lead: Natural Capital And Ecosystems Services at the Luc Hoffmann Institute. She previously led the development of green economy in the regional programme of WWF in the Greater Mekong and worked for the United Nations Environment Programme (UNEP), UN Convention on Combating Desertification (UNCCD), the UK Environment Agency, and New Forests Asia Ltd. Louise's research interests lie in environmental governance and how environmental economics theory and analysis methods contribute to improved public policy in practice.

Joydeep Ghosh has more than ten years of experience in research, consulting and teaching. His areas of research interest include economic modelling, climate change, agriculture and human capital, and he has several publications in national and international journals in these areas. Joydeep has worked in organizations like Ernst & Young (EY), International Food Policy Research Institute (IFPRI) and Institute of Economic Growth (IEG). Joydeep holds master's degrees in agricultural and applied economics from Virginia Tech, USA, and in Agribusiness from Washington State University, USA. He has a PhD in Economics from Gokhale Institute of Politics and Economics, India.

Nilanjan Ghosh is Senior Fellow (Professor) and Head of Economics at ORF Kolkata, and Senior Economic Advisor at the World Wide Fund for Nature, New Delhi. A natural resource economist and econometrician by training, He obtained his PhD from the Indian Institute of Management Calcutta. He has been working in the domains of ecological economics, developmental issues, water resources, and financial markets, and conducts his research by combining frameworks of neoclassical economics and institutions. His publications so far include 6 books and 35-odd peer-reviewed research papers in journals like Water Policy, Conservation and Society, Journal of Industrial Ecology, Journal of Index Investing and EPW, as well as book chapters. He has served the Indian Society for Ecological Economics (INSEE) in various capacities including Acting President, and has delivered the Presidential Address at The Society's Seventh Biennial Conference in 2013.

Ranjan Ghosh is a post-doctoral fellow and lecturer at the Department of Economics, Swedish University of Agricultural Sciences (SLU) in Uppsala, Sweden. He earned his PhD at Humboldt University Berlin and conducted an important part of his research at the Vincent and Elinor Ostrom Workshop, Indiana University, Bloomington, US. He completed his M.Sc in Economics from the Madras School of Economics, 2007. Prior to his doctoral program he worked as a researcher at TERI and Citigroup Analytics. He works on agri-food value chains, energy and resource economics. His prime interest lies in the methodology and applications of New Institutional Economics.

Emine Hanedar is an Economist at the Fiscal Affairs Department of the IMF. Prior to that she worked as a Senior Economist at the Strategy and Economic Policy Department and the European Department of the Dutch Ministry of Finance. Her work to date covers a wide range of macro and fiscal policy issues in particular in the area of fiscal adjustment, public debt (sustainability), public spending, tax policy, inequality and the European Monetary Union. She has contributed to numerous policy and research publications of the Dutch Ministry of Finance and has been published on various macro-fiscal issues.

Somnath Hazra has a Ph.D degree in Forest Economics with more than 14 years of NRM professional experience with different Indian research centers including UGC and 4 years teaching experience of PG (Environmental Economics) and UG Courses (Environmental Economics) in Rabindra Bharati University and experience in managing and executing development programmes in various capacities for Government, International Development organizations and Private Sector.. He has domain expertise in Climate Change, AR CDM, Sustainable forest management, Biodiversity Assessment, Forest Governance, Policy analysis, etc. He has written more than 30 research articles and 5 edited volumes on climate change, environmental economics and development economics. He was associated as a climate change and forestry consultant of different State Governments of India, Government of Kenya and other two African countries. He has developed Climate Change Action Plan for seven Indian States as forestry and climate vulnerability expert. He was Associated as Ecological Economist (consultant) of West Bengal Biodiversity Board, Government of West Bengal, India.

Ahmed Karmaoui has been working as the Team Investigator of various profession consultancy jobs and research activities on climate change adaptations in dryland. His recent research focuses on understanding the arid human-environment interactions. His research and teaching interests are environment science, land cover change, climate change impact, and local resource management. KARMAOUI has considerable experience working on interdisciplinary teams to address research questions related to challenges associated with coupling natural and human systems, including climate change adaptation.

Barun Deb Pal is currently an Assistant Professor at the Institute of Social and Economic Change, Bangalore. He has been working in the field of SAM based CGE modelling for the last 7 years. He has also worked on climate-smart agriculture and land-use planning models for South Asia as a key researcher at the International Food Policy Research Institute (IFPRI). He has a long professional affiliation with the National Council of Applied Economic Research (NCAER), working on climate change CGE modeling. He has published papers in journals of international repute with one of his publication being "A Social Accounting Matrix for India", published in 2012 in Economic Systems Research (Taylor and Francis). His current areas of research interest include various developmental issues and their linkages with climate change, low carbon agriculture, Infrastructure and public utility pricing.

Debajit Palit of TERI has around 18 years of experience working in the field of clean energy access, rural electrification policy and regulation, distributed generation, solar photovoltaics and biomass gasification. He has also written widely on energy access and rural electrification issues, particularly related to South Asia. He has authored a book on rural electricity distribution franchisees and has also edited a book on mini-grids for rural electrification of developing countries. He has a wide national and international experience, working in projects spread across India, Bangladesh, Bhutan, Cambodia, Myanmar, Nepal, and Philippines in Asia and Ethiopia, Kenya, Liberia, Mozambique, Sierra Leone and Uganda in Africa.

Sanjib Pohit is presently working as a Professor, AcSIR and a Senior Principal Scientist at the CSIR- National Institute of Science, Technology & Development Studies. He was educated at the Indian Statistical Institute. Previously, he held research positions (Senior Fellow/Chief Economist) at the National Council for Applied Economic Research (New Delhi, India) and was a visiting scholar at the University of Michigan (Ann Arbor, USA) and the Conference Board of Canada. Dr. Pohit has been a member of several committees of the Government of India and a Council Member of the Gerson Lehman group. He has been a consultant to various national and international bodies, including The World Bank, Asian Development Bank, The Energy & Resource Institute, OECD, CUTS, Price Waterhouse Coopers, ICRIER and RIS. Dr. Pohit is an experienced modeler in the area of trade and environment with 20 years of modeling experience. He has he worked in the area of institutional economics, transport economics, input-output models, FDI, informal trade, the automobile industry and South Asian integration. He has co-authored 8 books, and has published more than 100 articles in journals/books. He has presented his research at seminars and conferences in different parts of the world – Japan, Canada, USA, India, Bangladesh, Switzerland, the Netherlands, Singapore and Finland.

Basanta K. Pradhan is currently Professor and Head, Development Planning Center at the Institute of Economic Growth (since 2008). Previously, he was Chief Economist at NCAER (2002-2008) and visiting Assistant Professor at the State University of New York at Stony Brook (1988-89). He was a Distinguished visiting Fellow at the University of Canberra (Nov, 2011) and a Senior Research Fellow at University of Warwick (2001-02). Professor Pradhan has been a consultant to many international organizations like World Bank, UNDP, UNIDO, IDRC, etc. He has lead large research projects and has been principal author of major reports. His interests are mainly growth and distribution with particular focus on the Indian economy. He has developed SAM and CGE models to analyze various development issues. He has books, reports and academic journal papers to his credit. He has served as a member of various advisory and academic committees.

José Manuel Saiz-Alvarez, Ph.D. in Economics and Business Administration, Autonomous University of Madrid (Spain). Ph.D. in Sociology and Political Sciences, Pontifical University of Salamanca (Spain). Dr. Saiz-Alvarez is officially accredited by the Spanish Agency of Quality Evaluation and Accreditation. He has also studied in the USA at the Royal Complutense College at Harvard, and at University of South Florida; in France, at University Lumière-Lyon II, and in Estonia, at Tallinn University. Academic Director for Business Administration Doctoral Studies, Nebrija University (Spain). Visiting Professor at TEC de Monterrey (Mexico), EAN University (Colombia), and the Catholic University of Santiago de Guayaquil (Ecuador). Honorary Professor, Autonomous University of Madrid (Spain). President of FIEC Institute. Member of the Latin-American Family Business Net. Co-founder of the International Center of Research on Solidarity Economy, based at the Metropolitan University of Puerto Rico. He has been a researcher at the Eastern European Institute, Complutense University (Spain). Certificate of Recognition, Capitol House of Representatives of Puerto Rico. Diploma of Honor, Valahia University of Targoviste (Romania). Member of the Scientific Research Council, Professor Edward Lipinski School of Economics, Law and Medical Sciences at Kielce (Poland). Member of the Editorial Board and referee of numerous national and international journals. Who's Who in the World, from the 2011 Edition. He has given more than one hundred lectures in Europe and America, and is author of more than a hundred publications in his specialty. To date he has supervised more than 40 doctoral thesis from students from Argentina, Chile, Colombia, Ecuador, Guatemala, Italy, Mexico, Spain, USA, and Venezuela.

Sumit Sharma is a Fellow at the Centre for Environmental Studies group of TERI. Qualified by the graduate and post-graduate degrees from Delhi College of Engineering and Indian Institute of Technology-Delhi, respectively, he has been working in the group for last 12 years. He has worked on number of projects related to air quality management which involves air quality monitoring, emission inventorisation, air quality modelling (dispersion and receptor), and drafting air quality management plans. He has worked on the state of the art photo-chemical models for simulation of ground level ozone and other pollutants at urban and regional scales. He has a number of peer reviewed research publications to his name. He is also involved in sensitization of various stakeholders through workshops and building capacities through training programs.

Shaleen Singhal is Head of the Department of Policy Studies at TERI University. He has over 18 years of academic, research and consulting experience of working on sustainable urban development issues in India and the United Kingdom. Previously he had served the core faculty position in Sustainability Design at School of the Built Environment, University of Ulster, UK and was a member of the Built Environment Research Institute. With education profile spanning architecture, planning and regeneration, he has developed synergies across three disciplines for contribution to teaching and research. His doctoral study entitled: City Competitiveness, Regeneration, and Property-led Business Strategies, from University of Ulster received the 2009 Emerald/EFMD Outstanding Doctoral Research Award, competing with entrants from 37 countries. His recent publications emphasize the significance of low carbon urban development, infrastructure performance, ecology based planning and sustainable regeneration for cities. His doctoral students are adopting a multi-disciplinary approach to examine urbanization related themes. Dr. Singhal is the Indian lead collaborator of the 'Indian European Multi-level Climate Governance Research Network Programme'. He is a Fellow of the Higher Education Academy, UK.

Anurag Varma received his Master of Architecture in Architectural Conservation degree from School of Planning and Architecture, Delhi and his Bachelor of Architecture from the Lucknow University, India. Currently pursuing Doctoral studies at TERI University, Delhi his research focuses on the synergies between place-based cultural aspects, urban planning and sustainability issues in pilgrimage towns. As an Architect heading his own design practice and Consultant to other organizations, his professional expertise includes spatial planning, urbanism and architecture design of buildings in a heritage context. His professional works include spatial planning of Greenfield hill-settlements at Bhutan and India. As an Adjunct Professor at various Universities in India, he has been associated in design studios focusing on appropriate spatial responses in an urban context.

Index

F

G

H

I

J

L

M

N

O

P

R

S

T

U

V

W

Z

www.ingramcontent.com/pod-product-compliance
Lightning Source LLC
LaVergne TN
LVHW060406300926
849162LV00006B/1356
* 9 7 8 1 5 2 2 5 0 0 9 4 0 *